# Lecture Notes of the Institute for Computer Sciences, Social Informatics and Telecommunications Engineering 385

More information about this series at http://www.springer.com/series/8197

Mulugeta Admasu Delele ·
Mekuanint Agegnehu Bitew ·
Abebech Abera Beyene ·
Solomon Workneh Fanta ·
Addisu Negash Ali (Eds.)

# Advances of Science and Technology

8th EAI International Conference, ICAST 2020
Bahir Dar, Ethiopia, October 2–4, 2020
Proceedings, Part II

Springer

*Editors*
Mulugeta Admasu Delele
Bahir Dar University
Bahir Dar, Ethiopia

Abebech Abera Beyene ⓘ
Bahir Dar University
Bahir Dar, Ethiopia

Addisu Negash Ali ⓘ
Bahir Dar University
Bahir Dar, Ethiopia

Mekuanint Agegnehu Bitew ⓘ
Bahir Dar University
Bahir Dar, Ethiopia

Solomon Workneh Fanta ⓘ
Bahir Dar University
Bahir Dar, Ethiopia

ISSN 1867-8211          ISSN 1867-822X  (electronic)
Lecture Notes of the Institute for Computer Sciences, Social Informatics
and Telecommunications Engineering
ISBN 978-3-030-80617-0          ISBN 978-3-030-80618-7  (eBook)
https://doi.org/10.1007/978-3-030-80618-7

This Springer imprint is published by the registered company Springer Nature Switzerland AG
The registered company address is: Gewerbestrasse 11, 6330 Cham, Switzerland

# Preface

On behalf of the organizing team, it is our pleasure to introduce the proceedings of the 8th EAI International Conference on Advancements of Science and Technology (ICAST 2020), which took place at the Bahir Dar Institute of Technology, Bahir Dar University, Ethiopia, during October 2–4, 2020. The ICAST conference is an annual platform for researchers, scholars, scientists in academia, and practitioners in various industries to share know-how, experiences, challenges, and recent advancements in science and technology. In addition, the conference has continued to show promise in the application of research findings and innovations in all areas of science and technology. ICAST 2020 attracted 200 submissions of which 157 were sent out for peer review, where each paper was evaluated by, on average, three experts in the area. The technical program of ICAST 2020 consisted of 74 full papers in the oral presentation sessions during the main conference tracks. The conference was organized into six tracks: Track 1: Chemical, food, and bio-process engineering; Track 2: Electrical and computer engineering; Track 3: IT, computer science, and software engineering; Track 4: Civil, water resources, and environmental engineering; Track 5: Mechanical and industrial engineering; and Track 6: Material science and engineering. The six tracks were conducted as parallel sessions in six halls. In addition to the high-quality technical paper presentations, the technical program also featured three opening keynote speeches and seven session keynote speeches. The three opening keynote speakers were Prof. Desta Mebratu, University of Stellenbosh, South Africa; Dr. Hirpa G.Lemu, University of Stavanger, Norway; and Dr. Lara Allen, Centre for Global Equality, UK.

Coordination with the Steering Committee chair, Prof. Imrich Chlamtac, the Organizing Committee chair, Prof. Kibret Mequanint (The University of Western Ontario, Canada), the co-chairs, Dr. Abebech Abera, Dr. Mekuanint Agegnehu and Dr. Solomon Workneh, the Technical Program Committee chair, Dr. Mulugeta Admasu was essential for the success of the conference. We sincerely appreciate their constant support and guidance. It was also a great pleasure to team up with such an excellent Organizing Committee who worked hard in organizing and supporting the conference. We are grateful to the Technical Program Committee who were instrumental in organizing the peer-review process of the technical papers, which led to a high-quality technical program. In particular, the Technical Program Committee, led by Dr. Mulugeta Admasu, and the co-chairs, Dr. Belachew Bantyrga, Dr. Addisu Negash , Dr. Gebeyehu Belay, Dr. Hanibal Lemma, Dr. Zerihu Getahun, Dr. Elias Wagari and Prof. A. Pushparaghavan, were instrumental in organizing the peer-review process of the technical papers, which led to a high-quality technical program. We are also grateful to the conference manager, Radka Pincakova, for her support, and to all the authors who submitted their papers to the ICAST 2020 conference.

We strongly believe that ICAST 2020 provided a good forum for all researchers, developers, and practitioners to discuss all science and technology aspects that are relevant to advancements in this area. We also expect that future ICAST conferences will be as successful and stimulating as indicated by the contributions presented in this volume.

October 2020                                                    Kibret Mequanint
                                                        Mulugeta Admasu Delele

# Organization

## Steering Committee

Imrich Chlamtac      University of Trento, Italy
Seifu Tilahun      Bahir Dar University, Ethiopia
Kibret Mequanint      University of Western Ontario, Canada

## Organizing Committee

### General Chair

Kibret Mequanint      University of Western Ontario, Canada

### General Co-chairs

Abebech Abera      Bahir Dar University, Ethiopia
Mekuanint Agegnehu      Bahir Dar University, Ethiopia
Solomon Workneh      Bahir Dar University, Ethiopia

### Technical Program Committee Chair and Co-chairs

Mulugeta Admasu      Bahir Dar University, Ethiopia
Belachew Bantyrga      Bahir Dar University, Ethiopia
Addisu Negash      Bahir Dar University, Ethiopia
Gebeyehu Belay      Bahir Dar University, Ethiopia
Hanibal Lemma      Bahir Dar University, Ethiopia
Zerihu Getahun      Bahir Dar University, Ethiopia
Elias Wagari      Bahir Dar University, Ethiopia
Pushparaghavan A.      Bahir Dar University, Ethiopia

### Sponsorship and Exhibit Chair

Dagnachew Aklog      Bahir Dar University, Ethiopia

### Local Chair

Dagnenet Sultan      Bahir Dar University, Ethiopia

### Workshops Chair

Fikreselam Gared      Bahir Dar University, Ethiopia

### Publicity and Social Media Chair

Hailu Shimelis      Bahir Dar University, Ethiopia

**Publications Chair**

Mulugeta Admasu          Bahir Dar University, Ethiopia

**Web Chair**

Ephrem Dagne             Bahir Dar University, Ethiopia

**Posters and PhD Track Chair**

Nigus Gabbiye            Bahir Dar University, Ethiopia

**Panels Chair**

Zenamarkos Bantie        Bahir Dar University, Ethiopia

**Demos Chair**

Bantelay Sintayehu       Bahir Dar University, Ethiopia

**Tutorials Chairs**

Mulugeta Azeze           Bahir Dar University, Ethiopia

# Technical Program Committee

Abdulkadir Aman          Addis Ababa University, Ethiopia
Abebe Dinku              Addis Ababa University, Ethiopia
Abebech Beyene           Bahir Dar University, Ethiopia
Abraham Asmare           Bahir Dar University, Ethiopia
Addisu Negash Ali        Bahir Dar University, Ethiopia
Addiszemen Teklay        Bahir Dar University, Ethiopia
Amando P. Singun Jr.     University of Technology and Applied Sciences -
                         Higher College of Technology, Oman
Aklog Dagnachew          Bahir Dar University, Ethiopia
Assefa Asmare Tsegaw     Bahir Dar University, Ethiopia
Belachew Bantiyrga       Bahir Dar University, Ethiopia
Belete Yigezu            Addis Ababa Science and Technology University,
                         Ethiopia
Bereket Haile            Bahir Dar University, Ethiopia
Berhanu Assefa Demessie  AAiT/AAU
Berihun Bizuneh          National Taiwan University of Science and
                         Technology, Taiwan
Beteley Tekola Meshesha  Addis Ababa University, Ethiopia
Delele Worku             Bahir Dar University, Ethiopia
Hailu Shimles            Bahir Dar University, Ethiopia
  Gebremedhen
Abreham Debebe           Addis Ababa Science and Technology University,
                         Ethiopia
Anteneh Mohammed Tahir   Wollo University, Ethiopia

| | |
|---|---|
| Misganaw Alemu | Bahir Dar University, Ethiopia |
| Mulugeta Admasu Delele | Bahir Dar University, Ethiopia |
| Mulugeta Yilma | Adama University, Ethiopia |
| Nigus Gabbiye Habtu | Bahir Dar University, Ethiopia |
| Seifu Tilahun | Bahir Dar University, Ethiopia |
| Semu Moges | University of Connecticut, USA |
| Shalemu Sharew | National Taiwan University of Science and Technology, Taiwan |
| Shegaw Ahmed | Addis Ababa University, Ethiopia |
| Shimelis Kebede | Addis Ababa University, Ethiopia |
| Sirawdink Forsido | Jimma University, Ethiopia |
| Sisay G. Gebeyehu | Bahir Dar University, Ethiopia |
| Solomon Fanta | Bahir Dar University, Ethiopia |
| Solomon Kiros | Addis Ababa University, Ethiopia |
| Solomon T/Mariam Teferi | Addis Ababa University, Ethiopia |
| Temesgen Debelo Desissa | Bahir Dar University, Ethiopia |
| Temesgen Nigussie | Bahir Dar University, Ethiopia |
| Teshome Mulatie Bogale | Bahir Dar University, Ethiopia |
| Tessera Alemneh | Bahir Dar University, Ethiopia |
| Yetenayet Tola | Jimma University, Ethiopia |
| Zebene Kifile | Addis Ababa University, Ethiopia |
| Zenamarkos Bantie Sendekie | Bahir Dar University, Ethiopia |
| Zerihun Getahun | Bahir Dar University, Ethiopia |
| Zerihun, Workineh | Bahir Dar University, Ethiopia |

# Contents – Part II

## Late Track

# Contents – Part I

## Electrical and Computer Engineering

## IT, Computer Science and Software Engineering

# Civil, Water Resource and Environmental Engineering

# Study on Partial Replacement of Cement with Animal Bone Ash in Concrete at Elevated Temperatures

Solomon Dagnaw[1] and Tesfaye Alemu Mohammed[2(✉)]

[1] Civil Engineering Department, University of Gondar, Gondar, Ethiopia
[2] Civil Engineering Department, Addis Ababa Science and Technology University, Addis Ababa, Ethiopia
tesfaye.alemu@aastu.edu.et

**Abstract.** It is not uncommon to find inefficient waste disposal systems in third world countries like in Ethiopia where the human factor is crucial in generating wastes like animal bones. Animal bone ash constitutes high calcium, offering good binding characteristics to employ bone ash (BA) as a partial replacement of cement in concrete production. This study experimentally investigates use of animal bone ash (BA) as partial replacement of cement in structural concrete production at elevated temperature. Parameters studied in this study include elevated temperature intensity (300 °C, 600 °C and 900 °C), duration of temperature exposure (1 h and 3 h), cooling methods and various bone ash (BA) cement blending percentages (0%, 5%, 10%, 15% and 20%). A total of 237 concrete cylindrical test specimens was casted and tested to study behavior of concrete with cement replaced by bone ash (BA) at elevated temperatures. Experimental test results showed that weight, tensile and compressive strengths of bone ash blended cement concrete reduced with an increase in temperature and their respective test values depends on choice of cooling methods. Fast cooling exhibited an additional strength loss of 35% as compared to natural air cooling. Also, concrete residual compressive strength decreases sharply beyond 10% replacement of cement with bone ash (BA). This implies optimum threshold value of bone ash (BA) replacement of cement in concrete at elevated temperature is 10%.

**Keywords:** Elevated temperature · Cement partial replacement · Animal Bone ash (BA)

## 1 Introduction

As compared to other construction materials, concrete constituents larger proportion of built in structures and this trend is projected to rise twice in coming 30 years [1]. Cement is essential component of concrete making and its properties influence fresh and hardened mechanical property of concrete [2]. Construction boom in Ethiopia lead cement consumption to rise 10% per year during 1997–2007 years and 16.1% per year

M. A. Delele et al. (Eds.): ICAST 2020, LNICST 385, pp. 3–16, 2021.
https://doi.org/10.1007/978-3-030-80618-7_1

in last five years [3]. However, cement production involves release of large amount of carbon dioxide ($CO_2$) almost it accounts for more than 50% of combined industrial carbon dioxide ($CO_2$) emissions [4]. Studies indicated 0% increase in carbon dioxide ($CO_2$) emissions can be attained if alternative supplemental materials could be used to replace 30% of cement globally consumed cement [1, 5]. Potential cement substituting materials include animal bones ashes, rice hulk, fly ash, silica fume, textile and blast slags. Besides, these material wastes also create environmental pollution in third world countries like Ethiopia where there is no effective waste disposal systems.

Animal bone is rich in calcium constituting 97% of body's overall calcium deposit [6] and Portland cement, a crucial input for cement production, contains nearly 50% calcium oxide (CaO) [7]. Reports indicated in Ethiopia annually on average there is 400.5 million Kg animal bone wastes [8]. Animal bone calcium content and supply volume makes animal bone ash ideal replacement material for cement production industries here in Ethiopia.

Concrete in a built environment endures to uphold its strength and service requirements imposed by codes of practices. Yet, this concrete characteristic comes short and distress when concrete cis exposed to elevated temperatures of fire loading. Popularity of concrete as a construction material is attributed to its good fire resistance as compared to materials such as wood, aluminum and steel [9, 10]. However, this resistance to fire holds true up to a certain level of elevated temperature and duration of exposures. Chang et al. [11] reported behavior of concrete when exposed to a sustained fire is dependent on characteristics of concrete constituents such as aggregate type, cement paste characteristics, bond between cement paste and aggregate, rate of heating and cooling, temperature exposure time and loading types [12].

Various industrial by products and solid wastes have exhibited to enhance cement paste microstructure by densifying mix of cement paste and improving interfacial zone. Even if bone ash (BA) is not a pozzolanic material as investigated by different researchers so far, it can replace partially cement in concrete production at normal temperature due to higher percentage of CaO. However, effect of elevated temperature on concrete produced by substituting its ingredients with various waste materials particularly BA as cement substitution in concrete at elevated temperature has not been investigated by previous researchers.

This study filled in perceived void in literature by experimentally investigating effect of replacing cement with animal bone ash on mechanical properties of concrete at elevated temperature. Variables considered in this study include quantifying residual compressive and tensile strengths; marking concrete spalling and weight losses; two cooling methods such as fast and natural air cooling methods; and fire intensity exposure and duration times. In the end, this research:

- Investigates compressive and split tensile strengths of bone ash blended cement concrete at various temperature intensities and exposure times.
- Studies effect of cooling methods on bone ash (BA) modified concrete's compressive strength
- Determines optimum level of bone ash percentage cement replacement at elevated temperature

# 2 Materials and Methods

## 2.1 Materials

The animal bones solid wastes were obtained from solid waste disposal sites in Bahir Dar city, Ethiopia. Next, they were washed and sun dried after careful separation of flesh, tissues and fats. Then, bone samples were burned in an open air and ash from burned bones had been grinded using hammer mill and passing through 150 μm (No. 100) sieve as per [13].

Concrete mix batch was prepared proportioning cement, fine aggregate, coarse aggregate and water. Ordinary Portland Cement (OPC) cement of 42.5R grade manufactured by Dangote Cement Factory was used in concrete mix. The concrete making materials used in this research are cement, fine aggregate, coarse aggregate and water. The type of cement was 42.5R Ordinary Portland Cement (OPC) satisfying [14] grade, manufactured by Dangote Cement Factory. Lalibela sand having 2.65 specific gravity was employed in concrete mix as well. Also, coarse aggregate from Meshenti aggregate crushing plant having 25 mm maximum size and portable drinking water was used in preparing concrete mix batches. Material Property tests of aggregates are carried out according to ASTM Standards [15].

## 2.2 Experimental Procedures

**Mix Proportioning.** Nominal concrete mixing ratio of 1:1.7:2.7cement, fine aggregate and coarse aggregate and 0.44 water cement ratio [16] was employed. Concrete batch input constituent materials were mixed by weight. Bone ash partially replaced cement in various proportions such as 0%, 5%, 10%, 15% and 20%.

**Sample Preparation/Casting of Specimen.** Standard cylindrical molds of size of 200 mm height and 100 mm diameter made of cast iron were used to cast concrete specimens to test required mechanical properties of concrete. Required volumes of mix ingredients were measured and batch mixing were performed thoroughly to ensure that homogeneous mix was obtained. Mixing was done using standard pan type mixers of capacity 56 L. Initially, a dry mix constituting cement and bone ash, fine aggregate and coarse aggregate was mixed for three minutes and then water was poured and batch mixing applied for another 4 min. Before casting, slump of the concrete is measured by compacting concrete in 3 layers with twenty five (25) strokes of sixteen (16) mm rod applied to each layer. Interior surfaces of the steel molds were thinly coated with oil to prevent adhesion of concrete. Concrete was left in a mold and allowed to set for 24 h before cylindrical molds were removed. Then concrete cylinders were transferred to a curing tank and left in a tank for 28 days at room temperature.

**Heating and Cooling Down Process.** Target temperature was set using a knob and temperature was increased at time intervals until target temperatures achieved. The specimens were subjected to exposure tests in an electrical furnace for temperatures intensities of (300 °C, 600 °C and 900 °C) with a retention periods of 1 and 3 h for each temperature intensity. Two types of cooling methods were studied namely air cooling (intending to simulate the natural extinction of a fire) and water cooling (intending to simulate action of firemen in fire combat). Air cooling was achieved by keeping specimens to cool naturally whereas water cooling was attained by quenching specimens' right after exiting a furnace. In both cooling methods, specimens are stored for 24 h before testing was initiated.

**Test Techniques and Procedures.** Objective of this research is to investigate mechanical properties of concrete produced with cement being partially replaced by bone ash (BA) at elevated temperatures of 300, 600 and 900 °C. After, specimens were cooled down using air and water cooling methods, mechanical tests were conducted at room temperature (20 ± 5 °C). Concrete samples of 105 were casted and tested for determination of compressive strength and again another 84 samples were casted and tested in order to determine split tensile strength of concrete. Also, other 48 samples were casted and tested to evaluate effect of cooling conditions on compressive strength of concrete at various bones ash (BA) cement replacement. Totally, 237 cylindrical concrete specimens were casted and tested to achieve objective of this research.

*Compressive Strength Test.* Compressive strength test was performed according to [17] by using a hydraulic compression machine of capacity 2000 KN. After heating, specimens were left to cool down under water and natural air conditions. Extreme care was taken when handling heated concrete specimens. Specimens were weighed before and after heating to calculate weight losses. In this study, variations in color of concrete due to heating to various intensities of temperatures were determined. Specimens were loaded to failure; and ultimate loading capacities and their respective modes of failure were recorded.

*Split Tensile Strength Test.* Concrete tensile strength is determined by indirect test methods like split cylinder test. This is due to inconvenience to apply uniaxial tension to a concrete specimen. Split tensile strength test was carried out according to [18] by using a hydraulic compression machine of capacity 2000 KN.

# 3  Results and Discussions

In this section, materials chemical characterization, consistency setting time, slump test, compressive and tensile strength test results are presented.

## 3.1  Chemical Composition of Bone Ash

Calcined ash cementitious characteristic is revealed by its oxide composition. As shown in Table 1, bone ash (BA) chemical analysis contains iron oxide ($Fe_2O_3 = 0.78\%$), aluminum oxide ($Al_2O_3 = 1.24$) and silicon dioxide ($SiO_2 = 3.26\%$) and their respective total sum which was 5.28% is way less than 70% minimum threshold criterion for a material to be considered as pozzolan [19].

Therefore, bone ash (BA) oxide composition employed in this study fails to meet requirements of a pozzolanic material, rather, bone ash (BA) can be considered as a cementitious filler/additive. This is primarily due to its high 26% by weight CaO content. Table 1 below shows oxide composition of BA relative to OPC oxide composition limit as per [14].

**Table 1.** Chemical composition of bone ash (BA)

| Elemental oxides | BA (%) | OPC (%) |
|---|---|---|
| Calcium Oxide (CaO) | 26 | 60–67 |
| Silica Oxide ($SiO_2$) | 3.26 | 17–25 |
| Aluminum Oxide ($Al_2O_3$) | 1.24 | 3–8 |
| Iron Oxide ($Fe_2O_3$) | 0.78 | 0.5–6 |
| Magnesium Oxide (MgO) | 0.84 | 0.1–4.0 |
| Sodium Oxide ($Na_2O$) | 0.16 | 0.2–1.3 |
| Potassium Oxide ($K_2O$) | 0.21 | |
| Phosphate Oxide ($P_2O_5$) | 14.26 | – |
| Manganese Oxide (MnO) | 1.23 | 0.03 |
| Sulfur tri Oxide ($SO_3$) | 1.29 | 1.8–4.6 |
| Loss of Ignition (LOI) | 0.85 | 33 |

## 3.2 Properties of Animal Bone Ash Blended Cement Paste

Vicat apparatus was used to measure bone ash blended cement consistency. This test reveals cement paste mobility and flow when water cement ratio varies due to addition of bone ash (BA) replacement in various proportion. Cement paste was mixed to normal consistency as revealed by $10 \pm 1$ mm penetration using Vicat plunger (Table 2).

**Table 2.** Fresh concrete normal consistency with various percentage of bone ash (BA)

| Mix code | BA - 0% | BA - 5% | BA - 10% | BA - 15% | BA - 20% |
|---|---|---|---|---|---|
| Consistency | 28 | 28.75 | 29.5 | 30 | 31 |

Normal consistency test results indicate batch mixing water volume demands for various animal bone (BA) replacement percentages and consistency tests reveal bone powder blended mixes require additional water volumes as compared to similar cement only control batch mixes. Normal consistency test results 26%–33% fall within standard specification ranges [20]. Next, Table 3 presents consistency test results of various BA blended cement setting time.

Test results indicated initial and final setting time rise as percentage of bone ash replacement of cement increased this is due to diminished hydration process of cement as a results increase of bone ash replacement in various proportions. Also, as compared to control, bone ash (BA) blended batch mixes with 60 to 600 min setting time ranges satisfy setting time requisite of [14].

**Table 3.** Initial and final setting times of BA blended Cement paste

| Proportion of material | Initial setting time (minute) | Final setting time (minute) |
|---|---|---|
| 100%cement + 0%BA | 132.5 | 470 |
| 95%cement + 5%BA | 140 | 485 |
| 90%cement + 10%BA | 143 | 530 |
| 85%cement + 15%BA | 150 | 546 |
| 80%cement + 20%BA | 162 | 578 |

### 3.3  Workability of Bone Ash Blended Cement Concrete

Slump test was executed to determine workability bone ash blended batch mixes. A constant water cement ratio of 0.44 was used for concrete mixes and for various proportions of BA replacement slump test was measured to quantify workability changes. Table 4 presents slump test results of fresh concrete with various proportion of BA replacement. Results indicated as BA replacement proportion increases, a drop in concrete mix slump values was observed. Control mix with 0% BA scored 43 mm slump value where as 5%, 10%, 15% and 20% BA replacements exhibited 40 mm, 37 mm, 33 and 31 mm slump values respectively. Also, as compared to control, BP blended mixes demand high volume of water than cement in equal quantity. In various proportion of BA replacement, results showed BA absorbed more water leading to reduction in slump values. This is consistent with findings [21, 22] where concrete workability decrease constantly with BA incremental replacement in various proportions.

**Table 4.** Workability results of fresh concrete with varying replacements of BA

| Mix code | BA - 0% | BA - 5% | BA - 10% | BA - 15% | BA - 20% |
|---|---|---|---|---|---|
| W/C ratio | 0.44 | 0.44 | 0.44 | 0.44 | 0.44 |
| Slump (mm) | 43 | 40 | 37 | 33 | 31 |

### 3.4  Effect of Elevated Temperature on Compressive Strength of Concrete with BA as Cement Replacement – Air Cooling

In this section, compressive strength test results of cylindrical concrete specimens result are discussed by considering various factors such as intensity of temperature, exposure duration, bone ash contents and cooling methods. Table 5 and Fig. 1 below shows concrete compressive strength variations with BA content, intensity of temperature and exposure duration.

**Table 5.** Compressive strengths when concrete is exposed to different temperature intensities and durations

| Percentage replacement of cement with BA (%) | Compressive strength (MPa) | | | | | | |
|---|---|---|---|---|---|---|---|
| | RT | 300 °C 1 h | 300 °C 3 h | 600 °C 1 h | 600 °C 3 h | 900 °C 1 h | 900 °C 3 h |
| 0 | 38.95 | 38.09 | 35.95 | 23.75 | 20.44 | 11.68 | 9.95 |
| 5 | 36.47 | 35.18 | 34.53 | 22.80 | 19.41 | 11.02 | 9.51 |
| 10 | 34.18 | 32.96 | 32.65 | 22.67 | 19.29 | 10.52 | 9.07 |
| 15 | 29.36 | 27.89 | 27.55 | 17.72 | 15.23 | 7.5 | 7.21 |
| 20 | 28.72 | 26.77 | 25.14 | 14.78 | 12.25 | 6.14 | 5.17 |

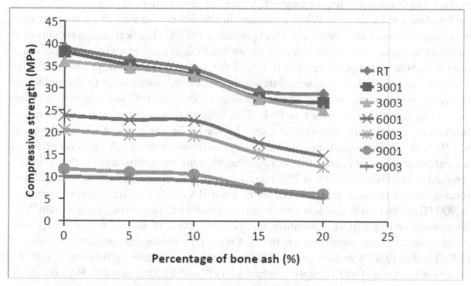

**Fig. 1.** Variation of compressive strength with percentage of BA and temperature (NB: The last digit in the legend of the figure represents the exposure duration. For example 3001 implies that at 300 °C for 1 h exposure duration)

As shown in Table 5, at room temperature when percentage of bone ash for replacement of cement increases from 0% to 20%, compressive strength of concrete decreases gradually and this is in conformity with report obtained by [22, 23]. The decrease was as a result of reduction of C-S-H in matrix due to OPC volume losses and lack of binding property of BA (small amount of silicate oxides). Although, specimens containing bone ash have lower 28 days compressive strengths as compared to control (0% BA), there is no significant difference between compressive strength of control samples and samples made with cement being replaced by bone ash up to 10% at 300 °C.

As Table 5 shows when time of exposure increases, reduction rate of compressive strength also increases for all levels of bone ash replacement at 300 °C. At 300 °C, with same exposure duration and for 5% and 10% replacement of cement with BA, reduction in residual compressive strength of concrete is gradual.

At 600 °C, bone ash blended cement concrete losses more than half of its strength as shown in Table 5. This is attributed to chemical transformation of cement paste like decomposition of Ca(OH)2, which is one of the most important compound in cement paste, resulting shrinkage of concrete. In addition this rapid reduction in compressive strength attributed due to degradation of calcium silica hydrates (C–S–H) which mainly occur at temperature above 400 °C–600 °C according to [24]. As percentage of bone ash in the mix increases from 5% to 20%, concrete compressive strength reduced by 5% to 30% at room temperature and this reduction in residual compressive strength increases up to 40% for temperature of 600 °C. At same exposure duration and for 5% and 10% replacement of cement with BA, decrease in residual strength of concrete is gradual and it becomes higher as the BA level of replacement increased further as it can be observed in Table 5. When exposure duration is considered, there is up to 10% reduction difference between 1 and 3 h exposures at 600 °C. The percentage reduction in residual compressive strength of concrete with bone ash as cement replacement becomes more than 80% at temperature of 900 °C and this is due to the disintegration of C-S-H at around 900 °C. When exposure duration is considered, there is up to 5% reduction difference between one and three hour exposure times at 900 °C and this is half of the value obtained at 600 °C which is 10%. This implies that effect of exposure duration diminishes as exposure temperature rises. As shown in Table 5 and Fig. 1 above, at 300 °C with 1 h exposure time, residual compressive strength of BA partially replaced cement concrete is comparable to concrete strength at normal temperature with maximum percentage reduction of 6.79% at 20% bone ash replacement whereas at 600 °C, reduction in compressive strength reaches 48.54% at same BA content & temperature duration. At 900 °C, reduction in residual compressive strength reaches about 78.62% with 20% BA content and 1h exposure duration. On the other hand, at 300 °C with 3 h exposure duration, residual compressive strength of BA partially replaced cement concrete reduced by 5.91% and 12.47% at 10% and 20% BA replacement respectively whereas at 600 °C, reduction in compressive strength reaches 44.41% and 57.35% at same BA content & temperature duration. At 900 °C, reduction in residual compressive strength reaches about 73.46% and 81% for the aforementioned bone ash contents and exposure time. These results indicate that temperature intensity has significant influence on compressive strength of concrete particularly BA blended cement concrete at temperatures 300 °C and above. In addition, it is observed that reduction of residual compressive strength becomes steeper above 10% BA content for all levels of temperatures.

## 3.5 Effect of Elevated Temperature on Split Tensile Strength of BA Partially Replaced Cement Concrete – Air Cooling

It is not uncommon to neglect concrete tensile characteristics in strength calculations at elevated and room temperatures. Nevertheless, concrete tensile strength is essential since concrete cracking is due to tensile stress and evolution of micro cracks resulting in structural damage of a member in tension. When concrete is exposed to fire afore-mentioned formation of cracks can be overwhelming because of spalling due to elevated temperature. Table 6 and Fig. 2 below shows split tensile strength variation as function of temperatures and percentages of replacement.

**Table 6.** Compressive strengths when concrete is exposed to different temperature intensities and durations

| Percentage replacement of cement with BA (%) | Split tensile strength (MPa) | | | | | | |
|---|---|---|---|---|---|---|---|
| | RT | 300 °C | 300 °C | 600 °C | 600 °C | 900 °C | 900 °C |
| | | 1 h | 3 h | 1 h | 3 h | 1 h | 3 h |
| 0 | 4.1 | 3.14 | 2.7 | 1.93 | 1.83 | 1.03 | 0.75 |
| 5 | 4.09 | 2.71 | 2.55 | 1.87 | 1.38 | 0.96 | 0.57 |
| 10 | 4.08 | 2.38 | 2.35 | 1.8 | 1.19 | 0.73 | 0.45 |
| 15 | 3.97 | 2.3 | 2.15 | 1.75 | 1.06 | 0.70 | 0.39 |

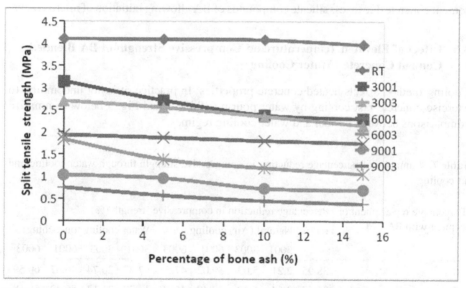

**Fig. 2.** Variation of split tensile strength with percentage of BA and temperature (NB: The last digit in the legend represents the exposure duration. For example 3001 implies that at 300 °C for 1 h exposure duration)

As shown in Table 6 and Fig. 2 above at both room temperature and 300 °C, when the percentage of bone ash for the replacement of cement increases from 0% to 15%, the split tensile strength of concrete also decreases gradually. At 300 °C in 3 h exposure, normal concrete losses about 34.15% of its initial tensile strength and this reduction become 45.84% when the percentage of BA is 15%.

At 600 °C, there is a high scale thermal damage in form of micro cracks and as a result BA partially replaced cement concrete had only 26.7% of its initial strength at 3 h exposure with 15% BA content. As shown in Table 6 at 1 h duration, the split tensile strength of concrete reduced by 9.33% at 15% replacement of cement with BA. At temperature of 900 °C and duration of 3 h, concrete with 15% BA had only about 10% of its original split tensile strength.

Generally, as it can be observed in Table 6 and Fig. 2 above as the temperature increases from 300 °C to 900 °C, the percentage reduction in residual tensile strength also increase for all percentage replacements of cement with BA. This linear variation of tensile strength as the compressive strength indicates that tensile strength also depends on the same parameters as the compressive strength. Again, the residual split tensile strength reduces as the exposure duration and Percentage of bone ash increases keeping the temperature intensity constant. Split tensile strength losses of bone ash (BA) blended concrete at elevated temperatures might be due to weak microstructure of BA blended cement concrete due to less silicate compounds of BA allowing initiation of micro cracks.

### 3.6 Effect of Elevated Temperature on Compressive Strength of BA Blended Cement Concrete - Water Cooling

Cooling method affects heated concrete properties. In practice, it is not uncommon to exercise concrete fast cooling by water pouring. Table 7 and Fig. 3 below summarize comparisons between normal and water cooling regimes.

**Table 7.** Summary of percentage reduction in compressive strength through water cooling and air cooling

| Percentage replacement of cement with BA (%) | Percentage reduction in compressive strength (%) | | | | | | | | |
|---|---|---|---|---|---|---|---|---|---|
| | RT | Natural (Air) cooling | | | | Water cooling (quenching) | | | |
| | | 3001 | 3003 | 6001 | 6003 | 3001 | 3003 | 6001 | 6003 |
| 0 | 38.95 | 2.21 | 5.03 | 39.02 | 47.52 | 7.47 | 20.74 | 46.67 | 60.59 |
| 5 | 36.47 | 3.54 | 5.32 | 37.48 | 46.78 | 14.78 | 21.14 | 56.32 | 58.68 |
| 10 | 34.18 | 3.57 | 5.91 | 34.67 | 44.41 | 24.93 | 32.91 | 59.74 | 67.79 |
| 15 | 29.36 | 5.01 | 6.16 | 39.65 | 48.13 | 40.57 | 47.34 | 74.76 | 82.66 |

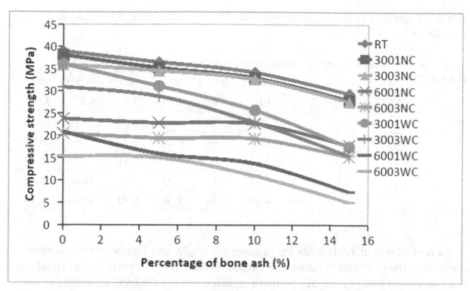

**Fig. 3.** Comparisons of residual compressive strength through water and air cooling (NB: NC = normal/ air cooling, WC = water cooling/quenching)

Relationship of cooling methods and compressive strength is presented in Table 7 and Fig. 3. As it can be observed on aforementioned table and figure by considering all contents of BA and exposure durations, at 300 °C in normal cooling regime the percentage reduction in compressive strength is from 2.21% to 6.16% where as in water cooling regime it is about 7.47% to 47.34%. Again at 600 °C in air cooling regime, the percentage reduction in compressive strength is from 34.67% to 48.13% and in water cooling regime it is about 46.67% to 82.66%.

In average as compared to air cooling, fast cooling results in up to 35% compressive strength loss. This loss could be attributed to a thermal shock formation as a result of sharp temperature drop in short period of time. Also, test results indicate compressive strength loss becomes steeper above 10% BA replacement for both cooling schemes. Similarly, further strength losses lessen as exposure temperature increases, implying for high temperature ranges (600 °C and 900 °C) effect of high temperatures is influential variable than effect of selected cooling method]. Concrete strength values gap with various cooling methods decreases as temperature increases. Overall, this research indicates cooling methods affects concrete compressive strength.

### 3.7  Effect of Heating on the Weight Loss of BA Blended Cement Concrete

Next, Table 8 below presents weight loss of specimens for various percentages of bone ash in different temperatures.

**Table 8.** Weight loss of concrete specimens for different percentages of bone ash at different temperatures

| Percentage replacement of cement with BA (%) | Percentage weight loss (%) | | | | | | |
|---|---|---|---|---|---|---|---|
| | RT | 300 °C 1 h | 300 °C 3 h | 600 °C 1 h | 600 °C 3 h | 900 °C 1 h | 900 °C 3 h |
| 0 | 0 | 3.62 | 5.97 | 5.09 | 8.24 | 9.89 | 10.10 |
| 5 | 0 | 3.77 | 6.64 | 6.36 | 8.79 | 9.4 | 9.72 |
| 10 | 0 | 3.94 | 6.92 | 7.17 | 9.11 | 9.26 | 10.34 |
| 15 | 0 | 4.12 | 7.11 | 7.35 | 9.40 | 10.06 | 10.43 |
| 20 | 0 | 4.94 | 7.49 | 8.50 | 9.73 | 10.39 | 10.78 |

As it is shown in Table 8 above, in general, weight loss increases with increasing temperature intensity and duration of exposure. Duration of temperature has significant effect on weight loss of bone ash partially replaced cement concrete especially at lower temperatures (300 °C), but its effect diminishes as temperature intensity increases. Temperatures of 600 °C and 900 °C cause hardened paste to lose its cementing property and thus significantly reduced hardened concrete mechanical properties. Due to temperature changes in concrete cause differential changes in concrete constituents, these results reduction of weight loss. Low temperature cannot remove free and capillary water and heat has low probability to transfer inner part of a concrete at this stage. Weight loss increases gradually as percentage of BA for cement replacement increases and highest loss occurred at 20% replacement of cement with BA. This is due to low binding property of bone ash as compared to cement. Also, unit weights decline as temperature surges. There is also weight loss of specimens caused by water loss. Air voids form in concrete as a result of water loss in cement paste. This results in deterioration of specimen structural integrity as temperature increases. Since BA is lightweight material as compared to OPC there is more reduction in weight as percentage of BA increases. Weight loss of specimens indicates concrete material mass loss of and subsequently excess air voids formation.

## 4 Conclusions

This research experimentally investigated behavior of concrete with bone ash partially replacing cement. Among other thing, variables including intensity of temperature, exposure duration, cooling method and various bone ash percentage replacements were studied. Next, findings inferred from this research are presented.

- Residual compressive strengths of normal concrete and concrete with BA as cement replacement (partial) have not shown significant loss in strength at 300 °C as compared to other temperature ranges. At 300 °C there is gradual compressive strength reduction up to 10% BA replacement where as 10% to 15% BA replacement, strength loss was doubled. Therefore, concrete produced by cement being partially replaced with 10% bone ash is stable up to temperature of 300 °C.

- The effect of exposure duration on concrete compressive strength with bone ash as cement replacement lessens for 900 °C as compared to 300 and 600 °C.
- The residual split tensile strength reduces as the exposure duration and percentage of bone ash increases keeping the temperature intensity constant.
- Fast cooling/water quenching results in further strength loss up to 35% as compared to air cooling.
- After exposure to elevated temperature, concrete with bone ash as cement replacement loses its weight and changes color. Also starting from 600 °C fine cracks begin to appear on its surface and the cracks became very pronounced at 900 °C.
- Overall as compared to control, usage of BA in concrete exposed to elevated temperatures results in compressive and tensile strengths losses. However as BA replacement up to 10% exhibited good concrete characteristics at elevated temperatures. Up to 10% BA replacement, as compared to control strength loss is statistically minute. This implies optimum threshold value of BA replacement of cement in concrete at elevated temperature is 10%. Therefore, a 10% replacement of cement with BA is a step forward in using waste materials as construction input materials and promoting green construction.

# References

1. EcoSmart: Environmental Impact: Cement Production and the $CO_2$ Challenge. http://www ecosmartconcrete.com/envirocement.cfm. Accessed 02 Mar 2012
2. Kassaye, A.F.: Study on the uses of Derba Ordinary Portland and Portland Pozzolana Cement for Structural Concrete Production. MSc thesis, Addis Ababa University (2014)
3. ESIA Summary Greenfield Derba Cement Project DMC: Establishment of 5,600Tpd Clinker Capacity Greenfield Cement Project and Operation of Captive Mines, Ethiopia (2008)
4. Badur, S., Chaudhary, R.: Utilization of hazardous wastes and by-products as a green concrete material through S/S process: a review. Rev. Adv. Mater. Sci. 17, 42–61 (2008)
5. Kocak, Y.: A study on the effect of fly ash and silica fume substituted cement paste and mortars. Sci. Res. Essays 5(9), 990–998 (2010)
6. Abdul, R.: Animal bone – a brief introduction. Int. J. Sci. Environ. Technol. 3(4), 1458–1464 (2014)
7. Kosmatka Steven, H., Kerkhoff, B., Panarese William, C.: Design and Control of Concrete Mixtures. 14th edn. Portland Cement Association, Skokie (2002)
8. Awol, A.: Using marble waste powder in cement and concrete production. MSc. thesis, Addis Ababa University (2011)
9. Karakurt, C., Topcu, I.B.: Effect of blended cements with natural zeolite and industrial by-products on rebar corrosion and high temperature resistance of concrete. Constr. Build. Mater. 35, 906–911 (2012)
10. Akca, A.H., Zihnioğlu, N.Ö.: High performance concrete under elevated temperatures. Constr. Build. Mater. 44, 317–328 (2013)
11. Chang, Y.F., Chen, Y.H., Sheu, M.S., Yao, G.C.: Residual stress-strain relationship for concrete after exposure to high temperatures. Cem. Concr. Res. 36(10), 1999–2002 (2006)
12. Hager, I.: Behaviour of cement concrete at high temperature. Bull. Pol. Acad. Sci. Tech. Sci. 61(1), 145–154 (2013). https://doi.org/10.2478/bpasts-2013-0013

13. ASTM C184-94e1: Standard Test Method for Fineness of Hydraulic Cement by the 150-μm (No. 100) and 75-μm (No. 200) sieves. ASTM International. West Conshohocken, PA (1994)

14. ASTM C150-05: Standard Specification for Portland Cement. ASTM International. West Conshohocken, PA (2005)

15. Dinku, A.: The need for standardization of aggregates for concrete production in Ethiopian construction industry. In: Third International Conference on Development Studies in Ethiopia, Addis Ababa, Ethiopia (2005)

16. ACI 211.1-91: Standard Practice for Selecting Proportions for Normal, Heavyweight, and Mass Concrete. An ACI Standard Reported by ACI Committee. 211, 38 (2009)

17. ASTM C39/C39M-18: Standard Test Method for Compressive Strength of Cylindrical Concrete Specimens. ASTM International. West Conshohocken, PA (2018)

18. ASTM C496/C496M-17: Standard Test Method for Split Tensile Strength of Cylindrical Concrete Specimens. ASTM International. West Conshohocken, PA (2017)

19. ASTM C618-19: Standard Specification for Coal Fly Ash and Raw or Calcined Natural Pozzolan for Use in Concrete. ASTM International. West Conshohocken, PA (2019)

20. ASTM C187-1: Standard Test Method for Normal Consistency of Hydraulic Cement. ASTM International. West Conshohocken, PA (2011)

21. Okoye, F.N., Odumodu, O.I.: Investigation into the possibility of partial replacement of cement with bone powder in concrete production. Int. J. Eng. Res. Dev. 12(10), 40–45 (2016)

22. W/amanuel, A.H., Quezon, E.T., Busier, M.: Effects of varying dosage replacement of cement content by animal bone powder in normal concrete mix production. Am. J. Civil Eng. Architect. 6(4), 133–139 (2018)

23. Falade, F., Ikponmwosa, E., Fapohunda, C.: Potential of Pulverized Bone as a Pozzolanic material. Int. J. Sci. Eng. Res. 3(7), 1–6 (2012)

24. Kowalski, R.: Mechanical properties of concrete subjected to high temperature. Architect. Civil Eng. Environ. 3(2), 61–70 (2010)

# Effect of Drainage Blanket on Reducing Uplift Pressure Under Chute Spillway: A Case Study on Megech and Ribb Dam Projects

Yirga Abebaye[1]([⊠]) and Mengiste Abate[2]

[1] Ethiopian Construction Design and Supervision Works Corporation, Addis Ababa, Ethiopia
[2] Bahir Dar University, Bahir Dar, Ethiopia

**Abstract.** Ribb and Megech dams have been designed by same designer, both dams have similar foundation, capacity and profile. However, Ribb dam spillway was designed and constructed with drainage blanket beneath the spillway channel slab. Whereas, the design and construction of Megech Dam Spillway was without this material. This study investigates the distribution of uplift pressure and seepage at control, chute and terminal section of the spillway's foundation of the two projects with and without drainage blanket using SEEP/W software and measured data. The result showed that on Ribb dam spillway up to 14% reduction of uplift pressure around control section and an average of 5% uplift pressure reduction at chute section of the spillway was found by using drainage blanket beneath the structure. However, providing drainage blanket beneath the stilling basin slab couldn't reduce the uplift pressure rather it allows the tail water to enter and surcharge the under-slab drainage system. If this drainage sand has been used on Megech dam spillway up to 12% uplift reduction around control section and an average of 3% reduction can be achieved at chute section of the spillway. Therefore, the provided drainage blanket beneath the spillway channel slab at control and chute section of Ribb dam spillway is necessary and good design. But this drainage system is not essential at the stilling basin of the spillway. Whereas, the control and chute section of Megech dam spillway without drainage blanket beneath channel slab is not safe against uplift pressure.

**Keywords:** Ribb · Megech · Spillway · Uplift pressure · Seepage · Numerical model

## 1 Introduction

Water resources are nowadays important to be controlled in the view of limited available water in accordance with the increasing demand for water. Hydraulic structures such as dams, reservoirs, barrages, weirs are those structures used for controlling water resources.

Ribb and Megech Dam Projects are located in Lake Tana sub Basin, in the upper Blue Nile Basin, Ethiopia. Ribb and Megech rivers in which these two dam projects

© ICST Institute for Computer Sciences, Social Informatics and Telecommunications Engineering 2021
Published by Springer Nature Switzerland AG 2021. All Rights Reserved
M. A. Delele et al. (Eds.): ICAST 2020, LNICST 385, pp. 17–35, 2021.
https://doi.org/10.1007/978-3-030-80618-7_2

are being developed are two of the main streams flowing in to Lake Tana. Both these Dam Projects are being constructed through the Ethiopian Government and they are multi-purpose by providing controlled discharge to irrigate 37,000 ha of land in Fogera and Denbia floodplains, expected to harvest fish, to control flood and Megech will also supply drinking water for Gondar Town [1, 2]. These show that the projects have crucial role for alleviating problems particularly in the study area and for the country at large. The design and supervision work of these two projects are conducted by Ethiopian Construction Design & Supervision Works Corporation, Water & Energy Design and Supervision Works Sector in association with TAHAL Consulting Engineers, while the construction is carried out by the Ethiopian Construction Works Corporation, Water Infrastructure Construction Sector.

For hydraulic structures constructed on permeable foundations, seepage occurs under the foundation of the structures due to the difference of water levels between upstream and downstream sides of the structures [3]. The effects of seepage on the foundation of hydraulic structures can be classified into three parts: uplift force, seepage discharge and exit gradient. Uplift force reduces the shear resistance between structure and its foundation, causes a reduction in stability of the structure against sliding or overturning. Increasing the seepage velocity at the downstream end of hydraulic structures, may cause the movement of soil particles and accordingly accelerates piping and soil erosion. The exit gradient is the main design criterion in determining the safety of hydraulic structures against the piping phenomenon [4].

The hydraulic engineer should carefully design the hydraulic structures such that it can perform its function safely. The most critical aspect of the design of such structures is the design concerning its foundation. The water seeping underneath the hydraulic structures endanger the safety of the structure and may cause failure. Therefore, the seepage under hydraulic structures can be considered one of the most important problems in the hydraulic structures safety [5]. Due to water under the spillway many catastrophic failures of the spillway which leads to the whole dam failure has been occurred in the world; for instance, Mt. Carmel Dam located in North Dakota, Big Sandy Dam Spillway: June 1983, and Hyrum Dam Spillway [6].

Ribb and Megech dam projects have appurtenance structures such as spillway, Intake tower and conduit which are very vital for the whole dam operation and safety. To achieve the projects final target, the necessary defensive design measures for the appurtenance structures should be taken into considerations which basically ensure safety and economy [7, 8]. The foundation, capacity and profile of Megech and Ribb dam spillways are almost the same. But beneath the chute, a drainage blanket typically consisting of drainage gravel (50 cm thick) and filter sand (30 cm) is provided at Ribb dam project to control seepage and relieve any hydrostatic pressures. Whereas, in Megech dam project, there is no any drainage and filter material provided beneath the chute slab except bedding sand placed for protection of the perforated transversal pipes which are located within 20 m interval parallel to the cutoff wall. The objective of this study was to analyze the effect of drainage blanket on reducing uplift pressure and seepage through the foundation of side channel chute spillway. This can be complemented through specific objectives; by analyzing the uplift pressure and seepage condition with and without drainage blanket beneath the spillway channel slab and by evaluating drainage system of the chute spillway. Hence, in this study the distribution of uplift pressure and the seepage condition through the spillways chute foundation of Megech and Ribb dam projects with and without drainage blanket was analyzed by using the numerical model, SEEP/W software (program) which is a sub-program of the Geo-Studio software. The measured uplift data were used for validation purpose. The study will have a good outcome in the future to take necessary defensive design measures under consideration for similar projects which will be conducted.

## 2 Materials and Methods

### 2.1 Study Area

The study was conducted on Megech and Ribb Dam which are located in Lake Tana Sub Basin, as shown in Fig. 1.

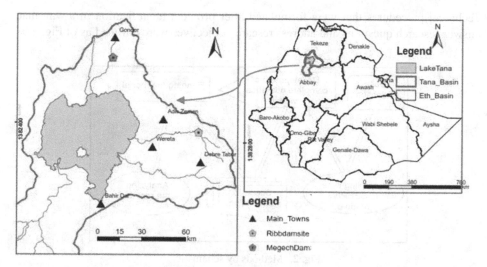

**Fig. 1.** Study area map

The mean annual rainfall at Megech and Ribb dam site is 1100 mm and 1400 mm respectively. The catchment area of Ribb is 685 km$^2$ and the dam maximum reservoir area is 10.02 km$^2$. Whereas, Megech has 424 km$^2$ catchment area and the maximum reservoir area is 8.7 km$^2$ [7, 8].

### 2.2 Materials

**Design Documents.** Laboratory test result certificates, as-built drawings, design documents, and technical specifications were used. Moreover, the engineering drawings for the spillway plan and section was considered.

**Digital Elevation Model.** A 30 m by 30 m resolution ASTER Global Digital Elevation Model which can be download from EOSDIS website (http://reverb.echo.nasa.gov/reverb) was used for topographic explanations of the study area by using ArcGIS.

**Geo-Studio (SEEP/W) Software.** The SEEP/W software (program) which is a subprogram of the Geo-Studio software was used to develop a numerical model that enables to simulate the distribution of uplift pressure and the seepage condition through the spillways chute foundation of Megech and Ribb dam projects with and without filter and drainage blanket. SEEP/W is a finite element package that can be used to model the fluid flow and pore-water pressure distribution within materials such as soil and rock [9]. Its comprehensive formulation makes it possible to analyze both simple and highly complex seepage problems [10].

### 2.3  Methods

Technical procedures that were formulated after problem identification in a way that answer research questions and address research objectives were outlined as of Fig. 2.

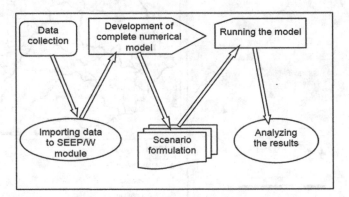

**Fig. 2.**  Methods by schematic

**Numerical Model Setup.**  After viewing the theoretical engineering basis, features and benefits for the SEEP/W program, the work procedures for the numerical model on the SEEP/W programs were done as follows:

*Construct the Model.* The first step to develop a numerical model in SEEP/W was defining the working area size, choosing the engineering units and setting the used scale. Sketching axes to define an evenly-spaced region for the axes, the number of increments along each axis was calculated by SEEP/W when the axes were generated. Then sketch model dimensions for drawing the problem region has been prepared.

*Analysis Parameters.* The first analysis parameter was the analysis type, the analysis type was selected as steady-state solution. Because under steady state conditions, the difference between input flux and output flux is zero at all times and solution to steady state, laminar-flow seepage problems can be obtained with the Laplace and Darcy equations. The analysis control was chosen as two-dimensional analysis. The coefficient of permeability of the foundation under the spillway chute had determined by Falling head and Packer test for both Megech and Ribb dam projects. Accordingly, the average hydraulic conductivity value has been fixed for Megech $4.71 * 10^{-6}$ m/s and for Ribb $4.74 * 10^{-6}$ m/s as per the tests result [11, 12]. Regions and finite elements were generated, the region boundary was drawn and number of elements in X and Y directions for region was chosen. The region was divided automatically by SEEP/W to number of elements.

*Boundary Conditions.* Boundary conditions in the study problem means the total head acting on upstream and downstream soil free surfaces. The total head acting on upstream side in this study problem is the normal pool level, and the total head acting on the downstream side is equal to zero since there is no stagnant tail water.

*Drawing Flux Section.* A flux section was required for the aim of studying problem to compute total seepage flow through floor of hydraulic structure model, flux section was drawn completely across elements which located under the hydraulic model floor in order to include flux through elements.

*Verification of the Studying Problem Data.* Before solution start, the problem data should be verified by SEEP/W to ensure that the data has been defined correctly, SEEP/W was performed a number of checks on the nodes and elements data, including filling any missing data, any missing node number, element overlap, initial water table, and appear these checks in the dialog box.

*Modelling Scenarios.* To analyze the distribution, impact of uplift pressure and pattern of the flow condition through the foundation of side channel chute spillway, model simulation with and without drainage sand beneath the chute slab were done for both Ribb and Megech Dam Spillways. During the model simulation the perforated transversal pipes which are located within 20 m interval parallel to each of the cutoff wall and the cutoff wall itself was considered. The effect and advantage of these drain pipes and cutoff walls was evaluated.

**Output and Results.** After the previous steps were done the output results can earn by seep/w as generating contour plot, displaying velocity vectors that represent the flow direction, displaying the computed flux across the specified section, displaying the numerical information for individual nodes and elements, and plotting graphs of the computed results.

**Validation of Model Results.** The simulated results obtained from SEEP/W software for different scenarios was compared as per the objectives and literatures stated on literature review portion of this study. Moreover, model results were validated with recorded data from installed Piezometer on the actual site.

## 3 Results and Discussion

### 3.1 Spillway Modelling and Model Result with and Without Drainage Sand

Figure 3 shows model simulation for Ribb Spillway cross-section with drainage blanket as designed and constructed and Fig. 4 displays model simulation of this Spillway cross-section without drainage blanket beneath the channel slab. In the same way the model is simulated for Megech Dam Spillway for the original design without drainage blanket beneath the chute slab and with sand blanket in place as of Fig. 9 and 10 respectively.

**Model Simulation for Ribb Dam Spillway as Designed**

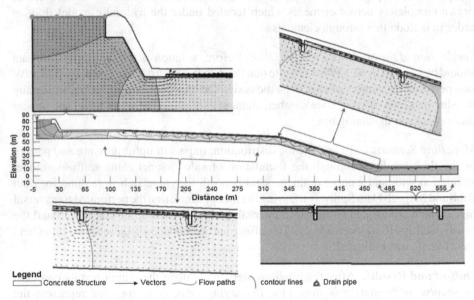

**Fig. 3.** Ribb spillway cross-section with drainage sand as designed and constructed

## Model Simulation for Ribb Dam Spillway without Drainage Sand

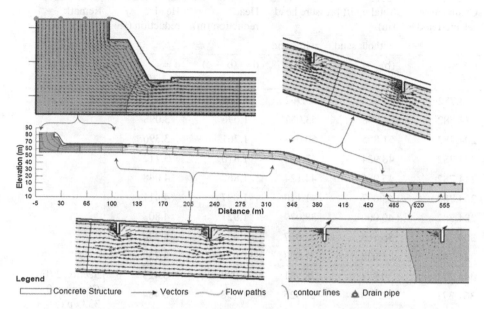

Legend

☐ Concrete Structure    ——→ Vectors    ——⁄ Flow paths    ╲ contour lines    ▲ Drain pipe

**Fig. 4.** Ribb spillway cross-section without drainage sand beneath channel chute slab

## Model Results Head Comparison of Ribb Spillway at Each Section
(See Table 1).

**Table 1.** Total uplift pressure head comparison of Ribb spillway with and without drainage sand blanket

| Chainage of selected nodes | Total uplift pressure head (m) | | Head reduction (m) | Head reduction (%) | Remark |
|---|---|---|---|---|---|
| | without sand | with sand | | | |
| (a) | (b) | (c) | d = (b − c) | e = (d * 100)/b | |
| 44.967 | 76.761 | 65.976 | 10.785 | 14.050 | Section 1 (From Chainage 0 + 000 up to 0 + 333) Chute with gentle slope (0.45%) |
| 64.968 | 73.355 | 65.623 | 7.732 | 10.540 | |
| 84.969 | 69.939 | 65.250 | 4.689 | 6.704 | |
| 104.970 | 66.518 | 64.879 | 1.638 | 2.463 | |
| 124.714 | 63.203 | 61.639 | 1.564 | 2.475 | |
| 144.782 | 60.451 | 58.914 | 1.536 | 2.542 | |

(*continued*)

**Table 1.** (*continued*)

| Chainage of selected nodes | Total uplift pressure head (m) | | Head reduction (m) | Head reduction (%) | Remark |
|---|---|---|---|---|---|
| | without sand | with sand | | | |
| (a) | (b) | (c) | d = (b − c) | e = (d * 100)/b | |
| 164.782 | 57.612 | 55.992 | 1.620 | 2.812 | |
| 184.782 | 54.748 | 53.052 | 1.696 | 3.098 | |
| 204.782 | 51.855 | 50.094 | 1.761 | 3.396 | |
| 224.782 | 48.934 | 47.118 | 1.816 | 3.712 | |
| 244.782 | 45.986 | 44.124 | 1.862 | 4.048 | |
| 264.782 | 43.007 | 41.110 | 1.897 | 4.411 | |
| 284.782 | 40.000 | 38.079 | 1.921 | 4.803 | |
| 304.782 | 36.963 | 35.027 | 1.936 | 5.238 | |
| 324.782 | 33.928 | 31.983 | 1.945 | 5.733 | |
| 344.271 | 30.971 | 28.981 | 1.989 | 6.423 | Section 2 (From Chainage 0 + 333 up to 0 + 468) Chute with steep slope (33.31%) |
| 364.271 | 27.723 | 25.925 | 1.798 | 6.484 | |
| 384.271 | 24.491 | 22.875 | 1.616 | 6.599 | |
| 404.271 | 21.286 | 19.841 | 1.444 | 6.785 | |
| 424.271 | 18.024 | 16.698 | 1.326 | 7.357 | |
| 445.241 | 14.626 | 13.625 | 1.001 | 6.845 | |
| 461.453 | 11.943 | 10.795 | 1.148 | 9.612 | |
| 479.145 | 10.574 | 10.165 | 0.409 | 3.868 | Section 3 (From Chainage 0 + 468 up to 0 + 568) stilling basin with 0% slope |
| 499.795 | 10.077 | 10.102 | −0.026 | −0.253 | |
| 516.477 | 9.899 | 10.100 | −0.201 | −2.033 | |
| 530.297 | 10.069 | 10.152 | −0.083 | −0.826 | |
| 544.157 | 10.320 | 10.422 | −0.102 | −0.987 | |
| 558.829 | 10.657 | 10.715 | −0.058 | −0.540 | |

The negative value at stilling basin section of the spillway indicates that the total head becomes greater when there is drainage blanket and perforated drain pipe beneath the stilling basin slab. The elevation head at this section is below the downstream river water level. The permeability of the drainage sand placed beneath the stilling basin slab is higher than the permeability of the downstream foundation. Due to this elevation head and permeability variation there is back water flow from downstream to stilling basin as shown on Fig. 9 which develops pore water pressure under the slab structure. The bedding slope of both transversal and longitudinal perforated pipe is horizontal which keeps the accumulated water to be stagnant rather than easily drain. That is why the total head becomes higher when there is drainage sand blanket beneath the stilling basin slab (Fig. 5).

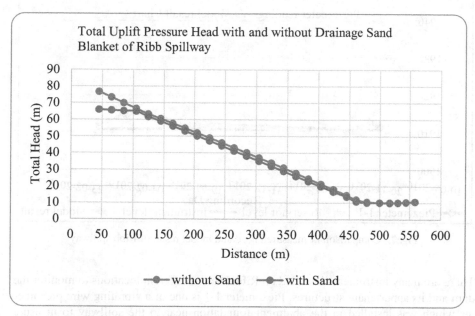

**Fig. 5.** Total uplift head comparison of Ribb spillway with and without drainage blanket

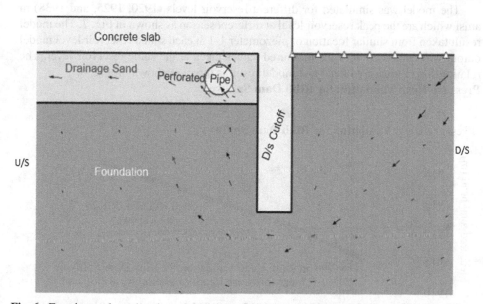

**Fig. 6.** Entering and surcharging of d/s tail water to the under-slab drainage system of stilling basin

## Comparison of Measured Head and Model Result of Ribb Spillway

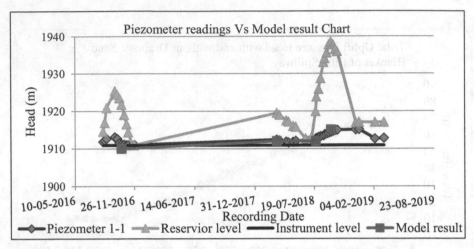

**Fig. 7.** Comparison of measured head and model result of Ribb spillway

There are many instruments installed on Ribb Dam at different locations to monitor the dam and its appurtenant structures. Piezometer 1-1 is one of a vibrating wire piezometer which was installed in the abutment foundation near to the spillway to measure ground water elevations and pore water pressures around spillway foundations. Data was recorded every week from this piezometer. More than three years data from piezometer 1-1 was taken for validation purpose of the numerical model.

The model was simulated for different reservoir levels (1920, 1925, and 1938) m amsl which are the peak reservoir level at different season as shown in Fig. 7. The model result taken from similar location of piezometer 1-1 at each stated reservoir level model output was compared with the measured values taken at the same reservoir level. The relationship of measured head and model result is direct as shown on Fig. 8.

**Pressure Head Validation for Ribb Dam Spillway**

### Pressure Head Validation for Ribb Dam Spillway.

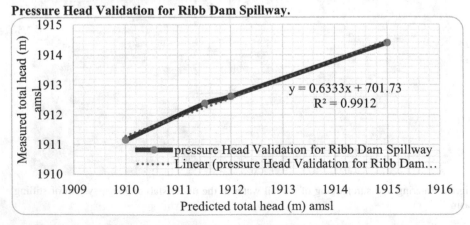

**Fig. 8.** Pressure head validation for Ribb dam spillway

## Model Simulation for Megech Dam Spillway as Designed

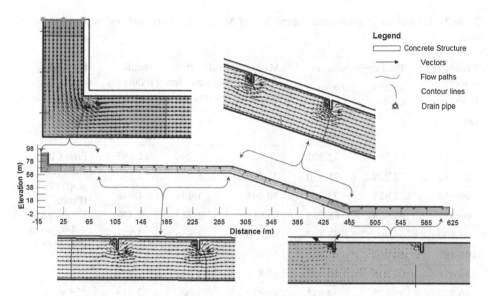

**Fig. 9.** Megech spillway cross-section without drainage sand as designed and constructed

## Model Simulation for Megech Dam Spillway with Drainage Sand

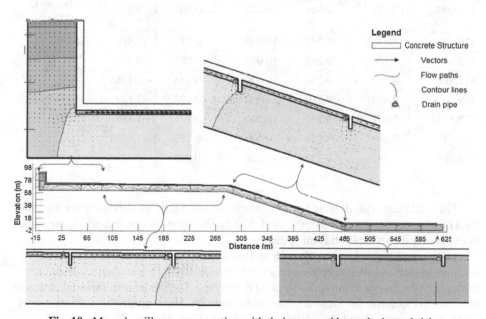

**Fig. 10.** Megech spillway cross-section with drainage sand beneath channel slab

(See Table 2).

**Table 2.** Total uplift pressure head comparison of Megech spillway with and without drainage sand

| Chainage of selected nodes | Total uplift head (m) | | Measured Total uplift head (m) | Head reduction (m) | Head reduction (%) | Remark |
|---|---|---|---|---|---|---|
| | without sand | with sand | | | | |
| (a) | (b) | (c) | (d) | e = (b − c) | f = (e * 100)/b | |
| 9.911 | 82.597 | 72.301 | 72.023 | 10.296 | 12.465 | First Chute |
| 29.732 | 77.729 | 71.830 | 71.220 | 5.900 | 7.590 | with gentle slope (1%) |
| 49.554 | 72.811 | 71.364 | 70.491 | 1.448 | 1.988 | (From |
| 66.311 | 69.928 | 68.215 | 69.018 | 1.713 | 2.450 | Chainage 0 |
| 85.500 | 66.999 | 65.143 | 66.796 | 1.856 | 2.771 | + 000 up to 0 + 284) |
| 106.187 | 64.067 | 62.204 | 66.460 | 1.863 | 2.909 | |
| 130.478 | 60.535 | 59.099 | 62.873 | 1.437 | 2.373 | |
| 296.232 | 35.875 | 34.815 | 40.812 | 1.060 | 2.955 | 2nd steep |
| 411.046 | 18.519 | 18.156 | 23.624 | 0.363 | 1.959 | Chute (33.42% |
| 429.690 | 15.582 | 15.277 | 18.838 | 0.306 | 1.962 | slope) |
| 448.551 | 12.618 | 12.413 | 13.621 | 0.205 | 1.624 | (Chainage 0 |
| 461.600 | 10.328 | 9.521 | 10.222 | 0.807 | 7.815 | + 284 up to 0 + 464) |
| 476.125 | 9.536 | 9.261 | 10.000 | 0.275 | 2.888 | Stilling |
| 495.988 | 9.168 | 9.251 | 10.000 | −0.083 | −0.905 | basin with 0% slope |
| 517.888 | 9.057 | 9.250 | 10.000 | −0.193 | −2.126 | (Chainage 0 |
| 539.544 | 9.057 | 9.250 | 10.000 | −0.193 | −2.129 | + 464 up to 0 + 610) |
| 557.131 | 9.079 | 9.250 | 10.000 | −0.171 | −1.885 | |
| 576.625 | 9.098 | 9.250 | 10.000 | −0.152 | −1.670 | |
| 599.085 | 9.282 | 9.252 | 10.000 | 0.030 | 0.319 | |

The total head with drainage sand beneath the stilling basin slab is higher than the total head under the slab without the sand. The justification for this scenario is the same as explained above for Ribb Dam spillway.

The ground water level at Megech spillway foundation was directly measured by using an apparatus called deep meter during borehole drilling for anchor bar installation throughout the length of the spillway at 20 m interval. The model result was taken from the selected location for ground water measurement. The measured head and model result were compared and the relationship is direct (Figs. 11 and 12).

**Pressure Head Validation for Megech Dam Spillway**

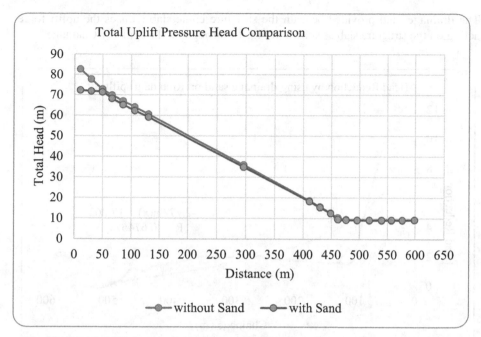

**Fig. 11.** Residual head comparison of Megech spillway with and without drainage blanket

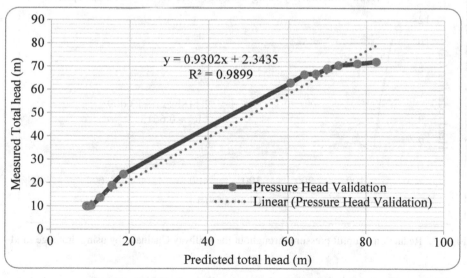

**Fig. 12.** Pressure head validation for Megech dam spillway

## 3.2 Uplift Pressure with and Without Drainage Sand

The simulated model results of both Ribb and Megech Dam Spillways with and without drainage sand beneath the spillway chute are compared as per the objective of this study.

The drainage sand provided beneath the structure chute slab reduces the uplift force acting on the structure slab as shown in Fig. 13 throughout the spillway Chainage.

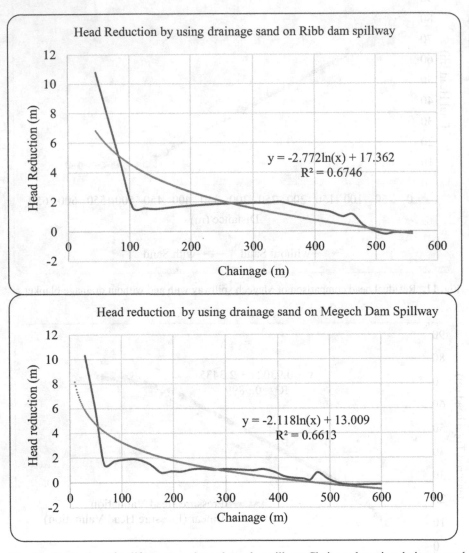

**Fig. 13.** Reduction of uplift pressure throughout the spillway Chainage by using drainage sand

Drainage blankets, drain pipes and cutoff walls are considered as effective measures to reduce seepage, uplift pressure and exit gradient under the foundation of hydraulic structures [4].

Cutoff walls were designed and constructed within 20 m interval throughout the spillway reach and perforated transversal drain pipes were installed parallel to each cutoff wall on both Ribb and Megech spillways. This arrangement causes the uplift reduction by providing drainage sand beneath the structure not same throughout the chute and ups and downs as shown in Fig. 13.

### 3.3 Distribution of Seepage and Uplift Pressure at Spillway Sections

**Seepage and Uplift Pressure at Control and Chute Sections.** The                    main seepage reduction zone for a chute spillway is typically located at the control section area [13]. The Control Section at Ribb Dam Spillway includes an impervious blanket constructed within the cross section of the approach channel, an impervious embankment constructed behind the abutment walls, a cutoff wall and a grout curtain which extends beneath control structure that makes the spillway safe against uplift pressure as shown in Fig. 14.

**Fig. 14.** Approach and control section of Ribb dam spillway

Whereas, the topographic condition of Megech dam spillway requires an impervious embankment which should be constructed behind the abutment walls or any other barrier to block the reservoir water entering to the back of the approach wall that may increase the uplift pressure under the near chute slab as shown on Fig. 15.

The seepage coming from reservoir under approach slab seeps to the foundation of spillway channel slab and intercepted by transverse perforated drain pipes that typically provided at 20 m intervals to intercept and convey seepage flows into a collection manhole located at either end of each of the drain pipes. From the coming seepage 42.24% of the seepage removes by the first transverse perforated pipe. In this case the first transverse perforated pipe in the chute section serves as pressure relief drains as shown in Fig. 16. The diameter of this first transverse perforated pipe is 25 cm which is more than enough to accommodate the coming seepage, $1.74E-05$ m$^3$/s. As it is stated on US Army Corps of Engineers Manual the perforated transverse drainpipes should not be less than 20 cm in diameter in order to minimize the chance of plugging and to facilitate inspection and

**Fig. 15.** Approach and control section of Megech dam spillway

maintenance. Therefore, the size of this pipe installed on Megech and Ribb dam spillway is acceptable.

A longitudinal pipe is used to connect the manholes and convey seepage water into the outlet channel. This drainage system reduces the seepage and uplift pressure from upstream to downstream gradually. Figure 16 shows the interception of the coming seepage by transverse perforated drainpipes and reduction of uplift pressure towards downstream.

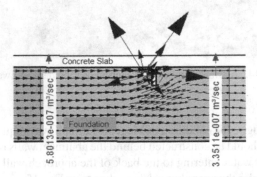

**Fig. 16.** Interception of Seepage flow under foundation of Megech dam spillway

**Seepage and Uplift Pressure at Terminal Section of the Spillway.** The first preference is to provide a narrow basin, where feasible, that can be designed to resist the entire uplift pressure that occurs due to the hydraulic jump by weight rather than relying on drains. Because drains may plug easily, difficult for maintenance and increase risk when they may not be fully functional [14]. However, for wide basins where it is determined that the drainage system is viable and cost effective, a separate (i.e. isolated from the chute under slab drainage system in order to prevent surcharging) under slab drainage system consisting of a drainage blanket (filter sand and/or drainage gravel) and perforated drainpipes may be incorporated. Water collected by the transverse drainpipes would normally be conveyed into manholes that would also permit access for inspection and maintenance. Although the under-slab drainage system will ordinarily be below the bed of the outlet channel, it may be possible in some cases to discharge some of the water by gravity from the manholes back into the stilling basin near the start of the jump. In other instances, pumping may be required. Careful attention to backfill provisions and cutoff requirements particularly along the sides and downstream end of the basin slab is required to prevent tail water from entering and surcharging the under slab drainage system (i.e. becomes a pump) [13].

Megech and Ribb Dam Spillway Stilling Basins are wide which leads the drainage system to be under slab drainage system consisting of a drainage blanket and perforated drainpipes that is viable and cost effective rather than providing a narrow basin that can be designed to resist the entire uplift pressure due to the hydraulic jump by weight. Although, the Stilling Basin at Ribb Dam Spillway is designed and constructed with a drainage blanket and perforated drainpipes as stated above, the drainage system is not isolated from the chute under slab drainage system in order to prevent surcharging that increases the uplift pressure under the stilling basin. Whereas, in the Megech dam spillway, there is no any drainage blanket provided beneath the stilling basin slab except the bedding sand placed for protection of the perforated transversal pipes which are located within 20 m interval parallel to the cutoff wall.

The model simulation result of both Megech dam spillway and Ribb Dam Spillway shows no reduction of uplift pressure in the stilling basin by using drainage blanket beneath the stilling basin slab rather it allows the tail water to enter and surcharge the under-slab drainage system as shown in Fig. 6. The slope of the stilling basin is 0% towards downstream and the ground level of the abutment behind the wall on each side (left and right) of the basin as well as the level of tail water is above the foundation of the stilling basin floor on both Megech dam spillway and Ribb Dam Spillway. Due to this elevation difference the drainage sand provided beneath stilling basin slab can't drain the develop water. This situation enforces the water developed under the stilling basin slab to be stagnant that increases the uplift pressure.

## 4 Conclusion and Recommendations

In this study, uplift pressure and seepage condition under side channel chute spillway was studied with and without drainage sand blanket beneath the chute slab considering the case of Megech and Ribb Dam Spillways. From the analysis, conclusion and recommendations were made.

### 4.1 Conclusion

The effect of drainage blanket on reducing uplift force varies on the different sections (control section, chute and stilling basin) of the spillway.

On Ribb dam spillway up to 14% reduction of uplift pressure around control section and an average of 5% uplift pressure reduction at chute section of the spillway was detected by using drainage sand beneath the structure. But no reduction of uplift pressure in the stilling basin by using drainage sand blanket beneath the stilling basin slab rather it allows the tail water to enter and surcharge the under-slab drainage system. Because the slope of the stilling basin is 0% towards downstream and the ground level of the abutment behind the wall on each side (left and right) of the basin as well as the level of tail water is above the foundation of the stilling basin floor. Moreover, the permeability of the drainage sand placed beneath the stilling basin slab is higher than the permeability of the downstream foundation. Due to this elevation and permeability difference the drainage sand provided beneath stilling basin slab can't drain the develop water. This situation en-forces the water developed under the stilling basin slab to be stagnant that increases the uplift pressure. Therefore, the provided drainage sand blanket beneath the spillway channel slab at control and chute section of Ribb dam spillway is necessary and good design. But this drainage system is not essential at the stilling basin of the spillway.

If this drainage sand has been used on Megech dam spillway up to 12% uplift reduction around control section and an average of 3% reduction can be achieved at chute section of the spillway. Therefore, the design and construction of control and chute section of Megech dam spillway without drainage sand blanket beneath channel slab is not safe against uplift pressure.

## 4.2 Recommendations

The stilling basin drainage system of Ribb dam spillway should be isolated from the chute under slab drainage system in order to prevent surcharging that increases the uplift pressure under the stilling basin. In addition to this careful attention to backfill requirements and the extent of cutoff walls is required to ensure that tail water is prevented from entering and surcharging the under-slab drainage system at the stilling basin.

The topographic condition of Megech dam spillway around control section requires an impervious embankment which should be constructed behind the abutment walls or any other barrier to block the reservoir water entering to the back of the approach wall that may increase the uplift pressure under the near chute slab.

Piezometers should be installed in the drainage blanket and deeper strata to monitor the performance of the drainage systems. If the drains become plugged or otherwise non effective, uplift pressures will increase which could adversely affect the stability of the structure.

If there will be an improved method to know the amount of water flowing into cracks and joints during spillway releases, the water can be considered in addition to ground water and the seepage from reservoir for better estimation of uplift force.

## References

1. T.C.E.L. MoWIE: Megech Dam_Final Planning Feasibility_Report_Volume 1-Rev, Addis Ababa, Ethiopia (2007)
2. T.C.E.L. MoWIE: Ribb Dam Feasibility Study Main Report_August_2007, Addis Ababa, Ethiopia (2007)
3. Garg, S.K.: Irrigation Engineering and Hydraulic Structyres.pdf, 9th 2005, Khanna (1976)

4. Shayan, K.: Effects of blanket, drains, and cutoff wall on reducing uplift pressure, seepage, and exit gradient under hydraulic structures, vol. 13, no. 4 (2015)
5. Moharrami, A.: Performance of Cutoff Walls Under Hydraulic Structures Against Uplift Pressure and Piping Phenomenon, no. February 2014 (2015)
6. G.C.I. Huzjak, R.J.: Water_Under_the_Spillway-Catastrophic_Failure_Prevented.pdf (2007)
7. T.C.E.L. MoWIE: Ribb Dam Detail Design (Final Report), Addis Ababa, Ethiopia (2006)
8. T.C.E.L. MoWIE: Megech Dam Detail Design (Final Report), Addis Ababa, Ethiopia (2010)
9. A. Geo-Slope International Ltd, C., Seepage Modeling with SEEP/W 2007, no. May, Canada (2009)
10. Broaddus, M.R.: Performing a steady-state seepage analysis using SEEP/W: a primer for engineering students (2015)
11. MoWIE: Ribb Dam Geological and Geothecnical Final Report, Addis Ababa, Ethiopia (2007)
12. MoWIE: Megech Dam Final Geotechnical and Geological Detail Design, vol. V (2008)
13. A.E. Alberta Transportation: Water Control Structures _ Selected Design Guidelines, no. November (2004)
14. Hussien, G.O.: Effect of under drain pipe on seepage analysis under hydraulic structures, no. March (2017)

# Optimization of Rock Bolt and Concrete Lining Combination: A Case of AKH Railway Tunnel Project

Sinodos S. Sefene[1](✉) and Henok F. Gebregziabher[2]

[1] Debre Markos University, Debre Markos, Ethiopia
sinodos_shetie@dmu.edu.et
[2] Addis Ababa Institute of Technology, Addis Ababa, Ethiopia

**Abstract.** Concrete lining and rock bolts are usually provided to support excavated tunnels on different ground conditions. These two support systems are worthy and need in-depth consideration as their impact on tunnel cost and deformation are critical. The optimum use of these support systems is a challenge that demands the best design solution. In order to facilitate the determination of the optimal combination of the two, an optimization scheme has been devised in this study using Finite Element Analysis (FEA) and MATLAB software for a specific under-construction tunnel in Karakore, Ethiopia. The tunnel displacements found from the FEA and the cost of tunnel construction were modeled using polynomial functions with a multi-objective optimization since the problem has two objectives. Considering displacement and cost functions, the optimum combination of rock bolt and concrete lining has been found. The result shows that the optimum combination can be found by increasing the number of rock bolts. The finite element analysis gives a total displacement of 6.34 cm in the best scenario case, which is slightly greater than the observed total displacement of about 6 cm. The total cost of rock bolt and concrete lining for the optimum combination becomes $30,700 per meter length of tunnel rock bolt and concrete lining construction.

**Keywords:** Rock bolt · Concrete lining · Optimization · Finite element method · MATLAB

## 1 Introduction

Based on the ground condition, rock bolts and concrete lining are provided as means of support for tunnels. These two support systems have an impact on the cost and the convergence of the tunnel. Designing the rock bolt for underground excavation considers the type of bolt (Smith 1993), bolt pattern, spacing, and size (Nguyena et al. 2015). In addition, bolt profile configuration affects load transfer capacity between the bolt and grout (Mostafa et al. 2015). The optimal profile geometry of the rock bolt is affected by the mechanical properties of the grout and the confining pressure (Cao et al. 2014). The bolt-grouting combined support system is proposed to prevent high stress (Chen et al.

© ICST Institute for Computer Sciences, Social Informatics and Telecommunications Engineering 2021
Published by Springer Nature Switzerland AG 2021. All Rights Reserved
M. A. Delele et al. (Eds.): ICAST 2020, LNICST 385, pp. 36–47, 2021.
https://doi.org/10.1007/978-3-030-80618-7_3

2016). By considering the different properties of rock bolt, the designer has to carry out an optimum rock bolt design.

The cause and effect of parameters are collected by using the fishbone diagram (Meyer et al. 2013). The fishbone diagram identifies many possible causes for an effect or problem. A Pareto chart is a type of chart that representing individual values in descending order by bars, and the cumulative total by the line. The purpose of the Pareto chart is to highlight the most influential factors (Visual-paradigm 2018).

The process of designing tunnel support lining involves the determination of design variables based on experience and intuition. The development of some standard methods for producing optimal designs would have practical significance. The subject of optimization of tunnel lining (Pérez-Romero et al. 2006) has been treated such as in topology optimization (Liu and Jin 2006; Yin and Yang 2000; Nguyen et al. 2014), shape optimization (Ghabraie et al. 2010), multi-objective optimization (Tonon et al. 2002) and modified colliding bodies optimization (Fazli 2017). Gamultiobj is one of multi-objective solver which is used to solve problems in several variables (Messac 2015). The optimum combination of rock bolt and concrete lining is found based on the principles of optimization that the objective function is optimized while performance and other constraints are satisfied (Arora 2004; Papalambros and Wilde 2000; Ravindran 2006).

The design of tunnels cannot proceed simply in the same way as a structure being exposed to well-defined loading conditions. In addition, there is no universally accepted tunnel design method; rather experience and engineering judgment play a great role. Besides the engineering judgment, the support system could be designed prudently to get an optimum solution so as to control the convergence of the tunnel (Kersten 2008).

Ethiopia has implemented many tunneling projects after launching the railway network throughout its corridors. Since there is little experience in the design and construction of tunnels in the country, this study aims at proposing an optimization method of tunnel support design which can be a contribution to the practical applications by considering the different configurations of rock bolt and concrete linings. This has been done by using numerical methods by employing the ground data taken from the Awash Kombolcha Haragebeya (AKH) railway tunnel project. Since there is a lack of refined parameters for seismic analyses, like site-specific ground motion data, the analysis considered only static conditions.

## 2  Design of Data for Optimization

Once the possible collections of parameters are determined through the fish-bone diagram (Meyer et al. 2013), the Pareto chart is developed. Pareto chart is used in the selection of those very influential parameters and narrows down the parameters to use in the design of the experiment (Visual-paradigm 2018). The number of rock bolt and concrete lining thickness have been selected as causal parameters. The effect of small change in parameter magnitude is first determined by using Eq. 1, while the cumulative result of parameters, known as the response, is found using Eq. 2. The parameters with higher coefficients are indicated to have more effect on the cost and settlement of the tunnel. Once the parameters are determined, the next step is the design of data for optimization.

$$a_i p_i = a_i p_{oi} + a_i \Delta p_i \tag{1}$$

where, $a_i$ = regression coefficients

$p_{oi}$ = operating mean parameter magnitude and

$\Delta p_i$ = small change in parameter magnitude.

$$Response = \sum_{i=1}^{n} a_i p_i \tag{2}$$

where, $a_i$ = regression coefficients and

$p_i$ = parameters (number of rock bolt and thickness of concrete lining).

The design of data for optimization involves the generation of the combination of parameters in which the study becomes easy to understand in a better way. For this particular research, two levels of design of data are used as shown in Table 1. The number of rock bolt is labeled as B and concrete lining thickness as L. The two parameters, B and L vary between 7 and 19 and 10 cm and 40 cm respectively, are taken based on practical considerations.

**Table 1.** Parameter combinations used in the analysis

| S. no | Combination code | Number of rock bolt | Lining thickness (cm) |
|-------|------------------|---------------------|-----------------------|
| 1 | $B_1L_1$ | 7 | 10 |
| 2 | $B_1L_2$ | 7 | 20 |
| 3 | $B_1L_3$ | 7 | 25 |
| 4 | $B_1L_4$ | 7 | 30 |
| 5 | $B_1L_5$ | 7 | 40 |
| 6 | $B_2L_1$ | 11 | 10 |
| 7 | $B_2L_2$ | 11 | 20 |
| 8 | $B_2L_3$ | 11 | 25 |
| 9 | $B_2L_4$ | 11 | 30 |
| 10 | $B_2L_5$ | 11 | 40 |
| 11 | $B_3L_1$ | 15 | 10 |
| 12 | $B_3L_2$ | 15 | 20 |
| 13 | $B_3L_3$ | 15 | 25 |
| 14 | $B_3L_4$ | 15 | 30 |
| 15 | $B_3L_5$ | 15 | 40 |

(continued)

**Table 1.** (*continued*)

| S. no | Combination code | Number of rock bolt | Lining thickness (cm) |
|---|---|---|---|
| 16 | $B_4L_1$ | 19 | 10 |
| 17 | $B_4L_2$ | 19 | 20 |
| 18 | $B_4L_3$ | 19 | 25 |
| 19 | $B_4L_4$ | 19 | 30 |
| 20 | $B_4L_5$ | 19 | 40 |

To achieve the objective of the research, the flowchart as shown in Fig. 1 was developed to show the algorism followed from the design of data optimization up to the numerical analysis for optimized design combination.

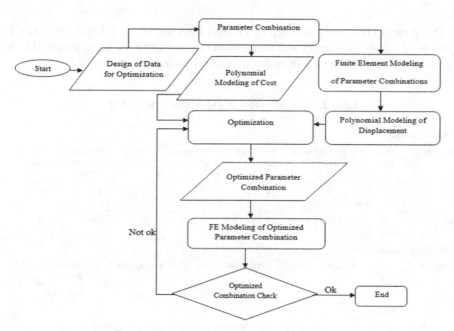

**Fig. 1.** Flowchart for conducting optimization

## 3  Parameter Optimization Process

After preparing the design data combinations, the numerical analysis was performed for each combination. The numerical analysis was done for a typical ground condition at 178 + 300 m chainage of the tunnel (T04) shown in Fig. 2. The ground has a Rock Mass Rating (RMR) value of 21–40 according to the engineering classification of rocks (Bieniawski 1989).

**Fig. 2.** Geographical location of tunnel T04

The ground condition and support systems data shown in Table 2 are taken as inputs for the numerical analysis. From a numerical computation using Plaxis 2D, the displacement of the tunnel has been determined for each combination.

**Table 2.** Ground condition and support system data

A. Ground condition

| Rock type | Excavation type | Overburden (m) | Unit weight, $\gamma$ (kN/m³) | Cohesion, C (kPa) | Friction angle, $\varphi$ | Modulus of elasticity, E (MPa) | Poisson ratio, v |
|---|---|---|---|---|---|---|---|
| A | Full excavation | 50 | 24 | 400 | 37 | 250 | 0.25 |
| B-C | Full excavation | 30 | 22 | 100 | 36 | 160 | 0.28 |

B. Rock bolt characteristics

| Length (m) | Bar diameter (mm) | Longitudinalspacing (m) | Ultimatecapacity (kN) | Axial stiffness, EA (kN/m) |
|---|---|---|---|---|
| 4 | 26 | 1 | 230 | $7.08 * 10^4$ |

C. Lining characteristics

| Support Type | Shotcrete | Lining |
|---|---|---|
| Thickness (m) | 0.2 | 0.3 |
| Modulus of elasticity, Ec (GPa) | 15 | 31 |
| Poisson's coefficient, v | 0.2 | 0.2 |
| Axial stiffness (MN/m) | 3000 | 9300 |
| Flexural stiffness (MNm²/m) | 10 | 69.75 |
| Self-weight (kN/m/m) | 5 | 7.5 |

The perimeter of the concrete lining was 34 m and the analysis was performed by considering plane strain conditions. The unit cost of rock bolt and concrete lining was $290 and $3100 respectively. The unit cost is adopted from the contractor for the year 2017 and is assumed to vary proportionally with time. Rock bolt cost includes all costs including installation (material, grout, equipment), whereas the concrete lining cost includes all costs up to casting (concrete material, formwork, and equipment). The calculated displacement of the tunnel from the numerical analysis together with the associated cost of the tunnel is shown in Table 3, for the chosen cases.

**Table 3.** Displacement and cost of tunnel

| S. no | Combination code | Number of rock bolt | Concrete lining thickness (cm) | Total displacement (mm) | Total cost of rock bolt and concrete lining ($) |
|-------|------------------|---------------------|-------------------------------|-------------------------|------------------------------------------------|
| 1 | $B_1L_1$ | 7 | 10 | 65.14 | 12,570 |
| 2 | $B_1L_2$ | 7 | 20 | 64.62 | 23,110 |
| 3 | $B_1L_3$ | 7 | 25 | 64.4 | 28,380 |
| 4 | $B_1L_4$ | 7 | 30 | 64.21 | 33,650 |
| 5 | $B_1L_5$ | 7 | 40 | 63.96 | 44,190 |
| 6 | $B_2L_1$ | 11 | 10 | 64.75 | 13,730 |
| 7 | $B_2L_2$ | 11 | 20 | 64.23 | 24,270 |
| 8 | $B_2L_3$ | 11 | 25 | 64.01 | 29,540 |
| 9 | $B_2L_4$ | 11 | 30 | 63.82 | 34,810 |
| 10 | $B_2L_5$ | 11 | 40 | 63.57 | 45,350 |
| 11 | $B_3L_1$ | 15 | 10 | 64.13 | 14,890 |
| 12 | $B_3L_2$ | 15 | 20 | 63.61 | 25,430 |
| 13 | $B_3L_3$ | 15 | 25 | 63.4 | 30,700 |
| 14 | $B_3L_4$ | 15 | 30 | 63.2 | 35,970 |
| 15 | $B_3L_5$ | 15 | 40 | 62.95 | 46,510 |
| 16 | $B_4L_1$ | 19 | 10 | 63.34 | 16,050 |
| 17 | $B_4L_2$ | 19 | 20 | 62.82 | 26,590 |
| 18 | $B_4L_3$ | 19 | 25 | 62.63 | 31,860 |
| 19 | $B_4L_4$ | 19 | 30 | 62.41 | 37,130 |
| 20 | $B_4L_5$ | 19 | 40 | 62.16 | 47,670 |

The numerical analysis results have been used in order to formulate a polynomial model for each parameter combination. The numerical results in column 5 are best fitted and correlated using a second-order polynomial surface model as shown in Eq. 3. The data from Column 3, 4 and 5 of Table 3 are used to derive the tunnel displacement function Q(x,y), whose graphical representation is shown in Fig. 3.

$$Q(x, y) = 66.09 + 0.000135x - 0.07211y - 0.005763x^2 - 1.239 * 10^{-9}xy + 0.0006522y^2 \tag{3}$$

where, x = number of rock bolt and
y = lining thickness in cm.

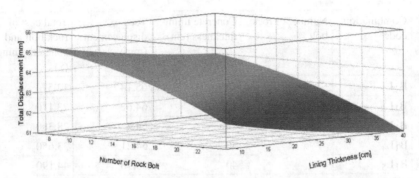

**Fig. 3.** Graphical presentation of tunnel settlement from numerical result

Similarly, the cost results are represented using the second-order polynomial model as shown in Eq. 4. The data from columns 3, 4 and 6 are used to derive the cost function F(x,y), whose graphical presentation is shown in Fig. 4.

$$F(x, y) = 290x + 1054y - 1.567 * 10^{-12}x^2 + 4.729 * 10^{-13}xy - 2.873 * 10^{-12}y^2 \tag{4}$$

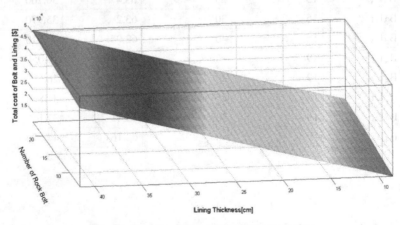

**Fig. 4.** Cost function graphical representation

where, x = number of rock bolt and
y = lining thickness in cm.

The two parameter correlation functions of Eq. 3 and 4 are used for optimization. The dimensionless relationship between the cost and displacement of the tunnel is shown in Fig. 5. While the cost of the tunnel is directly proportional to parameter increment, the displacement of the tunnel is inversely proportional to parameter increment.

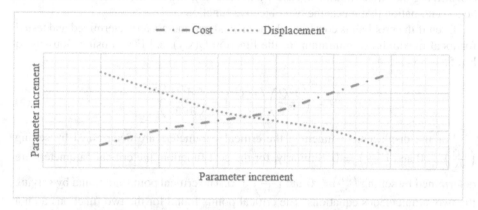

**Fig. 5.** Dimensionless relationship between cost and displacement

The Pareto front graph is derived from the two objective functions and plotted in Fig. 6, showing the relationship between the cost and displacement objective functions.

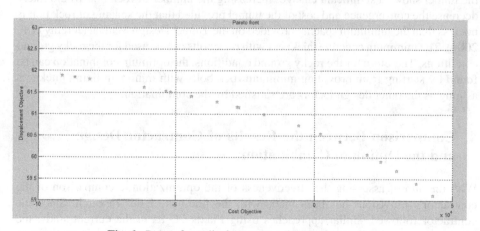

**Fig. 6.** Pareto front displacement and cost relationship

In the Pareto front, there is no single solution and for a nontrivial multi-objective optimization problem, no single solution occurs that simultaneously optimizes each objective (Emmerich and Deutz 2018). In that case, there exists a possibility of an infinite number of Pareto optimal solutions. Since the problem has two objective functions, multi-objective optimization is employed.

Considering the cost and displacement functions separately, the optimal result using MATLAB Gamulti Objective Solver obtained are 7 bolts with 10 cm thick lining and 19 bolts with 40 cm thick lining respectively. But these values are at the boundary of the constraints. Case scenario 1 (7 bolts with 10 cm lining) gives more settlement than the 20th case scenario, but it is cost-effective. On the other hand, case scenario 20, which shows less settlement than the other case scenarios is too costly. Therefore, considering the two extremities (case 1 and case 20), the optimum combination could be a combination that meets the two objective functions.

Even if the problem is constrained, the critical parameters are determined and tested for local maximum or minimum for the function Q(x,y) and F(x,y) using Boussinesq Eq. 5.

$$D = \left(\frac{\partial^2 Q}{\partial^2 x}\right)\left(\frac{\partial^2 Q}{\partial^2 y}\right) - \left(\frac{\partial^2 Q}{\partial x\, \partial_Y}\right)^2 \tag{5}$$

For the displacement function, the critical parameters are determined by setting $\left(\frac{\partial Q}{\partial x}\right) = 0$ and $\left(\frac{\partial Q}{\partial y}\right) = 0$. Similarly, for the cost function, the critical parameters are determined by setting $\left(\frac{\partial F}{\partial x}\right) = 0$ and $\left(\frac{\partial F}{\partial y}\right) = 0$. The critical points are found by solving the two simultaneous equations. The critical points found for the two functions do not lead to the optimum solution. The optimal combination of rock bolt and concrete lining with the constraints given is case scenario 13, which has 15 bolts and 25 cm thick lining, which can be considered as the optimum solution for this condition.

The variation of the number of rock bolt and lining thickness on the effect of cost of the tunnel shows a significant change. Increasing the number of rock bolt would likely decrease the convergence and cost of the tunnel provided that the spacing of rock bolt is not less than the minimum spacing provided on the Tunnel Design Manual (Jeremy et al. 2009). The minimum concrete thickness with rock bolts can be used for the rocky ground conditions. Therefore for the rocky ground conditions, the optimum combination can be found by starting from providing minimum rock bolts with minimum lining thickness as long as the other design factors are satisfied by the combination.

## 4    Comparison Between the Results of Contractor Design and the Optimum Combination

With the aim of assessing the effectiveness of the optimization, a comparison of the contractor's provisions has been made with the findings of this research. Since the contractor followed similar approaches using Plaxis 2D as in the current study, the displacements achieved by employing 11 rock bolts and 30 cm lining were close to one another. The optimization level of the selected support system as compared to the provisions of the contractor is compiled in Table 4.

The two design combinations show a variation in terms of number of rock bolt and thickness of concrete lining. The contractor design combination has less number of rock bolts than the optimized design combination, but thicker concrete lining than the optimized design combination. Because the rock bolts can reduce the convergence of

**Table 4.** Results of optimized and contractor design combination

| Design combination | Contractor (actual) | Optimized | Comment |
|---|---|---|---|
| Parameter combination | 11 rock bolts 30 cm lining | 15 rock bolts 25 cm lining | The observed total displacement after Support installations was 1.5 cm. The tunnel displacement before the installation of instrument is unknown. But this value usually is 3 to 4 times of the current observed instrument reading which becomes nearly 6 cm |
| Displacement | 6.38 cm | 6.34 cm | |
| Cost per meter (Longitudinal)($) | 34840 | 30700 | |
| Type of analysis and analysis software | FEA, Plaxis 2D | FEA, Plaxis 2D | |

the tunnel, the tunnel at an optimized design combination deforms less than the tunnel at the contractor design combination. The total displacement around the tunnel at optimum design combination is shown in Fig. 7. Since the observed displacement is lower than the predicted displacement from the numerical analysis, the optimized combination can be considered as effective.

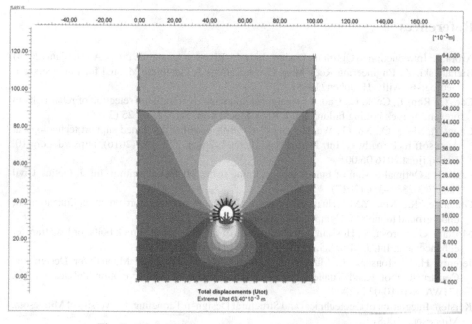

**Fig. 7.** Total displacement of the optimized combination

The design provided by the contractor is more expensive than the design combination optimized in this research. When the two design combinations are compared per meter of rock bolt and concrete lining construction, a difference of $4140 is observed.

## 5    Conclusion

In this research, optimization of rock bolt and tunnel lining combination has been performed by employing the numerical tools Plaxis 2D and MATLAB. The possibility of optimization of tunnel support has been assessed by taking a specific tunnel section from the Awash - Kombolcha - Haragebeya project, by modeling the cost of the tunnel using a polynomial function. The tunnel displacements found using the FEA were also modeled by using a polynomial function. The optimization potential has been illustrated by considering the displacement and cost functions per meter of tunnel length. The optimum combination was found at increased number of rock bolt and reduced lining thickness. The tunnel at the optimum design combination deforms less than the actual design. The optimized design gives a reduction in $4140 per meter length of the tunnel as compared to the provisions of the contractor.

**Declaration of Interest.** The authors report no conflicts of interest. The authors alone are responsible for the content and writing of this article.

## References

Arora, J.: Introduction to Optimum Design, 2nd edn. Elsevier Academic Press, Amsterdam (2004)

Bieniawski, Z.: Engineering Rock Mass Classifications A Complete Manual for Engineers and Geologists. Willy, Hoboken (1989)

Cao, C., Ren, T., Cook, C., Cao, Y.: Analytical approach in optimising selection of rebar bolts in preventing rock bolting failure. Int. J. Rock Mech. Min. Sci. **72**, 16–25 (2014)

Chen, Y., Meng, Q., Xu, G., Wu, H., Zhang, G.: Bolt-grouting combined support technology in deep soft rock roadway. Int. J. Min. Sci. Technol. **26**(5), 777–785 (2016). https://doi.org/10.1016/j.ijmst.2016.06.001

Fazli, H.: Optimal design of tunnel support lining using MCBO algorithm. Int. J. Optim. Civil Eng. **7**(3), 339–354 (2017)

Ghabraie, K., Xie, Y.M., Huang, X., Ren, G.: Shape and reinforcement optimization of underground tunnels. J. Comput. Sci. Technol. **4**, 51–63 (2010)

Mostafa, G., Korosh, S., Hossein, J.: Optimization of the fully grouted rock bolts for load transfer enhancement. Int. J. Min. Sci. Technol. **25**, 707–712 (2015)

Jeremy, H.C., Monsees, J., Munfah, N., Wisniewski, J.: Technical Manual for Design and Construction of Road Tunnels, s.l.: U.S. Department of Transportation Publication No. FHWA-NHI-10-034 (2009)

Kersten: Integration of Geotechnical and Structural Design in Tunneling. University of Minnesota, Minnesota (2008)

Liu, Y., Jin, F.: Bi-direction evolutionary structural optimization method for topology optimization of tunnel support. Eng. Mech. **23**, 110–115 (2006)

Messac, A.: Optimization in Practice with MATLAB® for Engineering Students and Professionals. Cambridge University Press, New York (2015)

Emmerich, M.T.M., Deutz, A.H.: A tutorial on multiobjective optimization: fundamentals and evolutionary methods. Nat. Comput. **17**(3), 585–609 (2018). https://doi.org/10.1007/s11047-018-9685-y

Nguyen, T., Ghabraie, K., Tran-Cong, T.: Applying bi-directional evolutionary structural optimisation method for tunnel reinforcement design considering nonlinear material behavior. Comput. Geotech. **55**, 57–66 (2014)

Papalambros, P., Wilde, D.: Principles of Optimal Design: Modeling and Computation. Cambridge University Press, Cambridge (2000). https://doi.org/10.1017/CBO9780511626418

Pérez-Romero, J., Oteo, C.S., de la Fuente, P.: Design and optimisation of the lining of a tunnel in the presence of expansive clay levels. Tunn. Undergr. Space Technol. **22**(1), 10–22 (2007). https://doi.org/10.1016/j.tust.2006.02.002

Ravindran, A.K.: Engineering Optimization: Methods and Applications. 2nd edn. Wiley, Hoboken (2006)

Meyer, R.A., Cannon, D.F., Kent, W.E.: The Fishbone (Ishikawa) diagram: a dynamic learning tool. Hospitality Tourism Educ. **8**, 45–47 (2013)

Smith, W.: Roof control strategies for underground coal mines. Inf. Circular **17**, 9351 (1993)

Nguyen, T., Ghabraie, K., Tran-Cong, T.: Simultaneous pattern and size optimisation of rock bolts for underground excavations. Comput. Geotech. **66**, 264–277 (2015). https://doi.org/10.1016/j.compgeo.2015.02.007

Tonon, F., Mammino, A., Bernardini, A.: Multiobjective optimization under uncertainty in tunneling: application to the design of tunnel support/reinforcement with case histories. Tunn. Undergr. Space Technol. **17**, 33–54 (2002)

Visual-paradigm: Pareto Chart Visual-paradigm Online Diagrams (2018). https://online.visual-paradigm.com. Accessed 12 Oct 2019

Yin, L., Yang, W.: Topology optimization for tunnel support in layered geological structures. Int. J. Numer. Methods Eng. **47**, 1983–1996 (2000)

# Regression Model for Predicting Water and Energy Demand: A Case Study of Addis Ababa City in 2050

Bedassa Dessalegn Kitessa[1]([⊠]), Semu Moges Ayalew[2], Geremew Sahilu Gebrie[1], and Solomon Tesfamariam Teferi[1]

[1] Addis Ababa Institute of Technology, Addis Ababa University, P.O. Box 385, Addis Ababa, Ethiopia
{bedassa.dessalegn,solomon.tesfamariam}@aait.edu.et
[2] School of Civil and Environmental Engineering, University of Connecticut, Storrs, USA

**Abstract.** Water and energy are so versatile that play great role in fulfilling the daily requirements of human life. Having knowledge on the future water and energy demand of the world, country, region and even a single city/town helps for planning and establishing water and energy policies. A regression model was used to estimate the energy and water demand considering the socio-economic drivers as parameters. An average population growth rate of 5.2% and a GDP growth rate of 11% were used as base scenarios to predict the residential, commercial and industrial energy demands. Population and GDP per capita based scenario was used to predict the transport (street-lighting) energy demand. The total energy demand for residential, commercial, industrial sectors and street-lighting was around 50 and 190 Peta Joule in 2030 and 2050 respectively. Additional, the energy requirement for water distribution, transmission, and water treatment was determined. Similarly, this scenario was used to determine residential, commercial and industrial water demand. The total water demand was predicted to be 0.4 and 0.68 billion cubic meters in 2030 and 2050 respectively.

**Keywords:** Socio-economic · Regression model · Water-energy demand

## Acronyms

| | |
|---|---|
| AA | Addis Ababa |
| AADMP | Addis Ababa Distribution Master Plan |
| AAWSA | Addis Ababa Water and Sewerage Authority |
| BCM | Billion Cubic Meter |
| BoFED | Bureau of Finance and Economic Development |
| CSA | Central Statistical Agency |
| DVRPC | Denver's Climate Resiliency Committee |
| EEP | Ethiopian Electric Power |
| EEU | Ethiopian Electric Utility |
| ETB | Ethiopia Birr |

M. A. Delele et al. (Eds.): ICAST 2020, LNICST 385, pp. 48–68, 2021.
https://doi.org/10.1007/978-3-030-80618-7_4

GDP        Growth Domestic Product
GTP II     Growth and Transformation Plan II
JICA       Japan International Cooperation Agency
MAE        Mean Absolute Error
MLP        Multilayer Perception
MUDHCo     Ministry of Urban Development, Housing and Construction
MW         Mega Watt
NRW        Non-Revenue Water
PJ         Peta Joule
RAE        Relative Absolute Error
RMSE       Root Mean Squared Error
UN         United Nation
UNDESA     United Nations Department of Economics and Social Affairs
USA        United State of America
WE         Water and Energy
WEKA       Waikato Environment for Knowledge Analysis

# 1 Introduction

The socio-economic drives such as population, per capita income, gross domestic product and technology affect highly the water-energy demand [1–3]. According to a UN report [4], the global population by 2050 is projected at 9.3 billion [5]. If one needs to extend the projections population beyond 2050, uncertain mortality and migration assumptions need to be considered. With continuing urbanization, the city population has grown rapidly and this led to an increase in water-energy demand [6]. Though the urbanization highly affects the water-energy demand, in developed countries where urbanization is not an issue, water-energy demands are highly influenced by GDP growth [7]. Energy is required to deliver an urban water supply at each stage (water transmission, treatment, distribution, etc.).

Availability and affordability of energy is a prerequisite for water supply (for pumping water in distribution, transmission, and water treatment) in Addis Ababa. In 2018, Legadadi and Gefersa water treatment plants consumed 6.76 GJ and 3.52 GJ respectively, while operating at an average of 22 h/day (Source: AAWSA). With a rise in population, urbanization, and commercial, industrial, institutional, residential activities, the demand for energy and water has been rising significantly in the city.

The growing population of Addis Ababa city, high urbanization rates and higher affluence stimulating consumption of goods and services are important trends driving the future development of impacts and city needs for energy resources. With 614 MW electricity demand in 2014, Addis Ababa's capital region accounted for around 42% of the country has an interconnected system peak load [8]. Energy demand forecasting is a systematic procedure for quantitatively defining future energy supply [9].

Deterministic and Stochastic Method are some of the prediction technique [9]. The deterministic method is a simple extrapolation of the historical demand not accounting for random variations of different driving parameters. As a result, it is less accurate in demand forecasting. In the Stochastic Method, the uncertainty of driving parameters like population number and economic growth is considered to give more value that is accurate.

Ethiopia's urban population will expect to triple by 2037 [10]. Studies done on the city's rate of urbanization have shown that the population to grow by 5% annually [10]. Moreover, the city's GDP is about ETB 90.9 billion ETB in 2015 and the GDP per capita income has grown from USD 788.48 in 2010 to USD 1,359 in 2015 [11].

Regression is the most widely used model and a stochastic approach for developing the relationship between variable y and variables x [12]. The trend line, energy and water are some of the domains in which linear regression is used. The goal of this model is to predict the response to n data points $(x_1, y_1)$, $(x_2, y_2)$ ... $(x_n, y_n)$ by a regression model.

WEKA [13] is a tool developed by Waikato University New Zealand and a collection of machine learning algorithms that are represented by the necessary actions that load the data and once the data is loaded there may be performed a regression on the dataset.

Water and Energy are basic for human life and it needs prediction of demand to plan the future water and energy supply. Electricity energy and water consumption in various sectors are investigated. Prediction tools are used for estimating water and energy consumption to predict water and energy demand. Water and Energy demand forecast can be divided into short-term, medium-term and long-term [14]. This paper aims to analyze water and energy consumption in Addis Ababa city to predict the long-term water and energy demand up to 2050 using the regression model (Stochastic Method). In the long-term, it is common to perform water and energy demand prediction using different drivers [14].

## 2 Methodology

The uncertainty effects of the demand drivers such as the GDP per capita, GDP and the population are considered in the stochastic prediction method. The data of these driving parameters are correlated to the historical consumption of water and energy data using a WEKA tool. Forecasting these three parameters are combined with the water-energy consumption using the regression equation, from the equation the future water and energy demand is predicted. The summary of the framework to predict the water and energy demand in 2050 for Addis Ababa city is indicated in Fig. 1.

### 2.1 Data Collection

Data including the GDP, GDP per capita and the population from CSA, water and energy consumption from AAWSA and EEU were collected respectively. The energy used for water depending on the data from AAWSA office is also used in this study. The commercial and industrial water demands are 53 and 47% of non-domestic water demand respectively [15]. Domestic or residential water demands include water required for drinking, cooking, bathing, washing utensils, washing clothes, flushing toilets, etc. Commercial water demand is affected by the number and types of commercial establishments. The water demand of Addis Ababa city is estimated from 2016 to 2030 by AAAWSA and considered as data to predict from 2030 to 2050 (Table 1).

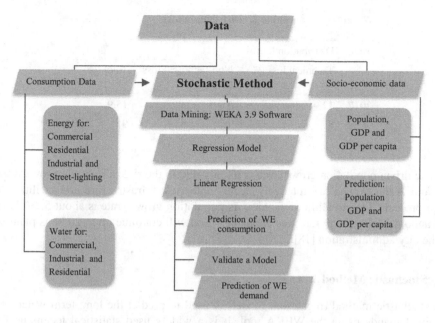

**Fig. 1.** Data and methodology framework

**Table 1.** Addis Ababa city water demand (BCM) (source: AAWSA, 2019)

| Water demand | Year | | | | | | | |
|---|---|---|---|---|---|---|---|---|
| | 2016 | 2018 | 2020 | 2022 | 2024 | 2026 | 2028 | 2030 |
| Industrial | 0.03 | 0.03 | 0.03 | 0.04 | 0.04 | 0.04 | 0.05 | 0.05 |
| Commercial | 0.03 | 0.03 | 0.04 | 0.04 | 0.04 | 0.05 | 0.05 | 0.06 |
| Residential | 0.11 | 0.12 | 0.14 | 0.16 | 0.17 | 0.19 | 0.21 | 0.23 |
| Total | 0.17 | 0.19 | 0.21 | 0.23 | 0.26 | 0.28 | 0.31 | 0.34 |

The real loss is equal to 75% of NRW [16]. According to AAWSA, the real loss is computed from 2016 to 2030 and assumed to be decreasing from 2030 to 2050 considering there will be technology improvement for loss reduction.

The energy consumption of Addis Ababa city for street-lighting, residential, industrial and commercial sectors was collected from EEU office. Energy distribution loss (e.g., power loss) is the other main factor that influences the energy demand. Therefore, considering the distribution loss is important in planning the energy demand of Addis Ababa city. Distribution network in Addis Ababa's capital region has the following problems: Lack of capacity, poor reliability and quality of supply and high losses which are approximately 19% loss in distribution system occurs due to lack of capacity and equipment deterioration (Source: AADMP Volume 1 Part 2). The EEP has a plan to improve the distribution loss described in Table 2 through AADMP project.

**Table 2.** Distribution loss

| Year | Distribution loss | | |
|------|-------------------|--------------------------|-----------|
|      | Technical loss (%) | Non-technical loss (%) | Total (%) |
| 2017 | 12.9 | 3 | 15.9 |
| 2034 | 8 | 1 | 9 |

The urban population growth rate is mainly due to the rise in migration toward the city and Addis Ababa has relatively better industries, infrastructure and facilities or mega-projects. Due to all these factors, its population growth rate is about 5.2% [17]. The annual GDP growth rate was about 11% and will continue up to 2050 as planned by the city administration [18].

## 2.2 Stochastic Method

The stochastic method (regression model) is used to predict the long-term water and energy demands using the WEKA tool. It is a widely used statistical technique for modeling the linear relationship between two or more variables. Regression is a used as a method in this study to develop a relationship between dependent variables denoted by y and independent variables denoted by x. The dependent variable is either water or energy consumption whereas the independent variables are the socio-economic drivers. Equation 1 gives the correlation between y and x of the regression model.

$$y = a_0 + a_1 x_1 + a_2 x_2 + a_3 x_3 + \ldots + a_n x_n \tag{1}$$

Where $a_1, \ldots, a_n$ and $a_0$ are regression coefficients and constant respectively and $x_1, \ldots, x_n$ are independent variables (population, GDP and GDP per capita) and whereas y is dependent variable (water and energy consumption).

The accuracy of the model is validated using evaluation parameters such as Mean Absolute Error (MAE) [19], Root Mean Squared Error (RMSE) [20], Mean Absolute Error (MAE) and Coefficient of determination ($R^2$).

The steps followed to stochastically predict the water and energy demands are given as follows:

*Parameter Forecast (GDP and Population):* To consider the effects of uncertainty drivers (e.g., GDP, GDP per capita and population) on the water and energy prediction, knowing the values of these parameters is required.

*Population Forecast:* To predict the future population of the city, the growth rate (%) and the present population (Po) should be known. Addis Ababa's population is 3.6 and 3.7 Million in 2017 and 2018 respectively (CSA data). The population growth rate is taken into consideration to forecast the population by Eq. (2).

$$P_t = P_0 + GR \times P_0 \tag{2}$$

Where $P_t$ is the annual population at a certain year, GR is the population growth rate (%) and $P_o$ is the present or current annual population.

*GDP Forecast:* The growth rate (%) of Addis Ababa GDP and the initial GDP should be taken into consideration to predict GDP using Eq. (3).

$$GDP_t = GDP_o + GR \times GDP_o \tag{3}$$

Where $GDP_t$ is the future gross domestic product, GR is the GDP growth rate (%) and $GDP_o$ is the initial GDP.

Finally; the equation between the main socio-economic drivers and water consumption was developed using the WEKA tool.

## 3   Result and Discussion

Since the population is the main driver of water and energy demand, its projection has been made using the population growth rate, Fig. 2. The result shows the current population, 4.5 million, will rise to about 18 million in 2050.

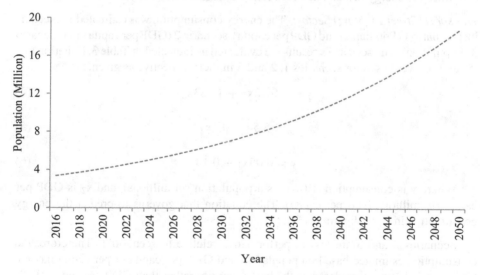

**Fig. 2.** Population forecast of Addis Ababa city

The city's GDP will grow annually on average by 11%, the GDP of the city up to 2050 was estimated and used to predict the water-energy demand, Fig. 3. In 2050 GDP is expected to reach 3600 billion ETB.

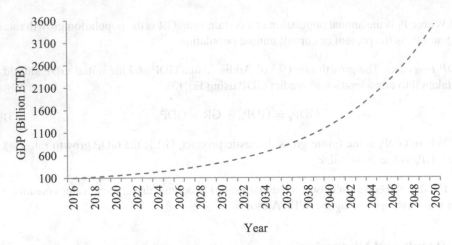

**Fig. 3.** GDP forecast using GDP growth rate

### 3.1  Energy Demand

With the rise in population, urbanization, commercial, industrial and institutional activities, the energy demand has been rising in Addis Ababa city.

*Transport (Street-Lighting) Sector:* The energy consumption was estimated for scenarios; scenario 1 (Population and GDP per capita), scenario 2 (GDP per capita) and scenario 3 (Population). The scenario's results are evaluated as indicated in Table 3. Equation (4), (5) and (6) were used for scenarios 1, 2 and 3 in their respective as given.

$$y = -0.42x_1 + 49.83x_2 \qquad (4)$$

$$y = 5.54 - 0.1x_2 \qquad (5)$$

$$y = 0.05x_1 - 0.13 \qquad (6)$$

Where y is consumption (PJ), $x_1$ is a population (in millions), and $x_2$ is GDP per capita (in millions ETB per capita). The equation that governs to predict the energy consumption in street-lighting is Eq. (4).

Scenarios 2 and 3 are less in performance relative to scenario 1. Therefore, the consumption estimated based on population and GDP per capita or per capita income (PCI) scenario was considered as the best scenario, rather than GDP per capita (PCI) scenario and population scenario. Besides, scenario 1 is the best fit by the model to observed energy consumption. Figure 4 indicates the energy consumption for street-lighting.

*Commercial Sector:* The energy consumption for the commercial was estimated for three scenarios and scenarios are evaluated as in Table 4. Equation (7), (8) and (9) were developed for scenario 1, 2 and 3 respectively as follows:

$$y = 2.96x_1 - 7.61 \qquad (7)$$

**Table 3.** Evaluation parameter for scenarios used in transport energy consumption

| Scenarios | Drivers | Parameter | | | | |
|---|---|---|---|---|---|---|
| | | $R^2$ | MAE | RMSE | RAE (%) | RRSE (%) |
| 1 | Population and PCI | 0.98 | 0.0016 | 0.002 | 18.6 | 18.3 |
| 2 | PCI | 0.92 | 0.0036 | 0.0043 | 41.27 | 39.84 |
| 3 | Population | 0.92 | 0.0036 | 0.0043 | 41.14 | 39.79 |

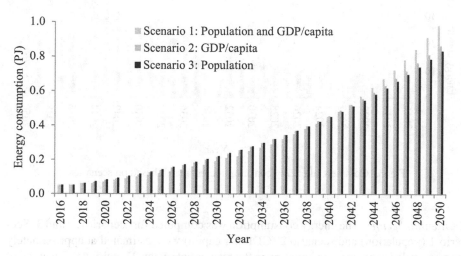

**Fig. 4.** Predicted energy demand for street lighting

$$y = 328.53x_2 - 7.06 \tag{8}$$

$$y = 1.48x_1 + 164.3x_2 - 7.34 \tag{9}$$

Where; y is consumption (PJ) for the commercial sector. The governing equation that fits historical data and used to predict future consumption is Eq. (8).

**Table 4.** Evaluation parameters for scenarios used in commercial energy consumption

| Scenarios | Drivers | Parameters | | | | |
|---|---|---|---|---|---|---|
| | | $R^2$ | MAE | RMSE | RAE (%) | RRSE (%) |
| 1 | Population | 0.98 | 0.076 | 0.093 | 13.66 | 15.41 |
| 2 | GDP per capita | 0.98 | 0.077 | 0.094 | 13.79 | 15.62 |
| 3 | Average | 0.98 | 0.072 | 0.092 | 13.57 | 15.51 |

Scenario 1 and 2 results were nearly equivalent to the averages of two scenarios (scenario 3) which represent the future energy consumption for the commercial sector, Fig. 5.

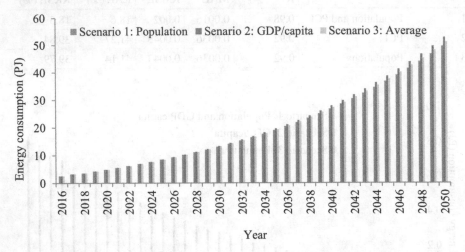

**Fig. 5.** Commercial energy consumption estimated based on scenarios

*Residential Sector:* The energy consumption was computed for scenario1, 2 and 3. Scenario 1 (population) and scenario 2 (GDP per capita) were estimated at approximately the same value of energy consumption in the residential sector. Therefore, the average of the two scenarios represents the residential energy consumption, because of the accuracy of estimation. The model has generated Eq. (10), (11) and (12) for scenarios 1, 2 and 3 respectively as follows.

$$y = 3.82x_1 - 9.27 \tag{10}$$

$$y = 424.68x_2 - 8.56 \tag{11}$$

$$y = 1.91x_1 + 212.34x_2 - 8.92 \tag{12}$$

Where; y is energy consumption (PJ) in the residential sector. Scenario 3 or Eq. (11) is used for the prediction of energy consumption in the residential sector. The performance of the scenario fit is given in Table 5.

Predicted residential sector energy consumption is indicated in Fig. 6.

**Table 5.** Evaluation parameter for scenarios used in residential energy consumption

| Scenarios | Drivers | Parameters | | | | |
|---|---|---|---|---|---|---|
| | | $R^2$ | MAE | RMSE | RAE (%) | RRSE (%) |
| 1 | Population | 0.95 | 0.20 | 0.25 | 25.90 | 31.01 |
| 2 | GDP per capita | 0.95 | 0.21 | 0.25 | 26.02 | 31.06 |
| 3 | Average | 0.95 | 0.21 | 0.23 | 31.52 | 31.06 |

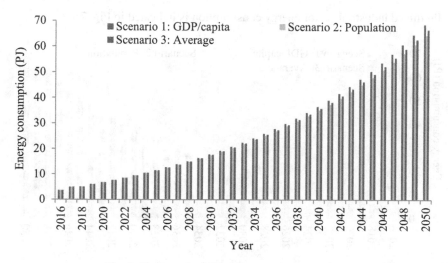

**Fig. 6.** Estimated residential energy consumption

*Industrial Sector:* The first two scenarios have nearly the same value; hence, their average has been taken to forecast energy consumption for the three scenarios respectively expressed in Eqs. 13, 14 and 15.

$$y = 4.01x_1 - 9.18 \tag{13}$$

$$y = 420.73x_2 - 7.69 \tag{14}$$

$$y = 2.01x_1 + 210.37x_2 - 8.44 \tag{15}$$

Where; y is consumption (PJ) for the industrial sector. The equation generated by a model based on scenario 3 or Eq. (15) is a general equation to predict future water consumption. The evaluation result for scenarios is shown in Table 6.

**Table 6.** Model performance of fit evaluation parameters

| Scenarios | Drivers | Parameters | | | | |
|---|---|---|---|---|---|---|
| | | $R^2$ | MAE | RMSE | RAE (%) | RRSE (%) |
| 1 | Population | 0.96 | 0.19 | 0.24 | 24.21 | 28.20 |
| 2 | GDP per capita | 0.95 | 0.21 | 0.26 | 26.46 | 31.07 |
| 3 | Average | 0.95 | 0.21 | 0.23 | 31.32 | 29.07 |

Predicted industrial sector energy consumption is indicated in Fig. 7.

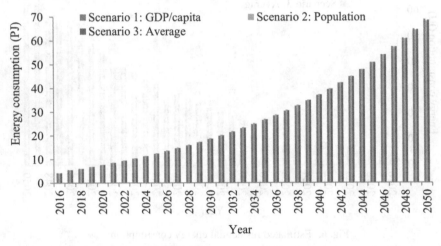

**Fig. 7.** Estimated industrial energy consumption based on scenarios

The energy demand was fitted using the coefficient of regression as shown in Table 7.

Where; $a_1$ and $a_2$ are fitting parameter coefficients for population and GDP per capita respectively.

Energy demand was estimated considering distribution loss. The distribution loss is 19% in 2016 and planned to improve distribution loss to 9% in 2034, AADMP [21] and it reaches 7% in 2050. The future energy demand is indicated in Fig. 8.

*Energy for Water:* Energy used for the urban water stage (distribution, treatment and transmission) was predicted. Consequently, energy demand for water sectors (residential, commercial and industrial) was also determined. Considering the 2016 year as a baseline, energy demand for water stages was predicted up to 2050 as indicated in Fig. 9.

The energy demand for water distribution (industrial, commercial and residential) is given in Fig. 10.

The power demand in AA capital region is expected to increase from 800 MW in 2014 to 3,600 MW in 2034 [21] and from 1212 MW in 2015 to 6109 MW in 2037 [22] with an annual growth rate of 8.1%. Figure 11 shows the values of the studies.

**Table 7.** Regression parameters in energy demand prediction

| Sectors | Scenarios | Parameters | Value | Constant | Value |
|---|---|---|---|---|---|
| Transport | 1 | $a_1$ | −0.5 | $a_0$ | 0.03 |
| | | $a_2$ | 49.8 | | |
| | 2 | $a_2$ | 5.5 | $a_0$ | −0.1 |
| | 3 | $a_1$ | 0.1 | $a_0$ | −0.1 |
| Commercial | 1 | $a_1$ | 3.0 | $a_0$ | 7.6 |
| | 2 | $a_2$ | 328.5 | $a_0$ | −7.1 |
| | 3 | $a_1$ | 1.5 | $a_0$ | −7.3 |
| | | $a_2$ | 164.3 | | |
| Residential | 1 | $a_1$ | 3.8 | $a_0$ | −9.3 |
| | 2 | $a_2$ | 424.7 | $a_0$ | −8.6 |
| | 3 | $a_1$ | 2.0 | $a_0$ | −8.9 |
| | | $a_2$ | 212.3 | | |
| Industrial | 1 | $a_1$ | 4.0 | $a_0$ | 9.2 |
| | 2 | $a_2$ | 420.7 | $a_0$ | −7.7 |
| | 3 | $a_1$ | 2.0 | $a_0$ | −8.4 |
| | | $a_2$ | 210.4 | | |

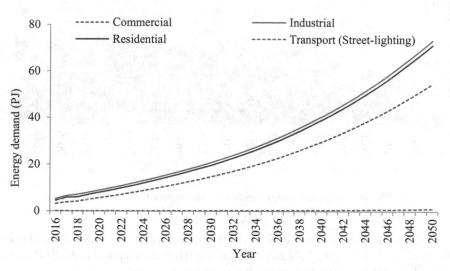

**Fig. 8.** Estimated energy demand for sectors

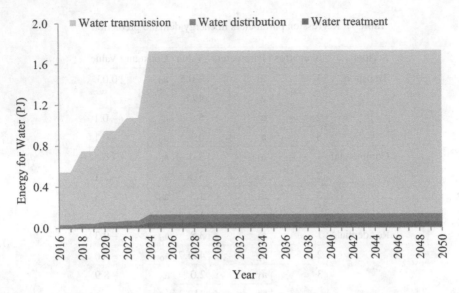

**Fig. 9.** Estimated energy demand

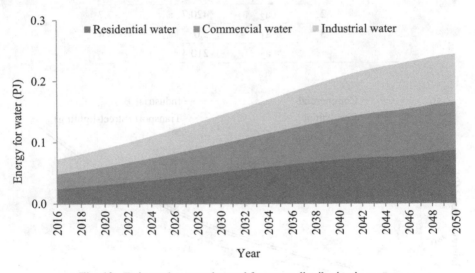

**Fig. 10.** Estimated energy demand for water distribution in sectors

The MAE, RMSE, RAE and RSE (%) of the predicted (Model) energy demand from 2016 to 2034 are 1.22, 1.42, 7.74 and 7.77% respectively as compared to the EEP study. The predicted energy consumption result becomes as indicated in Table 8.

The high value of model error corresponding to commercial, industrial, residential and street-lighting are 5, 10, 9 and 6% respectively, which are insignificant to the actual.

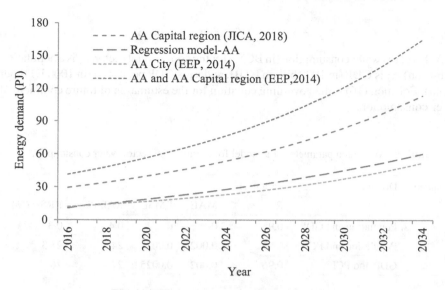

**Fig. 11.** Studies on energy demand prediction

**Table 8.** Energy (PJ) consumption results from a model and actual

| S/n | Commercial | | Industrial | | Residential | |
|-----|------------|-------|-----------|-------|------------|-------|
| | Observed | Model | Observed | Model | Observed | Model |
| 1 | 2.1 | 2.0 | 3.9 | 4.1 | 3.2 | 3.6 |
| 2 | 2.6 | 2.5 | 4.6 | 4.2 | 3.9 | 4.3 |
| 3 | 3.1 | 3.3 | 5.3 | 5.5 | 4.8 | 5.0 |
| 4 | 3.7 | 3.6 | 6.0 | 6.1 | 5.3 | 5.7 |
| 5 | 4.2 | 4.2 | 6.8 | 6.8 | 6.1 | 6.4 |

## 3.2 Water Demand

In African cities, urban water demands are non-homogeneous within the same urban area and levels of water service vary from standpipes to household connections (Wallingford, 2003). The water demands can be classified as domestic (residential) and non-domestic (commercial and industrial).

*Commercial Sector:* Water consumption was estimated using the best-fit independent variable (scenarios) as shown in Table 9. The generated equations by the model for prediction of consumption for scenarios 1, 2 and 3 are given using Eq. (16), (17) and (18) respectively.

$$y = 10.72x_1 - 0.03x_2 - 0.004 \tag{16}$$

$$y = -0.47x_1 + 0.001x_3 - 0.0017 \tag{17}$$

$$y = 0.025x_1 + 0.0006x_3 + 0.0095 \qquad (18)$$

Where; y is water consumption (in BCM) for the commercial sector, $x_1$ is a population (in billion), $x_2$ is GDP (in 1000 billion ETB), and $x_3$ is GDP per capita (in 1000 ETB per capita). Equation (16) is the governing equation for the estimation of future commercial water consumption.

**Table 9.** Validation parameter of a model for commercial sector water consumption

| Scenario | Drivers | Parameter | | | | |
|---|---|---|---|---|---|---|
| | | $R^2$ | MAE | RMSE | RAE (%) | RRSE (%) |
| 1 | Population and GDP | 0.98 | 0 | 0 | 0.4 | 0.37 |
| 2 | Population and PCI | 0.97 | 0.002 | 0.0023 | 24.3 | 23.3 |
| 3 | GDP and PCI | 0.96 | 0.002 | 0.0025 | 27 | 26 |

The estimated commercial sector water consumption is indicated in Fig. 12.

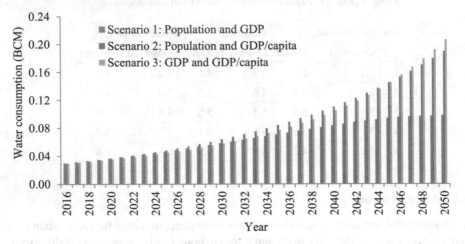

**Fig. 12.** Predicted water consumption for commercial

*Industrial Sector:* The water consumption a scenario with their statistical evaluation was determined as indicated in Table 10. Generated equations for independent variables considered in water consumption prediction are given by Eq. (19), (20) and (21) for scenarios 1, 2 and 3 respectively.

$$y = 9.38x_1 - 0.026x_2 - 0.0036 \qquad (19)$$

$$y = -0.13x_1 + 0.0007x_3 + 0.0068 \qquad (20)$$

$$y = -0.033x_2 - 0.0011x_3 - 0.002 \qquad (21)$$

Equation (19) is the governing equation for predicting future industrial water consumption.

**Table 10.** Evaluation parameter for the model in water consumption

| Scenarios | Drivers | Parameter | | | | |
|---|---|---|---|---|---|---|
| | | $R^2$ | MAE | RMSE | RAE (%) | RRSE (%) |
| 1 | Population and GDP | 1 | 0 | 0 | 0.39 | 0.37 |
| 2 | Population and PCI | 0.9 | 0.0022 | 0.0024 | 34.03 | 31.4 |
| 3 | GDP and PCI | 1 | 0 | 0 | 0.45 | 0.42 |

The regression model captured the industrial sector water consumption that was computed by AAWSA cases; when population and GDP are considered as a scenario (scenario 1). Therefore, scenario 1 is the best assumption for industrial water demand prediction. Estimated water consumption is shown in Fig. 13.

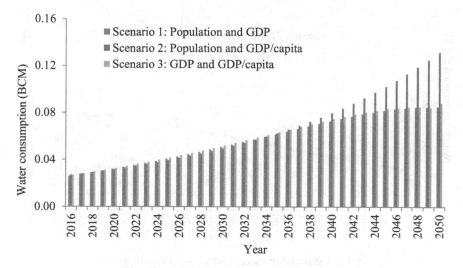

**Fig. 13.** Industrial sector water consumption

*Residential Sector:* Evaluations of a scenario for residential sector water consumption was determined as indicated in Table 11. The equation for scenarios 1 and 2 are given by Eqs. (22) and (23) respectively.

$$y = 50.73x_1 - 0.18x_2 - 0.047 \qquad (22)$$

$$y = -0.37x_1 + 0.0038x_3 - 0.0003 \tag{23}$$

Where; y is water consumption (in BCM) for the residential sector. For residential water consumption; Eq. (22) is the best for both fitting historical data and estimating future consumption.

**Table 11.** Metric evaluation parameter for model scenarios

| Scenarios | Drivers | Parameter | | | | |
|---|---|---|---|---|---|---|
| | | $R^2$ | MAE | RMSE | RAE (%) | RRSE (%) |
| 1 | Population and GDP | 1 | 0.0003 | 0.0003 | 0.9 | 0.8 |
| 2 | Population and PCI | 0.9 | 0.0026 | 0.0031 | 7.8 | 7.9 |

The model more captured the baseline residential water consumption, when population and GDP scenario (scenario 1) is considered. Scenario 1 is a paramount independent variable for industrial water consumption forecasting. The future water consumption for the residential is given in Fig. 14.

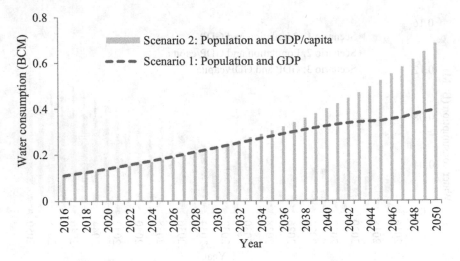

**Fig. 14.** Estimated residential sector water consumption

The regression parameters used to fit the water demand is indicated in Table 12.

Where; $a_1$, $a_2$ and $a_3$ are coefficients of regression for independent variables of population, GDP and GDP per capita respectively.

Distribution loss is understood in demand estimation and needs technology improvement for water loss reduction. The NRW should be less than 25% according to the World Bank recommends and is decreasing to 23% in 2030 for Addis Ababa [23] and decreases

**Table 12.** Regression parameters used in water demand prediction

| Sector | Scenario | Parameters | Value | Constant | Value |
|---|---|---|---|---|---|
| Commercial | 1 | $a_1$ | 10.7 | $a_0$ | −0.004 |
| | | $a_2$ | −0.03 | | |
| | 2 | $a_1$ | −0.5 | $a_0$ | −0.002 |
| | | $a_3$ | 0.001 | | |
| | 3 | $a_2$ | 0.03 | $a_0$ | 0.01 |
| | | $a_3$ | 0.001 | | |
| Industrial | 1 | $a_1$ | 9.4 | $a_0$ | −0.004 |
| | | $a_2$ | 0.03 | | |
| | 2 | $a_2$ | −0.1 | $a_0$ | 0.007 |
| | | $a_3$ | 0.001 | | |
| | 3 | $a_2$ | −0.03 | $a_0$ | −0.002 |
| | | $a_3$ | 0.001 | | |
| Residential | 1 | $a_1$ | 50.7 | $a_0$ | −0.05 |
| | | $a_2$ | −0.2 | | |
| | 2 | $a_1$ | −0.4 | $a_0$ | −0.0003 |
| | | $a_3$ | 0.004 | | |

to 22% in 2050. The real loss is 75% of NRW. The real loss for NRW of 23 and 22% is 17.5 and 16.75% respectively.

Water demand for sectors (residential, industrial and commercial) was estimated based on water loss and scenario-1 as indicated in Fig. 15.

The commercial water consumption growth rate decreased from 4.34% in 2030 to 0.72% in 2050. Also for industrial, it was decreased from 4.34% in 2030 to 0.47% in 2050. For the residential, the growth rate trend decreases from 4.49% in 2030 to 0.33% in 2045 and finally growth rate alter between 1.8% and 2.8% from 2046 to 2050. Commercial and industrial sector water consumption has a decreasing growth rate from 2030 to 2050. In 2030; the residential, commercial, and industrial water demand was 68.1%, 17% and 14.8% of total water demand respectively and in 2050 for the respective sector is 68.2%, 16.9% and 14.8% of total water demand.

According to AAWSA, the water demand for 2018, 2022 and 2025 is 0.29, 0.37 and 0.39 BCM respectively and consequently, the predicted demand in this paper is 0.27, 0.32 and 0.36 BCM for the respective year. This study result shows an insignificant gap with the AAWSA's result.

The estimated water consumption by the regression model using the training test data set and the actual data is given in Table 13.

From Table 13, the lower and higher value of the relative error of the model compared to the AAWSA case is 0.29 and 2.4% respectively, this shows the variation of insignificant value.

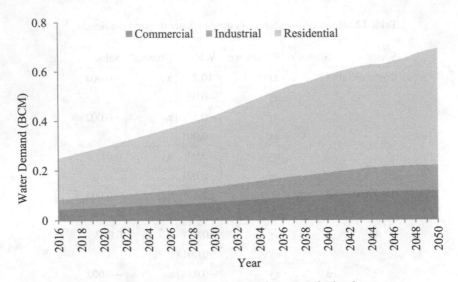

**Fig. 15.** Predicted water demand for sectors in the city

**Table 13.** The fit for the regression model using the training data set

| S/n | Total water consumption (BCM) | |
|-----|-------------------------------|------------------|
| | AAWSA | Predicted (Model) |
| 1 | 0.17 | 0.16 |
| 2 | 0.19 | 0.18 |
| 3 | 0.21 | 0.21 |
| 4 | 0.23 | 0.23 |
| 5 | 0.26 | 0.25 |
| 6 | 0.28 | 0.28 |
| 7 | 0.31 | 0.31 |
| 8 | 0.34 | 0.33 |

## 4  Conclusion

Energy and water consumption data were collected from EEU and AAWSA offices respectively. The energy used for water was also gathered from the AAWSA bureau, while socio-economic drivers were taken from CSA and BoFED. In this paper water and energy, demand was estimated for different scenarios based on socioeconomic drivers. A regression model was used to estimate water and energy consumption using the WEKA tool. Losses (Energy and water distribution) were considered in estimating water and energy demand. Energy used in water (for distribution, transmission water treatment) was estimated based on baseline data and quantity of water.

Socio-economic drivers were forecasted for population considering population growth rate and GDP growth rate. Energy demand was forecasted considering an average consumption estimated based on population scenario and GDP per capita scenario and distribution loss for the residential, commercial and industrial sectors, while street lighting sector demand is based on population and GDP per capita scenario. The average scenario (population scenario and per capita income scenario), considering the two scenarios give an acceptable estimation. These scenarios estimate almost equivalent results and taking the average scenario was appropriate. The population and GDP scenario was used to estimate the water consumption and demand for all sectors used in the study.

All scenarios used in water and energy consumption estimation were selected based on best-fit statistical evaluation parameters. The best-fit scenario to historical consumption is the best estimator of future water and energy consumption and demand. When population growth rate and GDP growth rate are capturing up to 2050 as a socio-economic driver, a regression model using the data mining tool (WEKA) is likely to use for the prediction of water and energy consumption. In the WEKA tool, it was conceivable to consider any parameters, which are supposed to be the drivers for water and energy demand. Considering water and energy distribution loss as an additional factor to the socio-economic factor in demand estimation, the water-energy demand for sectors was predicted in this paper. According to AADMP, the energy distribution loss is 15.9% in 2017 and planned to decrease to 9% in 2030 by improving disruption loss and it reaches 6.65% in 2050. In the years 2030 and 2050, the electrical energy demand was estimated to be 13.2 and 51.03 PJ for the commercial sector; 18.6 and 68.4 PJ for the industrial sector; 17.6 and 66.5 PJ for the residential sector whereas it was 0.19 and 0.98 PJ for the transport sector. Respectively, for the two years mentioned above, the water demand in billion cubic meters was estimated to be 0.071 and 0.12 for the commercial sector; 0.06 and 0.10 for the industrial sector; 0.28 and 0.47 for the residential sector.

**Acknowledgements.** The authors are greatly indebted to Addis Ababa Water and Sewerage Authority, Ethiopian Electric Utility for providing required data.

# References

1. Oyedepo, S.O.: Energy and sustainable development in Nigeria: the way forward. Energy Sustain. Soc. **2**(1), 1–17 (2012)
2. Stillwell, A.S., King, C.W., Webber, M.E., Duncan, I.J., Hardberger, A.: Energy-Water Nexus in Texas (2011)
3. Sefifi, H., Sepasian, M.S.: Electric Power System Planning. Springer, Heidelberg (2011)
4. UNFPA: State of the World Population: People and Possibilities in a World of 7 Billion. UNFPA, New York, USA (2011)
5. UNDESA: World Population to 2300. United Nation, New York, USA (2004)
6. Yin, Z., Jia, B., Wu, S., Dai, J., Tang, D.: Comprehensive forecast of urban water-energy demand based on a neural network model. Water-Open Access J.: MDPI (2018)
7. Csereklyei, Z., Humer, S.: Modeling primary energy consumption under model uncertainity (2012)
8. World Bank: Enhancing Urban Resilience: city strength resilient cities program (English). Addis Ababa (2015)

9.  Sulivan, R.: Power System Planning. McGraw-Hill (1977)
10. World Bank: Ethiopia Urbanization Review: Urban Institutions for a Middle-Income Ethiopia (2015)
11. BoFED: Poverty level assessment of Addis Ababa, Addis Ababa (2016)
12. Kaw, A., Eric Kalu, E.: Numerical Methods with Applications, 2nd edn. lulu.com (March 7, 2011), eBook (Mathematice for College) (2010)
13. Hall, M., Frank, E., Holmes, G., Pfahringer, B., Reutemann, P., Witten, I.: The WEKA data mining software: an update. ACM SIGKDD Explor. Newsl. **11**(1), 10–18 (2009). https://doi.org/10.1145/1656274.1656278
14. Genethliou, D., Feinberg, E.: Load Forecasting, New York (2012)
15. Getnet, A.: Evaluation of Addis Ababa Water Supply System Using Integrated Approach, Addis Ababa (2019)
16. World Bank: Challenge of Reducing Non-Revenue Water (NRW) in Developing Countries. PPIAF, Washington, DC (2006)
17. MUDHCo: National Report on Housing and Sustainable Urban Development, Federal Democratic Republic of Ethiopia (2015)
18. UN-Habitat: United Nations Human Settlements Programme, Addis Ababa, Ethiopia (2017)
19. Fortin, J.G., Anctil, F., Parent, L.-É., Bolinder, M.: Site-specific early season potato yield forecast by neural network in Eastern Canada. Precision Agric. **12**(6), 905–923 (2011). https://doi.org/10.1007/s11119-011-9233-6
20. Veenadhari, S., Misra, B., Singh, C.D.: Machine learning approach for forecasting crop yield based on climatic parameters. In: 2014 International Conference on Computer Communication and Informatics, Coimbatore, India (2014)
21. JICA: Addis Ababa Distribution Master Plan (2018)
22. EEP: Power Demand Forecasting, Addis Ababa (2014)
23. AAWSA: Consultancy service for Addis Ababa water distribution and operation management and hydraulic modeling (2019)

# Determination of Bio-methane Potential as Renewable Energy of Beverage Industrial Effluents at Mekelle, Ethiopia

Atsede Gidey Tesfay, Kinfe Kassa, and Daniel Reddythota[✉]

Faculty of Water Supply and Environmental Engineering, Arba Minch Water Technology Institute, Arba Minch University, Arba Minch, Ethiopia
daniel.reddy@amu.edu.et

**Abstract.** Industrial Effluents are a major challenge to be treated and disposed of without contamination of water and soil. Soft drinks Industrial effluents are having alcoholic compounds which are toxic to aquatic life as well as the environment. In the past, the increasing demands for energy and impending climate change have driven the search for renewable energy sources. Diminishing supplies of fossil fuels and production of pollution are the major challenges with the continued usage of fossil fuels. This paper aimed to give an account of biogas production from beverage industrial effluents as well as effluent treatment for environment safety. Besides, the study helped to compare the capacity of mixed substrates and pure beverage industrial effluents to release methane gas. The anaerobic digestion removed 68.95%, 65.30% and 71.74% of $BOD_5$, TS and VS, respectively from beverage industrial effluents. Mixed substrates comparatively produced more methane than beverage industrial effluents. Beverage industrial effluent released 323.5 ml of bio-methane with cumulative $CH_4$ yield of 76.15 ml per gram of VS which was added into the reactor per working volume of 1.8 L. Soft drink industry can establish a biogas plant to fulfil the energy needs of the industry.

## 1 Introduction

Industrial effluents, with limited treatment, are discharged into the environment causing damage to the surrounding soil, water and environment resources as well as the spread of diseases to the humans and livestock in Ethiopia [1]. Beverage as well as molasses-based distillery industries consume large volumes of freshwater and generate a huge amount of waste water [2, 3]. The primary sources of pollutants at alcohol & distillery industries are the spillage, cooling water from the condenser, and wastewater from fermenter [3, 4]. Raw Spent Wash (RSW) coming out of the distillery industry and 12–15 times by volume of the product alcohol, is one of the most difficult wastes to be disposed of due to its acidic reaction, dark brown colour and high ash content [5, 6]. It is having an extremely high concentration of organic and inorganic pollutants in terms of biological oxygen demand (BOD), chemical oxygen demand (COD), total solids (TS), sulfate, phosphate, phenols and various toxic metals [7].

© ICST Institute for Computer Sciences, Social Informatics and Telecommunications Engineering 2021
Published by Springer Nature Switzerland AG 2021. All Rights Reserved
M. A. Delele et al. (Eds.): ICAST 2020, LNICST 385, pp. 69–84, 2021.
https://doi.org/10.1007/978-3-030-80618-7_5

The prime contaminant in soft drink industry (SDI) is mostly sucrose due to the preparation of concentrated syrups, which causes an increase in the concentration of organic substances expressed in terms of Total Suspended Solids (TSS), Chemical Oxygen Demand (COD), sodium, nitrates and phosphates [8]. This wastewater has to be treated by a conventional method to save the soil, water and environment.

Bioconversion processes are one of the most attractive ways to find alternative sources of energy and control pollution from waste streams [9]. Moreover, biological processes for the treatment and recycling of wastewater are considered to be cheap and environmentally safe. Anaerobic digestion (AD), once considered as a strenuous process, has been now applied at the industrial scale [10]. In this context, biogas generated from alcohol and soft drink - based industrial wastewater will play a vital role in future. Biogas is a versatile renewable energy source, which can be used for substitution of fossil fuels. Methane-rich biogas can replace natural gas as a feedstock in the production of chemicals and materials [11]. Throughout the world, AD has become a major focus of interest in waste management. It is an environment-friendly process to produce energy in the form of biogas and manure as residue [1]. AD mitigates several other environmental problems like production of foul smell, the spread of pathogens and emission of greenhouse gases.

In this study two Bio-methane potential (Bmp) tests were conducted, The first Bmp test was conducted to measure methane yield of a mixed substrate (subs) (25%RSW+75% MSDIE; meaning thereby that 25% of the working volume was RSW & the remaining 75% was filled with MSDIE). The second Bmp test was conducted with pure MSDIE. The Bmp tests were conducted as laboratory-scale batch experiments using 2 L anaerobic reactors. Characteristics of Raw and Bmp test industrial effluents were analysed.

## 2  Methodology

Desta Alcohol and Liquor Industry (DALI) and Moha Soft Drink Industries (MSDI) are located at Qiha and Kedamay Weyane sub-cities of Mekelle city, respectively. DALI uses sugar cane molasses to produce ethanol for preparing the products like dry gin, denatured spirit, Vodka and processed alcohol. MSDI uses acidulants, stabilizers, preservatives, flavours, colourants (Sunset yellow, Caramel) and sugar to produce Mirinda Orange, Mirinda Tonic, Pepsi, 7Up and Sprite.

### 2.1  Sampling

Samples were collected from the outlet of DALI effluents (Raw spent wash (RSW)) as well as during fermentation of cane molasses. Samples from MSDI were collected from the outlet of the industrial effluents after screening. Since effluent generated from MSDI has different characteristics over time due to variation in product type, water consumption & operation type, samples were collected by grab time phase composite method. The samples were collected from DALI and MSDI two times for both trial-1 and trial-2 of Biomethane production (Bmp) tests and quality analysis to identify the bio-methane potential of these industrial effluents. To avoid any biochemical reaction, substrates were stored at 4 °C.

**A Sampling of Moha Soft Drink Industrial Effluents (MSDIE), Trial-1 and Trial-2.**
The samples from MSDI were collected at four stages i.e. during production, rinsing of final syrup, mixing and cleaning Internal part (CIP). CIP has two sub-stages one having three steps and another four steps. Mirinda and Pepsi production is for 5 days and 2 days, respectively in a week. CIP will be every Sunday. The sample volume was dependent upon the volume of the effluent from different products and operations generated every day. The samples of MSDI were collected after 25 days of the first Bmp test for trial-2 like the first sampling (Table 1).

**Inoculum Sampling.** The inoculums used to inoculate the Bmp reactors were collected from a mesophilic anaerobic digester obtained from DALI which was used to treat effluents of the industry. The inoculum was collected at different heights of sampling points at 2 m, 4 m, 6 m, 8 m and 10 m from the ground. An equal volume of inoculum (200 ml) was taken at each height of sampling point and it was mixed into one sample holder. The inoculum was sieved during sampling using 2 mm size mesh. It was taken four times, first for first Bmp test of mixed substrates of MSDIE & RSW and pure MSDIE, the second for control tests of both Bmp tests of mixed substrates & pure MSDIE, the third for the second Bmp test of mixed substrates & pure MSDIE and fourth for control test for second tests of mixed substrate & pure MSDIE. Inoculums were stored at Bmp test temperature or at ambient Temperature for less than five days to keep them fresh [12]. Sample of inoculums was stored for one day and then analysed for Total Solids (TS) & Volatile Solids (VS) putting on water a bath at a process temperature of 36.5 °C.

## 2.2 Analysis of Raw, Bmp Test Effluent and Inoculum

**Analysis of Basic Parameters.** The collected samples of DALI, MSDI industries and inoculum were analyzed using CP – 505, ORION STAR A211 and HI 5522, USA $P^H$ meters, respectively. The Physicochemical Sample analysis was undertaken by triple analysis. COD of all raw samples and effluents from the Bmp test were measured by using HI 839800 COD REACTOR & test tube heater 2008 series. COD values of the samples were measured with COD meter (AL200, COD Vario) after measuring the COD value of the blank sample. DO of the RSW was measured directly after sampling by using DO meter (HQ40d). DO was measured with triple analysis. BOD of all raw samples, inoculum & Bmp effluents including their control tests was analyzed two times for both trials in a triple manner. $BOD_5$ of the Bmp test effluent of all reactors which was filled with substrates & inoculum also measured after digestion.TS and VS are compulsory parameters for substrates (subs) as well as inoculum analysis. TS & VS was analyzed by Gravimetric method with Ovens BINDER D78532 Tuttlingen and Bahnhofstr 20, 28865 Lilienthal/Bremen, of Germany, respectively.

**Analysis of Inoculum.** pH & Temp of the sieved inoculum was measured at the industry laboratory. The DO, $BOD_5$, TS and VS of sieved inoculum was analysed using standard methods. Determination of VS of inoculum was important in Bmp test because it was helpful to fix the volume of the sample and the inoculum. The volume of inoculum used for all Bmp tests of all main and control experiments was calculated depending upon VS

**Table 1.** The volume of sample collected from various sources of MSDI, trial-1 & trial-2.

| Operation type | Time (min) | Flow rate ($m^3/h$) | Discharge ($m^3/d$) | Sample vol. (ml) | Time (min) | Flow rate ($m^3/h$) | Discharge ($m^3/d$) | Sample Vol. (ml) |
|---|---|---|---|---|---|---|---|---|
| Mirinda production | – | – | 585.15 | 2500 | – | – | 518.33 | 2500 |
| Pepsi production | – | – | 585.15 | 1000 | – | – | 518.33 | 500 |
| 7 up production | 11.61 ± 2.38 | 14.06 ± 0.78 | 8.162 | 7.874 | – | – | 518.33 | 500 |
| Rinsing of final syrup line, filler & mixer | – | – | 3 | 2.894 | 11.25 ± 2.2 | 13.96 ± 0.74 | 18.328 | 17.680 |
| Three steps CIP | – | – | | | – | – | – | |
| Caustic | 23.75 ± 4.79 | 14.65 ± 0.53 | 0.828 | 0.799 | 26.67 ± 1.86 | 14.6 ± 0.44 | 0.927 | 1.788 |
| Caustic rinse with cool water | 6.5 ± 1 | 14.55 ± 0.41 | 0.225 | 0.434 | 5.33 ± 1.03 | 14.65 ± 0.4 | 0.186 | 0.359 |
| Final rinse | 11.25 ± 2.5 | 14.8 ± 0.43 | 0.396 | 0.765 | 11.67 ± 2.58 | 14.6 ± 0.44 | 0.406 | 0.782 |
| Total | | | 1.450 | 1.998 | – | | 1.519 | 2.930 |
| Five step CIP | – | – | | | – | – | – | |
| Caustic | 29.5 ± 4.20 | 14.85 ± 0.47 | 1.043 | 1.006 | 27.5 ± 2.26 | 14.3 ± 0.68 | 0.936 | 1.806 |
| Caustic rinse with warm water | 25 ± 4.08 | 14.05 ± 0.99 | 0.836 | 0.807 | 26.5 ± 1.97 | 13.93 ± 0.84 | 0.879 | 1.696 |
| Sanitize | 56.25 ± 6.29 | 14.3 ± 0.81 | 1.915 | 1.847 | 53.33 ± 4.08 | 14.20 ± 0.82 | 1.803 | 3.479 |
| Final rinsing | 11.25 ± 2.50 | 13.65 ± 0.90 | 0.366 | 0.353 | 10.83 ± 2.04 | 13.83 ± 0.75 | 0.357 | 0.688 |
| Total | | | 4.160 | 4.013 | | | 3.975 | 7.67 |

of substrates and VS of inoculum. To know the performance of the anaerobic reactor, characteristics of the effluent from anaerobic digester was analyzed. This helped to know the per cent removal of TS, VS & $BOD_5$ of the raw effluent which was added to the reactor. Quality of Bmp effluent from mixed subs and per cent removal of the impurities was analyzed in terms of TS, VS & $BOD_5$. TS, VS & $BOD_5$ were analyzed like the raw effluent. Temp, $P^H$, Ash, DO & COD of the Bmp test effluents also analyzed like the raw industrial effluents.

*Determination of Volume Inoculum for Bmp Test.* To minimize acidification or inhibition problems the portion of VS from the inoculum should be greater than that from the subs; for easily degradable subs Inoculum and Substrates (I/S) ratio should be greater than or equal to four [12, 13].

## 2.3 Experimental Description

The Bmp tests were initialized to measure the methane potential of two different samples, one for mixed subs (25% RSW+75%MSDIE) with a working volume of 1.4 l and the second for pure MSDIE with a working volume of 1.8l. All Bmp tests including their control tests were conducted in duplicate. For main test trial-1 of mixed subs with total VS of 18.151 g, the volume of inoculum was 269.031 ml (VS = 16.867 g/l) and 283.175 ml of inoculum (VS = 17.86 g/l) was used for the second trial of mixed subs with total VS of 20.23 g. The volume of inoculum for the main test of MSDIE of trial-1 with total VS of 3.996 g was 59.228 ml (VS = 16.867 g/l) and 62.99 ml of inoculum (VS = 17.86 g/l) was used for the second trial of MSDIE with total VS of 4.5 g. The Original $P^H$ of the mixed substrates before pouring into the reactor and mixing with an inoculum of main tests of trial-1 & trial-2 was kept at the neutrality range (7.0 to 7.8) suitable for methanogenic activity [14]. The original $P^H$ was in the neutrality range (7.34 and 7.46, respectively). The original $P^H$ of MSDIE was 8.27 & 8.61 and adjusted to working $P^H$ of 7.38 & 7.32 of trial-1 & trial-2, respectively adjusted using 6M HCl & 2M NaOH.

**Bmp Test Experimental Setup and Operation.** The wastewater was first characterized according to the standard procedure before being poured into the digester. Bmp test was conducted in duplicate in batch operation using 2 L anaerobic reactors. Water-column based gas measuring method was applied. In particular, the method allowed produced methane passed as bubbles through 2M NaOH solution, that pushed the alkaline water level down in the column & the volume of displaced alkaline water was taken as the volume of biomethane. The Anaerobic batch digester was connected to a gas measuring cylinder. An 8 mm diameter L-shape glass tube used for gas flow was inserted into rubber stopper which was used to cover the opening of the reactor. The rubber stopper which was placed on the opening of gas measuring cylinder held two L-shape 8 mm glass tubes, one to receive gas from the reactor and other for flow of the displaced solution. A plastic tube was used to connect the glass tubes between the reactor & gas measuring cylinder.

To maintain the anaerobic condition, the oxygen present in the reactor was sucked by using a suction pump for a few minutes. To prevent the re-entry of the oxygen, rubber stoppers were placed immediately in the opening of the reactor & silicon gasket was applied to seal the rubber stopper. To obtain pure methane or to clean the biogas, the biogas produced from the anaerobic digestion (AD) of subs and inoculum was allowed to pass through the alkaline solution (2M NaOH) to absorb $CO_2$ using phenophetalin as an indicator. The gas measuring cylinder (inverted in the bucket) and the bucket were filled with a reddish colour alkaline solution.

After arranging the gas measuring set up, the reactor was submerged in a water bath (SY-2L4H WATER BATHS) maintaining the mesophilic temperature of 36.5 °C. To maintain the homogeneity of the subs or to maximize the contact between substrates and microorganisms, mixing should be applied in several ways: turning up and down once a day, using stirring magnet bar & using an external agitation system [14]. In this Bmp test manual up and downmixing was applied once in a day during each day of digestion. The water bath was filled with water periodically as and when its water level decreased. Biogas production was monitored for continuous 25 days (Fig. 1).

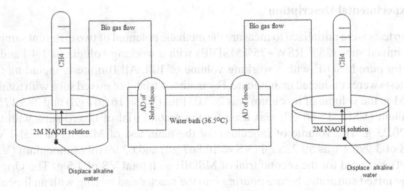

**Fig. 1.** Arrangement of Bio-methane production (Bmp) test

**Conducting Control Test.** The Bmp test for the control test was also conducted using similar volume (2 L) of the reactor, and due to equipment restriction it was conducted after the Bmp tests of the samples. The control test was conducted to measure the methane potential of the residual organic content present in the inoculum. The experimental setup and methane yield measurement were similar to that of the main experiment. The volatile solids (g) of the inoculum added to the control test of each sub was equal to the sample but the volume of inoculum was not equal due to inoculum characteristics varying with time. The volume of distilled water added for the control test was equal to the sample volume which was added to the main experiment. The control test trial-1 of mixed subs contained 18.15 g/L of VS, while the inoculum (308.69 ml) contained 14.70 g/L VS. The second trial of mixed subs contained 20.23 g/L of VS, while inoculums (237.08 ml) contained 21.33 g/l of VS. The control test trial-1 of pure MSDIE contained 3.99 g/L of VS, while the inoculum (67.959 ml) contained 14.70 g/L. The second trial of pure MSDIE contained 4.5 g/L of VS, while inoculums (52.736 ml) contained 21.33 g/l of VS. The $P^H$ of the control tests was adjusted to neutrality range similar to that of the main experiment.

## 2.4 Process of Biogas Production

The process of AD occurs in a sequence of stages involving distinct types of bacteria [15]. That can be described by four key steps, i.e., hydrolysis, acidogenesis, acetogenesis and methanogenesis [16]. In the first step hydrolysis, involves the breakdown of large organic polymer like carbohydrates, proteins, and fats chains into smaller molecules such as simple sugars, amino acids and fatty acids by hydrolytic bacteria, in the second step Acidogenesis, fermentative bacteria utilize & convert products of hydrolysis to organic acids & alcohol. In the next step acetogenesis; acetogenins consume hydrogen gas & produce acetic acid, carbon and energy sources. Finally, methanogens utilize and convert the intermediate products of the preceding steps into biogas ($CH_4$ and $CO_2$) and trace gases [17].

## 2.5 Electricity Production from Biomethane Capacity

Based on the collected data concerning the kind and amount of waste from the FAB industry, the potential for methane production was calculated. The methane potential was determined as [18]

$$Q = \sum_{i=1}^{n} RiLi \tag{1}$$

Where, Q is the methane production potential in the industry ($m^3$ of $CH_4$/year), Ri is the amount of the $i^{th}$ kind of waste generated in the industry (tonnes/year), and Li is the methane production efficiency from the $i^{th}$ kind of waste in a given branch ($m^3$ of $CH_4$/tonne).

# 3 Results and Discussion

In this section quality parameters of the Raw and Bmp test effluents of industrial effluents & inoculum results are listed and discussed. The bio-methane produced from the mixed subs & pure MSDIE was presented graphically and quality improvement i.e. removal of the raw effluents was expressed in terms of TS, VS & $BOD_5$.

## 3.1 Characteristics of Raw and Bmp Test Effluents

**Characteristics of RSW.** The quality parameters of RSW having dark brown colour were characterized as very high in terms of $BOD_5$, COD, TS, VS, ASH, Temp and $P^H$ (Table 2). The quality of RSW was comparable with the results of other studies [19–22]. The quality of RSW was very high compared to the quality of MSDIE.

**Characteristics of Raw and Bmp Test Effluent of Mixed Substrates.** The raw mixed substrates were characterized as medium to strong waste with 6470 m g/l of $BOD_5$, 17100 mg/l of COD, $P^H$ of 7.41 & VS of 13.71 g/l. The Bmp test effluent of mixed subs was characterized by medium strength with 2,185.32 mg/l of $BOD_5$, 10,100 mg/l of COD, $P^H$ of 7.43 & 4.12 g/l of VS (Table 3).

**Table 2.** Characteristics of Raw effluent of RSW

| Parameter | Before digestion |
|---|---|
| Temp (°C) | 52.9 ± 0.28 |
| $p^H$ | 4.2 ± 0.13 |
| DO(mg/l) | 2.00 ± 0.08 |
| BOD₅(mg/l) | 47,380 ± 1,456.61 |
| COD(mg/l) | 99,000 ± 4,242.64 |
| TS(g/l) | 76.43 ± 1.76 |
| Ash(g/l) | 28.67 ± 3.03 |
| VS(g/l) | 47.75 ± 2.98 |

**Table 3.** Characteristics of raw and Bmp test effluent of mixed substrates.

| Parameter | Before digestion | After digestion |
|---|---|---|
| Temp (°C) | 10.1 ± 0.17 | 33.58 ± 0.46 |
| $p^H$ | 7.41 ± 0.08 | 7.43 ± 0.06 |
| DO(mg/l) | 6.88 ± 0.47 | 0.15 ± 0.01 |
| BOD5(mg/l) | 6,470 ± 14.14 | 2,185.32 ± 139.72 |
| COD(mg/l) | 17,100 ± 989.95 | 10,100 ± 424.26 |
| TS(g/l) | 21.48 ± 0.76 | 9.12 ± 0.70 |
| Ash(g/l) | 7.77 ± 1.00 | 5.00 ± 1.28 |
| VS(g/l) | 13.71 ± 0.84 | 4.12 ± 1.4 |

**Characteristics of Raw and Bmp Test Effluent of Pure MSDIE.** Pure MSDIE have medium quality with 40.9 mg/l of BOD₅, 502 mg/l of COD, 2.36 g/l of VS & $P^H$. A comparatively low $P^H$ of 6.92 of MSDIE was measured during rinsing of syrup tanks, while a high $P^H$ of 12.63 was measured during cleaning with caustic. Use of caustic soda for cleaning & effluent from raw water treatment (RO) may be a reason to increase the $P^H$ and TS of MSDIE [21, 23]. The Bmp test effluent with 12.7 mg/l of BOD₅, 710 mg/l of COD, $P^H$ of 7.43 & 0.67 g/l of VS (Table 4) was characterized as low strength effluent.

## 3.2  Bmp Test Results and Quality Improvements

During the Bmp test, all trials of both substrates including their control tests produced high methane volume on the first day of the digestion (Table 5). This indicated that the I/S which was used in all Bmp test prevented the initial buildup of materials, meaning thereby, that the volume of inoculum added to the reactors was enough to degrade the VS present in both substrates.

**Table 4.**  Characteristics of raw & Bmp test effluent of MSDIE.

| Parameter | Before digestion | After digestion |
|---|---|---|
| Temp (°C) | 24.9 ± 0.17–55.13 ± 0.12 | 31.4 ± 1.37 |
| pH | 6.92 ± 0.08–12.63 ± 0.00 | 7.43 ± 0.03 |
| DO(mg/l) | 5.16 ± 0.03–6.64 ± 0.08 | 0.180 ± 0.01 |
| $BOD_5$(mg/l) | 40.9 ± 1.83 | 12.70 ± 1.49 |
| COD(mg/l) | 502 ± 25.46 | 710 ± 14.14 |
| TS(g/l) | 3.17 ± 0.57 | 1.1 ± 0.30 |
| Ash(g/l) | 0.807 ± 0.63 | 0.433 ± 0.22 |
| VS(g/l) | 2.36 ± 0.41 | 0.667 ± 0.23 |

**Table 5.**  Inoculum characteristics used for all Bmp tests

| Parameter | Trial-1 | | Trial-2 | |
|---|---|---|---|---|
| | For both subs | For control tests | For both subs | For control tests |
| Temp (°C) | 22.93 ± 0.06 | 24.4 ± 0.20 | 23.3 ± 0.25 | 24.66 ± 0.11 |
| pH | 7.81 ± 0.00 | 7.24 ± 0.01 | 7.71 ± 0.02 | 7.31 ± 0.17 |
| TS(g/l) | 38.53 ± 1.29 | 39.83 ± 1.40 | 48.57 ± 0.75 | 48.2 ± 2.23 |
| VS(g/l) | 16.87 ± 2.06 | 14.7 ± 1.49 | 17.86 ± 1.87 | 24.66 ± 2.42 |
| DO | 0.14 ± 0.01 | 0.13 ± 0.02 | 0.16 ± 0.01 | 0.15 ± 0.01 |
| $BOD_5$ | 2033.3 ± 237.98 | 2070.00 ± 96.44 | 1876.67 ± 66.58 | 2273.33 ± 166.53 |

**Bmp Test Results and Quality Improvements of Mixed Substrates.** There was an improvement in the quality of effluent from mixed subs under Bmp test. There was a removal of 57.55% of TS, 69.93% of VS and 66.22% of $BOD_5$ of mixed subs during AD. The percentage removal of COD of mixed subs was lower than documented pieces of evidence elsewhere [7, 15, 24], this could be due to the residual COD of inoculums.

Bio-methane was produced from the main experiment & control test of both trials during the whole digestion time. Comparatively higher methane volume was measured during the second trial of Bmp test for both main experiment & control test. This was due to the higher organic content of subs in the second trial compared to the first trial [21, 24]. The degassing of inoculum will be 2–5 days at process temperature [25]. But during the Bmp tests of control and both substrates, bio-methane was produced for more than ten days of digestion. The decline in degassing of inoculums by two to five days should deplete the residual organic content, which is present in the inoculum. The total yield of bio-methane production was 260.07 ml per gram of VS for mixed substrates. The cumulative methane production after 25 days was 4991 ml (Table 6).

**Table 6.** Bmp test result of mixed subs and its control tests of both trials in ml of $CH_4$.

| Time day | Trial-1 | | | Trial-2 | | | $CH_4$ product | | $CH_4$ yield | |
|---|---|---|---|---|---|---|---|---|---|---|
| | Subs | Inocu | Net | Subs | Inocu | Net | Ave net | Cumu | Ave Net | Cumu |
| 1 | 630 | 44 | 586 | 780 | 90 | 690 | 638 | 638 | 33.245 | 33.245 |
| 2 | 122 | 2 | 120 | 380 | 68 | 312 | 216 | 854 | 11.255 | 44.500 |
| 3 | 150 | 2 | 148 | 410 | 12 | 398 | 273 | 1127 | 14.225 | 58.725 |
| 4 | 220 | 44 | 176 | 330 | 26 | 304 | 240 | 1367 | 12.506 | 71.231 |
| 5 | 340 | 16 | 324 | 260 | 22 | 238 | 281 | 1648 | 14.642 | 85.874 |
| 6 | 280 | 14 | 266 | 250 | 10 | 240 | 253 | 1901 | 13.183 | 99.057 |
| 7 | 370 | 12 | 358 | 270 | 16 | 254 | 306 | 2207 | 15.945 | 115.002 |
| 8 | 220 | 6 | 214 | 355 | 12 | 343 | 278.5 | 2485.5 | 14.512 | 129.514 |
| 9 | 270 | 12 | 258 | 340 | 10 | 330 | 294 | 2779.5 | 15.320 | 144.834 |
| 10 | 300 | 10 | 290 | 265 | 14 | 251 | 270.5 | 3050 | 14.095 | 158.929 |
| 11 | 270 | 10 | 260 | 190 | 14 | 176 | 218 | 3268 | 11.359 | 170.288 |
| 12 | 250 | 10 | 240 | 110 | 12 | 98 | 169 | 3437 | 8.806 | 179.094 |
| 13 | 210 | 8 | 202 | 140 | 16 | 124 | 163 | 3600 | 8.494 | 187.588 |
| 14 | 190 | 10 | 180 | 215 | 14 | 201 | 190.5 | 3790.5 | 9.927 | 197.514 |
| 15 | 205 | 10 | 195 | 235 | 8 | 227 | 211 | 4001.5 | 10.995 | 208.509 |
| 16 | 190 | 4 | 186 | 155 | 2 | 153 | 169.5 | 4171 | 8.832 | 217.341 |
| 17 | 165 | 0 | 165 | 140 | 4 | 136 | 150.5 | 4321.5 | 7.842 | 225.184 |
| 18 | 145 | 0 | 145 | 110 | 10 | 100 | 122.5 | 4444 | 6.383 | 231.567 |
| 19 | 122 | 4 | 118 | 122 | 12 | 110 | 114 | 4558 | 5.940 | 237.507 |
| 20 | 98 | 20 | 78 | 126 | 10 | 116 | 97 | 4655 | 5.054 | 242.562 |
| 21 | 78 | 6 | 72 | 120 | 2 | 118 | 95 | 4750 | 4.950 | 247.512 |
| 22 | 64 | 4 | 60 | 82 | 0 | 82 | 71 | 4821 | 3.700 | 251.212 |
| 23 | 58 | 0 | 58 | 80 | 4 | 76 | 67 | 4888 | 3.491 | 254.703 |
| 24 | 46 | 0 | 46 | 76 | 4 | 72 | 59 | 4947 | 3.074 | 257.777 |
| 25 | 38 | 2 | 36 | 62 | 10 | 52 | 44 | 4991 | 2.293 | 260.070 |

The volume of methane produced during Bmp test of all substrates and their control tests is given in Figs. 2, 3, 4, 5, 6 and 7. The net gas produced in every day of Bmp test of a substrate was obtained by subtracting the $CH_4$ produced by inoculum. The average net $CH_4$ of subs was obtained for both trials (Fig. 2 and 3).

The yield of $CH_4$ was measured as the volume of $CH_4$ per gram of VS of the substrates and calculated by dividing total cumulative or average net methane volume of substrates by total gram of VS of the substrates present in Fig. 4. The cumulative $CH_4$ product of substrates was calculated by adding the average net $CH_4$ product in each day showed in Fig. 4.

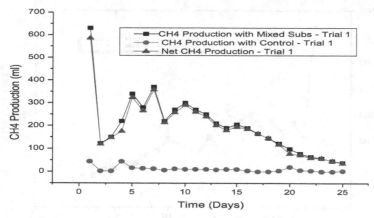

**Fig. 2.** CH₄ production (ml) of main experiment & control test of mixed subs vs. Time (day), trial-1

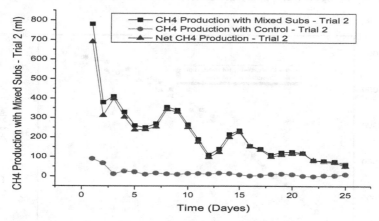

**Fig. 3.** CH₄ production (ml) of main experiment & control test of mixed subs vs. Time (day), trial-2

The cumulative methane production from mixed substrates was shown in Fig. 5. Methane production per gram of VS with time was shown in Fig. 5. The cumulative production of methane increased up to 25 days and after that, it was stopped the production.

**Bmp Test Results and Quality Improvements of Pure MSDIE.** There was an improvement in the quality of effluent from MSDIE under Bmp test. There was a removal of 65.27% of TS, 71.78% of VS and 68.95% of MSDIE during anaerobic digestion. The residual COD of inoculum might be the reason to increase the COD of Bmp test effluent. The percentage of impurity removal which was recorded during the Bmp test was comparable with other studies [26–28].

After 21 days of digestion, there was no bio-methane production from the main experiment, while methane production of control tests was stopped after the 10th day

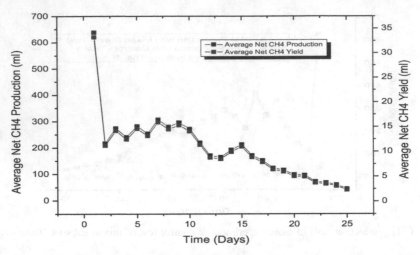

**Fig. 4.** Average net CH$_4$ production & CH$_4$ Yield of mixed subs vs. Time (day)

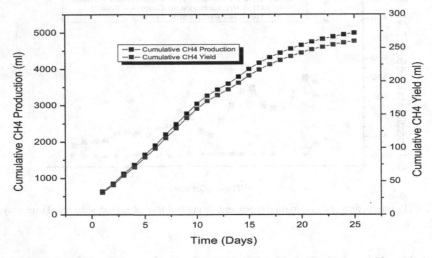

**Fig. 5.** Cumulative CH$_4$ production (ml) CH$_4$ yield (ml) of mixed subs vs. Time (day)

of digestion (Fig. 6). Comparatively higher methane volume was measured during the second trial of Bmp test for both main experiment & control test (Fig. 7). This was due to the higher organic content of subs in the second trial compared to the first trial [17, 26, 29]. The bio-methane yield was comparable with other results of Bmp test of MSDIE (Fig. 8). The cumulative bio-methane yield of MSDIE was 76.15 ml per gram of VS which was added at the startup of the digestion with a cumulative biomethane product of 323.5 ml (Fig. 9).

**Electricity Production.** In this research Moha soft drinks industry can establish the Anaerobic Digestion unit to produce biomethane which can convert into electricity to

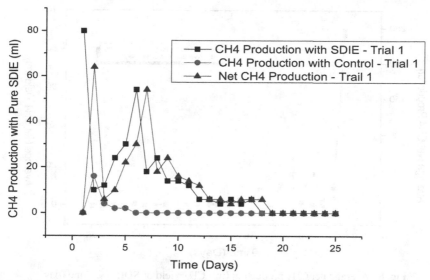

**Fig. 6.** $CH_4$ production (ml) of the main experiment of SDIE & its control test vs. Time (day), trial-1

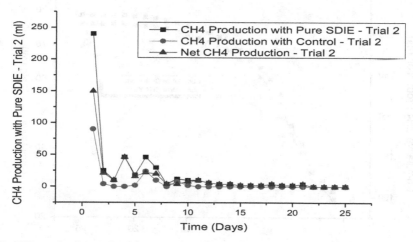

**Fig. 7.** $CH_4$ production (ml) of the main experiment of SDIE & its control test vs. Time (day), trial-2

fulfil the need of the industry. In this research used 2 L anaerobic digestion unit to produce methane, the highest cumulative production of biomethane after 25 days was 4991 ml means 4.991 kg or 4.991 $m^3$ of methane was produced. Theoretically (actual average) from 1 $m^3$ of biogas, 2.1 kWh electrical energy can be produced [18]. As per the records Moha soft drinks industry producing 17,000 cases of soft drinks per day and using 300000 L of water per day. The effluents might be approximately 283000 L per day. The production of biogas within a day will be 9408.335 $m^3$ (First-day methane

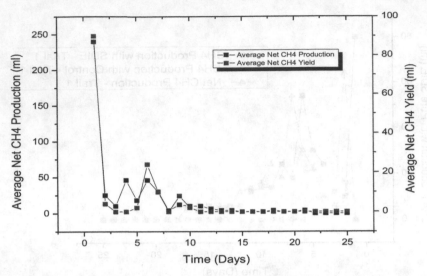

**Fig. 8.** Average net $CH_4$ production (ml) $CH_4$ yield of SDIE vs. Time (day)

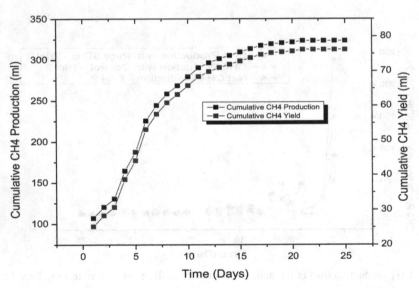

**Fig. 9.** Cumulative $CH_4$ productions (ml) & $CH_4$ yield (ml) of pure SDIE measured in ml of $CH_4$ vs. Time (day)

production was 33.245 ml). As per the Eq. 1, the electricity production capacity will be approximately 19757.50 kWh per day.

# 4   Conclusion

The parameters were measured during rinsing of syrup tanks & during washing of syrup tanks, filler & mixer using caustic soda respectively for Moha soft drinks industrial effluents. RSW was characterized as strong waste which was dark brown in colour. The Bmp test removed 57.55% of TS, 69.93% of VS and 66.22% of $BOD_5$ from mixed substrates and 65.27% of TS, 71.78% of VS & 68.95% of $BOD_5$ from MSDIE. The quality of Bmp effluent of MSDIE was within the standards of WHO to dispose of water bodies safely. The neutral range of pH was suitable for mesophilic activity was observed. Comparatively high bio-methane volume was produced from mixed substrates than MSDIE. The total yield of bio-methane production was 260.07 ml per gram of VS for mixed substrates. The cumulative methane production after 25 days was 4991 ml. The electricity production possibility from the effluents of Moha soft drinks industry will be 19757 kWh per day which can fulfil the energy needs of the industry.

# References

1. Nweke, C., Nwabanne, J., Igbokwe, P.: Anaerobic digestion treatment of soft drink wastewater. J. Environ. Hum. **2**(1), 25–35 (2015). https://doi.org/10.15764/EH.2015.01004
2. Chowdhary, P., Raj, A., Bharagava, R.N.: Environmental pollution and health hazards from distillery wastewater and treatment approaches to combat the environmental threats: a review. Chemosphere **194**, 229–246 (2018). https://doi.org/10.1016/j.chemosphere.2017.11.163
3. Haroon, H., Waseem, A., Mahmood, Q.: Treatment and reuse of waste water from beverage industry. J. Chem. Soc. Pak. **35**(1), 5–10 (2013)
4. Tshuma, J., et al.: Open access beverage effluent treatment technology. Am. J. Eng. Res. (Ajer) **5**(10/0109), 1–9 (2016). http://www.ajer.org
5. Ince, O., Kolukirik, M., Oz, N.A., Ince, B.K.: Comparative evaluation of full-scale uasb reactors treating alcohol distillery wastewaters in terms of performance and methanogenic activity. **144**, 138–144 (2005). https://doi.org/10.1002/Jctb.1154
6. Vaishali, A.P., Pooja, J.B., Yogesh, P.L., Mayuri, J.B.: Characterization of molasses spent wash and its decolorization using mushroom cultivation. Int. J. Res. Chem. Environ. **7**(1), 25–29 (2017). http://www.ijrce.org
7. Myra, L.T., David, L.H., Judith, C.T.: Treatment of mollasses based distillery waste water in a pilot scae anaerobic sequencing batch reactor (ASBR). Electron. J. Biol. **2**, 1–7 (2016)
8. Ally, Y.: Reduction of the environmental impact of a soft drink manufacturing plant. Unpublished master's thesis, University of KwaZulu-Natal, Durban (2015)
9. Cantrell, K.B., Ducey, T., Ro, K.S., Hunt, P.G.: Livestock waste to bioenergy generation opportunities. Biores. Technol. **99**, 7941–7953 (2008)
10. Metcalf and Eddy, Inc.: Wastewater Engineering, Treatment, Disposal and Reuse. 3rd edn, pp. 359–440, 1275–1280. McGraw-Hill, Inc., Singapore (1991)
11. Shin, S.G., Han, G., Lim, J., Lee, C., Hwang, S.: A comprehensive microbial insight into twostage anaerobic digestion of food waste-recycling wastewater. Water Res. **44**, 4838–4849 (2010)
12. Holliger, C., et al.: Towards a standardization of biomethane potential tests. Water Sci. Technol. **74**(11), 2515–2522 (2016). https://doi.org/10.2166/wst.2016.336
13. Moody, L.: Using Biochemical Methane Potentials & Anaerobic Toxicity Assays. Un Published Lecture Notes, Iowa State University, 15 April 2010

14. Esposito, G., Frunzo, L., Liotta, F., Panico, A., Pirozzi, F.: Bio-methane potential tests to measure the biogas production from the digestion and co-digestion of complex organic substrates. Open Environ. Eng. J. **5**, 1–8 (2012)

15. Papong, S., Rotwiroon, P., Chatchupong, T., Malakul, P.: Life cycle energy and environmental assessment of bio-CNG utilization from cassava starch wastewater treatment plants in Thailand. Renew. Energy **65**, 64–69 (2014). https://doi.org/10.1016/j.renene.2013.07.012

16. Muzenda, E.: Bio-methane generation from organic waste: a review. In: World Congress on Engineering and Computer Science (WCECS), vol. 2, pp. 22–24 (2014)

17. Wang, B., Achu, I., Nistor, M., Liu, J.: Determination of methane yield of celluloseusing different experimental setups. Water Sci. Technol. 598–564 (2014). https://www.researchgate.net/publication/264715634

18. Pazera, A., et al.: Biogas in Europe: food and beverage (FAB) waste potential for biogas production. In: 2nd International Scientific Conference Biogas Science, ACS Publications, Special Issue, Enegy fuels (2015). https://doi.org/10.1021/ef502812s

19. Mengistu, M.G., Simane, B., Eshete, G., Workneh, T.S.: A review on biogas technology and its contributions to sustainable rural livelihood in Ethiopia. Renew. Sustain. Energy Rev. **48**, 306–316 (2015). https://doi.org/10.1016/j.rser.2015.04.026

20. Mojapelo, N., Muzenda, E., Kigozi, R., Aboyade, A.O.: Bio-methane potential of the organic fraction of municipal solid waste. In: 6th International Conference on Green Technology, Renewable Energy & Environmental Engg (ICGTREEE), Cape Town (SA), 27–28 November, pp. 193–197 (2014)

21. Morosini, C., Conti, F., Torretta, V., Rada, E.C., Passamani, G.: Biochemical methane potential assays to test the biogas production from the anaerobic digestion of sewage sludge and other organic matrices. WIT Trans. Ecol. Environ. **205**, 235–243 (2016). https://doi.org/10.2495/Eq160221

22. Turinayo, Y.K.: Physicochemical properties of sugar industry and molasses based distillery effluent and its effect on water quality of River Musamya in Uganda. Int. J. Environ. Agric. Biotechnol. **2**(3), 1064–1069 (2017). https://doi.org/10.22161/ijeab/2.3.8

23. Redzwan, G., Banks, C.: An evaluation of soft-drink waste water treatment by anaerobic digestion. Malays. J. Sci. **26**(1), 23–34 (2007). https://www.researchgate.net/publication/262137873

24. Svensson, K., Kjørlaug, O., Jarle, S., Wittrup, J.: Biomass and bioenergy comparison of approaches for organic matter determination in relation to expression of bio-methane potentials. Biomass Bioenerg. **100**, 31–38 (2017). https://doi.org/10.1016/j.biombioe.2017.03.005

25. Angelidaki, I., et al.: Defining the biomethane potential (BMP) of solid organic wastes and energy crops: a proposed protocol for batch assays. Water Sci. Technol. **59**(5), 927–934 (2009). https://doi.org/10.2166/wst.2009.040

26. Nadais, M.H., Capela, I.: Synthetic soft drink waste water suitability for production of volatile fatty acids. Process Biochem. **50**(8), 1308–1312 (2016). https://doi.org/10.1016/j.procbio.2015.04.007

27. Narihiro, T., Kim, N.-K., Mei, R., Nobu, M.K., Liu, W.-T.: Microbial community analysis of anaerobic reactors treating soft drink wastewater. PLOS ONE **10**(3), e0119131 (2015). https://doi.org/10.1371/journal.pone.0119131

28. Sheldon, M., Erdogan, I.: Multi-stage EGSB/MBR treatment of soft drink industry wastewater. Chem. Eng. J. **285**, 368–377 (2016). https://doi.org/10.1016/j.cej.2015.10.021

29. Wannapokin, A., Ramaraj, R., Unpaprom, Y.: An investigation of biogas production potential from fallen teak leaves (Tectona grandis). Emergent Life Sci. Res. **3**(1), 1–10 (2017)

# Performance Evaluation of Pressurized Irrigation System (A Case of Kobo Girana Irrigation System, Ethiopia)

Kassa Abera[1]($\boxtimes$) and Michael Mehari[2]

[1] Department of Hydraulic Engineering, Wollo University, KioT, Kombolcha, Ethiopia
[2] Ministry of Water, Irrigation and Electricity, Addis Ababa, Ethiopia

**Abstract.** There are some pressurized irrigation projects launched in Ethiopia. Yet, there are no more research works on the performance evaluation of pressurized irrigation systems because of researchers believe that pressurized system has good performance. But practically, it is not true especially in developing countries such as Ethiopia, which has poor water resource management system. So to fill this gap, this research was studied on performance evaluation of Hormat Golina–4 drip irrigation systems in Kobo Girana Valley. The objective of this study was to evaluate the performance of Kobo Girana pressurized irrigation, specifically Hormat Golina-4 drip irrigation. The emitter discharge and soil moisture content were collected from seven experimental plots fields. The emitter flow was collected by using a total of 63 catch cans, 9 catch can per plot area and measured by using graduated cylinder. Hydraulic performance indicators such as application efficiency (Ea), irrigation adequacy (Pa), equity performance (PE), dependability performance (PD), delivery performance ratio (DPR) and distribution uniformity characteristics; percent of clogged emitters (Pc), emission uniformity (EU), emitter flow rate variation (qvar), coefficient of variation (Cv) and uniformity coefficient (Uc) were evaluated accordingly. The average values of the above discussed parameters in the scheme were found that Ea (61.41%), Pa (41.52%), PE (0.33), PD (0.23), DPR (2.21), Pclog (33.33%), EU (47.71%), pvar (71.03%), CV (45.31%) and UC (53.42%), respectively. Results showed that the overall performance level of Hormat Golina – 4 drip irrigation systems is low and poor.

**Keywords:** Performance · Evaluation · Pressurized irrigation · Drip system · Kobo Girana · Hormat Golina –4

## 1 Introduction

Ethiopia is one of the developing county which is highly dependent on rainfed agriculture. But due to high climate change variability and degradation of natural resources such as land and water potential, poverty and food insecurity increased from decade to decade. Therefore, one of the best solution to improve rainfed agriculture is development of different irrigation systems [1]. There is no consistent and reliable inventory and well

M. A. Delele et al. (Eds.): ICAST 2020, LNICST 385, pp. 85–97, 2021.
https://doi.org/10.1007/978-3-030-80618-7_6

– studied documented with regards to water and irrigation potential in Ethiopia [2]. Although, the Ministry of Water, Irrigation and Electric city (MoWIE) was indicated 560 irrigation potential sites on different major river basins in the region [3], the total area of irrigable land by twelve major river basins in the region is predicted as nearest to 3.7 million hectares which is based on the suitability of the topography [3]. However, only five percent of this area is irrigated with low performance [4]. Even though, Ethiopia has good rainfall distribution and ample water resources potential, still the agricultural system does not entirely benefit from the technologies and know-how of water resource management and irrigation development system [5].

Beside to major river basins in general and some of the planed irrigation plant in particular has been irrigated by pressurized irrigation system by extracting ground water like Kobo Girana pressurized irrigation system [6]. In Kobo Girana pressurized irrigation development program, 563 ha was irrigated by pressurized (drip and sprinkler) irrigation system but now only 439 ha is irrigated due to well yield reduction and lateral and emitter clogging problem. Performance evaluation and assessment of pressurize irrigation system is one of a technical analysis and classification of water resource management in irrigation and drainage schemes to assure that the input of resources (water and land), operational timetables, anticipated outputs and essential actions proceed as the intended. Solving the performance level of irrigation system using several techniques and planning is deliberated a key issue for addressing the requirement for increasing productivity of irrigated scheme under stress on water resources availability. Many irrigation schemes in developing countries such as Ethiopia, are highly characterized by poor performance level. The main reason for low performance is related to poor institutional structures and non-flexibility of the schemes arrangements [7].

In Ethiopia, irrigation development is still in infant stage due to many challenges, especially, pressurized irrigation system is not well adopted due to its high initial cost and requirement of skilled man power [2]. Adoption of innovated technologies by landholders is a dynamic learning process in developing countries such as Ethiopia. Because, adaptation of innovative technology is highly dependent on different conditions of the society such as, social, cultural and economic aspects, and also characteristics of the technology transformation methods. Therefore, adoption will arise after the landowner recognizes that the technology boosts the individual goals related to their income. The variety of goals is dependent among landowners, including socio-economic, and environmental objectives. Technology is more likely to be adapted when there is a high relative improvement and when they are easily trainable, simple to test and acquire about preceding to implementation.

Kobo Girana Valley Development Program implements large scale pressurized irrigation Project over the region with combination of Surface and Pressurized irrigation system and the source of irrigation water is from ground water. This sub basin has good ground water potential. The main problem of irrigation development in Hormat Golina-4 is inappropriate management of the innovated technology. This is principally due to lack of responsible skilled man power and inadequate institutional setup that are equipped with sufficient capacity [6]. Therefore, it requires a proper operation and watering of the field crop based on the design requirement to increase crop production and to improve water management problems for the sustainability of the system. So to check the effective functionality of each auxiliary structures of the system, performance evaluation of this project is necessary. With this background and justification, this study have been conducted to evaluate the performance of Kobo Girana pressurized irrigation scheme a case of Hormat – Golina 4 Drip irrigation system, with the objectives of assessing the current operation rules and recommending another possibilities for more effective usage of water, sustainability of the system, to improve crop productivity of the irrigable land and to duplicate the technology from government oriented system to small holder farmers by introducing the advantage and the productivity of pressurized irrigation system over surface irrigation system.

## 2 Methods and Materials

### 2.1 Study Area Description

Kobo Valley sub-basin pressurized and surface irrigation project is topographically located between 12°18′ to 11°56′ N and 39°23′ to 39°47′ E of latitude and longitude respectively. Kobo Girana Irrigation Development Project is located in North Wollo Zone Administration in Amhara region which is found at a distance of 50 km from Woldia Town and 410 km from Bahir Dar Town. The total area of Kobo Valley sub-basin is assessed, 1439 km² from which 29% is flat plain and the remaining area is dominated by large mountainous and undulating hilly. The project area is bounded by from North Southern Tigray Zone, from Soth Alawha sub-basin, from West Lasta Mountain and from East Zoble Mountain (Fig. 1).

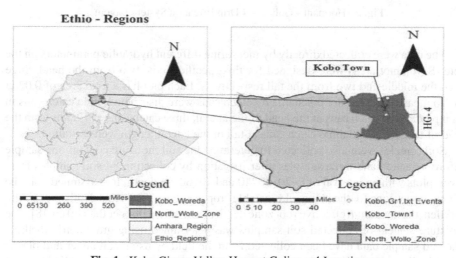

**Fig. 1.** Kobo Girana Valley, Hormat Golina – 4 Location

There are fourteen pressurized irrigation systems; three partially drip and partially sprinkler, eleven drip and forty surface irrigation sites in Kobo Girana Valley Development Program. There is a total of 563 ha irrigable land by drip irrigation system, but now only 439 ha is irrigated. From these Hormat Golina number four (HG-4) is one of a drip irrigation system which is located 3 km from the Kobo Town to south direction and it has a total irrigable area of 50ha and the total number of beneficiaries in this system are 695. Generally, there are 25 head controls and 200 valves to irrigate a total area of 50ha in HG – 4. The manifold has a length of 100 m in which the laterals connected by three – way connectors with a lateral length of 25 m. Each connector has a spacing of 3 m. The lateral and emitter spacing is 1 m and 0.3 m respectively. The width of the lateral is restricted by the operating valve. One head control can irrigate 2 ha at the same time and it contains eight valves each irrigated 0.25 ha (Fig. 2).

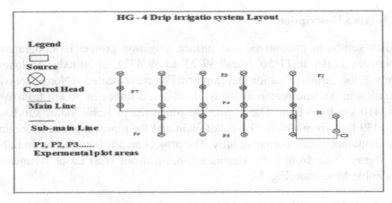

**Fig. 2.**  Hormant - Golina – 4 Drip Irrigation System Layouts

The data were collected directly by measuring different hydraulic parameters on the field. Seven plot areas were designed for this specific study, two from the head, three from the middle and two from the tail respectively. Each plot has a total area of 0.0225 ha. To measure the emitter discharge 63 catch cans were distributed; nine catch cans in each plot. Three catch cans at the head of the lateral, three catch cans at 12.5 m from the head of the lateral and three catch cans at tail of the lateral length were installed.

Soil samples were also collected to determine the soil moisture content one sample before irrigation and three samples after irrigation by collecting 84 soil samples from seven plots with an interval of 0–20, 20–40 and 40–60 cm depth. It is assumed that, the effective root zone for the irrigated vegetable crop is not more than this depth. According to Allen, the maximum effective root zone depth of onion is no longer than 60 cm [8]. The moisture content of collected soil samples was determined using gravimetric method. The soil sample data have been collected from the field by using soil auger and plastic bag. Finally, to determine moisture content, collected soil sample was applied to oven dry at 105 °C for 24 h using a catch can (Fig. 3).

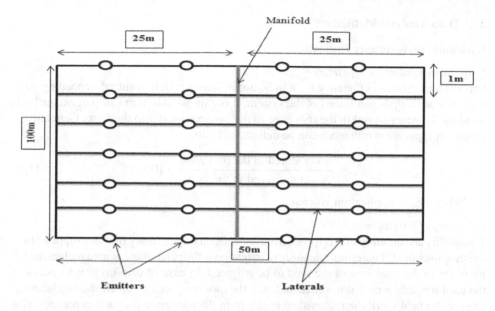

a) Lateral and emitter distribution layout of HG – 4

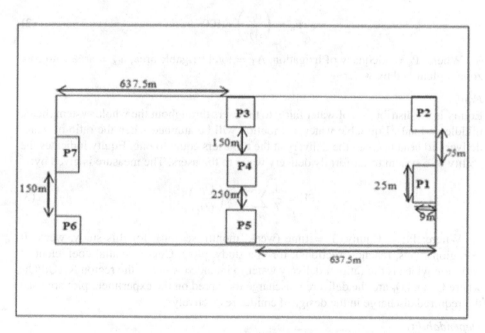

b) Soil sample location in the experiment plot area

**Fig. 3.** Experimental Plot Areas Layout of Hormat – Golina 4

## 2.2  Data Analysis Methods

### Hydraulic Performance Indicators

*Irrigation Application Efficiency*
Irrigation application efficiency is an indicator of losses which occurred depending on the input and output conditions of the system. It is expressed in terms of percentage by dividing the water stored in the root zone to the delivered water to the farm. Generally, irrigation application efficiency can be defined as bellow.

$$E_a = \frac{\text{water stored in the root zone}}{\text{water delivered to the farm}} * 100 \tag{1}$$

Where: $E_a$ = application efficiency.

*Adequacy of Irrigation*
The quality and quantity of crop production depends on the adequacy of water supplied to the irrigation field. Therefore, adequacy of irrigation is the percentage of area replenished by water to the total area of the field to be irrigated. In case of drip irrigation system, the total irrigable area is not wetted and only the root zone area is replenished by water. During the field work the replenished area within the root zone for each experimental plot were measured. Then, adequacy of Hormat Goliina – 4 drip irrigation system is estimated as shown below.

$$P_a = \left(\frac{a_{rz}}{A_T}\right) * 100 \tag{2}$$

Where: $P_a$ = adequacy of Irrigation, $A_T$ = total irrigable area, $a_{rz}$ = area with root zone replenished by water.

*Equity*
Equity is the distribution of water fairly to the users throughout the whole system (head, middle and tail). Equitable water distribution will be attained when the ratio of water delivery to head users to the delivery at the tail users equal to one. Equity indicates the ability of a system to uniformly delivery water to the users. The measure is given by:

$$PE = \frac{1}{T} \sum_T C_{VR}\left(\frac{Q_d}{Q_T}\right) \tag{3}$$

Where: PE = Equity, T = time (week, month, season); for this study, week, R = region (plots, reaches, sections); for this study, plots, $C_{VR}$ = spatial coefficient of variation which is the ratio of delivery water to intended water to the region R, (Qd/Qr) where $Q_d$ and $Q_r$ are the delivered discharge measured on the experiment plot area and the required discharge in the designed emitter respectively.

*Dependability*
Dependability is the degree of temporal variability in the ratio of delivered water to the required water over the region. The dependability parameter is defined as:

$$PD = \frac{1}{R} \sum_R C_{VT}\left(\frac{Q_d}{Q_r}\right) \tag{4}$$

**Table 1.** Water delivery performance indicators Range

| Parameters | Range | | |
|---|---|---|---|
| | Poor | Fair | Good |
| PD | >0.20 | 0.11–0.20 | 0.00–0.10 |
| PA | <0.80 | 0.80–0.89 | 0.90–1.0 |
| PE | >0.25 | 0.11–0.25 | 0.00–0.1 |

*Source: Molden and Gate (1990)*

Where: PD = dependability, T and R were defined before, $C_{VT}$ is temporal coefficient of variation at discrete location in a region R and a time span T.

*Delivery Performance Ratio (DPR)*

The most important and simple performance indicator in irrigation field is delivery performance ratio, which is the ratio of actual delivered discharge to designed discharge. [9]. The average monthly measured discharge for each emitter should be compared with intended (design) discharge by the form of Eq. (5) to get the DPR.

$$\text{Delivery Performance Ratio} = \frac{Q_{act}}{Q_{des}} \tag{5}$$

Where: Qact is the actual measured discharge in each emitter; Qdes is the intended design discharge.

On the actual field, all the emitters were not fully functional and then the total number of completely clogged emitters has been determined using [10] by Eq. (6).

$$P_{NC} = \left(\frac{Nc}{N}\right) * 100 \tag{6}$$

Where: PNc = number of clogged emitters in percent, Nc = number of clogged emitters in the plot, N = total number of emitters in the experiment plot. Drip irrigation is commonly limited to a small area coverage that gradually and commonly delivers water directly to the crop root zone in a droplet manner. Emitter clogging has often been accepted as inconvenient and one of the most significant worries for drip irrigation system projects, it causes to decreased system performance level and increased water pressure between irrigated and non-irrigated crops in the field [11].

**Uniformity Characteristics**

Uniformity refers to the extent of available water distribution over the delineated irrigation area.it is highly affected by water pressure distribution, pipe network arrangement, water quality, source of energy to boost water from the source, status of lateral and hydraulics nature of emitters [12].

*Distribution Uniformity (DU)*

The first one is distribution uniformity (DU) or emitter uniformity (Eu) which will be calculated by using [13] Eq. (7).

$$D_U = 100 * \left(\frac{q_{min}}{q_{aver}}\right) \tag{7}$$

Where: DU = Field distribution uniformity (%); qmin = minimum discharge rate obtained from measurement (l/h) and, qaver = average emitter discharge rates of the given plot (l/h).

*Emitter Flow Variation (qvar)*

Emitter flow variation is the important uniformity characteristics used to check the flow variation between emitters within the latera and it is calculated using equation of [14].

$$q_{var} = \left( \frac{q_{max} - q_{min}}{q_{max}} \right) \tag{8}$$

Where: $q_{var}$ = emitter flow variation, qmax = maximum flow rate in the emitter (l/h), qmin = minimum flow rate in the emitter (l/h).

*Coefficient of Variation*

Another uniformity parameter is coefficient of variation which is the variation of emitter flow rate from the mean. It is the ratio of standard deviation to mean as shown below by using Equation of [14].

$$Cv = \frac{Sd}{qav} \tag{9}$$

Where: Sd = standard deviation of emitter flow rates (l/h) and, $q_{av}$ = average emitter flow rate (l/h).

*Uniformity Coefficient*

Coefficient of uniformity (Uc) is defined as the coefficient of variation and expressed as the ratio of standard deviation to mean and it is determined using Eq. (10) as described below [15].

$$U_C = \left( 1 - \frac{S_d}{q_{av}} \right) * 100 \tag{10}$$

Where: $U_C$ = coefficient of uniformity (%); Sd = average standard deviation of all emitters flow (l/h), $q_{av}$ = average emitter flow rate (l/h).

# 3   Result and Discussion

## 3.1   Irrigation Application Efficiency

The average irrigation application efficiency of HG- 4 was obtained (using Eq. 1) 61.41%. According to Adapted from Irrigation Association, the current efficiency status of the scheme is poor. It is obvious that the application efficiency for drip irrigation is about 90–95%. But, this low efficiency was resulted due to the long service time of the lateral (above ten year), 33.33% of the emitters were completely clogged and 47.62% were discharging over the intended design discharge which is resulted from illegal penetration of the clogged emitters by the users using awl and nail (Table 2). The over discharging, 47.62% (Table 2) was resulted by modifying the manufactured emitter diameter by farmers when the emitter clogged by dust material or fertilizer. This increases the loss of water in the system.

**Table 2.** Irrigation Efficiency analysis and result

| Plot | Emitter discharge (L/hr) Along the lateral | | | Average discharge | | Area | SMD(mm) | Wd(mm) | Ea(%) |
|---|---|---|---|---|---|---|---|---|---|
| | Head | Middle | Tail | Qaver(L/hr) | V(m³) | A(m²) | | | |
| P1 | 2.60 | 3.13 | 0 | 1.91 | 21.65 | 225 | 50.76 | 96.21 | 52.76 |
| P2 | 2.33 | 0.42 | 1.64 | 1.46 | 17.05 | 225 | 48.74 | 75.78 | 64.32 |
| P3 | 0.94 | 0.64 | 0 | 0.53 | 13.06 | 225 | 48.77 | 58.06 | 84.00 |
| P4 | 0.27 | 1.76 | 0 | 0.68 | 13.67 | 225 | 49.34 | 60.74 | 81.23 |
| P5 | 1.90 | 2.58 | 0.33 | 1.61 | 18.71 | 225 | 34.10 | 83.15 | 41.01 |
| P6 | 1.34 | 3.23 | 2.17 | 2.25 | 26.18 | 225 | 47.98 | 116.35 | 41.24 |
| P7 | 2.32 | 1.74 | 0 | 1.35 | 15.78 | 225 | 50.98 | 70.14 | 72.68 |
| Average application efficiency in each reaches (%) | | | | | | Overall Ea (%) | | | |
| Reach | | Head | Middle | | Tail | 61.41 | | | |
| Average efficiency Ea (%) | | 58.54 | 68.75 | | 56.96 | | | | |

**Table 3.** Current Emitter status of HG – 4 on the selected plot areas

| Emitter status | No | Percent (%) |
|---|---|---|
| Normal discharging emitters | 12 | 19.05 |
| Over discharging emitters | 30 | 47.62 |
| Completely clogged emitters | 21 | 33.33 |
| Total | 63 | 100.00 |

## 3.2 Irrigation Adequacy

In Hormat – Golina 4 the maximum averaged replenished width at the root zone was 0.74 m which is 74% of the intended design width (1 m). Using Eq. 2, the adequacy of this scheme has been obtained 41.52%. This inadequate water is resulted due to clogging of emitters (33.33%) and improper penetration of emitters which reduces the water distribution from lateral head to tail (end) and the water availability reduced from head to tail reach. This implies that more water was loss at head reach and the pressure is reduced at the tail reach (Fig. 4).

## 3.3 Equity

Average overall equity of the delivery system of Hormat – Golina 4 is found to be 0.33 (Table 3). Therefore, based on the general criteria given in (Table 1), [9], (0.33 > 0.25), the overall result implies that the scheme equity is poor.

## 3.4 Dependability

The average dependability of this scheme was obtained 0.23 which is unsatisfactory, based on criteria's given in (Table 1) [9], (0.23 > 0.2) (Table 4).

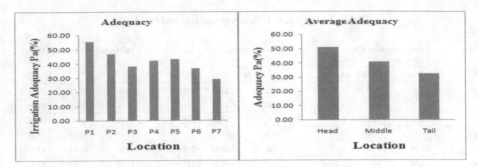

**Fig. 4.** Irrigation adequacy in each experiment plots and Reaches

**Table 4.** Equity and dependability result

| Parameter | Reaches | | | Average |
|-----------|---------|--------|------|---------|
|           | Head    | Middle | Tail |         |
| PD        | 0.23    | 0.25   | 0.22 | 0.23    |
| PE        | 0.21    | 0.46   | 0.32 | 0.33    |

Where: PD = dependability performance and
PE = equity performance.

## 3.5 Delivery Performance Ratio (DPR)

Delivery performance ratio is used to check the delivered quantity of water to crop in line with the intended designed emitter discharge. Accordingly, delivery performance ratio (DPR) of Hormat – Golina 4 was obtained 2.21. This value is greater than unity which is due to the farmers simply puncturing the clogged emitters without considering the standard emitter spacing and diameter which resulted high water loss (Fig. 5).

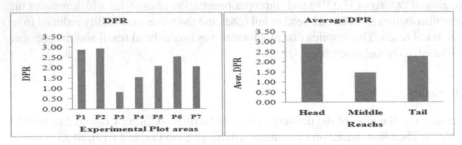

**Fig. 5.** Delivery Performance Ratio of experimental plots and reaches

### 3.6 Emitter Distribution Uniformity

**Distribution Uniformity (EU)**

Average distribution uniformity of Hormat Golina – 4 was 47.71% and which is classified as poor distribution uniformity (<70 for drip system) [15].

**Emitter Flow Variation (qvar)**

The overall flow rate variation of this scheme was found 71.03% which is unacceptable according to [16]. This unacceptable flow variation may come from the long period service of the lateral (ten years in case of HG – 4), poor water quality due to addition of fertilizer, temperature of the area, emitter manufacturing variation and emitter clogging as explained by [17] (Fig. 6).

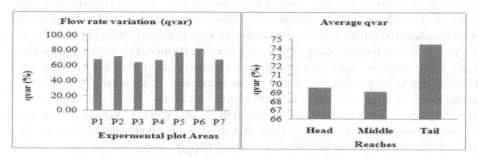

**Fig. 6.** Flow rate variations for experimental plot areas and reaches

**Coefficient of Variation (Cv)**

Average coefficient of variation at head, middle and tail respectively were obtained 35.76%, 50.79% and 49.38% respectively and the overall average coefficient of variation was 45.31% according to [15], which is unacceptable value.

**Uniformity Coefficient (Uc)**

The overall uniformity of the scheme has been found 53.42% and According to [18], this result felts to unacceptable. At the head reach the water pressure is high and as the head increased from head reaches to tail reach, the water pressure becomes low and it cannot be easily pass through the clogged emitters. Uniformity coefficient has inverse proportion with flow rate variation. This implies that as flow rate variation decreased, coefficient of uniformity will have increased.

## 4  Conclusion and Recommendation

### 4.1  Conclusion

This study was conducted in Kobo Girana Valley Development program, to evaluate the performance level of Hormat Golina – 4 drip irrigation systems with the objective of assessing hydraulic performance indicators and uniformity characteristics analysis. The result showed that the overall irrigation application efficiency of the system and emission uniformity of the emitters was 61.41and 47.71% respectively. This implies that the performance of the scheme is poor.

The major problems observed during the study were emitter clogging, water sharing problem with users at the head and at the tail, illegal penetration of clogged emitters by the users and luck of maintenance and improper collection of laterals after irrigation has completed. In this situation the scheme will not serve very well in the future unless the laterals changed.

## 4.2 Recommendation

For water scared areas, drip irrigation system is one of a vital method for both water saving and good crop production. But improper management of the system will result high investment cost. Mostly newly innovated technologies are directly copied and transferred from developed countries to developing countries without adequate training. As a result, the direct users of the technology simply practiced in traditional experience and which leads to low performance of the system. The system by itself may not be performed low, but due to poor management and maintenance practice the overall performance of the system will be low. This kind of problems was observed in Hormat Golina – 4 drip irrigation system. So, the concerned institutions are expected to give due emphasis for these innovated technologies, not only transferring it but adequate training must be given to the users. In a case of Hormat Golina – 4 drip irrigation system; 33.33% of the emitters were clogged and most of the laterals are highly damaged. So to increase the productivity of the scheme, the laterals need replacement unless it is difficult to continue by this condition and set a ground rule and penalty for users when they illegally penetrate the laterals.

## References

1. Awulachew, S.B., Merrey, D.J., Kamara, A.B., Koppen, B.V., Vries, F.P.D. Boelee, E.: Experiences and opportunities for promoting small–scale/micro irrigation and rainwater harvesting for food security in Ethiopia. Working paper 98 (IWMI): Colombo, Sri Lanka (2005)
2. Haile, G.G.: Irrigation in Ethiopia, a review. J. Environ. Earth Sci. **3**, 264–269 (2015). https://doi.org/10.15413/ajar.2015.0141
3. Awulachew, S.B., Yilma, A.D., Loulseged, M., Loiskandl, W., Ayana, M., Alamirew, T.: Wp123, Water Resource and Irrigation Development in Ethiopia (2007)
4. Ekwe, A.C., Onu, N.N., Onuoha, K.M.: Technical and Institutional Evaluation of Geray Irrigation Scheme in West Gojjam Zone, Amhara Region Ethiopia. J. Spat. Hydrol. **6**, 1–14 (2006)
5. Awulachew, S.B., Erkossa, T., Namara, R.E.: Irrigation potential in Ethiopia 59 (2010)
6. Tadesse, N., Nedaw, D., Woldearegay, K., Gebreyohannes, T., Steenbergen, F.V.: Groundwater management for irrigation in the raya and kobo valleys, Northern Ethiopia. Int. J. Earth Sci. Eng. **8**, 1104–1114 (2015)
7. Dejen, Z.A.: Hydraulic and operational performance of irrigation schemes in view of water saving and sustainability (2015)

8. Allen, R., Pereira, L., Raes, D., Smith, M.: Crop Evapotranspiration: - Guidelines for Computing Crop Water Requirements. Irrigation and Drainage Paper, 56. FAO, Rome (1998)
9. Molden, D.J., Gates, T.L.: Performance measure of irrigation water delivery systems. J. Irrig. Drain. Eng. **116**(6), 804–823 (1990)
10. Liu, H., Huang, G.: Laboratory experiment on drip emitter clogging with fresh water and treated sewage effluent. Agric. Water Manag. **96**, 745–756 (2009)
11. Zamaniyan, M., Fatahi, R., Boroomand-nasab, S.: Evaluation of emitters and water quality in trickle irrigation systems under Iranian conditions (2013)
12. Smajstrla, A.G., Boman, B.J., Pitts, D.J. Zueta, F.S.: Field evaluation of micro irrigation water application uniformity. Fla. Coop. Ext. Ser. Bul. 265. Univ. of Fla (2002)
13. Kruse, E.G.: Describing irrigation efficiency and uniformity. J. Irrig. Drain Div. ASCE **104**(IR1), 35–41 (1978)
14. Wu, I.P.: A Unit-plot for drip irrigation lateral and sub-main design. ASAE Paper, St. Joseph, MI 49085. No. 83-1595 (1983)
15. ASAE: Design, installation and performance of trickle irrigation systems. ASAE standards. Transactions of American Society of Agricultural Engineering. Ep 405, St. Joseph, Michigan, pp. 507–510 (1985)
16. Bralts, V.F.: Operational principles-field performance and evaluation. In: Trickle Irrigation for Crop Production, pp. 216–240. Elsevier, Amsterdam (1986)
17. Jensen, M.E.: Design and operation of farm irrigation systems. An ASAE Monograph No. 3. ASAE 2950 Niles Road. St. Joseph, Michigan 49085, USA (1983)
18. ASAE: Field evaluation of micro irrigation systems. EP458, pp. 760−765 (2003)

# Trend and Variability in Flood Discharge and Attribution to Climate Change in Wabi Shebele River Basin, Ethiopia

Fraol Abebe Wudineh[1]([⊠]), Semu Ayalew Moges[2], and Belete Berhanu Kidanewold[1]

[1] School of Civil and Environmental Engineering,
Addis Ababa University, Addis Ababa, Ethiopia
fraol.abebe@aait.edu.et
[2] Department of Civil and Environmental Engineering,
University of Connecticut, Mansfield, USA

**Abstract.** This study tried to investigate trends and variabilities in mean and extreme hydro-climatic variables in Wabi Shebele River Basin using data based statistical approach. Linear trend investigation and Mann-kendall trend significance tests are performed as a preliminary analysis to see trends on mean discharges and climate variables, while Quantile Perturbation Method (QPM) analysis is conducted to detect clear oscillating patterns and trends in extremes. The result indicates that less increasing trend in mean annual discharge in the basin up to 0.58 $Mm^3$/year, 1.49 $Mm^3$/year, 0.94 $Mm^3$/year and 11.06 $Mm^3$/year in Maribo, Wabi at Dodola, Robe and Erer river respectively. Similarly, less increasing trend is observed in annual rainfall in western and eastern upper basin whereas decreasing trend in middle and lower part of the basin. Mean temperature shows significant increasing trend in upper and middle part of the basin, but decreasing trend in lower basin. The QPM analysis in flood and precipitation extremes indicates there is five/5/ year frequency of significant anomalies and general increasing trends in floods. In early 1980s, significant negative perturbation was observed in Maribo, Robe and Erer rivers. The precipitation extreme anomalies increase at Adaba station and decrease at Robe (Arsi) station. The correlation between discharges and precipitation decreases from West upper to lower basin part of the basin. Average correlation value ($R^2$) of 0.23%, 0.027%, 0.02% and 0.08% are observed in Maribo, Robe, Tebel and Erer watersheds respectively.

**Keywords:** Peak over threshold · Temporal variability · Quantile Perturbation Method (QPM)

## 1 Introduction

Both changes and variability in the water resources have severely threatened the sustainable water resources development, particularly in the downstream part of the watershed. Therefore, determining the variability of stream runoff is essential task in water resources

© ICST Institute for Computer Sciences, Social Informatics and Telecommunications Engineering 2021
Published by Springer Nature Switzerland AG 2021. All Rights Reserved
M. A. Delele et al. (Eds.): ICAST 2020, LNICST 385, pp. 98–120, 2021.
https://doi.org/10.1007/978-3-030-80618-7_7

management and ecosystem restoration [1, 2]. The mean annual discharge provides a measure of the potential supply; intra-annual and multi-annual variation provides information which can be used to determine the probability of experiencing deficiencies under natural conditions and the amount of storage required [2–4]. In current situations, the hydrology of the earth is shifting with the potential to make floods and droughts more extreme [5]. There is now highly need for decision- makers to better understand the ongoing change and variation in hydroclimatic extremes in order to make preparations for the possibility of changing conditions.

The studies of changes have both a scientific and practical significance. The need to understand the impact that man is having on the 'nature' also another importance. The Wabi Shebele River Basin is one of frequently affected basin by hydrological extremes in Horn of Africa [6, 7]. For instance, in 1996, 1999 unexpected floods destroying homes and crops specially in three districts i.e., Kelafo, Mustahil and Burkur [8]. According to the local authorities, 34 people and 750 livestock died, with 70,000 affected by the floods in these areas. The flood of April 2005 was considered as the worst flood in past 40 years by locals, when 30,000 persons surrounded by flood waters and 6000 live stocks were washed away [7]. Ethiopian Ministry of Water, Irrigation and Electricity (MoWIE) study of Wabi Shebele River Basin master plan shows that severe hydrologic extremes in the basin especially in 1973, 1979, 1984–85 is caused by natural atmospheric variability [28]. Previous studies have focused on water resources potential assessment than trends and variabilities of hydroclimatic elements in the basin [9–12]. A few studies conducted on climate characteristics shows significant declines of annual and summer (June-September) rainfall total since 1982 in south eastern of Ethiopia, using progressive Man-kendall test on annual rainfall of Jijiga and Negele climate gauging stations [13]. Upper Wabi shebele basin at upstream of Melka Wekana is located in high rainy area, which its discharge is affected by rainfall conditions more similar to those of the high Ethiopian plateaus than to those of the downstream of Wabi Shebelle basin [9].

To understand the driving factors of changes in extreme discharges, it is important to look back to historical records and assess how variable the extreme discharges were temporally in the river basin. Also, it is useful to understand whether extreme events become more frequent or intense in the recent years. The statistics most commonly used to describe variability of river runoff are the standard deviation, and the coefficient of variation. Mann-Kendall test and Spearman tests are the most non parametric trend tests used in hydro climatic variables. However, the results of these statistical tests are often influenced by serial correlation and increase the chance of incorrectly rejecting the null hypothesis of no trend or vice versa in most hydro climatological data. To overcome this problem a rather novel approach named quantile perturbation method (QPM) [14–18] which is not dependent on the above-mentioned assumptions is utilized for analyzing temporal trend and variabilities in extreme hydroclimatic variables in this study. The study of temporal changes in extreme events identifies anomalies which can be attributed to different phenomena.

This study aims to assess temporal changes in extreme high discharges in Wabi Shebele River Basin and attribute to climate variables. Specifically, the study aims at: 1) analyzing variabilities in extreme hydro-climatic variables and 2) investigating the correlation in between extreme discharge anomalies and precipitation extreme anomalies for better communicating the science to water resource practitioners.

## 2 Materials and Methods

### 2.1 Study Area

Wabi Shebele River Basin is a transboundary basin in between Ethiopia and Republic of Somalia in horn of Africa. It originates from Bale mountain ranges of the Galama and Ahmar of Ethiopia, about 4000 m above sea level and drains portion of Somalia before draining to Indian Ocean. About 72% of the catchment (202,220 km$^2$) is lying in Ethiopia. In this study, Wabi Shebele basin is used to represent the catchment that is lying in Ethiopia within 4°45' N to 9°45' N latitude and 38°45' E to 45°45' E longitude (Fig.1). The climate of the basin is dependent on the altitude and strong latitudinal movement of the intertropical convergence zone (ITCZ) [11, 19]. The highlands are cool and densely populated while the lowlands are arid and sparsely populated with recorded rainfall of 1487 mm and 220m respectively [2, 28]. While having the largest area coverage, the basin's annual runoff is estimated to 3.4 BCM which is the lowest among the major river basins exist in Ethiopia [19]. The spatial variability of temperature is significant with mean, maximum and minimum value of 19.9 °C, 27.1 °C and 12.6 °C respectively. The mean annual evaporation of the basin ranges from around 1,000 mm in the north-west to 2800–3000 mm in the south-east.

### 2.2 Methods

**Data.** Meteorological data including precipitation and temperature were collected from the National Meteorological Agency (NMA). Daily rainfall and temperature (maximum and Minimum) records for 7 stations (Table 1), with a good spatial distribution, were used to see the characteristics of precipitation and temperatures in this study. These stations are selected based on quality of data, length of record, from different watersheds and rainfall regime. The distribution of rainfall between watersheds shows variations (Fig. 3). Significant variation occurs during the rainy season (i.e. June to September). Considerable variation is also observed from April to June and from September to October.

The discharge data in this study were collected from the Hydrology Department of the Ministry of Water, irrigation and Electricity (MoWIE). The measurements of river levels follow the guidelines of the World Metrological Organization (WMO) [20]. Five stations from upper, middle and lower part of the basin, relatively which have long record, one on main river and others on major tributaries of the basin were selected. The monthly database contains maximum and minimum discharges of each month in addition to the monthly average runoff, which assisted to construct the extremes time

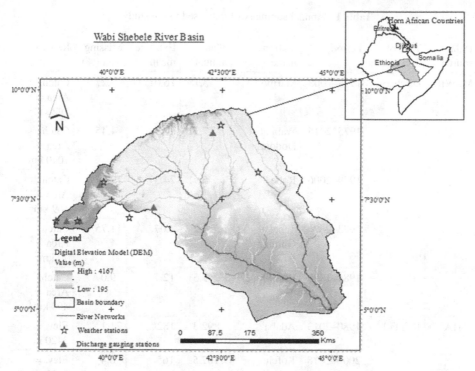

**Fig. 1.** Map of study area

series. Main characteristics of selected discharge gauging stations are described below (Table 1 and 2).

The number of missed data in discharge is maximum in dry season (October-January) in Wabi Shebele River Basin (Table 2). This may be due to inappropriate placing of discharge gauging station. Adane, [19] reported that some of gauging stations in Wabi Shebele River Basin are installed on raised structures anchored to bridges, while others are off setted in pockets of the main course of the stream. Due to these, most of the stations has shown that the stations are not reliable to capture the low discharge situation in the basin. Therefore, such type of gauging station placing problem may be the cause for missed data especially in dry season. For existing gaps in between data, multiple regression method with adjacent discharge data and rainfall data is used to fill.

**Peak Over Threshold Selection (POT).** In this study, three highest value for each year from wet season is used to see annual and monthly hydroclimatic variability. In case of daily precipitation analysis, at least 15 extreme measurements per year is selected. To see extreme variability in precipitation and discharge at weekly aggregation level, at least 5 POT values are selected. In case of extreme discharge, similar procedures in precipitation are followed to select monthly and annual extreme discharge.

**Table 1.** Annual summary of data used in the study.

| Data source | Type of data | Period | Station name | Mean annual | Extreme mean | Missing data (%) | Remark |
|---|---|---|---|---|---|---|---|
| MoWIE | Discharge | 1975–2008 | Maribo | 3.18 | 16.01 | 9.27 | Catch. Area = 192 km$^2$ |
| | | 1975–2015 | Wabi at Dodola | 7.32 | 36.14 | 4.45 | Catch. Area = 1040 km$^2$ |
| | | 1979–2006 | Robe | 5.91 | 24.3 | 19.97 | Catch. Area = 169 km$^2$ |
| | | 1983–2006 | Tebel at Gindhir | 1.2 | 2.07 | 11.75 | Catch. Area = 79 km$^2$ |
| | | 1984–1999 | Erer (upper) | 2.51 | 12.7 | 9.07 | Catch. Area = 494 km$^2$ |
| NMA | Rainfall | 1980–2013 | Adaba | 892.3 | 182 | 21.1 | Elev. = 2420 m |
| | | 2000–2018 | Kofele | 1107.5 | 165 | 6.4 | Elev. = 2620 m |
| | | 1980–2013 | Robe (Arsi) | 1113.7 | 201.5 | 1.7 | Elev. = 2400 m |
| | | 1980–2013 | Gindhir | 1090.7 | 201.5 | 11.51 | Elev. = 1920 m |
| | | 1980–2013 | Diredawa | 665.4 | 130.4 | 1.92 | Elev. = 1260 m |
| | | 1980–2011 | Jijiga | 585.5 | 112.6 | 2.87 | Elev. = 1775 m |
| | | 1980–2011 | Degahabour | 349.6 | 91.9 | 5.64 | Elev. = 1070 m |

Q = Discharge in $m^3 s^{-1}$, RF = Rainfall in mm.

**Trend Analysis.** Trends and variabilities in hydroclimatic data from year to year were determined by linear regressions and standard deviations. The statistical significance of trends in the data was determined by the Mann-Kendall test. Both "ZMK" and "p" values were obtained to characterize trends and statistical significance. "ZMK" is the standardized Mann-Kendall (MK) statistic which follows the standard normal distribution with a mean of zero and a variance of one, and "p" is the probability value of the MK statistic also referred to the statistical significance (%). The value of near to zero

**Table 2.** Seasonal summary of data used in the study.

| Type of data | Station/River | Season | Extreme mean | Font size and style |
|---|---|---|---|---|
| Discharge | Maribo | Dry | 10.47 | 11.43 |
| | | Wet | 16.01 | 4.9 |
| | Wabi at Dodola Bridge | Dry | 24.73 | 6.14 |
| | | Wet | 36.14 | 2.99 |
| | Robe | Dry | 6.52 | 18.3 |
| | | Wet | 20.98 | 22.4 |
| | Erer | Dry | 3.9 | 11.7 |
| | | Wet | 12.25 | 6.4 |
| Rainfall | Adaba | Dry | 56.86 | 23.2 |
| | | Wet | 178.88 | 21.3 |
| | Kofele | Dry | 96.86 | 10.5 |
| | | Wet | 155.14 | 4.6 |
| | Robe (Arsi) | Dry | 77.83 | 2.4 |
| | | Wet | 195.5 | 0.6 |
| | Diredawa | Dry | 56.9 | 1.8 |
| | | Wet | 178.9 | 1.3 |
| | Jijiga | Dry | 46.7 | 2.6 |
| | | Wet | 104 | 3.1 |
| | Degehabour | Dry | 33.9 | 4.8 |
| | | Wet | 78.2 | 6.5 |

Dry = October–March, Wet = April–September.

regression gradient means no trend (the null hypothesis), whereas the value of regression gradient very different from zero means large trend in data (the alternative hypothesis).

**Quantile Perturbation Method (QPM).** QPM is an empirical statistical analysis used to study trends and multi decadal oscillations in extremes [17]. It uses ranks of time series to detect frequency and perturbation of extreme discharge series in this paper. The perturbation is the ratio of similarly ranked data from the two series i.e. series in block length and refence series. The reference series is the long-term expected series while the other series is taken as the actual series within a particular block (sub-period). Then, for each block of years a single perturbation is calculated as the average of all perturbations above a particular threshold. Repeating the averaging over the different blocks assigns one factor to each block which eventually leads to a temporal variation of the perturbation factor. To identify periods of significant perturbations, the confidence interval is calculated and superimposed on the same plot. To calculate the confidence intervals, the values in the full time series at each site are randomly resampled to make a new series with different sequence, and the anomalies are recalculated for the resampled series based on the QPM method. The anomaly calculations are repeated 1000 times, leading to 1000 anomaly values for each block period. After ranking of the 1000 anomaly factors, the 25th and 975th values define the 95% confidence intervals for each block period. It is then graphically possible to identify periods of significant variations that the perturbation factors between the upper and lower limits of the confidence interval (the region of acceptance of the null hypothesis) are considered insignificant, whereas those outside the region of acceptance of the null hypothesis are defined as statistically significant.

Based on Tabbari et al., [21] recommendations, QPM is applied on different block length (5, 7 and 10-years) to select appropriate value of sub-period (block length) in between 5- and 15-years as preliminary analysis in the study. From preliminary analysis the block length which shows better oscillation patterns (high and low) of extreme value is selected for the whole time series variability analysis.

**Pearson's Correlation Coefficient.** Pearson's correlation coefficient is used to see the strength of linear relationship between two variables. If the two variables are linearly related, the correlation coefficient will be near 1 or −1. The sign depends on whether the variables are positively or negatively related. The correlation coefficient related to zero (0) if there is poor relationship between the variables. Between rainfall in the Wabi Shebele basin and runoff in main and tributary rivers were determined at daily and annual time scales. The effect of seasonality in precipitation on river discharge was investigated separately by using data from the wet period from April - September (6 months).

## 3 Results and Discussion

The spatial and temporal variabilities in hydro-climate of Wabi Shebele River Basin is observed using data based statistical approach. Linear regression test, Mann-Kendall trend test and quantile perturbation method (QPM) are used to investigate possible trends and oscillation patterns in river discharge and climate variables. The linear trend test and Mann-Kendall trend test are performed to see trends on mean discharges, total rainfall and mean temperatures and then compare with previous results, while the QPM analysis was used to see trends and variabilities in hydroclimatic extremes due to its capacity to detect clear oscillating patterns and trends in extremes.

As observed on Figs. 2 and 3, the Wabi Shebele basin rainfall is bimodal type taking place from February-May and June – September on high land area and from March-May and September – November in lowland. In western - eastern upper and middle basin, the months from June-September (Summer) is the periods in which largest precipitation record exist, the months from march -may (Spring) is the period in which significant precipitation record exist. But in lowland around Gindhir, Gode and Degehabour, the months from March-May (Spring) and September-November (Autumn) are periods in which largest and significant rainfall records exist respectively (Fig. 2). Therefore, in highland and lowland of Wabi Shebele River Basin has two regimes of wet and dry season categories are exist. The months in which less precipitation is record exist collectively categorized as dry season in both regions. Accordingly, the highland part of the basin around Adaba, Merero, Robe (Arsi), Seru, Deder, Harar and Jijiga have dry season in between October and March, and wet season in between April and September. Whereas the lowland area of the basin around Gindhir, Degehabour, Gode have wet season (March to May; September to November) and dry season (December to February; June to August). The low-lying areas of Wabi Shebelle Basin around Degehabour, Gode, Kebridehar, and Kelafo rains from March to May is caused by moisture from the Indian Ocean, while the October to November rains is associated with the retreat of the ITCZ in a southward direction [11]. The temperature situation of sub basins shows that wet season is the season in which maximum temperature record exist specially February up to May, and the dry is the season in which minimum temperature record exist (Fig. 2).

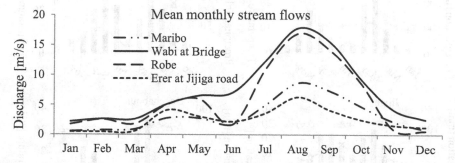

**Fig. 2.** Mean monthly discharge distributions at selected gauging stations in record length.

In all rivers, the discharge is recorded as maximum in wet season (July to September) season and minimum in dry season (October–March). Around 60% of the annual discharge in all rivers is from the heavy summer (June–September) rains, whereas around 19% of the annual discharge is from spring (February–May) rains.

### 3.1  The Trend Analysis

In this study linear regression test and Mann-Kendall trend test are performed to see trends and verify its significance on mean discharge, total rainfall and mean temperatures and then compare with previous results. A linear trend analysis to the annual mean runoff at all stations revealed an increasing trend at values of 1.45 $Mm^3$, 0.58 $Mm^3$ and 0.94 $Mm^3$ on Wabi at Dodola bridege, Maribo and Robe respectively. The verification analysis on trend using Mann-Kendall trend test (Table 3) shows insignificant trends for the selected stations at annual and seasonal discharge levels (Table 3). In some stations significant increasing trend in discharge are observed in wet season, for example, in Wabi river at Dodola bridge and Erer river at western and eastern upper basin.

Trends in mean river discharge follows similar trends with rainfall exist in western and eastern upper basin sample gauging stations (Table 3 and 4). The spatial and temporal distribution of rainfall governs amount and intra and inter annual variability of discharges. This indicates that, Wabi Shebele River flow exhibits typical characteristics of tropical rainfall-dependent discharge regimes. Similar result in discharges was obtained from trend analysis on mean river discharge in between 1975 and 2015 in Wabi Shebele River Basin shows less or insignificant trends (Table 3).

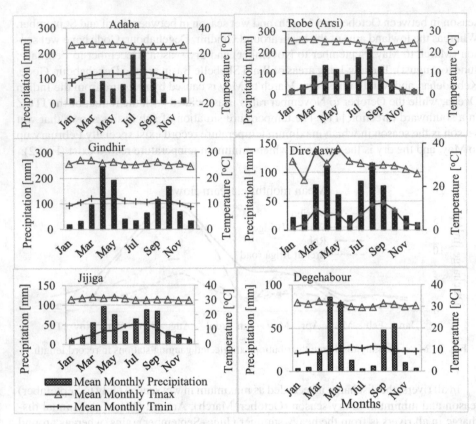

**Fig. 3.** Mean monthly precipitation and temperatures distributions at selected gauging stations.

**Table 3.** Statistical summary of trend test in mean annual discharge.

| Stations | Data type | Period | Average (Mm³) | St. dev. (Mm³) | Slope (Mm³/year) | S | α | $Z_{mk}$ | p-value |
|---|---|---|---|---|---|---|---|---|---|
| Maribo | Discharge | 1975–2008 | 100.2 | 24.32 | 0.581 | 587 | 0.05 | 1.48 | 0.092 |
| Wabi at Dodola Bridge | Discharge | 1975–2015 | 230.9 | 64.44 | 1.485 | 164 | 0.05 | 1.83 | 0.619 |
| Robe | Discharge | 1979–2006 | 48.5 | 28.19 | 0.944 | 74 | 0.05 | 1.44 | 0.086 |
| Tebel | Discharge | 1983–2006 | 3.00 | 1.66 | 0.179 | 192 | 0.05 | 4.73 | 0.001 |
| Erer | Discharge | 1984–1999 | 87.5 | 78.29 | 11.07 | 48 | 0.05 | 2.03 | 0.018 |

Trend analysis on annual, seasonal and monthly rainfall indicates less or insignificant increasing trends in record length (1980–2013) at western and eastern upper Wabi Shebele Basin on Bale, Arsi and Harar highlands. But, significant decreasing trends in rainfalls is observed at middle and lowland area of the basin around Arsi robe, Gindhir and Degehabour in Wabi Sheble basin (Table 4). The wet season (April to September) rainfall has shown insignificant increasing trend in the basin. The study conducted by EPCC [22] also indicates insignificant trend of summer rainfall which range from +4 up to −5 mm/decade and substantial decreasing trends in spring rainfall during the last three decades from 1975–2007 in the basin.

Temperature trend analysis shows significant increasing trends in most of gauging stations located in upper and middle part of the basin except lower part of the basin around Degahabour which shows significant decreasing trend (Table 5). The south-eastern part of the low-lying areas of the basin around Degehabur, Gode, Kebridehare, and Kelafo receives no rainfall in July and August and has two rainy seasons [11]. The first is from March to May, and the second is from October to November. As tried to explained under Sect. 2.2, max temperature in the basin is recorded in wet season and minimum temperature is in dry season. The temperature trend difference from other part of the basin probably tied to rainfall distribution difference from others.

Table 4. Statistics summary of trend in annual rainfall.

| Stations | Data type | Period | Average (mm) | St. dev. (mm) | Slope | S | α | $Z_{mk}$ | p-value |
|---|---|---|---|---|---|---|---|---|---|
| Adaba | Rainfall | 1980–2013 | 892.3 | 303.2 | 0.8 | 99 | 0.05 | 1.48 | 0.44 |
| Kofele | Rainfall | 2000–2018 | 1097.6 | 107.6 | −7.62 | −55 | 0.05 | −1.97 | 0.17 |
| Robe (Arsi) | Rainfall | 1980–2013 | 1113.7 | 339.8 | −19.3 | −169 | 0.05 | −2.52 | 0.04 |
| Gindhir | Rainfall | 1980–2013 | 1090.7 | 455.4 | −10.9 | −1 | 0.05 | −0.03 | 0.39 |
| Diredawa | Rainfall | 1980–2013 | 665.4 | 151.0 | 2.38 | 39 | 0.05 | 0.56 | 0.64 |
| Jijiga | Rainfall | 1980–2013 | 585.5 | 108.8 | 1.6 | 57 | 0.05 | 0.91 | 0.33 |
| Degehabour | Rainfall | 1980–2011 | 349.6 | 155.3 | −3.8 | −85 | 0.05 | −1.39 | 0.304 |

## 3.2  Trends and Variabilities in Annual Extremes

Quantile perturbation method (QPM) is used to see possible trends and variabilities in extreme discharge and climatic variables. The method has a capacity to explore clear oscillating patterns and trends in hydroclimatic extremes. The method also has also the option of identifying the statistical significance of the variability observed and thus the statistical significance of the variability identified. The mean perturbation is assigned to a year which is approximately in the middle of the block. The value of confidence interval is superimposed on the same plot of extreme perturbations to identify the periods of significant variations.

From preliminary analysis conducted, 5 (five) year block of periods shows better oscillation patterns (high and low) of extreme discharges and precipitation in comparison

**Table 5.** Statistics summary of trend in mean temperature.

| Stations | Data type | Period | Average (°C) | St. dev. (°C) | Slope | S | α | $Z_{mk}$ | p-value |
|---|---|---|---|---|---|---|---|---|---|
| Adaba | Temperature | 1980–2013 | 14.66 | 0.714 | 0.05 | 239 | 0.05 | 3.5 | 0.001 |
| Kofele | Temperature | 2000–2018 | 19.56 | 0.527 | 0.01 | 55 | 0.05 | 1.9 | 0.397 |
| Robe (Arsi) | Temperature | 1980–2013 | 14.85 | 0.689 | 0.06 | 339 | 0.05 | 5.0 | 0.001 |
| Gindhir | Temperature | 1980–2013 | 18.32 | 0.70 | 0.02 | 115 | 0.05 | 1.7 | 0.139 |
| Diredawa | Temperature | 1980–2013 | 25.54 | 0.40 | 0.03 | 330 | 0.05 | 4.9 | 0.002 |
| Jijiga | Temperature | 1980–2013 | 19.50 | 0.654 | 0.04 | 194 | 0.05 | 3.1 | 0.002 |
| Degehabour | Temperature | 1980–2011 | 19.30 | 6.333 | −0.3 | −161 | 0.05 | 2.8 | 0.005 |

to 7- and 10-years block lengths as shown on Fig. 4. Hence a 5-year block was used as block length of variability analysis in this study.

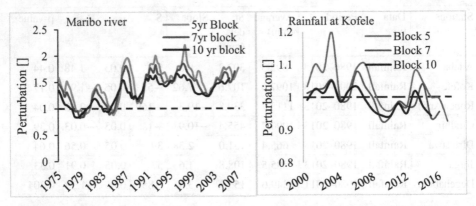

**Fig. 4.** Extreme perturbations at different block lengths on both discharge and precipitation.

**Extreme Discharge.** When considering extreme high discharges in annual time steps, most of perturbation values varies within confidence interval (Fig. 5). Among gauging stations increasing trend is observed on Maribo river. In early 1980s, significant negative perturbation up to −26.5%, −17.8%, −25% and −20% was observed in Maribo, Robe, Tebel and Erer watersheds respectively. Whereas, maximum significant perturbations up to 88.3%, 95.6%, 610% and 482% are observed respectively in watersheds in between 1986–1989. High oscillation pattern in annual extreme high discharges were observed in upper basin watersheds. Generally, extreme high discharge quantile perturbation shows increasing trend in Wabi Shebele River Basin from 1975 to 2015. The estimated confidence intervals are wide enough excluding the possibility of statistically significant change. Therefore, significant anomalies of extreme discharges can be due major driving factors like climate variables or catchment characteristics.

The oscillation pattern of extreme discharge quantiles changes within half a decade in both directions negatively and positively, which shows existence of external factors effects with in a given interval of years. For instance, the sea surface temperature change (SST) occurrence over the globe will occur within two to seven year interval in the form of El-Nino and La-Nino [23]. The effect this climate change indices is high over the world including our country. There is a consequence of flood and drought in Ethiopia during the occurrence year of these indices [24]. Most of positive significant anomalies of extreme discharge quantiles in Wabi Shebele River Basin occurred in moderate to very strong El-Nino years (Table 6). Contrary most of negative significant anomalies in the basin occurred in week to strong La Nino years. This indicates global climate change indices are a probable cause for changes of extreme discharge quantiles in Wabi Shebele River Basin. The impact of El Niño and La Niña are surprisingly increasing over the globe especially in developing countries like Ethiopia which their economies are dependent on regularly occurring seasonal weather conditions.

**Table 6.** Summary of QPM analysis in annual extreme discharge.

| Sub basin | Magnitude of highest anomaly (%) | Time of highest anomaly | Remark |
|---|---|---|---|
| Maribo | −10.7 | 1979 | WE |
| | −11.9 | 1984 | WL |
| | +95.6 | 1987 | SE |
| | 100.5 | 1992 | SE |
| | 120.5 | 1997 | VSE |
| Wabi at Dodola Bridge | −26.5 | 1979 | WE |
| | +61.5 | 1982 | VSE |
| | +85.3 | 1987 | SE |
| | −15.5 | 1990 | SL |
| | −20.1 | 2002 | ME |
| Robe | +610.5 | 1989 | SL |
| | +655.7 | 1999 | SL |
| Tebel | −53.2 | 1983 | VSE |
| | +846.9 | 1997 | VSE |
| | +1071.3 | 2002 | ME |
| Erer | −31.1 | 1985 | WL |
| | +482.5 | 1988 | SE |
| | +501.1 | 1996 | ML |

WE = Weak El Niño, SE = Strong El Niño, VSE = Very strong El Niño, WL = Weak La-Niña, SL = Strong La-Niña years.

The effects of El Niño southern oscillation had a variable impact on Horn African countries, ranging from drought to floods in history [25]. El Niño refers to the large-scale ocean-atmosphere climate interaction linked to a periodic warming in sea surface temperatures across the central and east-central Equatorial Pacific and La Niña represent periods of below-average sea surface temperatures across the east-central Equatorial Pacific [26]. The humanitarian impact of La-Niña is greater when it immediately follows an El-Niño. In 1988 El Niño year's floods affected 2.5 Million peoples, whereas the 1999 and 2011 drought years occurred following La-Niña events affected 31.5 Million and 14 Million peoples respectively in the region including Wabi Shebele basin [24].

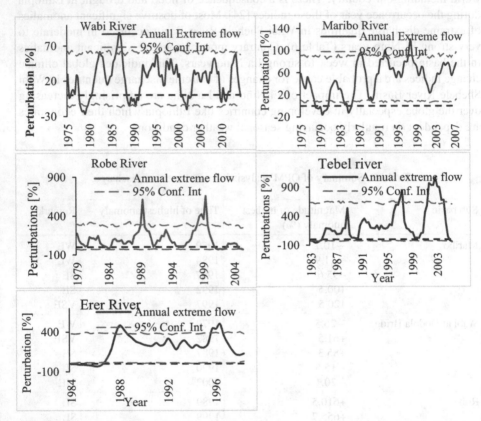

**Fig. 5.** Extreme discharge variability with confidence interval in Wabi Shebele River Basin.

**Precipitation Extremes.** The perturbation in precipitation extreme varies within confidence interval in most of stations of the basin taken in consideration. But unique result is observed on Adaba and Robe (Arsi) stations record (Fig. 6). An increasing and decreasing trend of precipitation extremes is observed in Adaba and Robe (Arsi) stations respectively. In early 1980s significant negative anomaly up to −10.4% is observed at Adaba station, but maximum positive perturbation of +38.2% is observed at Robe station. In 2000s significant positive anomaly of +137.8% is observed at Adaba and significant negative anomaly of −39.2% at Robe (Arsi) rainfall stations are observed. In the other side most rainfall stations indicate significant positive precipitation anomalies in early 1980s specially between 1982–1983 and immediate decreasing trend in between 1984 and 1985 (Table 7 and Fig. 6). Generally, most of rainfall perturbation analysis indicates decreasing trends in middle Wabi Shebele basin.

In Ethiopia, droughts and floods are occurred frequently at every 3–5 years for last 50-years [27]. The actual power generated from Melka Wakena Dam, the hydropower plant exist in this sub basin, shows power decrement in 1991, 1996 and 2000 by 32%, 21% and 38% relative to their Preceded years [20].

In other side western and eastern upper Wabi Shebele basin indicates significant positive anomaly in precipitation extremes in 2000s. This also coincided with the resent study result [7, 19, 24, 28, 29] which indicates several devastating floods in Wabi Shebele River Basin in recent years. The destructive flood in August 2005 on the basin affected 100,000, 154 deaths and the flood occurred starting November 2008, in basin caused around 52,000 human displacement from 14 kebeles (small admirative unit), 185 villages and 164-hectare farm lands washed away [29].

**Table 7.** Characteristics of highest anomaly in precipitation extremes.

| Station name | Magnitude of highest anomaly (%) | Time of highest anomaly |
| --- | --- | --- |
| Adaba | −14.4 | 1983 |
|  | +76.8 | 1990 |
|  | −18.3 | 2000 |
|  | 137.8 | 2009 |
| Kofele | +42.2 | 2006 |
|  | +47.9 | 2007 |
|  | −9.7 | 2017 |
| Robe (Arsi) | +38.2 | 1982 |
|  | +34.5 | 1987 |
|  | −47.1 | 1993 |
|  | −36.9 | 2001 |
| Gindhir | +170.7 | 1980 |
|  | −33.5 | 1994 |
|  | −42.5 | 2000 |
|  | −38.6 | 2003 |
| Diredawa | −20.06 | 1984 |
| Jijiga | +47.3 | 1986 |
|  | −19 | 2008 |
| Degehabour | +210.4 | 1982 |
|  | +215.5 | 1986 |
|  | −20.8 | 1990 |
|  | +201.2 | 2000 |

**Temperature Extremes.** There are a few limitations in the application of the frequency perturbation method for temperature compared to rainfall. First, the independence criterion is difficult to ascertain as there are correlation in daily value similar to river

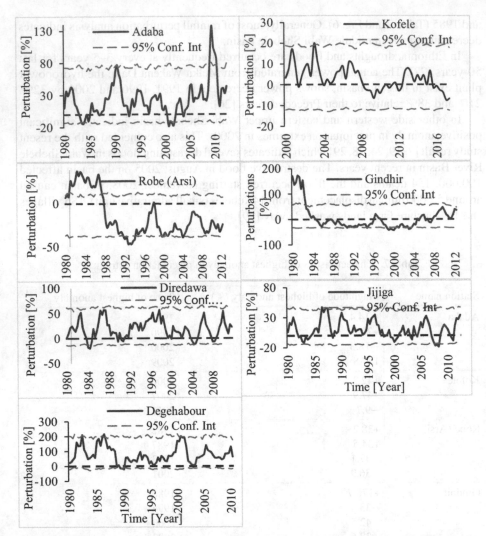

**Fig. 6.** Annual precipitation extreme perturbations using 5-year block length with 95% Confidence interval at seven /7/ gauging station of Wabi Shebele River Basin.

discharge. For this study, the independence criterion was ignored. Instead, only a threshold for the peaks was selected. Second, temperature significance periods were not based on 95% confidence intervals because there was no reasonable distribution valid for all the periods in temperatures [17]. Therefore, temperature anomalies were then analyzed based on the long-term average perturbation.

Extreme high temperatures in Wabi Shebele River Basin perturbation analysis shows general increasing trends in the basin particularly in upper and middle of the basin but less decreasing trend in lower part of the basin (Fig. 7). Starting 1990 significant increasing trends are observed in Adaba, Kofele, Robe gauging stations record.

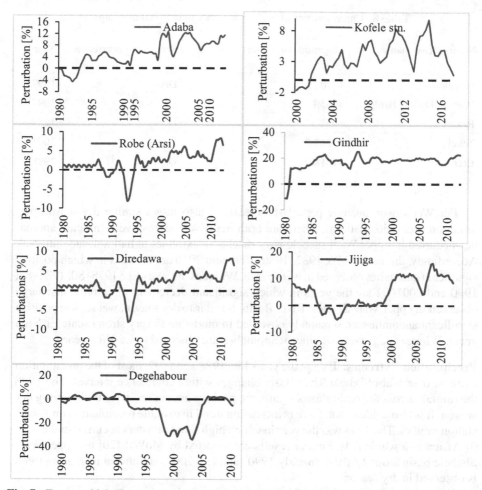

**Fig. 7.** Extreme high Temperature average perturbations using 5-year block length at selected gauging stations in Wabi Shebele Basin.

### 3.3   Trends and Variabilities in Seasonal Extremes

The QPM approach is applied to extreme value at seasonal aggregation level. Three maximum events are selected from each season to see temporal variability in extreme seasonal flood events. Two seasons, i.e. dry (October–March) and Wet (April– September), are used to see extreme quantiles in this study.

**Extreme Discharge.** QPM analysis conducted on seasonal extreme discharges indicates significant positive anomalies in dry season streamflow of upper Wabi shabele basin at five years interval in average i.e., 1977, 1982, 1987, 1997 and 2008. These years are directly coincided with weak to very strong El-Nino years.

**Table 8.** Characteristics of highest anomaly in seasonal discharges.

| Station/River name | Magnitude of highest anomaly (%) | Season of occurrence | Year |
|---|---|---|---|
| Maribo | +370 | Dry | 1997 |
| Wabi at Dodola Bridge | +265.1 | Dry | 1997 |
| Robe | +967.3 | Dry | 1989 |
| Tebel | +1029.7 | Wet | 2001 |
| Erer | +1318.9 | Dry | 1998 |

For Wet season quantile perturbation analysis also shows similar dry season perturbation oscillation patterns. There are both negative and positive significant anomalies occurred in upper Wabi shebele river discharge extremes at half a decade interval. Accordingly, the years 1976, 1982, 1986, 1995 and 2010 are the yeas in which positive significant anomalies observed in wet season. Whereas the years like 1978–80, 1984–85, 1990 and 2001–02 are the years in which significant decrement of extreme discharge observed in upper Wabi Shebele River Basin. Similar to dry season, wet season positive significant anomalies are separately observed in moderate to very strong scale El-Nino years. Whereas negatively significant anomalies are observed in La-Nina years.

**Precipitation Extremes.** Except the years like 1988 and 1997, most of the precipitation extreme over Wabi Shebele River Basin changes within confidence interval. The 1988 the rainfall across the basin shows significant positive anomalies in the basin during dry season. It is also evident that, there is increasing trend in extreme precipitation on Adaba station rainfall. The 1988 was the year in which high flood disasters occurred in the horn of Africa as a whole [24]. Similar results are reported by MoWR [20] on upper Wabi Shebele basin around Adaba. In early 1990s and late 2000s significant increasing trend is observed in dry season.

In wet season (April- September), the extreme precipitation anomalies obeyed two phases in Wabi Shebele River Basin, decreasing trend in between 1980–1990 and less increasing trend in between 1990 to 2013. Early 1980s and 1990s are years in which significant positive and negative anomalies are observed respectively in most of stations (Table 9).

**Temperature Extremes.** $Q$PM analysis on seasonal extreme high temperatures indicates increasing trend in both dry and wet season (Table 10). The size of positive trends decreases from western to eastern upper basin and indicates general decreasing trend in downstream of Wabi Shebele River Basin around Degehabour and Gode area. There is strong arguments in literatures that, with more water vapor and heat in the atmosphere, results for high storms [30–32].

**Table 9.** Characteristics of highest anomaly in seasonal extreme precipitation

| Station name | Magnitude of highest anomaly (%) | Season of occurrence | Year |
|---|---|---|---|
| Adaba | +666.6 | Dry | 1990 |
| Kofele | +32.9 | Wet | 2004 |
| Robe (Arsi) | +5948.9 | Dry | 1982 |
| Gindhir | +777.1 | Dry | 1992 |
| Diredawa | +1493 | Dry | 1997 |
| Jijiga | −23.7 | Wet | 1999 |
| Degehabour | +251.7 | Wet | 1985 |

**Table 10.** Characteristics of highest anomaly in seasonal extreme high temperatures.

| Station name | Magnitude of highest anomaly (%) | Season of occurrence | Year |
|---|---|---|---|
| Adaba | +15.8 | Wet | 2004 |
| Kofele | +11.9 | Wet | 2014 |
| Robe (Arsi) | +12.8 | Dry | 2002 |
| Gindhir | +18.9 | Dry | 1990 |
| Diredawa | +12.9 | Dry | 2012 |
| Jijiga | +17.9 | Wet | 2008 |
| Degehabour | −35.6 | Dry | 2003 |

### 3.4 Effect of Aggregation Level on Detected Anomalies

The effects of time aggregation on variability analysis is investigated based on QPM analysis on daily, monthly and annual anomalies in the study area. In extreme discharge perturbation analysis, anomalies at daily aggregation level is less than both monthly and annual perturbation (Fig. 8). Whereas, the precipitation extreme perturbation at daily aggregation level are higher than both monthly and annual aggregation level (Fig. 9) which coincided with the study result of Ntegeka and Willems [17]. This indicates that, the extreme discharge perturbation conducted by QPM at different aggregation level gives completely opposite result with the study result of Ntegeka and Willems [17] in which the perturbations of smaller aggregation level are greater than larger level. It is known that the first day discharge has significant effect on the next day or lack of independency in daily discharge may be the cause for less anomaly in small time aggregation level.

### 3.5 Correlation Analysis

Intergovernmental Panel on Climate Change (IPCC) [26] indicate that climate change "has detectably influenced" several of the water-related variables that contribute to

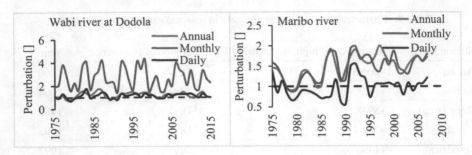

**Fig. 8.** Comparison between extreme discharge perturbations at different aggregation levels

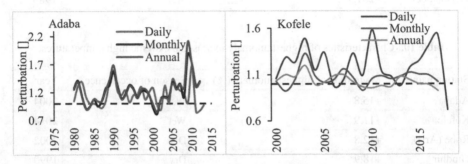

**Fig. 9.** Comparison between precipitation perturbations at different aggregation levels.

floods, such as rainfall and snowmelt [26]. In this study the rainfall variability in Wabi shebele basin was taken as one of the major driving factors for flood change in the basin. To confirm this hypothesis, Pearson's correlation analysis is conducted on extreme anomalies of discharge and precipitation in different watersheds of the basin (Table 11). The statistical significance of correlation value is checked using student test at 5% significance error.

The result indicates that oscillation pattern of both variables, i.e. extreme discharge and precipitation anomalies are similar even though the statistical correlation value shows a little bit small. From Table 8, it is evident that in dry season a better positive correlation value in between extreme discharge and precipitation up to 62%, 20%, 30%, 53% and 65% are observed at Maribo, Wabi at Dodola, Robe, Tebel and Erer watersheds respectively. Further in Wet season, low negative correlation value up to −42%, −42% and −9% are in Maribo, Wabi at Dodola and Robe watersheds respectively. Whereas positive wet season correlation value up to 31% was observed in Erer watershed. In general, statistical correlation using Pearson's correlation coefficient method shows, less than 50% correlation value in average in between extreme discharge and precipitation correlation. This implies that for change in extreme discharge in Wabi Shebele River Basin, there is other driving factors in addition to climate elements. There was study result by MoWR, [20], in upper Wabi Shebele River Basin (upstream of Melka wakena) strong flood only occurs when soil has been previously saturated with water after the first rainy phase. This is because of not very intense rainfall conditions and considerable perviousness of soil in sub basin.

**Table 11.** Annual and seasonal correlation coefficient between discharges and rainfall.

| Station name | Annual | Dry season (October–March) | Wet season (April–September) |
|---|---|---|---|
| Maribo | 0.03 | **0.62*** | 0.004 |
| Wabi at Dodola Bridge | −0.20 | 0.20 | -0.18 |
| Robe river | −0.09 | 0.3 | -0.13 |
| Tebel river | −0.18 | **0.53*** | -0.29 |
| Erer river | −0.14 | **0.65*** | -0.27 |

* = Statistically significant at 5% significant error

## 4  Conclusions

Temporal variabilities in hydro climate variables were examined for Wabi Shebele River Basin in between 1975–2015. The preliminary trend detection done on discharges at five sample rivers using linear trend regression test which is verified by Mann-Kendall significance test indicates less/insignificant increasing trends on mean annual discharge. Rain fall trend analysis conducted on total rainfall of different stations in the basin indicates significant decreasing trend in middle and lower part of the basin. The western and eastern highland area of the basin indicates less increasing trends in rainfall. The trend analysis conducted on mean temperatures indicates significant increasing trend in Wabi Shebele River Basin.

The temporal trend and variability analysis done on extreme high discharge using QPM approach indicates significant increasing trend in Maribo river from western upper basin and Erer river discharge from eastern upper basin. The other most extreme discharge anomalies vary within confidence interval. The dry and wet seasons anomalies mostly follow similar oscillation pattern with annual extreme discharge anomaly. Most of positive significant anomalies of extreme discharge quantiles in Wabi Shebele River Basin occurred in moderate to very strong El-Nino years. Contrary most of negative significant anomalies in this sub basin occurred in week to strong La Nino years. Therefore, we can conclude that global climate change indices may be the other influential factors for increments and decrements of extreme discharge quantiles in Wabi Shebele River Basin in addition to other driving factors in the sub basin. The precipitation extreme perturbations analysis shows increasing trend at all aggregation levels in western and eastern upper basin and decreasing trend in middle in between 1980 and 2018. QPM analysis on extreme high temperature indicates significant increasing trend with high oscillation pattern. The study conducted by EPCC [22] reveals similar result that substantial increasing trend in rainfall over south eastern highlands of Ethiopia and warming trend of about 0.4 °C/decade in the region which strengthen the current study.

The QPM analysis conducted to explore the effect of time aggregation level on extreme quantile perturbations indicates that, the perturbations for the annual aggregation level are generally greater than both monthly and daily perturbations in case of extreme discharge, which completely contradict to the result obtained in case of precipitation, in which extreme perturbation at daily aggregation level is greater than both monthly and annual perturbation. This indicates, the extreme discharge perturbation conducted by QPM at different aggregation level on extreme discharge gives completely opposite result with the study result of Ntegeka and Willems [17] done on precipitation extreme, which is the perturbations of smaller aggregation level are greater than larger level. The correlation analysis done between extreme discharge and precipitation indicates strong correlation of dry season extreme discharge and precipitation anomaly up to 65% in some watersheds, even though it falls below 50% in other sample watersheds.

Wabi Shebele River Basin is largest basin in Ethiopia with ungagged hydrologic characteristics. It is hard to characterize the whole basin extreme hydroclimatic variabilities with only five sub basins which most of it confined at upper highland area of the basin, while the basin has more than 11 sub basins with larger than 500 km$^2$ catchment area. Therefore, extension of river discharges and precipitations in ungagged sub basin using robust model and analysis can explore better information on trends, temporal variabilities, correlations and periodicities in extreme hydroclimate variabilities of the basin.

# References

1. Taye, M.T., Willems, P.: Temporal variability of hydroclimatic extremes in the Blue Nile basin, 10 March 2012
2. Meng, F., Liu, T., Huang, Y., Luo, M., Bao, A., Hou, D.: Quantitative detection and attribution of runoff variations in the Aksu River Basin, August 2016
3. Zhang, G., Guhathakurta, S., Lee, S., Moore, A., Yan, L.: Grid-based land-use composition and configuration optimization for watershed stormwater management. Water Res. Manag. **28**, 2867–2883 (2014). https://doi.org/10.1007/s11269-014-0642-y
4. Zuo, Q., Zhao, H., Mao, C., Ma, J., Cui, G.: Quantitative analysis of human-water relationships and harmony-based regulation in the tarim river basin. J. Hydrol. Eng. **20**, 05014030 (2014)
5. Charles, J.V., et al.: Global Change and Extreme Hydrology, no. 800, pp. 624–6242. National Academies Press, 500 Fifth Street, NW, Washington, D.C. (2000)
6. MoWR: Wabi Shebele River Basin Integrated, master Plan Project, Soils and Land Evaluation, Addis Ababa. II ed. Addis Ababa (2003)
7. Tadesse, T.: Seasonal prediction of hydro-climatic extremes in the greater horn of Africa under evolving climate conditions to support adaptation strategies. National Drought Mitigation Center, University of Nebraska-Lincoln (2014)
8. UNDP: Drought and Floods Stress Livelihoods and Food Security in the Ethiopian Somali Region. Assessment Mission Report, 5–17 October and 27 October–2 November (1999)
9. BECM-ORSTOM: Hydrological Survey of the Wabi Shebele Basin. Imperial Ethiopia Government National Water Resources Commission, Volume II (1973)
10. Houghton-Carr, H.A., Print, C.R., Fry, M.J., Gadain, H., Muchiri, P.: An assessment of the surface water resources of the Juba-Shabelle basin in southern Somalia. Hydrol. Sci. J. **56**(5), 759–774 (2011). https://doi.org/10.1080/02626667.2011.585470

11. Amer, S., Gachet, A., Belcher, W.R., Bartolino, J.R., Hopkins, C.B.: Groundwater exploration and assessment in the Eastern lowlands and associated highlands of the Ogaden Basin Area, Eastern Ethiopia. Phase 1 Final Technical Report, Prepared in cooperation with the United States Geological Survey (2013)

12. Ayalew, D.W.: Theoretical and empirical review of Ethiopian water resource potentials, challenges and future development opportunities. Int. J. Waste Resour. (2018). https://doi.org/10.4172/2252-5211.1000353

13. Seleshi, Y., Zanke, U.: Recent changes in rainfall and rainy days in Ethiopia. Accepted 26 Mar 2004

14. Chiew, F.H.S.: An overview of methods for estimating climate change impact on Runoff. In: 30th Hydrology and Water Resources Symposium, [CDROM ISBN 0858257904], Lauceston, Australia, 4–7 December 2006

15. Mpelasoka, F.S., Francis, H., Chiew, S.: Influence of rainfall scenario construction methods on runoff projections. CSIRO Land and Water, Australia (2009). https://doi.org/10.1175/2009JHM1045.1

16. Harrold, T., Chiew, F.H.S., Siriwardena, L.: A method for estimating climate change impacts on mean and extreme rainfall and runoff. In: Zerger, A., Argent, R.M. (ed.) MODSIM 2005. International Congress on Modelling and Simulation, pp. 497–504. Modelling and Simulation Society of Australia and New Zealand, Melbourne (2005)

17. Ntegeka, V., Willems, P.: Trends and multidecadal oscillations in rainfall extremes, based on a more than 100-year time series of 10 min rainfall intensities at Uccle, Belgium. Water Resour. Res. (2008). http://doi.wiley.com/10.1029/2007WR006471

18. Willems, P.: Multidecadal oscillatory behaviour of rainfall extremes in Europe. Clim. Change **120**(4), 931–944 (2013). https://doi.org/10.1007/s10584-013-0837-x

19. Adane, A.A.: Hydrological drought analysis, occurrence, severity, risks: the case of Wabi Shebele River Basin, Ethiopia. Ph.D. dissertation, University of Seigen, Germany (2009)

20. MoWR: Wabi Shebele River Basin integrated master plan study project. vol. VII Water resources, Part 2 Hydrology (2003)

21. Tabari, H., AghaKouchak, A., Willems, P.: A perturbation approach for assessing trends in precipitation extremes across Iran. J. Hydrol. **519**, 1420–1427 (2014). https://doi.org/10.1016/j.jhydrol.2014.09.019

22. Ethiopian Panel on Climate Change (EPCC): First Assessment Report, Summary of Reports for Policy Makers. Published by the Ethiopian Academy of Sciences (2015)

23. Siam, M.S., Wang, G., Demory, M.-E., Eltahir, E.A.B.: Role of the Indian ocean sea surface temperature in shaping the natural variability in the discharge of Nile River. Institute of Technology, 15 Vassar St. Cambridge, MA 02139 (2014)

24. Report of United Nations Office for the Coordination of Humanitarian Affairs Integrated Regional Information Networks (UNOCHA). Ethiopia Published on Relief Web. Journal, 19 November 2014

25. UNOCHA: The state of response to El-nino in the Horn of Africa (2015)

26. https://www.nrdc.org/stories/flooding-and-climate-change-everything-you-need-know

27. World Bank: Managing Water Resources to Maximize Sustainable Growth A World Bank Water Resources Assistance, Strategy for Ethiopia (2006)

28. Moges, S., Alemu, Y., McFeeters, S., Legesse, W.: Flooding in Ethiopia, Recent History and the 2006 Flood. Cambria Press, Amherst (2010)

29. IWMI: Share Bale Eco-Region Research Report Series no. 7 (2015)

30. Dettinger, M., Hidalgo, H., Das, T., Cayan, D.: Noah knowles: projections of potential flood regime changes in California. A Report California Climate Change Center, California (2009)
31. Williams, P., et al.: Recent summer precipitation trends in the Greater Horn of Africa and the emerging role of Indian Ocean sea surface temperature. India (2011)
32. Hall, J., et al.: Understanding flood regime changes in Europe, a state-of-the-art assessment, Germany, 13 April 2015

# Sizing of a Standalone Photovoltaic Water Pumping System of a Well in Ngoundiane Site

Amy Sadio[1], Senghane Mbodji[1,2](✉), Biram Dieng[1], Arona Ndiaye[1], Ibrahima Fall[1], and Papa Lat Tabara Sow[1]

[1] Resarch Team in Renewable Energies, Materials and Laser,
Alioune Diop University of Bambey, Bambey, Senegal
senghane.mbodji@uadb.edu.sn

[2] Semiconductors and Solar Energy Laboratory, Cheikh Anta Diop University, Dakar, Senegal

**Abstract.** In this paper, the sizing and design of a standalone photovoltaic water pumping system in Ngoundiane, a village located in Senegal is investigated. An intuitive sizing method is firstly applied to get approximate information on the sizes of the various components. In this method, the capacity of various components is separately computed and any relationship between them are considered. To improve the results, a new sizing approach based on numerical methods is developed using the Average Loss of Power Supply Probability (ALPSP) criterion. Empirical simple models are used to model the components of PV system. From the energy generated by PV array, the different states of charge of the battery storage are estimated. A simple algorithm has been elaborated to determine the different PV and battery combinations for various ALPSP levels. The proposed model has been applied to the meteorological average data in Ngoundiane site and conducted using MATLAB software. The results showed that the numerical method proposed allows a 50% reduction of the storage capacity when compared to the intuitive method. However, we noticed that the values of ALPSP are particularly high with a smaller value of 0.3, probably due to the underestimation of input parameters and the nature of meteorological data used in the model. In order to show the importance of the developed approach, a comparison with literature has been performed.

**Keywords:** Photovoltaic water pumping system · Numerical method · Average loss of power supply probability

## 1 Introduction

Solar energy is one of the cleanest among renewable resources and has lower maintenance costs compared to other alternatives, e.g. wind, biomass (Olcan et al. 2015). The use of solar photovoltaic energy for water pumping is a relative new technology with reasonable costs. Photovoltaic water pumping system is a very significant application of solar photovoltaic energy. Indeed, it is economically difficult to extend the electrical network in remote zones, which have some difficulties to accede to drinkable water.

© ICST Institute for Computer Sciences, Social Informatics and Telecommunications Engineering 2021
Published by Springer Nature Switzerland AG 2021. All Rights Reserved
M. A. Delele et al. (Eds.): ICAST 2020, LNICST 385, pp. 121–137, 2021.
https://doi.org/10.1007/978-3-030-80618-7_8

However, the main drawback of the solar energy is its random and intermittent nature, which require an exhaustive technico-economic study to obtain an optimal PV system. So different methods of sizing have been developed and presented in the literature. They differ in terms of simplicity and reliability and can be categorized as intuitive, numerical, analytical, Artificial Intelligence and hybrid methods (Sidrach-de-Cardona et al. 1998; Khatib et al. 2016; Sadio et al. 2018; Sadio et al. 2019; Anwar 2017; Hontoria et al. 2005).

Intuitive methods consist of using simple equations to calculate the different component sizes of the system. They include the most disadvantageous month and average data approaches. These methods establish no relation between the components of the system, and they are not accurate.

In analytical methods, the sizes of system components are expressed as a function of the reliability and the system cost by mathematical equations with coefficients depending on the geographic positions. These methods are simple and accurate; however, they are not so flexible.

The numerical methods are based on simulations that allow the calculation, for each period of time, of the energy balance of the system. These methods are more accurate and can evaluate the system reliability, which is quantified by the Loss of Power Supply probability (LPSP). The LPSP is also known as the Loss of Load Probability (LOLP), the Loss of Power Probability (LPP), and the Load Coverage Rate (LCR) (Sadio et al. 2018). It represents the load dissatisfaction rate (Sadio et al. 2018). It requires meteorological data recorded on a long time period. These data are not available in the most areas (Sadio et al. 2017).

The Artificial Intelligence techniques can be an alternative for overcoming the limits of the classic methods when meteorological data are not available (Jakhrani et al. 2012). They include the Genetic Algorithm and others. They can solve a complicated optimization problem with a great number of parameters to handle. They are accurate and reliable; they can also treat incomplete data but require lot of memories during computations. The hybrid methods are a combination of the positive aspects of the previous methods (intuitive, analytical, numerical and Artificial). Many researchers work in this field aim to improve results of PV systems sizing. Hence, Jakhrani et al. (2012) developed a novel analytical model for optimal sizing of standalone photovoltaic systems. These authors used different equations and load demands to determine the optimal section of PV array and useful capacity of storage, for various values of LPP. The technical and economic criteria used to evaluate the system performance are the cost and the LPP. The comparison of some results showed a similarity between the iso-reliability curves of the proposed model and the ones found in the literature. This method is very accurate with minimal cost. In the Cabral and Filho (2010) study, a stochastic method for the sizing of standalone photovoltaic systems is developed. Authors performed a comparative study between the proposed model and a determinist method, in order to verify the best way for modelling standalone photovoltaic systems. They concluded that the best method is the stochastic one. Indeed, these methods consider the variability of solar irradiation, load demand, and provide the most accurate result. The simulation showed that the determinist method leads to an oversizing with a LPSP of 0.0%. Khatib et al. (2016) reviewed the sizing methodologies of PV array and storage batteries in a standalone photovoltaic system. Several software used for the optimal sizing of standalone photovoltaic system have been presented. Compared to others, the authors concluded that the numerical sizing methods are more accurate and simpler. These methods consider the random variability of meteorological data. In Shen et al. (2009) work, the optimal sizing of solar array and battery in a standalone photovoltaic system, in Malaysia, is investigated. The sizing is based on the energy effectiveness model and LPSP. This model has been applied by using the solar irradiation data of year 1999, of Kuala Lumpur and a load demand assumed to be constant for all year. The results obtained from this method have been compared to the one calculated with a hybrid system. It has been shown that the hybrid system reduces the size of PV capacity. Nogueira et al. (2014) proposed the sizing and simulation of a photovoltaic/wind system, using batteries, applied on a small rural area located in the South of Brazil. The developed model is based on the LPSP and the time of critical period. Results showed that for a set LPSP, yielded energy decreases if the critical period increases and for a set critical period, the energy produced decreases if the LPSP raises. In the work presented by Al-Falahi et al. (2017), the recent size optimization methodologies for standalone solar and wind hybrid renewable energy system have been reviewed. They presented several energy systems combining hybrid PV/wind systems with other renewable (RES) or conventional (CES) sources. The authors reported that the combination with RES are widely used in standalone applications. Indeed, they ensure a continual electricity supply to the load. The drawback of CES is the high investment cost and emission of harmful gas. The authors discussed different techniques (classic and modern methods) and software tools (HOMER, IHOGA, TRNSYS), used to improve the hybrid system reliability. Kaushik et al. (2016) reviewed the modelling, design methodology, and sizing optimization of photovoltaic based on water pumping, standalone and grid connected system. They presented the technical and economic parameters and the different sizing methods used in optimization process of PV system.

Olcan et al. (2015) developed a multi-objective analytical model for optimal sizing of standalone photovoltaic water pumping systems. Supply probability and the life cycle cost are used as technical and economic criteria, respectively. This model integrates several improvements such as changing of tilt angles, accurate estimation of water demand, use of irradiation and temperature data sequences, etc. It allows a complete optimization of photovoltaic water pumping system. The comparison between the proposed model and calculation method showed most appropriate results of sizing than the calculation algorithms. Chaabene et al. (2009) investigated an energy management algorithm for an optimum control of a photovoltaic water pumping system. The algorithm aims to extend the period of operating of the pump by controlling a commutation unit that connect the system components in relation to the multi-objective management criterion. The implementation of this algorithm showed that the proposed approach allows the extension of the pumping period up to 5h per day and provides a 97% daily average improvement of the pumped water quantity. Bakelli et al. (2011) treated the optimal sizing of photovoltaic pumping system with water storage tank using LPSP concept. The developed model consists of three sub-model: sub-model of pumping system; technical sub-model based on LPSP; economic sub-model based on Life Cycle Cost (LCC). A set of configurations corresponding to the desired LPSP can be generated from this model. Benyoucef and

Hamidat et al. (2009) studied systematic procedures for sizing photovoltaic pumping system, using water storage tank. Results of this study showed that the performance of photovoltaic pumping system depends on the total height and the photovoltaic nominal power. Based on the literature the numerical sizing method have been the most accurate method used for sizing the solar PV system. In addition, a good size optimization algorithm must handle small step meteorological and load demand time series data (hourly or smaller) Anwer et al. (2017). In this study, the optimal sizing using intuitive and numerical methods for designing a standalone photovoltaic water pumping system of a well situated in the village of Ngoundiane in Senegal is investigated. Average data of solar irradiation and load demand of Ngoundiane site and Average Loss of Power Supply Probability (ALPSP) concept are used to validate the proposed method and assess the technical reliability respectively.

This work is divided into three parts. In first part, we evaluate the different input parameters. In second part, the two developed sizing methodologies are presented: an intuitive method using average data approach and a numerical method based on the determinist approach. In the third part, we exhibit the results and discussions. Finally, this paper is completed by a conclusion and some recommendations.

## 2    Materials and Methods

The main input parameters used in the design of photovoltaic water pumping system are the daily requisite water demand, the total pumping height and the available solar energy.

### 2.1    Estimation of Daily Water Demand

The well is situated in the village of Ngoundiane in Senegal. Ngoundiane is far from Thies by 30 km and is positioned to 14°50 North and 17°06 West. The well supplies water to the families and the livestock. The water requirement has been assessed during the period of high drink. Table 1 gives human and livestock water requirements:

**Table 1.** Domestic and livestock water requirements respectively (Hadj Arab et al. 2005).

| Human water flow | | Livestock water flow | |
|---|---|---|---|
| Family | 10 | Family | 10 |
| Number of persons per family | 10 | Number of animals per family | 20 |
| Used daily water quantity per person | 50 L | Mean used daily water quantity per animal | 45 L |
| Total | 3.5 m$^3$ | Total | 9 m$^3$ |

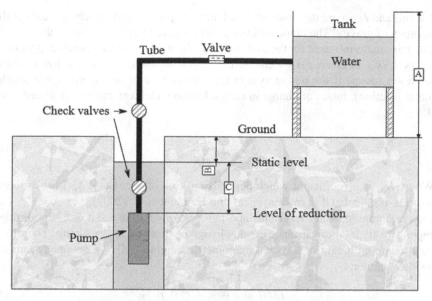

**Fig. 1.** Configuration of a water pumping system.

## 2.2 Determination of the Power Pumping Height

Figure 1 shows the configuration of a water pumping system.

During pumping, the water level inside the well tends to drop, so pumping is possible again when the regeneration of well balances the amount of water drawn (Kazem et al. 2013). The fall of the water level inside the well depends on some elements such as the kind of soil's permeability and thickness of water bearing.

The total pumping height ($h$) is the sum between static ($h_s$) and dynamic ($h_d$) heights:

$$h = h_s + h_d \tag{1}$$

For a well that have important variations of water level according to the flow, a corrective term is added and Eq. 1 is rewritten as follows (Hadj Arab et al. 2005):

$$h = h_s + \left(\frac{h_d + h_s}{Q_p}\right)Q_A \tag{2}$$

$Q_P$ (m$^3$/h) and $Q_A$ (m$^3$/h) are the flow of test and apparent flow respectively. The dynamic height is the distance between the water level in the well and the highest point from which the water is pumped. It can be calculated from Darcy-Welsbach formula (Ayop et al. 2018):

$$h_d = f\frac{L}{D}\frac{v^2}{2g} \tag{3}$$

$f$ is the coefficient of friction, it depends on the Reynolds number and the relative roughness that characterizes the surface of the pipe, $v$ (ms$^{-1}$) is the average speed of the fluid, $D$(m) and $L$(m) are the diameter and length of piping respectively, $g$(m/s$^2$) is the acceleration of gravity. The diameter D of piping is determined from Eq. 3 above.

The most materials used for the hydraulic canalization are metals (steel, copper) and polymers (PVC). In this paper we choose PVC because it is available with low cost and causes fewer losses. If the piping system have other kind of accessories (gate, angle, T-square, junction), losses of charge in each additional element can be calculated from Eq. 4:

$$h_d = k_{ac} \frac{v^2}{2g}$$

(4)

Where $K_{ac}$ is a coefficient which depends on kind of accessory. $K_{ac}$, for different accessories, is calculated from Benyoucef and Hamidat et al. (2009).

During pumping, water level falls and induces a hydraulic resistance, $R_h$, through the pipe. This hydraulic resistance creates losses of charge j in the piping. Therefore, the total pumping height or the total manometric height (TMH) is obtained from the following equation:

$$TMH = h + A + C + j$$

(5)

A and C correspond to the height of the tank and the level of water reduction, respectively. In our study, we do not take into account the support of the tank and the shutoff valve.

We measured the static level, reduction level, height of tank and losses of charge. Results are shown in Table 2.

**Table 2.** Results of the measurements of the static level, reduction level, dynamic level, height of tank and losses of charge.

| Statistic level | Reduction level | Dynamic level | Height of tank | Losses | HMT |
|---|---|---|---|---|---|
| 12 m | 24 m | 36 m | 5 m | 10 | 45.1 m |

## 2.3 Sunniness Level in Ngoundiane Site

Due to the non-availability of meteorological data in Ngoundiane site, irradiation and temperature data from Ndem village, Bambey, in the Diourbel region are used. The annual variation of the monthly daily irradiation average in Bambey zone is given in Fig. 2.

Annual average of daily solar irradiation of the zone of Bambey is of 5.85 kWh/m$^2$/day. Maximal value of irradiation is obtained at month of April with a value of 7.05 kWh/m$^2$/day while minimal value is recorded at month of December with a value of 4.88 kWh/m$^2$/day. The average temperature of this site varies between 25–30 °C.

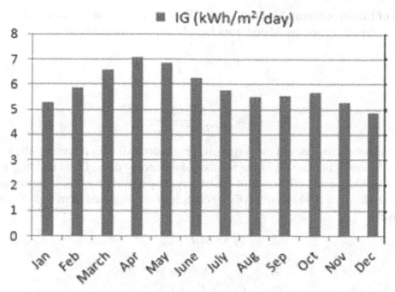

**Fig. 2.** Annual variation of monthly solar irradiation average of Bambey zone (Sadio et al. 2017).

### 2.4 Methods

In this section, the different stages of proposed sizing methods are presented. First, the hydraulic and energy consumption are estimated using Eqs 6 to 9. They express the required hydraulic ($E_h$) and electrical ($E_e$) energies and the hydraulic ($P_h$) and electrical ($P_e$) power to satisfy the load requirements respectively:

$$E_h = C_h \cdot V_e \cdot TMH \tag{6}$$

$$E_e = \frac{E_h}{\eta_{MP}} \tag{7}$$

$$P_h = \rho \cdot g \cdot Q \cdot TMH \tag{8}$$

$$P_e = \frac{P_h}{\eta_{MP}} \tag{9}$$

$V_e$ (m³) is the water quantity, $C_h$ (kg.S.h/m²) is the hydraulic constant and its expression is given by Eq. 10:

$$C_h = \frac{\rho \cdot g}{3600} \tag{10}$$

$\rho = 1000$ kg/m³ is the density of water, $\eta_{MP}$ is the efficiency of motor-pump couple and Q corresponds to the maximal pumping flow.

**Process of Intuitive Sizing Method.** Total PV module $(P_{PV})$ in $W_C$ and useful battery $(C_u)$ in $Ah$ capacities are calculated from Eqs. 11 and 12 respectively:

$$P_{PV} = \frac{E_e}{k \cdot E_I} \tag{11}$$

and

$$C_u = \frac{N_j \cdot E_e}{DOD \cdot U_s \cdot \eta_{bat}} \tag{12}$$

$k$ is the global efficiency of the system, it is estimated to 0.6, $E_I$ represents the average solar irradiation of the site, $N_j$ is the number of autonomy days, DOD and $\eta_{bat}$ are the Depth of Discharge and efficiency of the battery, respectively and $U_S$ is the voltage of the system. Residual $(C_r)$ and total $(C_{batl})$ capacities are deducted from Eqs. 13 and 14, respectively:

$$C_r = DOD \cdot C_u \tag{13}$$

and

$$C_{bat} = C_u + C_r \tag{14}$$

The number of PV module $(N_{PVs})$ in series and the number of string parallel $(N_{PVp})$ are determined, respectively, as follows:

$$N_{PVs} = \frac{U_S}{U_{PVu}} \tag{15}$$

and

$$N_{PVp} = \frac{P_{PV}}{P_{PVu}} \tag{16}$$

$U_{PVu}$ and $P_{PVu}$ are the individual voltage and capacity of a PV module respectively. The number of batteries in series and parallel are given by Eqs. 17 and 18 respectively:

$$N_{bats} = \frac{U_S}{U_{batu}} \tag{17}$$

$$N_{batp} = \frac{C_{batTol}}{C_{batu}} \tag{18}$$

$U_{batu}$ and $C_{batu}$ are the unitary voltage and capacity of a battery.

**Sizing of Other Components**

*Sizing of the Pump.* The choice of the pump depends on the flow and the total manometric height (TMH). The pump flow is obtained by the following formula:

$$Q = \frac{3.6 \cdot P_h}{g \cdot MTH} \tag{19}$$

Equation 19 can be rewritten as:

$$Q = \frac{3.6 \cdot P_e \cdot \eta_{MP}}{g \cdot MTH} \tag{20}$$

*Sizing of the Charge Controller.* The power of charge controller must be higher than the total PV power, its voltage must be identical to the PV array voltage. It must support an upper intensity to maximal current of PV array and load demand when they simultaneous operate.

The number, the total input and output current of charge controller are calculated from Eqs. 21, 22, and 23, respectively:

$$N_{Ch} = \frac{P_{PV}}{P_{Ch}} \tag{21}$$

$$I_{Che} = \frac{P_{Ch} \cdot N_{Ch}}{U_S} \tag{22}$$

$$I_{Chs} = N_{ch} \cdot I \tag{23}$$

$N_{ch}$ is the number of charge controller, $P_{ch}$ is the nominal power of one charge controller, $I_{Che}$ and $I_{Chs}$ are the input and the output currents of a charge controller respectively and $I$ is the operating current of the charge controller.

*Sizing of Inverter.* The nominal power of the inverter ($P_{inv}$) in *VA* is calculated from Eq. 24:

$$P_{inv} = \frac{1.2 \cdot P_e}{\cos \phi} \tag{24}$$

1.2 is the factor of oversizing and $\cos \phi$ is the power factor equal to 0.87.

*Sizing of the Conductor's Sections.* In this study, we use copper conductors that are sized to handle the intensity going through them. The section ($S$) of the wires between the different components is calculated as follows:

$$S = \frac{2 \cdot \rho \cdot L}{\Delta U} I_{max} \tag{25}$$

$\Delta U$ is the drop of voltage, $\rho$ is the resistance for copper, $I_{max}$ and $L$ are the maximal current and length of the wires between two components respectively.

*Sizing of Water Tank.* For a best evaluation of water demand, we apply standard method. In this method, the storage capacity of tank is included between 25% and 50% with an average of drink peak estimated to 33%. This volume is divided in three reserve: distribution reserve (DR), safety reserve (SR) which depends on the service level and fire reserve:

$$V_{res} = N_j \cdot C_d \tag{26}$$

## 2.5 Proposed Numerical Sizing Method

The new sizing approach based on numerical methods, in particular, the determinist approach proposed in this paper is detailed in this part. Average data of irradiation and temperature in Bambey zone are handled. Empirical simple models are utilized to model the different components. From hourly equations, which relate different components of the system, a simple algorithm is elaborated and adapted to the data nature of our site. The daily average energy $E_{PVav}$ produced by PV array, in kWh, is calculated from following mathematical expression (Sadio et al. 2018):

$$E_{PVav} = A_{PV} \cdot I_G \cdot \eta_{inv} \cdot \eta_{wire} \cdot \eta_r \left[ 1 - \beta \left( T_{amb} + \frac{G}{800} (T_{NOCT} - 20) - T_{ref} \right) \right] \quad (27)$$

$A_{PV}$ is the section of PV array, $\eta_{inv}$, $\eta_{wire}$ and $\eta_r$ represent the inverter, wires and reference efficiencies, respectively, $\beta$ is the temperature coefficient, $T_{amb}$ is the ambient temperature, $T_{NOCT}$ is the cell temperature in nominal conditions, which is measured under 800 W/m$^2$ of solar radiation, 20 °C of ambient temperature and 1 m/s of wind speed, $T_{ref}$ is the reference temperature and $G$ is the solar irradiance. The section of the PV array is given by Eq. 28:

$$A_{PV} = A_{PVu} \frac{P_{PV}}{P_{PVu}} \quad (28)$$

$A_{PV}$ is the unitary section of a module. The difference between average energy produced by PV array and daily load demand is given by Eq. 29:

$$\Delta E = E_{PVav} - \frac{E_e}{\eta_{inv}} \quad (29)$$

If $\Delta E$ is lower than zero, the average energy stored in the battery system is calculated as follows:

$$E_{batav} = E_{bat\,min} + \left( \frac{E_e}{\eta_{inv}} - E_{PVav} \right) \eta_{batc} \quad (30)$$

If $\Delta E$ is higher than zero, the average energy stored in the battery system is given by:

$$E_{batav} = E_{bat\,min} + \left( E_{PVav} - \frac{E_e}{\eta_{inv}} \right) \quad (31)$$

With $E_{batmin}$ is the minimum level of energy allowed in batteries. The discharge efficiency is considered to be equal to 1.

In order to protect batteries against damage and drastic reduction of their lifetime, the average energy stored in batteries is subject to the following restriction

$$E_{bat\,min} \leq E_{batav} \leq E_{bat\,max} \quad (32)$$

$E_{batmax}$ is the maximum level of energy allowed in storage system.

If the average energy generated by PV array is lower than load demand, and average energy stored in battery reaches the allowed minimum, it occurs an energy deficiency, called Average Loss of Power Supply (ALPS). It represents the missing energy to satisfy the load demand and is mathematically expressed by Eq. 33:

$$ALPS = E_e - (E_{PVav} + E_{batav} + E_{bat\,min})\eta_{inv} \tag{33}$$

The Loss of power supply probability is the ratio between ALPS and load demand. It is expressed by:

$$ALPSP = \frac{ALPS}{E_e} \tag{34}$$

It varies between 0 and 1. If ALPSP is equal to 0, the system will always be able to satisfy load demand. If ALPSP is equal to 1, the system will never meet requirements load.

From all these considerations, we elaborated a simple algorithm, which aims to calculate the storage capacity corresponding to each value of the PV capacity considering the different operating conditions of system. The different stages of the algorithm are shown in Fig. 3. This algorithm is run by using input data defined in our previous work (Sadio et al. 2018) and technical and economic parameters given in Table 3.

**Table 3.** Technical and economic parameters of the components.

| Designation | Characteristic | Unitary cost (Euros) |
|---|---|---|
| Module | 250 $W_C$/48 V | 362.95 |
| Pump system | Lorentz PS2-1800 | 1307.12 |
| Battery | 190 Ah/2 V | 151.00 |
| Charge Controller | MPPT 150 V/60 A | 510 |
| Inverter | 1000 VA, 48 V DC | 207.4 |

The different stage of proposed numerical method are shown in Fig. 3.
The algorithm of numerical sizing has been run using MATLAB software.

## 3 Results and Discussion

Figure 4 represents the variation of ALPSP in relation to PV capacity. It shows that the ALPSP decreases when PV capacity increases. Indeed, most large PV capacity allows to generate a great quantity of energy and reduce the energy deficiency.

Figure 5 shows different combinations of PV and battery capacities for various values of ALPSP called iso-reliability curves. The ALPSP varies between 0.3 and 0.9. The different combinations, which satisfy reliability levels of 0.9 and 0.3, are shown in Figs. 6 and 7, respectively. We remarked that the increase of ALPSP involves the one of

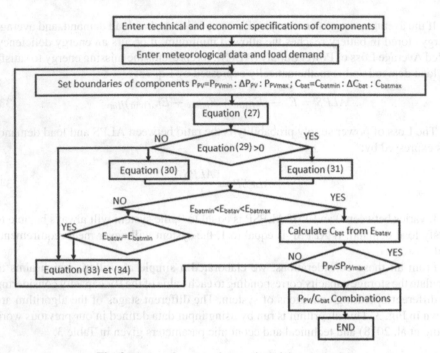

**Fig. 3.** Stage of proposed numerical sizing method.

components size. Indeed, to obtain small values of ALPSP and improve the reliability of system, PV and battery capacities must be important.

The smaller value of ALPSP provided by the model is 0.3 considered as great when referring in literature. This can be justified by the data nature because the use of average data reduces the accuracy of results. In addition, load water and TMH have been underestimated in sizing process.

In Fig. 7 we remarked that a PV capacity value of 8250 $W_P$ corresponds to a storage capacity of 820 Ah (Table 4).

We obtained a combination of 8250 $W_P$/1638 Ah and 8250 $W_P$/820 Ah for intuitive and numerical methods, respectively. The numerical method allows to reduce the storage capacity to 50%. Indeed, the different state of the battery has been calculated from the energy generated by the PV array; that is not possible in intuitive method where the capacities are computed separately and result in oversizing. However, we noticed a high value of ALPSP 0.3, which is due to the use of average data in sizing process and an underestimation of the input parameters.

In order to show the importance of the results in this paper, the proposed model is compared with some results of the literature (Khatib et al. 2016; Kazem et al. 2013; Hadj Arab et al. 2005).

In Khatib et al. (2016), we noticed the same variation for the iso-reliability curves with the proposed model, but the values are weaker. We explained this difference by the models used to model the different components in the system, which are more robust in Khatib et al. 2016. Indeed, we have not access to meteorological hourly (or smaller) data

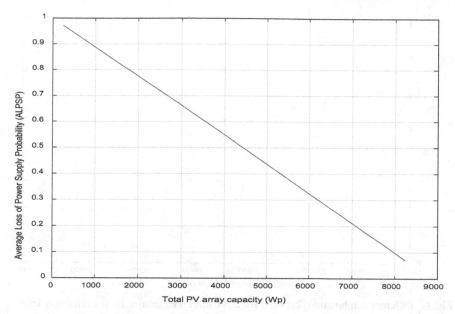

**Fig. 4.** Variation of ALPSP according to the total PV capacity.

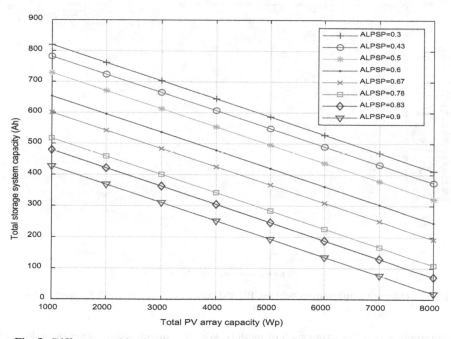

**Fig. 5.** Different combinations between PV and batteries capacities for various ALPSP.

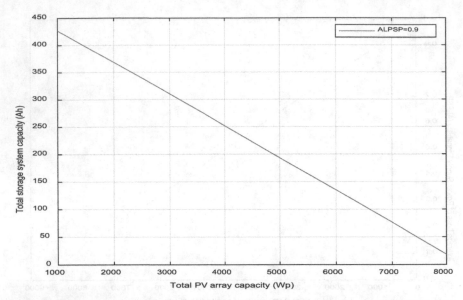

**Fig. 6.** Different combinations between PV and batteries capacities for 0.9 reliability level.

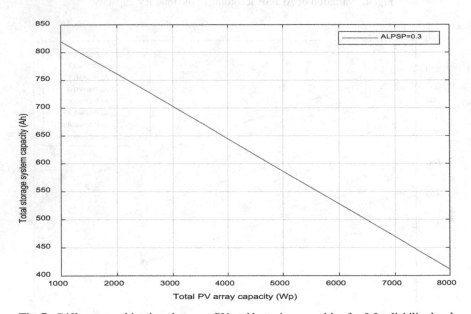

**Fig. 7.** Different combinations between PV and batteries capacities for 0.3 reliability level.

in Ngoundiane site for using such of models. We are constrained to use meteorological daily average, which not consider the uncertainty nature of these data and affect the accuracy of the results.

**Table 4.** Results of intuitive and numerical sizing methods.

| Designation | Intuitive method | Numerical method |
|---|---|---|
| Hydraulic energy (Wh/day) | 15669 | 15669 |
| Electric energy (Wh/day) | 26115 | 26115 |
| Hydraulic power | 2243.77 | 2243.77 |
| Electric power (W) | 3740 | 3740 |
| Pump flow ($m^3$) | 250 | 250 |
| Piping diameter (mm) | 19 | 19 |
| Total capacity of PV array (Wp) | 8250 | 8250 |
| Total number of PV array | 33 | 33 |
| Total capacity of storage system (Ah) | 1638 | 820 |
| Total number of battery | 216 | 120 |
| Total number of charge controller | 4 | 4 |
| Total number of Inverter | 6 | 6 |
| Volume of tank ($m^3$) | 250 | 250 |

In Kazem et al. (2013), we have small difference in the values of ALPSP. However, the battery capacity increases with the PV capacity in this paper. Contrary to our study where the PV and battery capacities are inversely proportional. What allows to find out a compromise between technical and economic criterion. In addition, with monthly data, a reliability of 0.3 is obtained, then by using machine learning to predict meteorological hourly data, the reliability can be increased and results can be strongly improved.

## 4    Conclusion

The optimal sizing of a photovoltaic water pumping system of a well implanted in Ngoundiane's village has been investigated in this paper. We have used the ALPSP to evaluate the technical performance of system. First, an intuitive method is applied by separately determining the capacity of components. Afterwards, a numerical sizing method is developed. The different components of the PV system have been modeled by using empirical simple model more adapted to the input parameters of Ngoundiane site. From these models a simple algorithm has been elaborated to find PV and battery combinations for various levels of reliability. ALPSP concept is used to evaluate the technical performance of system. After implementing this model in MATLAB, obtained results showed that the numerical sizing method allows to decrease the storage capacity to 50% when compared to the intuitive method. Nevertheless, the ALPSP values are seem high compared to the ones found in literature. This is due to an undervaluation of input parameters and the use of average data of meteorological variables in the model. These results can be improved by using hourly input data. It is also important to define an accurate input profile and to include all variables, which can affect the optimal operating of the system. In the future works, an accurate model to predict and generate hourly data of solar radiation will be performed by using machine learning. From this data, the dynamic behavior of components of PV system can be studied with precision and many parameters would be taken into account in the sizing model.

# References

Al-Falahi, M.D.A., Jayasinghe, S.D.G., Enshaei, H.: A review on recent size optimization methodologies for standalone solar and wind hybrid renewable energy system. Energy Convers. Manag. **143**, 252–274 (2017)

Ayop, R., Isa, M., Tan, C.W.: Components sizing of photovoltaic standalone system based on loss of power supply probability. Renew. Sustain. Energy Rev. **81**(2), 2731–2743 (2018)

Bakelli, Y., Azoui, B., Hadj, A.: Optimal sizing of photovoltaic pumping system with water tank storage using LPSP concept. Sol. Energy **2**, 288–294 (2011)

Benyoucef, B., Hamidat, A.: Systematic procedures for sizing photovoltaic pumping system, using water storage tank. Energy Policy **4**, 1489–1501 (2009)

Cabral, C.V., Filho, D.O.: A stochastic method for standalone photovoltaic system sizing. J. Electr. Syst. Inf. Technol. **9**, 1628–1636 (2010)

Chaabene, M., Kamoun, M.B.K., Sallem, S.: Energy management algorithm for an optimum control of a photovoltaic water pumping system. Appl. Energy **12**, 2671–2680 (2009)

Hadj Arab, A., Benghanem, M., Gharbi, A.: Dimensionnement de Systèmes de Pompage Photovoltaïque. Rev. Energ. Ren **8**, 19–26 (2005)

Hontoria, L., Aguilera, J., Zufiria, P.: A new approach for sizing standalone photovoltaic systems based on in neural networks. Sol. Energy **78**, 313–319 (2005)

Ibrahim Anwar, I., Tamer, K., Azah, M.: Optimal sizing of a standalone photovoltaic system for remote housing electrification using numerical algorithm and improved system models. Energy **126**, 392–403 (2017)

Jakhrani, A.Q., Othman, A.K., Rigit, A.R.H.: A novel analytical model for optimal sizing of standalone photovoltaic system. Sol. Energy **1**, 675–682 (2012)

Kaushik, S.C., Lamba, R., Rawat, R.: A review on modelling, design methodology and size optimization of photovoltaic based water pumping, standalone and connected grid system. Renew. Sustain. Energy Rev. **57**, 1506–1519 (2016)

Kazem, H.A., Khatib, T., Sopian, K.: Sizing of a standalone photovoltaic/Battery system at minimum cost for remote housing electrification in Sohar, Oman. Energy Build. **61**, 108–115 (2013)

Khatib, T., Ibrahim, I., Mohamed, A.: A review on sizing methodologies of photovoltaic array and storage battery in a standalone photovoltaic system. Energy Convers. Manag. **120**, 330–348 (2016)

Nogueira, C.E.C., Vidotto, M.L., Niedzialkoski, R.K.: Sizing and simulation of a photovoltaic/wind energy system using batteries, applied for a small rural property located in the South of Brazil. Renew. Sustain. Energy Rev. **29**, 151–157 (2014)

Olcan, C.: Multi-objective analytical model for optimal sizing of standalone photovoltaic water pumping systems. Energy Convers. Manag. **100**, 358–369 (2015)

Sadio, A., Fall, I., Mbodji, S., Sissokho, G.: Analysis of meteorological data for photovoltaic applications in Ngoundiane site. EAI Endorsed Trans. Collabor. Comput. **3**, e2 (2017)

Sadio, A., Fall, I., Mbodji, S.: New numerical sizing approach of a standalone photovoltaic power at Ngoundiane, Senegal. EAI Endorsed Trans. Energy Web Inf. Technol. **5**, e2 (2018)

Sadio, A., Fall, I., Mbodji, S., Sow, P.L.T.: A comparative study based on the Genetic Algorithm (GA) method for the optimal sizing of the standalone photovoltaic system in the Ngoundiane site. EAI Endorsed Trans. Energy Web Inf. Technol. **6**, e1 (2019)

Shen, W.X.: Optimally sizing of solar array and battery in a standalone photovoltaic system in Malaysia. Renew. Energy **34**, 348–352 (2009)

Sidrach-de-Cardona, M., Mora Lopez, L.I.: A simple model for sizing standalone photovoltaic system. Solar Energy Mater. Solar Cells **55**, 199–214 (1998)

# Mechanical and Industrial Engineering

# Influence of Nanoparticles Addition
# on Performance of CSOME in DI CI Engine

Megersa Lemma[1(✉)] and Ramesh Babu Nallamothu[2]

[1] Mechanical Engineering Department, Mizan Tepi University, Tepi, Ethiopia
[2] Mechanical Systems and Vehicle Engineering Department, SoMCME, Adama Science and
Technology University, Adama, Ethiopia
ramesh.babu@astu.edu.et

**Abstract.** In this work it is aimed to test the performance of cotton seed oil
biodiesel with cerium oxide ($CeO_2$) nanoparticles as additive. This work goes
through the various stages like production of biodiesel, addition of nanoparticles
with the biodiesel-diesel blends in different proportion using ultrasonicator, testing
the effect of nano additives on physiochemical properties of the fuel blend, testing
the stability of fuel blend with nano particles, testing the performance and exhaust
emission in diesel engine. The blends B10 (90% diesel and 10% biodiesel in
volume), B20 (80% diesel and 20% biodiesel in volume), B20+50ppm (80% diesel
and 20% biodiesel and 0.05 gm/l cerium oxide) in volume, B20+100ppm (80%
diesel and 20% biodiesel and 0.1 gm/l cerium oxide) in volume, B25 (75% diesel
and 25% biodiesel) in volume were prepared. From the performance test results,
the cotton seed oil fuel blended with cerium oxide shows increment in brake power
4.5kW 4.68kW and brake torque of 18.43 Nm and 18.52 Nm with 50 ppm and
100 ppm respectively. Addition of $CeO_2$ improved exhaust emission compared to
pure diesel (B0). The brake specific fuel consumption of cotton seed fuel blended
with cerium was decreased compared to the diesel. Generally, it may be concluded
from the experimental investigation that the cotton seed oil biodiesel fuel blended
with cerium oxide nanoparticle can become a good alternative to petro-diesel.

**Keywords:** Biodiesel · $CeO_2$ nanoparticles · Performance and emission ·
Stability of the blend · Ultrasonicator

## 1 Introduction

The growing industrialization and motorization of the world has led to a step up for the
demand of petroleum-based fuel. The petroleum-based fuels are obtained from restricted
reserves. These finite reserves are highly targeted in certain areas of the world. Therefore, those countries not having these resources face energy/foreign exchange crisis,
principally because of the import of crude petroleum. Hence, it's necessary to appear
for alternative fuels which might be produced from resources accessible domestically
among the country such as alcohol, biodiesel, vegetable oils etc. [1]. To solve this issue,
many researchers established with results that biodiesel is an alternate fuel.

M. A. Delele et al. (Eds.): ICAST 2020, LNICST 385, pp. 141–155, 2021.
https://doi.org/10.1007/978-3-030-80618-7_9

It is evident that two things are necessary, one is process of vegetable oil to biodiesel and the alternative is testing obtained biodiesel in diesel engine for its compatibility as fuel to diesel engine particularly the blend percentage which will offer results almost like diesel. Biodiesel is outlined as mono-alkyl esters of long chain fatty acids derived from renewable biolipids via transesterification method, that conform to ASTM D6751 specifications to be used in diesel engines [1]. The method of elimination all glycerol and fatty acid from the vegetable oil within the presents of catalyst are called as trans-esterification. It's basically a written record reaction. Triglycerides are first reduced to di glycerides. The di glycerides are afterwards reduced to mono glycerides. The mono glycerides are finally reduced to fatty acid esters [2].

The properties of biodiesel typically have higher density, viscosity, cloud point, cetane number, lower volatility and heating value The properties of biodiesel typically have higher density viscosity cloud point cetane number lower volatility and heating value compared with diesel fuel that affecting on engine performance and emissions. However, using optimised blend of nano particles and diesel will help to reduce these high properties or its blends could also be used in the present diesel engines with very little or no modification to the engine [4, 8]. With the following goals and method this work has been completed through fuel additives (nanofuel). Nanofuel could be a renewable and ecofriendly alternative diesel fuel for CI engine. What are more additives being an important a part of these days fuels, along with the carefully developed fuels composition. They contribute to efficiency responsibility associated long lifetime of an engine like using optimised blend of nano particles and diesel rather than conventional diesel fuel considerably reduces emission of particulate matters (PM), carbon monoxide (CO), sulphur oxides (SOx), and unburned hydrocarbons (HC). With the utilization of fuel additives within the blend of nanoparticles and diesel improves performance, combustion and additionally improves fuel properties that enhance the combustion characteristics. The impact of mixture of cerium oxide ($CeO_2$) and carbon nanotube (CNT) in single cylinder four-stroke water-cooled inconstant compression ratio engine using castor biodiesel blend with ethanol. When blended at 25ppm, 50ppm and 100 ppm of 32 nm sized $CeO_2$ and 100 nm sized CNT, brake thermal efficiency and cylinder pressure is increased. Moreover, such a blend of nano particles resulted in forward-looking peak pressure incidence with cleanser combustion means reducing emission [8]. This work study was designed to analyze the result of CSME blended with diesel beside cerium oxide ($CeO_2$) nanoparticle on the performance and exhaust gas characteristics of diesel engine. For investigation varied blends of cotton seed biodiesel with diesel were taken. The cerium oxide ($CeO_2$) nano particle was added with various proportions [5]. The researchers are targeted on single biodiesel with Nano fuels blends like soybean oil, rapeseed oil, pongamia pinnata oil, Cotton seed oil, Neem oil, Castor oil, Mahua oil, Mahua oil, jatropha oil, lineed oil, rice bran oil etc. and its blended with diesel [5, 6]. The stability of nano fluid is increase by ultrasonic bath stabilization or by adding chemical agent within the fluid [7].

Nanoparticles acts as a fuel accepted catalyst that improves specific properties of fuel once value-added to the base fuel depending upon the dosage level of it (i.e., flash point, fire point, kinematic viscosity, heating value and cetane number). This can be because of its better thermo physical properties. Particles that have size in between one nm to one hundred nm are thought about as nanoparticles. The size of nanoparticles varies from 1 to 100 nm [9–12]. The experimental on emission characteristics, performance with Hinge oil methyl ester (HOME) biodiesel fuel blended with multi walled carbon tube (MWCNT) at 25 ppm and 50 ppm concentration in single cylinder four stroke direct injection diesel engine [13–16]. In addition, the investigation of emission characteristics and performances of pure diesel and diesel-biodiesel blend and ethanol blends with 25 ppm cerium oxide ($CeO_2$) [17–19].

## 2   Materials and Methods

The cotton seed was obtained from awash. Methanol, potassium hydroxide, and distilled water were purchased from chemical marketing and suppliers companies (Ranchem chemicals Plc, Addis Ababa) for laboratory scale amount. Cerium oxide ($CeO_2$) nanoparticle were purchased from Nano Research Lab, India; diesel fuel was purchased from Oil Libya Adama. All chemicals used for the research were analytical grade. Characterisation of fuel blends were tested at Ethiopian petroleum supply and enterprise while the performance and exhaust emission test was conducted at Dilla University Mechanical Engineering laboratory on CT 110 Test Stand Diesel Engine (single cylinder, 4-stroke engine).

### 2.1   Extraction of Cotton Seed Oil

The raw Cotton seed were obtained from cotton ginning factory Awash and separated the seed from the lint before the oil extracted from the seed. The lint goes to textile industry and the seed for the oil extraction to Hundaf Engineer Food oil production Plc. There are some core procedures to be followed for extracting crude oil from cotton seed. The steps are like collection of all cotton seeds, de hulling and separation of the hulls (husk), cleaning the seed and drying, mechanical press, heat treatment and cooking and filtering. Figure 1 shows the pressing of cotton seed using screw press.

After the crude oil was extracted using screw press, the transestification was done at Adama Science and Technology University, Chemistry Department Laboratory.

**Fig. 1.** Extraction of oil from cotton seed by screw pressing.

## 2.2 Determination of Acid Value

### 2.2.1 Titration

In order to determine the percent of FFA in the oil, a process called titration is used. The vegetable oil is first mixed with methanol. Next, a mixture of sodium hydroxide (NaOH) and water is added till all of the FFA has been reacted. This can be confirmed by checking the pH of the mixture. If the oil samples have high FFA content (more than 1%) then the reaction consumes more alkali catalyst to neutralize the FFA. The FFA content in the oil was found as 0.59. The FFAs < 1, therefore transestirification process was used to prepare biodiesel. Figure 2 shows the titration of crude oil.

**Fig. 2.** Titration to find FFA in the oil

## 2.2.2  Laboratory Preparation of Biodiesel (Transestirification Process)

The biodiesel production using transesterification process involves various stages.

**Fig. 3.** Transesterification

**Fig. 4.** Glycerol Separation from methyl ester

**Fig. 5.** Washing biodiesel (soap is at bottom)

**Fig. 6.** Final washing of biodiesel

**Fig. 7.** Drying of biodiesel

**Fig. 8.** Prepared biodiesel

The figures Fig. 3, 4, 5, 6, 7 and Fig. 8 show the stages of biodiesel production like transesterification using hotplate with magnetic stirrer, separation of glycerine, washing of biodiesel with water (First washing and Final washing), biodiesel drying and finally the prepared biodiesel.

### 2.2.3 Mixing Nanoparticles with Fuel Blend

The cerium oxide nanoparticles were mixed with B20 at a proportion of 50 ppm and 100ppm using magnetic stirrer and ultrasonic cleaner for homogeneous dispersion of nanoparticles in the blend. Stable mixture was obtained adding CTAB surfactant.

Blending of nanoparticles was done using ultrasonic cleaner with a frequency of 40 kHz for about 30 mnts. Figure 9 shows the ultrasonic cleaner and the prepared blends. Figure 10 shows all fuel blends prepared.

**Fig. 9.** Ultrasonicator and fuel blends

**Fig. 10.** Prepared biodiesel blends

## 3   Experimental Setup

The performance and exhaust emission tests were conducted on CT 110 Test Stand for Small Combustion Engine. The specifications of the test stand are given in the Table 1. Figure 11 Shows the picture of the experimental setup.

**Table 1.** Specification of the CT 110 Test Stand with engine

| Engine model | 1B30-2 |
| --- | --- |
| Number of cylinders | 1 |
| Length × Width × Height | 370 mm × 330 mm × 450 mm |
| Company | Hatz |
| Weight | 35 kg |
| Fuel | CT 100.22 Diesel |

(*continued*)

**Table 1.** (*continued*)

| Bore | 80 mm |
|------|-------|
| Stroke | 69 mm |
| Crank length | 34.5 mm |
| Rod length | 114.5 mm |
| Output power at 3500 min-1 | 5.5 kW |
| Oil capacity | 1.1 L |
| Stop solenoid | 12 V |
| Compression ratio | 22: 1 |
| Engine type | Air-cooled single cylinder 4-stroke Diesel Engine |

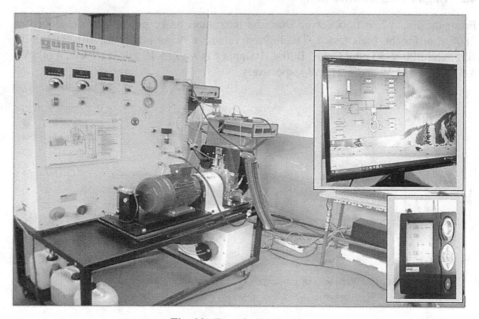

**Fig. 11.** Experimental setup

# 4 Result and Discussion

## 4.1 Characterization Results

The characterization results of the biodiesel produced from cotton seed oil and blend fuels that were certified from Ethiopian petroleum supply enterprise are shown in Table 2.

**Table 2.** The properties of biodiesel and blends.

| SNo | Properties | Test method ASTM | EPSE Diesel limits | Results | | | | | |
|-----|-----------|------------------|--------------------|---------|---|---|---|---|---|
| | | | | B100 | B10 | B20 | B25 | B20+50ppm CeO₂ | B20+100ppm CeO₂ |
| 1 | Density@15 °C (g/ml) | D4O52 | Report | 0.8563 | 0.8425 | 0.8467 | 0.8488 | 0.8477 | 0.8464 |
| 2 | Density@20 °C (g/ml) | D4052 | Report | 0.8465 | 0.8389 | 0.8432 | 0.8454 | 0.8442 | 0.8458 |
| 3 | Flash Point (PMCC, °C) | D93 | Min.60 | 182 | 85 | 86 | 89 | 87 | 86 |
| 4 | Cloud point (°C) | D2500 | Max.+5 | +3 | +1 | −1 | +2 | +1 | +1 |
| 5 | Total acidity (mgKOH/g) | D974 | – | 0.0985 | 0.0852 | 0.1009 | 0.0918 | 0.0930 | 0.1005 |
| 6 | Viscosity@40 °C (cSt) | D445 | 1.9–6 | 3.67 | 3.29 | 3.32 | 3.33 | 3.32 | 3.31 |

## 4.2  Engine Brake Power (kW)

From the Fig. 12, it is observed that, the maximum brake power was developed at 2808 rpm for the fuels tested. The highest values of brake power for B0, B10, B20, B25, and B20 + 50 ppm $CeO_2$, B20 + 100ppm $CeO_2$ are 5.18 kW, 4.67 kW, 4.60 kW, 4.31 kW, 4.53 kW and 5.21 kW respectively.

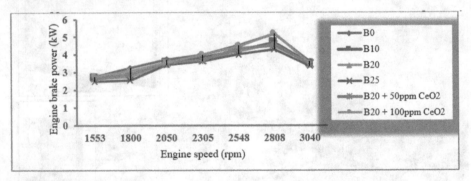

**Fig. 12.** Variation of Brake power (kW) with Engine speed (rpm)

## 4.3  Engine Brake Torque (Nm)

From Fig. 13, given below, it is observed that all fuel samples producing maximum torque at a speed of 2548 rpm. The maximum brake torque for the fuel samples B0, B10, B20, B25, B20 + 50 ppm $CeO_2$ and B20 + 100 ppm $CeO_2$ are 18.48 Nm, 18.35 Nm, 18.12 Nm, 17.83 Nm, 18.43 Nm, and 18.52 Nm respectively. B20 + 100 ppm $CeO_2$ had higher brake torque than other fuel blends. It is clearly observed that the addition of $CeO_2$ caused higher brake torque.

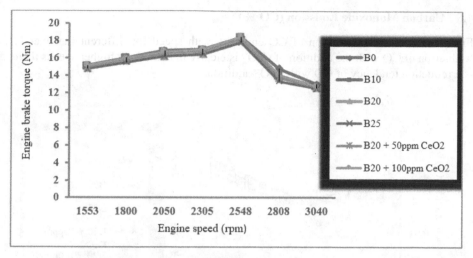

**Fig. 13.** Variation of Brake torque (Nm) with Engine speed (rpm)

## 4.4 Brake Specific Fuel Consumption Bsfc (kg/kWh)

Figure 14 below shows that there is a reduction of brake specific fuel consumption with addition of nanoparticles. Engine speed for neat diesel, biodiesel blend fuel and biodiesel blend fuel plus cerium oxide nano particles. The bsfc was observed to be reducing from 1553 rpm to 2548 rpm later starts increasing.

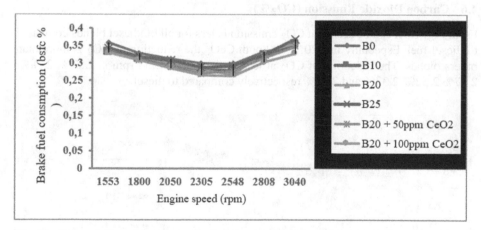

**Fig. 14.** The variation of brake specific fuel Consumption (kg/kWh) with engine speed (rpm)

## 4.5 Carbon Monoxide Emission (CO %)

Figure 15 shows the variation of CO emission with speed for different fuel blends. Reduction of CO with the addition of $CeO_2$ is clearly indicated. At higher speeds there is a reduction tendency of CO with $CeO_2$ addition.

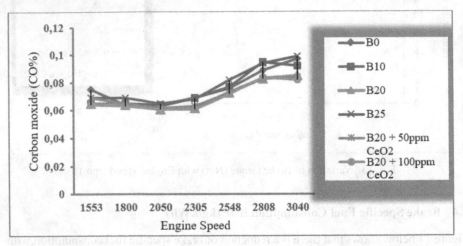

**Fig. 15.** Variation of carbon monoxide (%) with respect to engine speed (rpm)

## 4.6 Carbon Dioxide Emission ($CO_2$ %)

From Fig. 16, it can be seen that $CO_2$ emission is less for all biodiesel blends compared to diesel fuel. Especially in B20 + 100 ppm $CeO_2$ the reduction of $CO_2$ is more than others blends. The reduction of $CO_2$ at low engine speed 1553 rpm is 2.53%, 2.38%, 2.47% 2.52%, 2.32% and 2.28% respectively compared to diesel.

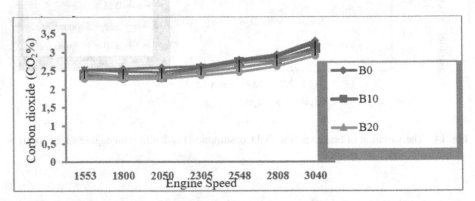

**Fig. 16.** Variation of carbon dioxide (%) respect to engine speed (rpm)

## 4.7  Hydrocarbon Emission (HC ppm)

B20 + 50ppm $CeO_2$ and B20 + 100 ppm $CeO_2$ fuel blends had less HC emission than others Fig. 17.

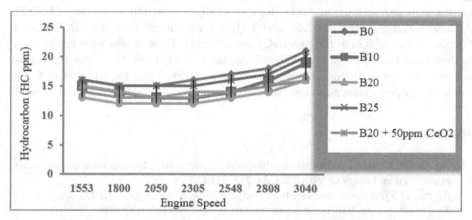

**Fig. 17.**  Variations of Hydrocarbon (HC) respect to Engine speed (rpm)

## 4.8  Emission Test for (O2%)

The oxygen ($O_2$) in case of fuel blended with cerium oxide nano particle is somewhat higher than other fuels. For a blend of B20 + 100 ppm $CeO_2$ the $O_2$ emission is 17.56%, 17.55%, 17.49%, 17.33%, 17.29%. 17.18%, 16.99% higher for engine speeds 1553 rpm, 1800 rpm, 2050 rpm, 2305 rpm, 2548 rpm, 2808 rpm, and 3040 rpm respectively, than diesel fuel (Fig. 18).

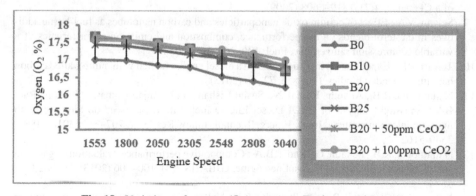

**Fig. 18.**  Variations of oxygen ($O_2$) respect to Engine speed (rpm)

## 5    Conclusion

Based on engine performance and exhaust emission tests, it can be concluded that diesel biodiesel fuel blends with $CeO_2$ can be used satisfactorily in diesel engine without any modifications of the engine. Transesterification reduced the viscosity of the oil considerably and addition of $CeO_2$ also caused slight reduction in viscosity (3.67cSt, 3.29cSt, 3.32cSt, 3.33cSt, 3.32cSt, and 3.31cSt for biodiesel, B10, B20, B25, B20 + 50ppm $CeO_2$, and B20 + 100ppm $CeO_2$ respectively). These results were nearly close to diesel and confirm with the biodiesel standards (ASTM D6751). From the engine performance test and emission test, it is clearly observed that the addition of $CeO_2$ caused better performance and less harmful emissions compared to conventional diesel.

## References

1. Agarwal, A.K.: Biofuels (alcohols and biodiesel) applications as fuels for internal combustion engines. Progr. Energy Combust. Sci. **33**, 233–271 (2007)
2. Akhtar, T.: Synthesis of biodiesel from triglyceride oil, Master's thesis (2011)
3. Arul Mozhi Selvan, V.R.A.: Effects of cerium oxide nanoparticle addition in diesel anddiesel-biodiesel-ethanol blends on the performance and emission characteristics of a CI engine. **4**, 1–6 (2009)
4. Benjumea, P., Agudelo, J., Agudelo, A.: Basic properties of palm oil biodiesel–diesel blends. Fuel **87**(10–11), 2069–2075 (2008)
5. Ghanshyam, S., Soni, P.D.: Performance and emission characteristics of CI engine using diesel and biodiesel blends with nanoparticles as additive - a review study. **3**(4), 2321–9939 (2015)
6. Mekhilef, S.S.: A review on palm oil biodiesel as a source of renewable fuel. Renew. Sustain. Energy Rev. **15**(4), 1937–1949 (2011)
7. Sajeevan, A.C.: Diesel engine emission reduction using catalytic nanoparticles: an experimental investigation (2013)
8. Selvan, V.A.M., Anand, R.B., Udayakumar, M.: Effects of cerium oxide nanoparticle addition in diesel and diesel biodiesel ethanol blends on the performance and emission characteristics of a CI engine. **4**(7), 1819–6608 (2009)
9. Selvan, V.A.: Effect of cerium oxide nanoparticles and carbon nanotubes as fuel-borne additives in diesterol blends on the performance, combustion and emission characteristics of a variable compression ratio engine. Fuel **130**, 160–167 (2014)
10. Tewari, P.D.: Experimental investigations on a diesel engine fuelled with multi-walled carbon nanotubes blended biodiesel fuels. **3**, 72–76 (2013)
11. Nallamothu, R.B., Anantha Kamal, N., Seshu Kishan, N., Niranjan Kumar, I.N., Appa Rao, B.V.: Emission Analysis of CRDI Diesel Engine fueled ith cotton seed oil biodiesel with multiple injection strategy. Int. J. Emerg. Technol. Innov. Res. **5**(9), 707–712 (2018). ISSN 2349-5162
12. Nallamothu, R.B., Fekadu, G., Rao, P.B.A.: Comparative performance evaluation of gasoline and its blends with ethanol in gasoline engine. GJBAHS **2**(4), 100–106 (2013). ISSN 2319-5584
13. Neway, S., Nallamothu, R.B., Nallamothu, S.K., Nallamothu, A.K.: Investigation on pollution caused by gasoline and diesel fuelled vehicles. Int. J. Eng. Trends Technol. (IJETT) **36**(7), 376–381 (2016). ISSN 2231-5381

14. Nallamothu, R., Anantha Kamal, N., Seshu Kishan, N., Niranjan Kumar, I., Appa Rao, B.: Effect of multiple injection strategy on combustion of cotton seed oil biodiesel in CRDI diesel engine. In: Narasimham, G. S. V. L., Babu, A Veeresh, Reddy, S Sreenatha, Dhanasekaran, Rajagopal (eds.) Recent Trends in Mechanical Engineering. LNME, pp. 107–119. Springer, Singapore (2020). https://doi.org/10.1007/978-981-15-1124-0_9
15. Nallamothu, R.B., Birbirsa, G., Niranjan Kumar, I.N., Appa Rao, B.V., Seshu Kishan, N.: A review on performance of biodiesel in engines with and without addition of nanoparticles. Int. J. Manag. Technol. Eng. IJMTE/1592 IX(I), January 2019
16. Nallamothu, R.B., Lemma, M., Niranjan Kumar, I.N., Appa Rao, B.V., Anantha Kamal, N., Seshu Kishan, N.: Performance of cotton seed biodiesel with nano additives in diesel engines: a review. J. Appl. Sci. Comput. VI(II), 142–147 (2019)
17. Nallamothu, R.B., Fekadu, G., Rao, P.B.A.: Comparative performance analysis of gasoline and its blends with ethanol in gasoline engine. Glob. J. Biol. Agric. Health Sci. GJBAHS 2(4), 100–106 (2013). ISSN 2319-5584
18. Firew, D., Babu, N.R., Didwania, M.: The performance evaluation of diethyl-ether (DEE) additive with diesel blends using diesel engine test rig. Int. J. Sci. Eng. Res. 7(6), 23–29 (2016). ISSN 2229-5518
19. Nallamothu, R.B., Nallamothu, A.K., Nallamothu, S.K.: Emission characteristics of CSOME in CRDI diesel engine with multiple injection strategy. In: Narasimham, G.S.V.L., Babu, A.V., Reddy, S.S., Dhanasekaran, R. (eds.) Recent Trends in Mechanical Engineering. LNME, pp. 97–108. Springer, Singapore (2021). https://doi.org/10.1007/978-981-15-7557-0_9

# Design, Analysis and Manufacturing of Multistage Evaporative Desert Cooling System

Somashekar Dasappa[1](✉), Mohammedkezal Mohammedabrar[1], Urmale Wegaso[1], and Adem Ali[2]

[1] Department of Mechanical Engineering, Samara University, Samara, Afar, Ethiopia
[2] College of Engineering and Technology, Samara University, Samara, Afar, Ethiopia

**Abstract.** This research described the development of a test setup and performance evaluation of a Multistage Evaporative Desert Cooling System (MEDCS) (Cooling - Humidification - Cooling -Dehumidification) by considering the advantage of indirect evaporative system and overcoming the disadvantages of direct evaporative cooling system using copper tubes and Honey comb cooling pads. In this research the maximum performance in multistage evaporative cooling at 2450 rpm. The best parameters are found at this rpm are temperature 23.6 °C, relative humidity 63%, specific humidity 0.13 kg of water vapors/kg of dry air, dry bulb temperature 38 °C, dew point temperature 10 °C, wet bulb temperature 13 °C and enthalpy 75 kJ/kg at average consumption of 8.07 L/h. In multistage evaporative cooling, after reached required relative humidity and specific humidity, by switching off direct evaporative cooling system we can maintain same room temperature by running indirect evaporative cooling technology without any addition of moisture.

**Keywords:** MEDCS · DEC · IEC · Copper tubes · Honey comb cooling pads · DBT · WBT · DPT · Humidity and water

## 1 Introduction

World is continuously trying to formulate new one. Somebody tries to find new one and tries to transform an ordinary one to implement a technology. This is the upshot of population growth and increase in the comfort of living which is directly proportional to energy consumption. In practice power scarcity is also occurred. These difficulties are corrected by modification by Evaporative Cooling Technology.

Energy request worldwide for structures cooling has expanded forcefully over the most recent couple of many years, which has raised worries over consumption of energy assets and adding to an unnatural weather change. Current energy request gauges remains at somewhere in the range of 40 and half of all out essential force utilization. In hot atmosphere nations, the most noteworthy portion of building energy use is primarily because of space cooling utilizing conventional HVAC frameworks. For instance, in the

M. A. Delele et al. (Eds.): ICAST 2020, LNICST 385, pp. 156–172, 2021.
https://doi.org/10.1007/978-3-030-80618-7_10

Middle East, it represents 70% of building energy utilization and around 30% of all out utilization. These days, a structure cooling has become a need for individual's life and assumes an essential part in guaranteeing indoor solace levels. Subsequently, improving the productivity of cooling innovations are basic, especially ones that have the potential, for example elite, low force utilization [7]. The evaporative cooling (EC) innovation depends on warmth and mass exchange among air and cooling water. Direct evaporative cooling (DEC) depends on mechanical and warm contact among air and water, while Indirect evaporative cooling (IEC) depends on warmth and mass exchange between two floods of air, isolated by a warmth move surface with a dry side where just air is cooling and a wet side where both air and water are cooling. Both DEC and IEC are described by high energy effectiveness yet additionally by critical water utilization rates. On account of IEC innovation, on the dry side of the warmth move surface (dry surface), is streaming the essential (or item) air that is chilling off. On the wet side of the warmth move surface (wet surface), is streaming the optional (or working) air in blend with water [8].

Direct Evaporative Cooling (Dec) - This framework is the most established and the least complex kind of evaporative cooling in which the open air is carried into direct contact with water, for example cooling the air by changing reasonable warmth over to dormant warmth. Shrewd methods were utilized huge number of years prior by old human advancements in assortment of setups, some of it by utilizing pottery container water contained, wetted cushions/canvas situated in the sections of the air. Direct evaporative coolers in structures shift regarding operational force utilization from zero capacity to high power utilization frameworks. DEC frameworks could be isolated: Active DECs which are electrically controlled to work and Passive DECs that are normally worked frameworks with zero force utilization. DEC is just appropriate for dry and hot atmospheres. In sodden conditions, the overall dampness can reach as high as 80%, such a high mugginess isn't reasonable for direct flexibly into structures, since it might cause distorting, rusting, and buildup of vulnerable materials [7].

Indirect Evaporative Cooling (Iec) - The essential thought of the backhanded evaporative coolers is cooling by diminishing air reasonable warmth without changing its dampness, which is an unmistakable favorable position over DEC frameworks. A typical IEC unit involves: a warmth exchanger (HX), little fan, siphon, water tank, and water circulation lines. Roundabout evaporative coolers are grouped into: Wet-bulb temperature IEC frameworks and Sub wet-bulb temperature ICE frameworks [7].

# 2   Literature Review

The accompanying examination sees are considered for accomplish our goal as follows 1) T. Ravi Kiran et al. - In his Study they has zeroed in on energy prerequisites of the world and further added that Energy utilization everywhere on the world is expanding quickly and there is a squeezing need to create approaches to monitor energy for people in the future. Scientists are compelled to search for sustainable wellsprings of energy and approaches to utilize accessible wellsprings of energy in a more proficient manner. Traditional refrigeration based fume pressure cooling frameworks devour an enormous part of electrical energy delivered generally by petroleum derivative. An epic dew point evaporative cooler (DPEC) can reasonably cool the approaching air near its dew point temperature. In this paper achievability of DPEC framework is explored for different Indian urban areas for places of business during day time. Initially the climate information of various urban communities of India is utilized to discover the appropriateness of dew point innovation for Indian structures by assessing the cooling limit of the cooling framework for every city. Also energy sparing capability of the dew point cooling framework w. r. t. to the regular pressure based cooling framework for various urban communities of India is assessed. 2) J.K. Jain et al. - The evaporative cooler uses perhaps the most established guideline of cooling known to Man, cooling of air by the dissipation of water. It is the most well-known type of house hold cooling found in bone-dry zones. The notoriety of evaporative cooling in such territories is because of its moderately low starting expense and operational expense contrasted with refrigerated cooling. Regular direct evaporative coolers comprise of a water store, a siphon that draws water from the supply and releases it through shower spouts straightforwardly into the air stream or through the cooling cushions. Present days the vast majority of the structures and workplaces utilize traditional cooling frameworks which depend on fume pressure refrigeration framework. These frameworks devour generous force and they might be unsafe to climate moreover. In agricultural nation like India, larger part of populace rely upon minimal effort cooling gadgets, for example, direct evaporative cooler. In this manner it is a lot of expected to create improved/more proficient coolers. A few specialists have made endeavour to create evaporative coolers by method of adding/adjusting plans. [2], they have brought up that in the districts where wet bulb temperature is low, two phase evaporative cooling framework, which joins roundabout and direct evaporative cooling offers energy and cost sparing potential. Discovered that most zones (especially northern area) of India where the wet bulb temperature is as a rule underneath 25°C, roundabout framework can accomplish comfort conditions like refrigerated frameworks. Also the solace offered by backhanded evaporative framework is better than that accomplished by direct evaporative framework. He expressed that when evaporative cooling innovation is assessed as an energy protection measure as opposed to the sole wellspring of cooling, the open doors for application become boundless. He found that the coefficient of execution of the consolidated evaporative cooling framework was at any rate 20% more prominent than those accomplished while utilizing either the aberrant evaporative cooling or direct evaporative cooling framework alone. He broke down the capability of circuitous evaporative cooling in each climatic condition. A focal cooled working through cutting edge evaporative cooling frameworks. He assessed the exhibitions of cellulosic cushions made out of Kraft and NSSC creased papers in three woodwind sizes, tentatively. He introduced their examination dependent on a few phase evaporative coolers, endeavored to contemplate the regenerative kind warmth exchanger, which uses tank water to additional cool the air in second stage. In the current work a warmth exchanger has been added to coordinate evaporative cooler. The regenerative evaporative cooler has been created and tried under Indian climatic conditions. Execution of regenerative framework has been assessed as far as by and large adequacy and COP. 3) Chuck Kutscher - The utilization of regular evaporative cooling has quickly declined in the United States regardless of the way that it has high potential for energy reserve funds in dry atmospheres. Evaporative frameworks are extremely serious as far as first cost and give critical decreases in working energy use, just as pinnacle load decrease benefits. Huge market obstructions, for example, the expense of the model evaporative cooling frameworks and purchaser impression of evaporative coolers being not able to keep up comfort conditions, actually remain and can be tended to through improved frameworks joining, including the accompanying: 1) Innovative segments, 2) Better plan of gracefully pipes and dampers, 3) Identification of best atmospheres for full cooling season comfort control and potential cutoff points forced by a blustery season, 4) Development of utility associations to turn out evaporative cooling framework plan boundaries for creation manufacturers. This examination researches the first of these methodologies, investigating inventive parts. The U.S. Branch of Energy (DOE) Building America research groups are examining the utilization of two promising new bits of private cooling hardware that utilize evaporative cooling as a portion of their framework plan. 4) Moien Farmahini Farahani, et al. - In His examination the aftereffects of an examination on a two-stage cooling framework have been considered. This framework comprises of a nighttime radiative unit, a cooling loop, and a backhanded evaporative cooler. During the night in summer, imperative chilled water for a cooling curl unit is given by nighttime radiative cooling and is put away in a capacity tank. During the following day, the water in the tank gives chilled water to the cooling loop unit and hot outside air goes through two-arranges: the cooling curl unit and a circuitous evaporative cooler. Three sources give optional air to the roundabout evaporative cooler. The sources are open air, the air leaving from the cooling loop, and the air leaving from the aberrant stage (regenerative). The examination has been led in climate conditions in the city Tehran. The outcomes got exhibit that the primary phase of the framework expands the adequacy of the circuitous evaporative cooler. Likewise, the regenerative model gives the best solace conditions. 5) R.H. Turne - In His examination he centers on possible utilizations of evaporative cooling (EC) and a related study of exploration prerequisites of EC as provided in private and little business structures. To set up this work, the writing in the field was evaluated and individuals dynamic in the field were reached. Sixteen suggestions are introduced and portrayed in the paper including institutional issues, suitable functions for EC frameworks, fundamental investigation and testing, legitimate applications, and equipment advancement needs. These suggestions speak to composite suppositions from the writing survey and telephone discussions as dissected by the writers. There are expected applications for EC frameworks and related exploration gives that are not completely perceived by most government organizations, service organizations, engineers, enterprises, chiefs, and the devouring public. Nonetheless, as energy costs ascend there will be expanding interest for operationally cheap cooling frameworks. Accordingly, data on the capability of EC frameworks could profit these gatherings. This paper centers on private and little business building utilizations of EC.

# 3   Objective of the Research

The main objectives of the research are 1. Dry Cold Air: We aim to reduce the moisture content and supplying cold dry air for human comfort. 2. Abatement sicknesses like Legionnaire's infection: Legionnaires' illness is a kind of pneumonia brought about by microscopic organisms. You typically get it by taking in fog from water that contains the microbes. The fog may originate from hot tubs, showers, or cooling units for huge structures. The microbes don't spread from individual to individual. 3. Size: We aim to reduce the size of the assembly by making it more compact. 4. Weight: The evaporative cooler system is too bulky. Its weight reduction is also one of the aims. It can be reduced by using polymers and fiber. 5. Power consumption and Cost: Cost is the biggest barrier in implementation of evaporative cooler. We aim to minimize it as far as possible and minimize power consumption. 6. Extended Usability: Till date evaporative cooler is limited in Afar region and industrial purposes. We aim to make it available for mass rural use as stated above in small capacities and low cost.7. Relative Humidity and Temperature: To maintain RH from 40% to 60% and Temperature from 22 °C to 27°C.

## 4   Working Principal of the Multistage Evaporative Desert Cooling

*Stage 1 - 2:* From state 1 the atmospheric dust and hot dry air enters through air filter, where dust is filtered and achieved clean hot dry air at state *2. Stage 3 - 4:* From state 3 the mild cold water pumped from the pump to honey comb pad. Where water enters through honey comb pad from top to bottom, while doing so the hot dry air mixed with cold water and reducing the temperature of the air. In this operation the moisture content in the air increased at state 7. But the mist air at state 7 is not good for human comfort because of increasing the humidity of the air and also causes ailments like Legionnaire's disease. To overcome this uncomfort we have to do dehumidification without decreasing the temperature of air. *Stage 5 - 6*: The cold water from the honey comb pad pumped from the pump to heat exchanger and dehumidification unit. *Stage 7 - 8*: The mist air enters at state 7 to heat exchanger and dehumidification unit (indirect). The heat exchanger is a combination of copper tubes and honey comb pad. The mist air while flowing through heat exchanger decreases the moisture content in the cold air by condensing the moisture on copper tubes and honey comb pads there by dehumidification process completed. The air is further cooled and reaches near to dew point temperature. There by the cold dry air is achieved at state 8 and this air is good for human comfort and health (Fig. 2).

## 5   Design and Theoretical Analysis

Design: The Multistage Evaporative Desert Cooling System consist of two heat exchangers equally spaced in which chilled water is supplied from the sump by using a high pressure submersible water pump of 40W. A fan of 18 W is fitted front side of the indirect heat exchanger, as shown in Fig. 1.

Assumption:

1) Inside diameter of the copper tube is 5 mm (As per available in market)
2) Gap between heat exchanger is 2 cm.
3) Ambient temperature is 38 °C.
4) Water temperature at starting of unit is 32 °C
5) Conductivity of Copper is 386 W/m$^2$

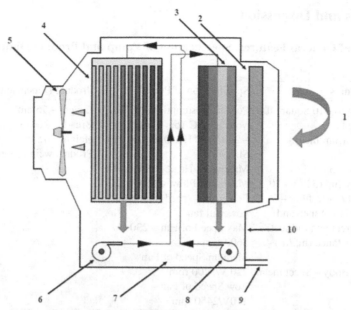

**Fig. 1.** Multistage evaporative desert cooling system. (Components - 1. Air Intake, 2. Air Filter 3. Honey comb pad 4. Heat Exchanger 5. Fan, 6. Submergible Water Pump, 7. Cement or Mud coated Water Sump, 8. Submergible Water Pump, 9. Drain or Out Let 10. Metal Body)

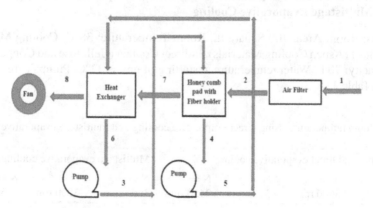

**Fig. 2.** Flow diagram of multistage evaporative desert cooling system

# 6  Results and Discussion

## 6.1  Detail of General Features, Specification of Pump and Product Dimension

| General Features | Specification of Pump | Product Dimensions |
|---|---|---|
| For rooms up to - 10 Square ft, Engg. Plastic Fan<br>Fan diameter (mm/inch) - 368/14<br>Speed Control- 3<br>Tank capacity (up to ltr.) – 70,<br>Mosquito net / Dust filter – Yes,<br>Cooling media – Aspen and cellulose (Direct and Indirect)<br>Air Throw Distance (mt./ft.) - 10/33<br>Stand – Yes, Body – Sheet metal | Power Consumption:-18 W,<br>Voltage:-AC 165<br>– 220 V/50 Hz, Outlet Nozzle Size:-½"<br>Maximum, Head:-1.85 m,<br>Maximum Flow: - 1100 L/H<br>Powerful 3-speed motor and powerful fan<br>Max Speed of Fan – 230 V / 3600 rpm<br>Medium Speed of Fan-220 V/3200 rpm<br>Low Speed of Fan - 110V/2450 rpm | Length – 75 cm<br>Breadth – 60 cm<br>Height – 75 cm<br>Product weight (kgs) – 15.5 |

## 6.2  Analysis of Room Temperature Using Direct Evaporative Cooling and Multistage Evaporative Cooling

Conditions: Room Area: 100 Square ft., Room Temperature: 38°C, Cooling Medium: Direct contact (Aspen Cooling Materials), Indirect Contact (Cellulose and Copper tube), Tank Capacity: 70 L, Water temperature at starting of unit is 33°C, Pump: Three Pumps Working (Table 1).

**Table 1.** Room temperature using direct evaporative cooling and multistage evaporative cooling

| Speed/Time | Direct evaporative cooling | | | Multistage evaporative cooling | | |
|---|---|---|---|---|---|---|
| | N = 3600 rpm | N = 3200 rpm | N = 2450 rpm | N = 3600 rpm | N = 3200 rpm | N = 2450 rpm |
| 0 | 38 | 38 | 38 | 38 | 38 | 38 |
| 30 | 37 | 37.8 | 37.8 | 37.6 | 37.9 | 37.8 |
| 60 | 35 | 37.2 | 37.2 | 36.9 | 37.3 | 37 |
| 90 | 33 | 35 | 36.4 | 36.1 | 36.5 | 35.5 |
| 120 | 32.6 | 33.6 | 35.5 | 35 | 34 | 34 |

*(continued)*

**Table 1.** (*continued*)

| Speed/Time | Direct evaporative cooling | | | Multistage evaporative cooling | | |
|---|---|---|---|---|---|---|
| | N = 3600 rpm | N = 3200 rpm | N = 2450 rpm | N = 3600 rpm | N = 3200 rpm | N = 2450 rpm |
| 150 | 32 | 32.3 | 34.1 | 34.2 | 33.5 | 33.5 |
| 180 | 31 | 31.1 | 33.1 | 33.5 | 32 | 32 |
| 210 | 29 | 29.4 | 31.7 | 32.1 | 30 | 30 |
| 240 | 28 | 28.3 | 30.5 | 31 | 29.5 | 29.5 |
| 270 | 27 | 27.6 | 28.6 | 29.4 | 28.3 | 28.3 |
| 300 | | 26.4 | 27.5 | 27.5 | 27 | 27 |
| 330 | | 25.1 | 26.2 | 25.9 | 26.6 | 26.6 |
| 360 | | | 25 | 25.4 | 25.4 | 26.1 |
| 370 | | | 24.8 | 24.7 | 24.7 | 25.7 |
| 400 | | | 24.7 | | 24.4 | 24.8 |
| 430 | | | | | 23.9 | 24.1 |
| 460 | | | | | | 23.8 |
| 490 | | | | | | 23.7 |
| 520 | | | | | | 23.6 |
| Avg Consumption of water | 15.56 L/H | 13.33 L/H | 10.5 L/H | 11.35 L/H | 10.24 L/H | 8.07 L/H |

## 6.3 Comparison of Direct and Multistage Evaporative Cooling @ 3600 rpm

The Fig. 3 shows the comparison of direct and multistage evaporative cooling. As time increases the consumption of water vapors also increases there by decrease in room temperature. In direct evaporative cooling, the initial operating temperature is 38 °C and final operating temperature is 27 °C by consumption of 70 Lts of water in 4.5 h. The average consumption of water is 15.56 L/H. In multistage Evaporative cooling, the initial operating temperature is 38 °C and final operating temperature is 24.7 °C by consumption of 70 Lts of water in 6.16 h. The average consumption of water is 11.35 L/H. There by we can conclude that, in multistage evaporative cooling the average consumption of water decreased by 5.21 L/H, room temperature decreased by 2.3 °C and operating time increased by 1.66 h.

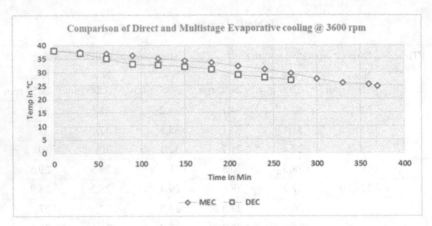

**Fig. 3.** Comparison of direct and multistage evaporative cooling @ 3600 rpm

The psychometric chart (Fig. 4) shows that the comparison of direct evaporative cooling system and multistage evaporative cooling system at 3600 rpm. The initial temperature at the beginning of experiment is 38 °C and corresponding relative humidity is 15%. The psychometric chart says that the relative humidity and temperature are higher in multistage evaporative cooling than direct evaporative cooling.

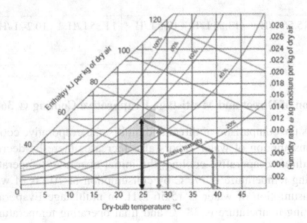

**Fig. 4.** Comparison of direct and multistage evaporative cooling @ 3600 rpm

## 6.4   Comparison of Direct and Multistage Evaporative Cooling @ 3200 rpm

The Fig. 5 shows the comparison of direct and multistage evaporative cooling.

As time increases the consumption of water vapors also increases there by decrease in room temperature. In direct evaporative cooling, the initial operating temperature is 38 °C and final operating temperature is 25.1 °C by consumption of 70 Lts of water in 5.25 h. The average consumption of water is 13.33 L/H. In multistage Evaporative cooling, the initial operating temperature is 38 °C and final operating temperature is 23.9 °C by consumption of 70 Lts of water in 6.83 h. The average consumption of water is 10.24 L/H. There by we can conclude that, in multistage evaporative cooling the average consumption of water decreased by 3.09 L/H, room temperature decreased by 1.2 °C and operating time increased by 1.58 h.

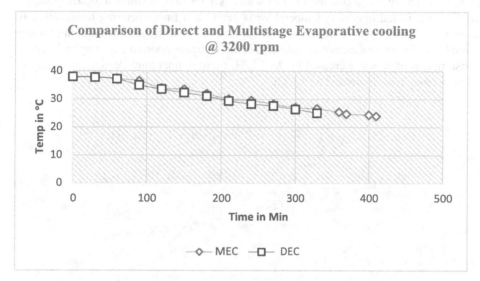

**Fig. 5.** Comparison of direct and multistage evaporative cooling @ 3200 rpm

The psychometric chart (Fig. 6) shows that the comparison of direct evaporative cooling system and multistage evaporative cooling system at 3200 rpm. The initial temperature at the beginning of experiment is 38 °C and corresponding relative humidity is 15%. The psychometric chart says that the relative humidity and temperature are higher in multistage evaporative cooling than direct evaporative cooling.

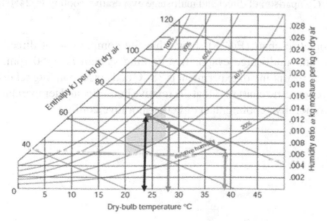

**Fig. 6.** Comparison of direct and multistage evaporative cooling @ 3200 rpm

### 6.5    Comparison of Direct and Multistage Evaporative Cooling @ 2450 rpm

The Fig. 7 shows the comparison of direct and multistage evaporative cooling.

As time increases the consumption of water vapors also increases there by decrease in room temperature. In direct evaporative cooling, the initial operating temperature is 38 °C and final operating temperature is 24.7 °C by consumption of 70 Lts of water in 6.67 h. The average consumption of water is 10.5 L/H. In multistage Evaporative cooling, the initial operating temperature is 38 °C and final operating temperature is 23.6 °C by consumption of 70 Lts of water in 8.66 h. The average consumption of water is 8.07 L/H. There by we can conclude that, in multistage evaporative cooling the average consumption of water decreased by 2.43 L/H, room temperature decreased by 1.1 °C and operating time increased by 1.99 h.

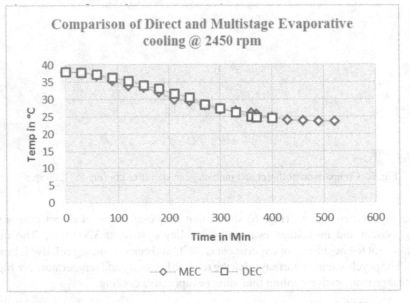

**Fig. 7.** Comparison of direct and multistage evaporative cooling @ 2450 rpm

The psychometric chart (Fig. 8) shows that the comparison of direct evaporative cooling system and multistage evaporative cooling system at 2450 rpm. The initial temperature at the beginning of experiment is 38 °C and corresponding relative humidity is 15%. The psychometric chart says that the relative humidity and temperature are higher in multistage evaporative cooling than direct evaporative cooling.

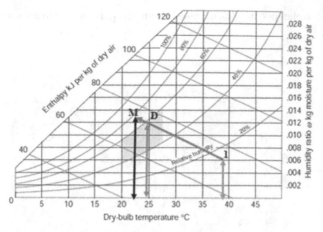

**Fig. 8.** Comparison of direct and multistage evaporative cooling @ 2450 rpm

## 6.6 Comparison of Direct Evaporative Cooling @ 2450 rpm, 3200 rpm and 3600 rpm

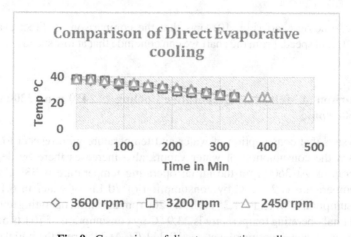

**Fig. 9.** Comparison of direct evaporative cooling

The Fig. 9 says that consumption of water and temperature with respect to time. As time increases the consumption of water vapors also increases there by decrease in room temperature. At 3600 rpm the initial operating temperature is 38 °C and final operating temperature is 27 °C by consumption of 70 Lts of water in 4.5 h. The average consumption of water is 15.56 L/H. At 3200 rpm the initial operating temperature is 38 °C and final operating temperature is 25.1 °C by consumption of 70 Lts of water in 5.25 h. The average consumption of water is 13.33 L/H. At 2450 rpm the initial operating temperature is 38 °C and final operating temperature is 24.7 °C by consumption of 70 Lts of water in 6.67 h. The average consumption of water is 10.5 L/H. From the above graph we can conclude that, by decreasing the speed of the cooling fan, the average consumption of water per hour decreases, room temperature decreases and operating time increases.

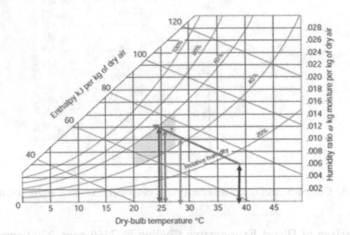

**Fig. 10.** Comparison of direct evaporative cooling

The psychometric chart (Fig. 10) says that the comparison of direct evaporative cooling at different speed. From the chart we can conclude that at low speed performance is maximum.

### 6.7   Comparison of Multistage Evaporative Cooling @ 2450 rpm, 3200 rpm and 3600 rpm

The Fig. 11 says that consumption of water and temperature with respect to time. As time increases the consumption of water vapors also increases there by decrease in room temperature. At 3600 rpm the initial operating temperature is 38 °C and final operating temperature is 24.7 °C by consumption of 70 Lts of water in 6.16 h. The average consumption of water is 11.35 L/H. At 3200 rpm the initial operating temperature is 38 °C and final operating temperature is 23.9 °C by consumption of 70 Lts of water in 6.83 h. The average consumption of water is 10.24 L/H. At 2450 rpm the initial operating temperature is 38 °C and final operating temperature is 23.6 °C by consumption of 70 Lts of water in 8.66 h. The average consumption of water is 8.07 L/H. From the above graph we can conclude that, by decreasing the speed of the cooling fan, the average consumption of water per hour decreases, room temperature decreases and operating time increases.

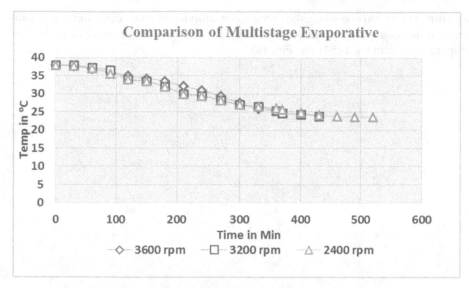

**Fig. 11.** Comparison of multistage evaporative cooling

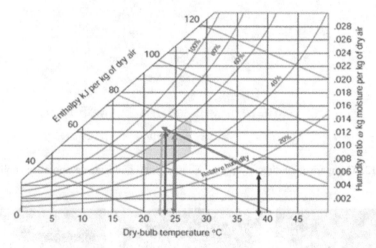

**Fig. 12.** Comparison of multistage evaporative cooling

The psychometric chart (Fig. 12) says that the comparison of multistage evaporative cooling at different speed. From the chart we can conclude that at low speed performance is maximum.

### 6.8 Comparison of Direct Evaporative Cooling and Multistage Evaporative Cooling @ 2450 rpm, 3200 rpm and 3600 rpm

From the Fig. 13 we can conclude that the performance of multistage evaporative cooling is effective than direct evaporative cooling. Multistage evaporative cooling in compare with direct evaporative cooling, the average consumption of water decreases, room temperature decreases and operating time increases. The best performance of multistage evaporative cooling at 2450 rpm (Fig. 14).

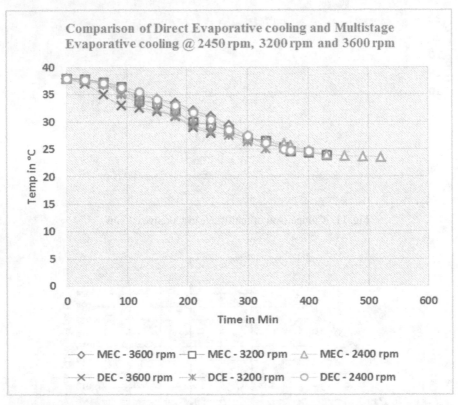

**Fig. 13.** Comparison of direct evaporative cooling and multistage evaporative cooling

**Fig. 14.** Multistage evaporative desert cooling system

# 7  Conclusion

1. The product is a combination of direct and indirect evaporative cooling.
2. The maximum performance in direct evaporative cooling at 2450 rpm. The best parameters are found at this rpm are temperature 24.7°C, relative humidity 43%, specific humidity 0.12 kg of water vapors/kg of dry air, dry bulb temperature 38°C, dew point temperature 9°C, wet bulb temperature 15 °C and enthalpy 75 kJ/kg at average consumption of 10.5L/h.
3. The maximum performance in multistage evaporative cooling at 2450 rpm. The best parameters are found at this rpm are temperature 23.6 °C, relative humidity 63%, specific humidity 0.13 kg of water vapors/kg of dry air, dry bulb temperature 38 °C, dew point temperature 10 °C, wet bulb temperature 13 °C and enthalpy 75 kJ/kg at average consumption of 8.07L/h.
4. It's very difficult to control relative humidity and specific humidity in direct evaporative cooling.
5. In multistage evaporative cooling, after reached required relative humidity and specific humidity, by switching off direct evaporative cooling system we can maintain same room temperature by running indirect evaporative cooling technology without any addition of moisture.
6. By using multistage evaporative cooling system human comforts parameter are achieved. They are relative humidity ranges from 40%–60% and temperature ranges from 22 °C–27 °C.
7. Compare to conventional cooling systems, the multistage evaporative cooling system consumes less water and it is suitable for dry places.
8. Its continuously circulates fresh air to the living room but air conditioning circulates same air again and again.
9. It consumes less power than air conditioning system and it is suitable for remote places.
10. The weight of multistage evaporative cooling system is lesser than air conditioning system thereby transportation and installation is easy.

**Acknowledgement.** This Project was sponsored by the Samara University, Samara, Afar, Ethiopia, under Research and Community Service - Vice president Office. The authors would like to thank the entire staffs of Department of Mechanical Engineering, College of Engineering and Technology – Dean Office and Research Directorate Office.

# References

1. Ravi Kiran, T., Rajput, S.P.S.: Cooling capacity and energy saving potential of dew point evaporative cooling system for Indian buildings. Int. J. Renew. Energy Res. 3(1), 73–78 (2012)
2. Jain, J.K., Hindoliya, D.A.: Development and testing of regenerative evaporative cooler. Int. J. Eng. Trends Technol. 3(6), 694–697 (2012)
3. Kutscher, C., Eastment, M.: Projected benefits of new residential evaporative cooling systems, NREL/TP-550-3934 October 2006. www.nrel.gov

4. Farahani, M., Heidarinejad, G., Delfani, S.: A two-stage system of nocturnal radiative and indirect evaporative cooling for conditions in Tehran. Energy Build. **42**(11), 2131–2138 (2010)
5. Turner, R.H.: Research requirements in the evaporative cooling field. Trans. ASME J. Solar Energy Eng. **103**, 89–91…3025
6. Yun, R., Hwang, Y., Radermacher, R.: Comparison of performance of a residential air conditioning system using microchannel and Fin-and-Tube heat exchanger. In: International Refrigeration and Air Conditioning Conference, Paper 752. http://docs.lib.purdue.edu/iracc/752. http://ag.arizona.edu/pubs/consumereriaz9145
7. Amer, O., Boukhanouf, R., Ibrahim, H.G.: A review of evaporative cooling technologies. Int. J. Environ. Sci. Dev. **6**(2), 111–117 (2015)
8. Porumb, B., Ungureşan, P., Tutunaru, L.F., Şerban, A., Bălan, M.: A review of indirect evaporative cooling technology. In: Sustainable Solutions for Energy and Environment, EENVIRO - YRC 2015, Bucharest, Romania, 18–20 November 2015 (2015)
9. Shrivastava, K., Deshmukh, D., Rawlani, M.V.: Experimental analysis of coconut coir pad evaporative cooler. Int. J. Innov. Res. Sci. Eng. Technol. **3**(1), 8346–8352 (2014)
10. Dubey, M., Rajput, S.P.S.: Development and performance evaluation of a semi indirect evaporative cooler. In: International Refrigeration and Air Conditioning Conference at Purdue, 14–17 July 2008
11. Mallappa, N., Amit, M., Ashish, M., Suhas, P., Vilas, S., Vaibhav, D.: Design AND fabrication of homemade air conditioner. Int. J. Eng. Res. Appl. **4**(4), 102–103 (2014). ISSN 2248-9622 (Version 6). www.ijera.com

# Analytical Analysis of Electric Vehicle Chassis Frame and Battery Thermal Management System

Dereje Arijamo Dolla[1](✉) and Ramesh Babu Nallamothu[2]

[1] Bule Hora University, Bule Hora, Ethiopia
[2] Adama Science and Technology University, Adama, Ethiopia

**Abstract.** The energy stored in the battery is the source of the energy to drive the electric vehicles. At the moment the size and the weight of the battery pack required for given mileage are very much high when compared to its counterpart IC engine. The main aim of this work is to modify the existing electric vehicle chassis frame for giving the provision of swapping battery rather than having permanent battery pack on the chassis frame. Specifically by taking RAV4 V5 EV as a baseline and all analysis was done on it, the static, dynamic and static impact (crush analysis) on finite element (ANSYS) is performed, battery thermal management system in the transient analysis by using EXCEL and ANSYS FLUENT is identified, and finally, prototype fabrication is carried out to demonstrate the shape of the chassis frame. According to study, the Material AISI 1020 and rectangular cross-section in 80 mm × 40 mm × 4mm is selected to the electric vehicle chassis frame and the modelling was done by using CATIA V5 and the analysis using ANSYS. Finally, the total deformation of chassis frame is 1.007 mm, equivalent stress is 115.88 MPa and the life of the chassis on full load is 130 days without deformation. The weight of the electric vehicle battery pack is decreased from 383.51 kg to 345.615 kg by modification of existing cooling plate and the chassis frame has a longer life than previous design because of the weight minimization of the battery pack on the existing vehicle.

**Keywords:** Batteries pack · Chassis frame · Electric vehicle · Swapping and BTMS

## 1 Introduction

In the last decades, with the increasing development of battery technologies and concerns for the environment, electric vehicles (EVs) technologies got rapid development. However, EV drivers have to face the problem of battery refuelling daily. Once the battery runs out, drivers can recharge it in the charging station. The battery takes 6–8 h to full charge in AC charging according to the manufacturer specified time. That means waiting a long time to refuel the battery in a permanently attached battery pack is as the main problem. And this study is going to develop swappable battery pack the electric vehicle

© ICST Institute for Computer Sciences, Social Informatics and Telecommunications Engineering 2021
Published by Springer Nature Switzerland AG 2021. All Rights Reserved
M. A. Delele et al. (Eds.): ICAST 2020, LNICST 385, pp. 173–189, 2021.
https://doi.org/10.1007/978-3-030-80618-7_11

and detail analysis on the frame study, battery thermal management system (BTMs) and weight minimization on the battery pack as case study on a baseline of RAV4 EV battery model, this existing vehicle uses permanently attached battery pack. As the main aim of this work is to design and modify of the existing RAV4 EV 2014 model electric vehicle [1] chassis frame for swapping mechanism of battery packs and check the thermal management system of the battery pack after design the chassis frame.

The following studies are separately done and taking this separate study as a gap and in this work going to merge those studies of the chassis frame and electric vehicle battery pack. The selection of structural steel AISI 1020 is done on the study of [2].

The battery and thus also the battery frame does not need to be considered in the weight limit of 400 kg for the empty vehicle [3]. Therefore, it is obvious to use the structure of the battery frame also for other functions, besides carrying the battery modules. The weight of the frame is still relevant because increased vehicle weight results in decreased vehicle performance and increased energy consumption. Although a frame made from steel profiles will be heavier than a frame made from aluminium extrusion profiles, it was decided to make the frame from steel because of cost reasons. The other one is Range anxiety [4] is a relatively new concept which is defined as the fear of running out of power when driving an electric vehicle [6–8]. To decrease range anxiety result that they got were that with bigger batteries this is still not the answer for the anxiety. So, swapping the battery pack is the best way to minimize this anxiety according to this work [9–11].

The other big issue in the electric vehicle battery pack is battery thermal management system (BTMS) [5] for optimal performance, safety and durability considerations, the battery must operate within the safe operating range of voltage, current and temperature as indicated by the battery manufacturer [12–14]. The voltage range is between the maximum voltage (3.65 V) and the minimum voltage (2 V), the temperature range is depending on the operating mode (charge and discharge) and varies between [−20 °C; 60 °C] and [0 °C; 40 °C] during discharge and charge, respectively. These ranges can change according to the cell chemistry and battery manufacturer. By adding an extra feature on study this work takes the temperature of Adama, Ethiopia and the analysis is done on locally [15, 16].

## 2 Material and Methods

### 2.1 Materials for Electric Vehicle Chassis Frame

The material AISI 1020 is selected for this electric vehicle chassis frame according to the literature discussion, the availability, cost and its mechanical properties that suit for chassis frame design and the rectangular cross-section was taken in reference of literature on related studies.

### 2.2 Steel AISI 1020 the Properties from ANSYS 15 Workbench

That the preferred material for this electric vehicle chassis frame is steel AISI 1020 and its mechanical properties is listed in Table 1 below.

**Table 1.** Table for material properties

| Properties of structural steel AISI 1020 which data's from ANSYS | |
| --- | --- |
| Compressive yield strength MPa | 250 |
| Tensile yield strength MPa | 250 |
| Tensile ultimate strength MPa | 460 |
| Reference temperature °C | 22 |
| Relative permeability | 10000 |

## 2.3 Specification for RAV4 EV 2014 Model

By taking this permanently attached battery pack of RAV4 EV 2014 model electric vehicle into swappable one to afford alternative rather than wasting time to charge the battery (by swapping the battery pack). The specification mentioned in Table 2 below. All the study is done on this specification.

**Table 2.** Specification for RAV4 EV 2014 model

| Mechanical and performance | RAV4 EV specification |
| --- | --- |
| Motor type (two drive modes; normal and sport) | AC induction motor with fixed gear open-differential transaxle |
| Power output | 154 hp (115 kw) max |
| Max. torque | 218 lb, -ft/273 lb, -ft |
| Max. speed | 85 mph/100 mph (160 kph) |
| Type | Lithium-ion (Li-ion) |
| Power output | 400 W max. |
| Voltage | 386 V max. |
| Weights and capacities | |
| Curb weight (lb) | 4032 |
| Seating capacity | 5 |
| Cargo volume (cu. Ft.) behind front/second row | 73.0/36.4 |
| Gross vehicle weight rating (GVWR) (lb.) | 5005 |
| Battery capacity (kwh) | 35.0/41.8 |
| Battery weight (lb.) | 845.5 |
| EPA-rated driving range | 103 miles |
| Charging time (normal/extended charge mode) | 12 A/120 V, 44 h/52 h<br>16 A/240 V. 12 h/15 h<br>30 A/240 V. 6.5 h/8 h |

## 2.4   Design, Modeling and Analysis of Chassis Frame

The software *CATIA* for model drawing, *ANSYS* for finite element analysis and *EXCEL* for transient analysis for battery thermal management system is used.

**Methodology**
The following Fig. 1 shows the working flow for this research work.

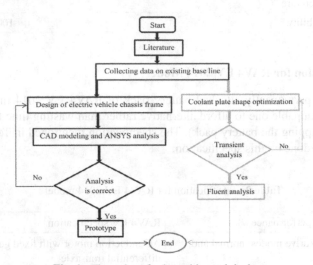

**Fig. 1.**   Flow chart for how this work is done

**Prototype Fabrication for Electric Vehicle Chassis**
The prototype Fig. 2 is only for the demonstration 1:1.5 scale of the actual one.

**Fig. 2.**   Chassis frame for designed electric vehicle

## 3 Design, Modeling and Analysis of the Chassis Frame

The chassis generally experiences four major loading situations; vertical bending, longitudinal torsion, lateral bending, and horizontal lozenging. Understanding these conditions is the key to designing a better chassis. When the chassis frame supported at its ends by the wheel axles and acted upon by an equivalent weight due to the vehicle's equipment, passengers and luggage around the middle of its wheelbase, the side members are caused to sag in the central region. This sagging is known as vertical bending [6].

General calculations for a considered load on baseline chassis frame is.

- Gross vehicle weight = 2270.22 kg
- Total load to be applied = 2270.22 × 9.81 = 22,270.86 N
- Considering an overload of 25% of the total load = 22,270.86 × 1.25 = 27,838.57 N.
- Chassis has two beams. So load acting on each beam is half of the Total load acting on the chassis. Load acting on the single frame = 27,838.57 N./2 = 13,919.285 N/Beam

### a. The calculation for the frame

The uniformly distributed load is 13,919.285 N/4,524 mm = 3.07 N/mm taking the reaction support A. as shown in Fig. 3.

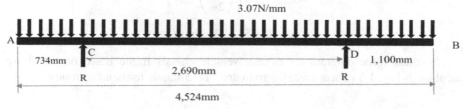

**Fig. 3.** Chassis as a simply supported beam with overhung

$$R_C + R_D = 13,919.285 \, \text{N} \tag{1}$$

$$RC = \frac{Wl(l - 2c)}{2b} \, [7] \tag{2}$$

$$Rc = 5,999.5 \, \text{N}$$

$$RD = 7,919.8 \, \text{N}$$

Where,

$R_c \, \& \, R_D = reaction\,forces\,at\,point\,C \,\& \,D$
$W = distributed\,load\,over\,the\,member,$

$l = length\ of\ the\ side\ member,$
$(a, b, c) = lengths\ between\ reaction\ support\ and\ edge$

*Mathematical analysis for shear force and bending moment*
Shear force

$V_A = Wa = 2,815.19\,\text{N}$
$V_C = RC - V_A = 3,184.31\,\text{N}$
$V_B = WC = 3,377\,\text{N}$

$$V_D = RD - V_B = 4,542.8\,\text{N}$$

Where: V is shear force,
Bending moment

$$M_{left} = -\frac{wa^2}{2} = -1,290,764.615\,\text{Nmm}$$

$$M_{right} = -\frac{wc^2}{2} = -1,857,350\,\text{Nmm}$$

$$M_{midd} = Rc\left(\left(\frac{Rc}{2w}\right) - a\right)$$

$$= 1,458,582.024\,\text{Nmm}$$

The shear force diagram for electric vehicle chassis frame based on the above calculations Fig. 4 for shear force diagram and Fig. 5 stands for bending moment.

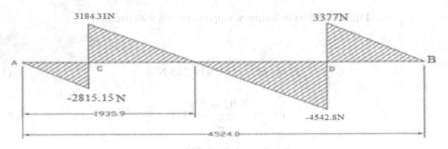

**Fig. 4.** Shear force diagram

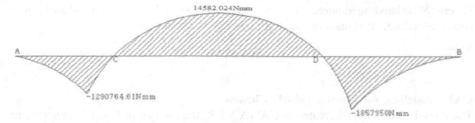

14582.024Nmm

−1290764.61Nmm

−1857350N mm

**Fig. 5.** Bending moment diagram for frame

From the above Fig. 4 and Fig. 5 taking that the distance or position of the shear stress occurs on the chassis frame and the position of bending moment. According to this reason position for both shear force and bending moment lies on the position 1935.9 mm distance from the front end of the chassis frame so this value is used to find the deflection (Y) in the following equation.

The calculation for stress generated

$$M_{max} = 1,458,582.024 \, \text{Nmm}$$

Moment of inertia around the x-x axis in the following Fig. 6.

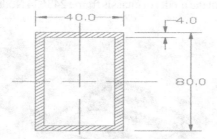

**Fig. 6.** Cross section for the chassis frame

$$I_{xx} = \frac{bh^3 - b_1 h_1^3}{12} = 711,338.667 \, \text{mm}^4$$

Deflection of the chassis frame

$$Y = \frac{wx(b-x)}{24EI}[x(b-x) + b^2 - 2\left(c^2 + a^2\right) - \frac{2}{b}c^2x + a^2(b-x) = 0.87 \, \text{mm}$$

The deflection of the total chassis frame is 0.87 mm from its normal position and the stress on the chassis frame is done in the following manner.

$$\frac{\sigma}{Y} = \frac{M}{I} = \frac{E}{R}$$

Where 'M' is bending moment, 'Y' is the distance between the xx section and the normal stress centerline; 'I' is mass moment of inertia in xx cross-section

$$\sigma = 104.62\,\text{MPa}$$

## CAD Modelling for Electric Vehicle Chassis

The chassis frame model created in CATIA V5 R20 as shown in Fig. 7 is imported to ANSYS 15. The meshed model of chassis frame is shown in Fig. 9 (Fig. 8).

**Fig. 7.** Designed electric vehicle chassis          **Fig. 8.** Designed 3D model

*Meshing.* The meshing of the model of chassis frame 243634 Nodes and 34528 elements.

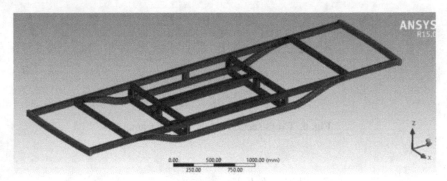

**Fig. 9.** Meshed model

*Loading and Boundary Conditions*

In this RAV4 EV 2014 model vehicle taking that of the existing vehicle load and the analysis is held by this load. The magnitude of the force on the upper side of chassis is 117720 N which is carried by the distributed load on chassis frame on Fig. 10.

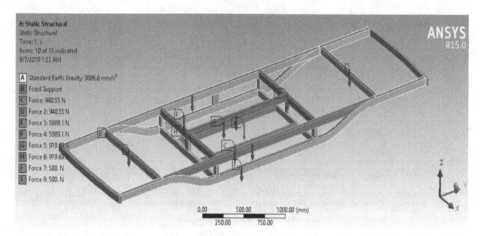

**Fig. 10.** Static loads (loads from the battery, passenger and luggage) on the chassis frame

## b. Battery thermal management system (BTMS)

### Shape Minimization of the Cooling Plate

The existing battery cell on rav4 EV is pouch type and its arrangement by two layers 7 batteries (170 mm) in vehicle track position and 7 batteries (position of 265 mm) in parallel to vehicle base and 7 batteries are out of normal arrangement then the total number the battery cell is 105. The mass of the single battery cell is 1.4285 kg and the mass of the cooling plate in one side of the battery cell before minimization is 1.1178 kg. Figure 11 shows that the noted scheme in visual.

### Transient Analysis for the BTMS

The derived differential equations, those represent the energy balance for the battery cell cooling plate, coolant plate and fluid equations are solved using the explicit finite difference method. The time derivative is replaced by the forward difference scheme. The transient temperatures are evaluated iteratively, using relations derived for the equation of energy balance [8]. The diameter of the copper coil and naming its top part of the plate (p1) and bottom plate (p2) respectively in Fig. 12, below.

*For p1 (Top Part of the Plate)*

$$E_{in} - E_{out} = \Delta E \tag{3}$$

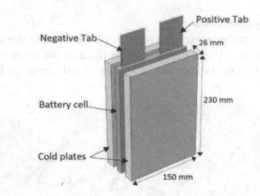

**Fig. 11.** Battery cell with its cooling plate

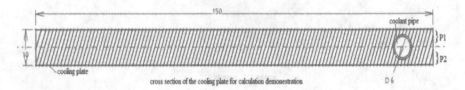

**Fig. 12.** Cross-section of the aluminium plate

$$heat\ coming\ from\ battery - heat\ transfer\ to\ fluid = \rho_p V_p C_p \frac{dT_{p1}}{dt}$$

By discretizing the above energy balance to get the following equation for the Sect. 1 or the above plate

$$heat\ generated - h_{fluid} A (T_p - T_f) = \rho_p V_p C_p \frac{dT_{p1}}{dt} \qquad (4)$$

**For Fluid**

$$-\dot{m}_f C_f \frac{\partial T_f}{\partial x} + h_f \pi D (T_{p1} - T_f) - h_f \pi D (T_f - T_{p2}) = \rho_f A_f C_f \frac{\partial T_f}{\partial t} \qquad (5)$$

**For p2 (Bottom Part of the Plate)**

$$h_f A (T_f - T_{p2}) - h_{air} A_s (T_{p2} - T_{air}) = \rho_{p2} V_{p2} C_{p2} \frac{dT_{p2}}{dt} \qquad (6)$$

The explicit finite-difference method is proposed to solve the system of equations. The time derivatives are replaced by a forward difference scheme, whereas the dimensional derivative is replaced by a backward difference scheme.

*For p1 (Top Part of the Plate)*

$$E_g - h_f A\left(T_p^t - T_f^t\right) = \rho_p V_p C_p (T_f^{t+\Delta t} - T_f^t) \tag{7}$$

*For Fluid*

$$-\dot{m}_f C_f \frac{\left(T_{fj}^t - T_{fj-1}^t\right)}{\Delta l} + h_f \pi D\left(T_{p1j}^t - T_{fj}^t\right) - h_f \pi D\left(T_{fj}^t - T_{p2j}^t\right) = \rho_f A_f C_f \left(\frac{T_{fj}^{t+\Delta t} - T_{fj}^t}{\Delta l}\right) \tag{8}$$

*For p2 (Bottom Part of the Plate)*

$$\rho_{p2} V_{p2} C_{p2} \left(\frac{T_{p2}^{t+\Delta t} - T_{p1}^t}{\Delta l}\right) = h_f A\left(T_f^t - T_{p2}^t\right) - h_{air} A_s (T_{p2}^t - T_{air}^t) \tag{9}$$

From the EXCEL transient analysis, the following figures founded it indicates that the temperature variation on the cooling plate in each minute. Some assumptions for the analysis are taken out.

These are

- The average speed of the vehicle 90 km/hr (25 m/s)
- The average temperature of the environment 25 °C in Adama city
- Assume that the driver drives the vehicle for 5 h (300 min) without rest
- Taking the elbow of the copper coil as the node, then the analysis has nine nodes

| | | | |
|---|---|---|---|
| $\rho_f$(kg/m$^3$) | = 997 | $k_f$(w/m.k) | = 0.607 |
| $\rho_{atr}$(kg/m$^3$) | = 1.225 | $h_f$ | = 257.32 |
| $\rho_p$(kg/m$^3$) | = 2700 | $E_g$(kw) | = 645 |
| $C_f$ (J/kg. k) | = 4185.5 | $T_{air}$ | = 25 |
| $C_p$ | = 921 | $D_p$ | = 0.007 |
| $h_{air}$ (W/m$^2$ k) | = 52.09 | L(m) | = 1.4 |
| $P_{rf}$ | = 6.14 | $\mu\_f$ | = 0.000891 |
| $f_{inlet}$ | = 20 $^{\circ}$C | $T_{initial}$ | = 25 $^{\circ}$C |

Constants and calculated values for the EXCEL input are as follow.

The values like Reynolds number, the volume of plate and volume pipe, volume of fluid and area are calculated values the constants took from thermodynamics table of cengle in 25 °C.

The Nusselt, Rayleigh, and Prandtl numbers are given by [8]:

$$R_l = \frac{\rho_{air} V_{air} L}{\mu} \tag{10}$$

$$R_l = 3.682 \times 10^5$$

*$P_r$ from thrmal property tables and charts*

$$N_u = 0.56 R_l^{1/2} P_r \tag{11}$$

$$N_u = 469.66$$

Where

$R_l$ = Renould number
$P_r$ = Prandtl number
$N_u$ = Nusselt number.

## CAD Modelling to the Cooling Plate

After performing the transient analysis by EXCEL, CAD modelling by CATIA v5 software and the analysis by ANSYS 15 for the fluent (CFD) is processed below in Fig. 13.

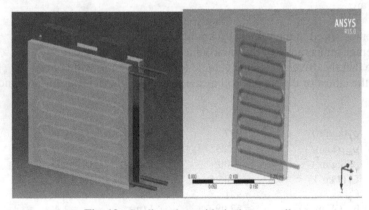

**Fig. 13.** Cooling plate with the battery cell

The maximum temperature registered in Fig. 14 is 319.2 K when it changed to degree Celsius it becomes

$$C^o = K - 273$$

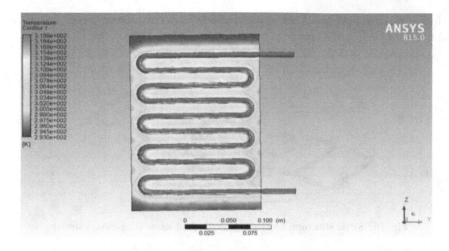

**Fig. 14.** Temperature contour result for the new cooling plate sectioned view

$$C^o = 319.2 - 273$$

$$C^o = 46$$

According to the excel result, we can see the effect of the fluent result on the cooling plate of the temperature of the entire plate with the coolant fluid temperature is 46.2 °C as shown on the above CFD analysis in figure Fig. 14. So, it is validated.

## 4   Result and Discussion

**a. Static structural analysis for electric vehicle chassis frame**

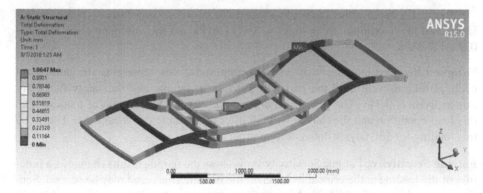

**Fig. 15.** ANSYS static result of total deformation

In the above figure Fig. 15, we understand that from the static structural analysis the total deformation is 1.0047 mm it is the maximum deformation in this loading.

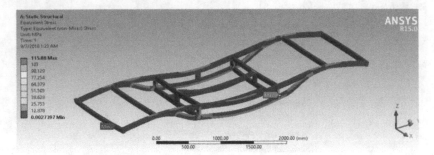

**Fig. 16.** Static structural analyses for equivalent stress (von-misses stress)

In the above figure, Fig. 16, the static structural analysis for equivalent stress (von-misses stress) is 115.88 MPa is the maximum stress and the minimum von-miss stress 0.00273 MPa.

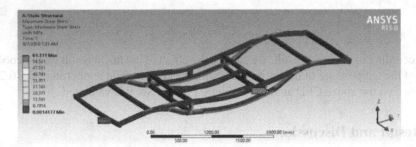

**Fig. 17.** Static analysis of maximum shear stress

Figure 17, express that the static structural analysis of shear stress on the chassis frame and the maximum shear stress is 61.111 MPa and the minimum shear stress is 0.001417 MPa.

**Fatigue Life.** The loading is of constant amplitude, this represents the number of cycle's1million cycle until the part will fail due to fatigue and the safety factor for this analysis is 0.743. The given load history represents 188,480 min of loading with this load condition and the chassis will fall after this minute this means that it stays by this loading for 130 days without deformation.

**Fatigue Sensitivity.** Fatigue Sensitivity shows how the fatigue results change as a function of the loading at the critical location on the model. This result may be scoped. Sensitivity may be found for life, damage, or factor of safety. And in the following ANSYS result based on the applied loading up to 72%, the frame has the same available life cycle after that when the percentage of loading is more the available life cycle decreased. The value only 72% is that much not good but based on the considering safety factor of chassis frame is 0.743 this safe and the taken personal Wight as 75 kg. Default values for the sensitivity options may be set through the Control Panel.

## b. Result for static impact analysis

The following Table 3 shows that results from the finite analysis.

**Table 3.** Result for static impact analysis

|  | Force applied (N) | Max. stress (Mpa) | Max. deformation (mm) | Factor of safety |
|---|---|---|---|---|
| Front | 19900 | 456.59 | 3.207 | 0.1889 |
| Rear | 8613 | 359.59 | 1.8599 | 0.2397 |
| Side | 8613 | 192.79 | 2.317 | 0.447 |

## c. Result for battery thermal management system

Figure 18 shows that the average temperature on plate facing on the battery cell (P1) of nine nodes in 300 min then the temperature is 38 °C to 47 °C smoothly increasing in each minute, the average fluid temperature of ten nodes is between 20 °C and 29.5 °C and the upper part of a plate (P2) average temperature is 21 °C to 28.08 °C. The correct mass flow rate for gating this temperature is the mass flow rate of 0.001 kg of the fluid. And the following graph describes the relations and features of the three case temperatures in nine nodes and 300 min.

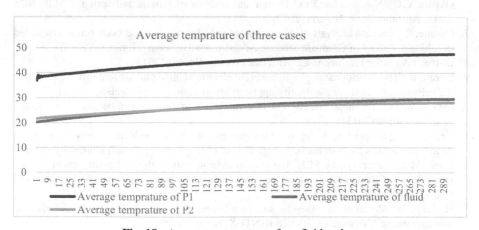

**Fig. 18.** Average temperature of $p_1$, fluid and $p_2$

# 5  Conclusions

The structural analysis includes the total deformation of the chassis frame on ANSYS 15 and the analytical work of the result. So, the total deformation on the ANSYS 15 workbench is 1.0047mm. And the von-misses stress is 115.55 MPa on the ANSYS result it shows the chassis is in safe mode. The maximum shear stress on the ANSYS is 61.111 MPa occurs on the right-rear part of the battery set. The fatigue life of the designed chassis frame is 130 days with a full load without deformation and sensitivity of the electric vehicle chassis frame able to 72% additional weight in 10e6 cycle beyond this percentage the sensitivity cycle tends to decrease.

That what is done in the BTMS is shape minimization of the cooling materials like a plate and cooper coil of the coolant the previous size of the cooling plate is 230 mm × 150 mm × 12 mm and the diameter of the coil is 9 mm and after shape minimization, the size changed to 230 mm × 150 mm × 10 mm and the copper coil diameter is 7 mm. the need of this minimization is to reduce the weight of the battery pack from 383.51 kg to 345.61 kg there is no problem happened on the entire structure of the battery because the transient analysis is done and the shape concerned with only the cooling plate, not the battery itself.

# References

1. Dealer, E.P.: Toyota RAV4 EV 2014 model owner's manual (2014)
2. Satinder, S., Beant, S.: Design optimization and statical crush analysis of chassis frame. Int. J. Automob. Eng. Res. (2014)
3. Eitzinger, S.: Chassis, drivetrain, and energy storage layout for an electric city vehicle (2011)
4. Knutsen, D., Willén, O.: A study of electric vehicle charging patterns and range. UPTEC STS13 015, pp. 1650–8319 (2013)
5. Samba, A.: Battery electrical vehicles-analysis of thermal. MOBI (the Mobility, Logistics and Automotive Technology Research Centre) (2015)
6. Okpala, C.C., Nwokeocha, T.O.: Design and analysis of chassis and spring. P.M.B. 5025 Awka, Anambra State, Nigeria (2017)
7. Damtie, E.: Strength analysis of three wheeled vehicle's chassis and body frame assembled in Ethiopia. School of Graduate Studies, Addis Ababa University, Ethiopia (2013)
8. Duffie, J.A.: Solar Engineering of Thermal Process. Canada (2013)
9. Lovatt, R.: The development of a lightweight electric vehicle chassis and investigation into the suitability of TiAl for automotive applications. Hamilton, New Zealand (2008)
10. Ottaviano, D.: Technical assessment and modeling of lithium-ion batteries for electric vehicles. Zurich (2012)
11. Unda, I., Papadopoulos, P., et al.: Management of electric vehicle battery charging in distribution networks. Institute of Energy School of Engineering Cardiff University (2012)
12. Khan, M.R., Swierczynski, M.J.: Towards an ultimate battery thermal management system. Department of Energy Technology, Aalborg University, Pontoppidanstræde 101, Aalborg DK-9220, Denmark (2017)
13. Haifeng, D., Zechang, S.: Design and simulation of liquid-cooling plates for thermal management of EV batteries. EVS28 KINTEX, Korea (2015)
14. Hua, J.: Progress in battery swapping technology and demonstration in China (2017)

15. Siraj, A., Babu, N.R., Reddy, K.S.: Static analysis of dump truck chassis frame made of composite materials. Int. J. Eng. Sci. Technol. **11**(2), 21–32 (2019). www.ajol.info/index. php/ijest
16. Amin, I.: Design and analyze the chassis of an electric vehicle for use in campus condition. University Technical Malaysia Melka (2009)

# Design and Experimental Test on Solar Powered Evaporative Cooling to Store Perishable Agricultural Products

Bimrew Tamrat[✉], Lijalem Ayele, and Raja Kathiravan

Faculty of Mechanical and Industrial Engineering, Bahir Dar Institute
of Technology, Bahir Dar University, Bahir Dar, Ethiopia

**Abstract.** This paper is dealt with the design and experimental test on solar powered evaporative cooling system which is maintaining inside temperature lower
than ambient temperature with higher level of relative humidity for the storage of
fresh Agricultural products such as tomato, carrot and green chili (pepper). The
experimental setup is a rectangular shaped storage space made of galvanized steel
for external cover, aluminum for internal cover insulated with fiber glass. Axial
fan supplies 0.78 m$^3$/s air at a speed of 0.93 m/s to wet pad and for recycling of
water through copper tube, an axial pump having flow rate of 0.054 kg/s is used
to remove the heat from the commodities. The results reveal that the shelf life
of the vegetables is increased 12 days when compared with ambient conditions.
The temperature range of the cooling cabinet is found 16.2 to 22.1 °C during the
hottest time of the day and the ambient temperature varied from 22.6 to 29.8 °C.
The relative humidity is found between 75 and 90% when the outside condition
is recorded between 66 and 80%. The maximum weight loss found after the sixth
day for carrot, tomato and pepper are 8, 10 and 16% in cabinet conditions and
50.6, 38 and 50% in ambient conditions respectively. The commodity decay is
found in an ambient condition is faster compared with the commodity stored in
the present cooling system. Evaporative cooling efficiency is found 82%.

**Keywords:** Solar powered evaporative cooling systems · Perishable products ·
Preservation · Relative humidity · Vegetables

## 1 Introduction

In Ethiopia the farmers are cultivating different types of fruits and vegetables such as
carrot, peppers, mango, tomato etc., after the harvest, the fruits and vegetables are stored
in high ambient temperature and below the required relative humidity by the farmers and
investors, that causes these fruits and vegetables spoilage and they may get economical
loss. Also, the post-harvest deterioration contributes towards a significant fraction of
the total loss in food grains, owing to poor storage facilities and lack of infrastructure.
By providing thermal cooling for this issue would be minimize the post-harvest losses
[1]. An issue of food losses leads to combat hunger and improve the food insecurity,

© ICST Institute for Computer Sciences, Social Informatics and Telecommunications Engineering 2021
Published by Springer Nature Switzerland AG 2021. All Rights Reserved
M. A. Delele et al. (Eds.): ICAST 2020, LNICST 385, pp. 190–203, 2021.
https://doi.org/10.1007/978-3-030-80618-7_12

especially in the poor and developing countries. Such losses not only affect the farmer societies, but also it leads waste of resources where employed during the production. The exact reasons and extent of such losses varies around the world and are most dependent on the specific conditions, as well as native factors predominant in a specific country [2].

The post-harvest deterioration contributes towards a significant fraction of the total loss in food grains, especially in the developing nations, due to existing poor storage facilities and lack of infrastructure. The quality of fruit and vegetables and their related shelf life are reduced by loss of moisture, decay, and physiological breakdown. Such deterioration is directly related to the storage temperature, relative humidity, air circulation, mechanical damage, and improper post-harvest sanitation [3]. An evaporative cooling process is operates using spontaneous processes of heat and mass transfer, where water and air are the working fluids to vary the temperature and moisture as per the local requirement. In water evaporation, an air flow is induced by the passage and thereby decreasing the air temperature. Based on the evaporative coolant system, waxing and hot water treatment have been found to be an efficient and economical means of reducing post-harvest storage loss [5]. Cold storage is one way of protecting the deterioration agricultural products such as fruits and vegetables using evaporative cooling technology. The purpose of the design is creating cold storage by adding cold air to it that increases the shelf life of the perishable agricultural products.

Design of evaporative cooling system powered by solar PV panel can be found everywhere at which the perishable agricultural products are highly produced. The present designed and developed evaporative cooling system is benefited for farmers, merchants, investors and consumers who are associated with the production and logistics chain of fruits and vegetables.

## 2 Design and Fabrication of Evaporative Cooling System

In this study, a solar powered evaporative cooling system was designed and constructed to preserve fresh vegetables of 80 kg storage capacity. The solar power evaporative cooling system basically consists of the solar energy conversion (PV panel, charge regulator, battery and invertor) cold storage space, cooling fan and the evaporative unit (cooling pad). the cooling system contains a rectangular shape with total storage space of $0.735 \text{ m}^3$, made of stainless steel for external cover, aluminum for internal cover and insulated between them by 0.05 m thick of fiber glass, a cooling fan provides air flow of 0.9 m/s velocity and consumes 35 W of power with a speed of 2800 rpm, cooling pad is made of natural fiber of 0.03 m thickness which is easily available in local. A water pump with discharge capacity of $5.4 \times 10\text{--}5 \text{ m}^3/\text{s}$ and power rating of 50 W is used to recirculate the water. A water reservoir of capacity 60 L is linked the cooling water with the cooling system at the bottom through pipe and to keep the cooling pad/mesh continuously wet. The cold storage consists of four shelves and water circulating pipe below each shelf used to remove heat generated by fruits and vegetables. The basic principle relies on solar powered cooling by evaporation, when the system is set in operation, the dry air from the suction fan passes over the wet surface (cooling pad) and evaporates the soaked water away from the cooling pad. When water evaporates, it draws latent heat from the air surroundings the cold storage, which produces considerable cooling effect in the storage chamber. The picture of solar powered evaporative cooling system developed by solid work modeling is shown in Fig. 1.

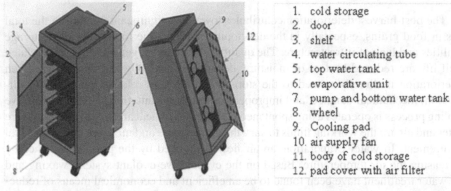

1. cold storage
2. door
3. shelf
4. water circulating tube
5. top water tank
6. evaporative unit
7. pump and bottom water tank
8. wheel
9. Cooling pad
10. air supply fan
11. body of cold storage
12. pad cover with air filter

**Fig. 1.** Solid work modeling of the cold storage

## 3 Heat Transfer and Heat Generation

The heat balance is calculated through the cabinet wall using the methods of heat transfer modes and the heat generation due to commodities respiration load, Air change load, Fruit and vegetable load, Power Loads.

### 3.1 Heat Transfer Through the Wall, $Q_w$

The conduction heat transfer through the wall or roof will depend on the thickness and thermal conductivity of the material used [27].

$$Q_w = \text{Heat gain} = UA_{os}(T_o - T_i) \tag{1}$$

Where $Q_w$ is Heat loss through wall, Aos is the outside surface rea of cold storage ($m^2$), U is The overall heat transfer coefficient (W/m² °C), Ti is the inside air temperature of cold storage (°C), To is outside atmosphere air temperature (°C).

### 3.2 Convection Heat Transfer Effect on Cold Storage, $Q_{cov}$

Heat transferred from the wall of cold storage to the cabinet air, it led to Newton's cooling law equation.

$$Q_{cov} = hA_c(T_w - T_c) \tag{2}$$

Where $Q_{cov}$ is convective heat transfer, h is convective heat transfer coefficient obtained from dimensionless number using film temperature in W/m² °C, $A_c$ is area of the cabinet in $m^2$, $T_w$ is wall temperature of cold storage in °C is $T_c$ is cabinet temperature in °C.

### 3.3 Heat Transfer Through Cooling Pad

The cooling pad is a plain porous wall bounded by two convective fluids (air) outside the pad surface and inside the cooler, each at different temperature, the elementary sensible heat flux in terms of overall temperature and thermal properties of the pad as shown in Fig. 2.

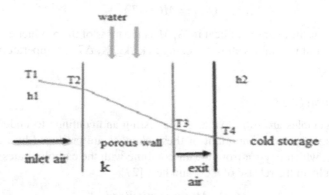

**Fig. 2.** Scheme of the heat transfer process across the porous evaporative cooling pad

Basic model equations

$$Q = h_1 A(T_1 - T_2) \tag{3}$$

$$Q = \frac{A(T_2 - T_3)}{X/K} \tag{4}$$

$$Q = h_2 A(T_3 - T_4) \tag{5}$$

The heat balance for the three equations gave

$$Q = \frac{A(T_1 - T_4)}{\frac{1}{h_1} + \frac{X}{K} + \frac{1}{h_2}} \tag{6}$$

Where $h_1$ and $h_2$ are the convective heat transfer coefficient, A is the area of the pad, k is the thermal conductivity of the pad, x is the thickness and T is the temperature.

### 3.4 Effect of Solar Radiation, $Q_{rad}$

Radiation is the energy emitted from a surface as particles or waves.

$$Q_{rad} = \varepsilon \sigma (T_c^4 - T_a^4) \tag{7}$$

Where $Q_{rad}$ is radiative heat energy, $\varepsilon$ is emissivity of the product kept in the cabinet, $\sigma$ is Stephen boltzmaan constant, $J/m^2 K^4$, $T_c$ is cabinet temperature (°C), $T_a$ is ambient temperature (°C).

# 4  Heat Generation

## 4.1  Fruit and Vegetable Load, $Q_{veg}$

Commodity is warmed in the warmer available in the conditioned space. The commodities loaded in the cold storage, than it is cooling up to the required temperature [18]. The heat transfer to the vegitables will be calculated using the following Eq. 8.

$$Q_{veg} = MC(\Delta T) \tag{8}$$

where $Q_{veg}$ is the quantity of heat in W, $M$ is the mass of the product in kg/day, C is the specific heat of vegetables above freezing in kJ/kg. K, $\Delta T$ is temperature difference in °C.

## 4.2  Respiration Load

Fruits and vegetables are still alive after harvesting and continue to undergo changes while in storage the more important of these changes are produced by respiration, a process during which oxygen from the air combine with the carbohydrates in the plant tissue and results in the release of $CO_2$ and heat [27].

$$Qr = M\,(respriationload) \tag{9}$$

Where $Qr$ is quantity heat in W, M is mass the product in kg.

## 4.3  Air Change Load, $Q_{ACH}$

Air that enters a storage space must be cooled. Air needs to be renewed, and consequently there is a need for ventilation. When air enters the refrigerated space, heat must be removed from it [21].

$$Q_{ACH} = (V) \times (ACH) \times (h_o - h_i) \times (\rho) \tag{10}$$

Where $Q_{ACH}$ is air change load due to door opening infiltration and ventilation in (W), V is volume of cold chamber in $m^3$, $\rho$ is density of commodity, $kg/m^3$, $h_o$ is enthalpy of air at $T_o$ in kJ/kg, $h_i$ is enthalpy of air at $T_i$ in kJ/kg, ACH is air change per hour.

## 4.4  Power Loads, $Q_{power}$

In cold storage applications use various equipment's such as fans and pump which add significantly to the heat gain [30].

$$Q_{power} = 2545 \times \frac{P}{Eff} \times FUM \times FLM \tag{11}$$

Where is $Q_{power}$ is power load in W, $P$ is horsepower rating from electrical power plans or manufacturer's data, Eff is equipment motor efficiency, as decimal fraction, FUM is Motor use factor (normally = 1.0), FLM is motor load factor (normally = 1.0).

The amount of heat must be removed from cold storage to cool the stored fruits and vegetables based on the storage capacity known as cooling load. Total Cooling load = heat transfer through cold storage cabinet wall + air change load + product load + respiration load + equipment load + convective heat transfer effect + effect of radiation.

### 4.5   Insulation Thickness Calculation

The insulation barrier of cold storage is defined as bulk materials with single- or multi-layer insulation. The complete insulation thickness formula containing insulation layers and interior/exterior wall structures is as below:

$$L = K [R - (\frac{1}{h_e} - \frac{1}{h_i})$$

(12)

Where K denotes insulation material thermal conductivity, R denotes wall structure thermal resistance, he and hi represent heat transfer coefficients of interior and exterior walls, respectively.

## 5   Fan Selection Based on the Cold Storage Size

The volume of air flow required to cool the cold storage [33] can be determined from equation

$$\dot{V} = k(\frac{Q}{\Delta T} - U \times A) \times s.f$$

(13)

Where, k is the coefficient factor, and the required air velocity (v) is given by (Table 1)

$$v = \frac{flow\ rate}{area\ of\ the\ pad}$$

(14)

**Table 1.**  Fan selection specifications.

| Items | | Letter | Specification |
|---|---|---|---|
| Cabinet | Size | H<br>W<br>D | 1.5m<br>0.7m<br>0.7m |
| | Total surface area | A | 4.1 m$^2$ |
| | Materials | | Steel, Aluminum & fiber glass |
| | Over all Heat transfer coefficient | U | 4.1 W/m. °C |
| Temperature difference | | $\Delta T$ | 14 °C |
| Total heat generation/cooling load | | Q | 711.42 W |
| Safety factor | | Sf | 1.15 |

## 5.1  Fan Power Consumption

Fan power consumption is directly proportional to system flow rate and static pressure. For theoretically perfect efficiency, the minimum power required to move air against resistance is defined as [34]:

$$P_f = \frac{V \times p}{6356} \qquad (15)$$

Where $p_f$ is horse power of fan, V is volumetric flow rate (cubic meter per minute), p is max static pressure of air, $N/m^2$.

## 5.2  Pumping Energy Requirements Analysis

The energy of a pump for a particular day can be determined in Eq. 16.

$$E = \frac{mgh}{\eta} \qquad (16)$$

Where $m$ is mass of water needed in kg, $g$ is acceleration due to gravity $(m/s^2)$, $h$ is height from the pump to top water tank (m), $\eta$ is efficiency of the system.

The flow rate of the pump can be calculated as in Eq. 16.

$$\dot{Q} = \frac{24}{PSH} x \, \dot{m}_{day} \qquad (17)$$

Where Q is water flow rate, m is amount of water per day, PSH is peak sunshine hour.

## 5.3  Power Requirements from Solar Panel

The amount of power required from the solar panel can be calculated from Eq. (18) by changing kWhr to kW.

$$P = \frac{E}{hr} = \frac{\frac{V}{hr} \times h}{367\eta} kw \qquad (18)$$

# 6  Selection of PV Array

The size of PV array has to have a relationship to the pump requirements. The depreciation of the panel due to ageing and environmental features (dust, etc.). Take the depreciation of 20% is allowed for:

$$P_{array} = 1.2P \qquad (19)$$

### 6.1 Solar Energy Analysis

Base condition: 2 fans (35 W each) for a day, 1 micro pump (50 W) for recirculating water through the cabinet [4].

- The total energy requirement of the system (total load) i.e. Total connected load to PV panel system is = No. of units × rating of equipment = (2 × 35) + 50 = 120 W
- Total watt-hours rating of the system = Total connected load (watts) × Operating hours, take the operating hour 10 h
- The battery required is calculated based on the operating hour and the voltage obtained from the solar panel which is 12V the battery current becomes

$$I = \frac{power}{voltage}$$

Inverter size is to be selected as:

- Total connected load to PV panel system = 200 W
- Inverter are available with rating of 600, 1000, 1500W etc.
- Therefore, the choice of the inverter should be 1000 W.

Evaporative cooling efficiency of the system is found from the experimental result by using the following formula 15.

$$\varepsilon = \frac{T_1 - T_4}{T_1 - T_w} \tag{20}$$

Where $\varepsilon$ is direct evaporation efficiency in %, $T_1$ is ambient temperature is °C, $T_4$ is cabinet temperature is °C, $T_w$ is wet-bulb temperature on pad is °C.

## 7  Result and Discussion

### 7.1  Experimental Setup

An experimental test was conducted with natural fiber as the cooling pad material with inlet air velocities of 0.93 m/s. The characteristic length of the pad is 30 mm, height 1.4 m and width 0.7 m. The pad was divided into two equal parts by area and an axial fan deliver air at the rate 0.00376 kg/s to the wet pad and water vapor could easily pass in to cold storage area. The experiment was performed as shown in Fig. 3.

### 7.2  Temperature and Relative Humidity Variation

The performance of evaporative cooling system with a sample load to be cooled was evaluated daily at intervals of two hours from 8:00 am and 12:00 pm for 12 days and tabulated in Table 2. Within these periods of evaluating the performance of the cooling system, the ambient temperature is found that it is increasing up to 12 noon and then it is decreasing but the cabinet temperature dropped from 21.5 °C at 2.00 pm and thereafter

**Fig. 3.** Pictures of experimental test set up of evaporative cooling

it is maintained an appreciable average temperature of 17 °C for the remaining testing period. However, the average temperature inside the cooling chamber varied from 16.2 °C to 22.1 °C while in the ambient air temperature varied from 22.6 °C to 29.8 °C. And the evaporative cooling chamber relative humidity is found between 75% and 90% while at outside relative humidity is measured and it is varied from 66% to 80%.

**Table 2.** The average temperature and relative humidity measured inside the cabinet and ambient air conditions for different local time.

| Local time | Ambient | | Cabinet | | |
|---|---|---|---|---|---|
| | Temperature (°C) | RH% | Temperature (°C) | RH% | WBT(°C) |
| 08 am | 23.7 | 71 | 16.2 | 75 | 16.5 |
| 10 am | 25.2 | 70 | 18.6 | 79 | 17 |
| 12 noon | 28.9 | 69 | 19.9 | 83 | 18.4 |
| 02 pm | 28.2 | 69 | 21.5 | 85 | 19 |
| 04 pm | 26.5 | 70 | 20.7 | 88 | 19.5 |
| 06 pm | 23 | 75 | 19.9 | 90 | 19.2 |

### 7.3 Physiological Weight Loss During Storage

It is observed that during the experiment, the commodity such as pepper, carrot and tomato, the weight loss is found that minimum for every day when stored in the evaporative cooling system chamber compared with an ambient storage and it is presented in Figs. 4 and 5.

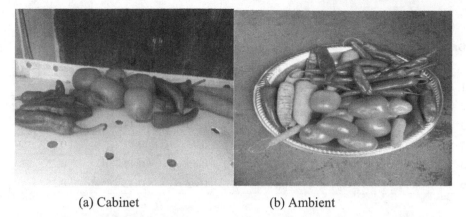

(a) Cabinet                              (b) Ambient

**Fig. 4.** Weight loss difference on seven days of cabinet and four days of ambient.

(a) Cabinet                              (b) Ambient

**Fig. 5.** Weight loss difference on seven days of cabinet and four days of ambient.

Table 3 shows the variation of weight loss of pepper, tomato and carrot right from the first day to sixth day.

Figure 6a, shows the variation of weight of carrot, tomato and pepper from the first day to the sixth day mentioned in circle, triangle and square respectively. The continuous line is for cabinet conditions and the dotted lines are corresponds to ambient conditions when the commodities were kept. The figures also show that there is an appreciable weight loss found when the commodities were kept in ambient conditions. This is meant that the evaporation is higher in ambient condition than in the cabinet condition so that the commodity decay very fast as compared as that of the commodity stored in an evaporative cooling system.

Figure 6b, shows the percentage weight loss calculated by every day with respect to the first day. It is found that the commodities kept in the cabinet condition are show that less weight loss compared to the commodities kept in the ambient conditions. Among the samples, a high weight loss happened on pepper due to skin resistance of moisture loss in both cabinet and ambient conditions. Also, it is found that the carrot and tomato kept

**Table 3.** Physiological weight loss measured in peppers, carrot and tomatoes

| Day | Carrot (kg) | | Tomato (kg) | | Pepper (kg) | |
|-----|---------|---------|---------|---------|---------|---------|
|     | Cabinet | Ambient | Cabinet | Ambient | Cabinet | Ambient |
| 1 | 0.75 | 0.75 | 1.00 | 1.00 | 0.50 | 0.50 |
| 2 | 0.75 | 0.71 | 1.00 | 0.91 | 0.45 | 0.35 |
| 3 | 0.73 | 0.65 | 0.98 | 0.79 | 0.43 | 0.30 |
| 4 | 0.71 | 0.50 | 0.90 | 0.73 | 0.43 | 0.25 |
| 5 | 0.69 | 0.43 | 0.92 | 0.65 | 0.42 | 0.25 |
| 6 | 0.69 | 0.37 | 0.90 | 0.62 | 0.42 | 0.25 |

in the cabinet conditions after four days there is no change in the weight loss because it may be the saturated conditions after that the carrot and tomato gets decayed. From this, it is concluded that the carrot and tomato can preserve up to five days by maintaining this cabinet condition. It can be extended some more days by maintaining the cabinet conditions with more humidity and less temperature. Whereas, in the ambient condition, it is found that the carrot and pepper are decayed after three days. Furthermore, in the case of tomato, the weight loss is increases in the first three days and then it comes to saturated during the next days because it losses it water content fastly by evaporation for the first three days and there is no evaporation is found in the forthcoming days. The maximum weight loss found after the sixth day for carrot, tomato and pepper are 8, 10 and 16% in cabinet conditions and 50.6, 38 and 50% in ambient conditions respectively. Till more experimental investigation to be carried out to get the optimum result.

Theoretical efficiency of the direct evaporative cooling using the standard values available in Metrological department of Ethiopia for Bahir Dar city and it is calculated 84%. From the actual experimental values it is found that 82%. The difference is due to the air leakage from the cabinet through which some heat is transferred to the system from ambient.

## 7.4 Feasibility Analysis

The time in which the initial cost out flow of a cold storage is expected to recovered from the cash inflows generated by the cold storage, which means the cost reduced by PV panel from grid power payment and cost by avoiding the spoilage of fruits and vegetables

$$payback\ period = \frac{initial\ cost}{cash\ inflow/year} \tag{21}$$

$$payback\ period = \frac{27,680birr}{15040.8birr/year} = 1.8\,yrs$$

From this solar powered evaporative cooling, reducing the spoilage of fruits and vegetables and also avoid grid power payment will pay back the total cost of the cold storage within 1.8 years.

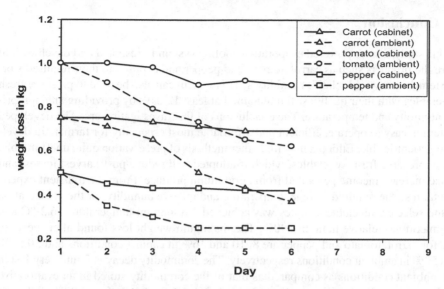

**a.** Variation of weight loss of carrot, tomato and pepper

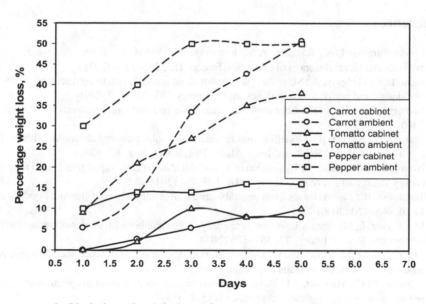

**b.** Variation of weight loss of carrot, tomato and pepper

**Fig. 6.** (a) Variation of weight loss of carrot, tomato and pepper (b) Variation of weight loss of carrot, tomato and pepper

# 8 Conclusion

In this study, a solar powered evaporative cooling system is designed and developed, to store the products such as carrot, tomato and pepper and exposed to their required storage temperatures and relative humidity's. This system can also be used to preserve fresh vegetables with their quality still maintained at least 12 days by providing an appropriate humidity and temperature. The conclusions of this investigation are: The developed system is easy to operate, efficient and affordable most especially for farmers in developing countries like Ethiopia may find other methods of preservation quite unaffordable. It can preserve fresh vegetables, which if adopted will reduce post-harvest losses, and hence increase income generated from agricultural produce. From the transient experimental test, the required storage temperature and relative humidity for the preservation of the selected vegetable samples was achieved a minimum temperature 16.2 °C and the maximum relative humidity 90%. The maximum weight loss found after the sixth day for carrot, tomato and pepper are 8, 10 and 16% in cabinet conditions and 50.6, 38 and 50% in ambient conditions respectively. The commodity decay is found very fast in the ambient conditions as compared as that of the commodity stored in an evaporative cooling system. Evaporative cooling efficiency by experimentally found 82%. Till more experiment should be conducted in future to get the optimum result.

# References

1. Chidambarama, L.A., Ramana, A.S., Kamaraja, G., Velraj, R.: Review of solar cooling methods and thermal storage options. Sol. Energy **15**, 3220–3228 (2011)
2. Basu, D.N., Ganguly, A.: Solar thermal–photovoltaic powered potato cold storage – conceptual design and performance analyses. Appl. Energy **165**, 308–317 (2016)
3. Camargo, J.R.: The use of fiber wood as evaporative pad packaging material, 18–21 August 2010
4. Prakash, V., KalWa, R.: Modelling and fabrication of solar powered air cooler with cooling cabin for household food items. Int. J. Mech. Eng. Robot. Res. **3**(3) (2014)
5. Islam, M.P., Morimoto, T.: Evaluation of a new heat transfer and evaporative design for a zero energy storage structure. Sol. Energy **118**, 469–484 (2015)
6. Tashtoush, B.: Natural losses from vegetable and fruit products in cold storage. Food Control **11**(6), 465–470 (2000)
7. Md. Parvez, I., Morimoto, T.: A new zero energy cool chamber with a solar-driven adsorption refrigerator. Renew. Energy **72**, 367–376 (2014)
8. Ma, L., Zhang, M., Bhandari, B., Gao, Z.: Recent developments in novel shelf life extension technologies of fresh-cut fruits and vegetables (2017)
9. Ndukwu, M.C., Manuwa, S.I.: Review of research and application of evaporative cooling in preservation of fresh agricultural produce **7**(85) (2014)
10. Patel, A.M., Patel, R.I.: Optimization of different parameter of cold storage for energy conservation **03**(02) (2012)
11. Al-Azri, N.A.: Development of a typical meteorological year based on dry bulb temperature and dew point for passive cooling applications. Energy Sustain. Dev. **33**, 61–74 (2016)
12. Susana, C., Fonseca, F.A.R.O., Jeffrey, K.: Brecht Modelling respiration rate of fresh fruits and vegetables for modified atmosphere packages: a review (2002)
13. Jahun, B.G., Abdulkadir, S.A., Musa, S.M., Umar, H.: Assessment of evaporative cooling system for storage of vegetables. Int. J. Sci. Res. **5**, 1197–1203 (2014)

14. Eggie, K.: Design and testing of an evaporative cooling system using an ultrasonic humidifier (2008)
15. Tewodros, Y.: Design and fabrication of a small-scale evaporative cooling system for perishable commodities (2017)
16. Liberty, J.T., Ugwuishiwu, B.O., Pukumab, S.A., Odoc, C.E.: Principles and application of evaporative cooling systems for fruits and vegetables preservation. J. Curr. Eng. Technol. 3(3), 1000–1006 (2013)
17. Bucklin, R.A., J.D.L., McConnell, D.B., Wilkerson, E.G.: Fan and pad greenhouse evaporative cooling systems (2016)
18. Deshmukh, G., Birwal, P., Datir, R., Patel, S.: Thermal insulation materials: a tool for energy conservation. J. Food Process. Technol. 8(4), 1–5 (2017)
19. Kraemer, R., A.P., Venn, J.: Design of a small-scale, low-cost cold storage system. Biosystems Design Project (BE 487)
20. Kharagpur, F.I.: Refrigeration and air conditioning, useful training material for mechanical engineering students/college, or as reference for engineer
21. Sue Bloomfied, R.: Batteries and solar power: guidance for domestic and small commercial consumers. BRE National solar centre (2016)
22. Vipin Das, N.M., Unnikrishnan, M., Jose, N., Rishikesh, P., Sukumaran, S.: Fabrication and analysis of solar powered air cooler. Int. J. Eng. Sci. (IJES) 5(1) (2016)
23. B1 Stellenhof, V.R.: Solar panel technical information guidlines solar flex
24. Bhatia, A.: Principles of evaporative cooling system. An approved continuing education provider (2012)
25. Mogaji, T.S., Fapetu, O.P.: Development of an evaporative cooling system for the preservation of fresh vegetables. Afr. J. Food Sci. 5(4), 255–266 (2011)
26. Jitendra Jayant, A.S.: Cooling load calculation for a potato cold storage plant. Int. J. Innov. Res. Eng. Sci. 3(5) (2016)
27. Ikegwu, O.J., Ekwu, F.C.: Thermal and physical properties of some tropical fruits and their juices in Nigeria. J. Food Technol. 7(2), 38–42 (2009)
28. Paltrinieri, G.: Handling of fresh fruits, vegetables and root crops. Food and Agriculture Organization of the United Nations (2014)
29. Bhatia, A.: Cooling Load Calculations and Principles. Continuing Education and Development, Inc.
30. Gross, K.C., Wang, C.Y., Saltveit, M.: The Commercial Storage of Fruits, Vegetables, and Florist and Nursery Stocks. Agricultural Research Service (2016)
31. Cengel, Y.A., Boles, M.A. (edn.): Thermodynamics an Engineering Approach (2007)
32. Mleziva, B.: Basic methods of fan selecting typical ventilation and cooling products based on their use (2012)
33. Mleziv, B.: Reducing power consumption by minimizing system pressure loss and choosing the right equipment. Fan Selection and Energy Savings, August 2010. Greenheck Fan Corp. Schofeld, W
34. Olukunle, J., Ndukwu, N.M., Manuwa, S.I., Oluwalana, B.: Mathematical model for direct evaporative space cooling systems (2013)
35. Kothandaraman, C.P.: Heat and Mass Transfer Data Book
36. Ebinuma, C.D., Camargo, J.R., Cardoso, S.: A mathematical model for direct evaporative cooling air conditioning system
37. Incropera, F.P.: Fundamental of heat and mass transfer (2007)
38. Kakac, S.: Heat Exchangers, Selection, Rating and Thermal Design. 2nd edn. Department of Mechanical Engineering. University of Miami. CRC Press LLC (2002)
39. Ranaware, N.D., Molawade, K.N., Mane, L.N.: A review on comparison between shell and tube heat exchanger. IJIERT 2(2), 2394–3696 (2015)
40. REGAL-BELOIT, Axial Flow Fan And Centrifugal Fan selection (2015)

# Effect of Oil Heat Treatment on Tensile and Bending Properties of Ethiopian Lowland Bamboo

Berhanu Abnet Mengstie[1](✉) and Eden Aragaw Addisu[2]

[1] Department of Mechanical Engineering, Bahir Dar Institute of Technology, Bahir Dar University, Bahir Dar, Ethiopia
[2] Department of Industrial Engineering, Bahir Dar Institute of Technology, Bahir Dar University, Bahir Dar, Ethiopia

**Abstract.** The main purpose of this study was analysis the effect of oil treatment of Ethiopian lowland bamboo on tensile and bending strength of bamboo. In this study Ethiopian lowland bamboo treated by oil in different treatment condition with hot oil and without hot oil. The treatment temperatures were 100, 130 and 160 °C with sun flower oil and treatment duration of 30, 60 and 90 min and bamboo immersed in oil for 2, 4 and 6 days without heat. After oil treatment of bamboo tensile and three point bending experimental test were investigated for treated and untreated bamboo samples. The experimental result showed that from all condition of oil heat treatment best tensile results were bamboo treated at 100 °C with sun flower oil for a duration of 60 min and for bending bamboos treated at 160 °C for a duration of 30 min. In addition to this bamboo treated without hot oil for a duration of 2, 4 and 6 days had good tensile and bending strength at long treatment duration.

**Keywords:** Bending strength · Ethiopian lowland bamboo · Oil treatment · Tensile strength

## 1 Introduction

Bamboo is a sustainable renewable material that is found globally. It is a cheap fast-growing plant and possesses high mechanical properties to compare with other woody materials. Bamboo is one of the resources which are highly distributed in Ethiopia.

Heat treatment, also known as thermal modification, is an effective way to improve the performance of materials (Li et al. 2015). Oil and heat treatment fluids are designed for rapid or controlled cooling of steel or other materials as part of hardening, tempering, or another heat-treating process. Oil has a major advantage over water due to its higher boiling range. The investigation of the thermal treatment of bamboo has led to the improvement of heat treatment with vegetable oils (Sukhairi et al. 2016).

There are studies on improving mechanical, chemical properties of bamboo through oil heat treatment in Moso bamboo, three species of Philippine bamboo (mechanical properties), and Semantan bamboo (chemical properties).

M. A. Delele et al. (Eds.): ICAST 2020, LNICST 385, pp. 204–215, 2021.
https://doi.org/10.1007/978-3-030-80618-7_13

Effects of different thermal modification media on the physical and mechanical properties of Moso bamboo (Yang et al. 2016). Yang, Lee, Lee, & Cheng study the employed thermal modification technology to modify Moso bamboo (Phyllostachys edulis) and explore its future development as a sustainable green material. The Moso bamboo exposure to linseed oil at 150, 170, 190, and 210 °C for a treatment duration of 1, 2, and 4 h. After treatment, the researchers were performing experimental for the case samples and finding of the author's shows both the modulus of rupture and modulus of elasticity values of the bamboo decreased as the treatment temperature increased.

Effects of hot oil treatment on the physical and mechanical properties of three species of Philippine bamboo (RD Manalo and MN Acda 2017). RD Manalo and MN Acda study the effects of hot oil treatment on physical and mechanical properties on three species of Philippine bamboo, viz. Bambusa blumeana, B. vulgaris, and Dendrocalamus asper were investigated after exposure to virgin coconut oil at 160 to 200 °C for 30 to 120 min. The results showed that there was a reduction strength property as indicated by the modulus of elasticity, modulus of rupture.

Properties of oil heat-treated four-year-old tropical bamboo Gigantochloa Levis (Sukhairi et al. 2016). The researchers treated Malesia bamboo by Palm oil at 140 °C, 180 °C, and 220 °C for the treatment durations of 30, 60, and 90 min. After treatment and experimental investigation, the result shows that heat-treated at 180°C for 60 min shows an overall quality in mechanical properties.

Previous research shows that bamboo mechanical properties are species-dependent. The objective of the study is how to improve Ethiopian low land bamboo mechanical properties and study the effect of treatment temperature and duration on bamboo tensile and bending strength.

This research aims to study the effect of oil heat treatment on the mechanical properties of Ethiopia lowland bamboo, which is one of the critical issues for the property improvement of bamboo and using bamboo in different bio structural engineering applications.

In addition, the research also studies the effect of oil on tensile and bending strength when the bamboo samples soaked in oil for a day without heat supply.

## 2  Methodology

To study the effect of oil heat treatment on mechanical properties Ethiopia lowland bamboo, 3 years old Ethiopian lowland bamboo harvested from Awi, Enjibra, Ethiopia. Ethiopian lowland bamboo is fast-growing and mature at age 3 years. also research showed that bamboo grows very rapidly usually takes 3–6 years to harvest (Xu et al. 2017). The bamboo samples were taken from the middle part and only internodes for practical and uniformity of samples.

After collecting bamboo culm, cut the middle part, and required internodes using wood workshop and ready for the oil treatment process. Bamboos were oil-treated in two cases. The first set bamboo treated with hot oil and second set bamboo treated without heat oil (simply soak bamboo in oil).

The oil treatment process uses a deep fryer electric (Nima, Japan) oil bath with sunflower oil as a heating medium. The sunflower oil selected because of readily available in the market, organic, and have a high flash point (217 °C).

## 2.1   Oil Treatment of Bamboo

In this study oil treatment of bamboo done in two ways firstly bamboo treated by heated oil and secondly bamboo treated without heat.

The first treatment with hot oil, the sunflower oil poured into the deep fryer electric (Nima, Japan) oil bath and heated up to a temperature of 100, 130 and 160 °C, and keep constant the temperature for a duration of 30, 60 and 90 min respectively. The treatment temperature and durations were selected based on kinds of literature results and by a preliminary test. In addition to this, the oil heat treatment technique was adopted from literature with some modifications.

To get a target and constant temperature a thermocouple was placed in the oil. The bamboo specimens then soaked in the heated oil. The bamboo samples get out of the oil bath after a treatment duration of 30, 60 and 90 min. Next to followed by the treatment temperature of 130 and 160 °C for a treatment duration of 30, 60 and 90 min. The oil treatment procedure developed by Berhanu et al. (Manalo 2017), (Salim et al. 2009), (Sukhairi et al. 2016), (Yang et al. 2016) used with some modifications.

Optimum temperature controlling method of oil heat treatment of bamboo procedure:

- For the oil heat-treatment of bamboo, the oil was firstly heated to the target temperature (100, 130 and 160 °C).
- Once the temperature was achieved, the bamboo specimens were soaked in the oil and treated for 30, 60 and 90 min of duration.
- To get a uniform target temperature a thermocouple was placed in the oil (Fig. 1).

The second oil treatment of bamboo is without heat, the sunflower oil poured into the steel tank and no heat supply. The bamboo samples were simply soaked in the oil. After a duration of 2, 4- and 6-days bamboo gets out from the tank.

After treatment of bamboo, all treated bamboo placed for one week in the same humidity. Next, prepared test samples based on test standards. For one test 3 samples were made. Among different standards for composites based materials, the tensile test of treated and untreated bamboo was carried out according to ASTM-D3039 (Intertek expert 2018.) and bending test was done based on ISO/TR22157–2: 2004 (E) (ISO/TR 2004) (Manak 1983).

All the mechanical tests were investigated using Computer Controlled Electro-Hydraulic Servo Universal Testing Machine which has a capacity of up to 100 KN, with 0.01 - 500 mm /min test speed. During the test, the following initial parameters were feed to the computer, displacement 0.2 mm/min, load speed 0.1 KN/s, and extension 0.01 mm/s.

## 3   Results

### 3.1   Tensile Test Result

The tensile strength of bamboo along the grain direction was tested. After a series of tests of bamboo for oil-treated and untreated bamboo for tensile load. Below table shows the average value of the three test results for each treatment temperature and duration (Tables 1 and 2).

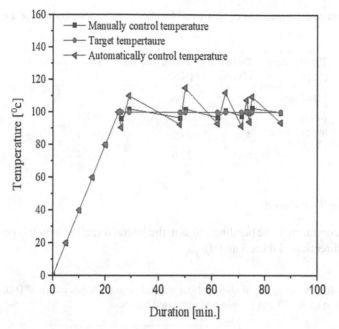

**Fig. 1.** Optimum temperature controlling method of oil heat treatment of bamboo.

**Table 1.** Result of tensile test of oil heat-treated bamboo at the temperature of 100, 130 and 160 °C for a duration of 30, 60 and 90 min and untreated bamboo.

| Temperature [°C] | Duration [Min.] | Maximum load [KN] | Tensile strength [MPa] |
|---|---|---|---|
| Untreated | – | 15.8 | 211.0 |
| 100 | 30 | 16.0 | 212.7 |
| | 60 | 19.7 | 262.2 |
| | 90 | 26.2 | 256.4 |
| 130 | 30 | 18.6 | 248.0 |
| | 60 | 18.3 | 243.9 |
| | 90 | 17.3 | 230.5 |
| 160 | 30 | 17.0 | 226.4 |
| | 60 | 15.9 | 211.9 |
| | 90 | 15.2 | 203.1 |

**Table 2.** Result of the tensile test of oil-treated bamboo at room temperature for a duration of 2, 4 and 6 days.

| Temperature [°C] | Duration [Days] | Maximum load [KN] | Tensile strength [MPa] |
|---|---|---|---|
| Untreated | – | 15.8 | 211.0 |
| Room temperature (27.5 °C) | 2 | 18.1 | 241.8 |
| | 4 | 19.7 | 262.4 |
| | 6 | 21.6 | 287.4 |

## 3.2 Bending Test Result

The loading condition of the bending test is in the lateral direction which is perpendicular to the grain direction (Tables 3 and 4).

**Table 3.** Result of bending test of oil heat-treated bamboo at the temperature of 100, 130 and 160 °C for a duration of 30, 60 and 90 min and untreated bamboo.

| Temperature [°C] | Duration [Min.] | Maximum load [N] | Bending strength [MPa] |
|---|---|---|---|
| Untreated | – | 1885.0 | 12.2 |
| 100 | 30 | 2016.0 | 22.1 |
| | 60 | 2865.2 | 28.0 |
| | 90 | 1382.3 | 14.9 |
| 130 | 30 | 2516.9 | 24.9 |
| | 60 | 2132.7 | 17.6 |
| | 90 | 1770.1 | 16.0 |
| 160 | 30 | 3615.0 | 29.1 |
| | 60 | 2340.9 | 15.0 |
| | 90 | 2075.3 | 14.9 |

**Table 4.** Result of the tensile test of oil-treated bamboo at room temperature for a duration of 2, 4 and 6 days.

| Temperature [°C] | Duration [Days] | Maximum load [N] | Bending strength [MPa] |
|---|---|---|---|
| Untreated | – | 1885.0 | 12.2 |
| Room temperature (27.5 °C) | 2 | 2725.1 | 17.2 |
| | 4 | 2976.4 | 19.6 |
| | 6 | 3098.0 | 20.6 |

# 4  Discussion

## 4.1  Effect of Oil Heat Treatment Temperature and Duration on Tensile and Bending Strength of Bamboo

The experimental result showed that the tensile strength of bamboo treated for 30 min at 100 °C oil less, maximum at 130 °C oil and drop at 160 °C oil. Also, bamboo treated for a duration of 60 and 90 min in 100 °C hot oil the tensile strength is higher than remaining treatment temperature (130 °C & 160 °C). For the remaining treatment temperature after 30 min treatment duration the tensile strength shows almost a linear drop. This shows bamboo oil heat-treated in short treatment duration and at low treatment temperature tensile strength is less, at high treatment temperature, and in short treatment duration tensile strength is good. Also, at high treatment temperature and long treatment duration tensile strength is poor.

Bamboo treated at a temperature of 100 °C oil with a treatment duration of 30, 60- and the 90-min experimental result showed a significant effect on the tensile strength of Ethiopian bamboo. In this treatment temperature, the bamboo was improved its tensile strength from 0.8% up to 24.26%. Bamboo treated at 100 °C oil had a maximum tensile strength at treatment duration of 60 min with 262.2 MPa. At this treatment temperature, the result showed that less improvement at 30 min, reached a peak at 60 min, and drop at 90 min in tensile strength (Fig. 2).

Next selected bamboo samples were oil treated in a temperature of 130 and 160 °C hot oil with a duration of 30, 60 and 90 min. Bamboos treated 130 and 160 °C hot oil the experimental result showed that high tensile strength at a treatment duration of 30 min as compared to other treatment durations.

The experimental result showed that bamboo treated at 130 °C hot oil with a duration of 30, 60 and 90 min the tensile strength increased to 9.24% up to 17.53% than untreated bamboo. Also, bamboo treated 160 °C oil for 30, 60 and 90 min the tensile strength increased up to 7.29% in a treatment duration between 30 min and 60 min. But bamboo treated for a duration of 90 min decrease to 3.75% than untreated bamboo (Fig. 3).

Bamboo simply soaked in oil for a duration of 2, 4- and 6-days, in this treatment condition the experimental result showed that a significant change in tensile strength as compared to oil heat-treated specimens and untreated bamboo. The improvement of tensile strength up to 36.21%.

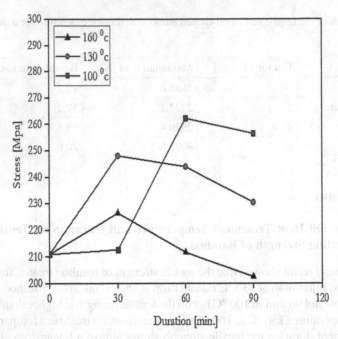

**Fig. 2.** Effect of oil heat treatment on tensile strength of Ethiopian bamboo.

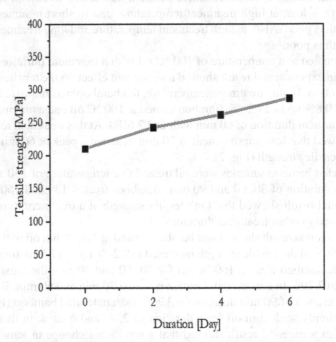

**Fig. 3.** Effect of oil treated without heat on tensile strength of bamboo.

The disadvantage of this treatment condition takes longer treatment duration as compared to oil heat-treated bamboo in the same tensile strength. This shows temperature (heat) is used to speed up the penetration of oil inside the bamboo culm.

When we compare the experimental result of bamboo treated with hot oil and without hot oil, the tensile strength of bamboo treated for a duration of 30, 60 and 90 min at a treatment temperature of 100, 130, and 160 °C the result showed that maximum improvement at one optimum treatment temperature and become drop at longer treatment duration. But bamboo treated by oil without heat or at room temperature for 2, 4 and 6 days the experimental result showed that almost linearly increased its tensile strength up to the end of a longer duration of 6 days (Fig. 4).

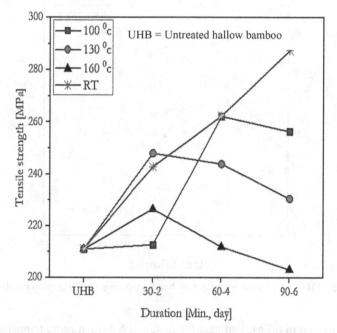

**Fig. 4.** Effect of oil treated with and without heated oil on tensile strength of bamboo

The bending experimental result showed that all treated bamboo had an improved strength. A similar tendency was observed with the tensile strength, indicating that the treatment temperature and duration affecting the bending strength of Ethiopian bamboo.

Bamboo treated at 100 °C oil had a maximum tensile strength at treatment duration of 60 min with 28.01 MPa. Bamboo treated at a temperature of 100 °C oil with a treatment duration of 30, 60- and the 90-min experimental result showed a significant effect on the bending strength of Ethiopian bamboo. In this treatment temperature, the bamboo was improved its bending strength 21.81% up to 128.83%.

Oil heat-treated bamboo at a temperature of 130 and 160 °C for a treatment duration 30 min had high bending strength as compared to other treatment temperatures and durations. The experimental result showed that oil heat-treated bamboo at 130 and 160 °C were 30.88% up to 62.33% and 22.39% up to 137.42% respectively increment in bending strength for a treatment duration of 30, 60 and 90 min.

The bending strength of bamboo treated at 100 °C for 60 min duration and 160 °C for 30 min duration almost the same. This shows that bamboo treated at a lower temperature for the long optimum duration and treated bamboo at high temperature for an optimum short duration the bending strength almost the same. But treat bamboo at a very high temperature for long-duration affects the microstructure of bamboo due to this experimental result showed that the bending strength bamboo treated for 90 min dropped (Fig. 5).

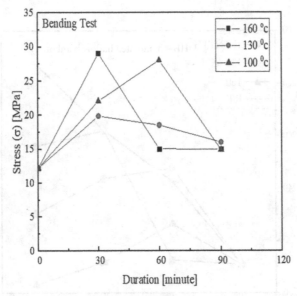

**Fig. 5.** Effect of oil heat treatment on bending strength of Ethiopian bamboo.

Bamboo treated in oil without heat for 2, 4, and 6 days at room temperature experimental result showed that almost a linear change increment in bending strength as the shown figure below (Fig. 6).

Bamboo specimens treated for 30 min with hot oil and 2 days without hot oil the bending strength test result showed greater for 30 min. This shows that the penetration of oil in the bamboo internode is less at a treatment duration of 2 days without hot oil. In another way, samples treated for 30 min with hot oil the temperature speeds up the penetration of oil (Fig. 7).

When we compare the result of oil heat-treated for 60 min and without heat oil-treated for 4 days the experimental result showed that bamboo treated 100 °C oil for 60 min had good bending strength. Bamboo treated at 130 and 160 °C oil for 60 min treatments the test result showed that the bending strength is less than bamboo treated at 100 °C oil with 60 min these shows to the effect of temperature. But without heat oil-treated bamboo for a day the bending strength increased.

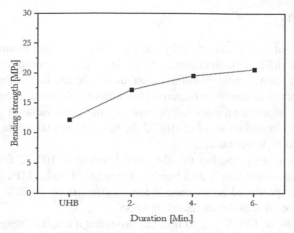

**Fig. 6.** Effect of oil treatment without heat on bending strength of bamboo.

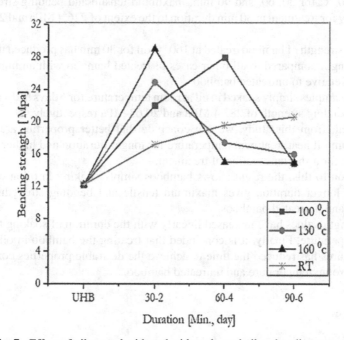

**Fig. 7.** Effect of oil treated with and without heated oil on bending strength

When we compare bamboo treated for 90 min oil heat and 6 days without heated oil the result the bending strength of 90 min bamboo in all treatment temperatures was dropped. Treatment for 90 min with hot oil, the temperature highly affects the microstructure of bamboo. The test result showed that oil heat-treated and without heat-treated bamboo had a significant difference in bending strength at longer treatment duration.

# 5 Conclusions

Results indicate that the uptake of oil by the Ethiopian low land bamboo is different from heated oil at different temperatures and soaking in oil at room temperature. The temperature of oil has a significant influence on the tensile and bending strengths of the bamboo. The effect of treatment in heated oil has minimized the duration to achieve the same value of the required properties. For example, the same value of tensile strength can be obtained by treatment in oil at 100 °C for 60 min. will take 4 days duration for treating in oil at room temperature.

Tensile and bending properties of oil-treated bamboo at 100 °C for 60-min duration have given maximum tensile and bending strengths of 262.2 MPa and 28.01 MPa respectively. It has produced an increase in tensile strength by 24.26% and 56.3% for bending strength relative to the untreated bamboo.

For a treat in oil at 130 °C for 30 min has produced a tensile strength of 248 MPa and a bending strength of 19.87 MPa. When samples are treated at the temperature of the oil at 160 °C for 30, 60, and 90 min, maximum tensile and bending strengths are obtained only for treatment at 30 min duration to the extent of 226.4 MPa and 29.06 MPa respectively.

Bending strength of bamboo treated at 160 °C oil for 30 min has produced the highest bending strength compared to all other cases of treated bamboo with an improvement of 137.42% relative to untreated bamboo.

Bamboo samples simply soaked in oil at room temperature for 6 days had a maximum tensile and bending strength of 287.4 MPa and 20.63 MPa respectively.

In general, from this study, we can conclude that better properties are achieved with minimum oil heat treatment temperature for longer duration and higher treatment temperatures for a shorter duration of treatment.

In addition to this, the result shows bamboos simply soaking in oil at room temperature for longer duration gives maximum tensile and bending strengths than oil heat-treated and untreated bamboos.

The strength values have increased linearly with the duration of soaking time in oil at room temperature. Finally, it is concluded that treating the bamboo in oil at different temperatures has reduced the time to achieve the desirable properties compared to treatment at room temperature and untreated bamboo.

# References

Manalo, R.D., Acda, M.N.: Effects of hot oil treatment on physical and mechanical properties of three species of philippine bamboo. For. Res. Inst. Malaysia **21**(1), 19–24 (2017)

Armandei, M., Fathi, I., Ghavami, K.: Experimental study on variation of mechanical properties of a cantilever beam of bamboo. Constr. Build. Mater. **101**, 784–790 (2015)

Arpa, E.: Advanced composites materials and their manufacture technology. Bioresour. Technol. **10**, 1–37 (2013)

Callister, W.D.J.: Fundamentals of Materials Science and Engineering, 7th edn., pp. 200–589. Wiley, New York (2007)

Costa, M.M.E., et al.: Influence of physical and chemical treatments on the mechanical properties of bamboo fibers. Proc. Eng. **200**, 457–464 (2017)

Bansal, R.K.: Text Book of Strength of Materilas, 3rd edn., pp. 125–130. Laxmi Publisher, New Delhi (2009)

Dubey, M.K.: Improvements in stability, durability and mechanical properties of radiata pine wood after heat-treatment in a vegetable oil. For. Res. Inst. Malaysia **2**, 10–15 (2010)

Embaye, K., Christersson, L., Ledin, S., Weih, M.: Bamboo as bioresource in Ethiopia : Management strategy to improve seedling performance ( oxytenanthera abyssinica ). Biores. Technol. **88**(2003), 33–39 (2003)

Gottron, J., Harries, K.A., Xu, Q.: Creep behaviour of bamboo. Constr. Build. Mater. **66**, 79–88 (2014)

Intertek expert: Tensile properties grips, vol. C, p. 2 (2018). Retrieved from iptl@intertek.com

Journal, P., Science, T.A., Sarawak, T.: The effects of oil boiling treatment on physical properties of bambusa vulgaris var. Striata (buluh gading). Pertinika J. Trop. Agric. Sci. **25**, 823–832 (2012)

Li, T., Cheng, D.L., Walinder, M.E.P., Zhou, D.G.: Wettability of oil heat-treated bamboo and bonding strength of laminated bamboo board. Ind. Crops Prod. **69**, 15–20 (2015)

Mahzuz, H.M.A., Ahmed, M., Dutta, J., Rose, R.H.: Determination of several properties of a bamboo of bangladesh. J. Civ. Eng. Res. **3**(1), 16–21 (2013)

Mallick, P.K.: Fiber- Reinforced Cmposites, 3rd edn., pp. 200–225. CRC Press, New York (2008)

Obispo, S.L.: Optimizing the mechanical characteristics of bamboo, construction and building materials. Master thesis, California Polytechnic State University, San Luis Obispo, pp. 100–125 (2012)

Panda, A., Dyadyura, K., Val, J., Harni˘, M., Zajac, J.: Manufacturing technology of composite materials principles of modification of polymer composite materials technology based on polytetrafluoroethylene. Ind. Crops Prod. **12**, 25–49 (2017)

Richard, M.J.: Physical, chemical, and mechanical properties of bamboo and its utilization potential for fiberboard manufacturing. LSU Master Thesis **1**, 121–125 (2013)

# Adaption of Water Ram Pump for Small-Scale Irrigation

Assefa Asmare Tsegaw[(⊠)]

Bahir Dar Institute of Technology, 6000 Bahir Dar, Ethiopia
assefaa@bdu.edu.et

**Abstract.** A hydraulic ram is a cyclic water pump powered by water hammer effect. The device uses to develop pressure permits a portion of water that powers pump to be elevated to a point higher than where the originally started. The ram is often useful, since it requires no outside source of power other than kinetic energy of flowing water. This paper deals with adaptation of water ram pump for small-scale irrigation. This research conducted making using of ANSYS, computational fluid dynamics. Different configurations of waste valves have been designed, checked and investigation results recorded. Investigations show that height testes effect on drive head, delivery head, pipe cross sections, design and arrangements of waste valve, flow rate and velocity. The final optimum ram pump has designed, developed and tested for small-scale irrigation and household purpose. It is observed that at a river flow rate of 9 L/min and head of 5 m, hydraulic ram pumps water at a flow rate of 0.7 L/min for 37M head. This typical test shows raising of water up to 740% with respect to height can be achievable. Moreover, this pump can extensively be utilized in rural areas where water is flowing in gorge areas for 7/24 at no expense of extra power utilized.

**Keywords:** Hydraulic ram · Elevation · Head · CFD · Kinetic energy · Waste valve

## 1 Introduction

Even though Ethiopia has plenty of water sources, the burden of fetching water for household and irrigation system is a hard work for women and children (Fig. 1) since rivers are flowing somewhat deep in valleys. Hydraulic ram pumps are one of the most historical and significant water delivery device which use power from the water flow to lift to some extent of elevation greater than the original sources of water [1–5]. They are used in rural areas where there is no electricity and other sources of supply of energy for small scale irrigations, household and other purposes. There is no need of external power to drive the pump [6–9].

© ICST Institute for Computer Sciences, Social Informatics and Telecommunications Engineering 2021
Published by Springer Nature Switzerland AG 2021. All Rights Reserved
M. A. Delele et al. (Eds.): ICAST 2020, LNICST 385, pp. 216–224, 2021.
https://doi.org/10.1007/978-3-030-80618-7_14

Even though the drive energy for hydraulic ram pumps is gravity, its different components and their special arrangements play significant role in lifting the water up [10–16]. A simple hydraulic ram pimp has five main components, namely, inlet pipe, check valve, waste valve, pressure chamber and delivery pipe. Inlet pipe is the pipe through which the water gets into the pump. The water then flows into the waste pipe and closes the waste valve. The water that closed the waste valve flows against the newly entering water and build up a higher pressure that exceeds the pressure on the delivery valve. This pressure differential lifts the water up to some elevations through the delivery valve [9, 17–19]. As some of the water is lifted up through the drive pipe, the remaining is also wasted through the waste valve. The check valve permits water to flow only in one direction and does not allow reverse flow.

Hydraulic ram pumps are simple in construction and have very small initial costs compared to power driven pumps. They also do not require fuel supply as they are driven by gravity only. Ram pumps are also environmentally friendly for they have zero emissions. Operating ram pumps and maintenance is also very simple as just cleaning the drive way [9, 10, 15, 20].

Water is the most essential resource for the agricultural growth in animal husbandry, irrigation and crop productions. Especially in countries like Ethiopia which mainly depends on agriculture, the increment in the supply of water will increase the growth of the sector. Water is also highly available in Ethiopia, despite of its accessibility. Most of the places where agricultural operations are made are highly mountainous. In contrast springs, rivers, and streams are found in valleys. To find water, farmers must go down, fetch some and then go back up the hill to use the water, which is very laborious. Even though, using power driven pumps is possible, the economical limitations remain as barriers because power driven pumps are expensive. Rural areas do not even have any other means of finding energy that can be manipulated to pump the water. These problems of extreme geographic and economic in-capabilities remain as threat for access of water.

Farmers in the rural areas of Ethiopia do not have access for both electricity and other means of obtaining energy. Though there are plenty of water sources, the people settle in higher place in pursue of loam lands. Thus, they are found at higher elevation compared to the rivers. Hydraulic ram pumps have a great potential of solving these problems [3].

The hydraulic ram pump gives a great benefit for growing crops cultivation and drinking water for animals. The adaption of this mechanism takes place especially for the low level of irrigation purpose to maximize the production capacity such as crops, vegetables, and animal breeding through the water lifting system.

**Fig. 1.** Traditional water transporting

## 2 Hydraulic Ram Pump Design

A hydraulic ram pump has been design based on the input parameters such as intake flow rate, intake head, intake temperature and pressure. Technical parameters in design consideration of ram pump is shown in Fig. 2 [21]. Figure 3 shows basic components of the hydraulic ram pump.

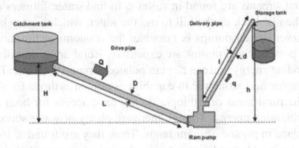

**Fig. 2.** Design consideration of ramp pump

$$\frac{L}{H} = 3 - 7, \quad \frac{L}{D} = 100 - 1000 \tag{1}$$

$$q = f \times \frac{H \times Q}{h} \tag{2}$$

Where:

L, Length of drive pipe
H, Supply head
h, Delivery head
D, Diameter of drive pipe
Q, Supply flow rate
f, Efficiency factor

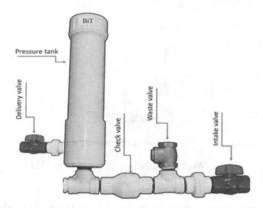

**Fig. 3.** Photo of manufactured hydraulic ram pump

## 3 Experimental Setup

Experimental setup of hydraulic ram pump testing is shown in the Fig. 4. On the left-hand side, the supply tank is placed at input heads of 4, 5 and 6 m. The input flow rate is kept constant at 9 L/min. The output flow rate and the output heads are measured in the right-hand side. The water that has been pushed up by the hydraulic ram pump is accumulated in the delivery tank placed higher than the supply tank.

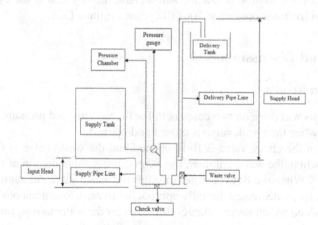

**Fig. 4.** Experimental setup

At first, the waste valve allows some of water to exit, subsequently it is the nonpumped water as shown in Fig. 5(a) will open due to gravity (or by help of a light spring) and water will flow down to the drive pipe source [23]. As the flow rushes, the water pressure at waste valve and the static pressure in the body of the ram pump will increase up to the resulting forces overcome the weight of the waste valve and start to close it.

As valve opening cuts, the water pressure in the ram pump body increases quickly and bangs the waste valve closed, as shown in Fig. 5(b) [4]. The dynamic column of

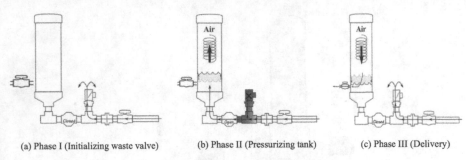

(a) Phase I (Initializing waste valve)     (b) Phase II (Pressurizing tank)     (c) Phase III (Delivery)

**Fig. 5.** Working principle of ram pump [22]

liquid in the intake pipe is no longer able to exit via the waste valve, so its velocity must suddenly diminution; this continues to cause a considerable rise of pressure which forces open the valve to the air-chamber.

As pressure surpasses the static delivery head, water will be forced up the pressure chamber, as shown in Fig. 5(c) [24]. Air trapped in the pressure chamber is instantaneously compressed to a pressure beyond the delivery pressure. Eventually, the water in the output pipe arises to a standstill and the static pressure in the tank then cascades to close the supply head. The output valve will then close, when the pressure in the air chamber beats that in the casing.

When the delivery valve shuts, the reduced pressure in the ram pump body will permit the waste valve to drop below its own weight, thereby letting the cycle start all over again. Most hydrams operate at 50–110 cycles a minute [25].

## 4   Results and Discussions

### 4.1   Simulation Results

The CFD analysis was done on two cases both for the velocity and pressure. Both cases ae investigated when the check valve is closed and opened.

Case 1: when the check valve is fully opened and the waste valve is fully closed: this is the case where the water hammer, the main driving phenomenon of the pumping system, happens. When the flow of water through the waste valve encounters a sudden encounter the velocity decreases, literally approaches to zero. Simultaneously the check valve is fully opened which means a larger flow area for the water to pass through which leads to a relatively lower velocity at a given mass flow rate. But it is still higher than the velocity near the waste valve (Fig. 6).

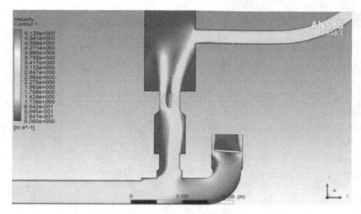

**Fig. 6.** Velocity contour when check valve is fully opened and waste valve is fully closed.

In this case, the pressure reaches its maximum due to the water hammers. This effect of the water hammer reaches back to check valve fully opening it to allow the fluid blocked by the waste valve to pass through the delivery valve (Fig. 7).

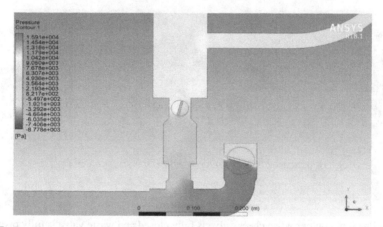

**Fig. 7.** Pressure contour when check valve is fully opened and waste valve is fully closed.

Case 2: when the check valve is fully closed and the waste valve is fully opened: in this case almost all the water coming through the drive pipe passes through the waste valve with almost the same velocity it enters the drive pipe except the effect of friction losses and minor head loses of elbow nature of the pipe at the end which have a cumulative effect of increasing velocity as shown below (Fig. 8).

The pressure throughout the whole pumping system varies with pipe area and against velocity. The respective angular positions of both the valves and corresponding pressure variation is related as follows.

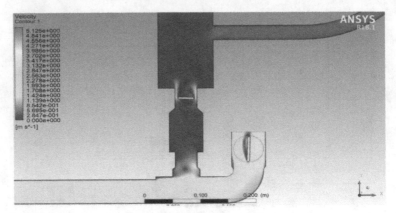

**Fig. 8.** Velocity contour when check valve is fully closed and waste valve is fully opened

Since there no obstacle applied to the flow of water through the waste valve, which literally means no water hammer, the pressure throughout the pumping system is almost uniform. The whole water is directly exhausted through the waste valve (Fig. 9).

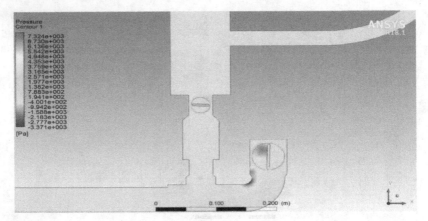

**Fig. 9.** Pressure contour when check valve is fully closed and waste valve is fully opened.

## 4.2 Test Results

As shown in Table 1, three successive tests have been made. On each of them, by varying the intake head, the output flow rate and the delivery head have been recorded.

For the same input flow rate of 9 L/min, by varying the input head, different results have been found. As the input head decreases, the output flow rate, the delivery head and the efficiency have also increased. The main reason is the potential energy that is gained by the increase in head.

**Table 1.** Test results

| Test | Input flow rate (L/min) | Input head (m) | Output flow rate (L/min) | Delivery head (m) | Efficiency (%) |
|------|-------------------------|----------------|--------------------------|-------------------|----------------|
| 1 | 9 | 4 | 0.6 | 25 | 40.32 |
| 2 | 9 | 5 | 0.7 | 37 | 57.20 |
| 3 | 9 | 6 | 0.75 | 45 | 60.5 |

## 5  Conclusions

Using the proper methods of designing, all components have been designed. Based on the design, using locally available materials the pressure chamber and its cups are manufactured. The remaining components such as gate valves, waste valves, union and nipples are purchased based on their corresponding specifications. From a vertical fall of 4 m and 5 m height and at an input flow rate of 9 L/min, it delivers minimum amount of water of 0.6 L/min and 0.7 L/min to a vertical lift of 25 m and 37 m. At 6 m head of input, with the same input flow rate, the 0.75 L/min and 45 m of output flow rate and delivery head are obtained. These test results infer that, as the input head increases, the delivery head also increases. The relation between the input head and the efficiency and the output flow rate are also similarly direct proportional. Hydraulic ram can assist farmers and other users by neglecting operating costs for their farms and livestock. It can be easily adapted by small scale farms be-cause of its low installation cost, neglecting its operating cost, and free from maintaining costs.

## References

1. Balgude, R.D., Rupanavar, S.P., Bagul, P.S., Ramteke, M.R.: Designing of hydraulic ram pump. Int. J. Eng. Comput. Sci. **4**, 11966–11971 (2015)
2. Celik, E.: Interactive ram pump display project. In: ASME 2012 International Mechanical Engineering Congress and Exposition, American Society of Mechanical Engineers Digital Collection, pp. 59–68 (2012)
3. Deo, A., Pathak, A., Khune, S., Pawar, M.: Design methodology for hydraulic ram pump. Int. J. Innov. Res. Sci. Technol. **5**, 4737–4745 (2016)
4. Diwan, P., Patel, A., Sahu, L.: Design and fabrication of hydraulic ram with methods of improving efficiency. Int. J. Curr. Eng. Sci. Res. (IJCESR) **3**, 5–13 (2016)
5. Folk, J.E.: Water powered ram pump. In: Google Patents (1993)
6. Hathorn, T.F., Maurice, T.J.: High speed reciprocating ram pump. In: Google Patents (1941)
7. Hatipoğlu, T., Nakay, İ, Köksal, E., Fığlalı, A.: Feasibility analysis of a hydraulic ram pump investment project. Arab. J. Geosci. **11**(9), 1–4 (2018). https://doi.org/10.1007/s12517-018-3491-9
8. Inthachot, M., Saehaeng, S., Max, J.F., Müller, J., Spreer, W.: Hydraulic ram pumps for irrigation in Northern Thailand. Agric. Agric. Sci. Proc. **5**, 107–114 (2015)
9. Jeffery, T., Thomas, T., Smith, A., Glover, P., Fountain, P.: Hydraulic ram pumps: a guide to ram pump water supply systems (1992)
10. Maw, Y., Hte, Z.: Design of 15 meter head hydraulic ram pump. Int. J. Sci. Eng. Technol. Research **3**, 2177–2181 (2014)

11. Mohammed, S.N.: Design and construction of a hydraulic ram pump. Leonardo Electron. J. Pract. Technol. **11**, 59–70 (2007)
12. Moody, P.E.: Underwater rapid-fire ram pump. In: Google Patents (1992)
13. Sheikh, S., Handa, C., Ninawe, A.: Design methodology for hydraulic ram pump (hydram). Int. J. Mech. Eng. Robot. Res. **2**, 170–175 (2013)
14. Yang, K., Li, J., Guo, Y., Guo, X., Fu, H., Wang, T.: Design and hydraulic performance of a Novel hydraulic ram pump (2014)
15. Young, B.: Design of hydraulic ram pump systems. Proc. Inst. Mech. Eng. Part A: J. Power Energy **209**, 313–322 (1995)
16. Young, B.: Design of homologous ram pumps (1997)
17. Mills, A.: The hydraulic ram (or impulse) pump. Phys. Educ. **49**, 211 (2014)
18. Young, B.: Generic design of ram pumps. Proc. Inst. Mech. Eng. Part A: J. Power Energy **212**, 117–124 (1998)
19. Thomas, T.: Disseminating ram-pump technology (1994)
20. Sobieski, W., Grygo, D., Lipiński, S.: Measurement and analysis of the water hammer in ram pump. Sādhanā **41**(11), 1333–1347 (2016). https://doi.org/10.1007/s12046-016-0560-1
21. Fatahi-Alkouhi, R., Lashkar-Ara, B., Keramat, A.: On the measurement of ram-pump power by changing in water hammer pressure wave energy. Ain Shams Eng. J. **10**, 681–693 (2019)
22. I. workshop, Hydraulic Ram Pump (2019)
23. Suarda, M., Sucipta, M., Dwijana, I.: Investigation on flow pattern in a hydraulic ram pump at various design and setting of its waste valve. In: IOP Conference Series: Materials Science and Engineering, p. 012008. IOP Publishing (2019)
24. Suarda, M., Ghurri, A., Sucipta, M., Kusuma, I.G.B.W.: Investigation on characterization of waste valve to optimize the hydraulic ram pump performance. In: AIP Conference Proceedings, p. 020023. AIP Publishing LLC (2018)
25. Nambiar, P., Shetty, A., Thatte, A., Lonkar, S., Jokhi, V.: Hydraulic ram pump: maximizing efficiency. In: 2015 International Conference on Technologies for Sustainable Development (ICTSD), pp. 1–4. IEEE (2015)

# Identification of Process Parameters and Optimization Techniques for AA 6061 in FSW: State-of-the-art

Eyob Messele Sefene[✉] 🆔 and Assefa Asmare Tsegaw

Bahir Dar Institute of Technology, Bahir Dar, Ethiopia
Eyob.Meseele@bdu.edu.et

**Abstract.** Friction Stir Welding (FSW) is a new method of solid state joining of metals and nonmetals as a substitute technology applied in high strength alloys that are challenging in joining processes in traditional ways. At this contemporary epoch, many transportation industries utilize friction stir welding by its light weight higher strength weld properties. However, many problems are associated and diminution on the weld quality by a shortage of skills. One of the key challenges is selecting an appropriate optimization techniques and process parameters for single and multiple response studies. The current scenario, focused on the determination and identification of appropriate process parameters and optimization techniques for welding of AA6061 material using friction stir welding. All process parameters and optimization methods are intensively studied from the previous kinds of literature and identified appropriate process parameters for AA6061 materials. Based on the results, process parameters namely rotational speed at 43.7%, traverse speed at 17.29%, tool tilt angle 7.46%, axial force of 7.09%, ratio of tool shoulder-to-pin size 3.69%, other parameters are 1.73% contributions for achieving higher mechanical properties (tensile and hardness) of AA6061.

**Keywords:** Process parameters · ANN · GA · GRA · RSM · Taguchi

## 1 Introduction

One of the methods of joining methods at solid state is friction stir welding. This technique termed as 'ecological sound' method because of energy effectiveness and environmentally friendly. Friction stir welding invented in Cambridge, UK by Wayne Thomas and his coworker in 1991 [1, 2]. This joining process is applied widely for similar and non-similar metallic and non-metallic materials in manufacturing sectors especially in transportation industries such as aerospace, rail ways, defense, wagons and other micro-electronics due to for many mechanical property advantages [3–9]. It provides numerous advantages over conventional welding such as a higher weld bead strength than weight ratio, it does not utilize consumable electrode and filler materials, less power consumption, significantly low HAZ, and there is no smoking during joining process [10–12]. At this contemporary epoch, the usage of magnesium alloy is exponentially increased due

M. A. Delele et al. (Eds.): ICAST 2020, LNICST 385, pp. 225–244, 2021.
https://doi.org/10.1007/978-3-030-80618-7_15

to higher strength-to-weight ratio. Magnesium is about 30% lighter than aluminum and four times lighter than steel with density of 1.8 g/cm$^3$ [12]. AA6061 is categorized under 6xxx series of aluminium alloy and the major constitutes element are magnesium and silicon, respectively. It has a good mechanical property, easily weldable, considered as a common alloy for general uses and in aerospace applications; it is used to construct wing and fuel silage parts [13–15]. The main aim of this study is to determine and identify appropriate process parameters and optimization techniques for the quality criteria on tensile and hardness strengths of AA 6061material by friction stir welding method.

## 2  Process Parameters of FSW

In design of experiments while optimization is going to be carried out, there are at least two main process parameters; controllable and fixed ones. Controllable parameters are those parameters where one can control based on the specified levels during execution of experiment. While, fixed parameters are parameters which will not altered throughout the experiments [16]. FSW process parameters namely controllable and fixed are summarized and shown in Fig. 1.

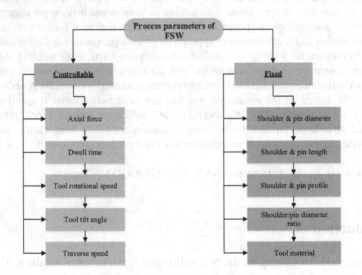

**Fig. 1.** Process parameters of FSW [17]

The above shown process parameters plays a dynamic role in affecting the quality criteria of point of interest plus the metallurgical properties of the weldment [17–20]. Therefore, to get admirable welding quality, optimization of the process parameters is the best alternative.

### 2.1  Control Process Parameters

**Axial Force:** Axial force which tends to hold pressurizing the weldment has a significant role in a proper mixing of heated materials. This force will impede formation of cavities in the retarding side of the weldment [21]. Higher axial force induces higher generation of heat in the base metals. Owing to the higher heat input, metal gets softened and extruded as flash, resulting tunnel defect in the middle of base metals. This force has no major alteration on microhardness at the nugget region. However, tensile strength corresponding to the axial force of the tool [22, 23].

**Dwell Time:** The duration of tool that plunged into the weld material at desired depth and a given rotational speed without translational motion is referred to this time. It is the most foremost joining process parameter for weldment strength next to rotational speed and welding speed or traverse speed [24].

**Tool Rotational Speed:** Prime motion imparted to the tool is one of the most dominant process parameters. This dominant process parameter is rotational speed of a tool. This rotational speed produces a substantial heat and string effect which will help to mix material flows. With the traverse movement of this tool with rotating at a certain number it moves the soften material from front to back and completing the weldment. It is the highest and most influential parameter [25, 26]. A higher rotational speed produces higher temperature and abandoned wider heat-affected zone on the base metals [27].

**Tool Tilt Angle:** The angle between the tool axis and the nominal axis of base metal referred as tilt angle. Tool tilt has a significant effect on generation of heat, metal follow movement, and consolidation. Tool tilt angle helps in impeding of flowing materials from being ejected [28]. The higher tool tilt angle may increase the wear rate of a tool and even further failure [29].

Traverse Speed: In some other words-welding speed. This parameter is one of the influential process parameters. On selecting of levels on influential process parameters, care shall be taken. The lower welding speed produces fine grain structure and exhibits with the best corrosion resistant [30] and also, the peak temperature and heat input of the joint increases during the process. On the other hand, higher welding speed will yield in higher mechanical properties of (hardness and tensile), but lower elongation of joint [31].

## 2.2  Fixed Process Parameters

Fixed process parameters are those of process parameters where no alteration is carried out throughout the experimental execution.

**Tool Profile (Pin):** The movement of heated and sot material will be governed by the shape and geometrical shape of the pin. This movement will significantly influence the plasticizing of material [32, 33].

**Tool Design**

- Geometric configuration shall be uncomplicated as to minimize the cost of a tool.

- It shall be able to move and stir substantial amount of material.

Tool design is a curial part of the design in this kind of joining process. Heat generation is dependent on a kind and type of tool configuration. This design section includes two main parts; shoulder and pin [34].

**Tool Geometry-Shoulder (D):** In solid state (friction stir) joining method, heat is generated through rotational speed with the help of tool shoulder geometry. The friction of sticking and sliding is depending on the tool shoulder geometry [35].

Tool geometry-pin length: one of the prime factors in friction stir joining method tool design is the design and choice of the pin length. For one sided friction welding process, the pin length and the thickness of base metal shall not be equal. If the length of the tool pin and the base metal is equal the weldment will not be effective. According to the study, the pin length must be at least less than 0.3 mm than the base metal. With this size of the pin, the shoulder should touch the base metal surface and root will be good [35].

**Tool Geometry-Pin Size (d):** One of the most notable process parameters is the pin size (diameter). This geometry will affect the weldment mechanical property and the weld cross sectional area. This is because the stirring in the weld is mainly caused by the pin dynamic motion [36]. It greatly affects the size of the weld region [37].

Tool geometry-D/d ratio: the ratio of the tool geometry shoulder diameter to pin diameter is one of the most essential process parameters in friction stir welding process [38].

**Tool Material:** In all the tool geometry, selection of tool material is very important. Since, friction stir welding is a process of joining by making use of heat generated in the tool and the base metal, selection of tool material is undoubtably very vital. A noble tool material shall have the following features:

- good strength and wear resistance
- good dimensional consistency
- good coefficient of friction between the base metal
- nonreactive with the base metal
- good machinability for ease of shaping
- good hot hardness
- affordable cost [35, 39].

## 3  Design of Experiment

Design of experiment (DOE) is an efficient way of executing experiment. In addition to this, this can help to analyzing and interoperating results [40, 41]. The method defines and examining all the possible combinations and situations in conducting experiments. Design of experiment commonly used for comparison, variable screening, transfer function identification, system optimization and robust design [40, 42].

## 3.1  Selection of Orthogonal Array

In the process of determination, the optimal process parameters, the combination of possible number of trials and parameter settings are arranged in systematic way to cut out the volume of experimental executions [43]. This orthogonal array is developed from Latin square. Before considering the type of orthogonal array there must be considering two points:

- number of controllable process parameters
- number of levels within the construable process parameters.

In addition to this, to choose sustainable OA, total degrees of freedom (DOF) are calculated. The DOF are the number of contrasts to make between design parameters. For example, a three-level design parameter counts for two degrees of freedom [45].

## 3.2  Optimization Methods of FSW for AA 6061

There are different and numerous kinds of optimization techniques employed in process parameters optimization of AA 6061 material. Some of them are discussed below.

**Artificial Neural Network (ANN):** ANN is biological inspired computational app-roach optimization technique. ANN is like human neural configuration which can learn from the past memory and envisaging to the future [46, 47]. This kind of optimization method is capable of solving un-anticipated dynamic problem. The performance of ANN is measured by the error between the outcome, training time, the complexity of the system [48]. ANN is widely used for medicine, finance, engineering, geology, physics and opti-mization process. The process is widely used in mono and multi-responses optimization processes. The basic steps involved in ANN are shown in Fig. 2.

**Genetic Algorism (GA):** GA is a search, computational and optimization algorithm inspired by natural evolution. This method was introduced by Jhon Holand in 1970 [51–54]. This algorithm employs Darwin theory of evolution and used layered coding to show the slicing process [55, 56]. GA espouses the productive strategy, which is based on the proper amount, to calculate the relative adaptive value of the individual and decide how much the probability is to put in to a mating pool and make the next round of optimization [57]. This optimization process used to analyze single and multiple responses optimiza-tion processes. The application areas of the GA are the parametric design of aircraft, robotic trajectory generation, strategy acquisition for simulated airplanes, scheduling medical diagnostics, identifying criminal suspects, data science and may more [58, 59].

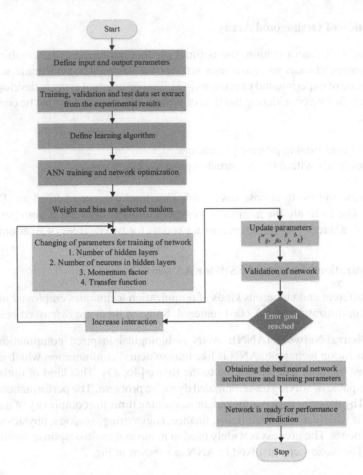

**Fig. 2.** Flowchart of artificial neural network [49, 50]

The flow step of genetic algorithm is shown in Fig. 3 below.

**Grey Relational Analysis (GRA):** GRA is a method for making decision based on Grey method. This method is developed by Deng Julong in 1989. This method utilized in advanced way of Taguchi optimization method. One of the drawbacks of Taguchi method is it considers only single response. However, GRA is useful in making of multiple response optimization [60–63]. Generally, this method converts multi response quality criteria in to single one. However, the drawback of this method is it is not suitable for mono response [64]. The procedures for establishment of this method is shown in Fig. 4.

**Response Surface Method (RSM):** RMS is a group of mathematical and statistical method designed by Box and Wilson in 1951. This technique utilized for the design of experiments describes the relationship between process variables and product quality characteristics [70–72]. This method can check the interaction between factors under

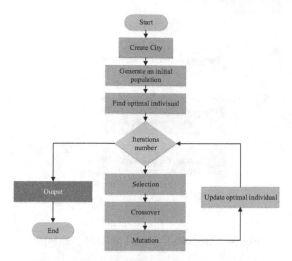

**Fig. 3.** Flowchart of Genetic Algorithm [51, 59]

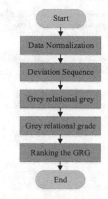

**Fig. 4.** Flowcharts of grey relational analysis method [65–69]

different conditions [73, 74]. In addition to this, it is suitable for single and multiple response optimization method [75]. The key pro of RMS is a reduced number of experimental trails required to assess multiple parameters and their interactions [76]. This method can be further applicable in many optimization fields [70, 71, 77] (Fig. 5).

**Taguchi Method:** This method is developed by the late Dr. Genechi Taguchi in 1940 [78, 79]. This method is for universal field of specialization [79, 80]. This method is applicable making use of orthogonal array scheme [79, 81]. Moreover, the method data interpretation is carried out by utilizing signal-to-noise ratio analysis. Signal-to-noise ratio is a measure of robustness of the system [82, 83]. Generally, the process is suitable for optimizing the mono response quality criterion. The flow step of this method is shown in Fig. 6 below.

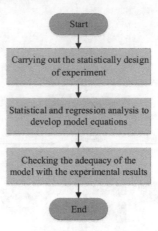

**Fig. 5.** Chronological steps of RSM [72, 74]

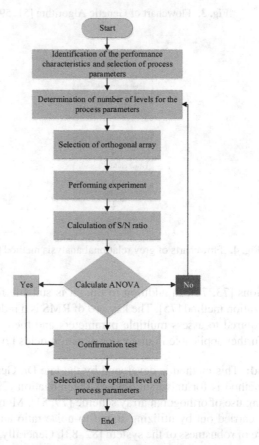

**Fig. 6.** Chronological flowcharts of Taguchi method [84–87]

# 4 Results and Discussions

## 4.1 Determination of Parameters

With all the possible combinations of all control process parameters filtered out by different mechanism; like fish bone diagram or cause and effect, experimental trails executed and results recorded. With making use of suitable optimization method, the possible combination of optimum parameters will be determined. Statistically determination of the analysis of variance will then conducted to find out the significance of control process parameters. Different scholars using ANOVA to identify parameters of how much percent contributing to the response of the study. Therefore, in the present study, reviewed and

**Table 1.** Determination of process parameters

Parameters with % contribution

| No | A.F | T.S | R.S | T.A | T.P.P | D/d | DT | DTP | PD | NºP | Error | Reference |
|----|-----|-----|-----|-----|-------|-----|----|-----|----|-----|-------|-----------|
| 1 | 38 | 11 | 51 | | | | | | | | 0 | [18] |
| 2 | 21.8 | 26.1 | 49.7 | | | | | | | | 2.4 | [88] |
| 3 | | 9.32 | 70.44 | | | 19.10 | | | | | 1.14 | [89] |
| 4 | | | 32.08 | 48.17 | | 17.53 | | | | | 2.19 | [90] |
| 5 | 6.9 | 18.43 | 74.67 | | | | | | | | | [91] |
| 6 | | 50.63 | 19.17 | 8.20 | | | 21.98 | | | | | [92] |
| 7 | 28.3 | 28.3 | 67 | | | | | | | | 3.3 | [93] |
| 8 | | 20.6 | 12.30 | 26.3 | | | | | | | 40.67 | [94] |
| 9 | | 33 | 62 | | | | | | | 5 | | [95] |
| 10 | 21.5 | 22.4 | 24.68 | | 26.23 | | | | | | 5.11 | [96] |
| 11 | | 34.8 | 47.30 | 8.79 | | | | | | | 9.04 | [97] |
| 12 | 21 | 33 | 41 | | | | | | | | 5 | [98] |
| 13 | | 6.14 | 53.0 | 36.9 | | | | | | | | [99] |
| 14 | | 38.0 | 24.4 | 33.8 | | | | | | | 3.8 | [100] |
| 15 | | 2.60 | 15.2 | | 74.49 | | | | | | 7.65 | [101] |
| 16 | 0.29 | 11.0 | 59.2 | | | | | | | | 29.39 | [102] |
| 17 | | 13.5 | 67.2 | 15 | | | | | | | 4.3 | [103] |
| 18 | 17.6 | 35.3 | 46.2 | | | | | | | | 0.64 | [44] |
| 19 | | 15.45 | 80.45 | | | | | | 3.92 | | 0.17 | [104] |
| 20 | 15 | 35 | 19 | | 23 | | | | | | 8 | [105] |
| 21 | | 23.8 | 65.2 | 6.3 | | | | | | | 4.7 | [106] |
| 22 | | 8.25 | 58.05 | | | | | 33.1 | | | 0.6 | [107] |
| 23 | | 0.03 | | | 38.12 | 58.6 | | | | | 3.23 | [108] |
| 24 | | | 96.24 | 0.06 | 0.41 | | | | | | 3.29 | [109] |

***Where:*A.F**: Axial force,**T.S**: Traverse speed, **R.S**: Rotational speed, **T.A**: Tilt angle, **T.P.P**: Tool pin profile, **D/d**: Shoulder diameter/tool diameter ratio, **DT**: Dwell time, **DTP**: Diameter of tool pin, **PD**: Plunge depth, **NºP**: Nº of pass.

determined the most significant process parameters that strongly improved the hardness and tensile strength of AA 6061 are study. Parameters collected from previous similar studies by looking at its percent of contributions on the above responses and make it an average to identify appropriate parameters for AA 6061 materials (Table 1 and Fig. 7).

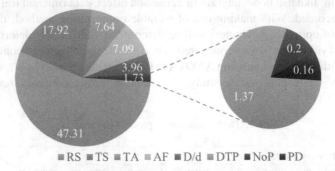

■ RS ■ TS ■ TA ■ AF ■ D/d ■ DTP ■ NoP ■ PD

**Fig. 7.** Determination of process parameters for FSW

Grounded to the above table and figure, rotational speed of 47.31%, traverses speed of 17.92%, tool tilt angle 7.64%, axial force 7.09% D/d ratio 3.96%, and other parameters are 1.73% contribute for getting a higher hardness and tensile strength of AA6061. The prime mover, rotational speed, welding speed, tool inclination angle, and central force are most critical and capital virtue process parameters for AA 6061 materials as per their weights (Table 2).

## 4.2   Determination of Optimization Techniques

**Table 2.** Determination of optimization techniques for 6061 AA materials

| No | Parameter | Optimization techniques | Material | Reference |
|----|-----------|------------------------|----------|-----------|
| 1 | R.S, W.S & A.F | ANN | 6061AA | [110] |
| 2 | R.S, & W.S | ANN | 6061AA & 7075AA | [111] |
| 3 | R.S, & W.S | ANN & RSM | 6061AA | [112] |
| 4 | R.S, W.S, & A.F | ANN & Taguchi | 6061AA & 2024AA | [44] |
| 5 | Sd, Sgd, Pl, P.A, Pd, & P.L | ANN & Taguchi | AA6061-T6 | [113] |
| 6 | R.S, W.S, A.F, & P.P | GA & RSM | 2024AA & 6061AA | [114] |
| 7 | R.S, W.S, and A.F | GA & RSM | 6061AA & 2014AA | [102] |

*(continued)*

**Table 2.** (*continued*)

| No | Parameter | Optimization techniques | Material | Reference |
|----|-----------|------------------------|----------|-----------|
| 8 | R.S, W.S, A.F, and P.P | GRA & RSM | 2024AA & 6061AA | [96] |
| 9 | R.S, W.S, A.F, Pl, Sd, & Pd | GRA & RSM | 6061AA | [115] |
| 10 | R.S, A.F, P.P, & Al.M | GRA & RSM | 6061AA & 7075AA | [116] |
| 11 | R.S, W.S, A.F, & P.P | GRA & RSM | AA6061-T6 & 2024AA | [117] |
| 12 | R.S, W.S, Pl, & Od | GRA & Taguchi | AA6061-T6 | [118] |
| 13 | R.S, W.S, & Td | GRA &Taguchi | 5083AA & 6061AA | [104] |
| 14 | Ts.P, A.F, R.S, W.S & T.A | GRA & Taguchi | 7075AA & 6061AA | [119] |
| 15 | R.S, W.S, & Pl | GRA & Taguchi | 6061AA | [120] |
| 16 | R.S, W.S, & P.P | GRA & Taguchi | AA6061-T6 & AA7075-T6 | [121] |
| 17 | R.S, W.S, & A.F | GRA & Taguchi | AA6061-T6 | [91] |
| 18 | R.S, W.S, A.F, & P.P | RSM | 6061AA & 7039AA | [122] |
| 19 | R.S, W.S, A.F, Pd, Th, & Sd | RSM | 6061-T6 | [123] |
| 20 | R.S, & W.S | RSM | 6061AA | [124] |
| 21 | R.S, W.S, T.A, Pl, Pd, & Sd | RSM | 6061AA | [125] |
| 22 | R.S, W.S, T.A, & P.P | RSM | AA6061-T6 | [126] |
| 23 | R.S, W.S, & A.F | RSM | AA6061-T6 | [4] |
| 24 | R.S, W.S, Sd, & T.A | RSM | AA5083-H12 & AA6061-T6 | [127] |
| 25 | R.S, W.S, & A.F | RSM | AA6061-T6 & AA7075-T6 | [128] |
| 26 | R.S, W.S, & T.A | Taguchi | AA6061-T6 & AA6951-T6 | [97] |
| 27 | R.S, W.S, & T.A | Taguchi | AA6061-T6 & AA5083-H321 | [100] |
| 28 | R.S, W.S, & Tsd | Taguchi | 6061-T6 | [129] |

(*continued*)

**Table 2.** (*continued*)

| No | Parameter | Optimization techniques | Material | Reference |
|----|-----------|------------------------|----------|-----------|
| 29 | R.S, W.S, & T.A | Taguchi | 6061-T6 & AA5083-H321 | [103] |
| 30 | R.S, W.S, & N.P | Taguchi | Al6061-Al7075 | [95] |
| 31 | R.S, W.S, and T.A | Taguchi | 6061-T6 and AA5083-H321 | [106] |
| 32 | R.S, W.S, & T.A | Taguchi | 5083AA & 6061AA | [94] |
| 33 | R.S, W.S, & A.F | Taguchi | 6061AA | [18] |
| 34 | R.S, W.S, & P.P | Taguchi | 6061AA | [130] |
| 35 | R.S, W.S, & T.A | Taguchi | AA6061-T6 & AA2024-T0 | [131] |
| 36 | R.S, W.S, & A.F | Taguchi | 6061AA | [88] |
| 37 | R.S, W.S, & T.A | Taguchi | 6061AA | [132] |
| 38 | R.S, W.S, & T.A | Taguchi | 6061AA | [133] |
| 39 | R.S, W.S, & A.F | Taguchi | AA6061-T4 | [93] |

*Where:* **R.S** = Rotational speed, **W.S** = Welding speed, **A.F** = Axial force, **P.P** = Pin profile, **T.A** = Tilt angle, **N.P** = Number of pass, **Tsd** = Tool shoulder diameter, **Pl** = Pin length, **Pd** = Tool geometry-Pin diameter, **Sd** = tool geometry-Shoulder diameter, **Th** = Tool hardness, **Sgd** = Shoulder groove depth, **P.A** = Pin angle, **P.L** = Pin lead, **Al.M** = Aluminum material, **Td** = Tool depth, **Od** = Offset distance, **Ts.P** = Thickness of plate.

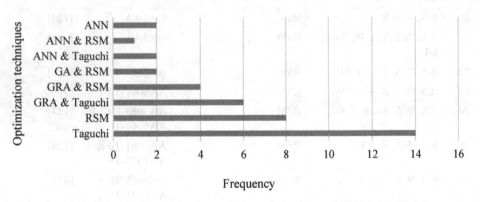

**Fig. 8.** Utilization of optimization techniques for welding of 6061 AA materials

Grounded on the above table and figure, scholars frequently used Taguchi and RSM tools respectively, to optimize a single response for 6061 AA materials. On the other hand, they used GRA, ANN, and GA for multi-objective response optimization (Fig. 8).

# 5    Conclusions

In this review research, process parameters of AA 6061 material optimization methods are extensively studied and summarized for further utilization. Based on the reviews the following conclusions are drawn out:

- Friction stir welding is significantly affected by choice of control process parameters. Hence, as a first step of optimization process sorting and selection of these possible process parameters are very crucial. They impart maximum hardness and tensile strength because the lower traverse speed and higher rotational speed, tilt angle, and axial forces are produced adequate heat for joining the base metal.
- Most of the researchers frequently used Taguchi and RSM optimization techniques respectively, to optimize welding parameters for 6061 AA materials. However, the Taguchi method is only used for mono objective responses. Correspondingly, RSM is used for complex optimization calculation processes, but it is suitable for the number of independent variables that are less than three. However, Taguchi and RSM techniques are simple and suitable to optimize *single responses.*
- ANN and GA are given dynamic results due to its biological approach algorithms but it's complicated and long processes related to Taguchi and RSM.
- Grey relational analysis and genetic algorithm coupled with Taguchi, RSM and ANN optimization techniques are preferable for *multi-objective response* optimization.

# Reference

1. Ma, Z., Feng, A., Chen, D., Shen, J.: Recent advances in friction stir welding/processing of aluminum alloys: microstructural evolution and mechanical properties. J. Crit. Rev. Solid State **43**, 269–333 (2018)
2. Bosneag, A., Constantin, M., Nitu, E., Iordache, M.: Friction stir welding of three dissimilar aluminium alloy: AA2024, AA6061 and AA7075. In: IOP Conference Series: Materials Science and Engineering, p. 022013. IOP Publishing (2018)
3. Saravanakumar, R., Krishna, K., Rajasekaran, T., Siranjeevi, S.: Investigations on friction stir welding of AA5083-H32 marine grade aluminium alloy by the effect of varying the process parameters. In: IOP Conference Series: Materials Science and Engineering, p. 012187. IOP Publishing (2018)
4. Elatharasan, G., Kumar, V.S.: An experimental analysis and optimization of process parameter on friction stir welding of AA 6061–T6 aluminum alloy using RSM. Proc. Eng. **64**, 1227–1234 (2013)
5. Boukraa, M., Lebaal, N., Mataoui, A., Settar, A., Aissani, M., Tala-Ighil, N.: Friction stir welding process improvement through coupling an optimization procedure and three-dimensional transient heat transfer numerical analysis. J. Manuf. Process. **34**, 566–578 (2018)
6. Zhang, C., Wang, W., Jin, X., Rong, C., Qin, Z.: A study on microstructure and mechanical properties of micro friction stir welded ultra-Thin Al-1060 sheets by the shoulderless tool. J. Metals **9**, 507 (2019)
7. Kumar, A., Milton, M.S.: A Comparison of welding techniques of aluminium alloys a literature review. J. Int. J. Sci. Res. Sci. Eng. **2**, 172–175 (2016)

8. Kumar, S., Kumar, S., Kumar, A.: Optimization of process parameters for friction stir welding of joining A6061 and A6082 alloys by Taguchi method. J. Mech. Eng. Sci. **227**, 1150–1163 (2013)
9. Roldo, L., Vulić, N.: Friction stir welding for marine applications: mechanical behaviour and microstructural characteristics of Al-Mg-Si-Cu plates. J. Trans. Maritime Sci. **8**, 75–83 (2019)
10. Dawood, H.I., Mohammed, K.S., Rajab, M.Y.: Advantages of the green solid state FSW over the conventional GMAW process. J. Adv. Mater. Sci. Eng. **2014**, 1–10 (2014)
11. Shaik, B., Gowd, G.H., Durgaprasad, B.: Experimental investigations on friction stir welding process to join aluminum alloys. Int. J. Appl. Eng. Res. **13**, 12331–12339 (2018)
12. Kundu, J., Ghangas, G., Rattan, N., Kumar, M.: Friction stir welding: merits over other joining processes. Int. J. Curr. Eng. Technol. **7**, 1175–1177 (2017)
13. Materials ASoT. Standard Test Methods for Tension Testing of Metallic Materials1. ASME Designation: E 8 – 042004, p. 1–24
14. Dixit, D., Mishra, A.: Friction stir welding of aerospace alloys. Int. J. Res. Appl. Sci. Eng. Technol. **7**, 863–870 (2019)
15. Kulekci, M.K.: Magnesium and its alloys applications in automotive industry. Int. J. Adv. Manuf. Technol. **39**, 851–865 (2008)
16. Roy, R.K.: A Primer on the Taguchi Method. 2nd edn. United States of America (2010)
17. Sagar Patel, P.K.M., Mirani, M.: A review- friction stir welding of AA6061 aluminum alloy using drilling machine. IJLTEMAS **III**, 33–37 (2014)
18. Nourani, M., Milani, A.S., Yannacopoulos, S.: Taguchi optimization of process parameters in friction stir welding of 6061 aluminum alloy: a review and case study. J. Eng. **3**, 144–155 (2011)
19. Prasath, S., Vijayan, S., Rao, S.K.: Optimization of friction stir welding process parameters for joining ZM 21 to AZ 31 of dissimilar magnesium alloys using Taguchi technique. Metallurgia Italiana 25–33 (2016)
20. Ugender, S.: Influence of tool pin profile and rotational speed on the formation of friction stir welding zone in AZ31 magnesium alloy. J. Magnesium Alloys **6**, 205–213 (2018)
21. Mendes, N., Loureiro, A., Martins, C., Neto, P., Pires, J.: Effect of friction stir welding parameters on morphology and strength of acrylonitrile butadiene styrene plate welds. J. Mater. Design **58**, 457–464 (2014)
22. Sreenivas, P., Kumar, A.: Effect of applied axial force on Fsw of AA 6082–T6 aluminium alloys. Int. J. Mech. Eng. Technol. **8**, 88–99 (2017)
23. Serier, M., Berrahou, M., Tabti, A., Bendaoudi, S.-E.: Effect of FSW welding parameters on the tensile strength of aluminum alloys. J. Arch. Mech. Technol. Mater. **39**, 41–45 (2019)
24. Jambhale, S., Kumar, S., Kumar, S.: Effect of process parameters & tool geometries on properties of friction stir spot welds: a review. Univ. J. Eng. Sci. **3**, 6–11 (2015)
25. Ugender, S., Jayakrishna, S., Francis, E.D.: Influence of welding speed, axial force and rotational speed on the formation of friction stir welding zone in AZ31 magnesium alloy. Int. J. Mech. Eng. Technol. **9**, 845–857 (2018)
26. Ko, Y.-J., Lee, K.-J., Baik, K.-H.: Effect of tool rotational speed on mechanical properties and microstructure of friction stir welding joints within Ti–6Al–4V alloy sheets. J. Adv. Mech. Eng. **9**, 1–7 (2017)
27. Iqbal, Z., Bazoune, A., Al-Badour, F., Shuaib, A., Merah, N.: Effect of tool rotational speed on friction stir welding of ASTM A516–70 steel using W–25% re alloy tool. Arab. J. Sci. Eng. **44**, 1233–1242 (2019)
28. Barlas, Z.: The Influence of tool tilt angle on 1050 aluminum lap joint in friction stir welding process. Acta Phys. Polonica A **132**, 679–681 (2017)
29. Krishna, G.G., Reddy, P.R., Hussain, M.M.: Effect of Tool tilt angle on aluminum 2014 friction stir welds. Glob. J. Res. Eng. **14**, 60–70 (2015)

30. Murugan, B., Thirunavukarasu, G., Kundu, S., Kailas, S.V.: Influence of tool traverse speed on structure, mechanical properties, fracture behavior, and weld corrosion of friction stir welded joints of aluminum and stainless steel. J. Adv. Eng. Mater. **21**, 1800869 (2019)
31. Barenji, R.V.: Effect of tool traverse speed on microstructure and mechanical performance of friction stir welded 7020 aluminum alloy. J. Mater.: Design Appl. **230**, 663–673 (2016)
32. Mohanty, H.K., Mahapatra, M.M., Kumar, P., Biswas, P., Mandal, N.R.: Effect of tool shoulder and pin probe profiles on friction stirred aluminum welds—a comparative study. J. Marine Sci. Appl. **11**, 200–217 (2012)
33. Moradi, M., Jamshidi Aval, H., Jamaati, R.: Effect of tool pin geometry and weld pass number on microstructural, natural aging and mechanical behaviour of SiC-incorporated dissimilar friction-stir-welded aluminium alloys. Indian Acad. Sci.**44**(1), 1–9 (2018). https://doi.org/10.1007/s12046-018-0997-5
34. Khan, N.Z., Siddiquee, A.N., Al-Ahmari, A.M., Abidi, M.H.: Analysis of defects in clean fabrication process of friction stir welding. Trans. Nonferrous Metals Soc. China **27**, 1507–1516 (2017)
35. Meilinger, Á., Török, I.: The importance of friction stir welding tool. Prod. Process. Syst. **6**, 25–34 (2013)
36. Venkateswarlu, D., Mandal, N., Mahapatra, M., Harsh, S.: Tool design effects for FSW of AA7039. Weld. J. **92**, 41–47 (2013)
37. Said, M.T.S.M.: The effect of pin size on friction stir welded AA5083 Plate lap joint. In: International Conference on Production, Automobiles and Mechanical Engineering, pp. 87–92 (2015)
38. Khan, N.Z., Khan, Z.A., Siddiquee, A.N.: Effect of shoulder diameter to pin diameter (D/d) ratio on tensile strength of friction stir welded 6063 aluminium alloy. Mater. Today: Proc. **2**, 1450–1457 (2015)
39. Joshi, S.K., Gandhi, J.D.: Influence of tool shoulder geometry on friction stir welding: a literature review. IJRSI **III**, 261–264 (2015)
40. Durakovic, B.: Design of experiments application, concepts, examples: State of the art. Period. Eng. Nat. Sci. **5**, 421–439 (2017)
41. Sharma, G.V.S.S., Rao, R.U., Rao, P.S.: A Taguchi approach on optimal process control parameters for HDPE pipe extrusion process. J. Ind. Eng. Int. **13**, 215–228 (2017)
42. Fukuda, I.M., Pinto, C.F.F., Saviano, A.M., Lourenço, F.R., Moreira, C.D.S.: Design of experiments (DoE) applied to pharmaceutical and analytical Quality by Design (QbD). Braz. J. Pharmaceut. Sci. **54** (2018)
43. Kasman, Ş: Optimisation of dissimilar friction stir welding parameters with grey relational analysis. Proc. Inst. Mech. Eng. Part B: J. Eng. Manuf. **227**, 1317–1324 (2013)
44. Amit Kumar, M.K.K., Singh, G.: Modeling and optimization of friction stir welding process parameters for dissimilar aluminium alloys. In: IConAMMA_2017, pp. 25440–25449. Materials Today, India (2018)
45. Ghetiya, N.D., Patel, K.M., Kavar, A.J.: Multi-objective optimization of FSW process parameters of aluminium alloy using taguchi-based grey relational analysis. Trans. Indian Inst. Met. **69**, 917–923 (2015)
46. Khaze, S.R., Masdari, M., Hojjatkhah, S.: Application of artificial neural networks in estimating participation in elections. Int. J. Inf. Technol. Model. Comput. **1**, 23–31 (2013)
47. Manickam, M.V., Mohanapriya, M., Patil, S.P.: Research study on applications of artificial neural networks and E-learning personalization. Int. J. Civ. Eng. Technol. **8**, 1422–1432 (2017)
48. Ihme, M., Marsden, A., Pitsch, H.: On the optimization of artificial neural networks for application to the approximation of chemical systems. J. Cent. Turbulence Res. Ann. Res. Briefs 105–118 (2006)

49. Arabzadeh, V., Niaki, S.T.A., Arabzadeh, V.: Construction cost estimation of spherical storage tanks: artificial neural networks and hybrid regression—GA algorithms. J. Ind. Eng. Int. 14(4), 747–756 (2017). https://doi.org/10.1007/s40092-017-0240-8

50. Tuntas, R., Dikici, B.: An investigation on the aging responses and corrosion behaviour of A356/SiC composites by neural network: The effect of cold working ratio. J. Compos. Mater. 50, 2323–2335 (2016)

51. Haldurai, L., Madhubala, T., Rajalakshmi, R.: A Study on genetic algorithm and its applications. Int. J. Comput. Sci. Eng. 4, 139–143 (2016)

52. Kristiadi, D., Hartanto, R.: Genetic algorithm for lecturing schedule optimization (case study: university of Boyolali). Indones. J. Comput. Cybern. Syst. 13, 83–94 (2019)

53. Donoriyanto, D., Anam, A.: Application of genetic algorithm method on machine maintenance. J. Phys.: Conf. Ser. 012225 (2018)

54. Hussain, A., Muhammad, Y.S., Nawaz, A.: Optimization through genetic algorithm with a new and efficient crossover operator. Int. J. Adv. Math. 2018, 1–14 (2018)

55. Sobey, A.J., Grudniewski, P.A.: Re-inspiring the genetic algorithm with multi-level selection theory: multi-level selection genetic algorithm. J. Bioinspir. biomimet. 13, 1–14 (2018)

56. Hou, S., Wen, H., Feng, S., Wang, H., Li, Z.: Application of layered coding genetic algorithm in optimization of unequal area production facilities layout. J. Comput. Intell. Neurosci. 2019, 1–18 (2019)

57. Lai, Y., Dai, Y., Bai, X., Chen, D.: Discrete variable structural optimization based on multidirectional fuzzy genetic algorithm. Chin. J. Mech. Eng. 25, 255–261 (2012)

58. Mohammadi, F.G., Amini, M.H., Arabnia, H.R.: Evolutionary computation, optimization and learning algorithms for data science. arXiv preprint arXiv (2019)

59. Chande, S., Sinha, M.: Genetic algorithm: a versatile optimization tool. BVICAM's Int. J. Inf. Technol. 1, 7–13 (2013)

60. Lin, S.-T.: Application of grey-relational analysis to find the most suitable watermarking scheme. Int. J. Innov. Comput. Inf. Control 7, 5389–5401 (2011)

61. Vijayan, S., Raju, R., Rao, S.K.: Multiobjective optimization of friction stir welding process parameters on aluminum alloy AA 5083 using Taguchi-based grey relation analysis. J. Mater. Manuf. Process. 25, 1206–1212 (2010)

62. Wang, L., Yin, K., Cao, Y., Li, X.: A new grey relational analysis model based on the characteristic of inscribed core (IC-GRA) and its application on seven-pilot carbon trading markets of China. Int. J. Environ. Res. Public Health 16, 1–16 (2019)

63. Kumar, A., Soota, T., Kumar, J.: Optimisation of wire-cut EDM process parameter by Grey-based response surface methodology. J. Ind. Eng. Int. 14(4), 821–829 (2018). https://doi.org/10.1007/s40092-018-0264-8

64. Hrairi, M., Daoud, J.I., Zakaria, F.: Optimization of incremental sheet metal forming process using grey relational analysis. Int. J. Recent Technol. Eng. 7 (2019)

65. Shivade, A.S., Shinde, V.D.: Multi-objective optimization in WEDM of D3 tool steel using integrated approach of Taguchi method & Grey relational analysis. J. Ind. Eng. Int. 10, 149–162 (2014)

66. Fang, G., Guo, Y., Huang, X., Rutten, M., Yuan, Y.: Combining grey relational analysis and a Bayesian model averaging method to derive monthly optimal operating rules for a hydropower reservoir. J. Water 10, 1–20 (2018)

67. Karthikeyan, R., Senthilkumar, V., Thilak, M., Nagadeepan, A.: Application of grey relational analysis for optimization of kerf quality during CO2 laser cutting of mild steel. J. Mater. Today: Proc. 5, 19209–19215 (2018)

68. Liu, C.-Y., Tong, L.-I.: Developing automatic form and design system using integrated grey relational analysis and affective engineering. J. Appl. Sci. 8, 1–22 (2018)

69. Khanna, R., Kumar, A., Garg, M.P., Singh, A., Sharma, N.: Multiple performance characteristics optimization for Al 7075 on electric discharge drilling by Taguchi grey relational theory. J. Ind. Eng. Int. **11**, 459–472 (2015)

70. Nair, A.T., Makwana, A.R., Ahammed, M.M.: The use of response surface methodology for modelling and analysis of water and wastewater treatment processes: a review. J. Water Sci. Technol. **69**, 464–478 (2013)

71. Raleng, A., Singh, A., Singh, B., Attkan, A.K.: Response surface methodology for development and characterization of extruded snack developed from food-by-products. Int. J. Bio-Resour. Stress Manage. **7**, 1321–1329 (2016)

72. Said, K.A.M., Amin, M.A.M.: Overview on the response surface methodology (RSM) in extraction processes. J. Appl. Sci. Process Eng. **2**, 8–18 (2015)

73. Wang, Y., Deng, L., Fan, Y.: Preparation of soy-based adhesive enhanced by waterborne polyurethane: optimization by response surface methodology. J. Adv. Mater. Sci. Eng. **2018**, 1–8 (2018)

74. Bal, M., Biswas, S., Behera, S.K., Meikap, B., Health, P.A.: Modeling and optimization of process variables for HCl gas removal by response surface methodology. J. Environ. Sci. Health **54**, 359–366 (2019)

75. Akçay, H., Anagün, A.S.: Multi response optimization application on a manufacturing factory. J. Math. Comput. Appl. **18**, 531–538 (2013)

76. Ramakrishna, G., Susmita, M.: Application of response surface methodology for optimization of Cr (III) and Cr (VI) adsorption on commercial activated carbons. Res. J. Chem. Sci. **4**, 40–48 (2012)

77. Riswanto, F.D.O., Rohman, A., Pramono, S., Martono, S.: Application of response surface methodology as mathematical and statistical tools in natural product research. J. Appl. Pharmac. Sci. **9**, 125–133 (2019)

78. Dar, A.A., Anuradha, N.: An application of Taguchi L9 method in black scholes model for european call option. Int. J. Entrep. **22**, 1–13 (2018)

79. Ishrat, S.I., et al.: Optimising parameters for expanded polystyrene based pod production using taguchi method. J. Math. **7**, 1–17 (2019)

80. Yılmaz, M., Keskin, M.E.: Optimal Okuma Şartlarının Taguchi Yöntemiyle Belirlenmesi. Acad. Platform J. Eng. Sci. **7**, 25–32 (2019)

81. Baligidad, S.M., Chandrasekhar, U., Elangovan, K., Shankar, S.: Taguchi's Approach: Design optimization of process parameters in selective inhibition sintering. J. Mater. Today: Proc. **5**, 4778–4786 (2018)

82. Li, Y., Shieh, M.-D., Yang, C.-C., Zhu, L.: Application of fuzzy-based hybrid Taguchi method for multiobjective optimization of product form design. J. Math. Probl. Eng. **2018**, 1–18 (2018)

83. Achuthamenon Sylajakumari, P., Ramakrishnasamy, R., Palaniappan, G.: Taguchi grey relational analysis for multi-response optimization of wear in co-continuous composite. J. Mater. **11**, 1–17 (2018)

84. Azadeh, A., Miri-Nargesi, S.S., Goldansaz, S.M., Zoraghi, N.: Design and implementation of an integrated Taguchi method for continuous assessment and improvement of manufacturing systems. Int. J. Adv. Manuf. Technol. **59**, 1073–1089 (2012)

85. Qadir, S., Dar, A.A.: Distance to default and probability of default: an experimental study. J. Glob. Entrep. Res. **9**, 1–12 (2019)

86. Reddy, A., Rajesham, S., Reddy, P., Kumar, T., Goverdhan, J.: An experimental study on effect of process parameters in deep drawing using Taguchi technique. Int. J. Eng. Sci. Technol. **7**, 21–32 (2015)

87. Vaibhav Khola, H.R., Masudi, M.: Optimization of process parameters on Inconel 718 using Taguchi's technique. Int. Res. J. Eng. Technol. **5**, 1272–1279 (2018)

88. Shunmugasundaram, M., Kumar, A.P., Sankar, L.P., Sivasankar, S.: Optimization of process parameters of friction stirs welding of aluminum alloys (6061) using Taguchi method. Int. J. Sci. Res. **5**, 1988–1994 (2016)

89. Borkar, B.R., Navale, S.B.: Process parameters optimization in FSW process using Taguchi method. IJARIIE **4**, 551–558 (2018)

90. Ugender, S.: Optimizing the process parameters of friction stir welded AA 6061–T6 alloy using Taguchi orthogonal technique. Int. J. Curr. Eng. Sci. Res. **1**, 48–55 (2014)

91. Gupta, S.K., Pandey, K., Kumar, R.: Multi-objective optimization of friction stir welding of aluminium alloy using grey relation analysis with entropy measurement method. Nirma Univ. J. Eng. Technol. (NUJET). **3**, 29–34 (2015)

92. Gomathisankar, M., Gangatharan, M., Pitchipoo, P.: A Novel optimization of friction stir welding process parameters on aluminum alloy 6061–T6. Mater. Today: Proc. **5**, 14397–14404 (2018)

93. Kumar, S., Pandey, G.K.N.: Application of Taguchi method for optimization of friction stir welding process parameters to joining of Al alloy. Adv. Mater. Manuf. Charact. **13**, 253–258 (2013)

94. Prasad, M.D., Kumar Namala, K.: Process parameters optimization in friction stir welding by ANOVA. Mater. Today: Proc. **5**, 4824–4831 (2018)

95. Ugrasen, G., Bharath, G., Kumar, G.K., Sagar, R., Shivu, P., Keshavamurthy, R.: Optimization of process parameters for Al6061-Al7075 alloys in friction stir welding using Taguchi's technique. Mater. Today: Proc. **5**, 3027–3035 (2018)

96. Vijayan, D., Rao, V.S.: Optimization of friction stir welding process parameters using RSM based Grey-Fuzzy approach. J. Eng. Technol. **2**, 12–25 (2017)

97. Surjeet Singh, K.S., Singh, I., Shivesh, C.: An experimental analysis and optimization of process parameters on friction stir welding of dissimilar AA6061-T6 and AA6951-T6 using taguchi technique. Int. Res. J. Eng. Technol. **04**, 3329–3235 (2017)

98. Kumar, P.R., Raj, R.G.: A review on friction stir weldment of AA6061 and AA1100 aluminium alloys. Int. J. Adv. Inf. Sci. Technol. **3**, 104–108 (2014)

99. Devaiah, D., Kishore, K., Laxminarayana, P.: Study the process parametric influence on impact strength of friction stir welding of dissimilar aluminum alloys (AA5083 and AA6061) using Taguchi technique. Inte. Adv. Res. J. Sci. Eng. Technol. **3**, 91–98 (2016)

100. Devaiah, D., Kishore, K., Laxminarayana, P.: Parametric optimization of friction stir welding parameters using taguchi technique for dissimilar aluminum alloys (AA5083 and AA6061). Int. Organ. Sci. Res. **7**, 44–49 (2017)

101. Chaitanya, V.K., Varma, S.R., Raju, P.R.M., Viswanadha Raju, V.K.: Influence of welding parameters on the mechanical properties of dissimilar AA7075-AA6061 friction stir welds. Int. J. Recent Technol. Eng. **8**, 81–88 (2019)

102. Hema, P., Raviteja, N., Ravindranath, K.: Prediction and parametric optimization on mechanical properties of friction stir welding joints of AA 6061 and AA 2014 using genetic algorithm. Int. J. Innov. Res. Sci. Eng. Technol. **5**, 3870–3877 (2016)

103. Devaiah, D., Kishore, K., Laxminarayana, P.: Optimization of process parameters in friction stir welding of dissimilar aluminium alloys (AA5083 and AA6061) using Taguchi technique. Int. J. Innov. Res. Sci. Eng. Technol. **5**, 15303–15310 (2016)

104. Bahar, D., Arvind, N., Yadav, V.V., Raju, P.: Multi objective optimization in friction stir welding using Taguchi orthogonal array and grey relational analysis. Int. J. Adv. Technol. Eng. Explor. **5**, 214–220 (2018)

105. Vijayan, D., Rao, V.S.: Friction stir welding of age-hardenable aluminum alloys: a parametric approach using RSM based GRA coupled with PCA. J Inst. Eng. India Ser. **95**, 127–141 (2014)

106. Devaiah, D., Kishore, K., Laxminarayana, P.: Optimal FSW process parameters for dissimilar aluminium alloys (AA5083 and AA6061) using Taguchi tech46nique. J. Mater. Today: Proc. **5**, 4607–4614 (2018)
107. Chanakyan, C., Sivasankar, S., Alagarsamy, S.V., Kumar, S.D., Sakthivelu, S.: Parametric optimization for friction stir welding with AA2024 and AA6061 aluminium alloys by ANOVA and GRG. Mater. Today **27**, 1–5 (2019)
108. Ugender, S., Ma: Taguchi optimization of process parameters in friction stir welding of aluminium 2014 & 6061 alloys. Int. J. Curr. Eng. Sci. Res. **2**, 34–40 (2015)
109. Kumar, S., Kumar, S.: Multi-response optimization of process parameters for friction stir welding of joining dissimilar Al alloys by gray relation analysis and Taguchi method. J. Braz. Soc. Mech. Sci. Eng. **37**, 1–10 (2014)
110. Hema, P.: Experimental investigations on AA 6061 alloy welded joints by friction stir welding. J. Aluminum Alloys Compos. (2019)
111. Chiteka, K.: Artificial neural networks in tensile strength and input parameter prediction in Friction Stir Welding. Int. J. Mech. Eng. Robot. Res. **03**, 145–150 (2014)
112. Khourshid, A.M., El-Kassas, A.M., Sabry, I.: Integration between artificial neural network and responses surfaces methodology for modeling of friction stir welding. Int. J. Adv. Eng. Res. Sci. **2**, 67–73 (2015)
113. Momeni, M., Guillot, M.: Effect of tool design and process parameters on lap joints made by right angle friction stir welding (RAFSW). J. Manuf. Mater. Process. **3**, 1–14 (2019)
114. Vijayan, D., Abhishek, P.: Multi objective process parameters optimization of friction stir welding using NSGA–II. In: IOP Conference Series: Materials Science and Engineering, p. 012087. IOP Publishing (2018)
115. Sankar, B.R., Umamaheswarrao, P.: Optimisation of hardness and tensile strength of friction stir welded AA6061 alloy using response surface methodology coupled with grey relational analysis and principle component analysis. Int. J. Eng. Sci. Technol. **7**, 21–29 (2015)
116. Samuela, G.D., Dhasb, J.E.R.: Multi-Objective Optimization of friction stir welded dissimilar aluminium composites using grey analysis. Int. J. Appl. Eng. Res. **12**, 1279–1289 (2017)
117. Vijayan, D., Seshagiri, R.: A parametric optimization of FSW process using RSM based grey relational analysis approach. Int. Rev. Mech. Eng. (IREME). **8**, 328–337 (2014)
118. Prasanna, P., Penchalayya, C., Rao, D.: Optimization and validation of process parameters in friction stir welding on AA 6061 aluminum alloy using gray relational analysis. Int. J. Eng. Res. Appl. (IJERA). **3**, 1471–1481 (2013)
119. Yunus, M., Alsoufi, M.S.: Multi-objective optimization of joint strength of dissimilar aluminum alloys formed by friction stir welding using Taguchi-grey relation analysis. Int. J. Eng. Technol. **6**, 10–17 (2016)
120. Gopu, P., Dev Anand, M.: Optimal parameter determination on friction stir welding process of AA6061 using grey Taguchi method. Int. J. Recent Technol. Eng. **8**, 46–50 (2019)
121. RaviKumar, S., KajaBanthaNavas, R., Sai, S.: Multiple response optimization studies for dissimilar friction stir welding parameters of 6061 to 7075 aluminium alloys. Mater. Today: Proc. **16**, 405–412 (2019)
122. Dhancholia, D.D., Sharma, A., Vyas, C.: Optimisation of friction stir welding parameters for AA 6061 and AA 7039 aluminium alloys by response surface methodology (RSM). Int. J. Adv. Mech. Eng. **4**, 565–571 (2014)
123. Kavitha, S., Rajkumar, S.: Identification of the most critical friction stir welding process and tool parameters to attain a maximum tensile strength of the AA6061-T6 aluminium alloy. Int. J. Res. Advent Technol. 128–136 (2018)
124. Iswar, M., Suyuti, M.A., Nur, R.: Optimizing the machining conditions on friction stir welding of aluminum alloy through design experiments. Innov. Sci. Technol. Mech. Eng. Ind. **030003**, 1–5 (2019)

125. Sankar, B.R., Umamaheswarrao, P.: Modelling and optimisation of friction stir welding on AA6061 Alloy. Mater. Today: Proc. **4**, 7448–7456 (2017)
126. Safeen, W., Hussain, S., Wasim, A., Jahanzaib, M., Aziz, H., Abdalla, H.: Predicting the tensile strength, impact toughness, and hardness of Friction Stir-Welded AA6061-T6 using response surface methodology. Int. J. Adv. Manuf. Technol. **87**, 1765–1781 (2016)
127. Ghaffarpour, M., Aziz, A., Hejazi, T.-H.: Optimization of friction stir welding parameters using multiple response surface methodology. J. Mater. Design Appl. **231**, 571–583 (2017)
128. Elatharasan, G., Kumar, V.S.: Modelling and optimization of friction stir welding parameters for dissimilar aluminium alloys using RSM. Proc. Eng. **38**, 3477–3481 (2012)
129. Hanapi, M., Haslam, M., Hussain, Z., Almanar, I.P., Abu Seman, A.: Optimization processing parameter of 6061-T6 alloy friction stir welded using Taguchi technique. Mater. Sci. Forum: Trans. Tech. Publ. 294–298 (2016)
130. Anuradha, M., Sailaja, C, Chittaranjan Das, V.: Effect of tool pin profile and optimization of process parameters on A6061 by friction stir welding using Taguchi method. Int. J. Mech. Eng. Technol. **8**, 615–621 (2017)
131. Chauhan, S.M.S.P.Y.B.: Optimization of friction stir welding process parameters for welding aluminum alloys. Int. J. Sci. Technol. Eng. **2**, 69–75 (2015)
132. Harikishore, R., Satyavinod, L.: Parametric optimization for friction stir welding of Al6061 alloy using Taguchi technique. Int. J. Sci. Res. **6**, 334–339 (2017)
133. Shinde, R.D., Rathi, M.G.: Optimization of FSW process parameter to achieve maximum tensile strength of aluminum alloy AA6061. Int. Res. J. Eng. Technol. **03**, 936–943 (2016)

# Modeling of Pore Parameters and Experimental Validation Using the Microstructure of 0.85Mo and 1.5Mo Prealloyed Sintered Steels

Samuel Tesfaye Mekonone[1]($\boxtimes$), Alberto Molinari[2], and Solomon Mesfin Demlie[3]

[1] Addis Ababa University, Addis Ababa, Ethiopia
samuel.tesfaye@aait.edu.et
[2] University of Trento, Trento, Italy
alberto.molinari@unitn.it
[3] University of Gondar, Gondar, Ethiopia

**Abstract.** Empirical models were developed to relate stress with a resistance of materials that helps to predict the response of materials. For porous materials, measuring the pore parameters is required to incorporate the intensification effect of the pore on the stress distribution. However, image analysis is the common practice employed to measure pore parameters, mathematical models may also use as an alternative method. Mathematical modeling of pore parameters for square, triangular, and rectangular geometric pore was developed. Pore parameters used to characterize circularity ($f_{circle}$), elongation ($f_{shape}$), and the pore size (equivalent diameters, $D_{eq.}$) were analyzed for those geometric pores. The analytical results were compared with the pore parameters measured on the microstructures of prealloyed sintered steels. The modeling results are in agreement with the experimental analysis.

**Keywords:** Pore parameters · Geometric models · Sintered steels · Microstructures · Image analysis

## 1 Introduction

Pinions, gears, bearings, and cams are among the mechanical components produced by powder metallurgy. Porosity is the inherent characteristic of the microstructure of these components that are processed by powder compaction and subsequent sintering processes. To evaluate their resistance to mechanical loading, characterization of pore parameters, such as size, distribution, and the shape is required to incorporate its effect on the stress distributions [1–4]. Measuring these parameters on the microstructures using image analysis, that is the direct techniques of quantitative characterization of PM materials, is well adopted and used to understand its effect on the mechanical behaviors [5–8]. Bending and contact fatigue are the major damage mechanisms of PM components that are determined by the presence of porosity in the microstructure [9–11]. Fatigue limit and fatigue life of PM materials are usually lower as compared with the

M. A. Delele et al. (Eds.): ICAST 2020, LNICST 385, pp. 245–260, 2021.
https://doi.org/10.1007/978-3-030-80618-7_16

pore-free materials. The reduction of mechanical properties relates to the decreasing of load bearing surface, and pore acts as a notch effect in the microstructures [12–16]. It is acting as stress or strain intensifying zones [17], and specifically elongated and large pore typically become the site of crack nucleation that reduces the fatigue limit and the material tends to fail at lower stress. The mechanism used to improve the mechanical properties is controlling the compaction and sintering process to reduce the size and volume of porosity and to prepare rounded pore morphology [18]. Therefore, understanding the size and shape of the pore is an important step in the process of PM materials that help to predict its response to the applied loads. Currently, there is a trend to link the size of the bigger pore, pore distribution, and pore shape parameters with mechanical properties (specifically contact fatigue and fatigue strength) [19]. Based on the conservative approach, contact fatigue crack nucleation was predicted by comparing the yield strength of diffusion alloyed PM materials with applied stress where the analysis of stress incorporates notch effect [20].

The derivation of contact stress considers the effect of bigger pores (10% of the pore population corresponds to the total pore population) as stress intensifying area and deteriorate load bearing sections, where the analysis needs a measurement of pore parameters. This research work aims to model pore geometries and evaluate the pore parameters that can be considered as required inputs for the analysis of stress distribution in the porous microstructures. Modeling of the pore with the following geometries was proposed.

1.  Square geometric pore ($\square$) – formed between four particles.
2.  Triangular geometric pore ($\triangle$) – formed between three particles.
3.  Rectangular geometric pore ( $\square$ ) – formed between four particles.

Then the model results are validated by comparing with the pore parameters measured using image analysis that was carried out on low alloyed PM steel microstructures. Quantitative characterization of pore shape and size is possible with a lack of precision and universal definition of terms [21]. But the Shape factor parameter such as $f_{shape}$ (characterizes pore elongation), $f_{circle}$ (characterizes pore circularity) is well adapted to characterize the porous microstructures.

## 2  Pore Modeling, Materials, and Experimental Methods

### 2.1  Mathematical and Geometric Modeling of Pore

Analytical modeling of pore geometry in porous material was complex due to the diversity of pores shapes, orientations, and sizes. However, a limited number research papers have reported the pore parameters analyzed based on atomistic and macroscopic modeling approaches of compaction and sintering of PM materials [22–25] According to the classical model, a sharp neck is created between two perfect spherical particles (represents the initial stage of the sintering), and from the geometry, the ratio of neck to particle size is related by $X/D > 0.3$, where X is neck size and D is the particle size [5]. But no relationship was developed between neck and particle size at the final stage of sintering (decreased in size and became rounded), however, it became a critical parameter that can determine the behavior of the final product, only limited analytical and numerical model available for the final stage of sintering. On the one hand, because of several geometries of pore evolution and on the other hand, this is influenced by compaction/sintering parameters. This results in the complex geometry of pore and microstructural evolutions which is not the easy task to study analytically or numerically. However, there is a strong relation between pore parameters of sintered microstructure and green body compaction pressure [5], neck formation between grains affected manly by sintering temperature, and time that can be incorporated in these work. The relationship between $R'$ (refers to neck size) and $R/r$ (refers to particle size) of the simple geometry and compared with the results of image analysis on the microstructure. The influence of the compaction/sintering parameter is not considered here in the models. Figure 1 illustrates the proposed pore models that are defined by the spaces between spherical particles.

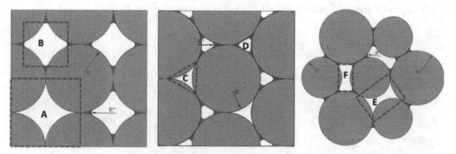

**Fig. 1.** The three types of pore models: square (A, B), triangular (C, D) and rectangular (E, F) geometric pores

The pore geometries, highlighted in the red in Fig. 1, are voids that are defined based on the number of contacts between spherical grains and grain size. These six pore geometries are characterized as follows:

- A and B are square geometric pores formed between four equal particles (it radius is R) with sharp ($R' = 0$) and rounded ($R' > 0$) edge, respectively;
- C and D are triangular pores formed between three equal particles (it radius is R) with sharp ($R' = 0$) and rounded ($R' > 0$) edge, respectively;
- E and F are rectangular geometric pores formed between different sized particles (its radius are R and r) with sharp ($R' = 0$) and rounded ($R' > 0$) edge, respectively.

Mathematical models are required to correlate the grain size and number of contacts with the proposed pore models that aim to analyzed and characterized the pore parameters. Three pore models as a square, triangular and rectangular geometries were defined in both cases of sharp and rounded edges. A sharp-edged pore model is, which is the simplest one, formed when the particles undergo a point contact, or the radius ($R'$) of the rounded edge is zero, and the size and shape of the three pore models vary with R and $R'$. The modes can be defined based on those dimensions except for rectangular geometries formed between particles with different sizes (R and r), which requires an additional characteristic that is the gap between particles of similar sizes. Besides, the morphology of these pore models is irregular in shape and with a certain error, it can be used to represent the voids in the microstructures of PM materials. The pore parameters ($f_{circle}$ and $f_{shape}$) are always less than 1 unless otherwise, all pore are perfect circles, which is not mostly realistic in PM microstructures. Circular pore morphology is the desired microstructures of PM materials because it provides good mechanical properties than irregular pores [11] and hence not considered here.

Figure 2 represents the pore geometries between three and four particles with triangles to formulate the area of the pore. Triangles were constructed by connecting the center of two particles and one of the rounded neck. α and β are angles of these triangles. The maximum and minimum diameter of the pore are highlighted as red and blue colors in the figure. The maximum diameter is the largest distance between two parallel lines, which passes through the edges or lines of pore without crossing the area of the pore. The minimum diameter is the smallest distance between two parallel lines, which passes through edges or lines of pore without crossing the area of the pore.

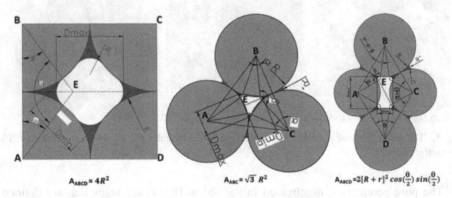

$$A_{ABCD} = 4R^2 \qquad A_{ABC} = \sqrt{3}\ R^2 \qquad A_{ABCD} = 2[R + r]^2 \cos\left(\tfrac{\theta}{2}\right) \sin\left(\tfrac{\theta}{2}\right)$$

**Fig. 2.** Geometrical relation of pores and circumscribed geometries

Square (ABCD), equilateral triangle (ABC), and rhombus(ABCD) circumscribe a square, triangle, and rectangular geometric pore models. The side length of a square (ABCD) and triangle (ABC) is 2R and the rhombus has R + r equal side lengths and the area of three geometries are $4R^2$, $\sqrt{3}R^2$ and $2[R + r]^2 \cos\left(\frac{\theta}{2}\right) \sin\left(\frac{\theta}{2}\right)$. These parameters use to drive for pore areas.

The area of the square geometric pore ($R' = 0$) valuated by subtracting the area of four circular sectors (characterized by the radius R and angle 90°) from an area of square ABCD. Area of the square geometric pore with the sharp neck ($A_{sharp\ neck,\ \square}$ ) is given by Eq. (1).

$$A_{sharp\ neck,\ \square} = (4 - \pi)R^2 \qquad (1)$$

Area of the triangular geometric pore with the sharp neck ($A_{sharp\ neck,\ \triangle}$) evaluated by subtracting the area of three circular sectors (characterized by the radius R and angle 60°) from an area of a bigger equilateral triangle ABC and is given by Eq. (2).

$$A_{sharp\ neck,\ \triangle} = \left(\sqrt{3} - \frac{\pi}{2}\right)R^2 \qquad (2)$$

Area of the rectangular geometric pore with the sharp neck ($A_{sharp\ neck,\ \square}$ ) evaluated by subtracting the area of four circular sectors (characterized by the radius R/r and angles $\theta/\pi - \theta$) from an area of rhombus ABCD is given by Eq. (3).

$$A_{sharp\ neck,\ \square} = 2(R + r)^2 cos\left(\frac{''}{2}\right) sin\left(\frac{\theta}{2}\right) - r^2(\pi - \theta) - R^2\theta \tag{3}$$

Figure 3 illustrates the triangles ABE constructed from the square, triangular, and rectangular geometric pore. with a side length of R + r, r + R', and R + R'. When the particle size is the same such as, R = r, square and rectangular geometric pore is the same. $A_3$ (grown neck area between particles) should be excluded from the rounded neck pore model by subtracting from the area of sharp neck pore.

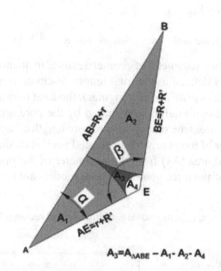

Fig. 3. Triangle ABE and its vertices are at the centers of particles and neck curvature

The pore geometries and dimensions mathematically correlated with the particle and neck size using Heron's formula and cosine rules. The angles of triangle ABE calculated from Eq. (4) and Eq. (5) (cosine rule).

$$cos\alpha = \frac{AE^2 + AB^2 - BE^2}{2AE * AB} \tag{4}$$

$$cos\beta = \frac{AE^2 + BE^2 - AB^2}{2AE * BE} \tag{5}$$

Area of triangle ($A_{ABE}$) is given by Eq. (6) (Heron's formula).

$$A_{\triangle ABE} = \sqrt{P(P - AB)(P - AE)(P - BE)} \tag{6}$$

Where P is the semi perimeter of the triangle and it is given by P = 2R + R' for square and triangular pore and P = R + r + R' for rectangular pore model.

A3 (as described by Fig. 3) was evaluated using Eq. (7).

$$A_3 = \begin{cases} \dfrac{R\sqrt{2RR' + R'^2} - \dfrac{R'^2(\pi - 2\alpha)}{2} - R^2\alpha, \ square \ or \ triangular \ pore}{\sqrt{RrR'(R + r + R')} - \dfrac{R^2(\pi - \alpha - \beta)}{2} - \dfrac{R'^2}{2} - \dfrac{r^2\alpha}{2}, \ Rectangular \ pore} \end{cases} \tag{7}$$

Therefore, the area of square/rectangular pore with rounded neck (A $_{round\ neck,\ \square}$) can be evaluated by subtracting 4 times of A3 from the total area of the pore with a sharp neck (Eq. (2)) and is given by Eq. (8).

$$A_{round\ neck,\ \square} = A_{sharp\ neck,\ \square} - 4*A_3 \tag{8}$$

Similarly, the area of triangular pore between three particles with round neck (A $_{round\ neck,\ \triangle}$) is given by Eq. (9).

$$A_{round\ neck,\ \triangle} = A_{sharp\ neck,\ \triangle} - 3*A_3 \tag{9}$$

Perimeter is an important parameter of geometries used to quantify the morphological parameters of a pore. It is defined as the total length or circumference of the pore. For the pore with a sharp neck (square and rectangular), the total perimeter is the sum of the arc length of four sectors (with radius R/r) shared by the pore area. And similarly, the perimeter of a triangular pore is the sum of the three arc length of sectors (the radius R and angle 60°). The perimeter of the pore with a rounded neck is determined by subtracting the perimeter of a shaded area (A3) from the perimeter of the pore with a sharp neck. The perimeter and area of the three geometric pore models are reported in Table 1.

**Table 1.** Perimeter and area of a square, triangular and rectangular pore models

| Pore model | pore perimeter, P | pore area, A |
|---|---|---|
| Square | $\begin{cases} 2\pi R, \quad R' = 0, \\ 4\left(\frac{\pi}{2} - 2\alpha\right)R + 4(\pi - 2\alpha)R', \ R' < 0 \end{cases}$ | $\begin{cases} (4 - \pi)R^2, \quad R' = 0, \\ (4 - \pi)R^2 - 4\left\{ R\sqrt{2RR' + R'^2} - \frac{R'^2(\pi - 2\alpha)}{2} - R^2\alpha \right\}, \ R' > 0 \end{cases}$ |
| Triangular | $\begin{cases} \pi R, \quad R' = 0, \\ 3\left(\frac{\pi}{3} - 2\alpha\right)R + 3(\pi - 2\alpha)R', \ R' < 0 \end{cases}$ | $\begin{cases} \left(\sqrt{3} - \frac{\pi}{2}\right)R^2, \quad R' = 0, \\ \left(\sqrt{3} - \frac{\pi}{2}\right)R^2 - 3\left\{ R\sqrt{2RR' + R'^2} - \frac{R'^2(\pi - 2\alpha)}{2} - R^2\alpha \right\}, \ R' > 0 \end{cases}$ |
| Rectangular | $\begin{cases} 2R + 2r(\pi -), \quad R' = 0, \\ 2R + 2r(\pi -) - 4r\alpha - 4R(\pi - \alpha - \beta) + \\ \quad 4R'\beta, \ R' < 0 \end{cases}$ | $\begin{cases} 2(R + r)^2 \cos\left(\frac{\theta}{2}\right)\sin\left(\frac{\theta}{2}\right) - r^2(\pi -) - R^2, \ R' = 0, \\ 2(R + r)^2 \cos\left(\frac{\theta}{2}\right)\sin\left(\frac{\theta}{2}\right) - r^2(\pi -) - R^2 - \\ 4\left\{ \sqrt{RrR'(R + r + R')} - \frac{R^2(\pi - \alpha - \beta)}{2} - \frac{r^2\alpha}{2} - \frac{R'^2\beta}{2} \right\}, \ R' > 0 \end{cases}$ |

The equivalent diameter of the pore model is given by Eq. (10).

$$D_{eq.} = 2\sqrt{\frac{A}{\pi}} \tag{10}$$

Where A, is the pore area (reported in Table 1).

$f_{shape}$ is defined by Eq. (11).

$$f_{shape} = \frac{D_{min}}{D_{max}} \tag{11}$$

Where, $D_{max}$ and $D_{min}$, are maximum and minimum diameters of the pore, highlighted as blue and red colors in Fig. 4 and Fig. 5. The maximum and minimum diameters of square and rectangular geometric pore between four particles are given by Eq. (12) and Eq. (13), which is derived from the detailed geometry as illustrated in Fig. 4.

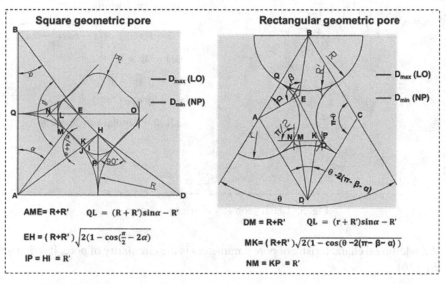

**Fig. 4.** Detail geometry of the square and rectangular geometric pore models

$$D_{min} = \begin{cases} 2IP + EH = 2R' + [R + R']\sqrt{2\left(1 - \cos\left(\frac{\pi}{2} - 2\alpha\right)\right)} \text{ ,for } \square \text{ model} \\ 2KP + MK = 2R' + [R + R']\sqrt{2(1 - \cos(\theta - 2(\pi - \beta - \alpha))} \text{ , for } \square \end{cases} \tag{12}$$

$$D_{max} = \begin{cases} AD - 2QL = 2[R + R'](1 - sin\alpha), \text{ for } \square \text{ } model \\ AD - 2QL = (R + R') + [r + R'](1 - 2sin\alpha) \text{ , for } \square \text{ model} \end{cases} \tag{13}$$

The minimum and maximum diameters of the triangular geometry pore is given by Eq. (14) and Eq. (15), which is derived from the detailed geometry as illustrated in Fig. 5.

$$D_{min} = D_{max}\sin\left(\frac{\pi}{3}\right) - IJ = D_{max}\sin\left(\frac{\pi}{3}\right) - R'\left[\sqrt{\tan^2\left(\frac{\pi}{3} - 2\alpha\right) - 1}\right] \tag{14}$$

$$D_{max} = 2NJ + FG = 2R'\tan\left(\frac{\pi}{3} - 2\alpha\right) + [R + R']\sqrt{2\left(1 - \cos\left(\frac{\pi}{3} - 2\alpha\right)\right)} \tag{15}$$

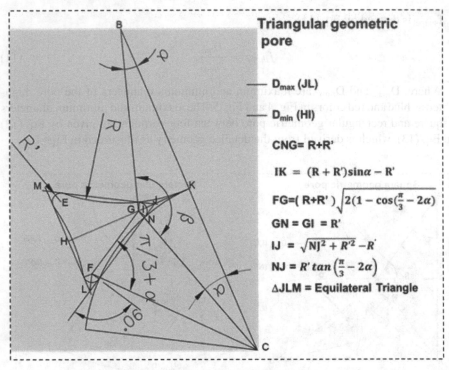

**Fig. 5.** Detail geometry of triangular pore

An additional characteristic of pore parameters is the circularity of pore. It is defined by Eq. (16).

$$f_{circle} = \frac{4\pi A}{P^2} \tag{16}$$

where A and P are the area and perimeter of pore models (reported in Table 1).

## 2.2 Materials and Experimental Methods

Two different Fe-Mo-C (interims of different Mo compositions) low prealloyed PM materials were used to study the pore characteristics. These powders compacted in double-action compaction then green compacts, which are rings, sintered at 1150 °C for 30 min, and maintained its final dimensions of 16 × 40 × 10 mm (inner diameter, outer diameter, and height, respectively). Density measurement was performed by the water displacement (WD) using a weighing balance accuracy of 0.0001 g and also calculated from the results of image analysis (IA) on the microstructures. Before microstructure preparation, the specimens were cleaned properly using toluene in the microwave, mounted in risen and gently ground from 220 to 1200.gride silica carbide polishing paper, and then polished using 3 and 1 μm alumina paste/slurry. For Image analysis, an optical microscope was used to prepare micrograph images on unattached spacemen. Seven images were taken on the contact surface (from 0–400 μm depth) of each material. To avoid the potential effect of shape parameter variation due to magnification over the microstructure, 20× magnification was selected [13]. Porosity, equivalent diameter, perimeter, aspect ratio, breadth, and length of pore were measured, and then $f_{circle}$, $f_{shape}$ were calculated.

## 3  Results and Discussion

In this section, pore size between grains, elongation, and circularity was discussed based on the analysis of the theoretical models developed using the relationship of grain sizes, number of grain contacts, and pore geometry. Again, these pore parameters were measured using image analysis applied on the microstructures of sintered steels that were used to validate the theoretical results. Figure 6 illustrates the correlation between the diameter of grain (2R) and the equivalent diameter ($D_{eq.}$) of the pore.

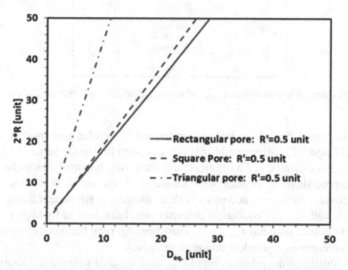

**Fig. 6.** Equivalent diameter versus particle size of square, triangular and rectangular pore models

The Equivalent diameter of rectangular, square, and triangular pore models varies linearly with the grain size. For a given grain diameter, the equivalent diameter of the triangular pore model is smaller than square and rectangular pore models. This variation shows that the triangular geometric pore may be suited to model only pores with smaller in sizes, while rectangular and square pore models are used for the bigger pores.

The circularity and shape of the pore models using triangular, rectangular, circular geometries were analyzed, and Fig. 7 represents $f_{circle}$ of the three pore models.

The area of rectangular, square, and triangular pore models is made to vary with the distance between grains (H) which is a function of the grain (R) and neck sizes (R'). Therefore, $f_{circle}$ of the triangular, rectangular, and square pore geometries is a function of the equivalent diameter that is dependent on grain (R) and neck (R/r nad R') sizes too. For the three models and sharp neck (R' = 0), $f_{circle}$ is constant and independent of the

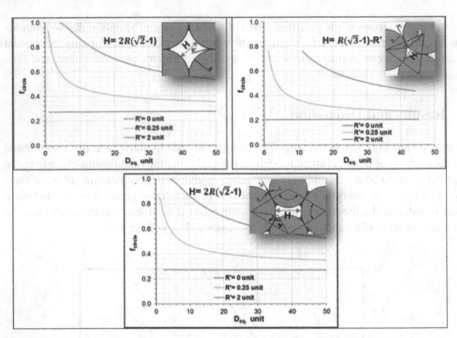

**Fig. 7.** Equivalent diameter versus $f_{circle}$ of square, triangular and rectangular pore models

pore size. The circularity of square/rectangular and triangular pore models with sharp corners is 0.21 and 0.27, respectively, that is the bottom line to the value of $f_{circle}$. When neck size increases (from 0 to 2 unit), $f_{circle}$ also increases that attributes to the formation of a rounded pore shape as the size of the length of the curved neck increases. But, at a constant neck size, circularity decreases with an increasing equivalent diameter of pore models. Pores with smaller equivalent diameter are characterized by higher circularity, and a perfect circular pore has $f_{circle} = 1$. However, the pore becomes elongated and its circularity decreases as equivalent diameter increases.

Figure 8 illustrates the relationship of $D_{eq.}$ and $f_{shape}$ of triangular, rectangular, and square pore models.

The horizontal bottom line indicates that the constant $f_{sahpe}$ of the pore with a sharp edge ($R' = 0$) and the values are 0.71, 071, and 0.87 for rectangular, square, and triangular pore models, respectively. $f_{shape}$ of the rectangular and square pore model is lower than the triangular pore model at the equal equivalent diameter and neck size. A similar trend was observed for $f_{circl}$ and $f_{shape}$ and both decreases with increasing equivalent pore size. Pores with smaller equivalent diameters are characterized by lower in irregularity and equivalent with a rounded geometry that results in a higher $f_{shape}$, then it equated to 1 as the geometry approaches a circular pore.

Again, the relationship between pore shape and circularity was analyzed, and Fig. 9 represents $f_{circle}$ versus $f_{shape}$ of triangular, rectangular, and square pore models with a variable gap between contacted grains and fixed height between bigger particles.

Since contacting grains that are used in the molding of the square and triangular pores are equal in size, the gap between grains (H) increases linearly with the grain size

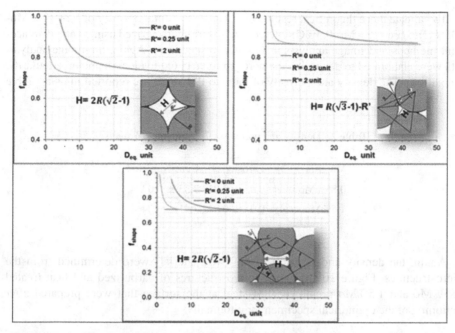

**Fig. 8.** Equivalent diameter versus $f_{shape}$ of square, triangular and rectangular pore models

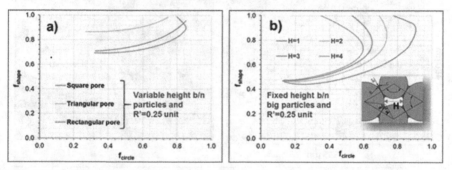

**Fig. 9.** $f_{circle}$ versus $f_{shape}$ of the three pore models: a) at a gap between grains (defined by, $H = 2R\left(\sqrt{2}-1\right)$ for rectangular and square models, and $H = R\left(\sqrt{3}-1\right) - R'$ for triangular pore), and b) at a different fixed height between bigger grains of the rectangular model.

(R), and it does not affect the relationship between $f_{circle}$ and $f_{shape}$. However, for the rectangular pore model, the size of the grains is not the same (characterized using R and r), such that the gap between grains depends on the size of the grain. At a fixed distance between larger grains, and as the gap between smaller particles is increasing, the relationship between $f_{circle}$ and $f_{shape}$ can be variable. Therefore, the relationship of circularity and elongation for the square, triangular and rectangular pore models shows similar trends of variations, and for rectangular pore geometry, the gap between particles is the determinate factor to $f_{circle}$ and $f_{shape}$ relation.

To validate these theoretical results, first density and total porosity of Fe-0.85%Mo-0.35%C and Fe-1.5%Mo-0.3%C sintered steels were characterized using water displacement methods and image analysis techniques, respectively. Again, the image analysis data were elaborated to determine the pore parameters (equivalent diameter, circularity, elongation). The density and porosity of the two PM steels are reported in using Table 2.

**Table 2.** Density and porosity of prealloyed PM steels

| Material | Porosity, $\varepsilon$ | Density, g/cm3 |
|---|---|---|
| 0.85%Mo steel | $0.06 \pm 0.01$ | $7.33 \pm 0.04$ |
| 1.5%Mo steel | $0.05 \pm 0.01$ | $7.41 \pm 0.04$ |

Again, the density and porosity of the two materials were determined from the microstructures. Figure 10 shows the microstructures of carburized and heat treated 0.85%Mo and 1.5%Mo prealloyed PM steel at the surface that were prepared after sectioning of the cylindrical specimen longitudinally.

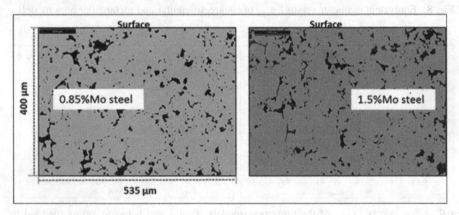

**Fig. 10.** Microstructure at the surface of carburized and heat treated low alloyed steels

To measure the pore parameters, image analysis was carried out on the surfaces of seven adjacent microstructures (each has a total area of $400 \times 535$ µm) on each PM steels. The average porosity and pore parameters were collected within 50 µm range up to the total depth of 400 µm. Average porosity 0.85% Mo and 1.5% Mo steels are 0.07 $\pm$ 0.01 and 0.07 $\pm$ 0.02, respectively.

Figure 11 represents $f_{circle}$ and $f_{shape}$ corresponding to 100% of pore populations measured by image analysis and three geometric pore models.

The results of pore models and image analysis shows that $f_{circle}$ decreases with increasing equivalent pore diameters. However, $f_{shape}$ determined from the model relatively higher than determined from the experimental results of the two materials. Image

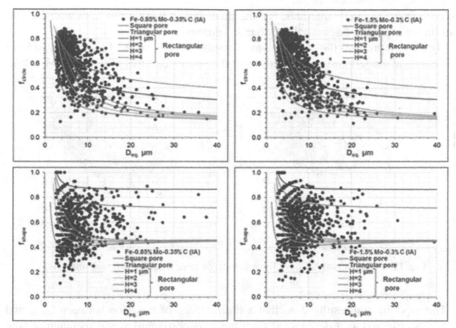

**Fig. 11.** $f_{circle}$ and $f_{shape}$ of the three pore model and image analysis of the micrograph 270 μm width by 400 μm depth.

analysis results of the irregular pore with lower circularity and shape are well fitted with a rectangular geometric pore model, whereas the pore with higher circularity and shape are well fitted with the square and triangular pore models. However, the pore morphology and sizes are statistical and the experimental results may not be expected to fit exactly with the model results, however, the results of $f_{circle}$ and $f_{shape}$ determined based on the two approaches are still comparable. Moreover, the rectangular pore model is agreed more with the smaller and larger size pore populations, and the square and triangular pore model agreed more with the smaller size and rounded pore populations. The large pore with rounded in morphology (large R and R', as it is illustrated using Fig. 7) of the pore model, may greatly approximate to explain the circularity of the pore characterized by image analysis. Therefore, the neck size, R', can be an important parameter of the pore modeling, which can be liked with sintering parameters. To model, the pore in the microstructure of PM materials depends on different processing parameters such that, R' can vary from zero to certain values. It is merely related to the type of materials and microstructures. Therefore, using larger R' may get higher priority and could get good agreement with a material having a larger pore size and rounded morphology. R' = 0.25 μm found to be the best fit with the microstructures of 0.85%Mo and 1.5%Mo steels.

$f_{shape}$ collected from the microstructures is more elongated in shape. On the contrary, the model shows rounded pore, $f_{shape}$ values are above 0.87 and 0.701 for triangular and square pore models, respectively. This indicates that the pore is not elongated as it is observed from the microstructures. But the small R′ can be selected to fit with the data from image analysis of densified and rounded porous materials.

Figure 12 represents the comparisons of results of $f_{circle}$ versus $f_{shape}$ analyzed from the theoretical models and image analysis of the microstructures of the two PM steels.

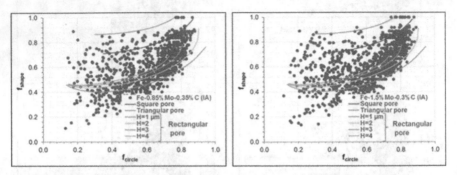

**Fig. 12.** $f_{circle}$ versus $f_{shape}$ of three geometric pore model and image analysis.

The experimental results show that a similar trend of variation between $f_{circle}$ and $f_{shape}$ was observed as it determined from the square, triangular, and rectangular pore models. The smaller pore size, which is characterized as rounded and regular pore, can be represented using square and triangular pore models, whereas the bigger pore, which is characterized as more irregular pore, can be represented using a rectangular pore model. Besides, a rectangular pore model with a neck size of R′ = 0.25 μm is comparable with the data of image analysis.

## 4   Conclusions

The theoretical model to characterize equivalent diameter, circularity, and elongation of pores between the contacts of three and four grains with sharp and rounded necks were analyzed. Based on the number of contacts between grains, grain size, and neck size, a mathematical model was formulated to determine the equivalent diameter and pore parameters ($f_{shape}$ and $f_{circle}$) of the pore formed between grains. To validate the model results, image analysis was carried out to measure porosity, equivalent pore diameter, pore area, and perimeter on the microstructure of Fe-0.85%Mo-0.35%C and Fe-1.5%Mo-0.3%C prealloyed PM material that used to analyze the pore parameters. The model is comparable with image analysis results and the following conclusion is drawn from the results,

- A pore model with a sharp neck is used to determine the lower limit of circularity ($f_{circle}$) and elongation ($f_{shape}$).
- The Square and triangular pore models represent the pore with higher circularity. But the rectangular geometric pore model is exactly fitted with irregular and larger pore size.

- Modeling of the pore parameters of a pore with a rounded neck shows better agreement with the results of image analysis, in particular, $f_{circle}$ and $f_{shape}$ of pore populations with smaller pore fits well with square and triangular pore models. Whereas the rectangular geometric pore model is well fitted with pore populations with irregular and larger pore size.
- As future work, the model is important to link the effect of pore size, shape, and morphology with the mechanical properties. In particular, nucleation of fatigue and contact fatigue cracks can be the prominent areas.

# References

1. Cristofolini, I., Molinari, A., Straffelini, G., Muterlle, P.V.: A systematic approach to design against wear for powder metallurgy (PM) steel parts: the case of dry rolling-sliding wear. Mater. Des. **32**(4), 2191–2198 (2011)
2. Metinöz, I., Cristofolini, I., Pahl, W., DeNicolo, A., Marconi, P., Molinari, A.: Theoretical and experimental study of the contact fatigue behavior of a Mo–Cu steel produced by powder metallurgy. Mater. Sci. Eng. A **614**, 81–87 (2014)
3. Mekonone, S.T., Pahl, W., Molinari, A.: Influence of the microstructure on the subsurface and surface damage during lubricated rolling-sliding wear of sintered and sinterhardened 1.5%Mo–2%Cu–0.6%C steel: theoretical analysis and experimental investigation. Powder Metall. **61**(3), 187–196 (2018)
4. Tesfaye, S., Molinari, A., Pahl, W.: Damage phenomena in lubricated rolling-sliding wear of a gas carburised 0.85%Mo low-alloyed sintered steel: theoretical analysis and experimental verification. Powder Metall. 1–9 (2017)
5. German, R.M.: Sintering Theory and Practice (1996)
6. German, R.M.: Powder Metallurgy Science, Met. Powder Ind. Fed. 105 Coll. Rd E Princet. N J 08540 U 1984 279 (1984)
7. German, R.M.: Powder Metallurgy of Iron and Steel. John Wiley Sons Inc 605 Third Ave N. Y. NY 10016 USA 1998 496 (1998)
8. Tomić, N.Z., et al.: Image analysis and the finite element method in the characterization of the influence of porosity parameters on the mechanical properties of porous EVA/PMMA polymer blends. Mech. Mater. **129**, 1–14 (2019)
9. Sonsino, C.M.: Fatigue design for powder metallurgy. Met. Powder Rep. **45**(11), 754–764 (1990)
10. Sonsino, C.M.: Fatigue design principles for sintered steel components. J. Strain Anal. Eng. Des. **41**(7), 497–555 (2006)
11. Benedetti, M., Menapace, C.: Tooth root bending fatigue strength of small-module sinter-hardened spur gears. Powder Metall. **60**(2), 149–156 (2017)
12. EUDIER, M. : The mechanical properties of sintered low-alloy steels. Powder Metall. **5**(9), 278–290 (1962)
13. Fleck, N.A., Smith, R.A.: Use of simple models to estimate effect of density on fracture behaviour of sintered steel. Powder Metall. **24**(3), 126–130 (1981)
14. Williams, S.H., Haynes, R.: Effect of porosity on the fatigue behaviour of sintered precipitated nickel powder. Powder Metall. **16**(32), 387–404 (1973)
15. Fleck, N.A., Smith, R.A.: Effect of density on tensile strength, fracture toughness, and fatigue crack propagation behaviour of sintered steel. Powder Metall. **24**(3), 121–125 (1981)
16. Hanejko, F., Rawlings, A., Narasimhan, K.S.V.: Surface densified P/M steel–comparison with wrought steel grades. In: Euro PM2005 Prague, pp. 509–511 (2005)

17. Chawla, N., Deng, X.: Microstructure and mechanical behavior of porous sintered steels. Mater. Sci. Eng. A **390**(1), 98–112 (2005)
18. Kubicki, B.: Stress concentration at pores in sintered materials. Powder Metall. **38**(4), 295–298 (1995)
19. Andersson, M.: The role of porosity in fatigue of PM materials. Powder Metall. Prog. **1**, 11 (2011)
20. Molinari, A., Metinöz, I., Cristofolini, I.: A conservative approach to predict the contact fatigue behavior of sintered steels. Powder Metall. Prog. **1**, 7 (2014)
21. Martin, W.D., Putman, B.J., Kaye, N.B.: Using image analysis to measure the porosity distribution of a porous pavement. Constr. Build. Mater. **48**, 210–217 (2013)
22. Brewin, P.R., Coube, O., Doremus, P., Tweed, J.H. (eds.): Modelling of Powder Die Compaction. Springer-Verlag, London (2008)
23. Samal, P., Newkirk, J. (eds.): Modeling and simulation of press and sinter powder metallurgy [1]. In: Powder Metallurgy. ASM International, pp. 179–190 (2015)
24. Rojek, J., Nosewicz, S., Maździarz, M., Kowalczyk, P., Wawrzyk, K., Lumelskyj, D.: Modeling of a sintering process at various scales. Proc. Eng. **177**, 263–270 (2017)
25. Pan, J.: Modelling sintering at different length scales. Int. Mater. Rev. **48**(2), 69–85 (2003)

# Design of Improved Nodal Classroom Chair for Ethiopian Higher Education Students to Transform Active Learning

Fetene Teshome Teferi(✉) ⓘ and Eyob Messele Sefene ⓘ

Faculty of Mechanical and Industrial Engineering, Bahir Dar Institute of Technology, Bahir Dar University, P.O. Box 26, Bahir Dar, Ethiopia

**Abstract.** A well-designed classroom chair is considered an important teaching resource to improve comfort and concentration in lecturing and peer activities of students. This research work focuses on the design of an improved classroom chair for engineering students to enhance active and conducive teaching-learning environment in Ethiopia universities. The motivation to do this research is the observed challenges and functional requirements in the classroom of many Ethiopian engineering institutes. Alternative conceptual nodal classroom chairs were sketched to reach to the final design of the classroom chair that can meet the specified requirements. The final designed nodal classroom chair was developed based on the assigned criteria's. The designed chair has four pivots to move the seat and table at the specified position to allow students during individual and peer activities. It is also developed considering the international furniture design guideline to maintain the ergonomic and anthropometric size of higher education students. In the final design of the nodal classroom chair, the critical dimensions of the average popliteal height of seat chair and table height are taken as 460 mm and 760 mm respectively based on the standard guidelines of British and EN 1729. An improved nodal classroom chair can be used to implement both lecture and Engineering drawing preparation with maximum size of A3 paper size.

**Keywords:** Nodal classroom chair · Design concept · Ergonomics · Active learning

## Nomenclature

RHS = Rectangular hollow steel.
SHS = Square hollow steel.
CHS = Circular hollow steel.
MDF = Medium-density fiber board.

## 1 Introduction

Ethiopia is the second-most populous country in Africa after Nigeria, with a population of 105 million. It is also one of the least developed countries in the world, ranked 173rd

M. A. Delele et al. (Eds.): ICAST 2020, LNICST 385, pp. 261–273, 2021.
https://doi.org/10.1007/978-3-030-80618-7_17

among 189 countries on the United Nations' Human Development Index [1]. Overall enrollments in secondary education in the nation of 105 million people are remarkably low by international standards. In 2013, the British Council projected that the number of tertiary students in Ethiopia will increase by an additional 1.7 million by 2025 [1]. Ethiopia has approximately 44 operational public universities right now. In addition to public universities, there are 32 public teacher training colleges, many TVET schools, and private colleges. In 2015, there were 729,028 undergraduate students, 37,152 students in master's programs, and 3,135 students in doctoral programs [1]. However, the number of students in higher education firms is increasing time to time. Ethiopia currently aspires to become a middle-income country by 2025 and wants to use higher education as its major tool of poverty reduction and economic development. The transformation of its agriculture-led economy to an industrial economy hinges on the availability of an educated workforce that can play a critical role in technology transfer and knowledge creation [2].

To realize such a vision, facilitating the required resources for teaching and learning process in higher education firms is highly essential. The most common resources used in the classroom are furniture, black and white boards, LCD projectors, well-ventilated classroom, and other teaching aids. To transform an interactive teaching-learning process, the development of a well-designed seating nodal chair has a significant influence. Hence, improved design classroom furniture allows students and teachers to vary their routines. This has many benefits, including encouraging peer-to-peer collaboration, connections with teachers, facilitating student engagement, and offering multiple options of teaching modes. By understanding the integral role of furniture and learning mode in transforming education, the authors are motivated to design an improved classroom nodal chair that would enhance teaching and learning environment.

## 1.1 Teaching Practices in Higher Education Institute of Ethiopia

In Ethiopia, the main course delivery methods in higher education universities include lectures, tutors, and experimental sessions according to the course guide book. The existing classroom furniture found in many universities are stationary armchairs, combined seats and desks, heavy chairs, and tables that do not allow students to interact easily. Students are even doing engineering drawings in such non-conducive working table. This situation hinders students' performance and understanding capacity of them. However, the instructors are interested to give peer group activities in the classroom, the arrangement of chair and tables for this purpose is time taker and tedious process. The design and development of portable, flexible furniture is required to enhance student-centered learning processes. The main objectives of designing and upgrading classroom chairs are to encourage interactive learning, provide comfortable sitting with larger work surfaces, improve functional relationships, increase flexibility to respond to future needs, increase classroom use rates, and increase students and teachers motivation in the learning and teaching process. Figure 1 below presents the teaching-learning scenario with an armchair seat in Bahir Dar Institute of Technology.

The armchair seat shown in Fig. 1 does not allow students to interact during group activities at the expected level, and also it is time taker to move and arrange thus chairs to apply different modes of teaching- learning processes.

**a.** Trainees sitting conditon during lecture time.    **b.** Trainees sitting conditions during group

**Fig. 1.** Existing classroom armchair at Bahir Dar Institute of Technology, Ethiopia.

## 1.2   Effect of Classroom Furniture on Active learning Environment

Active learning classrooms were identified as a top strategic technology and are more or less flexible depending on the type of furniture used. Furniture plays a vital role in the environment of active teaching and learning process. Proper usage of an ergonomically classroom chair is needed for the maintenance of good health, improvement in academic performance, active learning and motivation [3]. Improperly designed furniture, ill-fitted to the characteristics of a student can result in faster fatigue, defective posture, and the establishment of pathological states that could affect their performance in focusing in class [4, 5]. Classroom chairs could support body weight and enable postural movement and circulation [6]. On average, students spend a quarter of the day at school and 80% of the school time is mostly in the sitting position. Therefore, ergonomically precise sitting posture is an important factor for the elimination of musculoskeletal symptoms [7].

## 2   Methods and Design Considerations

### 2.1   Methods

To conduct this research work, the following methods and methodologies are applied.

1. A survey was conducted through observation and physical measurement of the avail classroom chairs which were used by students in higher education institute of Ethiopia, Bahir Dar institute of Technology to compile information for further improvement of the design of classroom chair. The existed overall dimension of armchair has 65 cm length, 65 cm width and 88c m height as shown below on Fig. 1.

   The armchair was fabricated from an oval shape steel pipe (20 mm * 30 mm * 1.25 mm), round steel pipe ( outer ø 22 mm and wall thickness 1.25 mm) and laminated plywood which has 10 mm thickness. The actual measured dimension of each part of the chair is shown below on Table 1.

   The available armchair which was shown on Fig. 1 is used for theoretical lecturing and also teaching technical drawing for extension engineering students in Bahir Dar

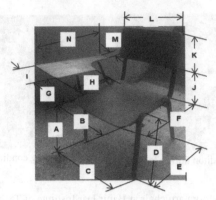

**Fig. 2.** Physical shape and dimension of armchair (Source: the picture was captured in Bahir Dar institute of Technology, February 2020).

**Table 1.** Measured dimensions of classroom armchair in Bahir Dar Institute of Technology.

| Measurement designation | Name of the measurement | Measurement values ( cm) |
|---|---|---|
| A | Popliteal height | 41 |
| B | Seat length ( buttock-popliteal length) | 45 |
| C | Base length | 52 |
| D | Stand height | 46 |
| E | Stand bottom width | 45 |
| F | Stand top width | 30 |
| G | Height between seat and arm table | 25 |
| H | Short length of arm table | 27 |
| I | Width of arm table | 28 |
| J | Height between seat and back support | 22 |
| K | Height of wooden back support | 25 |
| L | Length of wooden back support | 48 |
| M | Narrow width of arm table | 10 |
| N | Length of wooden arm table | 50 |

Institute of Technology. However the chair is not convenient for left-handed students and to prepare technical drawing (Fig. 2).

2. Literatures was assessed and reviewed from previous scientific research.
3. Developing alternative design concepts and screening out the best design.
4. Applying CATIA software for modeling and preparation of working drawing.

Generally, to fulfill the actual functional requirement of the designed chair, the current scenario of teaching -learning methods, used resources, and teaching aids are considered.

## 2.2  Design consideration

### 2.2.1 Design Requirements

The design of classroom chairs are done by considering students' requirements, functional requirements, and technical requirements to support interactive teaching and learning activities. The final design of this nodal chair should be ergonomically safe, robust, comfortable, moveable, and rotary in all directions of classmates to apply variable teaching methodology in the classroom. In addition the chair is not only lecturing purpose but also useful for practicing engineering drawing by using the size of A4 and A3 drawing paper. It also has material keeping case to handle books, bags, drawing instruments, water bottles, pencils, and pens to create conducive situations during teaching and learning process.

### 2.2.2 Ergonomic Consideration

Ergonomics is an engineering profession that applies theory, principles, data, and methods for understanding the interaction between humans and equipment to optimize conducive and safe working environments [8]. Anthropometry is a science that deals with body measurements, where the measure body length, shape, strength, and working capacity [9]. Ergonomic considerations in classroom chair design give many qualitative and quantitative advantages such as reducing developmental lead-time and cost, increasing user comfort and reliability [10, 11, 15]. The functional utility of the student's classroom furniture is a result of its physical design in relation to the physical structure and biomechanics of the human body. Hence, the key anthropometric dimensions shown in Fig. 3 (1–12) are considered in our chair design procedures (Table 2).

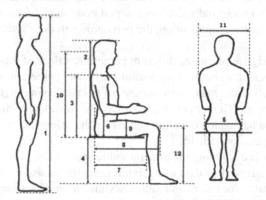

**Fig. 3.** Key anthropometric dimensions required for chair design [16].

The chair dimensions shown in Fig. 4 are a general-purpose chair to be used by any adult [12]. All elements of the chair must be planned. The seat height is determined by

**Table 2.** Anthropometric dimensions and their description.

| No | Designation | Descrption |
|----|-------------|------------|
| 1 | Stature | The vertical distance from the floor to the crown of the head |
| 2 | Sitting height | Height between seat and Top of the head in a normal relaxed posture |
| 3 | Sitting mid shoulder height | Height between the seat and level of the shoulder |
| 4 | Popliteal height | Height of the underside of the thigh immediately behind the knee |
| 5 | Hip breadth | Maximum horizontal distance across the hips |
| 6 | Elbow rest height | Distance between seat and lower most part of the elbow |
| 7 | Buttock-popliteal length | Horizontal distance from the most posterior point on the uncompressed buttocks to the back of the lower leg at the knee |
| 8 | Buttock knee length | Horizontal distance from the most posterior point on the uncompressed buttocks to most anterior point on the knee |
| 9 | Thigh clearance | The vertical distance from the seat surface to the maximum bulge on the anterior surface of the thigh was measured with a shortened anthropometer |
| 10 | Sitting eye height | Height of inner corner of the eye sitting in normal relaxed posture |
| 11 | Shoulder breadth | Maximum horizontal distance across the shoulders |
| 12 | Knee height | Height of uppermost point on the knee |

the popliteal height measurement "4" in Fig. 3. The popliteal height is the measure from the floor to the back part of the leg behind the knee joint while seated.

In designing for a known individual, one's own body dimensions may be measured and used. However, for mass application, the percentile values of a study population are usually required.

Therefore, in design application, different percentile values of different dimensions may be necessary even on a simple design solution. Lower percentile values are considered for accommodating the maximum number of people having higher values, where easy reach is the concern. Higher percentile values are considered where the maximum number of population having lower values cannot reach the level, as required in ensuring safety and ease of operation [13, 16, 17].

In This study, we are applying the general guidelines of British and European Standards for furniture design rather than using anthropometric measured data's. The British and European Standards for chairs and tables design for an educational institution was approved in January 2007. BS EN 1729 Part 1 (functional dimensions) ensures furniture to be appropriate size, shape and ergonomic design to maintain good posture and reduce Repetitive strain injury (RSI) and back pain in students. This size mark guide for higher education adult students indicates the fixed seat heights and table heights of suitable chair for the student's age as shown on Fig. 4 below [14].

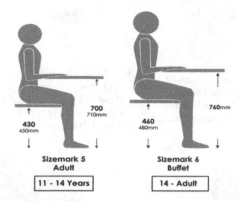

**Fig. 4.** Recommended chair and table size for design guide, EN1729 [14].

Since the fixed popliteal height and table height are mainly considered for improved nodal chair development. The average popliteal height of seat chair 460 mm and table height 760 mm indicated in Fig. 3 leads the author to generate a new design concept and to determine the average size of nodal classroom chair for engineering students to meet the specified objectives.

### 2.2.3 Design Concept Generation

The design idea of an improved nodal classroom chair is generated after analyzing all the requirements and observing the challenges faced in the classroom. For better interactive teaching and learning environments, the design should allow the chair to be moveable easily in any place of the class, and also the chair should allow the students to interact with their near classmates in all directions by rotating easily. In addition, the chair should function engineering students to do engineering drawing by handling all required materials safely and conveniently. In this stage, four different nodal classroom chair concepts were generated based on the major requirements. Each conceptual classroom chair design has its own design features and functions. The four conceptual chair designs are presented in Fig. 5 below with their brief descriptions.

The conceptual designs shown above on Fig. 5 are designed by targeting the specific purposes of comfort, ergonomic and safety, learning material handling, drawing practice, and peer learning. The nodal classroom chairs have four rotating pivots to allow rotary degrees of freedom for better interaction of students without wasting time. The designer considers the movability of the seat and table to adjust it to the convenient position during writing and drawing. The parts shown in the conceptual design from 1 to 9 are described as pen and pencil tray, table, seat frame, load support, base and material handler, foot (caster wheel), seat wood, and back seat respectively. The four conceptual designs are described below shortly.

**Concept Design 1(cd1).** The nodal classroom chair shown in Fig. 5a is designed to be fixed on the floor with fisher and screw. However, the seat and the table are easily

a. Nodal classroom chair conceptual design 1. ( 1. Pen and pencil case, 2. Table, 3. Seat frame, 4. Leg, 5. Material case, 6. Foot, 7. Laminated wood seat, 8. Back support)

b. Nodal classroom chair conceptual design 2. (1. Pen and pencil case, 2. Table, 3. Table stand, 4. Leg, 5. Material case, 6. Perforated hole for waste removal, 7. Caster wheel, 8. Seat, 9. Back support)

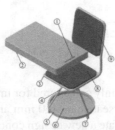

c. Nodal classroom chair conceptual design 3. (1. Pen and pencil case, 2. Table, 3. Table stand, 4. Leg, 5. Material case, 6. Perforated hole for waste removal, 7. Foot, 8. Seat, 9. Back support)

d. Nodal classroom chair conceptual design 4. (1. Pen and pencil case, 2. Table, 3. Table stand, 4. Leg, 5. Base, 6. Caster wheel, 7.seat, 8. Back support)

**Fig. 5.** Conceptual design of alternatives nodal classroom chairs (a–d).

rotated for convenient sitting and peer learning. In addition, this design includes learning material handling at the base of the chair.

**Concept Design 2(cd2).** The conceptual design shown in Fig. 5b is similar to conceptual design 1 except for the replacement of caster wheel to allow the movement of degree of freedom of the chair to go to at any place in the classroom for the intended purpose.

**Concept Design 3(cd3).** The additional features of conceptual design 3 over concepts 1 and 2 are teaching material drawer with table. This may help students to manage their learning materials easily and safely.

**Concept Design 4 (cd4).** The conceptual design 4 is similar to conceptual design with all features except the replacement of a fixed foot with a caster wheel. This might help students to move any place in the classroom to interact with other students or other planned purposes. The major differences between the four conceptual designs lie in the portability and teaching material handling convenience. However, the selection of a better design will be done using a design concept screening technique.

**2.2.4 Design Concept Screening**

The concept screening is a method used to sort out the number of concepts to reach to improved design concepts. This step was completed by comparing the merits and demerits of the generated concepts based on the specified selection parameters. In concept screening process, if any of the conceptual design of the chair is better than the other conceptual design and existed armchair, it is marked by a plus sign. On the other hand, a negative sign is used for the worst design than other alternative designs. The net score was calculated by summing up the positive and negative values. The concepts were ranked based on the total scores from highest to the lowest. Major selection criterions such as ergonomics and safety, ease of use, ease of manufacture, durability, and aesthetics are considered for refining purposes. Table 3 was used to rank the concepts and to choose the best one. The process follows the six basic steps to reach to final decision. These steps are preparing the selection matrix, rating the concepts based on selection criterions, ranking the concepts based on summed scores, combining, and improving the concepts, selecting one best concept and reflecting on the results, and the process.

**Table 3.** Design concept screening out matrix.

| No | Selection parameters | Alternative conceptual design | | | |
|---|---|---|---|---|---|
| | | Cd1 | Cd2 | Cd3 | Cd4 |
| 1 | Ergonomics and safety | + | + | + | + |
| 2 | Manufacturability | + | + | + | + |
| 3 | Material availability | + | + | − | − |
| 4 | Comfortably | + | + | + | + |
| 5 | Stability | + | − | + | − |
| 6 | Durability | + | + | + | + |
| 7 | flexibility | + | + | + | + |
| 8 | Aesthetic | + | + | + | + |
| 9 | Space saving | + | − | + | - |
| 10 | Maintainability | + | + | + | + |
| 11 | Cost | + | − | + | − |
| | Sum of "+"s | 11 | 8 | 10 | 7 |
| | Sum of "−"s | 1 | 3 | 2 | 4 |
| | Net score | 10 | 5 | 8 | 3 |
| | Rank | 1st | 3rd | 2nd | 4th |

*Cd = conceptual design

From Table 3 above, the design screening out matrix shows that conceptual design 1 is more preferable than other alternative design concepts depending on the assigned criterions. Thus final designed nodal classroom chair will be fixed on the floor and can be implemented on small area of classroom. On this chair, the students are able to draw any given working drawing with A4 and A3 paper. The chair also allows students to rotate in directions of their classmates for discussion and other peer activities.

## 2.2.5 Material Selection and Fabrication

The final design of the nodal classroom can be fabricated from locally available materials such as RHS, SHS, CHS, black sheet iron, and MDF wood, with the expected strength and functional requirements. The designed nodal classroom chair can be manufactured in small and medium metal manufacturing industries. The major manufacturing processes to be applied are cutting, pipe bending and rolling, welding, drilling, finishing, and assembling by using basic tools and machineries. Table 4 below presents the required raw materials and estimated cost to fabricate the final design nodal classroom chair.

**Table 4.** Main raw materials and estimated cost for nodal classroom chair fabrication.

| No | Item description with technical specification | Unit | Qty | Unit price (ETB) | Total price (ETB) |
|---|---|---|---|---|---|
| 1 | RHS (20*40*1.5) mm, length = 300 cm | pcs | 1 | 200.00 | 200.00 |
| 2 | Black sheet iron, dimension:(500*500*1) mm | pcs | 1 | 75.00 | 75.00 |
| 3 | SHS (25*25*1.5) mm, length = 400 mm | pcs | 1 | 24.00 | 24.00 |
| 4 | CHS: O. diameter = 43 mm, I. diameter = 35 mm, L = 100 mm | pcs | 1 | 10.00 | 10.00 |
| 5 | CHS: O. diameter = 33 mm, I. diameter = 28 mm, L = 200 mm | pcs | 1 | 20.00 | 20.00 |
| 6 | CHS: O. diameter = 50 mm, I. diameter = 44 mm, L = 100 mm | pcs | 1 | 15.00 | 15.00 |
| 7 | CHS: O. diameter = 27 mm, I. diameter = 23 mm, L = 160 mm | pcs | 1 | 10.00 | 10.00 |
| 8 | MDF Wood for table part:( 75 * 45 *1.6) cm | pcs | 1 | 45.00 | 45.00 |
| 9 | Laminated ply-wood for seat: (40 *45 *1.2) cm | pcs | 1 | 50.00 | 50.00 |
| 10 | Laminated ply-wood for back seat: (40 *25 *1.2) cm | pcs | 1 | 40.00 | 40.00 |
| 11 | Flat iron: (40 *4* 120) mm | pcs | 1 | 15.00 | 15.00 |
| 12 | Snap head bolt and nut: M6, length = 40 mm | pcs | 4 | 10.00 | 40.00 |
| 13 | Electrode, diameter 2.5 mm | pkt | 0.1 | 220.00 | 22.00 |
| 14 | Cutting tools | | | 100.00 | 100.00 |
| 15 | Paints | | | 150.00 | 150.00 |
| | Estimated total material cost | | | | 816.00 |
| | Labour cost | | | | 800.00 |
| | Overhead cost | | | | 200.00 |
| | Miscellaneous cost | | | | 200.00 |
| | Total selling price | | | | 2016.00 |

The modified nodal classroom chair was adapted from the existed acrylic modern classroom chair with desk which is used abroad. The nodal chair is possibly developed from available materials in the local market of Bahir Dar Ethiopia. The estimated selling price of the modified nodal classroom chair will be 2016.00 ETB. This price is lower when we compare to the price of armchair which is currently sold with 60USB (2100.00 ETB) used in the classroom of Bahir Dar Institute of Technology. It would also benefit the manufacturer of local enterprises and end users by reducing foreign currency.

### 2.2.6 Working Principles and Assembly Technique

The designed nodal classroom chair has an overall dimension of 50 cm * 50 cm * 85 cm. The popliteal height and table height from the floor is approximately 46 cm and 76 cm respectively, to meet the average ergonomical size of higher education students. The chair has three principal parts which are base sub-assembly, seat sub-assembly and table sub-assembly. The base assembly is fixed to the floor with fisher and screw by maintaining the perpendicularity of the post part. Next to base fixing, the table sub-assembly is fitted to the post of the base by sliding the table bush over it with close clearance assembly. Finally, the seat sub-assembly is fitted between the table hub and the base post with close clearance. These assembling techniques allow the seat and table to rotate in the required position of the student. Hence the movability of the chair facilitates student-centered learning easily by saving time and it also motivates students and teachers because of its conducive features for a variety of teaching pedagogy.

## 3    Result and Discussion

The final design of nodal classroom chair will play the vital role for facilitating student-centered learning. It has a capacity to rotate in all directions of classmate to share ideas and to perform peer activities in comfort seat. It is also designed by considering the basic criteria and requirements to minimize the existing challenges in the classroom. Figure 6 below presents the features of the final design of classroom chair and its assembly order.

The chair can be manufactured from available materials in the local market by maintaining its strength and functional requirement. The designed chair functioned as seat and comfortable table for both lecturing and also practicing of drawing for higher education engineering students. The major subassembly units can be assembled within a minute without using temporary fasteners.

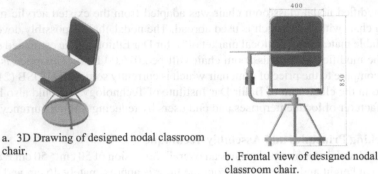

a. 3D Drawing of designed nodal classroom chair.

b. Frontal view of designed nodal classroom chair.

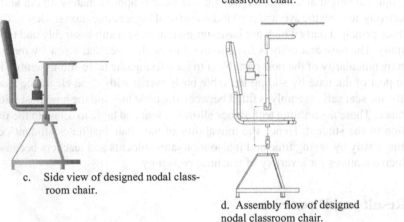

c. Side view of designed nodal classroom chair.

d. Assembly flow of designed nodal classroom chair.

**Fig. 6.** Final design features of nodal classroom chair (a–d).

## 4   Conclusion and Future Work

Classroom chairs is one of the basic inputs to run teaching –learning activities. Many studies indicated that well-designed classroom furniture has a positive influence on students to understand the subject matter and to keep them from fatigue problem. As developing comfortable educational classroom chair should also support the learning activities of the students. Therefore school furniture should be able to facilitate learning by providing a comfortable and stress-free workstation. It could help us to prevent discomfort, inappropriate sitting postures and occurring musculoskeletal disorders, conclusively increasing efficiency in schooling situations. Hence, the following conclusions are drawn from the final design works of nodal classroom chair.

1. The existing armchair in the classroom does not allow changing the traditional teaching pedagogy because of its inconvenience for required arrangements.
2. The newly designed nodal classroom chair is developed by following the international furniture design guide line to maintain the average anthropometric size of higher education students and also considers the functional requirements in the classroom in Ethiopia such as peer activities and practicing of engineering drawing.

3. The high degree of freedom of movement on the table and seat part of the designed chair allows students for better interaction between them for the given instruction and other activities.
4. In general, the screen out designed classroom chair is affordable, comfortable and fulfills the functional requirements of higher education students in Ethiopia if it is implemented as per the design specification.
5. In future studies, anthropometric measurements, cost reduction techniques on the designed nodal chair should be further studied to implement in all stage of Ethiopian students by including the major facilities on the classroom chair.

# References

1. Stefan Trines, Research Editor, WENR (2018) Education in Ethiopia
2. World Education Forum: Semonegna Education 1, Education Development Roadmap of Ethiopia: Embarking the differentiated higher education system by the year 2020 (2019)
3. Patron, D.D.: Classroom Ergonomics Implications for Health, Safety and Academic Performance. The Free Library, Huntington Valley 2009 (2013)
4. Lefler, R.K.: Office chair: choosing the right ergonomic office Deerfield, IL: Spine-health (2010)
5. Lane, K.E., Richardson, M.D.: Human Factors Engineering and School Furniture: A Circular Odyssey. Educ Facil Plan (1993)
6. Chaffin, D., Anderson, G.: Occupational Biomechanics, pp. 254–260. Wiley, New York (1991)
7. Aaras, A., Fostervold, K.I., Ro, O., Thoresen, M.: Postural load during VDU work: a comparison between various work postures. Ergonomics **40** (11), 1255–1268 (1997)
8. Dul, J., Weerdmeester, B.: Ergonomics for Beginners, p.160. Taylor & Francise-Library (2001)
9. Pheasant, S.: Body space: Anthropometry, Ergonomics, and the Design of Work, 2nd edn. Taylor & Francis, Bristol, PA (1996)
10. Brintrup, A.M., Ramsden, J., Takagi, H., Tiwari, A.: Ergonomic chair design by fusing qualitative and quantitative criteria using interactive genetic algorithms. IEEE Trans. Evol. Comput. **12**(3), 343–354 (2008)
11. Ismaila, S.O.: Anthropometric data of hand, foot, ear of university students in Nigeria. Leonard J. Sci. **15**, 15–20 (2009)
12. Cengage learning: Key anthropometric dimensions required for chair design. courtesy Guptil publications (2012)
13. Nag, P.K.: Ergonomics and Work Design, pp. 129–154. New Age International (P) Limited, New Delhi (1996)
14. GOPAK (n.d) Recommended chair and table design guide, EN1729
15. Teshome, F., Messle, E., Kolhe, K.P.: Development and testing of improved double skirt rocket stove for reducing emission level of carbon monoxide. In: ICAST 2019. Springer (2019)
16. Qutubuddin, S.Ma., Hebbala, S.S., Kumar, A.C.S.: Anthropometric consideration for designing students desks in engineering colleges. Int. J. Curr. Eng. Technol. **3**(4), 1179–1185 (2013)
17. Al-Hinai, N., Al-Kindi, M., Shamsuzzoha, A.: An ergonomic student chair design and engineering for classroom environment. Int. J. Mech. Eng. Robot. Res. **7**(5), 534–543 (2018)

# Modal Analysis of Adult Human Spine Vertebrae Using Numerical Method

Mekete Mulualem(✉)

Bahir Dar Institute of Technology, Bahir Dar, Ethiopia

**Abstract.** Human bodies are often exposed to vibrations when they are in the working place or vehicles. The low back pain and the degenerative diseases of the spine are more frequently found in humans exposed to vibration. In order to minimize these diseases, the occurrence of resonance conditions in the human spine body should be prevented; the determination of the natural frequency of each vertebra of the spine is the most required parameter to satisfy no occurrence of a resonant condition. This study aimed to determine the specific fundamental frequencies of the human spine vertebrae. In this paper, a detailed three-dimensional geometrical model of seated human spine vertebral is developed in Solidworks software based on actual vertebral geometry and the finite element model modal analysis is done by using ANSYS software. After FE modal analysis, the resonant frequencies of each vertebra of cervical (7), thoracic (12) and lumber (5) of the adult human spine are obtained and the fundamental frequencies of the vertebrae versus span of the spine are plotted. The result shows that the fundamental frequencies of all vertebra of the spine are different and the mini-mum fundamental frequency is 6.023 Hz for the thoracic spine (T4). In addition, it is revealed that for the whole spine vertebrae the fundamental frequency range is 6–19 Hz. The spine resonant condition may occur at any of this frequency range even though the fundamental frequency of the spine is 6.023 Hz.

**Keywords:** Human spine · Mode shape · Resonant state · Fundamental frequency

## 1 Introduction

Usually, the human body is subjected to a random movement when the person is in the working place, they face many different vibrations daily [1]. Means of transportation, machines, and human activities (e.g. people walking or dancing) may subject the human body to unwanted mechanical shaking or vibration. The exposure of a person for a certain degree of freedom body vibration will cause the comfort problem and health problems [2] as well [1].

Most workplaces where workers are exposed to whole-body vibration involves simultaneous motion in the fore-and-aft (x-), lateral (y-), and vertical (z-) directions [3]. The vertebral spine is the bendable pillar from tail to neck, a composition of individual bones that interlock with each other, the vertebrae. In the human vertebral column, there are

M. A. Delele et al. (Eds.): ICAST 2020, LNICST 385, pp. 274–285, 2021.
https://doi.org/10.1007/978-3-030-80618-7_18

33 vertebrae numbered and separated into sections: cervical, thoracic, lumbar, sacrum, and coccyx. [4], as shown in Fig. 1.

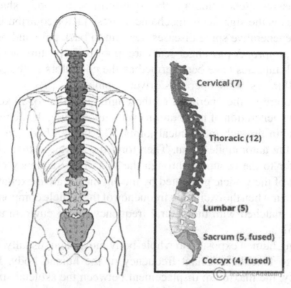

**Fig. 1.** The human spine vertebral structure (https://www.disabledworld.com/disability/types/spi nal/spine-picture.php)

Studies on the human body's reply to the whole-body vibration (WBV) have approved that low back pain (LBP) is a major health, social and economic problem with indeterminate etiology [5, 6]. There are no known effective means of low back pain (LBP) prevention and control methods, and it is the leading cause of disability below the age of 45 and also it is the greatest expensive cause of productivity losses [7]. The improvement of seat setups for comfort, taking of rest days from driving, checking for low back pain related health status before working as a driver, and following a better life culture are the commonly suggesting measures for the prevention of low back pain (LBP) [8].

Humans' low back pain (LBP) may arise from any causes which is the discomfort that the person feels between the top of the leg and the ribs [8]. The occurrence of (LBP) is highly related to occupational driving activity and some other related tasks. In the case of Indian Kolkata (Taxi) drivers, the study shows that the LBP has greatly affected their regular domestic, social activates and their ability to work too. Many of the drivers have reported that LBP has disabled them to conduct their regular activities such as the lifting of small water buckets, washing of their clothes at home, taking the bath properly, and carrying on of some duties involving controlled postures [9]. The car drivers subjected to uncontrolled vibration are more commonly exposed to low-back pain (LBP) and progressive diseases than in typical control groups [10–12] because of the continuous whole-body vibration (WBV) reasons to health risks for the lumbar spine [8, 9, 13]. The determination of the definite condition of car driver low back pain needs the study on the diverse vehicle drivers of Pondicherry, and the one - week occurrence of low back pain (LBP) was 23.9% of respondents [14]; due to their occupational exposure, the problem of LBP is mostly significant in auto-rickshaw ( ஆ‌ ) drivers [15].

As per various researches finding, the long-term whole-body shaking from the engines of vehicles is the significant mechanical stress factor contributing to the early and accelerated degenerative spine diseases, leading to back pain and prolapsed discs. In addition to this, improper passenger seat care, poor body posture while driving, and the fatigue of back muscles have been termed as the co-factors in the pathogenesis of musculoskeletal illnesses of the operators/driver's spine [8].

The vibrant nature of the operation of the engine and the road excitation are the main causes for the generation of in vibration every automobile, the generated vibration transfers to the cabin through mechanical joints. The human body has direct contact with the seats in the automobile cabin. Therefore, the vibration that comes from the engine will transfer to the occupant through the seat. The frequency of the vibration of any component of the vehicle generated by the engine is called excitation frequency. Resonance will occur when the excitation frequency of the vehicle component (especially the driver seat) is matched with the natural frequency of the environment component (human body) [16].

While assessing human exposure to whole-body movement, usually, the main focus of the studies is to find the resonant frequency of the human body. Because at the resonant frequency, the maximum displacement between the skeletal structure and the human organ will be takes placed, i.e. the biodynamic strain on the body tissue involved. Therefore, placing facts of the resonant frequency of the human body could help on the design of transport systems and industrial buildings so that the experience of vibration close to the body's resonant frequency may be minimized [17]. The force implemented at these special frequency points, where the peak of amplitudes, transforms more into vibration within the structure. The special frequency values, where the structure exhibit higher reactions against the implemented force, correspond to the natural frequencies of the structure [1].

In the case of the human body vibration scenario, the resonance occurs when the excitation frequency of the externally exerted force/load is closed to the fundamental frequency of the human spine. The most serious causes of lumbar degeneration and any related disease are the externally applied load/force and the deformation/strain in the lumbar during resonance [18]. Lumbar degeneration is a spine degenerative disorder and one of the common causes of low-back pain [19]. Therefore, to decrease the occurrence of lumbar degeneration, the occurrence of resonances needs to be prevented by applying curious optimization of any kinds of vibration sources via understanding the dynamic characteristics of the human body in such alike situations. To optimize the vibration source and subsequently prevent resonance, the excitation frequency of the vibration source should be maintained at extremely lower or higher than the natural/resonant frequency of the human lumbar spine, others human body's natural frequency as well. The excitation frequency of the vibration source of any system can be determined and adjusted by controlling and monitoring of the speed the energy source of the system. The challenge is the determination of the exact specific natural frequency of different human bodies.

The value of the excitation frequency of the structure under mechanical vibration is needed to be far from the natural frequencies of the structure; this condition may prevent the injuries caused by vibration. To achieve this condition and in the design of the vibration sources in working and living environments, the determination of the natural frequency of the structure is mandatory [19]. Even though works associated with the human body whole-body vibration (WBV) is rare [3], some investigations measured that the vertical direction natural/resonant frequency of the human lumbar spine in supine posture ranges within 1–6 Hz [11], an average of 4.4 Hz [20]. The extreme displacement effect(strain) for sitting posture, semi-supine, and standing has happened at between 4 and 6 Hz, (5–6 Hz) and 6.7 Hz, respectively [3].

There are various rationales in the analysis of human body natural frequencies based on the assumption of the human spine as a single mass system, the fundamental frequency of the spine is 8 Hz [21]. Different results of human body frequencies may be evaluated if the internal organs are taken to deliberation; it also depends on the position, orientation, and direction of the person subjected to vibration. By considering the partial lower spine finite element only, the natural frequency is determined as 3.5 Hz [19]. The human body is not rigid enough to have one natural frequency. The heart the muscles the bones the kidneys the liver and others have different compositions and densities and hence different natural frequencies. The realistic specific numerical natural frequency value of the human lumbar spine vertebrae has not been determined yet. Even though it is difficult to consider the actual human models due to their properties, geometries, joints, and other nonlinearity, it is possible to address the geometrical nonlinearity effect of the human spine by considering a realistic three-dimensional geometrical model of the spine vertebrae. Also, this study hypothesizes that it is not possible to have a single fundamental frequency for all spine vertebrae because of their geometrical unlikeness. Understanding of the frequency of the human body, specifically, the dynamic/vibrant response of the human spine is mandatory to provide insights into the relationship between vibration and spinal diseases. In order to provide comfortable and healthy travel by decreasing the vibration coming from the chassis of the intercity buses and any other related situations, this paper aimed to determine the fundamental frequency of each human spine vertebrae with the help of a detailed three-dimensional finite element model analysis based on the actual vertebral geometry. To determine the fundamental frequency of the human spinal cord, a complete three-dimensional FE model of the human spine was constructed with referring of the real vertebral geometry by using solidworks CAD modeling software package and the modal analysis was done via finite element method (FEM) with the help of Ansys 17.2 workbench software package. In addition, this study may be supportive in sympathetic further the nature of dynamics of the human spinal cord under the phenomenon of riding of the vehicle or any conditions when the whole body vibrates.

## 2 Materials and Methods

### 2.1 Natural Frequency and Mode Shape

In a free vibration state, there are numerous frequencies in which every structure has a trend to vibrate; these frequencies are usually called natural frequencies. Every natural frequency does have a related mode shape that the model could be assumed when it is vibrating at that frequency [22]. That information, mode shape, is the deformed shape of the structure that is associated with each natural frequency. Mode shape may also call as characteristic shape and fundamental shape. The deflection pattern of the structure associated with the first, second, third, ...natural frequency is called the first, second, third, ... mode shape; respectively.

Modes of vibration are the characteristic method in which vibration occurs. In a freely vibrating system, oscillation occurs in a certain characteristic frequency, i.e. Natural frequencies of the structure. The frequency of oscillation is termed as modal frequency (or natural frequency) and the shape made by the system is called mode shape. Mode shapes tell us how the structure tends to deform at the specific natural frequencies. The mode shapes tell us which regions would experience high stresses if the deformed shape is similar to the mode shape. Any structure does have its inherent modes. Modes of a structure are depending on its material properties (stiffness, mass, and damping factor), and the initial condition of the configuration of the structure. Every mode of the structure is defined by the natural frequency, mode shape, and modal damping; these are usually called modal parameters.

In structural engineering, it is crucial to determine the deterministic parameters such as strain, stress, frequencies, and corresponding mode shapes of a given set of design configurations. In the several applied engineering problem models that encompass any geometrical and physical factors, it is challenging to have a well-defined value of parameters due to the non-consistency of the mass distribution geometric properties or physical errors, as well as differences coming from the fabrication and assembly; and production procedures. In the same way, it is difficult to have well-defined geometrical and material properties and constraint parameters of the human spine. Due to the nonlinearities of the human body muscle-skeleton system and the nature of the excitation load, it is difficult to construct an accurate analytical mathematical model that could represent the transmission of dynamic loads from the vehicle structure to the occupant. Due to this reason, the utilization of the finite element analysis method is a helpful and valuable approach to address such dynamic response analyses. Since the FE modeling method could able to crack geometrical nonlinearity challenges easily relative to mathematical models.

## 2.2  Geometrical Model

The three-dimensional human spine CAD model can be constructed with the help of different methods, such as anatomy-based method, 3D scanner-based method, digital image-based method, etc. [23]. This study considered a resembled 50 percentile Chinese males' size which is a 75.5 kg of mass and 1.74 m of standing height and then the human spine body model has been developed as shown in Fig. 2, and the parametric data has been adapted from [23].

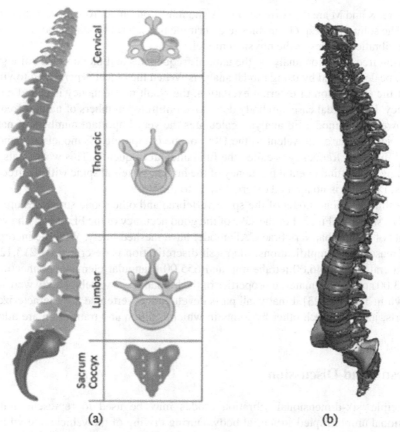

**Fig. 2.** (a) The vertebrae image (https://www.shutterstock.com/search/vertebrae), and (b) 3-Dimensional geometrical CAD model human spine

## 3 Finite Element Analysis

### 3.1 Modal Analysis

The modal analysis technique is used to determine the natural frequencies and corresponding mode shapes of an object. In addition to the determination of the vibration response of complicated structural dynamic problems, this technique is also being used for the identification, evaluation, and validation of the vibration phenomena, integrity assessment, structural modification, and damage detection [24] purposes.

The modal investigation of the human spine body is done to compute the natural frequencies and allied mode shapes. To analyze vibration mode and degree of freedom DOF that contribute to the primary resonance observed in the response of apparent mass, the frequencies and modes have been studied. The equation of motion for free un-damped vibration has been utilized, Eq. (1) [3].

$$[M]\{\ddot{x}\} + [K]\{\dot{x}\} = \{0\} \tag{1}$$

Where: K and M are the stiffness matrix and mass computed from the model, respectively. The solution to Eq. (1) enables to determine the natural/fundamental frequencies and the vibration modes of the physical model.

During free vibration analysis, the natural frequencies and mode shapes of a structure can be determined by using modal analysis. When the object is permitted to vibrate without the application of external excitation, the resulting frequency is called natural frequency. In an actual case, anybody does have unlimited numbers of natural frequencies, however, the modal FE analysis calculates the very important numbers of natural frequencies these are equivalent to the DOF of the computing FE model only and the resulted in lowest frequency is called the fundamental frequency. This work deals with the finding of the fundamental frequency of the human vertebral spine with the free-free analysis, i.e. there is no applied external force to the body.

The finite element model of the spine vertebrae and other bone structures are considered as shown in Fig. 3. For the sake of the good accuracy of the FE model, the whole elements of the lumbar vertebrae CAD model have meshed finely. With the incorporation of reasonable simplifications, the mesh discretization is described by 213,123.00 quadrilateral, 2,135,746.00 tetrahedral, and 655.00 triangular elements connecting by 222,333.00 nodes. The material properties of the human spine vertebral body were taken as shown in Table 1, [23]. Finally, all parts developed as vertebrae are characterized as stiff parts, joined to each other by joints in which rotation and translation are allowed [25].

# 4   Result and Discussion

In principle, six-dimensional vibration modes may be used to represent a three-dimensional uninterrupted structural body. During driving of the vehicle, the vibration of the driver will have six degrees of freedom for any occupants as well. Even though the occupants or the driver do have tri axial displacements, the spine mainly performs the vertical motion during full-body vibration or WBV [13, 26], due to the upward nature of the load. Due to its great influence effect on the modal analysis, the vertical direction displacement of the human spine body has been considered for both mode shape curve and natural frequency analyses.

## 4.1   Natural Frequencies of the Spine

Figure 4(b) shows the contour image of the modal analysis results of the vertebrae found in the lumbar, thoracic, and cervical spines. Figure 4(c) describes the natural frequency results of each vertebra of the whole region of the spine with the help of the spine vertebrae(x-direction) versus their fundamental frequency (y-direction) graph plot.

From the graph, Fig. 4(c) the minimum fundamental frequency is evaluated at the thoracic spine region for T4 and T5 with a value of 6.023 and 7.002 Hz, respectively. These minimum fundamental frequencies are the most common causes of spine discomfort and degenerative disease because the minimum fundamental frequency is significantly where the resonant condition occurs in any structure which is subjected or vibration.

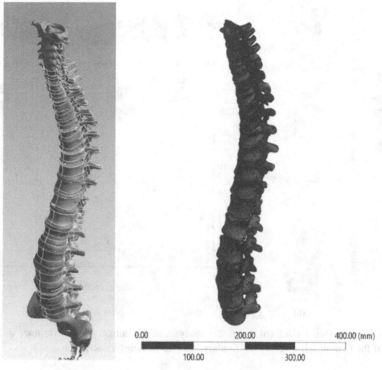

0.00    200.00    400.00 (mm)

100.00    300.00

**Fig. 3.** The meshed FE model

**Table 1.** The material property of human spine vertebrae.

| Structure/body | Elastic modulus E (MPa) | Poisson's ratio μ | Density ρ (kg/m³) |
|---|---|---|---|
| Human spine vertebrae | 12,000 | 0.3 | 1700 |

From Fig. 4, it can be stated that if the excitation frequency lies on one of the frequencies in the region (6–19 Hz), the driver or the occupant most likely feel discomfort since the resonance is occurring. At the condition of resonant, for vehicle drivers and the occupants, a small vertical force transmitting from the engine and road nature may able to create huge stress in the root of the vertebrae i.e. that make a big possibility to happen a bone fracture. Therefore, the excitation frequencies of any occupation which possibly create vibration should be maintained at very Farley low or high frequency of a range of (6–19 Hz).

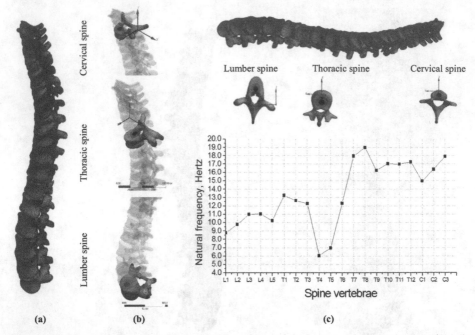

**Fig. 4.** (a) The meshed model, (b) the modal analysis of the human spine vertebrae, and (c) the vertebra of the human spine versus the fundamental frequencies value graph

## 4.2  Mode Shape of the Spine

Figure 5 shows the modal analysis, fundamental frequency, and corresponding mode shape, results of the L2, T8, and C3 vertebrae of a human spine. Figure 5(b) shows the contour image results of the total deformation and natural frequency of L2, T8, and C3 vertebrae; in the same way Fig. 5(c) describes the modal shape of these vertebrae at corresponding fundamental frequencies.

As shown in Fig. 5(b), the maximum vertical displacement is evaluated at the tip vertebra or process of the whole three regions of the spine (the lumbar, thoracic, and cervical spines) and the minimum displacement has occurred around the center of vertebras. This is happening because processes are the free ends and the central part of the vertebral body (spinal cord) is where the constraint is applied. From the basics of structural mechanics, when a structural member is subjected to a certain load, the maximum stress will occur at the region where minimum displacement has occurred and minimum stress will occur at the region where maximum displacement has occurred. This leads to say that the main cause of the vehicle's driver discomfort is the pain at the root or center of the vertebra of the whole spine. Since, these regions are where the maximum stress is occurring. From this, it is suggested that drivers sit with maintained leaned on the backrest of the seat, the occupants as well. Because maintained lend sitting of the drivers and passengers may prevent the occurrence of maximum stress at the root of the vertebra by distributing the exciting load towards the contacted region [23].

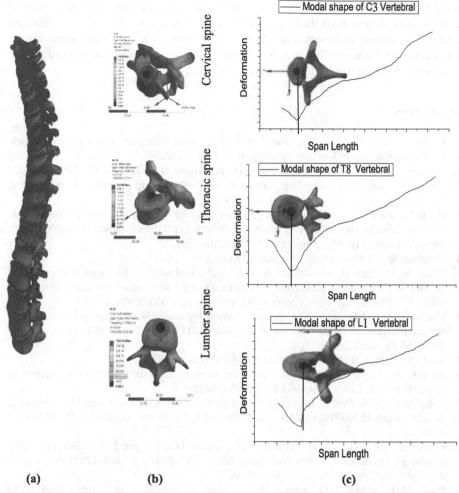

**Fig. 5.** (a) The meshed model of the spine, (b) the natural frequency results, and (c) the modal shape graphs of the L2, T8, and C3 vertebrae of the spine.

## 5   Conclusion

In general, this study concludes that even though the nature of the material of all vertebrae of a human spine is considered as the same, its fundamental frequency couldn't be a specific constant value because of their shape, size, and other geometrical non-uniformities. This study revealed that the minimum fundamental frequency of an adult human spine is around 6.023 Hz evaluated at the thoracic spine region, (T4). But it is not necessarily mean that the resonant phenomenon of the human spine vertebrae takes place at this specific excitation frequency, instead resonant of the human spine may occur in the frequency range of 6–19 Hz. Therefore, to reduce the occurrence of resonant of the human spine body, the excitation frequency of externally applied load should be maintained far from this range. This study didn't consider the influences of human factors such as BMI (body mass index), sex, and age on the natural or resonant frequency of human spine vertebrae. Besides, muscles were not included in the current spine FE model. Future studies may investigate the effects of human factors and muscle activations on the human spine's fundamental frequency.

# References

1. Karabulut, A., Nuri, O.: Investigation of vibration damping in the passenger seat constructions. Int. J. Electron. Mech. Mechatronics Eng. **6**, 1117–1122 (2016)
2. Marjanen, Y., Mansfield, N.: Validation and improvement of the ISO 2631-1 (1997) standard method for evaluating discomfort from whole-body vibration in a multi-axis environment, vol. Ph.D., p. 283 (2010)
3. Govindan, R., Saran, V.H., Harsha, S.P.: Low-frequency vibration analysis of human body in semi-supine posture exposed to vertical excitation. Eur. J. Mech. A/Solids 103906 (2019). https://doi.org/10.1016/j.euromechsol.2019.103906
4. Yenukoti, R.: Of Vertebral, no. August 2015 (2018)
5. Wang, W., Bazrgari, B., Shirazi-Adl, A., Rakheja, S., Boileau, P.É.: Biodynamic response and spinal load estimation of seated body in vibration using finite element modeling. Ind. Health **48**(5), 557–564 (2010). https://doi.org/10.2486/indhealth.MSWBVI-34
6. Mansfield, N.J., Maeda, S.: The apparent mass of the seated human exposed to single-axis and multi-axis whole-body vibration. J. Biomech. **40**(11), 2543–2551 (2007). https://doi.org/10.1016/j.jbiomech.2006.10.035
7. Study, E., Pain, L.B., Factors, O.: Redacted for Privacy (1987)
8. Jaiswal, A., Jaiswal, A.: Low back pain and work-related risk factors among drivers of Pondicherry. Int. J. Sci. Footprints **1**(2), 7–16 (2013)
9. Gangopadhyay, S., Dev, S.: Effect of low back pain on social and professional life of drivers of Kolkata. Work **41**(SUPPL.1), 2426–2433 (2012). https://doi.org/10.3233/WOR-2012-0652-2426
10. Frymoyer, J.W., Pope, M.H., Costanza, M.C., Rosen, J.C., Goggin, J.E., Wilder, D.G.: Epidemiologic studies of low-back pain. Spine (Phila. Pa. 1976) **5**(5), 419–423 (1980). https://doi.org/10.1097/00007632-198009000-00005
11. Pope, M.H., Wilder, D.G., Jorneus, L., Broman, H., Svensson, M., Andersson, G.: The response of the seated human to sinusoidal vibration and impact. J. Biomech. Eng. **109**(4), 279–284 (1987). https://doi.org/10.1115/1.3138681
12. Sakakibara, T., Kasai, Y., Uchida, A.: Effects of driving on low back pain. Occup. Med. (Chic. Ill). **56**(7), 494–496 (2006). https://doi.org/10.1093/occmed/kql045
13. Guo, L.X., Teo, E.C.: Prediction of the modal characteristics of the human spine at resonant frequency using finite element models. Proc. Inst. Mech. Eng. Part H J. Eng. Med. **219**(4), 277–284 (2005). https://doi.org/10.1243/095441105X34275
14. Alperovitch-Najenson, D., Santo, Y., Masharawi, Y., Katz-Leurer, M., Ushvaev, D., Kalichman, L.: Low back pain among professional bus drivers: ergonomic and occupational-psychosocial risk factors. Isr. Med. Assoc. J. **12**(1), 26–31 (2010)
15. Anwesh Pradhan, S.A., SoumitraDas, G.C.: Prevalence and risk factors of low back pain among auto-rickshaw drivers in urban Kolkata, India. Int. J. Curr. Res. Acad. Rev. **5**(5), 85–92 (2017). https://doi.org/10.20546/ijcrar.2017.505.011
16. Dahil, L., Karabulut, A., Uçan, O.N.: Investigation of vibration damping in the passenger seat constructions. Int. J. Electron. Mech. Mechatronics Eng. **6**(1), 1117–1122 (2016). https://doi.org/10.17932/iau.ijemme.m.21460604.2016.5/1.1117-1122

17. Randall, J.M., Matthews, R.T., Stiles, M.A.: Resonant frequencies of standing humans. Ergonomics **40**(9), 879–886 (1997). https://doi.org/10.1080/001401397187711

18. Guo, L.-X., Teo, E.-C., Lee, K.-K., Zhang, Q.-H.: Vibration characteristics of the human spine under axial cyclic loads: effect of frequency and damping. Spine (Phila. Pa. 1976) **30**(6), 631–637 (2005). https://doi.org/10.1097/01.brs.0000155409.11832.02

19. Ruoxun, F., Jie, L., Jun, L., Weijun, W.: Presentation of an approach on determination of the natural frequency of human lumbar spine using dynamic finite element analysis. Appl. Bionics Biomech. **2019** (2019). https://doi.org/10.1155/2019/5473891

20. Panjabi, M.M., Andersson, G.B., Jorneus, L., Hult, E., Mattsson, L.: In vivo measurements of spinal column vibrations. J. Bone Joint Surg. Am. **68**(5), 695–702 (1986)

21. Duarte, M.L.M.H., De Pereira, M.B., Misael, M.R., De Freitas Filho, L.E.A.: Is age more important than gender, Corporeal Mass Index (CMI) or Vision on whole-body human vibration comfort levels? In: Conference Proc. Soc. Exp. Mech. Ser., May 2006

22. Turcanu, D., Nicola, I., Prisecaru, T., Predoi, C.: The natural frequencies characteristics of a mechanical system using modal analysis. Rom. Reports Phys. **68**(3), 1326–1332 (2016)

23. Guo, L.X., Dong, R.C., Zhang, M.: Effect of lumbar support on seating comfort predicted by a whole human body-seat model. Int. J. Ind. Ergon. **53**, 319–327 (2016). https://doi.org/10.1016/j.ergon.2016.03.004

24. Khan, I.A., Awari, G.K.: Analysis of natural frequency and mode shape of all edge fixed condition plate with. Int. J. Innov. Res. Sci. Eng. Technol. **3**(2), 9277–9284 (2014)

25. Verver, M.M., Van Hoof, J., Oomens, C.W.J., Van De Wouw, N., Wismans, J.S.H.M.: Estimation of spinal loading in vertical vibrations by numerical simulation. Clin. Biomech. **18**(9), 800–811 (2003). https://doi.org/10.1016/S0268-0033(03)00145-1

26. Kiiski, J., Heinonen, A., Järvinen, T.L., Kannus, P., Sievänen, H.: Transmission of vertical whole body vibration to the human body. J. Bone Miner. Res. **23**(8), 1318–1325 (2008). https://doi.org/10.1359/jbmr.080315

# Performance Analysis of Beta-Type Stirling Cycle Refrigerator for Different Working Fluids

Muluken Z. Getie[1,2,3](✉) [ID], Francois Lanzetta[1] [ID], Sylvie Begot[1] [ID],
Bimrew T. Admassu[3] [ID], and Steve Djetel Gothe[1]

[1] FEMTO-ST Institute, Univ. Bourgogne Franche-Comte, CNRS
Parc technologique, 2 avenue Jean Moulin, F-90000 Belfort, France
`muluken.zegeye@bdu.edu.et`
[2] Bahir Dar Energy Center, Bahir Dar Institute of Technology, Bahir Dar
University, Bahirdar, Ethiopia
[3] Faculty of Mechanical and Industrial Engineering, Bahir Dar Institute
of Technology, Bahir Dar University, Bahirdar, Ethiopia

**Abstract.** The Stirling cycle refrigerators, which are the counterparts of the Stirling engines are of gas cycle machines. In the present paper, experimental investigation and numerical analysis of Beta-type Stirling refrigerator for domestic applications are conducted. The refrigeration performances such as input power requirement, cooling power, and coefficient of performance for moderate temperature applications have been analyzed using different working fluids (air, nitrogen, helium, and hydrogen). The numerical analysis is conducted to evaluate the performance of a machine with respect to different operating frequencies and charging pressures. The result of the analysis showed that air and nitrogen have better cooling power than helium and hydrogen in the operating ranges (15–25 bar and 6–12 Hz) of the cooling machine. On the other hand, the coefficient of performances in the case of helium shows a higher rate of increase with charging pressure than that of air and nitrogen.

**Keywords:** Beta type · Experiment · Moderate cooling · Different working fluid · Cooling power

M. A. Delele et al. (Eds.): ICAST 2020, LNICST 385, pp. 286–301, 2021.
https://doi.org/10.1007/978-3-030-80618-7_19

# Nomenclature

A= cross sectional area (m$^2$)

$C_p$= isobaric specific heat (J.kg$^{-1}$.K$^{-1}$)

$C_v$= isochoric specific heat (J.kg$^{-1}$.K$^{-1}$)

K = heat conductivity (W.m$^{-1}$.K$^{-1}$)

L =length (m)

M = mass of working gas (kg)

$\dot{m}$ = mass flow rate (kg.s$^{-1}$)

P = pressure (Pa)

Q = heat (J)

R = gas constant (J.kg$^{-1}$.K$^{-1}$)

T = temperature ($^\circ$C)

V = volume (m$^3$)

$V_d$= instantaneous swept volume of displacer (m$^3$)

$V_{swc}$= swept volume of compression (m$^3$)

W = work (J)

*Greek symbols*

ε = regenerator effectiveness

η = clearance effciency

γ = ratio of specific heats ($C_p$ /$C_v$)

θ = crank angle ($^\circ$)

ω = omera (rad.s$^{-1}$)

*subscripts*

c = compression space

cr = chiller

e = expansion space

g= gas

h = hot heat exchanger

leak = leakage

mean = mean value

r = regenerator

shut = shuttle

t = total


# 1   Introduction

Recently, due to the limitation of fossil fuels and their environmental impact, researchers in the area of motor have been forced to explore other types of machines that could substitute fossil fuel-driven engines. Stirling cycle engine is one of the alternatives as it runs with environmentally friendly gases. Stirling cycle machine is a type of external heat engine with a closed thermodynamic cycle. Robert Stirling invented the first Stirling machine in 1816as a heat engine to produce mechanical energy from heat energy. In this Stirling engine, the working fluid used to replace the steam engines was air. By reversing the cycle, the Stirling engine can operate as a heat pump or cooling machine. The Stirling cycle engine was first realized as a cooling machine in 1832 [1]. In 1862 Alexander Kirk developed a practical Stirling cycle cooler [2]. Subsequently, different researches have been conducted on Stirling cycle cooling machines and the detailed review is presented in [3].

The configurations of Stirling cycle machines are generally grouped based on piston and piston/displacer-cylinder arrangement as the Alpha, Beta, and Gamma configurations [4–6]. Different configurations have different mechanical designs but are working with the same thermodynamic cycles. Different configurations of the Stirling refrigerator have been investigated [7–11]. The optimal relationship between the cooling power and the coefficient of performance of the Stirling cycle refrigerating machine was conducted in different researches [12–14]. A general analytical model has been introduced for various applications of the Stirling refrigerator [15].

The V-type Stirling refrigerator was thermodynamically analyzed [16–18]. The impact of working fluids on the performance of a V-type Stirling cycle refrigerating machine for a charging pressure less than 5 bar was investigated [17]. The integral V-type

Stirling refrigerator was developed, tested, and proven as a domestic cooling machine [18]. The reported COP for such machines varied between 0.1 and 0.9 under different working parameters. The performance parameters, such as the input power demand and the coefficient of performance were examined under different turning speeds and charging pressures. An isothermal model was developed for an Alpha type Stirling cryocooler by considering various losses and the effects of various parameters on cooling performance were investigated [19]. From the research, it has been reported that heat conduction loss was the biggest heat loss and loss due to mechanical friction was the biggest work loss.

Batooei A. et al. conducted the optimization of the Stirling refrigerator based on the experimental and numerical methods for Gamma configuration [20]. The numerical method applied by this research is multi-objective optimization using non-ideal adiabatic conditions. The cooling capacity and the COP were experimentally investigated for helium and air as a working fluid. The experimental and numerical results from the research proved that the production of cold increases continuously with the rotational speed whereas COP has an optimum value. Theoretical and experimental evaluation of the Gamma-type Stirling refrigerator was conducted [21]. The optimum theoretical and experimental analysis coefficients of performances from the research were reported as 0.28 and 0.27 respectively.

Oguz et al. [22] conducted an experimental work for free-piston Stirling coolers. It has been reported that the COP values for coolers operating with ambient temperatures close to 30° C were found between 2 and 3 for cold head temperatures around 0° C and decreasing to around 1 for cold temperatures near to −40° C. The effect of parameters such as dead volume ratio, compression ratio, types of working fluids, and the phase angle on the performance of a Beta-type refrigerating machine was studied [23]. A 100 W Beta-type Stirling cycle refrigerator was designed and experimentally tested [24]. A thermodynamic model was developed and an experimental validation was conducted for optimizing Beta-type Stirling refrigeration machines using air as a working fluid [25]. Evaluation of the effect of geometrical parameters such as dead space volume and swept volume on the performance of the refrigerating machine was the special emphasis for this research. A Beta-type Stirling cooler was developed with a rhombic drive system [26]. In the same year, a similar configuration Stirling refrigerator was designed and fabricated to achieve a rapid transfer of heat from the system [27]. Helium and carbon dioxide have been used as a working fluid and the more efficient fluid was determined.

Generally, Stirling cycle machines are characterized by high thermal efficiency, low emissions, low vibration, low noise, the ability to use almost all types of thermal energy source, safe operation, low maintenance, and reversible working cycle. Furthermore, the findings of most researches done so far proved that Stirling cycle machines are promising alternatives for moderate temperature cooling applications. On the other hand, a limited number of researches have been conducted on these types of Stirling cycle refrigerators. Therefore, more studies are needed to enhance the performance of Stirling refrigerators in this application. In the present study, the developed numerical model is validated using an experiment and the effect of working fluid on the refrigerating performance is analyzed for moderate cooling applications. The analysis is conducted for air, nitrogen, helium, and hydrogen at different operating frequencies and charging pressure.

## 2 Mathematical Modeling

### 2.1 Adiabatic Modeling

The Stirling cycle machine consists of two variable volumes (compression and expansion) spaces physically separated by a regenerator and at different temperatures. For the Stirling cycle refrigerator, heat is absorbed from the low temperature heat source, and heat is stored and released in the regenerator (see Fig. 1). An ideal Stirling cycle refrigerator consists of four separate thermodynamics processes, which consists of two isothermal processes and two constant volume processes as shown in Fig. 2.

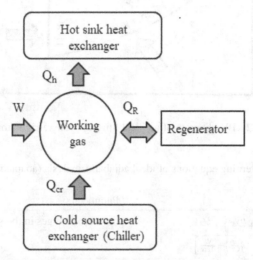

**Fig. 1.** Schematic diagram of Stirling refrigerator

In real Stirling cycle machines, the compression and expansion processes tend to be adiabatic. Therefore, the basis of this work is an ideal adiabatic analysis. For easy of analysis, the overall Stirling refrigeration machine is configured into five control volumes (two working spaces and three perfectly effective heat exchangers) serially connected, the model is similar to Urieli and Berchowitz model [6]. The governing equations of the adiabatic equation are shown in Table 1.

The ideal adiabatic equation is modified by incorporating shuttle heat loss and gas leakage to the crankcase. This is because these losses have a direct impact on working conditions (pressure and temperature) of working fluid and hence on the overall performance of the machine. So, differential equations of mass and energy conversations of the original ideal adiabatic analysis of the Stirling refrigeration machine have been modified including the effect of mass leakage and shuttle heat losses.

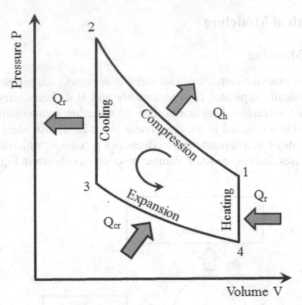

**Fig. 2.** PV- diagram of an ideal Stirling cycle refrigerator

**Table 1.** Governing equations of ideal adiabatic analysis (adapted from [6])

| Equation set | Parameters |
|---|---|
| $DP = \dfrac{-\gamma P\left(\frac{DV_c}{Tch} + \frac{DV_e}{Tcre}\right)}{\left[\frac{V_c}{TCh} + \gamma\left(\frac{Vh}{Th} + \frac{Vr}{Tr} + \frac{Vcr}{TCr}\right) + \frac{V_e}{Tcre}\right]}$ | Pressure changes in the system |
| $Dm = \left(\dfrac{pDV + VDp/\gamma}{RT}\right)$ | Mass accumulation |
| $DT = T\left(\dfrac{DP}{P} + \dfrac{DV}{V} - \dfrac{Dm}{m}\right)$ | Temperature change |
| $DQ = \dfrac{VC_v DP}{R} - C_p\,(T_{in}\dot{m}_{in} - T_{out}\dot{m}_{out})$ | Heat power in three heat exchangers |
| $D\,W = PDV$ | power |

The details of the analysis are presented in [28]. The final equations affected by the mass leakage and shuttle heat loss are presented in Eqs. (1, 2, and 3). The other equations remain unchanged as of the ideal adiabatic model.

$$DP = \frac{-\gamma P\left(\frac{DV_c}{Tch} + \frac{DV_e}{Tcre}\right) + \gamma R\frac{DQ_{shut}}{C_p}\left(\frac{T_{ch} - T_{cre}}{T_{ch}T_{cre}}\right) + \gamma RDm_{leak}}{\left[\frac{V_c}{TCh} + \gamma\left(\frac{Vh}{Th} + \frac{Vr}{Tr} + \frac{Vcr}{TCr}\right) + \frac{V_e}{Tcre}\right]} \tag{1}$$

$$Dm_c = \left(\frac{PDV_c + V_c Dp/\gamma}{RT_{ch}}\right) + \frac{DQ_{shut}}{C_p T_{ch}} \tag{2}$$

$$Dm_e = \left(\frac{pDV_e + V_eDp/\gamma}{RT_{cre}}\right) - \frac{DQ_{shut}}{C_pT_{ch}} \tag{3}$$

## 2.2 Modified Simple Analysis

The heat and power losses that do not have direct impact on the operating condition of a Stirling cycle machine are separately analyzed. These thermal and power losses are assumed as independent to each other and the total losses are the summation of the losses with the respective category. The losses incorporated in modified simple analysis are summarized in Table 2 as developed by the researchers' previous work [28].

**Table 2.** Summary of losses included in modified simple analysis [28]

| No | Types of losses | Equations |
|---|---|---|
| 1 | Heat losses due to internal conduction in the regenerator | $Q_{wrl} = k\frac{A}{L}(Twh - Twcr)$ |
| 2 | Loss due to regenerator ineffectiveness/external conduction | $Q_{rl} = \dot{m}c_p(1 - \varepsilon)(T_c - T_e)$ |
| 3 | Loss due to pressure drop in heat exchangers | $W_{fr} = \int_0^{2\pi}(\Delta P\frac{dV_e}{d\theta})d\theta,$ $\Delta P = \Delta p_h + \Delta p_r + \Delta p_{cr}$ |
| 4 | Heat conduction loss | $Q_{cond} = k\frac{A}{L}\Delta T$ |
| 5 | Pumping loss | $\dot{Q}_p = (1 - \eta)\dot{m}C_p(T_c - T_e)$ |
| 6 | Loss due to finite speed of piston | $W_{fin-sp} = 2\Delta p_{fin.sp}.V_{swc}$ |
| 7 | Mechanical Friction loss | $W_{mec.fr} = 2\Delta p_{mec.fr}.V_{swc}$ |
| 8 | Gas Spring hysteresis loss | $W_{gs} = \sqrt{\frac{1}{32}\omega\gamma^3(\gamma - 1)T_wP_{mean}Kg(V_d/2V_t)^2A_w}$ |

# 3   Experimental Setup

The considered experimental machine is a reversible thermal machine (motor and/or receiver) with Beta configuration and operates between two constant temperatures. This machine consists of expansion space, heater (acts as a chiller in case of the cooling machine), regenerator, cooler (acts as a hot heat exchanger in case of the cooling machine), compression space, piston, buffer space, and driving mechanisms. The power piston and displacer are arranged within a single cylinder. The displacer piston controls the variations of the expansion volume (cold room) and the power piston controls the compression space (hot room) for such Stirling refrigerating machine. The setup includes a regenerative Stirling refrigerator, cooling water system, the electric supplier, and a data acquisition system. The refrigerator is arranged with six thermometers and one pressure sensor for measuring the working conditions. The setup of the refrigerating machine is demonstrated in Fig. 3.

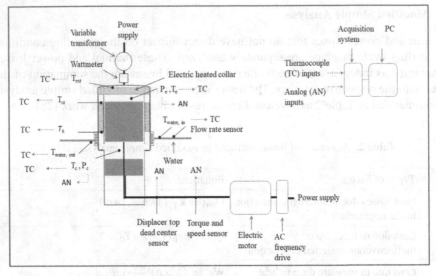

**Fig. 3.** Experimental setup of Stirling refrigerator

The hot heat exchanger and the chiller both have slot geometric arrangement and the configuration of the regenerator is an annular configuration with a stainless-steel woven screens' matrix. The main parameters and dimensions of the experimental device are shown in Table 3.

**Table 3.** Experimental engine specification

| No | Parameters | Value |
|----|-----------|-------|
| 1 | Hot heat temperature (°C) | 32 |
| 2 | Cooling temperature (°C) | −5 |
| 3 | Piston diameter (mm) | 60 |
| 4 | Displacer diameter (mm) | 59 |
| 5 | Piston stroke (mm) | 40 |
| 6 | Compression space swept volume (cm$^3$) | 103 |
| 7 | Expansion space swept volume (cm$^3$) | 113 |
| 8 | Working gas | Nitrogen |
| 9 | Frequency (Hz) | 7.5 |
| 10 | Charging pressure (bar) | 20 |

The refrigeration rotational speed varied between 435 to 725 rpm and the charging pressure is varied between 15–25 bar. The cooling capacity, coefficient of performance of the refrigerating machine, and minimum achievable no-load temperature of a Stirling refrigerator are determined experimentally. The thermal load was applied by two resistance heaters to the cold head of the Stirling cycle refrigerator, and steady-state characteristics of the refrigerator were measured. For a varied input voltage, different tests were carried out to determine the variation of the cooling performance with the cold head temperature of the coolers varied from −40 °C to 0 °C. The detailed experimental setup is presented in [28, 29]. The working gas considered in the experiment is nitrogen, which is assumed to behave like a perfect gas.

**Table 4.** Experimental results at a charging pressure of 17.5 bar (Nitrogen)

| Parameters | Experiment 1 | Experiment 2 | Experiment 3 |
|---|---|---|---|
| Electric power (W) | 1650 | 1640 | 1460 |
| Power loss electrical (W) | 285.2 | 280.5 | 251 |
| Power mechanical (W) | 1365 | 1359 | 1209 |
| Cold production (W) | 451 | 554 | 676 |
| Hot water power (W) | 1429 | 1472 | 1476 |
| Cooling temperature ($^\circ$C) | −15.1 | −4.3 | 10.5 |
| Temperature at exit head ($^\circ$C) | −10 | 1 | 16 |
| Speed(rpm) | 721 | 721.8 | 724 |
| Torque (Nm) | 18 | 18 | 16 |
| Mechanical COP | 0.33 | 0.41 | 0.56 |

Table 4 illustrates the three experimental results conducted at different electrical input power. In the Table, the electrical power loss, cooling production, the temperature of a gas at the cold side, and coefficient of performance of the machine are presented. As the gas temperature at the cold end increases, both cooling production and COP increases.

Figure 4 shows a no-load temperature distribution at different parts of the refrigerating machine with Nitrogen as a working gas. Initially, the refrigerator is set at ambient temperature and once the motor is switched on, the temperature of the cold side (expansion space) drops quickly and reaches a steady-state cold-end temperature. The minimum no-load temperature is achieved at a pressure of 25 bar and a frequency of 12.1 Hz is − 68 °C. The stabilization temperature is found after 20 min of operation. It is recognized that after the machine starts running, the buffer space temperature increases considerably from around 17.4 °C to 40 °C. This confirms that there is heat loss to the buffer space.

Figure 5 is a plot of temperature variation versus time in different parts of the refrigerating machine. The experiment was run for 90 min to confirm the trend of the cooling process for a long period using nitrogen as a working gas. The stabilization temperature at the cold end is −15.1 °C at a cooling load of 451 W, charging pressure of 17.5 bar,

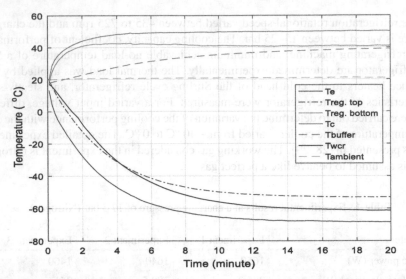

**Fig. 4.** No-load temperature variation at P = 25 bar and operating frequency = 12.1 Hz

and frequency of 12.1 Hz. Such Stirling refrigerator needs only 3 min to reach such a low temperature and the stabilization temperature is achieved after 40 min. The minimum temperature found is −24.9 °C and achieved 10 min after starting the operation. The buffer space temperature rises approximately by 10 °C from the ambient temperature. This result shows that there seems more gas leakage towards the buffer space that may result in heat loss. Furthermore, the stabilized temperature difference between the compression space (warm section) and the buffer space is less than 4° C.

As shown in Fig. 6, the temperature of water in the hot heat exchanger increases considerably. The heat power rejected with the flow of water at a hot heat exchanger could be given by the flow rate of water specific heat of the water and the change in temperature of water flowing in this heat exchanger.

$$\dot{Q}_h = \dot{m}_h C_p(T_{h,ex} - T_{h,in}) \qquad (4)$$

Where the mass flow of water ( $\dot{m}_h$ ) =3kg/min, specific heat of water (CP) = 4185 J.kg$^{-1}$K$^{-1}$, $T_{h,ex}$ is the temperature of water at the hot heat exchanger exit, and $T_{h,in}$ is the temperature of water at the entry of the hot heat exchanger.

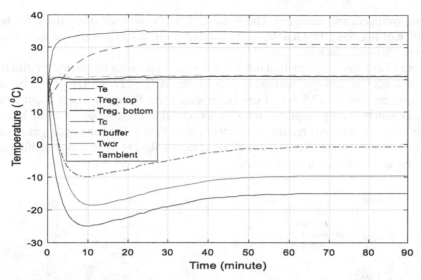

**Fig. 5.** Temperature distribution versus time at P = 17.5 bar, operating frequency = 12.1 Hz, and cooling load = 451 W

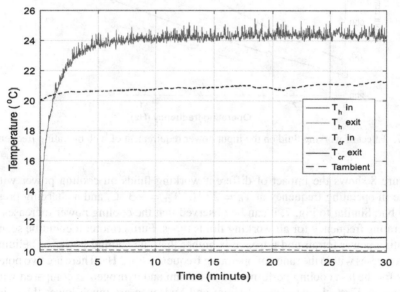

**Fig. 6.** The temperature of working fluid at 25 bar and 12.1 Hz

## 4   Results and Discussion

The numerical model is validated experimentally using the FEMTO 60 Stirling machine as described in the researchers' previous work [28]. In this part of the research, the simulation results of the analysis present the effect of different working fluids (air, helium, hydrogen, and nitrogen). The simulation was conducted using these fluids at the different operating frequencies and charging pressures to investigate the cooling performance of the machine.

Figure 7 illustrates the required input power versus operating frequency for different working fluids (air, nitrogen, helium, and hydrogen) at $T_h = 27\ °C$, $T_{cr} = -3\ °C$, and a charging pressure of 17.5 bar. It can be observed that the input power requirement increases with operating frequency for all working fluids. Furthermore, it could be seen that air and nitrogen fluids require more input power than helium and hydrogen. These results confirm that air and nitrogen operate at higher flow resistance than helium and hydrogen due to a higher mass flow rate.

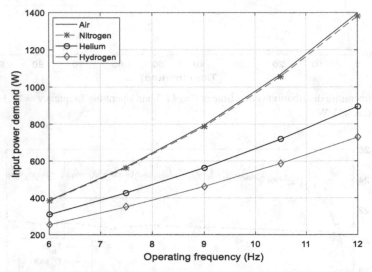

**Fig. 7.** Effect of working fluid on the input power requirement of with operating frequency

Figure 8 shows the impact of different working fluids on cooling power with an increase in operating frequency at $T_h = 27\ °C$, $T_{cr} = -3\ °C$, and a charging pressure of 17.5 bar. Similar to Fig. 7, it can be observed that the cooling power increases with the operating frequency for all working fluids types. Furthermore, it could be seen that the cooling power for air and nitrogen is higher than the cooling power of helium and hydrogen gases within the range of operating frequency 6–12 Hz. There are two potential reasons for the less cooling performance of helium and hydrogen as compared with air and nitrogen. First, the masses of helium and hydrogen are much lower than air and nitrogen, and hence a lower heat removal rate is observed and as a result lower cooling power. Second, helium and hydrogen have a higher thermal conductivity which leads to higher shuttle heat losses and these cause helium and hydrogen gases to produce lower cooling power than air and nitrogen. The shuttle heat loss has a complex effect on the cooling machine performance as it affects the working fluid pressure and temperature.

Figure 9 demonstrates the effect of different working fluids on the COP of a cooling machine with respect to operating frequency at $T_h = 27\ °C$, $T_{cr} = -3\ °C$, and charging

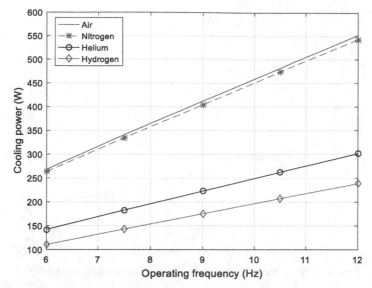

**Fig. 8.** Cooling capacity vs operating frequency at different working fluid types

pressure of 17.5 bar. It can be seen that air and nitrogen have better COP than helium and hydrogen within the range of operating frequency. Even though, both input power requirement and cooling power increase with operating frequency, COP decreases as a result of a higher rate of increase of flow friction and mechanical friction loss. The COP for air and nitrogen decreases radically with operating speed and this trend shows that at very high operating speed the COP for helium may be higher than the COP of air and nitrogen.

Figure 10 is a diagram demonstrating the required input power versus charging pressure for different working fluids at $T_h = 27$ °C, $T_{cr} = -3$ °C, and an operating frequency of 7.5 Hz. It can be observed that the input power requirement increases with pressure for all working fluids. Furthermore, it could be seen that air and nitrogen fluids require more input power than helium and hydrogen. This is because air and nitrogen operate at higher flow resistance than helium and hydrogen due to a higher mass flow rate for a given operating condition.

Figure 11 displays the influence of working fluids (air, nitrogen, helium, and hydrogen) on cooling power with respect to charging pressure at $T_h = 27$ °C, $T_{cr} = -3$ °C, and an operating frequency of 7.5 Hz. It can be observed that the cooling power increases with charging pressure for all working fluids. Furthermore, it could be observed that the cooling power for air and nitrogen is greater than the cooling power of helium and hydrogen due to a higher mass flow rate which leads to more heat removal rate.

Figure 12 displays the influence of working fluids on the COP of the refrigerating machine with charging pressure at $T_h = 27$ °C, $T_{cr} = -3$ °C, and an operating frequency of 7.5 bar. Air and nitrogen have by far better COP than helium and hydrogen. The COP for nitrogen increases from 53% to 73% as the charging pressure increases from 15 bar

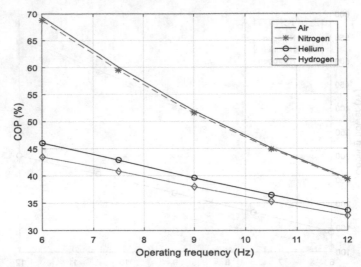

**Fig. 9.** COP vs operating frequency for different working fluid types

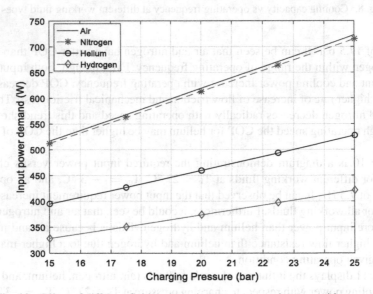

**Fig. 10.** Effect of different fluid types on input power requirement with pressure

to 25 bar. The COP for helium increases radically with charging pressure due to a lower rate of increase in flow friction losses as compared with air and nitrogen.

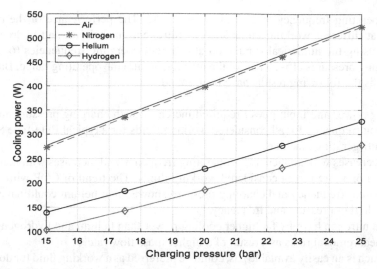

**Fig. 11.** Effect fluid types on cooling capacity of Stirling cycle refrigerator with pressure

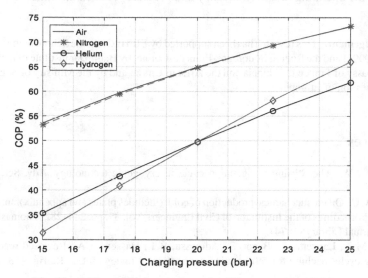

**Fig. 12.** COP vs charging pressure for different working fluids

## 5  Conclusion

In this research work, the experimental results are presented with and without load and performance analysis of the developed model is conducted for domestic cooling applications. The experimental investigation is used to determine the actual cooling power, coefficient of performance of the refrigerating machine, and minimum achievable no-load temperature of a particular Stirling cycle refrigerator. The minimum cold side no-load gas temperature was found with an experiment at a charging pressure of 25 bar and an operating frequency of 12.1 Hz is − 68 °C. The performance of the cooling machine at different working fluids such as nitrogen, air, helium, and hydrogen are analyzed using the numerical simulation at different operating frequencies (6–12 Hz) and charging pressures (15–25 bar) of the machine within the operating range. Based on the analysis the following results have been found:

- Cooling power and input power required increased with charging pressure and with operating frequency for all considered working fluids for a typical Beta-type Stirling cycle refrigerating machine.
- COP decreases with an increase in operating frequency and increases with increasing charging pressure for all considered working fluids. The trend of COP with respect to operating frequency and charging pressure showed that helium could have better COP at higher pressure and frequency.
- Air and nitrogen have by far higher cooling power than helium and hydrogen due to more heat removal rates as a result of a higher mass flow rate.
- Air, which is an easily available gas, could be preferred as a working fluid for domestic Stirling cycle cooling machines due to better comparative performance especially in most of the operating ranges (frequency and pressure) of such machine.

**Acknowledgement.** This research has been supported by EIPHI Graduate School (contract ANR-17-EURE-0002) and the Region Bourgogne-Franche-Comte, by Bahir Dar institute of technology, by the Embassy of France to Ethiopia and the African Union, and by the Ministry of Science and Higher Education of Ethiopia.

# References

1. Kohler, J.W.: The Stirling refrigeration cycle in cryogenic technology. Adv. Sci. **25**, 261 (1968)
2. Kirk, A. C.: On the mechanical production of cold. (includes plates and appendix). In: Minutes of the Proceedings of the Institution of Civil Engineers, vol. 37, pp. 244–282. Thomas Telford-ICE Virtual Library (1874)
3. Getie, M.Z., Lanzetta, F., Bégot, S., Admassu, B.T., Hassen, A.A.: Reversed regenerative Stirling cycle machine for refrigeration application: a review. Int. J. Refrig. **118**, 173–187 (2020)
4. Kirkley, D.: Determination of the optimum configuration for a Stirling engine. J. Mech. Eng. Sci. **4**(3), 204–212 (1962)
5. Reader, G.T., Hooper, C.: Stirling Engines. E. and F. Spon, New York, NY, USA (1983)
6. Urieli, I., Berchowitz, D.M.: Stirling Cycle Engine Analysis. A. Hilger Bristol (1984)
7. Ahmadi, M.H., Ahmadi, M.-A., Mohammadi, A.H., Mehrpooya, M., Feidt, M.: Thermodynamic optimization of Stirling heat pump based on multiple criteria. Energy Convers. Manag. **80**, 319–328 (2014)
8. De Boer, P.: Optimal performance of regenerative cryocoolers. Cryogenics **51**(2), 105–113 (2011)
9. Li, R., Grosu, L.: Parameter effect analysis for a Stirling cryocooler. Int. J. Refrig. **80**, 92–105 (2017)

10. Tyagi, S., Lin, G., Kaushik, S., Chen, J.: Thermo economic optimization of an irreversible Stirling cryogenic refrigerator cycle. Int. J. Refrig. **27**(8), 924–931 (2004)
11. Xu, Y., et al.: Operating characteristics of a single-stage Stirling cryocooler capable of providing 700 w cooling power at 77 k. Cryogenics **83**, 78–84 (2017)
12. Chen, J.: Minimum power input of irreversible Stirling refrigerator for given cooling rate. Energy Convers. Manag. **39**(12), 1255–1263 (1998)
13. Chen, J., Yan, Z.: The general performance characteristics of a Stirling refrigerator with regenerative losses. J. Phys. D Appl. Phys. **29**(4), 987 (1996)
14. Razani, A., Dodson, C., Roberts, T.: A model for exergy analysis and thermodynamic bounds of Stirling refrigerators. Cryogenics **50**(4), 231–238 (2010)
15. Ataer, Ö.E., Karabulut, H.: Thermodynamic analysis of the V-type Stirling-cycle refrigerator. Int. J. Refrig. **28**(2), 183–189 (2005). https://doi.org/10.1016/j.ijrefrig.2004.06.004
16. Guo, Y., Chao, Y., Wang, B., Wang, Y., Gan, Z.: A general model of Stirling refrigerators and its verification. Energy Convers. Manag. **188**, 54–65 (2019)
17. Tekin, Y., Ataer, O.E.: Performance of V-type Stirling-cycle refrigerator for different working fluids. Int. J. Refrig. **33**(1), 12–18 (2010)
18. Le'an, S., Yuanyang, Z., Liansheng, L., Pengcheng, S.: Performance of a prototype Stirling domestic refrigerator. Appl. Therm. Eng. **29** (2-3), 210–215 (2009)
19. Ahmed, H., Almajri, A.K., Mahmoud, S., Al-Dadah, R., Ahmad, A.: CFD modelling and parametric study of small-scale alpha type Stirling cryocooler. Energy Procedia **142**, 1668–1673 (2017)
20. Batooei, A., Keshavarz, A.: A gamma type Stirling refrigerator optimization: an experimental and analytical investigation. Int. J. Refrig. **91**, 89–100 (2018)
21. Katooli, M.H., Moghadam, R.A., Hajinezhad, A.: Simulation and experimental evaluation of Stirling refrigerator for converting electrical/mechanical energy to cold energy. Energy Convers. Manag. **184**, 83–90 (2019)
22. Oguz, E., Ozkadi, F.: An experimental study on the refrigeration capacity and thermal performance of free-piston Stirling coolers (2000)
23. Otaka, T., Ota, M., Murakami, K., Sakamoto, M.: Study of performance characteristics of a small Stirling refrigerator. Heat Transf. Asian Res. **31**(5), 344–361 (2002)
24. Gheith, R., Aloui, F., Nasrallah, S.: Experimental study of a beta Stirling thermal machine type functioning in receiver and engine modes. J. Appl. Fluid Mech. **4**, 33–42 (2011)
25. Hachem, H., Gheith, R., Aloui, F., Nasrallah, S.B.: Optimization of an air-filled beta type Stirling refrigerator. Int. J. Refrig. **76**, 296–312 (2017)
26. Cheng, C.-H., Huang, C.-Y., Yang, H.-S.: Development of a 90-k beta type Stirling cooler with rhombic drive mechanism. Int. J. Refrig. **98**, 388–398 (2019)
27. Suranjan, S., et al.: Determination of coefficient of performance of Stirling refrigeration. Int. J. Innov. Technol. Explor. Eng. (IJITEE) **8**, 2522–2529 (2019)
28. Getie, M.Z., Lanzetta, F., Bégot, S., Admmassu, B.T.: A non-ideal second order thermal model with effects of losses for simulating Beta-type Stirling refrigerating machine. Unpublished work (2021)
29. Djetel-Gothe, S., Lanzetta, F., Bégot, S., Gavignet, E.: Design, manufacturing, and testing of a Beta Stirling machine for refrigeration applications. Int. J. Refrig. **115**, 96–106 (2020)

# Yield Strength and Ductility Analysis on Steel Reinforcing Bars Used in Ethiopian Construction Industry

Tefera Eniyew[1]($\boxtimes$), Assefa Asmare[1], and Wim Dewulf[2]

[1] Department of Mechanical Engineering, Bahir Dar University, Bahir Dar Institute of Technology, Bahir Dar, Ethiopia
[2] Department of Mechanical Engineering, KU Leuven – University of Leuven, Leuven, Belgium

**Abstract.** One of the most utilized materials in the construction sectors having enormous compressive strength but weak in tension is concrete. This weakness overcomes with addition of the steel reinforcing bars whose properties must comply standards. Thermomechanical treated steel is an ideal material available at affordable cost to reinforce concrete as it has good ductility with high modulus of elasticity and same thermal expansion with concrete. The Ethiopian construction industry uses locally manufactured and imported rebar available from an open market. Locally produced reinforcing steel bars are milled from imported billets or local billets manufactured from scraps collected as obsolete products. Reinforcing bars produced from Ethiopian metal industries are selected next to the imported one without justifiable reasons. This paper dealt with evaluation of yield strength and ductility of rebar based on the compulsory Ethiopian standard to comply the quality of these locally manufactured rebar in order to build customers confidence. The Strength of four samples 14 mm diameter rebar three from locally produced and one the imported taken from the construction site were tested using universal testing machine. Additionally tension test data of different rebar collected from Amhara Design Supervision and Consultancy Work Enterprise were analyzed. Based on the results obtained, some of reinforcing bars from imported and locally produced have faced rejection.

**Keywords:** Tensile testing · Mechanical properties · Yield strength · Ductility

## 1 Introduction

Steel is virtually useful in all sectors of economy and the steel manufacturing industries are the most important sectors to determine the level of economic development of any nation [1]. It is an ideal material available at low cost to reinforce concrete as it is having good ductility with high modulus of elasticity [2]. Currently Ethiopian construction industries are boomed with the requirement of different construction materials, due to the rapid population and economic growth. The needs of materials of the construction sector is satisfied by importing various materials from abroad and/or locally produced

M. A. Delele et al. (Eds.): ICAST 2020, LNICST 385, pp. 302–314, 2021.
https://doi.org/10.1007/978-3-030-80618-7_20

products. One of the most utilized construction materials with high annual consumption is the reinforced steel bar. There are newly established steel rolling mills engaged to manufacture rebar from imported billets and/or by recycling end of life (EOL) steel products. Ribbed reinforcing bar is used for concrete structures in range of residential, commercial and infrastructure applications. Steel reinforcing bar is a crucial construction material to improve the tensional and flexural strength of concrete [3]. Due to the possibility to determine the properties of reinforcing bar before application, it plays a key role in the construction industry. Steel reinforcing bars used in the construction industry of different countries are obtained from both internal and external sources [3]. In the Ethiopian context, the internal sources are mini mills located in limited areas of the country. Imported steel bars coming into the country Ethiopia are mainly from Turkey, India, China, Russia and Ukraine [4]. The most common type of rebar is carbon steel, typically consisting of hot-rolled round bars with deformed patterns called thermo-mechanical treated (TMT). The properties of rebar can be modified by alloying with suitable elements, depending on their application area. For example, corrosion resistance is an essential property of material used in marine, and regions with high humidity content and in seismic zones, the specific ultimate tensile to yield stress (UTS/YS) ratio should be maintained close to 1.25 [5].

Steel reinforcing bars can be made from the virgin material or by secondary manufacturing process (recycling). Recycling of steel reduces the amount of energy consumed and environmental pollution in addition to the reduction of natural resources depletion. Most of the Ethiopian steel industries are engaged to manufacture reinforcing bars from steel scraps of different end of life steel products or imported billets. The collected ends off life steel products may have different chemical compositions and may need characterization in each foundry works. To minimize the complexity of material characterization, it is better to sort collected steel products using different sorting mechanism to predetermine the chemical composition of charged materials. The scrap materials are collected from different application areas stored on different places might be attacked by contaminants and their chemical composition may be affected. The chemical composition with the adverse manufacturing process will have higher influence on the mechanical properties obtained from products made by recycling process. The current state of the art can show that design of reinforced concrete in the developing countries may not be fully reliable. In the developing countries specially African where imported steel is very expensive, milling companies have taken up the challenge to re-cycle obsolete vehicle and machine metal parts for the production of structural and reinforcing steel [2]. The property of steel is greatly affected by its chemical composition, heat treatment and the method of manufacturing. The existing desired mechanical properties of rebar can be achieved through conventional rolling process by appropriate modification of chemical composition [6]. Most commonly yield strength, ultimate strength, Young's modulus of elasticity, Poisson's ratio and percentage elongation determine the mechanical properties of reinforcement bar. Thermo-Mechanical Treated bars are manufactured by rolling and in-line controlled cooling process is another alternative to get strength with ductility [7]. Based on the Ethiopian Building Code Standard, the yield strength of reinforcing bars limits to 400 to 600 MPa [8]. The world average specification for high yield steel bar is 460-500MPa which is difficult to achieve by conventional manufacturing process [6].

Thermo- mechanical Treated (TMT) rebar is an appropriate material for reinforcing concrete structures due to its similarity in thermal expansion with concrete, ability to bond well with concrete and ability to shoulder most of the tensile stress acting on the structure [9]. Today TMT bars are manufactured by rolling and in-line controlled cooling process. The industry level technology is patented under the names of Tempcore (western Europe) and Thermex (United states) [10] both with similar controlled cooling processes. Steel rebar with high strength combined with ductility, weldability and toughness can be obtained by applying Tempcore process for its fabrication [11]. In Tempcore hot rolled deformed bars are quenched at the end of rolling mill by applying high pressure jets of cold water on the red hot steel surface and this process hardens a crust near the steel surface while the bar core remains with high ductility [10]. The composition of martensite and ferrite/pearlite micro-structure of thermos- mechanically treated bar is shown in Fig. 1.

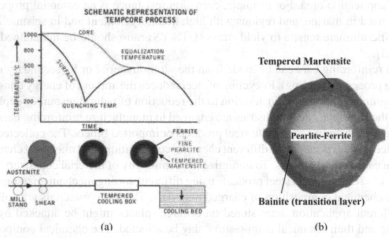

**Fig. 1.** Schematic representation of Tempcore process (a) TMT temperature profile with respect to time and (b) Typical TMT cross section observed in laboratory [10]

Thermo-mechanical-treatment is common in the manufacturing of most steel types, thermo- mechanical treated steel rebar has a ductile core and hard outer layer, the composite action gives sufficient ductility and yield strength [10]. TMT, the modified manufacturing process (i.e., in the cooling stage to control the microstructure formation) of steel led to a better performance than mild steel rebar at reduced cost of production. The TMT manufacturing process of rebar results in tempered martensitic at the periphery, ferrite-pearlite core, and a bainite transition layer. The pearlite core gives ductility to the bar and the martensitic layer gives the tensile strength and increases the corrosion resistance. Such type combination of microstructure can be considered dual phase (DP) steel belongs to the family of high strength low alloy steels [12, 13]. If the composition of structure constitute 20 to 30 percent of martensitic and the presence of a concentric and uniformly thick martensitic peripheral ring can assure the quality of the bar [7].

Even though the slight change of chemical composition of reinforcing bar affects the properties of steel, the tests in most construction sites have been restricted to tensile and bend tests [11, 14]. Since strength and ductility related capacities in reinforced concrete (RC) flexural members are largely controlled by steel reinforcing bars. Besides metallurgical/chemical compositions of the steel used, required properties especially those controlling the inelastic portion of the stress-strain curve which largely depends on the method of rebar manufacturing [15].

Different codes can be applied to specify the limits on the properties and testing procedures of the steel rebar based on the countries requirement. Worldwide, the most commonly utilized codes are ASTM A615, BS4449, ISO 6935-2 and EN 10080. Most of the developing countries adapt one of the above standard codes and contextualized to their requirement. In the case of Ethiopia, the standard agency adopts ISO 6935-2 standard for reinforcing bar and nominated as Compulsory Ethiopian Standard coded as CES- 101-2013. ASTM standards include a 550 MPa and in Germany the existing grades have 520 MPa minimum, and there are no grades with less strength [16].

Introduction of 600 MPa as minimum grade was considering as in ISO standard in some Asian countries. Contractors and consultants argued on that using high strength rebar will reduce rebar overcrowding in anti-seismic design, particularly in column-beam crossings, and reducing total steel mass needed for the overall construction [16]. Countries may use common terms yield strength, ultimate tensile strength, elongation and ratio of UTS with YS with different values are used to measure the conformity of rebar to their specific application (Fig. 2).

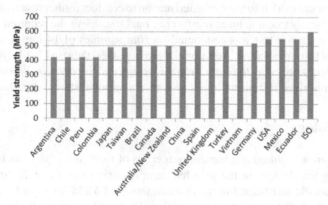

**Fig. 2.** Minimum yield strength for reinforcing bars (in MPa), on different standards [16]

According to Charles and Kankam typical stress–strain curves for standard steel bars used in reinforced concrete construction when loaded monotonically in tension exhibit an initial elastic portion which is a yield plateau and its length is a function of the strength of steel. Extending in the yield plateau region there is strain hardening range in which stress again increases with strain and finally, a range in which the stress drops off before fracture occurs. High strength, high-carbon types of steel generally have a much shorter yield plateau than lower strength low carbon steel [2].

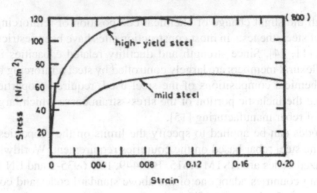

**Fig. 3.** Typical stress–strain curves for steel reinforcement [2]

There is no adequate information provided on the manufacturing process of reinforcing bar in Ethiopia. Additionally the strength analysis of the reinforcing bars used in Ethiopian construction industry is not recorded properly and the domestic trade of the reinforcing bar practiced an open market system. The open market system of the reinforcing bar did not provide enough information to the customer about the characteristic strength and chemical composition of reinforcing bars available on the market (Fig. 3).

This research provides information on the conformity of mechanical properties of steel reinforcing bars used in Ethiopian construction industry considering their yield strength and ductility based on the compulsory Ethiopian standard (CES-1 2013). The main purpose of the work is to have justified reason to conduct further research to improve the quality of locally manufactured reinforcing bars to achieve the required mechanical properties. The tension test was conducted on four samples of 14 mm diameter rebar using universal testing machine. Additionally tensional test data on 12, 14, 16, 20, 24 and 32 mm diameters were collected from Amhara Design and Supervision Works Enterprise which is an authorized institution found in Amhara regional state Bahir Dar- Ethiopia.

## 2   Methodology

The most common required mechanical properties of reinforcing bars can be evaluated by conducting tensile test on the selected samples using Universal Testing Machine (UTM). The tensile test helped in the determination of Yield Strength (YS), Ultimate Tensile Strength (UTS), Percentage Elongation (PE) and Percentage Reduction in Area (PRA) [1]. In this paper the experimental data collection methods for the tension test are categorized in to two tasks. On both cases the yield strength analysis is used to determine the load carrying capacity of different structures and ratio of UTS to YS & elongation values were analyzed to determine the level of ductility in respect to the compulsory Ethiopian Standard (CES -101-2013) and Ethiopian Building Code Standard (EBCS) to justify the failure or conformity of bars to use as reinforcement for concrete in the Ethiopian construction industry.

**Task 1: Conducting Tension Test on 14 mm Diameter Reinforcing Bar.** The Ethiopian construction industry uses imported and locally manufactured steel reinforced bars. The local manufactured reinforced bars are from two sources, one is recycled from the steel scraps and the other is from imported billets. The reinforcing bars used in Ethiopian construction are graded as B300, B400, B500 and B600 with its ductility grade A to D. Three samples of 14 mm diameter with 200 mm gauge length of local manufactured rebar from three different industries and one sample from imported one (turkey) are taken for tension test to determine their strength. The sources/manufacturers of the selected reinforcing bar are nominated as AIS, HSM, ES and Tur to assure the security. These sources/factories are selected based on the products availability on the market at the time of supervision. From 14 mm diameters of reinforcing bars, three required specimens for each sample are selected from the market in random way. A total of twelve specimens, three from each sample are selected. The samples are denoted as AIS 1, 2 & 3, ES 1, 2 & 3, HSM 1, 2&3 and Tur 1, 2 & 3. The number 1, 2, or 3 will not show quality difference, it is simply for the purpose of identification of specimens as shown in Table 1. Each sample was tested with universal testing machine for tensional strength that gives information about tensile strength, yield strength and ductility. The test result of UTM machine manipulated with MaxTest.exe program. The program delivers the amount of load applied, yield strength, ultimate tensile strength, elongation and stress- strain diagram of the test. The sequence of test is arranged in the form of lottery as shown in Table 1. All results of force, stress, strain and elongation are recorded on Table 2.

**Task 2: Analysis of Yield Strength and Ductility of Reinforcing Bar Tension Test Data Collected from Amhara Design and Supervision Works Enterprise (ADSWE).** To have enough data to draw conclusion on the conformity of rebar in Ethiopian construction industry, the tension test data on 12, 14, 16, 20, 24 and 32 mm diameter reinforced bars were collected from AMHARA DESIGN AND SUPERVISION WORKS ENTERPRISE (ADSWE). The test was conducted from February to June 2019 using universal tensile testing machine on 200 mm gauge length reinforcing bars. Amhara Design and Supervision Works Enterprise (ADSWE) was established as public enterprise in the regional sate of Amhara- Ethiopia to realize the objective of the wellbeing of people through providing excel consultancy service. ADSWE is an authorized organization by Amhara regional state to conduct tension test on reinforcing bars.

In ADSWE three specimens was tested on each sample, the average result is used for analysis. The average value of the three specimens for each thirty nine samples were collected from seven local steel reinforcing bars manufacturing industries and 22 samples imported from turkey except one sample from Ukraine. The yield strength, ultimate tensile strength, ratio of UTS to YS and elongation results are used to check the conformity of reinforcing bars in terms of result and ductility.

## 3 Result and Discution

### 3.1 Results

Tension test results conducted by universal testing machine on 14 mm diameter rebar, three samples from local manufactured and one sample imported from turkey, are tabulated as shown in Table 2 below. The recorded data is taken directly from the summary of

**Table 1.** Sequence of test for candidate materials

| No | Nomination symbol | Gauge length mm | Nominal diameter | Total length mm | Remark |
|----|----|----|----|----|----|
| 1 | ES1 | 200 | 14 | 360 | Local |
| 2 | HSM3 | 200 | 14 | 360 | Local |
| 3 | TUR2 | 200 | 14 | 360 | Imported |
| 4 | HSM2 | 200 | 14 | 360 | Local |
| 5 | TUR3 | 200 | 14 | 360 | Imported |
| 6 | AIS1 | 200 | 14 | 360 | Local |
| 7 | AIS2 | 200 | 14 | 360 | Local |
| 8 | TUR1 | 200 | 14 | 360 | Imported |
| 9 | ES3 | 200 | 14 | 360 | Local |
| 10 | AIS3 | 200 | 14 | 360 | Local |
| 11 | HSM1 | 200 | 14 | 360 | Local |
| 12 | ES2 | 200 | 14 | 360 | Local |

tension test result tabulated by the program **MaxTest.exe** integrated with UTM machine. Most of the stress strain diagrams of the conducted tension test samples show similar pattern. It includes the elastic limit, plastic limit and fracture point of all tension test with different values. Figure 4 shows how samples were breaking during the tension test at the fracture point.

Data collected from Amhara design and supervision works enterprise (ADWSE) is tabulated as shown from Table 3, Table 4, Table 5, Table 6, Table 7 and Table 8 based on their nominal diameter.

## 3.2 Discussion

The results obtained from tension test were evaluated based on Ethiopian standards such as CES 101–2013 and ECBS-2- 2013 Standards. In the case of strength the maximum yield strength did not restricted in most of the steel grades. The minimum yield strength is specified as 400 MPa in Ethiopian building code standard [8]. From the tested samples, products from two companies nominated as AIS1 and ES1 did not satisfy the requirements of the Ethiopian Standards.

In the case of ductility requirement, ratio of UTS/YS and Elongation are taken together in to consideration to check conformity of reinforcing bars. By considering elongation with the ratio UTS/YS together, most of locally manufactured bars are failed to satisfy the requirement, for example AIS2 and AIS3 bar have yield strength 576 and 594 respectively and have UTS/YS 1.16 requires minimum elongation at fracture 14% where as 11% elongation is recorded here. So the reinforcing bars are failed to satisfy CES- 101 in addition to the previously rejected one (AIS1 and ES1). Reinforcing bars nominated as HSM1, HSM2 and HSM3 have 596, 553 and 564 MPa yield

**Table 2.** Recorded data from tension test result of 14 mm diameter reinforcing bar from four different sources.

| Sr. No | Sample | Yield strength ReH (MPa) | Ultimate Tensile Strength Rm (MPa) | Elongation after fracture (%) | Remark |
|--------|--------|--------------------------|------------------------------------|-------------------------------|--------|
| 1 | AIS 1 | 375 | 530 | 23 | Local |
| 2 | AIS 2 | 579 | 672 | 11 | Local |
| 3 | AIS 3 | 594 | 692 | 11 | Local |
|   | **Average** | **516** | **631.33** | **15** | |
| 4 | ES 1 | 349 | 493 | 32.5 | Local |
| 5 | ES 2 | 565 | 630 | 12 | Local |
| 6 | ES 3 | 463 | 592 | 24 | Local |
|   | Average | 459 | 571.66 | 22.83 | |
| 7 | HSM 1 | 596 | 676 | 13 | Local |
| 8 | HSM 2 | 553 | 654 | 13 | Local |
| 9 | HSM 3 | 564 | 659 | 13 | Local |
|   | **Average** | **571** | **663** | **13** | |
| 10 | TUR 1 | 608 | 703 | 14 | Imported |
| 11 | TUR 2 | 602 | 696 | 13 | Imported |
| 12 | TUR 3 | 631 | 719 | 12.5 | Imported |
|   | **Average** | **613.66** | **706** | **13.16** | |

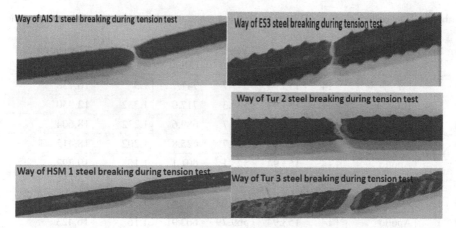

**Fig. 4.** The how steel samples were break during tension test

strength respectively. Referring their UTS/YS ratio the required elongation is 14% but they obtained 13% elongation, so they are failed to achieve the requirement of CES-101-2013.

**Table 3.** Data collected from ADSWE tension test data for 12 mm diameter bar from February to June

| Sr. No | Origin of bar | Dia. | Cr.A (mm$^2$) | YS (Mpa) | UTS (Mpa) | UTS/YS | Elongation (%) |
|--------|---------------|------|---------------|----------|-----------|--------|----------------|
| 1 | Turkey | 12 | 113.10 | 532.5 | 638.2 | 1.198 | 11.961 |
| 2 | ES | 12 | 113.10 | 567.566 | 729.333 | 1.285 | 15.182 |
| 3 | Apollo | 12 | 113.10 | 538.653 | 631.316 | 1.172 | 14.286 |
| 4 | Apollo | 12 | 113.10 | 529.044 | 619.828 | 1.172 | 15.500 |
| 5 | BIGS | 12 | 113.10 | 478.969 | 673.622 | 1.406 | 10.926 |
| 6 | BIGS | 12 | 113.10 | 478.969 | 673.622 | 1.406 | 10.926 |
| 7 | EK | 12 | 113.10 | 420.229 | 609.159 | 1.450 | 20.931 |
| 8 | HSMA | 12 | 113.10 | 571.692 | 690.033 | 1.207 | 11.640 |
| 9 | ZG | 12 | 113.10 | 508.236 | 678.362 | 1.335 | 14.607 |
| 10 | Turkey | 12 | 113.10 | 516.165 | 612.350 | 1.186 | 15.049 |
| 11 | Turkey | 12 | 113.10 | 495.710 | 656.191 | 1.324 | 14.013 |
| 12 | Turkey | 12 | 113.10 | 557.457 | 657.026 | 1.179 | 13.815 |
| 13 | Turkey | 12 | 113.10 | 577.587 | 674.627 | 1.168 | 14.111 |
| 14 | Turkey | 12 | 113.10 | 528.278 | 653.109 | 1.236 | 16.084 |
| 15 | Turkey | 12 | 113.10 | 431.724 | 651.285 | 1.508 | 15.051 |
| 16 | Turkey | 12 | 113.10 | 563.115 | 666.510 | 1.183 | 13.935 |

**Table 4.** Data collected from ADSWE tension test result for 14 mm bar from February to June

| Sr. No | Origin of bar | Di. | Cr.A (mm$^2$) | YS (Mpa) | UTS (Mpa) | UTS/YS | Elongation (%) |
|--------|---------------|-----|---------------|----------|-----------|--------|----------------|
| 1 | ES | 14 | 153.94 | 547.7 | 741.7 | 1.3 | 16.738 |
| 2 | BiGS | 14 | 153.94 | 538.3 | 717.0 | 1.332 | 12.850 |
| 3 | ZG | 14 | 153.94 | 559.7 | 689.6 | 1.232 | 18.604 |
| 4 | Apollo | 14 | 153.94 | 520.7 | 625.8 | 1.202 | 18.412 |
| 5 | Apollo | 14 | 153.94 | 523.1 | 601.1 | 1.15 | 19.392 |
| 6 | ZG | 14 | 153.94 | 538.2 | 685.8 | 1.27 | 20.675 |
| 7 | ZG | 14 | 153.94 | 524.92 | 655.34 | 1.25 | 19.537 |
| 8 | Apollo | 14 | 153.94 | 569.79 | 662.91 | 1.16 | 16.423 |
| 9 | Turkey | 14 | 153.94 | 543.00 | 729.29 | 1.34 | 14.794 |

Imported reinforcing bars nominated as TUR2 obtained 602 MPa yield strength and 1.15 UTS to YS ratio. The required elongation 14% but the recorded one 13%, it fails

**Table 5.** Data collected from ADSWE tension test result for 16 mm bar from February to June

| Sr. No | Origin of bar | Di. | Cr.A (mm$^2$) | YS (MPa) | UTS (MPa) | UTS/YS | Elongation (%) |
|---|---|---|---|---|---|---|---|
| 1 | AIS | 16 | 201.062 | 339.56 | 490.30 | 1.44 | 30.80 |
| 2 | AIS | 16 | 201.062 | 564.58 | 685.09 | 1.21 | 16.30 |
| 3 | Apollo | 16 | 201.062 | 499.94 | 606.42 | 1.21 | 20.34 |
| 4 | BIGS | 16 | 201.062 | 576.36 | 650.98 | 1.12 | 14.62 |
| 5 | BIGS | 16 | 201.062 | 495.11 | 608.20 | 1.22 | 20.52 |
| 6 | BIGS | 16 | 201.062 | 577.50 | 657.45 | 1.13 | 16.02 |
| 7 | BIGs | 16 | 201.062 | 585.44 | 678.89 | 1.15 | 15.88 |
| 8 | EK | 16 | 201.062 | 380.56 | 582.57 | 1.53 | 25.66 |
| 9 | EST | 16 | 201.062 | 504.45 | 643.40 | 1.27 | 21.06 |
| 10 | ZG | 16 | 201.062 | 527.03 | 702.37 | 1.33 | 17.66 |
| 11 | ZG | 16 | 201.062 | 534.39 | 673.04 | 1.25 | 21.67 |
| 12 | Turkey | 16 | 201.062 | 513.69 | 613.96 | 1.19 | 21.78 |
| 13 | Turkey | 16 | 201.062 | 522.99 | 635.62 | 1.21 | 18.54 |
| 14 | Turkey | 16 | 201.062 | 546.22 | 607.60 | 1.11 | 14.35 |
| 15 | Turkey | 16 | 201.062 | 536.20 | 645.55 | 1.20 | 15.05 |
| 16 | Turkey | 16 | 201.062 | 549.18 | 654.01 | 1.19 | 18.04 |

**Table 6.** Data collected from ADSWE tension test results for 20 mm bar from February to June

| Sr. NO | Dia. (mm) | Origin of the Bar | YS (Mpa) | UTS (Mpa) | Ratio UTS/ YS | Elongation (%) |
|---|---|---|---|---|---|---|
| 1 | 20 | Turkey | 523.60 | 639.41 | 1.221 | 20.137 |
| 2 | 20 | BIGS | 568.43 | 662.94 | 1.166 | 17.132 |
| 3 | 20 | HSMA | 560.52 | 691.07 | 1.232 | 13.564 |
| 4 | 20 | Apollo | 415.81 | 569.62 | 1.369 | 23.124 |
| 5 | 20 | Apollo | 540.60 | 654.73 | 1.211 | 18.518 |
| 6 | 20 | HSM | 472.67 | 646.99 | 1.368 | 16.537 |
| 7 | 20 | Turkey | 524.28 | 651.19 | 1.242 | 18.769 |
| 8 | 20 | Turkey | 500.29 | 614.82 | 1.228 | 21.170 |
| 9 | 20 | HSMA | 520.97 | 643.90 | 1.235 | 17.446 |
| 10 | 20 | HSMB | 415.63 | 623.72 | 1.500 | 15.901 |

to satisfy the requirement of CES- 101-2013. The imported TUR1 has yield strength 608 MPa and UTs to YS ratio 1.15 required elongations is 14% and also the recorded

**Table 7.** Data collected from ADSWE tension test result for 24 mm bar from February to June

| Sr. NO | Dia. (mm) | Origin of Bar | YS (Mpa) | UTS (Mpa) | Ratio UTS/YS | Elongation (%) |
|--------|-----------|---------------|----------|-----------|--------------|----------------|
| 1 | 24 | Turkey | 547.63 | 645.46 | 1.18 | 20.486 |
| 2 | 24 | ZG | 528.26 | 675.29 | 1.28 | 24.866 |
| 3 | 24 | BIGS | 452.48 | 561.12 | 1.24 | 27.895 |
| 4 | 24 | Apollo | 520.20 | 631.86 | 1.21 | 22.222 |
| 5 | 24 | KSMG | 502.32 | 638.57 | 1.27 | 29.312 |
| 6 | 24 | Turkey | 596.38 | 694.37 | 1.16 | 17.940 |

**Table 8.** Data Collected from ADSWE tension test result for 32 mm bar from February to June

| Sr. NO | Dia. (mm$^2$) | Origin of Bar | YS (MPa) | UTS (MPa) | Ratio UTS/YS | Elongation (%) |
|--------|---------------|---------------|----------|-----------|--------------|----------------|
| 1 | 32 | Turkey | 378.13 | 756.54 | 2.00 | 12.20 |
| 2 | 32 | BIGS | 566.68 | 731.64 | 1.29 | 13.35 |
| 3 | 32 | UHRAINE | 518.76 | 633.85 | 1.22 | 11.19 |
| 4 | 32 | Turkey | 459.18 | 594.30 | 1.29 | 16.93 |

one is 14%, it satisfies the requirement. The imported TUR3 has yield strength 631 MPa and UTS/YS ratio 1.14 required elongation is 10% and the recorded one 12.5% it also satisfies the need of CES- 101-2013.

Data collected from Amhara design and supervision works enterprise as referred from Table 3, Table 4, Table 5, Table 6, Table 7 and Table 8 shows all the required information in terms of ultimate tensile strength, yield strength and ductility. On the 12 mm diameter reinforcing bar all the samples satisfied the minimum yield strength (400MPa), because all the samples record more than 400 MPa. But in terms of ductility the amount of elongation and ratio of UTS to YS 50% of samples are failed to satisfy the requirement. From the same statistics 8 samples of the turkey products was examined and 4 of them are failed to satisfy the requirement. From 14 mm diameter samples only one sample from the local manufactured reinforcing bar was failed to satisfy the requirement in terms of elongation or ductility. Again from the collected data all 16 mm diameter reinforcing bar samples were passed all the requirements. According to the data collected from ADSWE samples with their nominal diameter less than 16 mm record failure to satisfy the requirements specified on CES-101-2013 and EBCS-2 2013 Ethiopian standards, most of the failed reinforcing bars were luck to achieve ductility. This may happen one due to the absence sufficient amount of temperature at the core of the bar required for self-tempering process of the reinforcing bar on the quenched surface. Two it may be due the presence of high amount of carbon or alloyed elements that form carbides harder than iron carbide. Re-bar with smaller diameter may cool in the fast rate without retain enough amount of temperature for self-tempering process due their surface area to volume ratio. Whereas rebar with larger diameter may able to retain enough amount of temperature at the core region and make self-tempering process. Because of the capability to store sufficient amount of self-tempering temperature at the core area during the quenching process, rebar with larger diameter are able to achieve the required ductility and they were satisfied CES- 101-2013.

## 4 Conclusion

From the tension test results conducted by universal testing machine and tension test data collected from ADSWE the following conclusions are drawn:

1. The quality of the reinforcing bar will not be assured by the origin of the country. According to the data collected from the tension test and ADSWE tension test data both the imported and local manufactured had faced rejection based on the requirements set by the Ethiopian Standard Agency (CES -101- 2013).
2. Most of the samples satisfy the required yield and ultimate tensile strength but they were failed to achieve ductility. This shows achieving higher strength without scarifying ductility is difficult in conventional manufacturing process especially at the smallest diameter reinforcing bar.
3. Reinforcing bars with higher diameter satisfied minimum yield strength and ductility better than reinforcing bars with smaller diameter. This might happen due to the composition of ferrite–pearlite and martensitic structure formed during the cooling process. The ferrite- pearlite and martensitic structure will depend on self-tempering process due to the temperature difference at the surface and core of the reinforcing bar. The core temperature during cooling is higher in larger diameter bars due to the difference in surface area to volume ratio. Materials with smaller diameter bars have larger surface area to volume ratio than larger diameters and smaller diameters release temperature in the fast rate than larger diameter bars.

## References

1. Kareem, B.: Tensile and chemical analyses of selected steel bars produced in Nigeria. Res. Gate (2009)
2. Charles, M.A.-A., Kankam, K.: Strength and ductility characteristics of reinforcing steel bars milled from scrap metals. Mater. Des. Mater. Des. 23(2002), 537–545 (2002)
3. Ejeh, S.P., Jibrin, M.U.: Tensile Tests on Reinforcing Steel Bars in the Nigerian Construction Industry (2012)
4. Jica, R.: Basic Metal and Engineering Industries: Policy Framework and the Firm-level Study (2010)
5. Panigrahi, S.S.B.K., Sahoo, G.: Effect of alloying elements on tensile properties, microstructure, and corrosion resistance of reinforcing bar steel. J. Mater. Eng. Perform. 18(8), 1102 (2009)
6. Balogun, S., Esezobor, D., Adeosun, S., Sekunowo, O.: Challenges of Producing Quality Construction Steel Bars in West Africa: Case Study of Nigeria Steel Industry (2009)

7. Gokul, P.N., Sarvani, A.O.N., Radhakrishna, S.P.: Variations in microstructure and mechanical properties of Thermo-Mechanically-Treated (TMT) Steel Reinforcement Bars (2015)
8. EBCS: Ethiopian Building Code Standards, Design of Concrete Structures (2013)
9. Souvik Das, J.M., Bhattacharyya, T., Bhattacharyya, S.: Failure analysis of re-bars during bending operations (2014)
10. Sooraj, G.P.R., Nair, A.O., Sethuraj, R., Nandipati, S., Radhakrishna, G.P.: Variations in microstructure and mechanical properties of Thermo-Mechanically-Treated (TMT) steel reinforcement bars (2018)
11. Salman, F.D.A.: Variability of Chemical Analysis of Reinforcing Bar Produced in Saudi Arabia
12. Yu Cao, J.A., Karlsson, B.: The influence of temperatures and strain rates on the mechanical behavior of dual phase steel in different conditions (2014)
13. Vladimir Torganchuk, A.B., Kaibyshev, R.: Effect of rolling temperature on microstructure and mechanical properties of 18%Mn TWIP/TRIP steels
14. Andrey Belyakov, R.K., Torganchuk, V.: Microstructure and Mechanical Properties of 18%Mn TWIP/TRIP Steels Processed by Warm or Hot Rolling (2017)
15. Rai, S.K.J.D.C., Chakrabarti, I.: Evaluation of Properties of Steel Reinforcing Bars for Seismic Design (2012)
16. Jorge Madias, M.W., Behr, G., Valladares, V.: Analysis of International Standards on Concrete Reinforcing Steel Bar (2017)

# Optimization of Treatment Parameters to Enhance Bending Strength of Bamboo

Andualem Belachew Workie and Assefa Asmare Tsegaw[✉]

Bahir Dar Institute of Technology, P. O. Box: 26, Bahir Dar, Ethiopia
assefaa@bdu.edu.et

**Abstract.** Bamboos are evergreen perennial flowering plants in the subfamily Bambusoideae of the grass family poaceae. The word "bamboo "comes from kannada term bamboo, which introduce to English through Indonesia and Malay. Bamboo is the most amply found with remarkable mechanical property. The investigation essence on optimization of treatment parameters to enhancement bending strength of bamboo. Treatment conditions taken at: 50 °C, 100 °C and 150 °C with palm oil for 30 min, 50 °C, 100 °C and 150 °C with boil water for 30 min. Soaking with water for 30 min, 1 h and 1.5 h, baking with for 30 min, 1 h and 1.5 h, baking for 20 min, 40 min and 60 min at 150 °C and exposing to smoking for 30 min, 60 min and 90 min. the optimum result obtained on specimens treated in water soaking for 90 min; boild in oil with 150 °C for 30 min boiling in water for 30 min at 150 °C; smoking for 90 min and baking at 150 °C for 60 min results the best performance on bamboo sample ultimately. Optimization confirmed with predicted bending strength and achieved 73.11% of enhancement.

**Keywords:** Bambusoideae · Bamboo · Optimal · Bending strength · Taguchi

## 1 Introduction

Bamboo plays a major role in the economy of rural people and industry [1–3].They are widely used for house for house constructions, bridges, fencing basketry, furniture,mats, agriculture tools, handles for tools,musical instruments, fishing rods, scaffoldings,weaving materials, pole and post, paper and pulp making, food for humans and livestock [4–7]. Bamboo can even use for medical areas as a benefit inspired by the bending and energy absorption characteristics [8].

Natural available plant bamboo has high strength, variety of purposes [2, 9]. Comparing between steel and bamboo with respect to its mechanical property specially, bending, is much lower [10]. Bamboo can be preserved either by using chemicals (chemical treatment) or without using chemicals (traditional treatment) to prolong their durability [11].

Investigation of mechanical behavior of bamboo can be done with FEM, Taguchi design of experiment and other methods, which can comfort to the design data and circumstance [12].

© ICST Institute for Computer Sciences, Social Informatics and Telecommunications Engineering 2021
Published by Springer Nature Switzerland AG 2021. All Rights Reserved
M. A. Delele et al. (Eds.): ICAST 2020, LNICST 385, pp. 315–325, 2021.
https://doi.org/10.1007/978-3-030-80618-7_21

Nevertheless, based on specific specie of this natural plant (bamboo) sufficient available data is very rare [13] when compared to other known species or known structural materials. Henceforth, this study paves away to further studies.

### 1.1 Objective

General objective of the study is optimizing the treatment parameters to enhance bending strength and examine extent in which process parameters improve mechanical properties of dendrocalamus membranous munro bamboo.

## 2 Methodology, Materials and Methods

### 2.1 Methodology

This study takes an experimental investigation of process parameters of treating bamboo for enhancing its mechanical properties.

### 2.2 Materials

Dendrocalumose membranous munero bamboo is one of the most extracted bamboo species in Awi zone was used for the purposes using traditional or non-chemical preservation. Methods like water soaking, heating and cooling in oil, baking, heating and cooling in water and smoking are the main methods that followed by people to enhance the mechanical properties of harvested bamboos before their multipurpose uses.

First, bamboo specimens with length of 260mm and 4mm in diameter treated to decrease their sensitivity to moisture and improve their durability. Treatment conditions taken at; 50 °C, 100 °C and 150 °C with palm oil for 30 min, 50 °C, 100 °C and 150 °C with boil water for 30 min, soaking with water for 30 min, 1 h and 1.5 h, baking with 20 min, 40 min and 60 min at 150 °C and exposing to smoking for 30 min, 60 min and 90 min.

### 2.3 Testing Equipment

For this research specimen bending specimen 47DIN5010 bamboos was used [14]. Universal bending testing machine Germany version 50110-1:2013 was used to measure the bending strength of the natural bamboo (Fig. 1).

### 2.4 Design of Experiment (DOE)

To come up with the required process optimization of point of interest, statistical method is one of the key tools. DOE is one of this kind. DOE is profuse tactics for exploring multi-factor prospect where effect of every process parameters each and combination of interrelation investigated. DOE offers a good understanding in finding of robust system. Taguchi practices for superiority quality to improve products and processes. Analysis

**Fig. 1.** Universal testing machine

carried out making use of Taguchi's design of experiment due to its small number of experiments to execute.

Likely fixed and control process parameters sorted out and summarized as shown in Table 1 and 2. Taguchi method mainly uses possible combinations of experimental trial making use of Latin square [8], which has properties of orthogonal array representation. Depending up on number of control factors and its unique properties of $L_{27}$ $(3^5)$ orthogonal array is suitable [15].

**Table 1.** Fixed factors

| Fixed factors | Value |
|---|---|
| Thickness | 3.5 mm |
| Condition | Dry |
| Length | 260 mm |

Improving required (point of interest) quality fall in to three categories: larger the better, smaller the better and nominal the best type [16]. Based on quality criteria improvement signal-to-noise quantification shall be evaluated. Henceforth, improving quality endeavored check as determination to make best use of the signal to noise (S/N) ratio.

The aim of this study is to enhance flexural strength of natural bamboo can categorized in maximum-the-better criterion. Consequently, signal-to-noise ratio ($\eta$) calculated as:

$$\eta = -\log\left[\sum_{i=1}^{r} 1/y_i^2\right] \tag{1}$$

**Table 2.** Control process parameters

| Control factors | | Level | | |
|---|---|---|---|---|
| | | 1 | 2 | 3 |
| A | Water soaking, [min] | 30 | 60 | 90 |
| B | Boiling in oil. [°C] | 50 | 100 | 150 |
| C | Boiling in water. [°C] | 50 | 100 | 150 |
| D | Smoking [min] | 30 | 60 | 90 |
| E | Baking [min] | 20 | 40 | 60 |

Where r is trial and $y_i$ observations under different noise situations. A level that make the most of signal-to-noise ratio for factors that will be substantial result. Hence, optimal conditions for flexural strength process easily determined. Value of $\eta$ at is optimal conditions calculated using Eq. (2) [15].

$$\eta_{opt} = m + \sum (m_i - m) \qquad (2)$$

Where $\eta_{opt}$ is S/N ratio at best situations, m is overall average value for trials, and mi is the $\eta$ under best settings for ith factor. Depending up on how close average of combination of best parameters and expected one, $\eta_{opt}$; in general, within 90%, it can have said to be important factors are not missed, there is no interaction between the factors and design is remains at its robustness.

## 3   Experimental Setup

The optimum marks obtained on specimens treated in water soaking for 90 min; boiled in oil with 150 °C for 30 min; boiling in water for 30 min at 150° C; smoking for 90 min and baking at 150 °C for 60 min.

An experiment result on parameters optimization for flexural strength has measured five times and intended using Eq. (1) for individual experimental conferring to number of measurements. Besides to this, average of each of control factors signal-to-noise ratio was calculated and summarized in Table 5 (Table 3).

**Table 3.** Experimental setup according to Taguchi's DOE

| Exp. | A,[min] | B.[min] | C.[min] | D.[min] | E.[min] |
|------|---------|---------|---------|---------|---------|
| 1 | 30 | 50 | 50 | 50 | 50 |
| 2 | 30 | 50 | 50 | 30 | 40 |
| 3 | 30 | 50 | 50 | 30 | 60 |
| 4 | 30 | 100 | 100 | 60 | 20 |
| 5 | 30 | 100 | 100 | 60 | 40 |
| 6 | 30 | 100 | 100 | 60 | 60 |
| 7 | 30 | 150 | 150 | 90 | 20 |
| 8 | 30 | 150 | 150 | 90 | 40 |
| 9 | 30 | 150 | 150 | 90 | 60 |
| 10 | 60 | 50 | 100 | 90 | 20 |
| 11 | 60 | 50 | 100 | 90 | 40 |
| 12 | 60 | 50 | 100 | 90 | 60 |
| 13 | 60 | 100 | 150 | 30 | 20 |
| 14 | 60 | 100 | 150 | 30 | 40 |
| 15 | 60 | 100 | 150 | 30 | 60 |
| 16 | 60 | 150 | 50 | 60 | 20 |
| 17 | 60 | 150 | 50 | 60 | 40 |
| 18 | 60 | 150 | 50 | 60 | 60 |
| 19 | 90 | 50 | 150 | 60 | 40 |
| 20 | 90 | 50 | 150 | 60 | 40 |
| 21 | 90 | 50 | 150 | 60 | 60 |
| 22 | 90 | 100 | 150 | 90 | 20 |
| 23 | 90 | 100 | 50 | 90 | 40 |
| 24 | 90 | 100 | 50 | 90 | 60 |
| 25 | 90 | 150 | 100 | 30 | 20 |
| 26 | 90 | 150 | 100 | 30 | 40 |
| 27 | 90 | 150 | 100 | 30 | 60 |

Samples with different parameters combinations are shown in Fig. 2 below.

**Fig. 2.** Bamboo samples at different parameters combinations

# 4   Result and Discussion

## 4.1   Bending Strength Analysis

Experimental results on parameters optimization in improving bending strength of bamboo measured and summarized as shown in Table 4. Furthermore, response of S/N ratio calculated using Eq. (1) for each trial according to number of measurements recurrence. In addition to this, average of each of control factors S/N ratio was calculated and summarized in Table 5.

**Table 4.** Experimental results

| Exp | A | B | C | D | E | Flexural strength [M pa] | S/N | Mean [M pa] |
|-----|---|---|---|---|---|--------------------------|---------|-------------|
| 1 | 1 | 1 | 1 | 1 | 1 | 6.6 | 16.3909 | 6.600 |
| 2 | 1 | 1 | 1 | 1 | 2 | 9.46 | 19.5178 | 9.460 |
| 3 | 1 | 1 | 1 | 1 | 3 | 12.782 | 22.1320 | 12.782 |
| 4 | 1 | 2 | 2 | 2 | 1 | 17.6 | 21.9103 | 17.600 |
| 5 | 1 | 2 | 2 | 2 | 2 | 27.082 | 28.6536 | 27.082 |
| 6 | 1 | 2 | 2 | 2 | 3 | 40.48 | 32.1448 | 40.480 |
| 7 | 1 | 3 | 3 | 3 | 1 | 64.064 | 36.1323 | 64.064 |
| 8 | 1 | 3 | 3 | 3 | 2 | 66.572 | 36.4658 | 66.572 |
| 9 | 1 | 3 | 3 | 3 | 3 | 123.772 | 41.8524 | 123.772 |
| 10 | 2 | 1 | 2 | 3 | 1 | 34.958 | 30.8709 | 34.958 |
| 11 | 2 | 1 | 2 | 3 | 2 | 37.796 | 31.5489 | 37.796 |
| 12 | 2 | 1 | 2 | 3 | 3 | 41.866 | 32.4372 | 41.866 |
| 13 | 2 | 2 | 3 | 1 | 1 | 31.878 | 30.0978 | 31.878 |
| 14 | 2 | 2 | 3 | 1 | 2 | 37.026 | 31.3701 | 37.026 |
| 15 | 2 | 2 | 3 | 1 | 3 | 44.704 | 33.0069 | 44.704 |

*(continued)*

**Table 4.** (*continued*)

| Exp | A | B | C | D | E | Flexural strength [M pa] | S/N | Mean [M pa] |
|-----|---|---|---|---|---|--------------------------|-----|-------------|
| 16 | 2 | 3 | 1 | 2 | 1 | 38.852 | 31.7883 | 38.852 |
| 17 | 2 | 3 | 1 | 2 | 2 | 40.37 | 32.1212 | 40.37 |
| 18 | 2 | 3 | 1 | 2 | 3 | 53.328 | 34.5391 | 53.328 |
| 19 | 3 | 1 | 3 | 2 | 2 | 57.926 | 35.2575 | 57.926 |
| 20 | 3 | 1 | 3 | 2 | 2 | 63.426 | 36.0453 | 63.426 |
| 21 | 3 | 1 | 3 | 2 | 3 | 72.05 | 37.1527 | 72.05 |
| 22 | 3 | 2 | 1 | 3 | 1 | 56.826 | 35.0909 | 56.826 |
| 23 | 3 | 2 | 1 | 3 | 2 | 61.6 | 35.7916 | 61.600 |
| 24 | 3 | 2 | 1 | 3 | 3 | 68.299 | 36.6886 | 68.299 |
| 25 | 3 | 3 | 2 | 1 | 1 | 64.548 | 36.1977 | 64.548 |
| 26 | 3 | 3 | 2 | 1 | 2 | 67.936 | 36.6420 | 67.936 |
| 27 | 3 | 3 | 2 | 1 | 3 | 74.558 | 37.4499 | 74.558 |

**Table 5.** Control variables signal-to-noise ratio

| Level | Water soaking | Heating in oil | Boiling in water | Smoking | Baking |
|-------|---------------|----------------|------------------|---------|--------|
| 1 | 28.69 | 29.04 | 29.34 | 29.20 | 30.75 |
| 2 | 31.97 | 31.97 | 32.32 | 32.51 | 32.02 |
| 3 | 36.26 | 35.91 | 35.26 | 35.21 | 34.16 |
| Delta | 7.57 | 6.87 | 5.92 | 6.01 | 3.41 |
| Rank | 1 | 2 | 3 | 4 | 5 |

## 4.2 Optimum Levels

Optimum process parameters and their levels are determined according to experimental outputs and Table 5 reveals optimum blends of control factors grounded on its uppermost average value of S/N ratio. Hence, the optimum blend and stages are A3B3C3D3E3, short listed and shown in Table 6. Moreover, from the normal probability plot (Fig. 4) it can deduce that the experiment doesn't interact between control parameters.

## 4.3 Confirmation Experiment

From validate test, it is obvious an enhancement of bending strength from 92.8968Mpa to 127.053Mpa with a minimum error of 2.73%. it shows about 73.11% increment.

Total Error = (error/total) *100%
Total allowance error = (0.3158/11.5513) *100% = 2.73%

Percentage error (% error) = [(Experimental Value-Theoretical value)/theoretical value] *100 (Fig. 3).

**Table 6.** Optimum process parameters

| Factor | | level | value |
|---|---|---|---|
| A | Water soaking, [min] | 3 | 90 |
| B | Heating in oil, [°C] | 3 | 150 |
| C | Boiling in water, [°C] | 3 | 150 |
| D | Smoking, [min] | 3 | 90 |
| E | Baking, [min] | 3 | 60 |

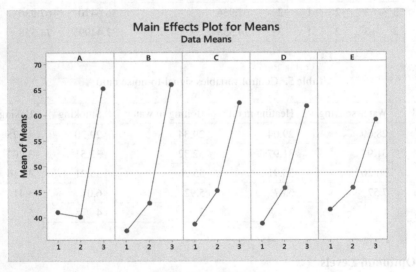

**Fig. 3.** Plot of S/N ratio

## 5  Analysis of Variance (ANOVA)

To find among all the process parameters which one is the influential one, statistical approach analysis is carried out. One of the methods is Anova. Anova tests by comparing variance. Hence, in this experimental investigation the main effects, significant factors are identified using F ratio test. Royl et al. [17] suggest one factor can pool as an error if its influence with respect to sum of square (SS) is less or equal to 10%. It indicates the significance of the individual control factors and their interactions. As shown in Table 5 all parameters have p-values less than 0.1, which means those variables, have higher influence on the bending strength of natural bamboo in high regard (Table 7).

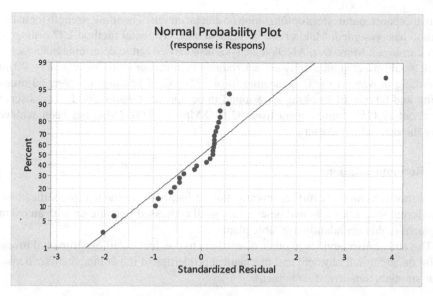

**Fig. 4.** Normal probability plot

**Table 7.** Analysis of variance (ANOVA)

| Source | DF | Seq SS | Adj SS | Adj MS | F-value | p-value | Contribution | Significance |
|--------|-----|--------|--------|--------|---------|---------|--------------|--------------|
| Water soaking | 2 | 25.351 | 25.351 | 12.6755 | 51.01 | 0.000 | 27.22% | significant |
| Boiling in oil | 2 | 24.096 | 24.096 | 12.0482 | 48.49 | 0.000 | 25.87% | significant |
| Boiling in water | 2 | 16.385 | 16.385 | 8.1927 | 32.97 | 0.000 | 17.59% | significant |
| Smoking | 2 | 16.033 | 16.033 | 8.0166 | 32.26 | 0.000 | 17.21% | significant |
| Baking | 2 | 7.300 | 7.300 | 3.6500 | 14.69 | 0.000 | 7.84% | significant |
| Error | 16 | 3.976 | 3.967 | 0.2485 | | | 4.27 | |
| Total | 26 | 93.142 | | | | | 100% | |

# 6  Conclusions and Recommendations

## 6.1  Conclusion

Optimalizations is done for enhancing the bending strength and increased from 92.8668Mpa to 127.053Mpa with a minimum error of 2.7%. The confirmatory test was done by taking the optimal parameters and the result is 108.52Mpa which is between the critical intervals and shows that the improvement of the response variable is accepted and also shows that the method that was used to optimize was valid. The study found that all the factors had significant influence on the response variables.

In this paper, parameters optimization on enhancement of bending strength for natural bamboo has presented. Making use of Taguchi's experimental method L27 orthogonal array employed. Moreover, ANOVA analysis also carried out to determine main factors, which would affect significantly surface roughness improvement. Consequently, 90 min of soaking in water 150 °C of heating in oil, 150 °C of heating in water, 60 min of baking and 60 min of smoking have found to be optimal parameters. It was observed that about 73.11% improvement from 92.8968Mpa to127.053Mpa has been achieved using the optimal parameters.

## 6.2 Recommendations

The author recommends further investigation of bamboo mechanical properties based on different fiber thickness and other issues shall addressed to come up with an overall judgment of this abundantly available plant.

The author also advices to other researchers to conduct detail experimental investigation on additional physical and mechanical properties of the composite like: density, shear strength, tensile test and other.

## References

1. Chen, G.Q., Hua, Y.K.: A study of new bamboo-based composite panels (I). J. Bamboo Res. 10(3), 83–87 (1991)
2. Chen, T.Y., Sawada, Y., Kawakai, S., Tanahashi, M., Sasaki, H.: Studies on bamboo fiberboard. Forest Prod. Ind. 8(4), 11–18 (1989)
3. Deshpande, A.P., Rao, M.B., Rao, C.L.: Extraction of bamboo fibers and their use as reinforcement in polymeric composites. J. Appl. Polym. Sci. 76(1), 83–92 (2000)
4. Bai, X., Lee, A.W., Thompson, L.L., Rosowsky, D.V.: Finite element analysis of MOSO bamboo-reinforced southern pine OSB composite Beams. Wood Sci. Technol. 31(4), 403–415 (1999)
5. Chung, K., Yu, W.: Mechanical properties of structural bamboo for bamboo scaffoldings. Eng. Struct. 24, 429–442 (2002)
6. Ghavami, K.: Ultimate load behaviour of bamboo-reinforced lightweight concrete beams. Cement Concr. Compos. 17, 281–288 (1995)
7. Lima, H.C., Willrich, F.L., Barbosa, N.P., Rosa, M.A., Cunha, B.S.: Durability analysis of bamboo as concrete reinforcement. Mater. Struct. 41, 981–989 (2008)
8. Amada, S., Ichikawa, Y., Munekata, T., Nagase, Y., Shimizu, H.: Fiber texture and mechanical graded structure of bamboo. Compos. B Eng. 28, 13–20 (1997)
9. Zou, M., Song, J., Xu, S., Liu, S., Chang, Z.: Bionic design of the bumper beam inspired by the bending and energy absorption characteristics of bamboo. Appl. Bionics Biomech. 2018, 8062321 (2018)
10. Gatenholm, P., Felix, J.: Methods for improvement of properties of cellulose polymer composites. In: Wolcott, M.P. (eds.) Wood fiber/polymer composites: fundamental concepts, process, and material options, Forest Products Society, Madison (1993)
11. Chen, G.Q., Hua, Y.K.: A study of new bamboo-based composite panels (II). J. Bamboo Res. 10(4), 72–78 (1991)
12. Chand, N., Shukla, M., Sharma, M.K.: Analysis of mechanical behavior of bamboo (dendrocalamus strictus) by using FEM. J. Nat. Fibers 5, 127–137 (2008)

13. Meena, R.K., Bhandhari, M.S., Barhwal, S., Ginwal, H.S.: Genetic diversity and structure of Dendrocalamus hamiltonii natural metapopulation: a commercially important bamboo species of northeast Himalayas. 3 Biotech **9**(2), 60 (2019)
14. American Society for Testing and Materials (ASTM). 1994. Standard methods of evaluating the properties of wood based fiber and particle panel materials. ASTM D1037-94. ASTM, Philadelphia, Pa.
15. Van Lint, J.H., Wilson, R.M.: A Course in Combinatorics," Cambridge University Press, USA, New York (2001)
16. Taguchi, G., Chowdhury, S., Wu, Y.: Taguchi's Quality Engineering Handbook. Wiley, United States of America (2004)
17. Roy, R.K.: Design of Experiments Using the Taguchi Approach: 16 Steps to Product and Process Improvement. Wiley-Interscience, United Staes of America (2001)

# Investigation on Damping Capability
# of Indigenous Wood Species in Ethiopia

Fasikaw Kibrete[1] and Hailu Shimels[2(✉)]

[1] Department of Mechanical Engineering, University of Gondar, Gondar, Ethiopia
[2] Department of Mechanical Engineering, Bahir Dar Institute of Technology, Bahir Dar
University, Bahir Dar, Ethiopia

**Abstract.** Damping capacity is a measure of a material's ability which absorb
vibration energy by converting into heat energy. Materials which have high damping ability can suppress excessive vibrations to a reasonable limit. Therefore, this
paper investigates the damping characteristics of five indigenous wood species
(*Cordia Africana, Juniperus Procera, Afrocarpus Gracilior, Syzygium Guineense*
and *Acacia Decurrens*) found in Ethiopia through analytical, numerical and experimental approaches. The experimental testing was performed using piezoelectric
accelerometer in association with LabVIEW for a perfectly clamped-free cantilever beam based on the impact hammer excitation. The damping ratio was computed using logarithmic decrement method from the decay curve measured. Based
on the investigation, the damping factor for all species of woods was almost equal
to 0.020 at room condition, and it is definitely greater than most other crystalline
materials. Thus, wooden materials are better suitable for engineering applications
in terms of vibrations if the other strength properties are satisfactory.

**Keywords:** Damping capacity · Logarithmic decrement · Natural frequency ·
Vibration · Wood

## 1 Introduction

Vibrational motion is a repetitive type motion of the bodies with a defined time interval.
The main causes of vibrational motion are unbalanced centrifugal forces, elastic nature
of system, external excitations, misalignment and dry friction between contact surfaces
[1]. Some vibrational motions are important with a desired amplitude and frequency
for musical instruments, geological investigations, drilling of geotechnical wells and
harvesting crops, but most vibrations are unwanted in many engineering applications
since it results wastage of energy, high stresses, unwanted noise, rapid wear and catastrophic failure due to its excessiveness [2]. Hence, it needs to be dampened. Therefore,
the interest of many researchers lies in dampening excessive vibrations using vibration
damping materials [3]. These materials have high energy dissipation capability, and play
a significant role in reducing noise, vibration and dynamic stresses of the mechanical
and structural systems, and in prolonging its lifetime under cyclic loading or impact [4,
5].

© ICST Institute for Computer Sciences, Social Informatics and Telecommunications Engineering 2021
Published by Springer Nature Switzerland AG 2021. All Rights Reserved
M. A. Delele et al. (Eds.): ICAST 2020, LNICST 385, pp. 326–340, 2021.
https://doi.org/10.1007/978-3-030-80618-7_22

Damping capacity is the ability of a material's ability to absorb mechanical energy by converting it into heat during mechanical vibration [6]. It can be expressed using several parameters, including specific damping capacity, amplification factor, inverse quality factor, loss factor and logarithmic decrement. Based on their damping capacity, materials can be categorized as low damping or high damping materials. Low damping materials have higher amplitude of vibration and are required for increasing sensitivity in sensors and certain precision instrumentation, and for proper functioning as in the case with parts of musical instruments, tuning fork and bells. On the other hand, high damping materials are very desirable to suppress mechanical vibration, noise and transmission of waves. These materials are used in many engineering components like turbine buckets, propeller blades, crankshafts, automotive bumper or in other devices where a component can resonate at some frequency to minimize the resonant amplitude, and thus minimizes the dynamic stresses to which the component is exposed [7, 8].

Particularly, woods have been put forward as a high damping material due to its composite polymeric nature consisting of crystalline cellulosic microfibrils embedded in a more or less amorphous matrix [9]. The cellular network converts mechanical energy into heat by frictional and viscoelastic resistance. Because of the high internal friction created by the cellular pore network, wooden materials are advantageous for many engineering applications to exhibit adequate damping ability so that any excessive vibration is dampened to an acceptable limit in practice [10, 11].

Even if wood has numerous engineering applications and Ethiopia has plenty of higher plant species, it is not used as a standardized engineering material probably because of lack of substantial work which describes the physical and mechanical properties of every species. Particularly, the damping capacity are not studied, known and documented by the researchers, forest products processors and different stakeholders still now because of the complexity of damping determination methods, less concern and limited knowledge [12, 13]. Therefore, it becomes relevant to conduct research on the damping properties of *Cordia Africana (Wanza), Juniperus Procera (Tsid), Afrocarpus Gracilior (Zigba), Syzygium Guineense (Dokma)* and *Acacia Decurrens (Girar).*

## 2 Analytical Analysis for Free Transverse Vibration of Cantilever Beam

Transverse vibrations of cantilevered beams have been the subject of numerous studies based on different beam theories [14–16]. Of existing beam theories, Euler-Bernoulli beam theory is used in this investigation because the lateral dimensions of the beam are less than one-tenth of its length. This theory assumes that the rotation of the differential element is negligible compared to translation and the angular distortion due to shear is small in relation to bending deformation [17].

### 2.1 Free Transverse Vibration Analysis of Cantilever Beam Without Damping

Figure 1 shows a cantilever beam which undergoes free vibration with the transverse displacement of $y(x, t)$.

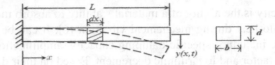

**Fig. 1.** Cantilever beam under free vibration.

The beam vibration is governed by partial differential equations in terms of spatial variable x and time variable t. Thus, the governing equations of motion for the free transverse vibration for Euler-Bernoulli beam is given by [18];

$$\frac{EI}{\rho A}\frac{\partial^4 y(x, t)}{\partial x^4} + \frac{\partial^2 y(x, t)}{\partial x^2} = 0 \tag{1}$$

where E is the Young's Modulus, $\rho$ is the mass density of beam material, $I = bd^3/12$ is the second moment of inertia of the beam, $A = bd$ is the cross-sectional area of the beam, and b and d are the width and depth of the beam cross-section, respectively.

For uniform beam, i.e. EI is constant, Eq. (1) can be reduced to;

$$C^2\frac{\partial^4 y(x, t)}{\partial x^4} + \frac{\partial^2 y(x, t)}{\partial x^2} = 0 \tag{2}$$

where $C = \sqrt{EI/\rho A}$ is a constant.

The governing equation is solved using the method of separation of variables, and the transverse displacement response $y(x, t)$ is written as a function of position and time as;

$$y(x, t) = W(x)T(t) \tag{3}$$

where $W(x)$ is the space function which is described as;

$$W(x) = C_1 \cosh \beta x + C_2 \sinh \beta x + C_3 \cos \beta x + C_4 \sin \beta x \tag{4}$$

and T(t) is the time-dependent amplitude described as;

$$T(t) = B_1 \sin \omega t + B_2 \cos \omega t \tag{5}$$

where $\beta = \sqrt[4]{\frac{\rho A \omega^2}{C^2}}$ is a constant, $\omega = \beta^2\sqrt{\frac{EI}{\rho A}}$ is the is the circular natural frequency, $B_1$ and $B_2$ are constants evaluated from the initial conditions; and real constants $C_i$ are evaluated om the boundary conditions of the beam. Therefore, the transverse deflection of the cantilever beam at the free end is calculated as;

$$y(x, t) = W(x) * \left[\frac{y_o}{W(L)} \cos \omega_n t\right] \tag{6}$$

where $W(x) = \frac{(\cosh \beta x - \cos \beta x)(\sin \beta x + \sinh \beta x) + (\sinh \beta x - \sin \beta x)(\cos \beta x + \cosh \beta x)}{(\cos \beta x + \cosh \beta x)}$, and $\omega_n$ is the natural frequency of the beam.

It is fact that continuous systems have an infinite degree of freedom. Therefore, an infinite number of natural frequencies of the cantilever beam are given by;

$$\omega_i = (\beta_i L)^2 \sqrt{\frac{EI}{\rho A l^4}} \tag{7}$$

where the values of $\beta_i l$ are 1.875104, 4.69409 and 7.85475 for the first three consecutive modes. Based on Eq. (7), the natural frequencies of a vibrating body depend on its geometry and material properties, and its determination is of vital importance for predicting resonant damages.

## 2.2   Free Transverse Vibration Analysis of Cantilever Beam with Damping

The governing equation of free transverse vibration of cantilever beam has been deeply investigated by many researchers, in particular, to take into account the effect of damping on the dynamic behavior of the beam. Even a large amount of literature is available on the subject of damping, there is no any single well-established empirical formula which represents the damping of the beam. Therefore, for a cantilever beam undergoing small deformation, linear beam theory is used for a given excitation. Based on the theory, the behavior of the first mode of vibration can be approximated to the behavior of a single degree of freedom spring mass damper system (see Fig. 2).

**Fig. 2.**  Spring mass damper system for single degree of freedom.

With these assumptions, the vibration of such a linear system is described by the popular equation as;

$$\ddot{x} + 2\zeta\omega_1\dot{x} + \omega_1^2 x = 0 \tag{8}$$

where $\omega_1$ is the fundamental natural frequency, $\zeta$ is the damping factor, and $x, \dot{x}$ and $\ddot{x}$ are the system response in terms of displacement, velocity and acceleration, respectively. The fundamental natural frequency $\omega_1$ is given by;

$$\omega_1 = \sqrt{k/m} \tag{9}$$

The damping value at the first natural frequency of each sample is quantified using an equivalent damping factor which is obtained from the time history graph using the logarithmic decrement method. It correlates damping with the fundamental natural frequency and the mass of the beam. Thus, the damping factor is given by;

$$\zeta = \frac{c}{2\sqrt{km}} = \frac{c}{2m\omega_1} \tag{10}$$

where $k$ is the stiffness, $c$ is the damping coefficient, and m is the mass. Therefore, the general solution to the equation is obtained as follows;

$$x(t) = A.e^{-\zeta\omega_1 t}\cos(\omega_d.t + \phi) \tag{11}$$

where A is the amplitude of vibration determined from initial conditions, $\phi$ is a phase angle that depends on the initial velocity, and $\omega_d$ represent the damped natural frequencies of the system for the first mode. Therefore, the undamped and damped natural frequencies are related to each other as;

$$\omega_d = \omega_1\sqrt{1 - \zeta^2} \tag{12}$$

If the tip of the cantilever beam is driven to an initial displacement and then left free to oscillate, the vibration is analytically obtained for the following initial conditions: $x(0) = x_0$ and $x_0 = 0$. In this case, the value of the vibration amplitude is calculated as;

$$A = \frac{x_0}{\sqrt{1 - \zeta^2}} \tag{13}$$

and the phase angle can be

$$\phi = \tan^{-1}\left(\frac{-\zeta}{\sqrt{1 - \zeta^2}}\right) \tag{14}$$

# 3   Numerical Analysis for Free Transverse Vibration of Cantilever Beam

There are numerous numerical methods which are used for the free transverse vibration analysis of cantilever beam due to advancement in computational techniques and availability of software. Out of many, finite element analysis is an efficient numerical tool to solve problems of continuous systems [19]. In this paper, the numerical analysis is carried out using ANSYS software.

## 3.1   Numerical Analysis Without Damping

Many practical problems encountered in engineering applications are mathematically modeled by differential equations. In most problems, it is difficult to get an accurate solution. Thus, an approximate solution is applied to solve such problems. Therefore, the finite element method based on the Galerkin's method of residual approach is used in this study. This approach is a most popular and powerful method for finding approximate solutions of differential equations by transforming into an appropriate integral equation [20, 21].

By applying the Galerkin's method, therefore, the governing equations of motion of the free transverse vibration stated in Eq. (1) is modified as [22];

$$\int_0^L \left(\frac{EI}{\rho A}\frac{\partial^4 y(x, t)}{\partial x^4} + \frac{\partial^2 y(x, t)}{\partial x^2}\right)w dx = 0 \tag{15}$$

where $L$ is the beam length and $w(x)$ is the Galerkin's weighting function. For n number of elements of length $l$, Eq. (15) can be modified as;

$$\sum_{i=1}^{n} \left[ \int_0^l \rho\, A \frac{\partial^2 y}{\partial x^2} w\, dx + \int_0^l EI \frac{\partial^2 y}{\partial x^2} \frac{\partial^2 w}{\partial x^2} dx \right] = 0 \tag{16}$$

Therefore, Eq. (16) can be modified as;

$$\sum_{i=1}^{n} \left( [m]\{\ddot{d}\} + [k]\{d\} \right) = 0 \tag{17}$$

where $\{d\}$ represents the nodal displacements, $\{d"\}$ denotes the second derivative of nodal displacement with time at the nodes. The mass $[m]$ and stiffness $[k]$ matrices are given by;

$$[m] = \rho\, A \int_0^1 [N]^T[N] \ dx = \frac{\rho\, A}{420} \begin{bmatrix} 156 & 22l & 54 & -13l \\ 22l & 4l^2 & 13l & -3l^2 \\ 54 & 13l & 156 & -22l \\ -13l & -3l^2 & -22l & 4l^2 \end{bmatrix} \tag{18}$$

and,

$$[k] = EI \int_0^l [\ddot{N}]^T[\ddot{N}]dx = \frac{EI}{l^3} \begin{bmatrix} 12 & 6l & -12 & 6l \\ 6l & 4l^2 & -6l & 2l^2 \\ -12 & -6l & 12 & -6l \\ 6l & 2l^2 & -6l & 4l^2 \end{bmatrix} \tag{19}$$

By considering the effect of all the elements, Eq. (17) is further modified to;

$$[M]\{\ddot{D}\} + [K]\{D\} = 0 \tag{20}$$

where $[M]$ and $[K]$ are the system mass and stiffness matrices and, $\{D\}$ and $\{\ddot{D}\}$ are the displacement and acceleration vectors of all the nodes of the entire beam, respectively. This equation represents the equation of motion for the free undamped vibration and its solution is given by;

$$\{D\} = \{\phi\}e^{i\omega t} \tag{21}$$

where $\omega$ and $\phi$ are the natural frequency (eigenvalue) and mode shapes (eigenvector) of vibration, respectively.

Substituting Eq. (21) into Eq. (20) and it results;

$$\left[ [K] - \omega^2[M] \right]\{\phi\} = 0 \tag{22}$$

The solutions of Eq. (22) give the natural frequencies of the system. The positive values of $\omega$ is the first lowest frequency called fundamental natural frequency.

## 3.2 Numerical Analysis with Damping

In the above derivations, the effect of damping is not considered since the direct formation of the damping matrix is very difficult in actual practice. But in ANSYS there are different ways which introduce the effect of damping, each of them being suitable for a particular case. In this investigation, therefore, the damping matrix [c] is determined by using Rayleigh damping theory in which the damping matrix is a function of mass [m] and stiffness [k] matrices that can be linearized with $\alpha$ and $\beta$ as constants. The damping matrix can be determined as [23];

$$[c] = \alpha[m] + \beta[k] \tag{23}$$

where $\alpha$ and $\beta$ are the Rayleigh damping coefficients which can be determined from specified experimental damping factor. In many practical cases, the resonance frequencies are relatively high. Therefore, the damping component related to the mass (the term involving $\alpha$) is negligible. In such case, the $\beta$ damping from $i^{th}$ mode can be evaluated from known values of $\zeta_i$ and $\omega_i$ which represents material damping. Thus;

$$\zeta_i = \frac{\beta\omega_i}{2} \tag{24}$$

For the first natural frequency of the cantilever beam, the damping factor can be calculated as;

$$\zeta = \frac{\beta\omega_1}{2} = 1.758 \ \beta\sqrt{\frac{EI}{\rho Al^4}} \tag{25}$$

## 3.3 Natural Frequencies and Mode Shapes Using Numerical Method

In order to prove the correctness of the results obtained from the analytical analysis in terms of the spacing between natural frequencies, a finite element model of the beam mounted in a cantilever configuration was developed using ANSYS APDL. In the pre-processor of the main menu, the beam 2 node 188 element was selected to perform the numerical analysis using ANSYS APDL on to which the boundary conditions for cantilever are imposed. The Young's modulus, density and Poisson's ratio values of the materials were given as input parameters. Using modeling option, the beam was generated as 2D entity of the beam. In meshing tool option, the beam was uniformly meshed into 10 equal parts and each element had 2 nodes (i.e., a total of 11 nodes in the system). It was assumed that 2 DOFs per node (translation along y-axis and rotation about z-axis), therefore the DOFs of each element were 4 and the DOFs of the system are 22. Therefore, the size of both element stiffness and mass matrices were (4x4), and the size of system stiffness and mass matrices were (22x22). In this work, Block Lanczos mode-extraction methods is used since it is preferable for large symmetric problems, and has fast convergence. The number of modes to extract and expand was equal to five. Finally, the results were obtained from General Post Processor.

Using Eq. (18) and (19), therefore, the size of the system stiffness and system mass matrices can be expressed as;

System stiffness matrix, [K] =

$$\frac{EI}{l^3} * \begin{bmatrix}
12 & 6l & -12 & 6l & 0 & 0 & 0 & 0 & 0 & 0 & 0 & 0 & 0 & 0 & 0 & 0 & 0 & 0 & 0 & 0 & 0 & 0 \\
6l & 4l^2 & -6l & 2l^2 & 0 & 0 & 0 & 0 & 0 & 0 & 0 & 0 & 0 & 0 & 0 & 0 & 0 & 0 & 0 & 0 & 0 & 0 \\
-12 & -6l & 24 & 0 & -12 & 6l & 0 & 0 & 0 & 0 & 0 & 0 & 0 & 0 & 0 & 0 & 0 & 0 & 0 & 0 & 0 & 0 \\
6l & 2l^2 & 0 & 8l^2 & -6l & 2l^2 & 0 & 0 & 0 & 0 & 0 & 0 & 0 & 0 & 0 & 0 & 0 & 0 & 0 & 0 & 0 & 0 \\
0 & 0 & -12 & -6l & 24 & 0 & -12 & 6l & 0 & 0 & 0 & 0 & 0 & 0 & 0 & 0 & 0 & 0 & 0 & 0 & 0 & 0 \\
0 & 0 & 6l & 2l^2 & 0 & 8l^2 & -6l & 2l^2 & 0 & 0 & 0 & 0 & 0 & 0 & 0 & 0 & 0 & 0 & 0 & 0 & 0 & 0 \\
0 & 0 & 0 & 0 & -12 & -6l & 24 & 0 & -12 & 6l & 0 & 0 & 0 & 0 & 0 & 0 & 0 & 0 & 0 & 0 & 0 & 0 \\
0 & 0 & 0 & 0 & 6l & 2l^2 & 0 & 8l^2 & -6l & 2l^2 & 0 & 0 & 0 & 0 & 0 & 0 & 0 & 0 & 0 & 0 & 0 & 0 \\
0 & 0 & 0 & 0 & 0 & 0 & -12 & -6l & 24 & 0 & -12 & 6l & 0 & 0 & 0 & 0 & 0 & 0 & 0 & 0 & 0 & 0 \\
0 & 0 & 0 & 0 & 0 & 0 & 6l & 2l^2 & 0 & 8l^2 & -6l & 2l^2 & 0 & 0 & 0 & 0 & 0 & 0 & 0 & 0 & 0 & 0 \\
0 & 0 & 0 & 0 & 0 & 0 & 0 & 0 & -12 & -6l & 24 & 0 & -12 & 6l & 0 & 0 & 0 & 0 & 0 & 0 & 0 & 0 \\
0 & 0 & 0 & 0 & 0 & 0 & 0 & 0 & 6l & 2l^2 & 0 & 8l^2 & -6l & 2l^2 & 0 & 0 & 0 & 0 & 0 & 0 & 0 & 0 \\
0 & 0 & 0 & 0 & 0 & 0 & 0 & 0 & 0 & 0 & -12 & -6l & 24 & 0 & -12 & 6l & 0 & 0 & 0 & 0 & 0 & 0 \\
0 & 0 & 0 & 0 & 0 & 0 & 0 & 0 & 0 & 0 & 6l & 2l^2 & 0 & 8l^2 & -6l & 2l^2 & 0 & 0 & 0 & 0 & 0 & 0 \\
0 & 0 & 0 & 0 & 0 & 0 & 0 & 0 & 0 & 0 & 0 & 0 & -12 & -6l & 24 & 0 & -12 & 6l & 0 & 0 & 0 & 0 \\
0 & 0 & 0 & 0 & 0 & 0 & 0 & 0 & 0 & 0 & 0 & 0 & 6l & 2l^2 & 0 & 8l^2 & -6l & 2l^2 & 0 & 0 & 0 & 0 \\
0 & 0 & 0 & 0 & 0 & 0 & 0 & 0 & 0 & 0 & 0 & 0 & 0 & 0 & -12 & -6l & 24 & 0 & -12 & 6l & 0 & 0 \\
0 & 0 & 0 & 0 & 0 & 0 & 0 & 0 & 0 & 0 & 0 & 0 & 0 & 0 & 6l & 2l^2 & 0 & 8l^2 & -6l & 2l^2 & 0 & 0 \\
0 & 0 & 0 & 0 & 0 & 0 & 0 & 0 & 0 & 0 & 0 & 0 & 0 & 0 & 0 & 0 & -12 & -6l & 24 & 0 & -12 & 6l \\
0 & 0 & 0 & 0 & 0 & 0 & 0 & 0 & 0 & 0 & 0 & 0 & 0 & 0 & 0 & 0 & 6l & 2l^2 & 0 & 8l^2 & -6l & 2l^2 \\
0 & 0 & 0 & 0 & 0 & 0 & 0 & 0 & 0 & 0 & 0 & 0 & 0 & 0 & 0 & 0 & 0 & 0 & -12 & -6l & 12 & -6l \\
0 & 0 & 0 & 0 & 0 & 0 & 0 & 0 & 0 & 0 & 0 & 0 & 0 & 0 & 0 & 0 & 0 & 0 & 6l & 2l^2 & -6l & 4l^2
\end{bmatrix}$$

System mass matrix, [M] =

$$\frac{\rho A}{420} * \begin{bmatrix}
156 & 22l & 54 & -13l & 0 & 0 & 0 & 0 & 0 & 0 & 0 & 0 & 0 & 0 & 0 & 0 & 0 & 0 & 0 & 0 & 0 & 0 \\
22l & 4l^2 & 13l & -3l^2 & 0 & 0 & 0 & 0 & 0 & 0 & 0 & 0 & 0 & 0 & 0 & 0 & 0 & 0 & 0 & 0 & 0 & 0 \\
54 & 13l & 312 & 0 & 54 & -13l & 0 & 0 & 0 & 0 & 0 & 0 & 0 & 0 & 0 & 0 & 0 & 0 & 0 & 0 & 0 & 0 \\
-13l & -3l^2 & 0 & 8l^2 & 13l & -3l^2 & 0 & 0 & 0 & 0 & 0 & 0 & 0 & 0 & 0 & 0 & 0 & 0 & 0 & 0 & 0 & 0 \\
0 & 0 & 54 & 13l & 312 & 0 & 54 & -13l & 0 & 0 & 0 & 0 & 0 & 0 & 0 & 0 & 0 & 0 & 0 & 0 & 0 & 0 \\
0 & 0 & -13l & -3l^2 & 0 & 8l^2 & 13l & -3l^2 & 0 & 0 & 0 & 0 & 0 & 0 & 0 & 0 & 0 & 0 & 0 & 0 & 0 & 0 \\
0 & 0 & 0 & 0 & 54 & 13l & 312 & 0 & 54 & -13l & 0 & 0 & 0 & 0 & 0 & 0 & 0 & 0 & 0 & 0 & 0 & 0 \\
0 & 0 & 0 & 0 & -13l & -3l^2 & 0 & 8l^2 & 13l & -3l^2 & 0 & 0 & 0 & 0 & 0 & 0 & 0 & 0 & 0 & 0 & 0 & 0 \\
0 & 0 & 0 & 0 & 0 & 0 & 54 & 13l & 312 & 0 & 54 & -13l & 0 & 0 & 0 & 0 & 0 & 0 & 0 & 0 & 0 & 0 \\
0 & 0 & 0 & 0 & 0 & 0 & -13l & -3l^2 & 0 & 8l^2 & 13l & -3l^2 & 0 & 0 & 0 & 0 & 0 & 0 & 0 & 0 & 0 & 0 \\
0 & 0 & 0 & 0 & 0 & 0 & 0 & 0 & 54 & 13l & 312 & 0 & 54 & -13l & 0 & 0 & 0 & 0 & 0 & 0 & 0 & 0 \\
0 & 0 & 0 & 0 & 0 & 0 & 0 & 0 & -13l & -3l^2 & 0 & 8l^2 & 13l & -3l^2 & 0 & 0 & 0 & 0 & 0 & 0 & 0 & 0 \\
0 & 0 & 0 & 0 & 0 & 0 & 0 & 0 & 0 & 0 & 54 & 13l & 312 & 0 & 54 & -13l & 0 & 0 & 0 & 0 & 0 & 0 \\
0 & 0 & 0 & 0 & 0 & 0 & 0 & 0 & 0 & 0 & -13l & -3l^2 & 0 & 8l^2 & 13l & -3l^2 & 0 & 0 & 0 & 0 & 0 & 0 \\
0 & 0 & 0 & 0 & 0 & 0 & 0 & 0 & 0 & 0 & 0 & 0 & 54 & 13l & 312 & 0 & 54 & -13l & 0 & 0 & 0 & 0 \\
0 & 0 & 0 & 0 & 0 & 0 & 0 & 0 & 0 & 0 & 0 & 0 & -13l & -3l^2 & 0 & 8l^2 & 13l & -3l^2 & 0 & 0 & 0 & 0 \\
0 & 0 & 0 & 0 & 0 & 0 & 0 & 0 & 0 & 0 & 0 & 0 & 0 & 0 & 54 & 13l & 312 & 0 & 54 & -13l & 0 & 0 \\
0 & 0 & 0 & 0 & 0 & 0 & 0 & 0 & 0 & 0 & 0 & 0 & 0 & 0 & -13l & -3l^2 & 0 & 8l^2 & 13l & -3l^2 & 0 & 0 \\
0 & 0 & 0 & 0 & 0 & 0 & 0 & 0 & 0 & 0 & 0 & 0 & 0 & 0 & 0 & 0 & 54 & 13l & 312 & 0 & 54 & -13l \\
0 & 0 & 0 & 0 & 0 & 0 & 0 & 0 & 0 & 0 & 0 & 0 & 0 & 0 & 0 & 0 & -13l & -3l^2 & 0 & 8l^2 & 13l & -3l^2 \\
0 & 0 & 0 & 0 & 0 & 0 & 0 & 0 & 0 & 0 & 0 & 0 & 0 & 0 & 0 & 0 & 0 & 0 & 54 & 13l & 156 & -22l \\
0 & 0 & 0 & 0 & 0 & 0 & 0 & 0 & 0 & 0 & 0 & 0 & 0 & 0 & 0 & 0 & 0 & 0 & -13l & -3l^2 & -22l & 4l^2
\end{bmatrix}$$

The system stiffness and mass matrices are used to find out the eigenvalues and eigenvectors of the vibration. The eigenvalues and eigenvectors can be real or complex depending on the damping value. However, the damping effect is generally neglected in the determination of eigenvalues and eigenvectors of a lightly vibrating system. Therefore, real eigenvalues and eigenvectors are derived from the assumed equation of motion of undamped vibration. This assumption fairly holds good in most of the practical cases where damping is less pronounced.

## 4 Experimental Analysis

In both analytical and numerical approaches, the starting three natural frequencies were calculated, and there was also a need to determine the damping ratio. But it is impossible because of no empirical formula for assessing damping. Therefore, experimental analysis was established for the determination of damping ratio using logarithmic decrement method from the time response graph.

### 4.1 Materials, Specimen Preparations and Physical Conditions

Five species of woods such as *Cordia Africana (Wanza), Juniperus Procera (Tsid), Afrocarpus Gracilior (Zigba), Syzygium Guineense (Dokma)* and *Acacia Decurrens (Girar)* were selected to perform the experimentation. These species of woods were collected around Bahir Dar and their age were estimated as above 30 years. The material properties of these wood under at 12% moisture content are tabulated in Table 1.

**Table 1.** Material properties of the selected wood species [12, 13].

| Species | Density (kg/m$^3$) | Young's modulus (N/mm$^2$) | Poisson's ratio |
|---------|--------|-----------------|-----------------|
| Cordia Africana | 410 | 6996 | 0.39 |
| Juniperus Procera | 540 | 9081 | 0.47 |
| Afrocarpus Gracilior | 520 | 6704 | 0.45 |
| Syzygium Guineense | 740 | 11229 | 0.43 |
| Acacia Decurrens | 816 | 14310 | 0.46 |

For this experiment, five specimens of each species were prepared along the grain with a dimension of $240 \times 12 \times 3$ mm$^3$ based on ASTM E-756 vibrating beam technique. Based on the standard, uniform cantilever beam configuration having a specimen dimension of $240 \times 12 \times 3$ mm$^3$ were selected for all wood species because it is a simple, fast, cost efficient and time saving technique [24–26].

After preparation, all the specimens were first dried in order to reach equilibrium in adsorption. Since the oven-drying method is the most universally accepted method for determining moisture content, drying was performed for 48 h in an oven dry set at 60 °C to prevent cracking of specimens [27, 28]. Then, the samples were conditioned at a temperature of $20 \pm 2$ °C and a relative humidity of $65 \pm 5\%$ until experimentation.

### 4.2 Experimental Set-Up

The experimental set-up for the free transverse vibration testing of the selected wood materials was shown in Fig. 3.

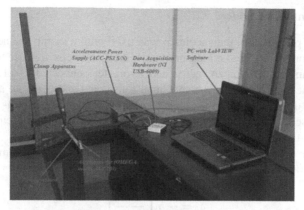

**Fig. 3.** Experimental set-up for the cantilever beam vibration testing.

The accelerometer (OMEGA modal ACC103) is attached with a cantilever beam at the free end and connected to NI data acquisition (NI USB-6009) to acquire, store and analyze vibration data received from sensor using LabVIEW.

Figure 4 and Fig. 5 shows the block diagram and front panel of the main LabVIEW program to measure the exponentially decay curves and the natural frequencies. Before running the program, the voltage sensitivity of ACC103 accelerometer was given as an input which is equal to $0.001019 \frac{volt}{m/s^2}$.

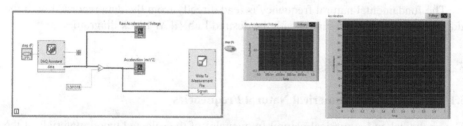

**Fig. 4.** LabVIEW block diagram and front panel for showing time domain.

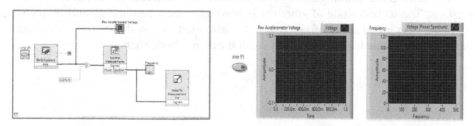

**Fig. 5.** LabVIEW block diagram and front panel for showing frequency domain.

## 4.3  Experimental Procedures

After specimen preparation, the specimen was fixed with a clamp at one end and free at the other. In order to take the measurements, the specimens were disturbed initially using impact hammer. The piezoelectric accelerometer connected to a LabVIEW program attached at the free end of the specimen sense data and generate a signal by the data acquisition device. Finally, the computer displays the required plots. The plots are subsequently used to evaluate of logarithmic decrement, damping factor and natural frequency of all the specimens from the time history curve.

Based on the decay graph, the logarithmic decrement ($\delta$) can be estimated using the expression;

$$\delta = \frac{1}{n} . ln\left(\frac{X_1}{X_{n+1}}\right) \tag{26}$$

where $x_1$, $x_{n+1}$ and n are the first cycle amplitude, last cycle amplitude and the number of cycles, respectively. Since the logarithmic decrement is more accurate with the increasing number of cycles n, the peak amplitudes in this investigation are obtained for six decrements i.e., $n = 6$ [29, 30].

Based on the calculated logarithmic decrement, the damping factor ($\zeta$) is analyzed as;

$$\zeta = \frac{\delta}{\sqrt{4\pi^2 + \delta^2}} \tag{27}$$

The fundamental natural frequency is read directly from the data recorded with the aid of accelerometer associated with the desired LabVIEW block diagram.

## 5  Result and Discussion

### 5.1  Analytical and Numerical Natural Frequencies

The analytical and numerical natural frequencies of the selected wood materials at the first three modes of vibration are tabulated in Table 2.

The first mode is bending mode of vibration where beam tends to bend about the root sections. The second mode of vibration is bending mode where the natural frequency is greater than initial mode of vibration. The third mode shape shows the first twisting mode which has the highest frequency in all the above mode shapes.

**Table 2.** Comparison of analytical and numerical natural frequencies at the first three modes.

| Species | Modes | Analytical Natural Frequency (Hz) | Numerical Natural Frequency (Hz) |
|---|---|---|---|
| Cordia Africana | 1 | 34.754 | 34.788 |
| | 2 | 217.803 | 222.37 |
| | 3 | 609.854 | 648.51 |
| | 1 | 34.502 | 34.525 |
| Juniperus Procera | 2 | 216.222 | 220.72 |
| | 3 | 605.428 | 643.51 |
| | 1 | 30.209 | 30.229 |
| Afrocarpus Gracilior | 2 | 189.320 | 193.27 |
| | 3 | 530.10 | 563.52 |
| | 1 | 32.774 | 32.796 |
| Syzygium Guineense | 2 | 205.393 | 209.69 |
| | 3 | 575.106 | 611.44 |
| | 1 | 35.233 | 35.256 |
| Acacia Decurrens | 2 | 220.803 | 225.40 |
| | 3 | 618.255 | 657.19 |

## 5.2 Experimental Damping Factor and Natural Frequency

From the acceleration vs time plots the damping factor is analyzed using the logarithmic decrement method. Therefore, the value of the damping factor of all the selected wood species materials is shown in Table 3.

**Table 3.** Experimental damping factor.

| Species | Damping Factor |
|---|---|
| Cordia Africana | 0.020 |
| Juniperus Procera | 0.019 |
| Afrocarpus Gracilior | 0.019 |
| Syzygium Guineense | 0.020 |
| Acacia Decurrens | 0.020 |

Based on the amplitude vs frequency graphs, the fundamental natural frequency of the selected wooden materials at a given dimension is shown in Table 4.

**Table 4.** Experimental fundamental natural frequency.

| Species | Fundamental Natural Frequency (Hz) |
|---|---|
| Cordia Africana | 35.2 |
| Juniperus Procera | 35.8 |
| Afrocarpus Gracilior | 33 |
| Syzygium Guineense | 33.8 |
| Acacia Decurrens | 40.2 |

Therefore, the analytical and numerical natural frequency of the selected woods at the first mode of vibration are tabulated with the experimental results as shown in Table 5.

**Table 5.** Comparison of fundamental natural frequencies.

| Species | Analytical Fundamental Natural Frequency (Hz) | Numerical Fundamental Natural Frequency (Hz) | Experimental Fundamental Natural Frequency (Hz) |
|---|---|---|---|
| Cordia Africana | 34.754 | 34.788 | 35.2 |
| Juniperus Procera | 34.502 | 34.525 | 35.8 |
| Afrocarpus Gracilior | 30.209 | 30.229 | 33 |
| Syzygium Guineense | 32.774 | 32.796 | 33.8 |
| Acacia Decurrens | 35.233 | 35.256 | 40.2 |

# 6 Conclusions

In this paper, the analytical and numerical analysis of a cantilever beam of five different wood species materials were studied upon for finding out the first three natural frequencies. The analyses assumed the Euler-Bernoulli beam theory by considering the beam model as a discrete system. There was also a need for analytical and numerical damping estimation, but it was impossible because of no empirical formula. Therefore, the experimental testing was performed using piezoelectric accelerometer in association with LabVIEW for a perfectly clamped-free cantilever beam based on the impact hammer excitation. The damping ratio was computed by using logarithmic decrement method. The experimental testing also verifies the natural frequencies obtained theoretically at the first mode of vibration. Therefore, the following conclusions are drawn on the basis of result.

- The natural frequencies as determined by the analytical and numerical methods has almost good agreement. But the experimentally measured fundamental natural frequency shows slight variation with the theoretically calculated. The variation is caused due to the assumptions made in both analytical and numerical analysis.
- By comparing the obtained natural frequencies of five wood species, it is seen that *Acacia Decurrens* recorded the highest natural frequency while *Afrocarpus Gracilior* recorded the lowest for the same cross section and length.
- The average value of damping factor for the selected wood species with a given dimension is almost equal to 0.020 at room temperature. This is definitely greater than for most other crystalline materials like metals and its alloys. Thus, woods are better suited for mechanical and structural applications subjected to vibrations if the other strength properties are satisfactory.

## 7 Future Work

In the present investigation, the free vibrational characteristics and damping properties of five species of wood materials were conducted by considering the sample as a cantilever beam for mathematical simplicity. The influence of moisture content and density on material damping were only considered. Therefore, it will be interesting to dig deeper into the following issues for further investigations.

1. The present analysis can be extended for forced vibration conditions and different beam configurations.
2. The investigation can be extended for several wood species with the increased number of specimens.
3. It can also be extended by considering various parameters affecting the damping capacity of materials.

## References

1. Anekar, N.: Design and testing of unbalanced mass mechanical vibration exciter. Int. J. Res. Eng. Technol. **3**(8), 107–112 (2014)
2. Visnapuu, A.: Damping Properties of Selected Steels and Cast Irons (1987)
3. Chung, D.: Review: materials for vibration damping. J. Mater. Sci. **36**(24), 5733–5737 (2001)
4. Hui, L., Xianping, W., Tao, Z., Zhijun, C., Qianfeng, F.: Design, fabrication, and properties of high damping metal matrix composites-a review. Materials **2**, 958–977 (2009)
5. Orban, F.: Damping of materials and members in structures. J. Phys. Conf. Ser. **268**(1), 1–15 (2011)
6. Sawant, H.: Experimental verification of damping coefficient by half power band width method. Int. J. Res. Aeronaut. Mech. Eng. **2**(7), 8–13 (2014)
7. Zhang, J., Perez, R.J., Lavernia, E.J.: Documentation of damping capacity of metallic, ceramic and metal-matrix composite materials. J. Mater. Sci. **28**(9), 2395–2404 (1993). https://doi.org/10.1007/BF01151671
8. Leite, E., Souza, T., Rabelo, G.: Estimation of the dynamic elastic properties of wood from Copaifera langsdorffii Desf using resonance analysis. Cerne **18**(1), 41–47 (2012)

9. Mclean, J., Arnould, O., Beauchêne, J., Clair, B.: The viscoelastic properties of some Guianese woods. In: Plant Biomechanics Conference – Cayenne, pp. 498–504 (2009)

10. Owal, D., Sanap, B.: Experimental investigation of damping performance of viscoelastic materials. Int. J. Curr. Eng. Technol. **5**, 18–21 (2016)

11. Ashby, M.F., Shercliff, H., Cebon, D.: Materials Engineering, Science, Processing and Design. 1st edn. Elsevier Ltd., University of Cambridge, UK (2007)

12. Desalegn, A., Demel, T., Gezahegn, A.: Commercial Timber Species in Ethiopia: Characteristics and Uses - A Handbook for Forest Industries, Construction and Energy Sectors, Foresters and Other Stakeholders. Addis Ababa University Press, Addis Ababa (2012)

13. Mamo, K.: Vegetative Propagation of Selected Indigenous Trees of Ethiopia (2002)

14. Gawande, H.: Investigations on effect of notch on performance evaluation of cantilever beams. Int. J. Acoust. Vib. **22**(4), 493–500 (2017)

15. Rezaee, M., Fekrmandi, H.: A theoretical and experimental investigation on free vibration vehavior of a cantilever beam with a breathing crack. Shock Vib. **19**(2), 175–186 (2012)

16. Duan, Y., Wang, J., Liu, Y., Shao, F.: Theoretical and experimental study on the transverse vibration properties of an axially moving nested cantilever beam. J. Sound Vib. **333**(13), 2885–2897 (2014)

17. Harris, M., Piersol, G.: Shock and Vibration Handbook. 5th edn. McGrawHill, New York, USA (2002)

18. Romaszko, M., Sapiński, B., Sioma, A.: Forced vibrations analysis of a cantilever beam using the vision method. J. Theor. Appl. Mech. **53**(1), 243–254 (2015)

19. Tripathy, K., Mishra, K., Mohanty, S.: Model analysis of variation of taper angle for cantilever and simply supported beam. IJIRSET **4**(11), 11353–11360 (2015)

20. Jafari, M., Djojodihardjo, H., Ahmad, K.: Vibration analysis of a cantilevered beam with spring loading at the tip as a generic elastic structure. Appl. Mech. Mater. **629**, 407–413 (2014)

21. Musa, A.: Galerkin method for bending analysis of beams on non-homogeneous foundation. J. Appl. Math. Comput. Mech. **16**(3), 61–72 (2017)

22. Gunakala, S.R., Comissiong, D.M.G., Jordan, K., Sankar, A.: A finite element solution of the beam equation via MATLAB. KMUTNB. Int. J. Appl. Sci. Technol. **2**(8), 80–88 (2012)

23. Song, Z., Su, C.: Computation of Rayleigh damping coefficients for the seismic analysis of a hydro-powerhouse. Shock Vib. **2017**, 1–11 (2017)

24. Wang, Z., Li, L., Gong, M.: Measurement of dynamic modulus of elasticity and damping ratio of wood-based composites using the cantilever beam vibration technique. Constr. Build. Mater. **28**, 831–834 (2012)

25. Hujare, P., Sahasrabudhe, A.: Experimental investigation of damping performance of viscoelastic material using constrained layer damping treatment. Procedia Mater. Sci. **5**, 726–733 (2014)

26. Chandan, K., Patil, A.: Experimental modal frequency and damping estimation of viscoelastic material by circle fit method. Int. J. Curr. Eng. Technol. **6**(6), 2199–2204 (2016)

27. Brémaud, I.: Acoustical properties of wood in string instruments soundboards and tuned idiophones: biological and cultural diversity. J. Acoust. Soc. Am. **131**(1), 807–818 (2012)

28. Ross, J.: Wood handbook: wood as an engineering material. USDA Forest Service, Forest Products Laboratory, General Technical Report FPL- GTR-190, Forest Products Laboratory of U.S. Department of Agriculture (2010)

29. DeVisscher, J., Sol, H., DeWilde, W.: Identification of the damping properties of orthotropic composite materials using a mixed numerical experimental method. Appl. Compos. Mater. **4**(1), 13–33 (1997)

30. Faizah, R., Priyosulistyo, H., Aminullah, A.: An investigation on mechanical properties and damping behaviour of hardened mortar with rubber tire crumbs (RTC). In: MATEC Web of Conferences, vol. 258, pp. 1–6 (2019)

# Characterization of Sisal-Glass Fiber Reinforced Epoxy Hybrid Composite

Abebe Zeleke[1](✉) and Hailu Shimels Gebremedhen[2]

[1] Department of Mechanical Engineering, Debre Tabor University, Debre Tabor, Ethiopia
[2] Faculty of Mechanical and Industrial Engineering, Bahir Dar Institute
of Technology, Bahir Dar, Ethiopia

**Abstract.** Mathematical modeling of a unidirectional hybrid composite is performed using classical lamination theory. The effects of varying volume fractions of sisal and glass fibers on the mechanical properties of the hybrid composite are studied. Experimental results were obtained for seven samples of composite materials. Impact, tensile and three-point bending tests were performed for studying different characteristics of the hybrid composites. Variability in mechanical properties due to different volume fractions of the two fibers was studied. It is found that there was significant variability in tensile strength, flexural strength, and impact resistance properties of the hybrid composite materials due to the variation in volume fractions of sisal and glass fibers. Generally, the hybrid composite samples have better mechanical properties compared with pure sisal epoxy and glass-epoxy composite materials.

**Keywords:** Hybrid composites · Natural fiber · Synthetic fiber · Vacuum molding · Mechanical properties

## 1 Introduction

A composite material is a composition of two or more materials combined for a better mechanical and physical property. A composite material consists majorly two components, namely called a fiber and matrix. The matrix is the weak component of a composite material which helps to connect the fiber components while the fiber components are the strong and stiff part of the a composite material [1–4].

Composite materials can be used as a substitution for commonly used metallic materials [3, 6] due to their low density, higher strength- weight ratio and modulus to weight ratio [3, 5–7]. Due to better properties of fiber reinforced composite materials, composite materials are widely used in place of metallic materials in the automotive and aircraft industries for structural components to decrease the chance of structural damage, to reduce the vehicle weight which results in fuel efficiency, and to give more beauty to the vehicle body [8, 9, 11, 12].

Hybrid composites which are composed of two or more reinforcing fibers into a single matrix material usually have two or more reinforcing fibers by retaining the advantage

© ICST Institute for Computer Sciences, Social Informatics and Telecommunications Engineering 2021
Published by Springer Nature Switzerland AG 2021. All Rights Reserved
M. A. Delele et al. (Eds.): ICAST 2020, LNICST 385, pp. 341–356, 2021.
https://doi.org/10.1007/978-3-030-80618-7_23

of fiber components of the hybrid composites. The development of hybrid composites can be performed by combining different natural fibers together, or by a combination of different synthetic fibers, or by combining both natural and synthetic fibers [13, 14].

The reinforcing phase for the composite materials can be made from natural fibers, such as plant, animal as well as synthetic fibers such as glass, carbon, or aramid fibers [3, 5]. The matrix material,,used for the development of composite materials can be distinguished into plastic,which helps the fiber to be in a stable shape, metal, and ceramic matrix [1, 3, 16, 17]. The most commonly used resins in the production of polymer composite materials are epoxies, polyesters, nylons, phenolics, Polyamide-imide, Polyimides [3]. Matrix flow during the manufacturing process through the fiber architecture determines the contents of voids, fiber distribution, fiber wetting, dry area, and others in the final composite laminate, which also affect its properties and performance [18–22].

In synthetic/natural fiber reinforced hybrid composites a hybrid that consists of natural fiber and synthetic fiber can be combined targeting for the enhancement of the mechanical and thermal properties of natural fiber-reinforced composites. The hybridization of synthetic fibers with natural ones provides a balance between practical costs and the finest mechanical properties compared with those of single natural fiber materials [21]. For example, synthetic fibers such as carbon fiber or glass fiber have higher strength and stiffness, as well as enough resistance to water absorption compared to natural fibers. On the other hand, natural fibers are hydrophilic due to their porous structure, and their composites may swell because they may absorb large amounts of water. As a result, hybridization of chemically treated natural fibers and synthetic ones has been recommended as a solution since hybridization bids an effective method by adding another kind of hydrophobic fiber to the hydrophilic fiber composites [26, 27, 30].

Making a hybrid composite material by combining natural and synthetic reinforcing fibers will help to get superior mechanical properties, as well as cost-reduction advantages. For example, tensile strength, elastic modulus, impact strength, and rigidity in a laminar hybrid composite increases while the toughness property decreases due to the hybridization of cotton and glass fibers [25, 26]. Flax fiber is generally known for its damping properties and carbon fiber is registered for its brilliant performance and mechanical properties. So, by hybridizing these two fibers it has been used on an industrial level for manufacturing tennis rackets and bicycle frames. In this combination, hybrid flax-carbon composite has better impact absorption performance compared with flax fiber-reinforced composite material [27]. The studies on the hybrid flax-glass composite material show that the tensile strength and Young's modulus of flax fiber laminates increase due to the addition of more stiff glass fiber [28]. The hybrid kenaf–Kevlar epoxy composites have superior impact performance as compared to the other hybrid composites [29]. Making a hybrid composite of coir and glass fibers significantly improves tensile strength, impact resistance, flexural strength, and reduces moisture absorption of the composite material [30].

This research work will attempt to investigate the physical and mechanical properties of sisal-glass epoxy hybrid composite material, by varying the contents of sisal and glass fibers. The comparison is also made with the pure sisal epoxy and glass epoxy composites.

The novelty of this paper is the vacuum mold method was used for the manufacturing of the composite samples. The analysis was made by varying the contents of both sisal and glass fibers from 15% to 35% at a 5% volume fraction difference in order to obtain the finest proportions of the natural and synthetic fiber combination for the best physical and mechanical properties.

## 2  Materials and Experimental Methods

### 2.1  Materials

The materials used for this research work are sisal and E-glass fibers as a reinforcement, Epoxy resin as the matrix. The sisal fiber is extracted and collected from the local area around Bahir Dar city. The remaining materials E-glass and Epoxy resin are collected from the product suppliers. The resin system consists of KADILUX RM501 (epoxy resin) and KADILUX RM504 (hardener) which were provided by KADISCO Epoxy and Paint factory. The corresponding resin to hardener ratio was 2:1. printing area is 122 mm × 193 mm. The text should be justified to occupy the full line width, so that the right margin is not ragged, with words hyphenated as appropriate. Please fill pages so that the length of the text is no less than 180 mm, if possible.

### 2.2  Chemical Treatment

Natural fibers cannot be used directly to manufacture a composite material due to their hydrophilic surface in nature. However, to improve adhesion property between the fibers and the matrix by reducing their hydrophilic nature many researchers have found different types of chemical treatments. Alkali treatment, silane treatment, benzoylation treatment, peroxide treatment, isocyanate treatment, and acetylation treatment are the most widely used surface treatment methods [31]. Among those chemical treatments, alkaline treatment is one of the most common and simplest methods used for the chemical treatment of natural fibers. In alkali treatment, the natural fibers needed to be submerged in NaOH solution for a certain amount of time (as seen in Fig. 1.). Alkali treatment is used to disorder the hydrogen bonding and to remove the lignin, wax, and oil contents from the outer surfaces of natural fibers. This will create surface roughness by breaking down the cellulose into monomers and the hydroxyl group gets ionized to the alkoxide [31, 32].

### 2.3  Development of the Hybrid Composite

In order to swell raw sisal fibers and to separate fiber bundles into smaller fibers by removing more lignin amount, the sisal fiber was treated with a 2% NaOH solution for 12 h at room temperature. Then the sisal fibers were washed at first with tap water and then with distilled water several times to remove any NaOH sticking to the fiber surface. Lastly, these fibers were dried for 3 days in sunlight to completely remove the moisture.

The vacuum molding method was used to manufacture the hybrid composites in an open aluminum sheet mold at high pressure using a vacuum pump. Vacuum molding

**Fig. 1.** Sisal fiber surface treatment using NaOH.

has an advantage for improving the strength of composite laminates by reducing manufacturing defects when compared with other manufacturing techniques. The effects of the vacuum method on the reinforcements are good formability, good surface quality, high strength, wear-resistance, and density of the laminate is significantly lower than the commonly used compression molding technique. The fiber volume fraction (50%) was kept constant, is determined based on the literature survey, in order to avoid resin leakage to the pump during the vacuum bagging process [33, 34].

Hybrid fiber mat laminas of different ratios of sisal and E-glass (listed in Table 1) were mixed with epoxy resin for the preparation of composites. The epoxy resin was

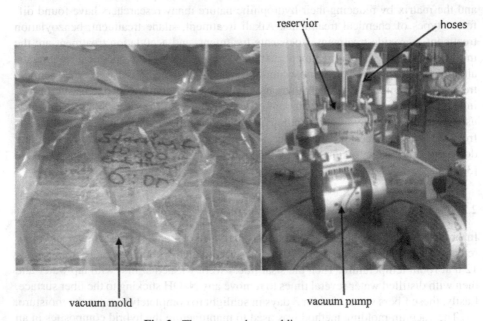

**Fig. 2.** The vacuum bag molding set-up.

prepared by mixing the resin and hardener at a ratio of 2:1 for 2 min. Figure 2 shows the vacuum molding set up used to manufacture the composite laminates. Each sample contains four layers of laminas prepared with a dimension of 200mm x 200mm molding size. The bottom surfaces of the aluminum sheet were cleaned and coated with wax for easy release of the composite samples from the mold. After arranging the fiber mats uniformly, they were mixed with the epoxy resin and compressed for 12 h in the mold using a vacuum pump. Finally, the composite samples cured for 72 h in sunlight before subjected to experimental tests.

**Table 1.** Samples of the hybrid composite at a different volume ratio of sisal and E-glass fibers.

| Samples | Fiber volume fraction | Resin volume fraction |
|---------|----------------------|----------------------|
| Sample 1 | 25% sisal + 25% E-glass | 50% |
| Sample 2 | 20% sisal + 30% E-glass | 50% |
| Sample 3 | 15% sisal + 35% E-glass | 50% |
| Sample 4 | 30% sisal + 20% E-glass | 50% |
| Sample 5 | 35% sisal + 15% E-glass | 50% |

The main materials and devices used for the vacuum mold are a vacuum pump, breather materials, a vacuum bag, and a vacuum tap.

## 2.4 Experimental Tests

**Density Measurement.** The densities of the hybrid composites were calculated using the Archimedes principle. In this method, the test specimens were tightly warped with cling warp to avoid the sucking of water. Cling wrap is used since it could easily take on the geometry of the test specimens and allow for precise volume measurement. Once the cling wrap is completed the waterproof specimens are dipped into a measuring container filled with water. After the specimen was fully immersed in the water the rise in the water level was recorded to get the specimen volume. From the mass and volume of the specimens, the density was determined using Eq. (1).

$$\rho = \frac{m}{v} \tag{1}$$

Where $\rho$ is the density of the composite, m is the mass of a single specimen and v is the volume of the displaced water when a specimen is immersed. The density of different samples obtained is depicted in Table 2.

**Table 2.** The density of the composite materials.

| Composite samples | Density (g/cm3) | Density (kg/m3) |
|---|---|---|
| Sample 1 | 1.1205 | 1120.5 |
| Sample 2 | 1.0696 | 1069.6 |
| Sample 3 | 1.1389 | 1138.9 |
| Sample 4 | 1.2189 | 1218.9 |
| Sample 5 | 1.0019 | 1001.9 |

The density of the composites ranges from 1 g/cm3 to 1.3 g/cm3. Increasing the glass fiber content in the hybrid composites promote an increase in density, as shown in Table 2 due to the higher density of glass fibers relative to the sisal fibers.

**Impact Test.** The Charpy impact test is carried out based on the national standard JBS-500B impact testing machine. In this experiment, an automatic drop pendulum hammer

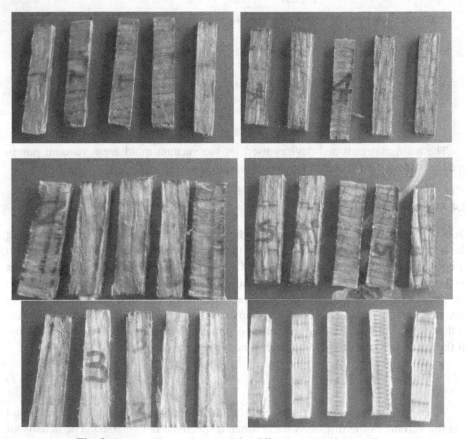

**Fig. 3.** Impact test specimens of the different composite samples.

Charpy impact testing machine was used to perform an impact test on a specific composite specimen at an impact speed of 5.4 m/s. The dial gauge displays the impact strength values of the composite material in Joules. All the test specimens have a dimension of 65 x 10 x 5 mm (length x width x thickness) based on ASTM D256 standard [35]. The Charpy impact test specimens of different composite samples are shown in Fig. 3.

Then the impact energy of five specimens from each sample was recorded and the average values of the impact energy were taken and reported for each sample. Figure 4 illustrates the Charpy impact pendulum testing machine.

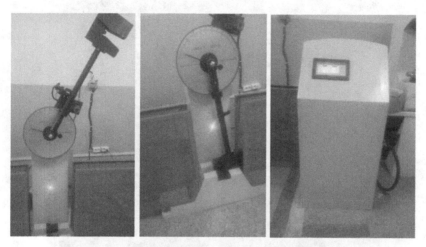

**Fig. 4.** The Charpy impact pendulum testing machine.

**Tensile Test.** Tensile test specimens of the different samples were subjected to a tensile test and the test was conducted as per **ISO 527–1 standard.** Prepared tensile test specimens of the different composite samples are shown in Fig. 5. The tensile properties

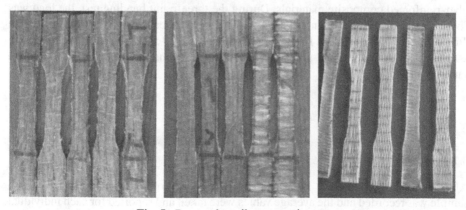

**Fig. 5.** Prepared tensile test specimens.

of the seven composite samples were studied by testing the specimens using the WAW-600D tensile testing machine. Figure 6. shows the tensile and three-point bending test set up. The cross-head speed for tensile testing was 10 mm/min and each specimen was loaded up to failure. The dimensions of the specimens for tensile testing were 120 x 20 x 5 mm (length x width x thickness). Five specimens of each sample were tested for tensile testing and the average values were taken and reported for each sample of the composite.

**Fig. 6.** WAW-600D universal tensile testing machine.

**Flexural Test.** Flexural test specimens of the different samples were subjected to a three-point bending test and the test was conducted as per ISO 14125 standards for fiber-reinforced composite materials. During the three-point bending test, the load was applied at the middle between the supports with a cross-head speed of 10 mm/min. The dimensions of the specimens for flexural testing were 120 x 20 x 5 mm (length x width x thickness). Prepared three-point bending test specimens of the different composite samples shown in Fig. 7.

## 3   Results

### 3.1   Impact Strength

After the completion of the impact test impact energy of five specimens from each sample was recorded and the average values were taken and reported for each individual sample. Table 3 shows the impact test results. The impact test results show that increasing

**Fig. 7.** Prepared three-point bending test specimens.

the volume fractions of glass fiber in the hybrid composite marks in the enhancement of impact resistance properties. But impact resistance properties decrease when the volume fractions of sisal fiber in the hybrid composite increases.

**Table 3.** Impact energy of the seven composite samples.

| Composite samples | Impact energy (J) | Impact energy (J/m$^2$) |
|---|---|---|
| Sample 1 | 14.6633 | 45117.9487 |
| Sample 2 | 15.7933 | 48594.8717 |
| Sample 3 | 13.83 | 42553.8461 |
| Sample 4 | 10.4867 | 32266.6667 |
| Sample 5 | 8.8167 | 27128.2051 |
| Sample 6 | 15.1533 | 46625.6410 |
| Sample 7 | 11.27 | 34676.9231 |

From the impact test results, it can be concluded that the glass-epoxy composite material has the highest impact damage resistance property. Relatively the pure sisal epoxy composite material has lower impact resistance property. For an equal amount of sisal and glass fibers i.e., 25% sisal and 25% glass fiber the impact energy is 14.6633 J.

when the glass fiber content is increased by 5% the hybrid composite shows 4% enhancement in its impact resistance property compared with the glass epoxy composite material and 8% improvement when compared with the hybrid composite containing an equal amount of sisal and glass fibers. But when the glass fiber content is increased from 30% to 35% the impact resistance property of the hybrid composite is again decreased by 12%. In the hybrid composite, the impact resistance property decreases by 40% as the sisal fiber content is increased by 10% i.e., impact energy decreases from 14.6633 J to 8.8167 J. Figure 8 and Fig. 9 shows the variation of impact energy at different contents of sisal and glass fibers.

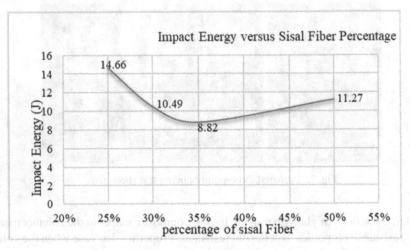

**Fig. 8.** Impact energy versus sisal fiber percentage.

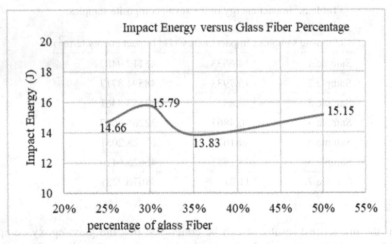

**Fig. 9.** Impact energy versus glass fiber percentage.

## 3.2  Tensile Strength

After the tensile test, it was found that sample 5 of the hybrid composite performed best under tensile load amongst all. Sample 5 has a tensile strength of 72.1334 MPa and a yield strength of 37 MPa. The tensile strengths of the seven composite samples are depicted in Table 4. The tensile test results show that increasing the volume fractions of both sisal and glass fibers in the hybrid composite marks in an increase of the tensile strength. At equal percentages of sisal and glass fibers which is sample 1, the tensile strength is 53.7669 MPa. However, when the volume fraction of glass fiber content is increased from 25% to 35%, and sisal fiber content is decreased from 25% to 15% the tensile strength is increased by 7%. Whereas, when the volume fraction of sisal fiber content is increased from 25% to 35%, and glass fiber content is decreased from 25% to 15%, tensile strength rises to 72.1334 MPa which is an increment of 34%.

**Table 4.** Tensile test results.

| Composite samples | Yield strength (MPa) | Tensile strength (MPa) |
|---|---|---|
| Sample 1 | 29.7 | 53.7669 |
| Sample 2 | 32.93 | 54.3067 |
| Sample 3 | 33.9 | 57.3667 |
| Sample 4 | 39.9 | 70.7667 |
| Sample 5 | 37 | 72.1334 |
| Sample 6 | 27.6 | 52.5888 |
| Sample 7 | 36.9 | 63.0667 |

The yield strength increases by 14% when the volume fraction of glass fiber content is increased from 25 to 35% and sisal fiber content is decreased from 25% to 15%. On the other hand, the yield strength increases from 29.7 to 39.9 MPa as volume fractions of sisal fiber content is increased from 25 to 30% and glass fiber content is decreased from 25% to 15%. But as the volume fractions of sisal fiber increased by 5% the yield strength of the hybrid composite decreases from 39.9 to 37 MPa.

Based on the tensile test results it can be concluded that the sisal-glass epoxy hybrid composite material shows an increase in tensile strength up to 37% when compared to composites made from only pure glass fiber and the tensile strength increases up to 17% when compared to pure sisal epoxy composite material. Generally, the sisal-glass fiber epoxy hybrid composite material has a better tensile and yield strength than either the pure glass epoxy or pure sisal epoxy composite materials. Figure 10 and Fig. 11 illustrates the variation of the ultimate tensile strength and the yield strength of the seven composite samples.

## 3.3  Flexural Strength

The flexural properties of the seven samples are studied by testing the specimens using the WAW-600D universal tensile testing machine shown in Fig. 6. the same machine

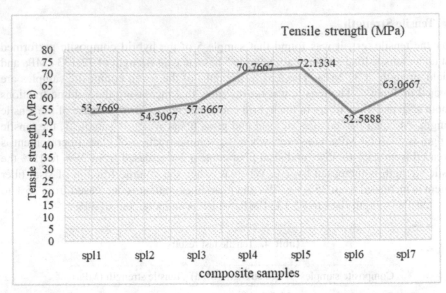

**Fig. 10.** The variation of the tensile strength for different amounts of sisal and glass fibers.

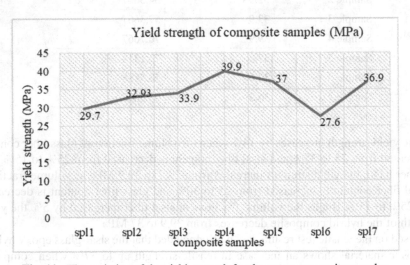

**Fig. 11.** The variation of the yield strength for the seven composite samples.

used for the tensile test. After the test, it was found that sample 4 of the hybrid composite performed best under the bending load amongst all and has a flexural strength of 87 MPa. The bending strengths of the seven samples of the composites are tabulated in Table 5. The flexural test results show that increasing the volume fractions of both sisal and glass fibers in the hybrid composite marks an increase of the flexural strength.

At equal percentages of sisal and glass fibers, the flexural strength is 80.2 MPa. It is notable that when the volume fraction of sisal fiber content is increased from 25 to 30%, the flexural strength of the composite is increased from 80.2 MPa to 87 MPa which is an 8% increment. But when the volume fraction of sisal fiber content is increased from 30 to 35%, the flexural strength of the composite is decreased from 87 MPa to 85.6 MPa which is a 2% decrement. On the other hand, when the volume fraction of glass fiber content is increased from 25 to 35%, the flexural strength increases to 84.6667 MPa which is a 6% increment.

**Table 5.** Three-point bending test results.

| Samples | Fiber volume fraction | Flexural strength (MPa) |
|---|---|---|
| Sample 1 | 25% sisal + 25% E-glass | 80.2 |
| Sample 2 | 20% sisal + 30% E-glass | 81.2 |
| Sample 3 | 15% sisal + 35% E-glass | 84.6667 |
| Sample 4 | 30% sisal + 20% E-glass | 87 |
| Sample 5 | 35% sisal + 15% E-glass | 85.6 |
| Sample 6 | Pure E-glass fiber | 64.8 |
| Sample 7 | Pure Sisal fiber | 62.4667 |

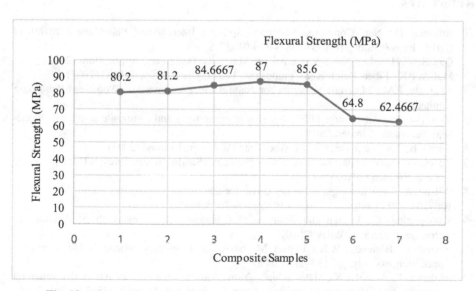

**Fig. 12.** The variation of the flexural strength for the seven composite samples.

Based on the flexural test results the sisal-glass epoxy hybrid composite material shows an increase in flexural strength up to 31% when compared to composites made from only pure glass fiber. The flexural strength increases by up to 39% due to the hybridization effect when compared to pure sisal epoxy composite material. Generally, the sisal-glass epoxy hybrid composite material has better flexural strength than either the pure glass epoxy or pure sisal epoxy composite materials. The results plotted in Fig. 12 shows the variation of the flexural strength for different composite samples.

## 4   Conclusion

Based on the observations from the experiments, the hybrid composite sample 2 possesses maximum impact strength and can hold up to 15.7933 J followed by pure glass-epoxy composite sample which is holding the impact strength of 15.1533 J. Sample 5 of the hybrid composite which contains 35% sisal fiber and 15% glass fiber by volume has the poorest impact resistance capacity with a maximum impact load of 8.8167 J. The tensile test results show that increasing the volume fractions of both sisal and glass fibers in the hybrid composite results in an increase of both tensile and yield strength. The sisal-glass epoxy hybrid composite material shows an increase in tensile strength up to 37% when compared to composites made from only pure glass fiber and the tensile strength increases up to 17% when compared to pure sisal epoxy composite material. The sisal-glass epoxy hybrid composite material shows an increase in flexural strength up to 31% when compared to composites made from only pure glass fiber. The flexural strength increases by up to 39% due to the hybridization effect when compared to pure sisal epoxy composite material.

## References

1. Brigante, D.: New Composite Materials. Springer International Publishing Switzerland (2014). https://doi.org/10.1007/978-3-319-01637-5
2. Gay, S.W., Hoa, D., Tsai, S.V.: Composite Materials: Design and Applications (2002)
3. Mallik, P.K.: Fiber- Reinforced Composites, 3 ed. Taylor & Francis, LLC (2007)
4. AL-Oqla, F.M.: Materials Selection for Natural Fiber Composites. Woodhead Publishing Limited (2017)
5. Vassilopoulos, A.P.: Fatigue life prediction of composites and composite structures. Woodhead Publishing Limited (2010)
6. Harris, B.: Fatigue in composites. Woodhead Publishing Limited (2003)
7. Kazemahvazi, S.: Impact Loading of Composite and Sandwich Structures. KTH Engineering Science, Sweden (2010)
8. Wilson, A.: Vehicle weight is the key driver for automotive composites. Reinf. Plast. **61**(2), 100–102 (2017). https://doi.org/10.1016/j.repl.2015.10.002
9. Kassapoglou, C.: Design and Analysis of Composite Structures with Applications to Aerospace Structures. Wiley (2010)
10. Atkins, T., Binienda, W.K.: Impact Mechanics of Composite Materials for Aerospace Application, no. July, pp. 117–118 (2008)
11. Ishikawa, T., Amaoka, K., Masubuchi, Y., Yamamoto, T.: Overview of automotive structural composites technology developments in Japan. Compos. Sci. Technol. **155**, 221–246 (2018). https://doi.org/10.1016/j.compscitech.2017.09.015

12. Safri, A., Thariq, M., Sultan, H., Jawaid, M.: Impact behaviour of hybrid composites for structural applications : a review, 133, pp. 112–121 (2018). https://doi.org/10.1016/j.compos itesb.2017.09.008.

13. Jawaid, M., Khalil, H.P.S.A.: Cellulosic/synthetic fibre reinforced polymer hybrid composites : a review. Carbohydr. Polym. 86(1), 1–18 (2015). https://doi.org/10.1016/j.carbpol.2011. 04.043

14. Kutyinov, V.F.: Composite Materials in Aerospace Design. Springer (1994)

15. Jones, R.M.: Mechanics of Composite Materials, 2nd ed. Taylor and Francis (1999)

16. Tauchert, T.R., Adibhatla, S.: Design of laminated plates for maximem stiffness. J. Compos. Mater. (1984). https://doi.org/10.1177/002199838401800105

17. Selver, E., Ucar, N., Gulmez, T.: Effect of stacking sequence on tensile , flexural and thermomechanical properties of hybrid flax/glass and jute/glass thermoset composites (2017). https://doi.org/10.1177/1528083717736102

18. Turan, F.: The effect of stacking sequence on the impact and post-impact behavior of woven/knit fabric glass/epoxy hybrid composites, 103, 119–135 (2013). https://doi.org/10. 1016/j.compstruct.2013.02.004

19. Gemi, L.: Investigation of the e ff ect of stacking sequence on low velocity impact response and damage formation in hybrid composite pipes under internal pressure. Comp. Study. 153, no. July, pp. 217–232 (2018). https://doi.org/10.1016/j.compositesb.2018.07.056

20. Subagia, I.D.G.A., Kim, Y., Tijing, L.D., Sang, C., Kyong, H.: Composites : part b effect of stacking sequence on the flexural properties of hybrid composites reinforced with carbon and basalt fibers. Compos. PART B 58, 251–258 (2014). https://doi.org/10.1016/j.compositesb. 2013.10.027

21. Panthapulakkal, S., Sain, M.: Injection-Molded Short Hemp Fiber/Glass Fiber- Reinforced Polypropylene Hybrid Composites — Mechanical , Water Absorption and Thermal Properties (2006). https://doi.org/10.1002/app

22. Kalantari, M., Dong, C., Davies, I.J.: Multi-objective robust optimisation of unidirectional carbon/glass fibre reinforced hybrid composites under flexural loading. Compos. Struct. 138, 264–275 (2016). https://doi.org/10.1016/j.compstruct.2015.11.034

23. Czél, G., Jalalvand, M., Wisnom, M.R.: Design and characterisation of advanced pseudo-ductile unidirectional thin-ply carbon/epoxy – glass/epoxy hybrid composites. Compos. Struct. 143, 362–370 (2016). https://doi.org/10.1016/j.compstruct.2016.02.010

24. Bandaru, A.K., Vetiyatil, L., Ahmad, S.: The effect of hybridization on the ballistic impact behavior of hybrid composite armors. Compos. Part B 76, 300–319 (2015). https://doi.org/ 10.1016/j.compositesb.2015.03.012

25. Flynn, J., Amiri, A., Ulven, C.: Hybridized carbon and flax fiber composites for tailored performance. JMADE (2016). https://doi.org/10.1016/j.matdes.2016.03.164

26. Mustafa, B., Mehmet, S.: Development of natural fiber reinforced laminated hybrid composites. 628, pp. 15–20 (2013). https://doi.org/10.4028/www.scientific.net/AMR.628.15

27. Altilia, S.D., et al.: Damage tolerance of carbon/flax hybrid composites subjected to low velocity impact *, 91, pp. 144–153 (2016), https://doi.org/10.1016/j.compositesb.2016.01.050

28. Saidane, E.H., Scida, D., Assarar, M., Sabhi, H., Ayad, R.: Composites : part a hybridisation effect on diffusion kinetic and tensile mechanical behaviour of epoxy based flax – glass composites. Compos. Part A 87, 153–160 (2016). https://doi.org/10.1016/j.compositesa.2016. 04.023

29. Yahaya, R., Sapuan, S.M., Jawaid, M., Leman, Z., Zainudin, E.S.: Measurement of ballistic impact properties of woven kenaf – aramid hybrid composites. Measurement 77, 335–343 (2016). https://doi.org/10.1016/j.measurement.2015.09.016

30. Shrivastava, R., Telang, A., Rana, R.S., Purohit, R.: Mechanical properties of Coir/G Lass fiber epoxy resin hybrid composite. Mater. Today Proc. 4(2), 3477–3483 (2017). https://doi. org/10.1016/j.matpr.2017.02.237

31. Li, X., Tabil, L.G., Panigrahi, S.: Chemical treatments of natural fiber for use in natural fiber-reinforced composites: a review. J. Polym. Environ. **15**(1), 25–33 (2007). https://doi.org/10.1007/s10924-006-0042-3

32. Rokbi, M., Osmani, H., Imad, A., Benseddiq, N.: Effect of chemical treatment on flexure properties of natural fiber-reinforced polyester composite. Procedia Eng. **10**, 2092–2097 (2011). https://doi.org/10.1016/j.proeng.2011.04.346

33. Karthick, R., Adithya, K., Hariharaprasath, C., Abhishek, V.: Evaluation of mechanical behavior of banana fibre reinforced hybrid epoxy composites. Mater. Today Proc. **5**(5), 12814–12820 (2018). https://doi.org/10.1016/j.matpr.2018.02.265

34. Hafizal Hamidon, M., Sultan, M.T.H., Ariffin, A.H.: Investigation of mechanical testing on hybrid composite materials. Fail. Anal. Biocomposites, Fibre-Reinforced Compos. Hybrid Compos, pp. 133–156 (2019). https://doi.org/10.1016/B978-0-08-102293-1.00007-3

35. Brasileiro, C.: Impact Tests in Polyester Matrix Composites Reinforced with Continuos Curaua Fiber. (1), pp. 3580–3588 (2014)

# Mechanical Vibration Analysis of Fiber Reinforced Polymer Composite Beams Using Analytical and Numerical Methods

Nigatu D. Tilahun[1,2] and Hirpa G. Lemu[3(✉)] (iD)

[1] Addis Ababa Science and Technology University, Addis Ababa, Ethiopia
[2] Debre Berhan University, Debre Berhan, Ethiopia
[3] University of Stavanger, Stavanger, Norway
Hirpa.g.lemu@uis.no

**Abstract.** In this study, the free and forced vibration analysis of fiber reinforced plastic composite beam has been conducted using numerical method (finite element analysis) and mathematical modeling in MATLAB. Mechanical and physical properties of the beam material are found using strength of material and semiempirical approach to get the equivalent properties. The beam is configured as cantilever beam with dimensions of 191 mm × 33 mm × 5.66 mm for all analyses of the vibration. For modal analysis of the vibrations, different effects such as fiber volume ratio, fiber materials, angle of orientation and stacking sequence of laminates are studied. From these effects, stacking sequence of laminates have highest influence on variation of stiffness and natural frequencies with unique fiber volume ratio and same fiber material. Forced vibration analysis was carried out using the same beam configuration as modal analysis, but with different stacking sequence of layers with harmonically exited loads. It has been observed that the vibration resonance occurred close to the natural frequencies of the beam.

**Keywords:** Beam of composites · Vibration analysis · Natural frequency · Numerical analysis · Resonance frequency

## 1 Introduction

There are several areas where fiber reinforced plastic (FRP) composites are dynamically loaded when structured as cantilevered beams such as those used in wind turbine blades, helicopter blades, fans, aeronautical and aerospace industries as well as in other fields of modern engineering technologies [1]. While designing such types of structures, it is necessary to make not only strength and deflection analysis, but also vibrational performance of the beams as initial step to determine their natural frequencies and resonance. Equivalent physical and mechanical properties like Young's modulus and density of FRP composite materials are influenced by different parameters such as fiber materials, fiber volume ratio, fiber angle and stacking sequence of layers. Mainly the

M. A. Delele et al. (Eds.): ICAST 2020, LNICST 385, pp. 357–369, 2021.
https://doi.org/10.1007/978-3-030-80618-7_24

natural frequencies of a beam depend on effective modulus of elasticities and density of FRP composite beam.

The free vibration of a laminated composite beam is commonly studied using classical laminate theory for different boundary conditions and length-to-thickness ratios for several layers, for instance using MATLAB [2]. In a study reported by Murat [3], a new method was applied for numerical modelling of free vibration on cantilever composite beam having a series of open and non-propagating cracks. In the study, mass and stiffness matrices of the composite beam for vibration analysis purpose was established. The mode shapes and natural frequencies of a number of cantilever carbon fiber reinforced polymer composites (CFRPCs) and glass fiber reinforced polymer composites (GFRPCs) were numerically found using the commercial finite element analysis software (ANSYS) [1]. In this study, the vibration characteristics of elliptic cylinder shells made of laminated composite with general boundary conditions were examined. The hypothetical model was recognized by means of the improved variation principle and multilevel partition method based on the first-order shear deformation model [4]. Modal analysis of laminated functionally graded carbon nanotube (FG-CNT) reinforced composite plates by using kp-Ritz based method on the first-order shear deformation theory (FOSDT) was investigated by Lei et al. [5].

Furthermore, Mohandes and Ghasemi [6] have studied and reported that the free vibration of thin circular cylindrical shell laminated with fiber metal reinforced by single walled carbon nanotubes using different boundary conditions. Kumar et al. [7] presented the investigation of free vibrations of the composite by piezoelectric materials. A FOSDT was used to present the undamped natural frequencies of symmetrically cross–ply laminated beams of the stacking sequence (0/90/90/0) using finite element method (FEM) [8, 9]. Babuska et al. [10] presented the theory and derivation of an element stiffness matrix for bend-twist coupled composite laminated beams. The exactness of the stiffness matrix terms was compared with those generated by finite element model in ABAQUS of an idealized beam geometry.

Madhu and Kumaraswamy [11] have also studied modal analysis by using finite element analysis software for laminated cantilever composite plates to find the modal frequencies. Teter and Gawryluk [12] presented a free vibration of a rotor with three active composite blades completed by different methods. The rotor blades structured using unidirectional laminate of glass–epoxy. Elshafei [13] presented finite element model that was established to examine the response of orthotropic and isotropic beams, structural element for aeronautics applications using MATLAB code. Ganesa and Thirumavalavan [14] offered free vibration of glass fiber reinforced composite. The glass fibers were treated with hydrochloric acid and sodium hydroxide solutions. The damping of fiber reinforced composites depends on the diameter, structure, and orientation of fiber in matrix. In the previous investigations, damping of structural composite beams had been investigated to estimate the natural frequencies and damping ratios [15, 16]. Tita et al. [17] proposed a method to estimate the dynamic damped behavior of fiber reinforced composite beams in flexural vibrations. A set of experimental dynamic tests were presented in order to study the modal shapes and natural frequencies.

Composite materials have vast variety of mechanical and physical properties such as density, modulus of elasticity and strength by alternating fiber volume ratio, fiber and matrix materials, angle of orientations and staking sequence of layers. These properties have effects on the equivalent properties of composite beam, natural frequencies and resonance of the beam. The literature review indicates that there still exists a need to justify the effects of those properties on the natural frequency and stiffness of the beam.

The objective of the study reported in this article is to investigate the mechanical and vibrational performance of cantilevered FRP composite beam subjected to transverse and distributed loads. The beam configuration is selected because FRP composites are widely used in this type boundary conditions and loading modes in several applications such as helicopter rotors and wind turbine blades.

## 2   Materials and Methods

The study of vibration analysis of FRP composite beam reported in this article is conducted using both numerical and analytical approaches. The steps followed include (1) identifying fiber and matrix material properties, (2) formulating physical and mechanical properties of composite materials using strength of material and semi-empirical approach and (3) coding in MATLAB and (4) conducting numerical analysis of free and forced vibration of continuous fiber composite plates and beams using ABAQUS/CAE 2017.

The elastic properties such as the longitudinal ($E_{11}$ or $E_1$), transversal ($E_{22}$ /$E_2$ and $E_{33}$/$E_3$) and shear ($G_{12}$) modulus and major Poisson's ratio ($v_{12}$) of composite materials are expressed as a function of the fiber and matrix volume ratios and their respective elastic properties as follows:

$$E_{11} = V_f \times E_{1f} + V_m \times E_m \tag{1}$$

$$E_{22} = E_{33} = \frac{E_{2f} \times E_m}{V_f \times E_m + V_m \times E_{2f}} \tag{2}$$

$$G_{12} = G_m \frac{(1 + V_f)G_{12f} + V_m G_m}{V_m \times G_{12f} + (1 + V_f) \times G_m} \tag{3}$$

$$v_{12} = V_f v_{12f} + V_m v_m \tag{4}$$

Where: $E_{1f}$ and $E_m$, arc longitudinal fiber and matrix moduli, respectively, $E_{2f}$ is the transverse modulus of the fiber, $v_{12f}$ and $v_m$ are the longitudinal Poisson's ratio of the fiber and the matrix respectively; $G_{12f}$ and $G_m$ are the shear moduli of the fiber and matrix, respectively. Table 1 shows the physical and mechanical properties of typical fiber and matrix materials used in the analyses.

**Table 1.** Typical Properties of Fibers and matrix (adopted from [18].

| Materials | $E_1$(GPa) | $E_2$(GPa) | $G_{12}$(GPa) | $v_{12}$ | Density (kg/m$^3$) |
|---|---|---|---|---|---|
| Graphite | 230 | 22 | 22 | 0.3 | 1800 |
| E-Glass | 85 | 85 | 35.42 | 0.2 | 2500 |
| Aramid (Kevlar-49) | 124 | 8 | 3 | 0.036 | 1400 |
| Epoxy | 3.4 | 3.4 | 1.308 | 0.3 | 1200 |

Modal analysis of composite is conducted on composite beam vibration model as per ASTM standards. According to ASTM E756–05 [19], the composite beams are modeled with dimension of 191 mm × 33 mm × 5.66 mm as shown in Fig. 1. For numerical analysis in ABAQUS/CAE, vibration analysis of the composite beam, an element size of 0.5 mm was selected.

For analysis of convergency, different values of the element size and number of elements are taken in order to get optimum output. The mesh sizes are 8 mm, 6 mm, 4 mm, 3 mm, 2 mm, 1.5 mm, 1 mm, 0.75 mm, 0.5 mm and 0.3 mm. The beam was simulated for quasi-isotropic stacking sequence consisting of layers having fiber orientations of 0°, +45°, −45°, and 90° symmetrically or [0°/+45°/−45°/90°]s to show the convergences of natural frequencies of the cantilevered beam. From these element sizes, the natural frequencies for all analyzed modes converged after the element size of 0.5 mm. For other vibration analysis of composite beam, the element size is selected as 0.5 mm from the convergency analysis for all numerical analysis.

To show the effects of orientation angle of fiber, the analysis was done with 10° interval from 0° to 90° (with $V_f = 0.6$ of glass-epoxy). In order to demonstrate the effects of the fiber volume ratio on natural frequency results for unidirectional laminates, glass-epoxy composite beam was used. Fiber volume ratios from 0.1 to 0.9 were employed with 0.1 interval. For the analysis of natural frequency under the effects of different fiber materials, E-glass, graphite and aramid (Kevlar-49) fibers with epoxy matrix of 0.5 fiber volume ratio and Quasi-Isotropic Laminates or [0/ ± 45/90]s are used. As given in Table 2, different staking sequences of laminates were employed to identify laminates that have higher value of natural frequency for first five number of modes. For this analysis, E-glass epoxy is used with $V_f = 0.6$.

Forced vibration of FRP composite beam under harmonic excitation uses the same composite beam configuration and element size. In the steady-state, the dynamics inputs are the lower and upper frequency, start mode, end mode and damping ratio. For this study, lower and upper frequency are 0 and 2000 respectively and structural average damping ratio value of 0.055 [15–17] was used. To study the effects of different loads on the resonance and corresponding frequencies of the glass-epoxy composite beams, end force in z (EFz), distributed load in z (DLz) and end force in y (EFy) directions are applied with the magnitude of 10 N (illustrated in Fig. 2).

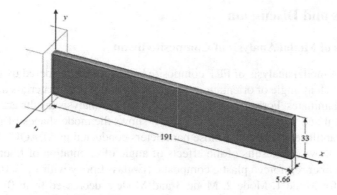

**Fig. 1.** Cantilever beam configuration.

**Table 2.** Laminates with different staking sequences.

|        | Laminates                          | Stacking sequence                   |
|--------|------------------------------------|-------------------------------------|
| SCAL   | Symmetric Cross-Ply Laminates      | [0/90/0/90]s                        |
| SAPL30 | Symmetric Angle-Ply Laminates      | [30/–30/30/–30/30]                  |
| SAPL45 | Symmetric Angle-Ply Laminates      | [45/–45/45/–45/45]                  |
| SBL    | Symmetric Balanced Laminates       | [30/–30/45/–45]s                    |
| ANBL   | Antisymmetric Balanced Laminates   | [30/45/–45/–30]                     |
| ASBL   | Asymmetric Balanced Laminates      | [30/45/–30/–45]                     |
| ANCPL  | Antisymmetric Cross-Ply Laminates  | [0/90/0/90/0/90/0/90]               |
| ANAPL30| Antisymmetric Angle-Ply Laminates  | [30/–30/30/–30/30/–30/30/–30]       |
| ANAPL45| Antisymmetric Angle-Ply Laminates  | [45/–45/45/–45/45/–45/45/–45]       |
| QIL    | Quasi-Isotropic Laminates          | [0/ ± 45/90]s                       |
| CS     |                                    | [0/ ± 30/90]s                       |

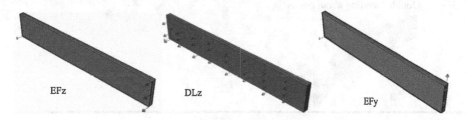

**Fig. 2.** Applied harmonic loads

## 3    Results and Discussion

### 3.1    Results of Modal Analysis of Composite Beam

The results of modal analysis of FRP composite beams were considered using different parameters such as angle of orientation, fiber volume ratio, fiber materials and stacking sequence of laminates. For some of these parameters, the analysis results are done using both analytical and numerical analysis. Table 3 shows the mode shapes of the analysis of the FRP cantilever beam under those parameters conducted in ABAQUS/CAE.

Figure 3 shows the results of the effects of angle of orientation of fiber on natural frequency of fiber reinforced plastic composite (E-glass Epoxy with $V_f = 0.6$). Natural frequencies for Mode 1, Mode 2, Mode 3 and Mode 5 decreased from 0° to 70° and slightly increased from 70° to 90° angle of orientation due to value of axial modulus. But for Mode 4 or twisting mode the natural frequency has peek value at 30° angle of orientation.

**Table 3.** Mode shapes of cantilever FRP composite beam

| Mode | Type and mode shape | Mode | Type and mode shape |
|------|---------------------|------|---------------------|
| 1 | Single Bending about z-axis | 4 | Twisting |
| 2 | Single Bending about y-axis | 5 | Triple Bending about z-axis |
| 3 | Double Bending about z-axis | | |

As illustrates in Fig. 4, natural frequency is increased from fiber volume ratio of 0.1 to 0.9 for all modes. But graphs show that for bending modes (Mode 1, Mode 2, Mode 3 and Mode 5) concave downward and for twisting mode (Mode 4) concave upward directions.

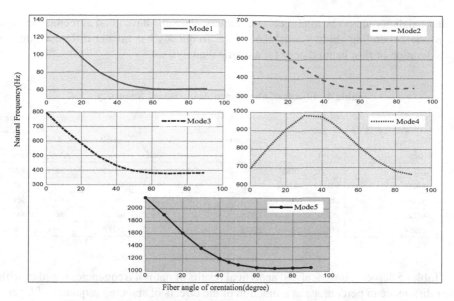

**Fig. 3.** Effects of angle of orientation for unidirectional laminates.

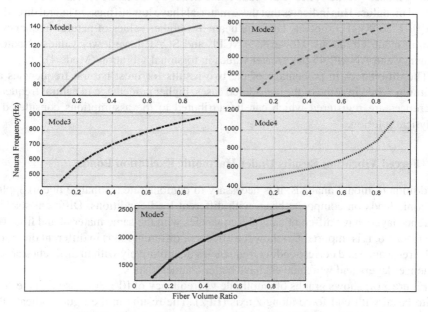

**Fig. 4.** Effect of fiber volume ratio on natural frequency

Fiber materials (E-glass, graphite and aramid or Kevlar-49) with epoxy matrix effects on natural frequency to be discussed which is done using both numerical and analytical solutions. The results in Table 4 shows that Graphite-Epoxy has greatest value of natural frequency for all mods compared to Glass-Epoxy and Aramid-Epoxy due to its higher axial modulus. The analytical and numerical results have good agreement except for Mode 2 (bending about y-axis) the natural frequency has greater difference due to consideration of thin beam theory for analytical analysis.

**Table 4.** Effects of fiber materials on natural frequency

| Mode | Natural frequency (Hz) | | | | | | | | |
|------|------------------------|--------|--------|--------|--------|--------|--------|--------|--------|
| | Glass-Epoxy | | | Graphite-Epoxy | | | Aramid-Epoxy | | |
| | Num. | Analyt | %diff | Num | Analyt | %diff | Num | Analyt | %diff |
| 1 | 102.83 | 102.192 | −0.6244 | 176.76 | 175.94 | − 0.467 | 140.73 | 139.91 | −0.588 |
| 2 | 478.27 | 595.819 | 19.7289 | 775.66 | 1025.8 | 24.385 | 620.99 | 815.72 | 23.87 |
| 3 | 636.96 | 640.43 | 0.5412 | 1075.2 | 1102.6 | 2.485 | 859.52 | 876.79 | 1.969 |
| 4 | 832.22 | 807.96 | −3.0023 | 1203.5 | 1225.5 | 1.7952 | 977.23 | 983.99 | 0.687 |
| 5 | 1755.4 | 1793.2 | 2.10796 | 2887.7 | 3087.3 | 6.4652 | 2321.5 | 2455 | 5.438 |

Tables 5 depicts numerical and analytical results of natural frequencies together with their difference in percentage as a function of the effects of stacking sequence of layers. The results show that SAPL45 and ANAPL45 have lower value natural frequency in bending modes (Mode 1, Mode 2, Mode 3 and Mode 5) because of their lower effective flexural modulus. This indicates that these materials have low stiffness in lateral direction. CS ([0/ ± 30/90]s) composite laminate beam has higher values of natural frequency in bending mode vibrations. However, ANCPL and SCAL have lower values of natural frequency and ANAPL45 has greater values in torsional vibration (Mode 4).

The differences in percentage of the two results for most natural frequencies are minimum, while in some of the considered cases, higher percentage in natural frequency differences are registered which can be attributed to the assumptions considered in analytical solution.

## 3.2 Forced Vibration Results Under Harmonic Excitation Loads

In addition to modal analysis, it is necessary to demonstrate resonance due to applied harmonic loads on composite beam with different load conditions. Different stacking sequence layers have different natural frequencies with the same material and fiber volume ratio. So, it is important to show the effects of different loads in different directions on the resonance and corresponding frequencies quantitatively with in different stacking sequences layers and which layers have better characteristics.

Figure 5 (a) shows graphs of amplitude vs frequency of [0/±30/90]s laminate composite beam with end force along z-axis (EFz). The results in the figure indicate that the resonance of the vibration occurs close to the first mode natural frequency of the composite beam for both analytical and numerical solutions. The numerical results of the amplitude have values in both positive and negative direction because they consist of real and complex solutions. Furthermore, slight vibration resonance is observed in the numerical analysis results close to 3rd mode natural frequency.

**Table 5.** Numerical analysis results of stacking sequence effect on natural frequency

| Layup | Results | Natural frequency (Hz) | | | | |
|---|---|---|---|---|---|---|
| | | Mode 1 | Mode 2 | Mode 3 | Mode 4 | Mode 5 |
| SCAL | Numerical | 112.35 | 560.62 | 696.4 | 687.88 | 1917 |
| | Analytical | 112.491 | 655.867 | 704.97 | 637.061 | 1973.9 |
| | %Diff | 0.12552 | 14.5224 | 1.2157 | − 7.9772 | 2.88262 |
| SAPL30 | Numerical | 91.258 | 533.96 | 565.04 | 1013.7 | 1569.1 |
| | Analytical | 88.268 | 514.637 | 553.166 | 964.21 | 1548.9 |
| | %Diff | −3.3874 | − 3.7548 | − 2.1466 | − 5.1327 | − 1.3042 |
| SAPL45 | Numerical | 69.664 | 394.99 | 434.21 | 1056.9 | 1215.8 |
| | Analytical | 66.9851 | 390.55 | 419.789 | 1062.3 | 1175.4 |
| | %Diff | − 3.9992 | − 1.137 | − 3.4353 | 0.50833 | − 3.4371 |
| SBL | Numerical | 91.868 | 473.25 | 570.3 | 1032.1 | 1585.5 |
| | Analytical | 89.2672 | 520.463 | 559.428 | 1024 | 1566.4 |
| | %Diff | − 2.9135 | 9.07126 | − 1.9434 | − 0.791 | − 1.2194 |
| ANBL | Numerical | 80.001 | 444.4 | 493.28 | 982.79 | 1371.3 |
| | Analytical | 82.4821 | 480.903 | 516.906 | 862.885 | 1447.4 |
| | %Diff | 3.00805 | 7.59044 | 4.57073 | − 13.896 | 5.2577 |
| ASBL | Numerical | 74.854 | 448.54 | 464.65 | 849.3 | 1268.2 |
| | Analytical | 73.8364 | 430.495 | 462.725 | 904.172 | 1295.6 |
| | %Diff | − 1.3782 | − 4.1917 | − 0.4161 | 6.06873 | 2.11485 |
| ANCPL | Numerical | 100.11 | 560.31 | 621.42 | 680.28 | 1714.3 |
| | Analytical | 100.223 | 584.34 | 628.088 | 637.061 | 1758.7 |
| | %Diff | 0.11285 | 4.1123 | 1.06159 | − 6.7842 | 2.52459 |
| ANAPL30 | Numerical | 95.141 | 535.26 | 590.57 | 1019.1 | 1638.7 |
| | Analytical | 92.7393 | 540.706 | 581.187 | 1030.1 | 1627.3 |
| | %Diff | − 2.5897 | 1.0072 | − 1.6144 | 1.06786 | − 0.7005 |
| ANAPL45 | Numerical | 70.756 | 395.3 | 441.21 | 1097.2 | 1236.8 |
| | Analytical | 67.9381 | 396.106 | 425.761 | 1132.7 | 1192.1 |
| | %Diff | − 4.1477 | 0.20343 | − 3.6285 | 3.1341 | − 3.7497 |
| QIL | Numerical | 108.5 | 509.24 | 674.14 | 893.53 | 1860 |
| | Analytical | 108.096 | 630.243 | 677.428 | 865.886 | 1896.8 |
| | %Diff | − 0.3735 | 19.1995 | 0.48535 | − 3.1926 | 1.94011 |
| CS | Numerical | 115.96 | 569.6 | 716.2 | 857.37 | 1971.9 |
| | Analytical | 115.307 | 672.286 | 722.618 | 816.492 | 2023.4 |
| | %Diff | − 0.5661 | 13.2742 | 0.8882 | − 5.0065 | 2.54522 |

As illustrate in Fig. 5 (b), the resonance of [0/± 0/90]s laminate composite beam due to distributed load in z-axis (DLz) is similar to that of the end load (EFz) given in Fig. 5 (a), though the magnitude of the amplitudes are different. Similarly, the resonance response of [45/–45/45/–45/45] laminate composite beam (Fig. 6) has been conducted with end force in y-axis direction (EFy). The results of the amplitude indicate that the vibration resonance occurs close to the 2nd mode or natural frequency of the composite beam in both the analytical and numerical solutions.

For the sake of comparison, results for different stacking sequences are analyzed and plotted in a single figure (Fig. 7). It is observed that the resonance amplitude of the beams with end force in z direction is higher for [45/–45/45/–45/45] laminate compared to the other laminates. Furthermore, lower resonance values are observed for [0/±30/90]s laminate with the same fiber volume ratio, load and beam configuration. This indicates that [45/–45/45/–45/45] laminate is easily exposed to failure due to higher resonance near to its 1st mode natural frequencies and it is less stiff compared with the other stacking sequences.

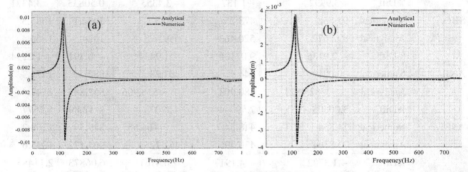

**Fig. 5.** Resonance of CS ([0/±30/90]s) composite beam due to (a) end force along z, EFz and (b) distributed load along z, DLz.

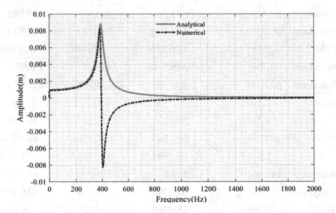

**Fig. 6.** Resonance of SAPL45 ([45/–45/45/–45/45]) composite beam due to EFy.

This analysis demonstrates that the resonance for specified design of applied cyclic load frequency on the composite beam can be controlled by alternating different stacking sequences, fiber volume ratios and using different fiber materials. The results also show

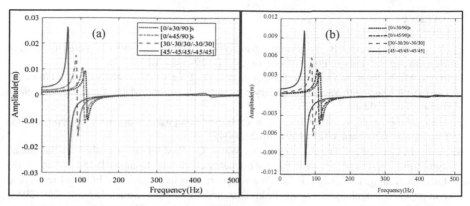

**Fig. 7.** Resonance of different laminate composite beam due to (a) EFz load and (b) EFy load.

that applied loads on different directions have different resonance frequencies on the same beam configurations because of different modes of natural frequencies. So, fiber reinforced plastic composite beams are better in controlling vibrations compared to isotropic beams because of fiber reinforced plastic beams that have variety of mechanical and physical properties and better opportunity to select the appropriate properties. As a result of resonances, the first mode natural frequencies of beams lead to failure of beams when designed with frequencies close to the natural frequencies due to same direction applied load compared to other modes.

## 4 Conclusions

This article presents analytical and numerical results of free and forced vibration analysis of FRP composite beam. The results of natural frequencies were obtained using different parameters such as fiber volume ratio, fiber materials, fiber angle and stacking sequence of layers for the first five modes. The results indicate that as the fiber volume ratio is increased, the natural frequencies also increases for all modes. It is also observed that graphite-epoxy composite beam has greater value of natural frequencies compared to aramid-epoxy and glass-epoxy. In general, the natural frequencies for bending modes mainly depend on the equivalent flexural modulus in longitudinal directions ($E_{1f}$) of composite beams. Comparison of analytical and numerical solutions of natural frequencies have sjown best agreement for Mode 1, Mode 3, Mode 4 and Mode 5 for all fiber materials and stacking sequences of laminates. According to numerical results, the first mode of natural frequencies in each direction are more critical for resonance. Furthermore, it has been observed that distributed and end concentrated harmonic loads with unique direction and magnitude have similar impact on the amplitude of the beam, but concentrated load increases the magnitude of amplitude and resonance.

# References

1. Pingulkar, P., Suresha, B.: Free vibration analysis of laminated composite plates using finite element method. Polym. Polym. Compos. **24**(7), 529–538 (2016)
2. Balci, M., Nalbant, M.O., Kara, E., Gündoğdu, Ö.: Free vibration analysis of a laminated composite beam with various boundary conditions. J. Autom. Mech. Eng. (IJAME). **9**(1), 1734–1746 (2014)
3. Kisa, M.: Free vibration analysis of a cantilever composite beam with multiple cracks. Compos. Sci. Technol. **64**(9), 1391–1402 (2004)
4. Zhao, J., Choe, K., Shuai, C., Wang, A., Wang, Q.: Free vibration analysis of laminated composite elliptic cylinders with general boundary conditions. Compos. B **158**, 55–66 (2018)
5. Lei, Z.X., Zhang, L.W., Liew, K.M.: Free vibration analysis of laminated FG-CNT reinforced composite rectangular plates using the kp-Ritz method. Compos. Struct. **127**, 245–259 (2015)
6. Mohandes, M., Ghasemi, A.: A new approach to reinforce the fiber of nanocomposite reinforced by CNTs to analyze free vibration of hybrid laminated cylindrical shell using beam modal function method. Eur. J. Mech./A Solids **73**, 224–234 (2018)
7. Kumar, G.A.Y., Kumar, K.M.S.: Free vibration analysis of smart composite beam. Mater. Today: Proc. **4**(2), 2487–2491 (2017)
8. Osman, M.Y., Suleiman, O.M.E.: Free vibration analysis of laminated composite beams using finite element method. Int. J. Eng. Res. Adv. Technol. **3**(2), 1–9 (2017)
9. Torabizadeh, M.A., Fereidoon, A.: A numerical and analytical solution for the free vibration of laminated composites using different plate theories. Mech. Adv. Compos. Struct. **4**(1), 75–87 (2017)
10. Babuska, P., Weibe, R., Motley, M.R.: A beam finite element for analysis of composite beams with the inclusion of bend-twist coupling. Compos. Struct. **189**, 707–717 (2018)
11. Madhu, S., Kumaraswamy, M.: Experimental investigation and free vibration analysis of hybrid laminated composite beam using finite element method. Int. J. Res. Appl. Sci. Eng. Technol. (IJRASET), **5**(VI), 40–53 (2017)
12. Teter, A., Gawryluk, J.: Experimental modal analysis of a rotor with active composite blades. Compos. Struct. **153**, 451–467 (2016)
13. Elshafei, M.A.: FE modeling and analysis of isotropic and orthotropic beams using first order shear deformation theory. Mater. Sci. Appl. **4**, 77–102 (2013)
14. Ganesa, P., Thirumavalavan, S.: Free vibration behaviour of glass fiber reinforced polymer composite. Middle-East J. Sci. Res. **20**(6), 734–737 (2014)
15. Naghipour, M., Taher, F., Zou, G.P.: Evaluation of vibration damping of glass-reinforced polymer-reinforced glulam composite beams. J. Struct. Eng. **131**(7), 1044–1050 (2005)
16. Kulkarni, P., Bhattacharjee, A., Nanda, B.K.: Study of damping in composite beams. Mater. Today: Proc. **5**(2), 7061–7067 (2018)

17. Tita, V., de Carvalho, J., Lirani, J.: A procedure to estimate the dynamic damped behavior of fiber reinforced composite beams submitted to flexural vibrations. Mater. Res. **4**(4), 315–321 (2001)
18. Kaw, A.K.: Mechanics of composite materials. CRC Press, Taylor & Francis Group (2006)
19. Duffy, K.P., Lerch, B.A., Wilmoth, N.G. Kray, N., Gemeinhardt, G.: Mechanical and vibration testing of carbon fiber composite with embedded piezoelectric sensors, **8341**, 1–14 (2012)

# Statistical Analysis of Ethiopian Wind Power Potential at Selected Sites

Abdulbasit Mohammed[1], Hirpa G. Lemu[2(✉)] [iD], and Belete Sirahbizu[1]

[1] Addis Ababa Science and Technology University, Addis Ababa, Ethiopia
[2] University of Stavanger, Stavanger, Norway
Hirpa.G.Lemu@uis.no

**Abstract.** The intent of the study reported in this paper is to make analysis of the wind speed data and annual wind energy potential at Abomsa Metehara and Ziway in Ethiopia. The wind speed data was collected from National Metrology Agency of Ethiopia, and then monthly and annual mean wind speed, wind power potential, wind energy potential and Weibull distribution parameters for these three sites have been analyzed and assessed. In the results, the monthly mean wind speeds, the measured and Weibull estimated of most probable monthly wind velocity, wind velocity carrying maximum energy, monthly wind power and wind energy density for these three sites at site locations have been estimated. Based on monthly and annually mean wind speeds at stations, annually and monthly mean wind velocities at 40 m, 60 m, 80 m, 100 m and 120 m heights via wind shear law have been extrapolated. At these heights, annual mean wind velocity carrying maximum energy, annual most probable wind velocity, annual mean wind power and annual wind energy density for these sites have been estimated. Additionally, the annual cumulative distribution function and probability density function of wind speed for the selected sites have been obtained using the Weibull distribution functions.

**Keywords:** Mean wind speed · Wind power density · Weibull parameters · Wind-driven water pump

## Abbreviations

| | |
|---|---|
| $ED_{ci}$ | Individual corrected measured energy density |
| $ED_{cw}$ | Weibull corrected estimation of wind energy density |
| $f(v)$ | Probability of observing wind speed (v) |
| $F(v)$ | Cumulative of observing wind speed (v) |
| $h_1; h_2$ | Height of data measured; the selected height |
| N | Number of collected data |
| n | Exponent of Weibull scale parameter at h2 |
| $P_{Dci}$ | Individual corrected measured wind power density |
| $P_{Dcw}$ | Weibull corrected estimation of wind power density |
| T | Period or time |
| v | Wind speed |

© ICST Institute for Computer Sciences, Social Informatics and Telecommunications Engineering 2021
Published by Springer Nature Switzerland AG 2021. All Rights Reserved
M. A. Delele et al. (Eds.): ICAST 2020, LNICST 385, pp. 370–381, 2021.
https://doi.org/10.1007/978-3-030-80618-7_25

$V_1; V_2$    Wind velocity at stations $(h_1)$; corrected wind velocity $(h_2)$
$v_m$    Mean wind speed
$V_{mE}$    Wind speed carrying maximum energy
$V_{mP}$    Most probable wind speed
$Z$    Is the roughness height of terrain

**Symbols**

$\alpha$    Weibull shape parameter
$\alpha_{h2}$    Weibull shape parameter at $h_2$
$\beta$    Weibull scale parameter
$\beta_{h1}$    Weibull scale parameter at $h_1$
$\beta_{h2}$    Weibull scale parameter at $h_2$
$\rho$    Air density
$\mu$    Weibull location parameters
$\gamma$    Wind shear exponent
$\sigma$    Standard deviation
$\Gamma(x)$    Gamma function

# 1 Introduction

Fossil fuels, as resources energy, are important for power generation which plays significant role in global economic development [1]. Contrary to the important role fossil fuels play, this source of energy has certain key limitations such as limited amount of available reserves and carbon emissions. The last mentioned one of the known unwanted environmental effects of use of fossil fuels as source of energy. As a result, recent focus is directed towards use of renewable energy sources and improving the efficiency and the management of energy sources [1, 2]. Among the available renewable energy sources, wind energy is the forefront energy resource for remote rural areas, for example for power generation and for water pumping purposes. Nowadays, many countries see wind energy as an alternative source of energy in order to mitigate the negative effects of fossil fuels. The operation of wind energy system is influenced by several factors such as size of generated power, wind shaft position and the wind regime [3]. Furthermore, wind speed potential analysis of a region is crucial to choose the proper wind energy conversion system. In order to map the existing potentials, wind speed frequency distribution is used and displayed using diverse distribution functions such as Gamma, lognormal, Rayleigh and Weibull. Ftrom these distribution functions, two parameter of Weibull distribution are used to model the wind speed in many regions of the world in recent years. This is because this method provides very good fit wind distribution [3].

Ethiopia is a country benefitting from wind energy resources in every region [4]. Wind energy potential in Ethiopia is estimated to be enormous due to local peculiar landscape. However, the country started to utilize the potential only very recently. One of the reasons for low utilization of wind energy in Ethiopia is the absence of reliable and accurate wind energy resource data. Development of reliable and accurate wind atlas helps to identify candidate sites for wind energy applications and facilitates the planning and implementation of wind energy projects [5]. However, the whole land area of the country practically falls under various wind resource categories without excluding land areas that could possibly be eliminated for reasons of accessibility, economics or environmental parameters [6]. In this work, the analysis of wind speed data and assessment of their wind energy potential for three selected sites was conducted. For 1-year (October 2018 to September 2019), every three hours a day, the wind data valid for a height of 10 m were collected from the National Meteorological Agency (NMA) of Ethiopia and daily mean wind speed were determined which was used as input parameter. The geographical location of the selected sites are Metehara (longitude 39°55'8.4"E, Latitude 8°51'31.2"N and altitude 944 m a.s.l), Abomsa (Longitude 39°49'58.8"E, Latitude 8°28'0.12"N and altitude 1630 m a.s.l) and Ziway (Longitude 38°56'51"E, Latitude 7°58'57.9"N and altitude 1705 m a.s.l).

Based on these collected data, the monthly and annual average wind velocities and their predicting wind power and energy output have been estimated at stations height and at extrapolated heights of 40 m, 60 m, 80 m, 100 m and 120 for the three selected sites. Weibull parameters, probability density and cumulative distributions function and most probable monthly wind velocity, wind velocity carrying maximum energy were considered.

## 2    Review of Previous Studies in Ethiopia

Some of previous reports that contributed to analysis of wind speed data and energy potential assessing at different sites in Ethiopia are Getachew et al. [7] who investigated the wind energy potential at four different sites in Ethiopia, i.e. (1) Addis Ababa (09:02N, 38:42E), (2) Adama (08:32N, 39:22E), (3) Bishoftu (8:44N, 39:02E) and (4) Mekele (13:33N, 39:30E). The data are compiled from various sources to make analysis using a software tool for data measured at the specified height (i.e. 10 m). The result showed a reasonable wind energy potential with average wind speed of about 4 m/s and mean wind speed of less than 3 m/s. Benti et al. [4] investigated the wind power potential of Ambo area in West Ethiopia using real wind speed data. A 6-year wind speed data (2010–2015) at 10 m height was obtained from the NMA of Ethiopia and statistically analyzed. According to the result, Ambo has an average wind speed of 3.2 m/s at the targeted height, where the wind gets maximum value of 4.5 m/s in February and minimum speed of 2.0 m/s in June and July. Wind data at 30 m and 50 m was extrapolated. Kumar et al. [8] analyzed wind speed data for energy production in Adama area. To design a small scale energy production from wind turbines, it is essential to get the probability density function, the cumulative density function and the cut-in wind speed of the targeted location. Bayray et al. [5] reported that wind data collected at 10 m over a period of one year from measuring masts in six different sites in Tigray, Ethiopia.

The data was analyzed and evaluated for the wind energy potential of the area by using different statistical software. Gaddada et al. [9] studied the wind resource assessment in the selected locations in Tigray, Ethiopia. Based on the wind assessed, three commercial wind turbines were chosen for technical assessment of electric power generation in eight selected locations. Girma [10] studied the wind speed distribution and estimated and comparative study of Weibull to Rayleigh distribution function has been analyzed for Dire Dawa and Hawasa in Ethiopia. Dulla et al. [11] examined wind energy potential of six sites i.e. Hawassa, Dilla, Wolayita soddo, Hossana, Wolkite and Butajira in southern Ethiopia. Weibull distribution function was used to analyze daily wind speed in five years, as well as the daily temperature and pressure of the areas. All sites have more than 50% chances that the wind speeds are greater than 4 m/s.

As the above review of literature shows, previous studies were based on wind speed data collected at a specified height, i.e. 10 m, and extrapolated the values in order to determine the wind speed for multiple numbers of heights to get more wind speeds and assess their wind power potential. If actual rotors of the wind turbines are placed more than 10 m height, it can be possible to estimate the variations of wind speed extracted at any different heights. Unlike the previous studies, this study focuses on specifically three selected location sites in Ethiopia i.e. Abomsa, Metehara and Ziway to analyze the wind speed potential and assesses their wind power and wind energy potential of these three selected sites at different heights.

## 3 Mathematical Formulation

The Weibull distribution approximates the probability laws of many natural phenomena. It has been used to represent wind speed distributions for application in wind loads studies. This method has greater flexibility and simplicity. Furthermore, it also gives a good fit to experimental data for wind energy applications. Weibull probability density function for three parameters is expressed as [12]:

$$f(v) = \left(\frac{\alpha}{\beta}\right)\left(\frac{v - \mu}{\beta}\right)^{\alpha-1} exp\left[-\left(\frac{v - \mu}{\beta}\right)^{\alpha}\right] \tag{1}$$

Where, $v$ is the wind speed, $\alpha$, $\beta$ and $\mu$ are the shape, scale and location parameters respectively. As $v \geq 0$, then $\mu = 0$ and Eq. (1) becomes [1–4]:

$$f(v) = \left(\frac{\alpha}{\beta}\right)\left(\frac{v}{\beta}\right)^{\alpha-1} exp\left[-\left(\frac{v}{\beta}\right)^{\alpha}\right] \quad v \geq 0,\ \alpha, \beta > 0 \tag{2}$$

Where $f(v)$ is the probability function of observing the wind speed $v$ whose descriptive parameters can be obtained. Then, the cumulative distribution function $F(v)$ is given as [12, 13]:

$$F(v) = \int_0^\infty f(v)dv = 1 - exp\left[-\left(\frac{v}{\beta}\right)^{\alpha}\right] \tag{3}$$

The mean value $v_m$ and standard deviation $\sigma$ of the wind speed, shape $\alpha$ and scale parameter $\beta$ of the Weibull distribution can be expressed as [1, 4, 13]

$$v_m = \beta\Gamma\left(1 + \frac{1}{\alpha}\right) \tag{4a}$$

$$\sigma = \beta\left[\left\{\Gamma\left(1 + \frac{2}{\alpha}\right) - \left[\Gamma\left(1 + \frac{1}{\alpha}\right)\right]^2\right\}\right]^{\frac{1}{2}} \tag{4b}$$

$$\alpha = \left(\frac{\sigma}{V_m}\right)^{-1.0860} \tag{4c}$$

$$\beta = \frac{\bar{v}}{\Gamma\left(1 + \frac{1}{\alpha}\right)} \tag{4d}$$

The measured standard deviation can be estimated from

$$\sigma = \left\{\left(\sum_{i=1}^{N} v_i - v_m\right)/N\right\}^{0.5} \tag{5}$$

## 3.1 Wind Speed Extrapolation

In most locations, wind speed varies with height, a phenomenon known as wind shear. The variation of wind speed as a function of height can be obtained using wind shear power law given as Eq. (6a) and the wind shear exponent as Eq. (6b) [12–14]:

$$V_2 = V_1\left(\frac{h_2}{h_1}\right)^{\gamma} \tag{6a}$$

$$\gamma = \left[0.096\left(log_{10}^{(Z)}\right) + 0.016\left(log_{10}^{(Z)}\right)^2 + 0.24\right] \tag{6b}$$

Where $h_1$ is 10 m, $h_2$ is the selected height, $V_1$ is the wind velocity at stations (10 m), $V_2$ is the corrected wind velocity ($h_2$), $\gamma$ is the wind shear exponent and Z is the roughness height of terrain, which is 1.5 m for the selected sites. The corresponding shape and scale parameters are expressed as [2]:

$$\alpha_{h_2} = \frac{\alpha_{h_1}}{1 - 0.0881 \ln\left(h_2/h_1\right)} \tag{7a}$$

$$n = 0.37 - 0.0881 \ln \beta_{h_1} \tag{7b}$$

$$\beta_{h_2} = \beta_{h_1}\left(h_2/h_1\right)^n \tag{7c}$$

## 3.2 Wind Energy Potential Assessment

The individually corrected measured wind power density and energy density at any height can be considered as [13, 14]

$$PD_{Ci} = \frac{1}{2}\rho v_m^3 \tag{8a}$$

$$ED_{Ci} = \frac{1}{2}\rho v_m^3 \times T \tag{8b}$$

Where T is the time duration. The corrected estimation of wind power density and wind energy density at any height for the selected sites with Weibull distribution can be expressed as given in Eq. (9a, 9b) [4, 14]:

$$PD_{CW} = \frac{1}{2}\rho\beta^3\Gamma(1+3/\alpha) \tag{9a}$$

$$PD_{CW} = \frac{1}{2}\rho\beta^3\Gamma(1+3/\alpha)T \tag{9b}$$

The most probable wind velocity $V_{mP}$ and wind velocity carrying maximum energy $V_{mE}$ with Weibull distribution can be expressed as [14]:

$$V_{mP} = \beta\left(\frac{\alpha-1}{\alpha}\right)^{\frac{1}{\alpha}} \tag{10a}$$

$$V_{mE} = \beta\left(\frac{\alpha+2}{\alpha}\right)^{\frac{1}{\alpha}} \tag{10b}$$

## 4  Discussion of Numerical Results

The collected wind speed data for Abomsa, Metehara, and Ziway at 10 m height over whole 1-year (October 2018 to September 2019) has been investigated. The wind data was collected during the daytime (06:00 – 18:00) within 3 h interval. The daily average of wind speed data were determined and monthly and annual average of wind velocities, standard deviation, wind power densities, and wind energy densities were estimated based on the measured wind velocities. From numerical results, the monthly mean wind speeds for the three selected sites at a height of 10 m are compared and illustrated in Fig. 1. As seen from Fig. 1, the average monthly distribution of wind speed values fluctuate between the lowest value of 2.01 m/s at Abomsa to the highest value of 4.14 m/ s at the Ziway site. And also Fig. 2 demonstrates the daily average wind speed variations for the three sites at 10 m height. It can be seen that the daily average wind speed fluctuations are different in 1-year.

Tables 1, 2, 3 and 4 show the monthly variation of the mean wind speed characteristics ($V_m$, $V_{mp}$ and $V_{maxE}$), the mean power density and mean energy density as well as the annual values of these parameters at 10 m height. As given in Table 2, the monthly mean wind speed of the selected sites varies from 2.01 m/s in August to 3.82 m/s in January (for Abomsa), from 2.53 m/s in March to 3.37 m/s in June (for Metehara) and from 2.66 m/s in April to 4.14 m/s in June (for Ziway). And also, annual mean wind speed for these sites is 2.80, 2.88 and 3.36 m/s respectively.

The least monthly value most probable wind speed is (1.84 m/s in August) and the wind speed carrying maximum energy is (2.86 m/s in September) in Abomsa and the highest value of most probable wind speed is 4.10 m/s in June and the wind speed carrying maximum energy is 5.54 m/s in November in Ziway site. The measured and estimated monthly mean power density varies between (7.95–37.52 W/m$^2$ and 7.81–37.63 W/m$^2$)

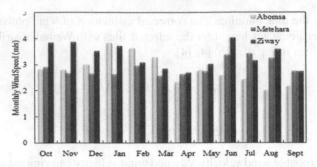

**Fig. 1.** Plot of monthly variations in mean wind speeds for the three sites at 10 m height.

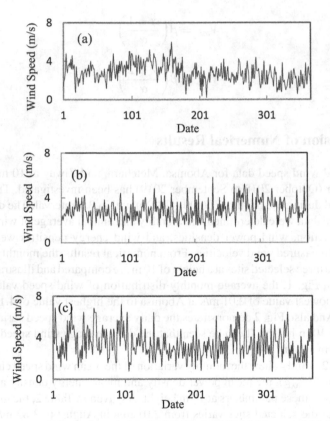

**Fig. 2.** Daily average wind speeds variation for (a) Abomsa, (b) Metehara and (c) Ziway at 10 m height

in Abomsa, (12.80–29.29 and 12.72–29.49) in Metehara and (16.46–58.87 W/m² and 16.72–59.50 W/m²) in Ziway respectively as shown in Table 2 and 3.

The smallest monthly value of the Weibull shape factor (α) for Abomsa is 2.50 and the highest value is 6.32 in January. The annual shape factors for Abomsa, Metehara and

**Table 1.** The monthly mean wind speed ($V_m$ $V_{mp}$ and $V_{mE}$) for three selected sites

| Year | Month | Abomsa | | | Metehara | | | Ziway | | |
|---|---|---|---|---|---|---|---|---|---|---|
| | | $V_m$ (m/s) | $V_{mp}$ (m/s) | $V_{mE}$ (m/s) | $V_m$ (m/s) | $V_{mp}$ (m/s) | $V_{mE}$ (m/s) | $V_m$ (m/s) | $V_{mp}$ (m/s) | $V_{mE}$ (m/s) |
| 2018 | Oct | 2.82 | 2.80 | 3.66 | 2.93 | 3.07 | 3.32 | 3.82 | 3.63 | 5.26 |
| | Nov | 2.81 | 2.94 | 3.18 | 2.72 | 2.82 | 3.20 | 3.92 | 3.64 | 5.54 |
| | Dec | 2.99 | 3.09 | 3.61 | 2.63 | 2.68 | 3.32 | 3.56 | 3.52 | 4.65 |
| 2019 | Jan | 3.82 | 4.00 | 4.29 | 2.63 | 2.73 | 3.14 | 3.67 | 3.42 | 5.15 |
| | Feb | 3.63 | 3.78 | 4.24 | 2.92 | 2.99 | 3.57 | 3.05 | 3.02 | 3.96 |
| | Mar | 3.27 | 3.18 | 4.38 | 2.53 | 2.56 | 3.17 | 2.91 | 2.99 | 3.55 |
| | Apr | 2.33 | 2.25 | 3.13 | 2.65 | 2.58 | 3.53 | 2.66 | 2.554 | 3.61 |
| | May | 2.76 | 2.88 | 3.17 | 2.75 | 2.73 | 3.58 | 3.01 | 2.95 | 3.99 |
| | Jun | 2.58 | 2.64 | 3.17 | 3.39 | 3.47 | 4.15 | 4.14 | 4.10 | 5.41 |
| | July | 2.42 | 2.36 | 3.22 | 3.36 | 3.45 | 4.11 | 3.20 | 3.07 | 4.36 |
| | Aug | 2.01 | 1.84 | 2.86 | 3.23 | 3.34 | 3.89 | 3.64 | 3.53 | 4.89 |
| | Sept | 2.16 | 2.12 | 2.86 | 2.75 | 2.83 | 3.35 | 2.72 | 2.49 | 3.89 |
| Annual average | | 2.80 | 2.77 | 3.67 | 2.88 | 2.86 | 3.73 | 3.36 | 3.43 | 4.15 |

**Table 2.** Monthly measured wind powers and energy densities for three selected sites

| Year | Month | Abomsa | | Metehara | | Ziway | |
|---|---|---|---|---|---|---|---|
| | | $PD_{ct}$ (W/m$^2$) | $ED_{ct}$ (kWh/m$^2$) | $PD_{ct}$ (W/m$^2$) | $ED_{ct}$ (kWh/m$^2$) | $PD_{ct}$ (W/m$^2$) | $ED_{ct}$ (kWh/m$^2$) |
| 2018 | Oct | 18.35 | 13.65 | 17.16 | 12.76 | 50.52 | 37.59 |
| | Nov | 15.00 | 10.80 | 14.34 | 10.32 | 56.47 | 40.66 |
| | Dec | 19.71 | 14.66 | 14.51 | 10.80 | 37.18 | 27.66 |
| 2019 | Jan | 37.52 | 27.92 | 13.35 | 9.93 | 45.95 | 34.18 |
| | Feb | 33.58 | 22.56 | 18.78 | 12.62 | 23.98 | 16.12 |
| | Mar | 29.94 | 22.27 | 12.80 | 9.52 | 18.58 | 13.82 |
| | Apr | 10.65 | 7.67 | 16.28 | 11.72 | 16.46 | 11.85 |
| | May | 14.60 | 10.86 | 17.64 | 13.13 | 23.37 | 17.39 |
| | Jun | 13.16 | 9.48 | 29.29 | 21.09 | 58.87 | 42.39 |
| | July | 12.15 | 9.04 | 28.35 | 21.09 | 28.86 | 21.47 |
| | Aug | 7.95 | 5.915 | 24.58 | 18.29 | 41.34 | 30.76 |
| | Sept | 8.51 | 6.124 | 15.85 | 11.41 | 19.74 | 14.21 |
| Annual average | | 18.43 | 161.40 | 18.58 | 162.73 | 35.11 | 307.57 |

Ziway are 3.13, 3.22 and 3.81, respectively. The value of the least monthly scale factor ($\beta$) is obtained as 2.26 m/s in Abomsa (August), and the highest value of 4.63 m/s in

Ziway (June). The annual scale factors are 3.13 m/s, 3.21 m/s and 3.72 m/s for Abomsa, Metehara and Ziway respectively (Table 4).

**Table 3.** Estimated Monthly wind powers and wind energy densities for three sites

| Year | Month | Abomsa | | Metehara | | Ziway | |
|---|---|---|---|---|---|---|---|
| | | $PD_{ct}$ (W/m$^2$) | $ED_{ct}$ (kWh/m$^2$) | $PD_{ct}$ (W/m$^2$) | $ED_{ct}$ (kWh/m$^2$) | $PD_{cw}$ (W/m$^2$) | $Ed_{cw}$ (kWh/m$^2$) |
| 2018 | Oct | 18.60 | 13.84 | 17.18 | 12.780 | 50.89 | 37.86 |
| | Nov | 15.05 | 10.83 | 14.42 | 10.380 | 57.41 | 41.33 |
| | Dec | 19.87 | 14.79 | 14.58 | 10.848 | 37.82 | 28.14 |
| 2019 | Jan | 37.63 | 28.00 | 13.33 | 9.920 | 46.49 | 34.59 |
| | Feb | 33.87 | 22.76 | 18.86 | 12.671 | 23.51 | 15.80 |
| | Mar | 30.46 | 22.67 | 12.72 | 9.467 | 18.60 | 13.84 |
| | Apr | 11.07 | 7.973 | 16.08 | 11.578 | 16.72 | 12.04 |
| | May | 14.61 | 10.87 | 17.37 | 12.921 | 23.46 | 17.45 |
| | Jun | 13.11 | 9.439 | 29.49 | 21.231 | 59.60 | 42.92 |
| | July | 12.23 | 9.101 | 28.74 | 21.384 | 29.38 | 21.86 |
| | Aug | 7.81 | 58.08 | 25.05 | 18.639 | 42.26 | 31.44 |
| | Sept | 8.607 | 61.97 | 15.68 | 11.291 | 19.57 | 14.09 |
| Annual average | | 18.45 | 161.65 | 19.70 | 172.613 | 29.15 | 255.367 |

**Table 4.** Monthly standard deviation, shape and scale parameters for three sites

| Year | Month | Abomsa | | | Metehara | | | Ziway | | |
|---|---|---|---|---|---|---|---|---|---|---|
| | | $\alpha$ (–) | $\beta$ (m/s) | $\sigma$ (m/s) | $\alpha$ (–) | $\beta$ (m/s) | $\sigma$ (m/s) | $\alpha$ (–) | $\beta$ (m/s) | $\sigma$ (m/s) |
| 2018 | Oct | 3.21 | 3.15 | 0.97 | 5.97 | 3.16 | 0.57 | 2.718 | 4.30 | 1.52 |
| | Nov | 5.97 | 3.03 | 0.55 | 4.70 | 2.97 | 0.66 | 2.55 | 4.42 | 1.64 |
| | Dec | 4.25 | 3.29 | 0.80 | 3.61 | 2.94 | 0.81 | 3.14 | 3.98 | 1.24 |
| 2019 | Jan | 6.32 | 4.11 | 0.71 | 4.45 | 2.89 | 0.67 | 2.59 | 4.13 | 1.52 |
| | Feb | 4.95 | 3.95 | 0.84 | 3.96 | 3.22 | 0.83 | 3.20 | 3.40 | 1.05 |
| | Mar | 2.94 | 3.67 | 1.21 | 3.58 | 2.81 | 0.78 | 4.02 | 3.21 | 0.81 |
| | Apr | 2.89 | 2.61 | 0.87 | 2.97 | 2.97 | 0.97 | 2.82 | 2.98 | 1.02 |
| | May | 5.42 | 2.99 | 0.59 | 3.19 | 3.07 | 0.95 | 3.02 | 3.37 | 1.09 |
| | Jun | 3.89 | 2.85 | 0.74 | 3.95 | 3.74 | 0.96 | 3.15 | 4.63 | 1.44 |
| | July | 2.98 | 2.71 | 0.89 | 3.97 | 3.71 | 0.95 | 2.80 | 3.59 | 1.24 |
| | Aug | 2.50 | 2.26 | 0.84 | 4.24 | 3.56 | 0.86 | 2.91 | 4.08 | 1.36 |
| | Sept | 3.04 | 2.42 | 0.78 | 4.05 | 3.03 | 0.76 | 2.48 | 3.07 | 1.17 |
| Annual average | | 3.13 | 3.19 | 0.98 | 3.22 | 3.21 | 0.98 | 3.81 | 3.72 | 0.98 |

Figure 3(a) and (b) show the annual cumulative distribution function (CDF) and probability density function (PDF) of wind speed for three sites respectively. The CDF is used to estimate the time when the wind speed is within a certain speed interval. As Fig. 3(b) shows, the most frequent expected wind speed in Ziway, Abomsa and Metehara are about 3.5, 2.8 and 2.8 m/s respectively.

The measured wind speed is extrapolated, because data was collected at a limited number of heights (10 m), for determining the wind speed for multiple numbers of heights to get more wind speeds and assess their wind power potential. And also by considering, if actual rotors of the wind turbines are placed more than 10 m height, we estimated the variations of wind speed extracted at any different heights such as 40 m, 60 m, 80 m, 100 m and 120 m.

The estimated values of extrapolation of annual average wind speed, the wind powers, energy densities, mean wind speed characteristics ($V_{mp}$ and $V_{mE}$) and scale and shape parameters at different selected heights for three selected sites presented in Table 5. Generally, the three site's wind speeds are suitable for lifting water, or for battery charging purposes. And also the wind speed for Ziway is suitable for small wind farms.

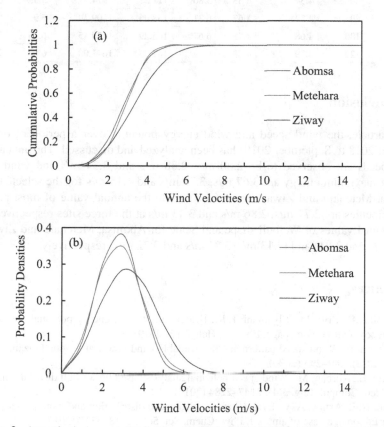

**Fig. 3.** Annual wind speed distribution (a) CDF and (b) PDF for three selected sites

**Table 5.** Extrapolated value of annual parameters for three sites at selected heights

| Sites | H (m) | $V_m$ (m/s) | $\alpha$ (-) | $\beta$ (m/s) | $PD_{cw}$ (W/m$^2$) | $Ed_{cw}$ (kWh/m$^2$) | $V_{mp}$ (m/s) | $V_{mE}$ (m/s) |
|---|---|---|---|---|---|---|---|---|
| Abomsa | 40 | 3.41 | 3.56 | 4.55 | 54.29 | 475.58 | 4.15 | 5.15 |
| | 60 | 3.62 | 3.72 | 5.07 | 74.57 | 653.26 | 4.66 | 5.69 |
| | 80 | 3.77 | 3.83 | 5.48 | 93.46 | 818.71 | 5.06 | 6.12 |
| | 100 | 3.89 | 3.92 | 5.82 | 111.38 | 975.68 | 5.40 | 6.46 |
| | 120 | 3.99 | 4.01 | 6.11 | 128.57 | 1126.25 | 5.69 | 6.76 |
| Metehara | 40 | 3.51 | 3.67 | 4.65 | 57.62 | 504.76 | 4.26 | 5.23 |
| | 60 | 3.72 | 3.83 | 5.18 | 79.00 | 692.06 | 4.79 | 5.78 |
| | 80 | 3.87 | 3.94 | 5.59 | 98.88 | 866.17 | 5.20 | 6.21 |
| | 100 | 4.00 | 4.04 | 5.94 | 117.71 | 1031.16 | 5.54 | 6.56 |
| | 120 | 4.10 | 4.12 | 6.24 | 135.76 | 1189.27 | 5.83 | 6.86 |
| Ziway | 40 | 4.09 | 4.34 | 5.29 | 82.06 | 718.85 | 4.98 | 5.77 |
| | 60 | 4.34 | 4.53 | 5.86 | 111.22 | 974.32 | 5.55 | 6.35 |
| | 80 | 4.52 | 4.67 | 6.31 | 138.06 | 1209.39 | 5.99 | 6.81 |
| | 100 | 4.68 | 4.78 | 6.67 | 163.29 | 1430.45 | 6.35 | 7.18 |
| | 120 | 4.79 | 4.88 | 6.99 | 187.33 | 1641.00 | 6.67 | 7.50 |

# 5 Conclusion

In this article, the wind speed and wind energy potential over a period of one year (October 2018 to September 2019) has been analyzed and discussed. The annual mean wind speeds are observed to be 2.80 m/s, 2.88 m/s and 3.34 m/s and wind speeds carrying maximum energy are 3.67 m/s, 3.73 m/s and 4.15 m/s for the selected site in Abomsa, Metehara and Ziway respectively, while the annual value of most probable wind velocities are 2.77 m/s, 2.86 m/s and 3.43 m/s at the three sites respectively. The mean annual values of Weibull shape and Scale for Abomsa, Metehara and Ziway are (3.13, 3.22 and 3.81) and (3.13 m/s, 3.21 m/s and 3.72 m/s) respectively.

# References

1. Khchine, E., Sriti, M., Elyamani, E.K.: Evaluation of wind energy potential and trends in Morocco. Journal homepage, Elsevier, Heliyon 5 (2019)
2. Kainkwa, R.: Wind speed pattern and the available wind power at basotu Tanzania. Renew. Eng. **21**(2), 289–295 (2000)
3. Dokur, E., Kurban, M.: Wind speed potential analysis based on weibull distribution. Balkan J. Electr. Comput. Eng. **3**(4), 2147–2284 (2015)
4. Benti, N.E., Asfaw, A.A.: Evaluations of wind speed distribution and wind power potential over Ethiopia: a case of ambo. J. Phys. Chem. Sci. **5**(4), 2348–3327 (2017)
5. Bayray, M., et al.: Wind energy data analysis and resource mapping of Geba catchment. North Ethiop. Wind Eng. **37**(4), 333–346 (2013)

6. Mulugeta, B.A., Aleksandar, S., Dragan, K., Slobodan, S.: Wind Energy Resource Development in Ethiopia as an Alternative Energy Future Beyond the Dominant Hydropower. Debre Markos University, Ethiopia (2013)
7. Getachew, B., Björn, P.: Wind energy potential assessment at four typical locations in Ethiopia. Appl. Energy, Elsevier **86**(3), 388–396 (2009)
8. Kumar, P., Kumar, A., Nanduri, R.: Analysis of wind speed data for energy production at central Ethiopia, Adama. Int. J. Recent Res. Sci. Eng. Technol. **1**(2) (2015)
9. Gaddada, S., Kodicherla, K.: Wind energy potential and cost estimation of wind energy conversion systems (WECSs) for electricity generation in the eight selected locations of Tigray region (Ethiopia). Renewables: Wind, Water and Solar **3**(10) (2016). https://doi.org/10.1186/s40807-016-0030-8
10. Girma, D.: Analysis of wind speed distribution: comparative study of weibull to rayleigh probability density function - a case of two sites in Ethiopia. Am. J. Mod. Energy **2**(3), 10–16 (2016)
11. Dulla, H., Eyob, T., Legesse, A.: Assessment of wind power potential of six sites in Southern Ethiopia. J. Appl. Phys. Sci. Int. **7**(4), 193–198 (2016)
12. Bagiorgas, H.S., Mihalakakou, G., Matthopoulos, D.: A statistical analysis of wind speed distributions in the area of Western Greece. Int. J. Green Energy **5**(1), 120–137 (2008)
13. Oyedepo, O., Adaramola, S., Paul, S.: Analysis of wind speed data and wind energy potential in three selected locations in south-east Nigeria. Int. J. Energy Environ. Eng. **3**(7), 1–11 (2012). https://doi.org/10.1186/2251-6832-3-7
14. Rasham, A.M.: Analysis of wind speed data and annual energy potential at three locations in Iraq. Int. J. Comput. Appl. **137**(11), 0975–8887 (2016)

# Nature Inspired Design in Fiber Orientation Trends for Reinforcement of Composites

Yohannes Regassa[1(✉)], Hirpa G. Lemu[2] , and Belete Sirabizuh[1]

[1] Addis Ababa Science and Technology University, Addis Ababa, Ethiopia
yohannes.regassa@aastu.edu.et
[2] University of Stavanger, Stavanger, Norway

**Abstract.** In this paper, review of the literature in the practice and method of nature-inspired design has been reported. Engineering design enhancement that has been achieved by natural phenomena mimicking and adapting it to develop new products is the designers' initiative as cost-effective design methods. The use of spider web geometry practice and trends as a technique for orienting fiber to reinforce composite has been reviewed rigorously and reported in this paper. An Orb web possesses many unique features to be mimicked for engineering structures. Spider web develops a self-stressing nature, which offers its excellent inelasticity and provides webs a mechanism for competent and economical means for harmonizing the local and global induced stresses in the structure. These make a spider web a model of engineering material with exceptional properties of combining a unique strength and toughness, because the mechanical properties of the fiber-reinforced composites are intensely swayed by the fiber orientation. Spider web-oriented types of fiber orientation are not yet widely used for the engineered composite product except for some cable-stayed bridges load suspensions. Lastly, a significant research gap between engineering design cognition and natural phenomena are identified for forthcoming researchers and concluding remark on natural emulating design practice has been lightened.

**Keywords:** Fiber orientation · Nature-inspired design · Polymer composite · Spider-web · Biomechanics

## 1 Introduction

Nature-inspired developments are clustered into three groups of inspirations as (1) graphic, (2) notion and (3) computational type [1]. A graphic inspiration agrees with the shape of several creatures or their structures, and to mimic similar roles and methods. A notion of inspiration arises when a designer or an engineer uses a philosophy established in nature, and a computational level stimulated by mechanisms or organisms occurring in nature. Biomaterials are the construction materials used by nature to build all living matters. The structures of most of these biomaterials have evolved to maximize the performance of the function provided. Humanmade biomaterials or processes are made through emulating natural phenomena. The silks that form spiders' webs excellent

© ICST Institute for Computer Sciences, Social Informatics and Telecommunications Engineering 2021
Published by Springer Nature Switzerland AG 2021. All Rights Reserved
M. A. Delele et al. (Eds.): ICAST 2020, LNICST 385, pp. 382–394, 2021.
https://doi.org/10.1007/978-3-030-80618-7_26

examples of these natural biomaterials that contribute to early human fishing net production. Spider silk is the model for engineering materials for its exceptional properties combining a unique strength and toughness.

Apart from the notable material properties, spider webs are natural models of a particular class of pre-stressed structures that are termed as tensegrity (tensional integrity) structures [2]. Such structures are characterized by unique geometry and mechanics that are used for very efficient structures because of their geometries with optimal distribution of structural mass and play significant parameters for the present as well as the toughness of a tensegrity creation of it. A self-stressing nature, which offers its inelasticity, provides spider webs the mechanism for competent and economical means for harmonizing the induced stresses. A sympathetic for the interaction of material properties and structural geometry may lean to light on our ability to design the next generation of ultra-lightweight, large area space structures. Orb-weaving spiders construct orb webs by depositing protein-based silk materials through their spinnerets for catching prey, sensing vibration, and protecting offspring. They are primarily a collection of structural radial filaments and gluey spiral threads with circular geometry, as illustrated in Fig. 1 [3].

**Fig. 1.** Schematic diagram of a spider's web.

The objective of this article is to investigate the practice and method of nature-inspired design and identifying a significant research gap between engineering design cognition and natural phenomena. Spider web geometry for fiber orientation to reinforce the composite was a focus area of this review work. Although there are many varieties of the web making spiders, orb webs make spired is chosen among the exiting varieties. Orb web possesses many unique features mimicked for engineering structures, and many scholars suggested its adaptation techniques.

## 2   Methods

As a method of research, beyond physical observation and examination of the environment and locally available spider web, the researchers have reviewed the latest published articles. Those reviewed research materials used for:

1. evaluating trends of using nature-inspired design methods,
2. pointing out the most used types of fiber orientation for reinforcing the composite structure.
3. assessing the effect of fiber orientation on mechanical strength.
4. evaluating the application of nature-inspired design for product development and innovations.
5. reviewing tools used for modeling and simulation of a spider web.

To conduct the review work for this article, the following keywords were used while searching the databases: 'fiber orientation', 'spider web geometry', 'modeling of spider web', 'mechanics of spider web', 'effect of fiber orientation on mechanical strength', 'nature inspired-design', 'application of nature-inspired design' and standard and published articles, conference papers and handbooks from indexed publishers were used.

## 3   State-of-the-Art on Polymer Composite

### 3.1   Fiber Orientation for Polymer Composites

Figure 2 illustrates the alignment of a single fiber measured by a unit vector **p** directed by the angles $(\theta, \phi)$. Such geometrical representation can be used to describe the motion of cylindrical fibers with a large aspect ratio $(R_p = l/d > 10)$, where $l$ is the length, and d is the diameter of fiber. At higher fiber concentrations, fiber to fiber connections result in variation of fiber orientation whose status is determined upon the volume fraction $(\phi_f)$ of fibers in the composite and for the dilute state. For instance, in the case when $\phi_f \ll (d/l^2)$, the interactions between fibers are rare. For the semi-dilute states, i.e. when $(d/l^2) \ll \phi_f \ll (d/l^2)$, contacts between fibers are quite common. Nevertheless, fiber to fiber interactions are purely hydrodynamic, and the change in orientation due to mechanical contact between fibers has no significant effects on fiber interaction [4].

The appropriate fiber orientation is primarily determined by the loading condition which can be either uniaxial, biaxial, shear, or impact state of loading on the structures. Countless scholars carried out experiments to explore the impact of fiber orientation on fiber structure of random mat, unidirectional 0/90, and woven fabric. State [5] investigated that the mechanical behavior of plain knitted and twill weaved fiber and revealed that a twill woven fiber ensures excellent mechanical properties as compared to the woven mat. Woven mat fiber affords a proper equilibrium in mechanical properties, and it is the favorite form of standard fiber mat for an engineered composite product by hand methods.

Nevertheless, the impact of hybrid fiber orientation for ultimate tensile strength (UTS) of unidirectional and biaxial strength of fiber reinforcements is not studied yet [6].

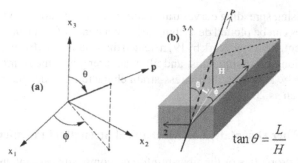

**Fig. 2.** (a) Geometry of fiber orientation, (b) extracting the (L, φ) values for each fiber on the 1–2 plane, and calculating the out-of-plane angle, θ, from its state height, H.

Hybrid fiber orientation promotes a composite with high strength for different loading conditions and headway for composite structure reliability. Fiber orientation with 0°, 90°, +45°, and or −45° is a standard method for designing fiber orientation and it is a common practice to produce composite structures. Figure 3 (adapted from [7]) shows practical fiber orientations 0/90, +45/−45 and/or orientation types that are frequently used by engineers.

The deviation of fiber orientation is defined by a curve relating the cumulative fraction of fibers to their alignment angle. A numerical study has shown that a single parameter exponential equation can best define the experimental cumulative curves of fiber alignment [8]:

$$X = 1 - e^{-\lambda\alpha} \tag{1}$$

where X is the cumulative fraction of fibers aligned between (−α) to (+α), α is the angle from alignment axis, and λ is a single experimental factor.

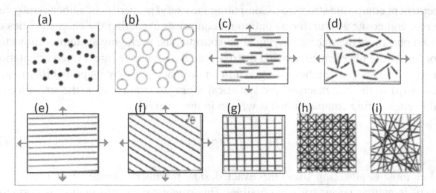

**Fig. 3.** Practiced fiber orientations: (a) and (b) homogeneous particle distribution in a matrix. (c) and (d) aligned (anisotropic) and random (quasi-isotropic) discontinuous fibers. (e) and (f) aligned (unidirectional) continuous fibers: θ = 0°, θ = 90°; 0° < θ < 90°. (g) bidirectional or cross-ply continuous fibers. (h) Multidirectional fibers and (i) Continuous random.

Since the raising spreading curves trail a common mathematical law, the continuous calculated curves can be plotted describing the dependence of mechanical properties on the fiber alignment. Research work by [9] revealed that composites having deficient levels of fiber orientation, tensile modulus, and ultimate strength of the reinforced sheets are predicted precisely. However, their stress-strain characteristics deviate from theoretical curves by as much as 20–30%.

## 3.2 Effect of Fiber Orientation on Mechanical Strength of Polymer Composite

The mechanical properties of the fiber-reinforced composites are intensely swayed by fiber orientation. In early theories, researchers used the strength of misaligned or planar random fiber for predicting the composite's strength based on the assumption that strength is an additive property [10]. These imply that the strength of random fiber orientation is equivalent to the average strength, with respect to alignment or orientation, of a set of unidirectional composites of the same composition. Pipes et al. [11] tested the strength of these concepts for glass-epoxy composites. They determined that strength is not an additive property, and the modest integration technique is insufficient for visualizing the strength of multi-directional composites. Unevenly aligned fibers, whose axes do not match with the loading direction, drive fewer to the strength of the composite than correctly aligned fibers. Since fibers are the principal stress-bearing structures in composites, the kind of fiber, state of fiber, and the used orientation affected properties the structures. The mechanical and physical performance of short fibers are hugely affected by the flaw induced during processing of fiber alignment for structural construction of composites.

A module of research conducted on woven and random mat fibers revealed that a woven fiber yields greater flexural strength than other forms. In contrast, a comparatively random mat indicates meager characters for all loading situations of woven and unidirectional fibers. Likewise, auxiliary factors like knitting and winding types, wrap and weft as well textile values can affect the mechanical properties of woven fiber reinforcement of composite structures. Computing the useful properties of a fiber-reinforced polymer composite as a uniform continuum comprises averaging the characteristics of the two phases. If the fiber scattering is anisotropic, the averaging system is subjected according to the fiber orientation and distribution. Such averages are termed orientation averages. The fiber orientation $p$ is given in an ordinary sense by its probability distribution $\psi(p)$ so that the macroscopic statistical averaged stress tensor (the stress tensor used in engineering computations) is written in the form of:

$$\Sigma = \int T(p)\psi(p)\partial p \tag{2}$$

For most engineering uses, the exact design for fiber orientation at each point of $\psi(p)$ is neither necessary nor possible. This orientational information is correctly approximated with the use of the second-order and fourth-order orientation tensors [12] as:

$$\underline{\underline{a}} = \int \underline{p} * \underline{p}\, \psi\left(\underline{p}\right)\partial p; \quad \underline{\underline{a_4}} = \int \underline{p} * \underline{p} * \underline{p} * \underline{p}\psi \tag{3}$$

The strengthening of a 2-phase composite can be approximately expressed by [7]

$$\sigma_c = V_\alpha\, \sigma_\alpha + V_\beta\, \sigma_\beta \tag{4}$$

where $V_\alpha$, $V_\beta$ and $\sigma_\alpha$, $\sigma_\beta$, are the equivalent volume fractions ($V_\alpha + V_\beta = 1$) and yield strengths (flow stress) of the two phases $\alpha$ and $\beta$ respectively. Such modeling approach assumes that one phase (the dispersoid or phase dispersed in a matrix) is much harder or stronger than the other (the matrix phase) [13].

Fibers oriented in the longitudinal direction have an excellent mechanical property than those oriented in transverse direction, and fibers oriented longitudinally (i.e., perpendicular to the fracture surface) are less exposed for new fracture conditions. Rupture and withdrawal of fibers occurres mostly while the fibers are aligned in the longitudinal direction, although for crossways oriented fibers, the crack growths in the path of fiber orientation. 0°/90° oriented fibers are used as blockades to inhibit the spreading of stress all over the matrix. Such a condition causes a higher concentration of localized stress and results in equally meager and non-linear mechanical properties on the structures [14].

# 4   Nature Inspired Design Process and Fiber Orientation

## 4.1   Nature Inspired Design Process

Nature-Inspired design is a design strategy that is established on nature theories for practically acquiring design wisdom from nature and to honor it as a model of design sustainability. The design process through the imitation of natural phenomena yields robust design. Contemporary design practices emphasis on eco-efficiency as a critical method in the arena of viable for product design advancement. This method predominantly aims at enhancing engineering products and services for the required design. Nature driven design needs interpretation of how nature performs. Though several scholars have discovered different design philosophies through natural inspiration, yet a consideration for nature as a source of sustainable engineering design does not mature well, to implement it to the practical value for sustainable production of design adaptation from nature.

For novel design through the nature-inspired system, the design spiral [15] is used as sustainable means of knowledge acquiring method to abide by nature principle for practical adaptation on product development. This design spiral involves

- Distilling the design function by identifying what the design is intended to do,
- Translating the design to biological systems and identifying how nature can do the intended function,
- Discovering natural models and creating taxonomy of natural strategies,
- Emulating nature's strategies, and
- Evaluating the design against life's principles.

This design spiral method is implemented through the principles of scoping, design generation and engineering work and evaluation [15]. While scoping involves (re)defining the design problem, the design idea generation retrieves inspirations and engineering solutions from nature. Then guidelines and sustainability criteria are developed for product engineering.

Nature-inspired design spiral dictates many features for designing and developing of justifiable products. Viewed from the product development process, the design spiral is goal-driven [15], i.e. it is directed for a workable end results that are inspired by natural methods. In addition, every approach in the spiral integrates philosophies intended at the command of closed-loop physical systems. As the design procedure is focused on culti-vating invention systems for the physical world, it emphasizes eco-friendly sustainability and addresses economic viability.

Bio imitation can be a practical tool to resolve the technical and common engineering design challenges at different levels. Biology has motivated designers since primitive man created spears from the teeth of animals and copied the operative sneak-and-pounce hunting method of huge hunters. However, the growth of a practical basis for decod-ing natural schemes into engineering design is a modern method for the enhancement of humanmade structures. The arrangements of systems, methods, and procedures in nature have extensively helped inventors, scientists, architects, and engineers for the discovery of enhanced and advanced solutions for their respected fields [1]. The airplane structures, different construction machinery, robotic arm, and many other products are engineered products through mimicking nature. Many researchers have been attracted to conduct different studies on spider web modeling and its mechanics. However, there is a very lim-ited document about mechanical properties of spider webs and practical implementation of such geometry.

From the biosphere of natural fiber, spider silk questioned for its unique properties of high strength and notable rapture elongation. Spider nets are one of the superior types of pre-stressed systems termed as tensegrity (tensional integrity) structures [16]. Due to the optimal spreading of structural mass, the spider web owns a unique combination of geometry that resulted in highly efficient systems mimicked for engineering structures. Spider's web geometry plays the primary role in describing the existence as well as the stiffness of a tensegrity structure. Such tensegrity arrangements are categorized as space structures. Today's human netting tools that are used for fishing are imitated from the spider web and are evidences for the early human practice of nature-inspired design.

## 4.2   Modeling Methods of Spider Web as Fiber Orientation

Figure 4 illustrates a research conducted by Thomas [17] to extract basic parameters for modeling and defining of spider web. The method illustrated in the figure was used for accurate definition and analysis of some parameters of research interest on a spider web such as:

1. Web area - the area fenced by the outermost gluey spiral,
2. Number of spans on the web,
3. Quantity of sticky spiral turns on the web,
4. Quantity of non-sticky spiral turns on the web,
5. Ratio between number of sticky and non-sticky spiral turns and
6. Web dimension or the distance between successive sticky spiral turns measured along a radius in the eastern, southern, and western regions of the web.

To formulate the spider web geometry, the length as the spiral moves a distance from the inside point to the outer side turn was divided by the number of turns minus one (Fig. 4) [17].

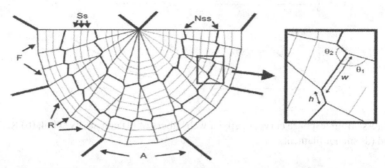

**Fig. 4.** A simplified Nephila orb web. Where A is the anchor filaments, F is frame filaments, R is the short radii, Ss and Nss are sticky and non-sticky spiral filaments respectively, h is for height (length of Nss spiral and radius junction) and width (w) of the Nss zigzag spiral pattern and the angle between the Nss and the radius ($\theta_1$) and the angle between the Nss spiral and the junction ($\theta_2$).

For each web, they [17] designated the area crossed by the eight southern-most radii and measured the following parameters from the seven fenced segments of each of the Ns spiral turns. Lost or radically altered directions in the segments were designation overlooked, and those measurements are summarized as;

1. The height to width ratio of the Nss spiral, zigzag shape (h/w) and the zigzag index of the Nss spiral can be calculated by the addition of the two angles of the Nss spiral, which it makes with its intersection at the radius divided by 180°, (i.e. $(\theta_1 + \theta_2)/180$).
2. Nss spiral was detectable by its zigzag/weave shape, where the distance of the intersection between the radius and the Nss spiral was used to build the height of the weave profile and the inter-radial length built the width of the web.
3. The intersection contained the Nss spiral fibers covering about the radius with smaller sticky silk filaments used to avoid slipup condition between the non-sticky spiral and the radius.
4. From uniaxial tensile test results (Fig. 5) [17]), it has been observed that there exists high non-linear stress-strain with high initial Young's modulus (stiffness) followed by a lower post-modulus curve.

Few efforts have been proposed to model spider orb webs with a proper analytical explanation for non-broken web type. Orb webs possess a stronger radial threads compared with the spiral threads because they are free of stress concentrations. This makes spider web unique for use as nature-based design to be mimicked for localized damage maintenance. Orb spiders optimize their web either by increasing the number of spiral threads for dense web (for trapping small insects) or modify it by adjusting the number of radial filaments. Familiarizing the environmental conditions or decreasing the cost of

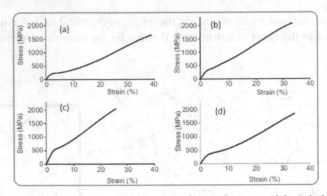

**Fig. 5.** Stress-strain response curves of spider webs fibers of (a) non-sticky spiral, (b) Radial, (c) frame, and (d) anchor filaments.

making the web without decreasing the damage tolerance of the web is also one of the techniques of optimization [18].

The 2D based modeling techniques conducted by Yuko et al. [19] for orb-web consisted of $R$ radial threads and $S$ spiral threads. In this study, the nodes are designated by a set of (r, s) as shown in Fig. 6. A 2D vector **Xr** indicates the location of this set, where r = 0, 1, 2,...., R−1 and s = 1,2, ......, S, $X_{r,0} = (0,0)$ is independent of r. The (r, s) element of the radial and spiral threads connect two adjacent nodes $X_{r,s}$ and $X_{r, s-1}$ and another set of adjacent nodes $X_{r, s}$, and $X_{r-1, s}$ respectively. The natural length of all (r, s) radial threads is equal to K while that of the (r, s) spiral thread $k_s$ depends on s because of geometrical restrictions:

$$k_s = \alpha sK \equiv 2sK \sin(\pi/R) \tag{5}$$

which means, without any tension, the node position is given in $(\theta, r)$ coordinates by

$$X_{r,s} = 2r\pi/R, sK) \tag{6}$$

The spring constant of the radial thread is independent of the element and represented:

$$\bar{U} = U/K \tag{7}$$

While that of spiral thread depends on the **s** and is designated in Eq. (8) because the spring constant is inversely proportional to the natural length.

$$\bar{u}_s = u/k_s \tag{8}$$

An effort for modeling and conducting a finite element analysis (FEA) was reported in [20] for an ideal web with a diameter of spiral contour 25 cm and this model contained four types of filaments (spiral, radial, frame, and anchorage) as given in Fig. 7. Different mechanical and physical properties characterize these threads. The finite element analysis and post-processing (FEMAP) software was used to model the spider web and ABAQUS non-linear FE code was used for detail analysis. The mechanical and physical properties of the spider thread are given in Table 1 [20].

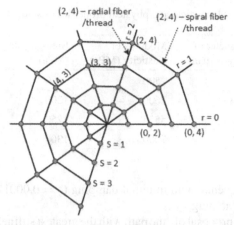

**Fig. 6.** Model of orb-web of spider consisting of 10 radial and 4 spiral threads (R = 10, S = 4).

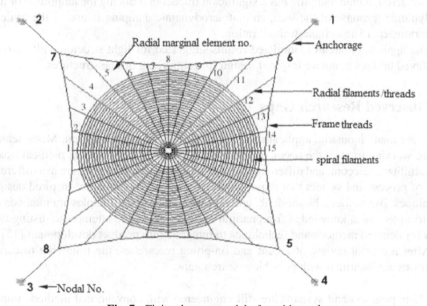

**Fig. 7.** Finite element model of a spider web.

The conclusion drawn from the study on the FEA of spider web are the following:

1. Initial tensions of the threads have significant effects on the transverse toughness of spider webs, and the broken threads contribute to the local effects. Within the localized damage, the spider web can function as a net for grasping prey without significant defects.

2. The impact load due to insect was simulated, and the web responds dynamically. The steady-state response magnifies approximately 3700 times to static response at

**Table 1.** Mechanical and physical properties of spider threads.

| Types of threads | Diameter of threads (μm) | Modulus of elasticity (MPa) | Breaking stress (MPa) | Initial tension (μm) |
|---|---|---|---|---|
| Spiral | 2.4 | 500 | 800 | 10 |
| Radial | 3.93 | 2600 | 1200 | 132 |
| Frame | 7.23 | 5555 | 1250 | 924 |
| Anchor | 8.03 | 7000 | 1300 | 1320 |

its first natural frequency with minimal damping ($\zeta = 0.0001$) and about 15 times (i.e. 0.1526) with damping.

3. For spider web, the proposal of "the path with the greatest stiffness carries the greatest load" is valid in such net structures.
4. The aerodynamic damping has a significant impact in reducing the amplitude of the dynamic response of the web, so that aerodynamic damping is one of the critical parameters to absorb the web vibration.
5. The application area of simulated results suggested for light structures like cable-stayed bridges as nature inspired design for reinforcing bridge structures.

## 5   Observed Research Gaps

There are many industrial applications created by nature-inspired design. Many scholars are working to meet the needs of aviation, automotive, construction, medical treatment, military, telecom, and different engineering area by emulating nature at a different level of process and system that require product design through nature-inspired design techniques. Biomimicry, biomimetic, and bio-inspired design principles are methods of acquiring technical knowledge from natural systems. There are attempts to distinguish them for detailed methods and techniques to integrate into product development [15].

After a careful review of recent and on-going researches, the following research directions are identified with possible research gaps.

1. Many products and systems are still engineered with conventional methods imply that there are limitations to meet the dynamics of industries and human needs.
2. Poor initiatives are observed in using and cultivating nature-inspired principles for fiber orientation to reinforce composite structures.
3. Limited tools, equipment, and machinery are available for real trucking and mimicking of nature for engineering application and production.
4. Though the iterations and evolutions that took place through billions of years have nature cultured in terms of optimal design, many optimization methods and processes are not still nature emulated.
5. Graphic inspirational methods are the most practiced methods to copy building designs or engineering systems. These are limited to copying the visual appearance of nature as it is. Conceptual inspiration, on the other hand, is a technique for

acquiring knowledge of nature's rules, principles, or patterns to be integrated for engineering systems. It is not well-practiced as of visual methods.

6. Design and production by computational inspirations (algorithmic bio-mimicry) are very limited in industrial applications and much more enforcement is required for evolutionary technologies.

7. Limited applications of web-like structures are employed to predict mechanical behavior and accurately to detect and locate damages for non-linear stress response-oriented design.

8. To date, there is a small claim to use nature mimicry for fiber orientation to reinforce the composite structures.

# 6  Concluding Remarks

Enhancement for engineering design-by-analogy or nature-inspired design has been the foundation of many pioneering designs for all human history. However, the visual, conceptual, and computational methods of inspiration to mimic nature remains much to be understood for endless innovation of products and processes for engineering applications. Fiber orientation plays a significant role in determining the mechanical properties of composite structures.

A spider web performs with a very flaw-tolerant system and provides opportunities for beating failure with lacking failing. Even if a few threads are damaged, the crack or failure propagation is localized. This reduced damage can be repaired, rather than replacing, and this is one of the unique features to mimic from nature of the spider web design for robust and damage-tolerant design of mechanical structures. To better understand the mechanical performance of the spider web structure, more advanced analysis and simulation works are sought. Due to their non-linearity, FEMAP and ABAQUS are proposed as practical tools for modeling and simulation of spider web.

From this study, spider web fiber orientation for composite reinforcement is suggested for practical applications using the analogy of nature-inspired design. An effort has been done to visualize the broader nature-inspired design techniques for modeling and analysis. The common practice regarding fiber orientation for product development assessed with the current knowledge of designer thought and the practiced approaches for the nature-inspired design are examined for further integration techniques. Then the future direction for nature-inspired design is proposed from the superior design-by-analogy viewpoint.

# References

1. Park, K.: The design characteristics of nature inspired architecture. In: Seoul World Architects Congress, pp. 2–7 (2017)
2. Ko, F.K., Jovicic, J.: Modeling of mechanical properties and structural design of spider web. Biomacromol **5**(3), 780–785 (2004)
3. Demont, M.E., Mcconnell, C.J., Carmichael, J.B.: Measuring the from physical Properties of silk from a spider's web. Am. Biol. Teach. **58**(8), 475–477 (1996)

4. Nguyen Thi, T.B., Morioka, M., Yokoyama, A., Hamanaka, S., Yamashita, K., Nono-mura, C.: Measurement of fiber orientation distribution in injection-molded short-glass-fiber composites using X-ray computed tomography. J. Mater. Process. Technol. **219**, 1–9 (2015)
5. Onyeka, F.C., Nwoji, U.G., Mbanusi, E.C.: Mechanical properties of bamboo props and their utilization as sustainable structural material. Int. J. Innov. Sci. Eng. Technol. **6**(10), 384–406 (2019)
6. Moakher, M., Basser, P.J.: Fiber orientation distribution functions and orientation tensors for different material symmetries. In: Hotz, I., Schultz, T. (eds.) Visualization and Processing of Higher Order Descriptors for Multi-Valued Data. MV, pp. 37–71. Springer, Cham (2015). https://doi.org/10.1007/978-3-319-15090-1_3
7. Murr, L.E.: Classification of composite materials and structures. In: Murr, L.E. (ed.) Hand-book of Materials Structures, Properties and Performances, pp. 1–13. Springer, Cham (2014). https://doi.org/10.1007/978-3-319-01815-7_23
8. Harper, L.H., Turner, T.A., Warrior, N.A., Rudd, C.D.: Characterisation of random carbon fibre composites from a directed fibre preforming process: The effect of fibre length. Compos. Part A Appl. Sci. Manuf. **37**(11), 1863–1878 (2006)
9. Fu, S.-Y., Lauke, B.: Effects of fiber length and fiber orientation distributions on the tensile strength of short-fiber-reinforcemented polymers. Compos. Sci. Technol. **56**(2), 1179–1190 (1996)
10. Omidi, M., Bokni, H.D.T., Milani, A.S., Seethaler, R.J., Arasteh, R.: Prediction of the mechan-ical characteristics of multi-walled carbon nanotube/epoxy composites using a new form of the rule of mixtures. Carbon **48**(11), 3218–3228 (2010)
11. Lim, S.H., White, J.L.: Development and characterization of orientation of anisotropic disk and fibrous particles in a thermoplastic matrix. J. Reol. **34**, 343 (1990). https://doi.org/10.1122/1.550132
12. Köbler, J., Schneider, M., Oswald, F., Andrä, H., Müller, R.: Fiber orientation interpolation for the multiscale analysis of short fiber-reinforced composite parts. Comput. Mech. **61**(6), 729–750 (2018)
13. Sanal, I., Zihnioglu, N.Ö.: To what extent does the fiber orientation affect mechanical performance? Constr. Build. Mater. **44**, 671–681 (2013)
14. Geethamma, V.G., Joseph, R., Thomas, S.: Short coir fiber-reinforced natural rubber com-posites: effects of fiber length, orientation, and alkali treatment. J. Appl. Polym. Sci. **55**(4), 583–594 (1995)
15. de Pauw, I., Kandahar, P., Karana, E., Peck, D., Wever, R.: Nature-inspired design: Strate-gies towards sustainability strategies towards. In: ERSCP-EMSU Conference, Delft, The Netherlands, 25–29 October 2010
16. Lin, L.H., Sobek, W.: Structural hierarchy in spider webs and spider web-type systems. Struct. Engineer **76**(4), 59–64 (1998)
17. Hesselberg, T., Vollrath, F.: The mechanical properties of the non-sticky spiral in Nephila orb webs (Araneae, Nephilidae ). J. Exp. Biol. 3362–3369 (2012)
18. Gole, R.S., Kumar, P.: Spider's silk: investigation of the spinning process, web material, and its properties. In: Biological Science and Bio-Engineering, IIT Kanpur. http://citeseerx.ist.psu.edu/viewdoc/download
19. Aoyanagi, Y., Okumura, K.: Simple model for the mechanics of spider webs. Phys. Rev. Lett. **104**, 1–4 (2010)
20. Alam, M.S., Wahab, M.A., Jenkins, C.H.: Mechanics in naturally compliant structures. Mech. Mater. **39**(2), 145–160 (2007)

# Testing Scenarios of Strategic Production Configuration Using Fuzzy Logic

Matthias Brönner[1]([envelope]) [iD], Dominik Fries[2], Julia Pelka[1], and Markus Lienkamp[1]

[1] Institute of Automotive Technology, Technical University Munich,
Boltzmannstr. 15, 85748 Garching, Germany
`Broenner@ftm.mw.tum.de`
[2] EVUM Motors GmbH, Joseph-Dollinger-Bogen 26, 80807 München, Germany

**Abstract.** Strategic production configuration in developing economies requires verified knowledge of the production system and its environment. In order to model these reproducibly, we use a fuzzy logic based model in this paper. This allows for simulation of dependencies within strategic production configuration. The results are transparent and reproducible and support strategic decisions-making. Thus, this method clarifies the correlations between business strategy, product, assembly and production system in developing economies. To evaluate the impact of local conditions on location configuration, we test scenarios such as changing competitive priorities, locations in different countries and product adaptation. The scenarios are tested within the aCar mobility project, a project in which an electric vehicle was designed for local value creation in Africa. The results allow for identifying similarities and differences in strategic recommendations, and therefore to develop a suitable production configuration. Thus, the key findings of this paper are the highlighting of effects of scenarios on the production strategy in developing economies. It becomes evident that for a sustainable strategy the possible scenarios of the development must also be taken into account in the early decision making process.

**Keywords:** Production strategy · Fuzzy logic · Production configuration

## 1 Introduction

The United Nations define 17 Sustainable Development Goals, aiming at a sustainable change of less developed regions [28]. Many of the goals are directly and indirectly linked to local employment in these regions. The automotive industry, with its wide-ranging value creation networks, is one of the industries that may change regions through local value creation [6]. Meanwhile, many countries are promoting the development of a local vehicle industry [23], through trade barriers for the import of new and used vehicles or local content requirements [2]. If

M. A. Delele et al. (Eds.): ICAST 2020, LNICST 385, pp. 395–407, 2021.
https://doi.org/10.1007/978-3-030-80618-7_27

automobile manufacturers plan a local assembly site, either for financial reasons or for reasons of sustainability, they must handle a small and strongly fluctuating demand [21]. With different boundary conditions in African countries, locations must also be planned individually in order to avoid over-dimensioning and thus investment risks. Additionally, with the market development, customer requirements may change [23]. This must be taken into account when planning an assembly plant [2].

Due to the effort involved in planning an assembly plant in Africa, we have developed a simulation model based on fuzzy logic to enable application-specific production site configuration. We use this simulation to evaluate the impact of changing boundary conditions, e.g. customer priorities, on the production site configuration. The results are not to be understood as fixed values, but rather as input for further strategic planning.

## 1.1   Theoretical Background

In this section, we explain the content of a production strategy as well as the impact of the surrounding conditions. This highlights the difference between the development of a sales-oriented strategy and one to be applied in developing economies. Further, we describe the current approach of the automotive sector. We conclude in the demand of a simulation model, that includes the surrounding conditions into decision making.

A production strategy is the part of the corporate strategy that includes the strategic and operational planning of value creation [11]. In strategic planning, the purpose is to plan a cost-, quality-, time-optimal and flexible production [9]. The optimum of these decisions are not the extreme values, but trade-off decisions [24]. Trade-off decisions weight in between the extreme values, such as a fully automated production and a purely manual assembly. The appropriate decisions are essential for the competitive advantage [11], while having an efficiency limit [25]. For example, an increasing number of variants challenges cost efficiency in production. Content of a production strategy besides plant and equipment also includes production planning and control, laboratory and staffing, product design and engineering as well as organization and management [16,24].

This content is also valid for production strategies in less developed countries. Mefford and Bruun (1998) also show the relevance of trade-off decisions in these regions in their production strategy development process [16]. There, the competitive priorities of cost, time, quality and flexibility apply. These are influenced by the external influences of business costs, laboratory availability, competitive hostility, market dynamics and government regulation. Consequently, these must be taken into account in production strategy planning. Using the example of production strategies in Ghana, Ehie and Muogboh (2016) show the impact that the environmental conditions have on the decisions made there [9]. In particular, the political influence on competitive priorities should not be underestimated in developing economies [9]. In addition, the degree of adaptation of the products to the local conditions must be considered. Saranga et al. (2018) found in their study of the Indian market that specially developed products are often more efficient than adapting existing products [22].

Automotive manufacturers often use a multistage-approach, to enter new markets in less developed regions. First stage, in small and volatile markets, vehicles are imported as Fully Build Up (FBU) vehicles. There is no local added value, which is why import duties of up to 100% of the vehicle value have to be paid [14]. In the second stage, Semi Knocked Down (SKD) vehicles are shipped from the main factory [1]. These vehicles are partially pre-assembled and shipped as a kit. The Completely Knocked Down (CKD) strategy offers more locally added value, with larger assembly volumes in the target market. Therefore the CKD concept is dependent on a functioning logistics concept [8]. The SKD assembly is often the preliminary stage of the CKD assembly and is demanded e.g. by the Nigerian government after 5 years of SKD assembly [4]. A local production and associated development offers the largest share of local added value, which is only realized with appropriate market size [15]. For the local added value of vehicles, assembly site planning is therefore essential at the beginning of a planning process. Relevant parameters of such planning of small-scale vehicle production sites, with the focus on electric vehicles, are summarized in [5].

In summary, for local production strategies, the environmental conditions must be integrated more than in existing approaches. In these, the selection of the strategy is primarily focused on customer requirements and sales potential (see [11,12,24]. However, in order to be able to make a well-founded decision regarding the production strategy, it is necessary to compare different scenarios with each other without much effort. For this reason simulations are used in early planning phases [13,17,27]. Due to the qualitative nature of the planning and uncertain data set at the beginning, a fuzzy logic based planning is appropriate [29]. Fuzzy logic allows for linking decision relationships using *If... Then...* Rules. With this, expert knowledge can be translated into mathematically logical models for decision-making. Classical fuzzy systems can be extended by a recurring traceability [3,10,27]. The schematic procedure of a recurrent fuzzy system is visualized in Fig. 1.

So far, a procedure was missing that integrates the existing dependencies between external influences and internal possibilities of a strategy into a simulation model. In [7] we present such a procedure, which we use in this paper to simulate the effects of different scenarios and discuss their results using the example of a small series car manufacturer.

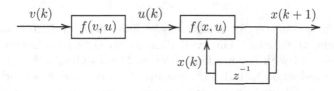

**Fig. 1.** Recurring fuzzy system

## 2    Model Description and Method

Based on the described theoretical background, we have developed a model to support production and assembly strategic decisions for small series production in Africa. The justification for choosing fuzzy logic as a method and the model structure are explained in detail in our publication [7]. In the following, a short summary of the model and this paper's focus, the procedure for testing different scenarios, are presented.

### 2.1    Model

Our model links country, product- and company-specific input factors with production configuration parameters. The link is made by *If...Then...* Rules implemented in a Matlab Simulink (2019b) model using the integrated Fuzzy Logic Designer. The model is described in detail in [7] and published under an open source license in Github[1]. The framework of the model is shown in Fig. 2. As illustrated, this framework can be used to set $m$ input parameters with $n$ output parameters in dependency.

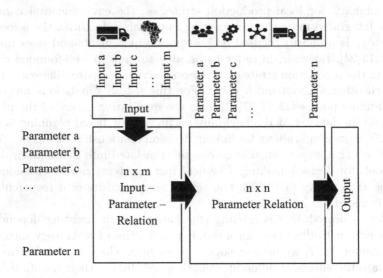

**Fig. 2.** Framework for production strategy simulation

The model parameter for our use case have been evaluated by industry experts for our application. The evaluation involved two workshops. Our first workshop was held with experts from EVUM Motors GmbH, a company planning vehicle production facilities in developing economies. A second workshop was organized in Ghana, Kumasi with entrepreneurs, vocational training staff

---

[1] https://github.com/TUMFTM/Production_Strategy_Development.

and scientists. Among the attendees (n = 7), 29% stated experience in corporate, business or production strategy, 57% have experience in production, manufacturing and assembly, 29% in qualification and training and 14% in engineering. The rule base of the model is based on dependencies mentioned in the literature, which were evaluated and weighted by (n = 5) experts. The selection of the experts was based on their knowledge of the vehicle and project, as well as their experience in production in a developing economy. The number of experts interviewed is based on the selection according to these criteria.

The output values of the model are between 1 and 10, whereby the output range is output dependent (Table 1). For example, in the case of the output value automation degree, an output value of 1 expresses a manual (very low automated) production and 10 a fully production assembly.

**Table 1.** Output parameters

| Output parameter | Parameter range | |
|---|---|---|
| Degree of automation | Low | High |
| Production system | Push | Pull |
| Depth of value added | Buy | Make |
| Production/assembly line structure | Workshop | Flow |
| Standardization of processes | Low | High |
| Linkage of processes | Low | High |
| Operating material flexibility | Special | Multi-functional |
| Equipment operating time | Temporary | Series operation |
| Warehouse concept | No stock | Large stock |
| Quality control | Low | High |
| Design stability | Freeze | Continuous improvement |
| Additional worker training | Low | High |
| Integration of society and politics | Low | High |
| Manufacturing technology | Conventional | Innovative |
| Production network | World factory | Local for local |
| Scalability of technology | Low | High |
| Number of expatriates (ramp up) | Low | High |
| Additional incentives | Low | High |

## 2.2   Method

This model is used to analyze the impact of different scenarios for the configuration of production or assembly. For this purpose, we define the reference and test scenarios first. Then, the respective input parameters of the scenarios are simulated. Finally, the results are compared and an overall recommendation is derived.

## 3    Application Case and Testing

Before defining the test scenarios, the use case is described. We simulate a strategy of a small series electric vehicle manufacturer, who plans to enter the markets in various countries in sub-Saharan Africa. The standard product is an all-wheel electric vehicle with a simple structure (ladder frame, folded exterior and interior). The vehicle is to be manufactured economically with locally added value. In addition to local final assembly of the purchased components, local production of the interior and exterior is also planned. This use case is derived from the aCar Mobility project[2].

### 3.1    Reference Scenario

To examine the effects of the test scenarios, we first define a reference scenario. As reference, we simulate a local production site in Kenya, as Kenya is the second largest economy in East Africa with a strong focus on agricultural value creation. For this application as well as the following cases, we use the input values summarized in Table 2.

The production location in Kenya has a low degree of automation and therefore prefer manual work tasks (Fig. 3). The production system is primarily a pull system, with a medium depth of added value. The resources should be flexible and planned for smaller series in terms of operating time. For the warehouse concept, low stock levels should be planned, as delivery times are not prioritized high. Quality controls have to be planned due to employee qualification, despite low quality priority. To secure a stable ramp up, the number of expatriates during this phase should be high. Training for new staff needs to be planned and motivation needs to be ensured in order to avoid fluctuation. It is crucial to involve local authorities in the planning process.

### 3.2    Scenario 1: Changing Competitive Priorities

With the development of the markets, customer priorities change. In India, for example, customer behavior is currently changing from purely cost-driven vehicle purchasing decisions to price-performance decisions [22]. As a result of this change, new automobile manufacturers such as Geely and BYD have emerged in India and China [23]. A successful product which was developed to satisfy this change of priorities is the Renault KWID in India [18,23].

For this reason, *Scenario 1* examines different customer priorities and their impact on the configuration of assembly or production. *Priorities 1* examines

---

[2] www.http://www.acar.tum.de/en/home/.

**Table 2.** Input parameters of test scenarios

| Input parameter | Kenya (Reference) | Priorities 1 | Priorities 2 | Country 1 | Country 2 | Multiple products 1 | Multiple products 2 |
|---|---|---|---|---|---|---|---|
| Volume | 1 | 1 | 1 | 5 | 10 | 1 | 1 |
| Market entry strategy | 5 | 5 | 5 | 5 | 5 | 5 | 5 |
| Qualification level of employees | 1 | 1 | 1 | 4 | 8 | 1 | 1 |
| Importance of economies of scale | 1 | 1 | 1 | 1 | 1 | 1 | 1 |
| Importance of delivery time | 1 | 3 | 5 | 1 | 1 | 1 | 1 |
| Importance of product cost | 10 | 7 | 5 | 10 | 10 | 6 | 4 |
| Importance of quality | 1 | 3 | 5 | 1 | 1 | 1 | 1 |
| Importance of flexibility | 3 | 3 | 3 | 3 | 3 | 5 | 7 |
| Importance of innovation | 1 | 3 | 5 | 1 | 1 | 3 | 6 |
| Importance of environmentaly friendly products | 10 | 10 | 10 | 10 | 10 | 10 | 10 |
| Importance of committed social responsibility | 10 | 10 | 10 | 10 | 10 | 10 | 10 |
| Type of product | 7 | 7 | 7 | 7 | 7 | 5 | 3 |
| Product complexity | 2 | 2 | 2 | 2 | 2 | 5 | 8 |
| Labor cost | 3 | 3 | 3 | 4 | 8 | 3 | 3 |
| Market demand | 6 | 6 | 6 | 6 | 6 | 6 | 6 |
| Supplier market competition | 2 | 2 | 2 | 5 | 8 | 2 | 2 |
| Intra corporate resources | 3 | 3 | 3 | 3 | 3 | 3 | 3 |
| Availability of local workforce | 10 | 10 | 10 | 8 | 6 | 10 | 10 |
| Fluctuation of local workforce | 10 | 10 | 10 | 8 | 6 | 10 | 10 |
| Energy supply | 2 | 2 | 2 | 5 | 8 | 2 | 2 |

the change from pure cost-motivation of the customer to more quality and faster delivery times. With *Priorities 2* we simulate customers who rate delivery time, quality and costs as equal. The results of this and the following simulations are summarized in Fig. 3.

The simulation of *Scenario 1* and its variations demonstrates that, compared to the reference configuration, the scalability requirements have to be adjusted. Furthermore, the requirements on the warehouse concept increase and the production system changes to pull processes. Quality controls, on the other hand, increase in both cases compared to the reference scenario and decrease in the case of equal evaluation of competitive priorities. Unaffected by customer priorities are for example the depth of added value, operating material (operating time and flexibility), training, integration and the number of expatriates to be calculated.

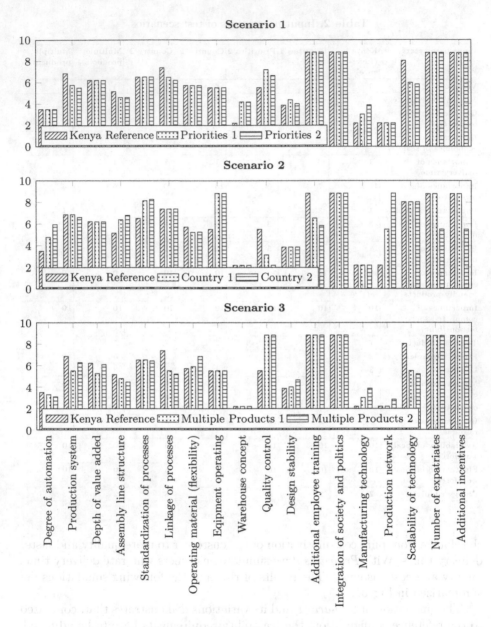

**Fig. 3.** Results of the test scenarios

## 3.3    Scenario 2: Different Countries

The effort to adapt a production to new locations is economically challenging, even with constant product requirements [2]. But, differences between the
African countries are significant, as they differ in market size and thus in the

possible sales volume [4]. The extent to which suppliers are available in the African countries and which quantities and quality can be supplied differs. Concurrently, the number of deliverable components is decisive for their costs [4]. Further, essential for the strategic decision of Nigerian manufacturers, is the availability of a skilled workforce [9].

Therefore, in *Scenario 2* the extent to which these planned production volumes impacts the production configuration is tested. Additional differences are the availability and qualification of skilled employees and their fluctuation. Furthermore, the influence of the availability of local suppliers is investigated.

The scenario of different countries has a decisive influence on the degree of automation, the operating time of the equipment and the production network. In addition, the necessary expenses for employee training are reduced. Furthermore, in the case of *Country 2* the number of expatriates and the necessary incentives are lower than in the reference scenario Kenya.

### 3.4 Scenario 3: Multiple Products

Especially in new markets, customer behavior is constantly changing [9]. The desire for individualization arises with the change in customer requirements. This makes adapted, customer-specific vehicles more important [22]. For this reason, it can be of interest to vehicle manufacturers to assemble several vehicle variants on site. Concurrently, the product complexity and the location flexibility increase [2].

The multiple products scenario examines the impact of multiple products at one site. Therefore, requirements in flexibility and innovation is increasing, while the cost focus is decreasing. Concurrently, we assume a rise in product complexity.

The simulation indicates the change of the linkage of the processes and increasing quality controls. The focus of scalability and assembly line design decreases with the trend towards fewer flow processes. Regardless of the product variants, for example, the training requirements, integration of local authorities and the number of expatriates required do not change.

## 4  Discussion

The findings of the simulation can be summarized for the application case as follows. The degree of automation is mainly altered by the change in volume for various countries. In contrast, the production system hardly changes and must be planned as a pull system. In this system, the processes should be largely linked. If the number of variants increases and customer priorities are uncertain, processes should be decoupled in order to ensure an assembly flow. This assembly line design is sensitive to the input changes in *Scenarios 2* and *3*. In *Scenario 2* the assembly line design should be planned more as a flow system, while in *Scenario 3* there is a slight shift towards workshop assembly.

The depth of value added is dependent on the number of variants and, largely independent of the volume, but mainly with a focus on purchased components. In all scenarios, the operating material flexibility is largely constant in the middle range, while the equipment operating time requirement increases significantly in *Scenario 2*. As a result, it can be concluded that the operating time of the equipment is to be configured as a long-term series equipment from a medium planned volume. The orientation of the production network also depends on the volume. If local demand increases, the strategy changes from a network production to a local for local production site.

The required employee training only decreases with increasing qualification in *Scenario 2*, but must still be planned as intensive. In contrast, the integration of local authorities is indispensable in each of the tested scenarios. With increasing customer demands (*Scenarios 1* and *3*) regarding quality, the assembly and manufacturing technology should be selected in order to meet these requirements. The number of expatriates required for a problem-free ramp-up decreases as the qualifications of the available employees increase (*Scenario 2*).

Figure 4 summarizes the variance of results.

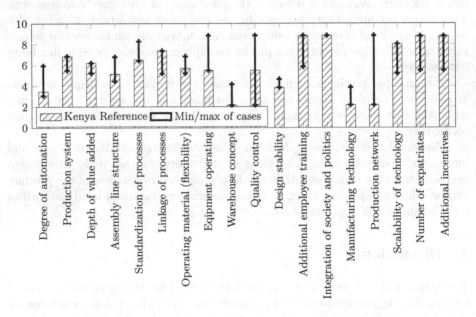

**Fig. 4.** Comparison of the extrema of the test scenarios

For this reason, a sensitivity analysis is carried out to describe the effect of individual parameter changes on the overall system. This allows a separation into important and less important factors [20, 26] For this purpose we use Morris analysis, which uses a grid search to identify these dependencies [19]. The method developed by Morris varies each time step by one factor and outputs two sensitivity measures [26]. Using this method, the highest average value is based on the qualification level of the employees on the motivation through external stimuli. The second largest average value is based on the size of the plant. This correlation also shows the highest standard deviation. Overall, the qualification level of the employees represents three of the four largest mean values. Other high combinations of mean value and standard deviation are, for example, market demand on the production system, the type of product on the flexibility of operating resources, the volume and market entry strategy on the duration of use of operating resources, the importance of innovation on production technology, and the importance of product costs on quality control and design stability.

## 5   Conclusion

The simulation results indicate that a factory must be planned individually for each location. Surrounding conditions such as political conditions, sales volumes, purchasing power, educational level and others influence the production strategy. This is illustrated by the variance of the simulation results. Including these boundary conditions in strategic planning reevaluates trade-offs in the decision-making process.

In conclusion, the influence of changing competitive priorities on the design of a production can be considered as low. Within this change, the corresponding manufacturing technologies and quality concepts should take into account the increased demands on quality and the storage concept should guarantee reliable delivery times. The differences between countries are mainly reflected in the degree of automation, which changes with the available employees, wages and sales volume. However, the degree of automation can still be classified as medium. This simulation reveals that employee qualifications affect the quality processes, despite constant customer demands for quality. Product diversification influences above all quality and technological decisions.

Nevertheless, commonalities can be determined for the application cases. The depth of value added (of the vehicle manufacturer) tends to be low, the focus is on supplier components. Although delivery difficulties are to be expected due to the challenging infrastructure, the warehouse must nevertheless be designed for low inventory levels. Only when customer requirements for delivery times increase does the inventory need to be increased. In general, expatriates to support the ramp-up are essential for a successful start, as is the integration of the population and government. In addition, if several locations are planned, the focus should be on a training concept that allows to reduce the training effort. Due to the lack of experience in the manufacturing industry, these should be provided for most employees. Changing demand and customer requirements also affect the demand for the flexibility of a location. Thus, this should be taken into account in the early planning stages.

In this paper, we demonstrate, that different scenarios can be simulated in the early stages of assembly and production strategy planning by using fuzzy logic model. This allows for future scenarios to be tested and the focus of further configuration planning to be adjusted. Since this model was designed using the expert rules for the application case, the rule base needs to be adapted for further applications. In future research, this model could be extended by a monetary evaluation in order to estimate the additional financial expenditure required for different strategies.

# References

1. Identification of critical success factors for emerging market entry planning processes in the automotive industry. In: 2015 IEEE International Conference on Industrial Engineering and Engineering Management (IEEM) (2015). https://doi.org/10.1109/IEEM.2015.7385936
2. Abele, E., Meyer, T., Näher, U., Strube, G., Sykes, R.: Global Production: A Handbook for Strategy and Implementation. Springer, Heidelberg (2008). https://doi.org/10.1007/978-3-540-71653-2
3. Adamy, J., Kempf, R.: Regularity and chaos in recurrent fuzzy systems. Fuzzy Sets Syst. **140**(2), 259–284 (2003). https://doi.org/10.1016/S0165-0114(02)00526-2
4. Black, A., Makundi, B., McLennan, T.: Africa's automotive industry: potential and challenges. In: Working paper Series 282 (2017). https://www.afdb.org/fileadmin/uploads/afdb/Documents/Publications/WPS_No_282_Africa's_Automotive_Industry_Potential_and_Challenges.pdf
5. Brönner, M., Ampofo, J., Fries, D., Lienkamp, M.: Configuration parameters within electric vehicle production strategies in Sub-Saharan Africa - The 'ACAR Mobility' Case (2019). 7th CIRP Global Web Conference, Towards Shifted Production Value Stream Patterns Inference of Data, Models and Technology (in press)
6. Brönner, M., Hagenauer, M.S., Lienkamp, M.: Sustainability - recommendations for an electric vehicle manufacturing in Sub-Saharan Africa. In: Procedia CIRP 81, pp. 1148–1153 (2019). 52nd CIRP Conference on Manufacturing Systems (CMS), Ljubljana, Slovenia, 12–14 June 2019. https://doi.org/10.1016/j.procir.2019.03.283
7. Brönner, M., Wolff, S., Jovanovic, J., Keuthen, K., Lienkamp, M.: Production strategy development: simulation of dependencies using recurrent fuzzy systems. Systems **8**(1), 1 (2020). https://doi.org/10.3390/systems8010001
8. Dombrowski, U., Weckenborg, S., Rennemann, T.: Ckd auf basis von produktionsprinzipien. Integrierte Prozesse kontinuierlich verbessern. Industrie Manag. **4**, 36–40 (2010)
9. Ehie, I., Muogboh, O.: Analysis of manufacturing strategy in developing countries: a sample survey of Nigerian manufacturers. J. Manuf. Technol. Manag. **27**(2), 234–260 (2016). https://doi.org/10.1108/JMTM-07-2014-0094
10. Gorrini, V., Bersini, H.: Recurrent fuzzy systems. In: Proceedings of 1994 IEEE 3rd International Fuzzy Systems Conference, pp. 193–198. IEEE, 26–29 June 1994. https://doi.org/10.1109/FUZZY.1994.343687
11. Hayes, R.H., Wheelwright, S.C.: Restoring Our Competitive Edge: Competing Through Manufacturing, Printing edn, vol. 13. Wiley, New York (1984)
12. Hill, A., Hill, T.: Manufacturing Operations Strategy, 3rd edn. Palgrave Macmillan, Basingstoke(2009)
13. Jia, G.Z., Bai, M.: An approach for manufacturing strategy development based on fuzzy-QFD. Comput. Industr. Eng. **60**(3), 445–454 (2011). https://doi.org/10.1016/j.cie.2010.07.003

14. Lee, K.H. (ed.): First Course on Fuzzy Theory and Applications. AISC, vol. 27. Springer, Heidelberg (2005). https://doi.org/10.1007/3-540-32366-X
15. Leontiade, J.: Planning strategy for world markets. Long Range Plan. **3**(2), 40–45 (1970). https://doi.org/10.1016/0024-6301(70)90007-5
16. Mefford, R.N., Bruun, P.: Transferring world class production to developing countries: a strategic model. Int. J. Prod. Econ. **56–57**, 433–450 (1998). https://doi.org/10.1016/S0925-5273(98)00085-1
17. Michaeli, P.: Methodik zur Entwicklung von Produktionsstrategien am Beispiel der Triebwerksindustrie, Forschungsberichte IWB, vol. 328. Utz, Herbert, München (2017)
18. Midler, C., Jullien, B., Lung, Y.: Rethinking Innovation and Design for Emerging Markets: Inside the Renault KWID Project. CRC Press, Boca Raton (2017)
19. Morris, M.D.: Factorial sampling plans for preliminary computational experiments. Technometrics **33**(2), 161 (1991). https://doi.org/10.2307/1269043
20. Saltelli, A.: Sensitivity Analysis in Practice: A Guide to Assessing Scientific Models, Reprint Wiley, Hoboken (2007)
21. Sampath, P.G.: Industrial development for Africa: trade, technology and the role of the state. Afr. J. Sci. Technol. Innov. Dev. **6**(5), 439–453 (2014). https://doi.org/10.1080/20421338.2014.970438
22. Saranga, H., George, R., Beine, J., Arnold, U.: Resource configurations, product development capability, and competitive advantage: an empirical analysis of their evolution. J. Bus. Res. **85**, 32 – 50 (2018). https://doi.org/10.1016/j.jbusres.2017.11.045
23. Saranga, H., Schotter, A.P., Mudambi, R.: The double helix effect: catch-up and local-foreign co-evolution in the Indian and Chinese automotive industries. Int. Bus. Rev. **28**(5) (2019). https://doi.org/10.1016/j.ibusrev.2018.03.010
24. Skinner, W.: Manufacturing - missing link in corporate strategy (1969). https://hbr.org/1969/05/manufacturing-missing-link-in-corporate-strategy
25. Slack, N., Chambers, S., Johnston, R.: Operations Management. Pearson Education, London (2016)
26. Spielmann, V.: Unsicherheits-und sensivitätsanalysen von kompartiment-modellen und computer-voxel-phantomen für interne strahlenexposition der patienten durch radiopharmazeutika in der nuklearmedizin (2017)
27. Stahl, B., et al.: Modeling cyclic interactions within a production environment using transition adaptive recurrent fuzzy systems. In: IFAC Proceedings Volumes, vol. 46, no. 9, pp. 1979–1984 (2013). https://doi.org/10.3182/20130619-3-RU-3018.00534
28. United Nations General Assembly: Transforming our world: the 2030 agenda for sustainable development: A/res/70/1 (2015). https://www.unfpa.org/sites/default/files/resource-pdf/Resolution_A_RES_70_1_EN.pdf
29. Velasquez, M., Hester, P.T.: An analysis of multi-criteria decision making methods. Int. J. Oper. Res. **10**(2), 56–66 (2013)

# Material Science and Engineering

# Preparation and Characterization of Shoe Polish from Cactus (*Opuntia Ficus Indica*) Powder and Charcoal Powder

Tessema Derbe[1]([✉]), Tassew Alemayehu[2], and Dinku Senbeta[3]

[1] Department of Chemistry, Wachemo University, P.O. Box: 677, Hossana, Ethiopia
[2] Department of Chemistry, Adigrat University, P.O. Box 50, Adigrat, Ethiopia
[3] Department of Biology, Adigrat University, P.O. Box 50, Adigrat, Ethiopia

**Abstract.** Shoe polish is a type of waxy paste that used in gloss, rub resistance, fading resistance and dust resistance by providing a thin film on the surfactants of the shoe. In this research work, new shoe polish was prepared from 5-g cactus powder and 5-g charcoal powder in 75:25 mL wax to olive oil ratio in the presence of denatured alcohol and benzene at an optimized procedure. Furthermore, the prepared shoe polish was subjected to different quality analysis parameters such as viscosity, density, melting point, reflexive index, pH value, ash content, conductivity and moisture content with the comparison of purchased shoe polish (Kiwi). As the results of these tested parameters indicated, the prepared shoe polish has shown a comparable result with purchased shoe polish (Kiwi). The functional group of the prepared shoe polish was also identified using FTIR analysis and the FTIR peaks confirmed the presence of a long-chain ester group in the shoe polish. Besides, the practical use of the prepared shoe polish and purchased shoe polish were examined by polishing some selected leather shoes with these shoe polishes; the prepared shoe polish exhibited a very good gloss, dust adsorption resistance, fading resistance and rub resistance just after three wearing days. Thus, the prepared shoe polish is fulfilled the quality parameters and replaceable the commercially available shoe polish on the market.

**Keywords:** Bee wax · Cactus · Kiwi · Olive oil · Shoe

## 1 Introduction

Shoe polish could be either liquid or paste which is used to restore the original luster and smoothness of the polished surface [1, 2]. It cleans and prevents deteriorating as well as fading of the polished surface due to the presence of surface tension forces between shoe surface and applied polish [3]. It used to shine waterproof, restore the appearance of leather footwear and keep the shoes looking new [4, 5]. Shoe polish not only used for footwear but also applied to all leather materials such as handbags, carpets, leather jackets, belts, and others to clean, protect and shine the adsorbents [2, 6].

Shoe polish shows many unique properties [7]. It forms a basis for decorative and protective properties on polished shoe by forming gloss [8]. It prevents precipitation

© ICST Institute for Computer Sciences, Social Informatics and Telecommunications Engineering 2021
Published by Springer Nature Switzerland AG 2021. All Rights Reserved
M. A. Delele et al. (Eds.): ICAST 2020, LNICST 385, pp. 411–422, 2021.
https://doi.org/10.1007/978-3-030-80618-7_28

of dust particles on the surface of polished shoe through quick-drying [9]. It serves as a barrier between polished surface and moisture-filled environment through formation of thin-layer. The polish must look smart and nice after polishing has applied on the adsorbents by forming decorative [2, 3].

Inline the above unique properties of shoe polish, polishing of the shoes daily is necessary for overall grooming. Furthermore, researchers and psychologists had proved that a person who polishes his/her shoes feels happy, confident, encouraged and cheerful. On the other hand, a person who didn't polish his/her shoes well feels defensive, guilty, withered and shy. In this regard, most people have tried to polish their shoes using soap and pure water. Nonetheless, this activity is not advisable since it evaporated very fast and the shine disappeared within a short time. This handy shine is not good for shoes since low wax content of soap and pure water polishes do not nourish durability for the shoe rather it damages at all [2, 6].

Based on the above circumstance facing in, researchers synthesized and characterized the shoe polishes using chemical sources [2, 6, 10]. Nevertheless, synthetic shoe polishes contain toxic colorant agents like aniline that causes sores, neurological retards, allergic reactions and cancer [2, 6]. Hence, replacing of this toxic chemical via environmentally friendly and nontoxic natural ingredient like cactus powder is too crucial. Therefore, this research was designed to prepare and characterize shoe polish from Cactus (*opuntia Ficus indica*) powder and charcoal powder.

## 2  Methodology

### 2.1  Chemicals and Solvents

Cactus powder, stearic acid, benzene, isopropanol, house- Made ethanol (known as 'areke' in Amharic language), olive oil, bee wax, charcoal powder, and paraffin wax were used during the entire work.

### 2.2  Sampling Method

Mature fresh leaves of cactus (*opuntia Ficus indica*) were collected from the side of Adigrat city. The collected leaves were washed with water and were put in clean polyethylene plastic bags. The bee wax sample was purchased from Diemma Honey and Bee Development Privet Factory at Adigrat city. The paraffin wax was obtained from Adigrat electronic supermarket. The charcoal was also purchased from the Meda Agame market, Adigrat city.

### 2.3  Preparation of Wax

The collected 15-g of paraffin wax was melted with stearic acid at high temperature to give a fine solution. 10 mL of white spirit was added and stirred for 15 min. The mixture was allowed to cool and was poured into a container for storage. In another way, the purchased bee wax was weighted and sliced into smaller parts using a knife. 10-g of sliced bee wax was added into double boiling water and waited till the wax was melted completely. A few drops of olive oils were added to prevent the re-solidification of the melted wax; finally stored for preparation of shoe polish.

## 2.4 Preparation of Shoe Polish

The first step in the preparation of shoe polish is melting of wax with the highest melting point in an electric heater (70 °C). Following this, 75 mL of the melted wax and 25 mL of olive oil were added into the reactor. Into this, five gram of cactus powder was added. The mixture was heated around 80 °C with continuously stirring. Into this heated emulsion mixture, 5–10 mL distilled water was added and the mixture was heated around 85 °C. Five gram of charcoal powder was added into the reactor by continually stirring and heated for half an hour. The mixed mass was poured into the shoe polish containers (Cans). In each cans, a few drops of odour agent (benzene) were added. And then a few drops of denature alcohol alternatively 'Areke' was added to prevent pathogens. The polish was allowed to stay undisturbed for a night and was stored for further analysis.

As shown in Fig. 1, new shoe polish was prepared from environmental available resources mainly cactus powder alternatively cactus jell (moisturizing agent), charcoal powder (colorant agent), waxes (adhesive agents) in the presence of smelling agent (benzene) and denatured alcohol (anti-pathogens and drying agent).

## 2.5 Instruments and Equipment

Double boiling reactor, hydrometer, Fourier Transform-Infrared Spectroscopy (FTIR) (model: IR prestige 21), Blenders, Preservers, Cans, Viscometer, pH meter (model: APF/Qcto/025), Conductivity meter (Model: Seven compact 5230), Refractometer (model: DR6200/02), Precision Balance (model: Cap124s), Vacuum Oven (model: Ov Ao31xx35), Muffle Furnace (model: P330MB2) were used throughout this work.

## 2.6 Quality Analysis of Shoe Polish

Most of the quality analysis and characterization of the prepared shoe polish were conducted at Addis's pharmaceutical factory PLC at Adigrat; northern Ethiopia.

### pH Value
By taking 20 mL of dissolved prepared and purchased shoe polishes, the acidity or alkalinity was determined using a digital pH meter (model APF/Qcto/025) [11, 12].

### Melting Point
The prepared shoe polish was loaded into the sealed melting point apparatus [13]. And the sample was heated and the temperature range was recorded from the initial phase change to final complete phase changes. And then the average result was taken.

### Density
The density of the prepared shoe as well as the purchased shoe polish (Kiwi) were determined using a hydrometer.

### Moisture Contents
The moisture content of the prepared shoe polish and the purchased shoe polish (Kiwi)

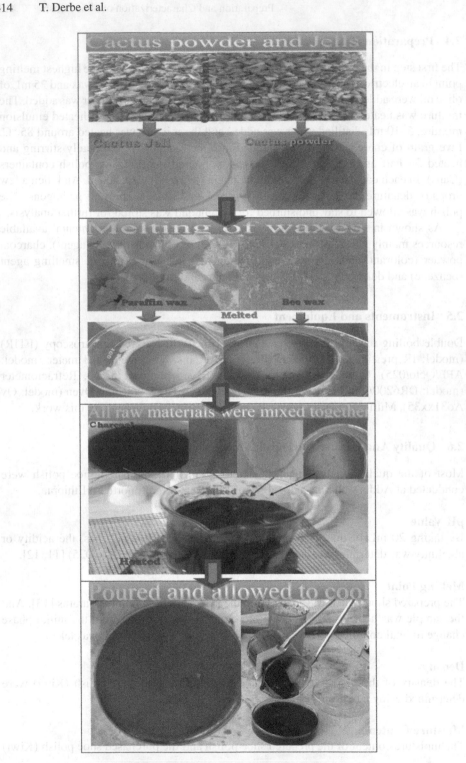

**Fig. 1.** Steps of shoe polish preparation

were determined using a vacuum oven (model: Ov Ao31xx35) and the percentage of moisture content was calculated by using equation [14, 15].

$$Moister = \frac{W_3 - W_1}{W_2 - W_3} X\,100\%$$  (1)

Where W3 = weight of sample and watch glass; W1 = weight of the sample after drying and W2 = weight of the sample before drying.

## Ash Content

The ash content of both prepared shoe polish and the purchased shoe polish (Kiwi) were determined using the Muffle furnace (model: P330MB2) [15]. 1g of both the prepared and the purchased shoe polishes were weighted using precision balance (model: Cap124s). The sample was put into 2 g crucible and the crucible was ignited in the muffle furnace for 3 h and then the crucible was placed in the desiccators. Finally, the sample was cooled to room temperature and weighed. The percentage of moisture content (ASh) was calculated using the equation [16, 17].

$$(\%ASh = 100\% - \%Loss\ of\ ignition)$$  (2)

$$\%Loss\ of\ Ignition = \frac{W_3 - W_2}{W_2 - W_3} x100\%$$  (3)

Where W3 = weight of the sample after drying; W2 = weight of sample and crucible and W1 = weight of a sample after drying.

## Viscosity Test

Both the purchased shoe (Kiwi) and the prepared shoe polishes were dissolved by iso-propanol in a separate beaker. 5 mL dissolved solution was taken and the viscosity was determined in a standard jacketed pipette viscometer in the unit of poise [12]. The instrument was equipped to hold the shoe polish solution at an approximately constant temperature. The temperature of the shoe polish was 25 °C and the determination was made as soon as the solution has uniformly reached the required temperature.

# 3  Result and Discussion

## 3.1  Quality Analysis of Shoe Polish

The prepared shoe polish was subjected to different quality analysis parameters such as viscosity, density, melting point, reflexive index, pH value, ash content, conductivity and moisture content. The analyzed parameters were compared with purchased shoe polish (kiwi) that purchased from the supermarket as shown below (Fig. 2 and Table 1).

## pH Value

The pH value of both the prepared shoe polish (sample) and the purchased shoe polish (Kiwi) were measured using a digital pH meter (model APF/Qcto/025) with standard method [13]. As shown in Figure 2 and Table 1, the prepared shoe polish has a pH value of 4.46 ± 0.43 which is relatively basic than purchased shoe polish (Kiwi) which has 4.25 ± 0.50 pH value. This indicates that the prepared shoe polish is less scratching the polished shoes or any other absorbent surfaces than the purchased shoe polish (Kiwi); the acidic adsorbate highly affect the durability and shining of the shoe surface.

## Melting Point

The melting point of the prepared shoe polish and purchased shoe polish (Kiwi) was measured using a thermometer. The melting points of the prepared shoe polish shows 45–48 °C which is ranged. This ranged melting point indicates the presence of different constituents in the prepared shoe polish such as bee wax, cactus powder, olive oil, denatured alcohol, and charcoal powder. Similarly, the purchased shoe polish (Kiwi) shows 42–45 °C which is not sharp. Both the prepared and the purchased shoe polishes show variable melting points; this might be the presence of different constituents in the shoe polishes.

## Viscosity

The viscosity was determined in a purchased jacketed pipette viscometer in the absolute unit of "centipoise (CP)". This method is commonly referred to as the Brookfield method [13, 18] and is described in ASTM D2983. The viscosity of this prepared shoe polish was 3.87 ± 0.09 which is comparable with purchased (Kiwi) 3.15 ± 0.37 at 25 °C as shown in Fig. 2 and Table 1. The flow of the prepared and purchased shoe polishes is almost similar and corresponds to each other.

## Moisture Content

The moisture content of the prepared shoe polish and the purchased shoe polish (Kiwi) were evaluated using a vacuum oven (model: Ov Ao31xx35). As it has seen in Fig. 2 and Table 1, the moisture content of prepared shoe polish is 58.24% ± 0.23 which is less moisturized than the purchased shoe polish (Kiwi) 69.38% ± 0.82. This might be due to the presence absorbent nature of charcoal powder which cases strong hydration in the prepared shoe polish. The other provable reasons might be due to drying time; uneven drying and over-drying of the prepared shoe polish in the drying oven [15].

## Ash Content

The ash content of the prepared shoe polish and the purchased shoe polish (Kiwi) were determined using Muffle furnace (model: P330MB2) as stated in the method section. The percentage ash content of the prepared shoe polish is 1.1% ± 0.11 while the purchased shoe polish (Kiwi) is 0.3% ± 0.05 (Fig. 2 and Table 1). As the result revealed that the prepared shoe polish contains a relatively large number of inorganic constituents than the purchased shoe polish (Kiwi). This might be due to the presence of porous charcoal powder.in prepared shoe polish; this leads high inorganic residue during ignition.

## Refractive Index

The reflexive indexes of both the prepared and the purchased shoe polishes were analyzed using the Refractometer (model: DR6200/02). As the results revealed that 1.37692 ± 0.20 for purchased shoe polish (Wiki) and 1.37687 ± 0.03 for the prepared shoe polish which is almost equivalent (Fig. 2 and Table 1). Thus, they are comparable in the shining and attractiveness on the shoe after polishing has applied.

The parameters analyzed above can affecting the quality of shoe polishes. Shoe polishes having high moisture content, high reflexive index, and less conductive are more acceptable and shining as well as water repellent. This leads to quick dryable and dust repellent after polishing has been applied on the shoe surface [6, 4].

**Table 1.** Comparisons of prepared shoe polish with purchased shoe polish (Kiwi)

| Parameters | Purchased (Kiwi) | Prepared |
|---|---|---|
| pH | 4.25 ± 0.50 | 4.46 ± 0.43 |
| Density (g/mL) | 0.67 ± .094 | 0.84 ± 0.067 |
| Viscosity (cp) | 3.15 ± 0.37 | 3.87 ± 0.09 |
| Melting point (°C) | 42 ± 0.23 | 48 ± 0.56 |
| Moisture content (%) | 69.38 ± 0.82 | 58.24 ± 0.23 |
| Reflexive index | 1.37692 ± 0.20 | 1.37687 ± 0.03 |
| Conductivity($\mu$S/cm) | 0.443 ± 0.11 | 0.623 ± 0.10 |
| Ash content (%) | 0.3 ± 0.05 | 1.1 ± 0.11 |

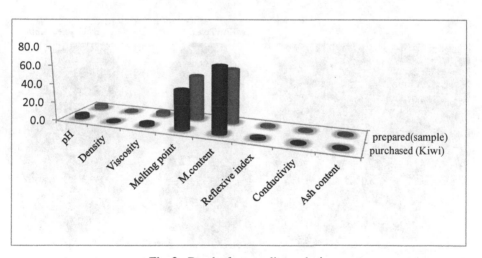

**Fig. 2.** Results from quality analysis

**Practical Test of Shoe Polish**

By considering the comparable results that had obtained above, some shoes have polished via prepared shoe polish and purchased shoe polish, and then some practical tests of the polished shoe such as rub resistance [6], fading resistance [2], and dust adsorption resistance were tested just after three days wearing time. The level of dust adsorption resistance was examined by simple observation and compared with the purchased shoe polish (Kiwi). The polished shoe was also rubbed with glass paper to test the rub resistance; the change was examined and compared with the purchased shoe polish. The polished shoe was also tested for fading resistance by exposing it to the sun for 24 h and the change is observed (Table 2).

**Table 2.** Some practical use of shoe polishes

| Tests | Prepared shoe polish | Purchased shoe polish |
|-------|---------------------|----------------------|
| Drying time | Moderate | Very good |
| Rub resistance | Very good | Moderate |
| Fading resistance | Very good | Very good |
| Gloss/shining | Very good | Very good |

The prepared shoe polish exhibited a very good gloss, dust absorption resistance, fading resistance and rub resistance on the applied leather shoes as shown below Fig. 3 in fact, the prepared shoe polish can be also applied to all leather materials such as handbags, carpets, belts, wallets and related surface adsorbents.

**Fig. 3.** Practical test of shoe polish

## 3.2 FTIR Spectroscopy Analysis

**Purchased Shoe Polish (Kiwi)**
As shown in Fig. 4, the peak at 2952.02 cm$^{-1}$ indicates the presence of alkyl C-H stretching since most absorption peaks of C-H single bonds occur in the range of 2960–2850 cm$^{-1}$ [19]. The peak at 1735.93 cm$^{-1}$ indicates the presence of carbon-oxygen double bonds which is a carbonyl group (C = O stretching) [18]. The sharp peaks at 1371.17cm$^{-1}$ and 1462.04 cm$^{-1}$ indicate the presence of =C-H stretch since the most = C-H absorptions [18] occur in the range of 1480–1350 cm$^{-1}$. The peak at 1170.79 cm$^{-1}$ indicates the presence of C-O stretching; the most carbon to oxygen single bonds (C-O) absorption occurs in the range of 1300–1000 cm$^{-1}$ [19]. Thus, the FTIR absorption peaks and analysis possibly confirm the presence of the ester group in the purchased shoe polish Kiwi (Fig. 4).

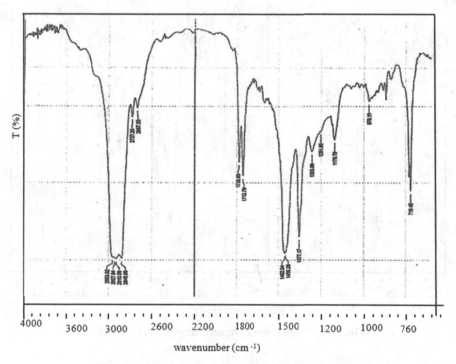

**Fig. 4.** FTIR analysis of purchased shoe polish (Kiwi)

**Prepared Shoe Polish (Sample)**
As shown in Fig. 5 below, the peak at 2953.02 cm$^{-1}$ indicates the presence of alkyl C-H stretching since 2960–2850 cm$^{-1}$ is the most absorption range for C-H single bonds stretching [18]. The peak at 1749.44 cm$^{-1}$ indicates the presence of a carbonyl group (C = O stretch). A sharp peak at 1448.54 cm$^{-1}$ indicates the presence of =C-H bending

since the most =C-H absorption [19] occurs in the range of 1480–1350 cm$^{-1}$. The peak at 1170 cm$^{-1}$ also indicates the presence of C-O stretch; the most C-O absorption occurs in the range of 1300–1000 cm$^{-1}$ [19]. Thus, the FTIR absorption peaks and analysis confirms the presence of a long chain aliphatic ester group in the prepared shoe polish (Fig. 5). This might be due to the presence of bee wax which has a long chain of alcohols; it is a secondary alcohol which can be dehydrogenated to ketone or carboxylic groups and further to ester groups during preparation of this shoe polish from bee wax and cactus powder as listed in methodology section [5, 9]. The presence of ester group in this prepared shoe polish being serving an additive in terms of lubrication and resistance of hydrolysis [8, 9]. Furthermore, the presence of ester group in shoe polish plays an important role in quick-drying and good smell during and after polishing of the shoe.

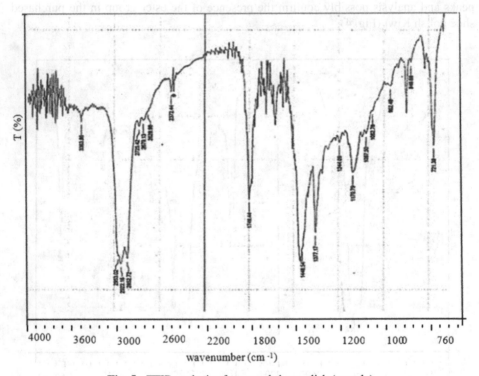

**Fig. 5.** FTIR analysis of prepared shoe polish (sample)

## 4   Conclusion

In conclusion, the shoe polish was prepared from cactus powder and charcoal powder in the presence of bee wax and olive oils at small scale. The prepared shoe polish was tested with different quality parameters such as viscosity, density, melting point, reflexive index, pH value, ash content, conductivity and moisture content, and compared with purchased shoe polish (Kiwi). The tested parameters indicated that the prepared shoe polish is comparable with purchased shoe polish (Wiki). The functional group of both the prepared and purchased shoe polishes were identified using FTIR analysis and the peaks confirmed that the presence of long chain ester groups in both prepared and purchased shoe polishes. Furthermore, the practical use of prepared shoes polish and purchased shoe polish (Kiwi) such as rub resistance, fade resistance, dust adsorption, and drying time were tested through polishing of some selected leather shoes; resulted in the prepared shoe polish is very good and analogous with the purchased shoe polish (Kiwi). Thus, the work suggests the stakeholders to prepare and to use this shoe polish since it meets all the tested quality parameters and practical parameters in the comparison of well-known shoe polish (Kiwi). Moreover, the prepared shoe polish is low cost and eco-friendly which can replace the market available shoe polishes and create a new promising job opportunity for the community.

**Acknowledgement.** The researchers want to express their thanks to the College of Natural and Computational Science, Department of Chemistry, Adigrat University, and Addis pharmaceutical factory PLC, Adigrat; for giving laboratory facilities. Researchers extend their appreciation to Adigrat University for giving funding opportunities in terms of financial.

**Competing of Interests.** The authors declare that they have no competing of interests.

# References

1. Gumel, S.M., Umar, A.: Comparative study of performance of shoe polishes formulated from polyethylene and carbon black. Chem. Search J. **2**, 42–44 (2011)
2. Byrne, L.M., Cole, M.D., Milligan, F., Thorpe, J.W.: Shoe polish stains on fabric: a comparison of different shoe polish types. Forens. Sci. **34**, 53–60 (2011)
3. Kamalu, C., Osoka, E.: Formulation of black leather shoe polish from hydrogenated castor oil. J. Res. Eng. **2**, 50–54 (2005)
4. Muehlethaler, C., Ng, K., Gueissaz, L., Leona, M., Lombardi, J.R.: Raman and SERS characterization of solvent dyes: an example of shoe polishes analysis. Sci. Dir. 1–14 (2016)
5. Rajaram, J., Rajnikanth, B., Gnanamani, A.: Preparation, characterization and application of leather particulate-polymer composites. J. Polym. Environ. **17**, 181–186 (2009)
6. Ameh, C.U.: Thermophysical properties of shoe polish manufactured from pure water sachet. Assump. Univ. J. Technol. **15**, 129–132 (1994)
7. Milligan, F., Cole, M.D., Thorpe, J.W.: The examination of black wax shoe polish stains after ageing and weatherin. J. Forens. Sci. Soc. **34**, 23–27 (1994)
8. Taiwo, A.F., Ameh, C.U.: Preliminary studies on properties of shoe polish formulated from wax produced from waste water sachets. Int. J. Eng. Innov. Technol. **2**, 120–123 (2013)
9. Oviawe, A.P., Ukponmwan, D.O., Okei, F.C.: Physiochemical studies of neutralizeres and their effects on stability of cosmetic emolusion. Trend Appl. Sci. Res. **4**, 327–333 (2006)
10. Cole, M.D., Thorpe, J.W.: Analysis of black shoe polish marks on clothing. J. Forensic Sci. Soc. **32**, 237–244 (1992)
11. Tarun, J., Susan, J., Suria, J., Susan, V.J., Criton, S.: Evaluation of pH of bathing soaps and shampoos for skin and hair care. Indian J. Dermatol. **59**, 442–444 (2014)
12. Manjula, D., Jenita, J.J.L., Premakumari, K.B., Shanaz, B.: Formulation and evaluation of flaxseed hair gel: a natural hair tamer. Int. J. Res. Pharm. Chem. **8**, 487–490 (2018)

13. Pixton, S.W., Warburton, S.: Determination of moisture content and equilibrium relative humidity of dried fruit-sultanas. J. Stored Prod. Res. **8**, 263–270 (1973)
14. Bouraoui, M., Richard, P., Fichtali, J.: A review of moisture content determination in foods using microwave oven drying. Food Res. Int. **26**, 49–51 (1993)
15. Borsaru, M., Charbucinski, J., Eisler, P.L., Youl, S.F.: Determination of ash content in coal by borehole logging in dry bore-holes using gamma-gamma methods. Geoexploration **23**, 503–518 (1985). Elsevier Science Publishers
16. Liu, J., Pan, Y., Yao, C., Wang, H., Cao, X., Xue, S.: Determination of ash content and con-comitant acquisition of cell compositions in microalgae via thermogravimetric (TG) analysis. Sci. Dir. **12**, 149–155 (2015)
17. Chamberlain, J., Gibbs, J.E., Gebbie, H.A.: Determination of refractive index spectra by Fourier spectrometry. Infrared Phys. **9**, 185–209 (1969)
18. Amir, M.: Application of Fourier transforms infrared (FTIR) spectroscopy for the identification of wheat varieties. J. Food Sci. Technol. **50**, 1018–1023 (2013)
19. Li, W., et al.: Green waxes, adhesives and lubricants. Rev. Philos. Trans. Roy. Soc. **368**, 4869–4890 (2010)

# Graphitic Carbon Nitride with Extraordinary Photocatalytic Activity Under Visible Light Irradiation

Gebrehiwot Gebreslassie[1](✉) (iD), Pankaj Bharali[2], Gebremedhin Gebremariam[3],
Assefa Sergawie[1], and Esayas Alemayehu[4]

[1] Department of Industrial Chemistry, College of Applied Sciences, Addis Ababa Science and
Technology University, 16417 Addis Ababa, Ethiopia
`gebrehiwot.gebreslassie@aastu.edu.et`
[2] Department of Chemical Sciences, Tezpur University, Napaam, Tezpur 784028, India
[3] Department Chemistry, College of Natural and Computational Sciences, Mekelle University,
231 Mekelle, Ethiopia
[4] Faculty of Civil and Environmental Engineering, Jimma University, 378 Jimma, Ethiopia

**Abstract.** Catalytic activities of graphitic carbon nitride ($g\text{-}C_3N_4$) are restricted
thanks to inadequate visible light absorption and high rate electron–hole recombination. In this work, we synthesized porous $g\text{-}C_3N_4$ using polycondensation
process. Structural and physico-chemical characteristics of the prepared $g\text{-}C_3N_4$
materials were studied via XRD, DRS, PL, FTIR, Raman spectroscopy, SEM, BET
and CHN elemental analyzer. The prepared samples exhibited surprising catalytic
activity for the photo-oxidation of rhodamine-B (RhB) in visible light irradiation.
From the fabricated $g\text{-}C_3N_4$ materials, the $g\text{-}C_3N_4$-550 showed photodegradation
efficiency of 100% towards the RhB pollutant in water within 30 min. No appreciable decrease of the photocatalytic efficiency of $g\text{-}C_3N_4$ was observed up to five
consecutive cycles, confirming the synthesized $g\text{-}C_3N_4$ was highly stable. Thus,
this work gave a simple process for large scale production of highly visible light
responsive and stable $g\text{-}C_3N_4$ materials used for environmental remediation.

**Keywords:** Graphitic carbon nitride · Porous materials · Photodegradation

## 1 Introduction

Recently, photocatalysts have been broadly intended for the elimination of carbon-
based pollutants from aqueous media in addition to from the atmosphere owing to their
properties of transforming light energy to chemical energy for facilitating decompose
various toxic contaminants [1, 2]. All-embracing efforts have been made by numerous researchers on the way to prepare semiconductor materials for the photocatalytic
response with an suitable band gap, counting metal-containing oxide, oxynitride and
sulfide [3, 4]. Nevertheless, the search to unconventional photocatalyst with a relatively
simple fabrication process and extraordinary activity is still underway [5].. Graphitic

carbon nitride (g-C$_3$N$_4$) is one of the new class photocatalyst under exploration [6]. Triazine units (C$_3$N$_3$) and heptazine (C$_6$N$_7$) form the basic building blocks of g-C$_3$N$_4$ and are linked by planar amino groups to form prolonged networks. Tri-s-triazine rings are more stable building blocks of g-C$_3$N$_4$ than triazine [7]. The g-C$_3$N$_4$ has a 2D structure like to that of graphene and has chemical compositions of C, N, and with H atoms as impurity [8, 9]. Fascinating properties of g-C$_3$N$_4$ include proper band gap to absorb visible light, exceptional two-dimensional structure, nontoxic nature, biocompatibility, superb thermal stability, tunable electronic structure and simple process for mass production. As a result, g-C$_3$N$_4$ is currently in focus to its applications as a metal-free catalyst for photodegradation of different organic CO$_2$ reduction and fuel cells [10, 11]. The use of g-C$_3$N$_4$ has been restricted by its many drawbacks such as: (a) low surface area, (b) high rate of electron–hole recombination, and (c) medium band gap (2.7 eV, absorbs visible light less than 465 nm) [12].

Unlike photocatalysts containing metal that need expensive precursors for synthesis, the g-C$_3$N$_4$ can be prepared via thermal condensation of nitrogen-rich organic chemicals i.e. thiourea, melamine, cyanamide, urea, and dicyandiamide [8, 13]. Of these, cyanamide is costly and volatile, and its derivatives (melamine or dicyanamide) has low solubility. Thus, preparation of g-C$_3$N$_4$ using cyanamide and melamine precursors, is either costly or tough to operate [14]. For this reason, inexpensive and non-toxic urea is preferred source for g-C$_3$N$_4$ fabrication for targeted structural and photcatalytic properties [15]. For instance, Lee et al. [16] had prepared meso-porous C$_3$N$_4$ from urea by a thermal polymerization procedure using silica nano-spheres as template and used for phenol removal. Recently, Fang et al. [17] reported g-C$_3$N$_4$ synthesized by directly heating urea for 2 h at 600 °C.

Herein, we report simple preparation of porous g-C$_3$N$_4$ through direct pyrolysis of the urea precursor at temperature alternating from 470 °C to 550 °C. This energy-saving process takes just 1 h to complete (Fig. 1). Several authors had reported that the temperature requirement of the g-C$_3$N$_4$ synthesis from urea were from 400 °C to 650 °C while the reaction time varied from 2 h to 4 h [14, 18, 19]. Undoubtedly, the

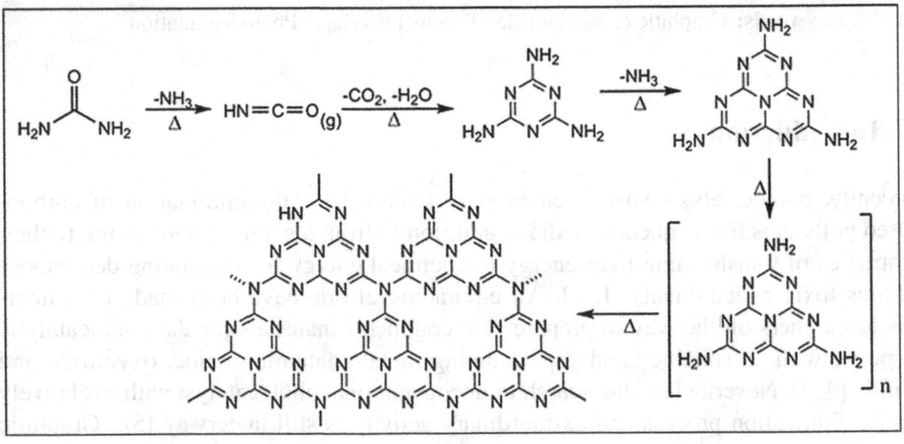

Fig. 1. Reaction diagram of the prepared g-C$_3$N$_4$ materials.

energy consumption was higher in those efforts. Following Fig. 1, the g-$C_3N_4$ obtained from heating of urea at 550 °C revealed extraordinary photodegradation towards RhB pollutant in aqueous solution. Notably, complete degradation of RhB ($C_o = 10$ mg $L^{-1}$) was achieved within 30 min in visible light treatment, using only 55 mg dose of catalyst. This can be attributed to the narrower band gap (2.5 eV), lower photogenerated electron-hole recombination rate and enhanced adsorption capability of the photocatalyst (due to large specific surface area 114.5 $m^2$ $g^{-1}$). Such a simple preparation method combined with superior photodegradation performance and confirmed long-term photostability may accelerate the use of g-$C_3N_4$ in practical environmental remediation protocols.

## 2  Experimental Part

### 2.1  Materials

Urea ($CH_4N_2O$, 99.5%), and nitric acid ($HNO_3$, 68%) were bought from Merck, India. Rhodamine B (RhB, 99.9%) was got from Rankem Fine Chemicals Pvt. Ltd., India. All the materials were used as obtained.

### 2.2  Preparation of g-$C_3N_4$

Graphitic carbon was prepared by poly-condensation of low-priced urea. In brief, optimized weight of urea (6 g) was kept in a ceramic crucible with cover and placed in a furnace and heated up to three different temperatures (470, 510 and 550 °C) for 1h. Thereafter, the crucible was permitted to cool to ambient temperature naturally. Then, products were ground into powder and washed with 0.1 M $HNO_3$ and distilled water. Finally, the products were dried at 60 °C and labeled as g-$C_3N_4$-470, g-$C_3N_4$-510 and g-$C_3N_4$-550 (tagged with the temperatures of preparation, for easy identification). The average weight of the g-$C_3N_4$ powders obtained from 6 g urea at 470, 510 and 550 °C were 0.535, 0.420 and 0.367 g, respectively.

### 2.3  Characterization Techniques

The crystallinity and orientation of the samples were studied using a D8 Focus Powder diffractometer (Bruker AXS, Germany). DRS results were noted using a UV–V is spectrometer (UV-2450, Shimadzu, Japan) within 200 nm to 900 nm. PL spectra were recorded using a Fluorescence spectrometer (LS 55, PerkinElmer) in 365 nm. IR spectra were recorded in FT-IR mode using a Frontier MIRFIR spectrometer (PerkinElmer), scanned over 400 to 4000 $cm^{-1}$ in transmission mode. The Raman results were measured using Raman spectrometer (EZRRAMAN-N, EnwareOptronics, USA). Measurement was conducted in excitation laser 785 nm, NA0.3, spot size 3 μm, exposure time 10 s, pixel resolution 1.45 $cm-1$ per pixel, spectral region 3000–100 $cm^{-1}$. The elemental analysis was performed using a CHN Analyzer (2400 Series 2, PerkinElmer, USA). Nitrogen adsorption-desorption isotherm measurements were performed on a surface area analyzer (NOVA 1000E, Quantachrome). Before analysis, the sample was pretreated by degassing for 4 h at 150 °C to remove any adsorbed species. The specific surface area of the photocatalyst was calculated from $N_2$ adsorption-desorption isotherm measurements using BET equation. Poresize distribution was got from the desorption branches through Barrett–Joyner–Halenda (BJH) method. Scanning electron microscopy was performed using a SEM (JSM 6390LV, JEOL, JAPAN). Elemental mapping was performed using JOEL JSM 6390LV equipped with EDS.

## 2.4  Photocatalytic Test

The photocatalytic ability of the g-$C_3N_4$ was assessed by RhB degradation in visible light irradiation. Normally, 55 mg of g-$C_3N_4$ photocatalyst was suspended in RhB solution (100 mL, 10 mg $L^{-1}$). The solution was stirred for 30 min in dark to confirm the formation of an adsorption-desorption equilibrium. Then, the mixture solution was illuminated with 10 W LED lamp (Havells, India). 3 mL aliquots were withdrawn at given time intervals of irradiation. The absorbance of the solution was measured using the UV–Vis spectrophotometer (Carry 60 UV-Vis, Agilent) at 554 nm corresponding to the maximum absorption wavelength of RhB after separated the photocatalyst using a centrifuge. The effects of amount catalyst, dye concentration, type of catalyst and catalyst stability were studied. The degradation efficiency was calculated using Eq. 1. Here, De is the degradation efficiency; $C_o$ is the initial concentration of the RhB before irradiation and C represents the concentration of RhB after irradiation at time t. C and $C_o$ values of RhB solution was calculated using Beer–Lambert ($A = \varepsilon bC$). First, we have been prepared calibration curve using RhB standard solutions and $\varepsilon$ was obtained from the slope of A vs. C calibration curve. Then, the initial concentration ($C_o$) and concentration at a time t (C) of RhB were calculated using $C_o = A_o/\varepsilon b$ and $C = A/\varepsilon b$, respectively.

$$D_e = \frac{C_o - C}{C_o} \times 100 \qquad (1)$$

## 2.5  Detection of the Reactive Species

Main active species were detected by active species trapping experiments. The detection process was same with the photocatalysis experiment. formic acid (FA, $h^+$ scavenger)p-benzoquinone (BQ, $\bullet O_2^-$ radical scavenger), and 2-propanol (2-PA, $\bullet OH$ radical scavenger) were added into photocatalytic system before the photocatalytic reaction happened in visible light illumination and the concentration of the scavengers was controlled to be fixed at 5 mol $L^{-1}$.

## 2.6  Recyclability and Stability Study

Recyclability and stability study were conducted by recovering and reused the g-$C_3N_4$ after photocatalysis reaction completed. Typically, after first photodegradation reaction completed, the g-$C_3N_4$ photocatalyst was recovered by centrifugation (5,000 rpm, 10 min) in an 800B centrifuge. Then, recovered g-$C_3N_4$ was washed 3 times by distilled water to remove adsorbed RhB and dried for 30 min. Thereafter, the dried g-$C_3N_4$ was reused for next photocatalytic reaction cycle. The stability study was conducted at optimum conditions; irradiation time (30 min), dosage of photocatalyst (55 mg) and concentration of RhB (10 mg $L^{-1}$).

# 3    Results and Discussion

## 3.1    Material Characterization

**Crystal Structure, Surface Texture and Microstructure Analysis.** In order to identify the factors affecting the main reaction of converting urea into g-$C_3N_4$, we examined the effect of covered or opened crucible and temperature effect. In covered crucible yellow colored solid was produced at a temperature above 400 °C as shown in Fig. 2a. Alternatively, when the crucible was open, no solid was produced and all the urea got decomposed into gaseous products. This is because in the opened crucible all the gases quickly escaped from the system without further reaction and condensation. Formation of $NH_{3(g)}$ at low temperatures during the pyrolysis reaction inside the covered crucible is essential as self-supporting atmosphere to initiate the polymerization of the intermediates into g-$C_3N_4$. The release of the $H_2O_{(g)}$ and $CO_{2(g)}$ during further condensation at high temperature contributed to exorcize the oxygen from the g-$C_3N_4$ product [20, 21]. In the covered crucible, the g-$C_3N_4$ solid could be produced up to annealing temperature of 550 °C (Fig. 2b). No solid was observed at temperatures greater than 550 °C, which showed that the g-$C_3N_4$ was completely decomposed during pyrolysis, even in a covered crucible, if the reaction temperature exceeded 550 °C.

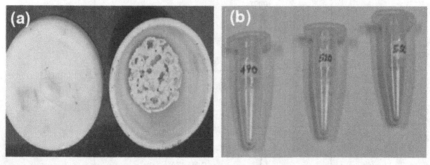

**Fig. 2.**    (a) Photo of g-$C_3N_4$ prepared in a covered crucible with 6 g urea at 550 °C. (b) Photo of g-$C_3N_4$ samples prepared at 470, 510 and 550 °C, respectively.

Afterward, we studied the temperature effect on the structure of g-$C_3N_4$. Figure 3 demonstrates the XRD results of g-$C_3N_4$-470, g-$C_3N_4$-510 and g-$C_3N_4$-550 samples. The small angle peaks at $2\theta = 12.65°$ attributed to (100) planes of g-$C_3N_4$ and conforming to in-planar ordering of the nitrogen-linked tri-s-triazine units. For the two samples, g-$C_3N_4$-470 and g-$C_3N_4$-510, the 12.65° peak did not show any shift. On the other hand, the XRD peak at 12.65° shifted to 12.74° for the g-$C_3N_4$-550 sample (prepared at 550 °C). The strongest peak at $2\theta = 27.26°$ of the g-$C_3N_4$-470 sample shifted to 27.37° (in g-$C_3N_4$-510) and to 27.52° (in g-$C_3N_4$-550). These observations bring out the influence of preparation temperature on the XRD patterns. The interlayer stacking of the (002) planes in the g-$C_3N_4$ is strongly affected when the preparation temperature varied from 470 to 510 to 550 °C, causing the position shift of the strongest XRD peak. The slight shift of the (100) and (002) diffraction peaks toward higher diffraction angles is associated to increased sample preparation temperature. It was reported by Praus et al. [22] that the increasing condensation temperature improved the polycondensation of g-C$_3$N$_4$. The crystallite size (D$_{hkl}$) were calculated by Scherrer's equation (Eq. 2).

$$D_{hkl} = \frac{\kappa \lambda}{\beta \cos \theta} \tag{2}$$

$$d_{hkl} = \frac{\lambda}{2 \sin \theta} \tag{3}$$

Where, $\lambda$ is the wavelength of the X-rays ($\lambda = 0.154$ nm), $\beta$ is the broadening diffraction peak at its FWHM, $\theta$ is the angle of diffraction and $\kappa$ is a constant (i.e. 0.94). The average g-C$_3$N$_4$ crystallite sizes were estimated from the highest diffraction peaks (002) plane as D$_{002}$ = 5.92 nm, D$_{002}$ = 6.20 nm and D$_{002}$ = 7.13 nm, corresponding to g-C$_3$N$_4$-470, g-C$_3$N$_4$-510 and g-C$_3$N$_4$-550 samples, respectively. The interlayer distance (d$_{khl}$) was calculated by using Eq. 3. The calculated interlayer spacing of the (002) planes was d$_{002}$ = 0.32 nm and that of the (100) planes was d$_{100}$ = 0.69 nm; these values are identical to g-C$_3$N$_4$-470, g-C$_3$N$_4$-510 and g-C$_3$N$_4$-550 samples. These results are in accordance with those previously reported results [22].

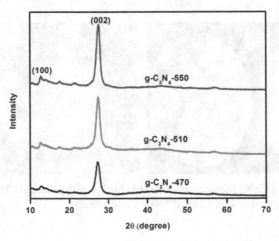

**Fig. 3.** XRD patterns for g-C$_3$N$_4$-470, g-C$_3$N$_4$-510 and g-C$_3$N$_4$-550 materials.

FT-IR analysis was accustomed characterize the molecular group in the prepared g-C$_3$N$_4$ samples. As presented in Fig. 4, the broad absorption bands at 3086, 3155 and 3252 cm$^{-1}$ point out the presence of N−H and −NH$_2$ bonds. The distinctive skeletal vibrations of nitrogen hetero-cycles which match to stretching vibrations of C = N and C−N appear in between 1640 to 1235 cm$^{-1}$. The intensive bands at 1461, 1572, 1537 and 1640 cm$^{-1}$ are ascribed to stretching of C = N. In addition, the stretching vibrations of C−N are characterized by the bands at 1235, 1316 and 1407 cm$^{-1}$ [23]. In addition, the band at 812 cm$^{-1}$ is recognized to heptazine units breathing mode, which found the energetically favored structure entities of g-C$_3$N$_4$ [24].

Furthermore, the surface textural properties of the g-$C_3N_4$ photocatalyst were characterized using nitrogen adsorption–desorption experiments. Specific surface area of g-$C_3N_4$-550 was calculated using BET method while the porosity property of the samples was calculated using the BJH method. As presented in Fig. 5a, the g-$C_3N_4$-550 possesses characteristic of mesoporous materials. The surface area of the g-$C_3N_4$-550 sample was found to be 114.5 $m^2$ $g^{-1}$. The BJH pore-size distribution graph (Fig. 5b) expresses that the g-$C_3N_4$–550 has pore-size distribution between 1 and 130 nm with pore diameter and pore volume of 3.98 nm and 1.43 $m^3$ $g^{-1}$, respectively.

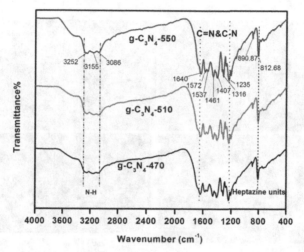

**Fig. 4.** The FTIR Spectra of the g-$C_3N_4$-470, g-$C_3N_4$-510 and g-$C_3N_4$-550 samples.

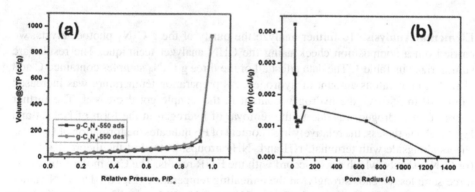

**Fig. 5.** (a) $N_2$ adsorption–desorption isotherm of the g-$C_3N_4$-550 sample. (b) The BJH pore-size distribution of the g-$C_3N_4$-550 sample.

Surface morphology and textural properties of the photocatalyst was investigated using a SEM. SEM images of g-$C_3N_4$-550 sample with different morphologies are represented in Fig. 6a–c. The agglomerated sheet like g-$C_3N_4$-550 was clearly observed.

EDS examination of g-$C_3N_4$ showed that the g-$C_3N_4$ consists of only C and N, which indicating that there is no impurity in the prepared g-$C_3N_4$ samples (Fig. 6d).

The Raman spectra results of g-$C_3N_4$ products were displayed in Fig. 7. As shown in Fig. 7, the Raman peaks at 712 and 1380 $cm^{-1}$ are the features of typical g-$C_3N_4$. The spectral region of 1250–400 $cm^{-1}$ is representative of skeletal vibrations of nitrogen based aromatic rings [25]. On the other hand, the common peak at 970 $cm^{-1}$ confirmed skeletal vibration of heptazine. The strongest peak at 1380 $cm^{-1}$, observed in all the three samples, approves with the conversion urea to g-$C_3N_4$. The distinctive peak of g-$C_3N_4$ at about 712 $cm^{-1}$ was also observed in all samples [26].

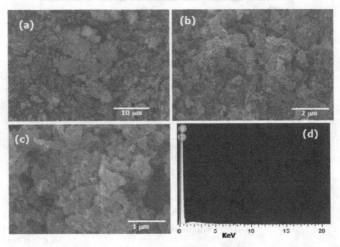

**Fig. 6.** (a-c) SEM images of the g-$C_3N_4$-550 sample at different magnifications. (d) The EDS spectrum for elemental compositions of the g-$C_3N_4$-550 sample.

**Elemental Analysis.** To further analyze the purity of the g-$C_3N_4$ photocatalysts, we carried out a composition check using the CHN analyzer technique. The results are summarized in Table 1. The data attest all of the three g-$C_3N_4$ samples contained C and N with a momentous amount of hydrogen. As preparation temperature was increased from 470 to 550 °C, the hydrogen content in the sample got decreased. The further decrease of hydrogen was due to the removal of hydrogen in the form of $NH_{3(g)}$ and $H_2O_{(g)}$. Nonetheless, the relatively high content of $H_2$ indicates the formation of $C_aN_bH_c$ sheets alongside with terminal -NH and -$NH_2$ groups, instead of the theoretical $C_3N_4$ (or $C_6N_8$) sheets, which are in accord with the FTIR results. The C:N molar ratio in the three samples depends strongly on the annealing temperature (Fig. 8). The C:N values of g-$C_3N_4$-470, g-$C_3N_4$-510 and g-$C_3N_4$-550 are 0.65, 0.67 and 0.72, respectively. This indicates that as the annealing temperature increases the C:N ratio increases (due to the removal of hydrogen from the sample). The maximal C:N ratio was found to be 0.72, which is almost proximate to the theoretical value of 0.75 for g-$C_3N_4$ [27]. Due to incomplete condensation of the urea, even at a temperature of 550 °C, the formula of g-$C_{6.3}N_{8.7}H_{2.5}$ (or, g-$C_{2.5}N_{3.5}H$) is more realistic than the g-$C_3N_4$. Regardless of this, graphitic carbon nitride is denoted as g-$C_3N_4$ for the sake of clarity and simplicity.

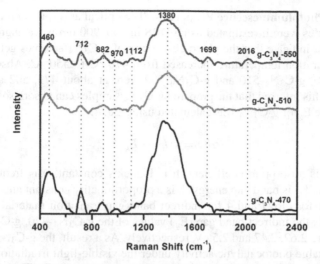

**Fig. 7.** The Raman spectra of the three g-C₃N₄ samples.

**Table 1.** CHN analysis and empirical composition of the g-C$_a$N$_b$H$_c$ samples.

| Catalyst | C (wt%) | N (wt%) | H (wt%) | a | b | c |
|---|---|---|---|---|---|---|
| g-C₃N₄-470 | 33.97 | 64.02 | 2.01 | 5.66 | 9.14 | 3.98 |
| g-C₃N₄-510 | 35.51 | 63.51 | 1.70 | 6.01 | 8.95 | 3.53 |
| g-C₃N₄-550 | 37.65 | 61.07 | 1.28 | 6.27 | 8.72 | 2.53 |

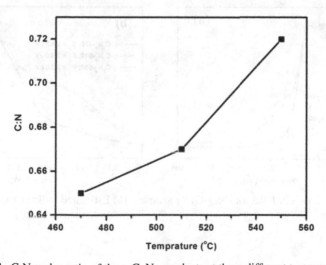

**Fig. 8.** C:N molar ratio of the g-C₃N₄ products at three different temperatures.

**Optical and Photoluminescence Properties.** The optical absorption properties of the prepared samples were investigated using DRS in 200–900 nm wavelength range. The plots in Fig. 9a indicate that the photo-absorption of g-C₃N₄ samples gets red-shifted after the preparation temperature increased from 470 °C to 550 °C. Absorption edge of g-C₃N₄-470, g-C₃N₄-510 and g-C₃N₄-550 were at about 473, 502 and 498 nm, respectively. This inferred that the prepared g-C₃N₄ samples can absorb solar energy up to 503 nm. The $E_g$ of g-C₃N₄ was calculated using Eq. 4.

$$\alpha h\nu = k(h\nu - E_g)^{\frac{n}{2}} \tag{4}$$

Where, $\alpha$ is absorption coefficient, h is Planck's constant, $\nu$ is frequency of the absorbing light, $E_g$ is band gap energy; k is a proportionality constant and n is constant number (i.e. 1 for direct and 4 for indirect band gap transition material). As can be seen in Fig. 9b, the indirect band gap ($E_g$) values of the g-C₃N₄-470, g-C₃N₄-510 and g-C₃N₄-550 are 2.62, 2.47 and 2.5 eV, respectively. As a result, the g-C₃N₄ is expected to own remarkable photocatalytic activity under the visible-light irradiation.

The recombination rate of $e^-/h^+$ pairs was examined from PL emission intensity. Figure 10 displays the PL spectra of the g-C₃N₄-470, g-C₃N₄-510 and g-C₃N₄-550 photocatalysts. The spectrum intensity for the g-C₃N₄-550 is lower than the corresponding g-C₃N₄-470 and g-C₃N₄-510 samples. One may understand that the recombination rate of $e^-/h^+$ pairs in g-C₃N₄-550 is lower than that of the g-C₃N₄-470 and g-C₃N₄-510 materials. Hence, the photogenerated charge carriers in the g-C₃N₄-550 could have longer lifetime and they can freely participate in the photocatalytic reactions. Thus, based on the obtained results from DRS and the PL, the g-C₃N₄-550 sample is predictable to exhibit catalytic enhancement than the g-C₃N₄-470 and g-C₃N₄-510.

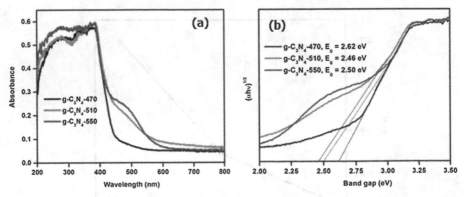

**Fig. 9.** (a) The UV–VIS DRS for the g-C₃N₄ samples. (b) Estimated indirect band gaps of the g-C₃N₄ samples.

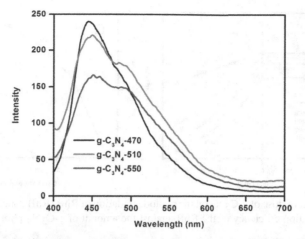

**Fig. 10.** The photoluminescence (PL) spectra of the g-C3N4-470, g-C3N4-510 and g-C3N4-550 samples at an excitation wavelength of 365 nm.

## 3.2 Photocatalytic Activity

**Effect of Catalyst Dosage.** Investigation were accomplished by changing the amounts of g-C$_3$N$_4$-550 photocatalyst, keeping the RhB concentration fixed (10 mg L$^{-1}$, 100 mL). During adsorption-desorption experiment in dark place, decreasing in dye concentration was observed as the catalyst loading increases from 15 to 65 mg in the first 15 min (Fig. 11a). This is due to the amount of the dye adsorbed on the catalyst increases as the catalyst dose increases (i.e. active sites increase). Then, the dye concentration is constant during 15 to 30 min and adsorption-desorption equilibrium reached 30 min. After visible light irradiation, the rate of reaction increased when the amount of g-C$_3$N$_4$ photocatalyst increased from 15 to 55 mg, beyond which it showed a reduction (Fig. 11a). As displayed in Fig. 11b, the efficiency of RhB degradation increased as the catalyst dose increased. The enhanced degradation may be attributed to an increase of the number of active sites of catalyst which accelerates the photoreaction. The lower rate (when the catalyst dosage is increased beyond 55 mg) is due to the scattering of the light in the reaction mixture, which delays light penetration through the solution containing the RhB. Similarly, with a higher dose of catalyst, the possibility of deactivation of the activated molecules by the ground state molecules (through collision) is very high and this causes a decreases in the rate of reaction [28]. Thus, the optimum dosage of the g-C$_3$N$_4$ photocatalyst for the RhB degradation reaction may be taken as 55 mg.

**Effect of Initial RhB Concentration.** The influence of initial concentration of RhB on degradation rate was investigated by varying RhB concentration from 5 mg L$^{-1}$ to 15 mg L$^{-1}$, keeping amount of g-C$_3$N$_4$-550 (55 mg per 100 mL of the reaction mixture) constant. The degradation efficiency was almost the same even if the RhB concentration increased from 5 to 10 mg L$^{-1}$. However, it is decreased after RhB concentration increased beyond 10 mg L$^{-1}$ (Table 2). Thus, the optimum RhB concentration in the reaction mixture was taken as 10 mg L$^{-1}$.

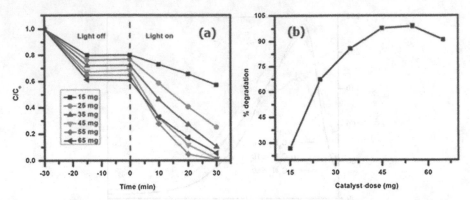

**Fig. 11.** (a) Effect of dose of g-$C_3N_4$ on the photodegradation of RhB (RhB concentration: 10 mg $L^{-1}$) (b) Degradation efficiency of the RhB against the amount of g-$C_3N_4$ photocatalyst within 30 min.

**Table 2.** Effect of RhB concentration on the degradation rate.

| g-$C_3N_4$ dose (mg) | RhB concentration (mg $L^{-1}$) | RhB volume (mL) | %degradation | Time (min) |
|---|---|---|---|---|
| 55 | 5 | 100 | 100% | 30 |
| 55 | 10 | 100 | 100% | 30 |
| 55 | 15 | 100 | 64% | 30 |

**Effect of Catalyst Type.** The photocatalytic performance of the g-$C_3N_4$ catalysts prepared at different condensation temperatures (g-$C_3N_4$-470, g-$C_3N_4$-510 and g-$C_3N_4$-550) were tried for the degradation of RhB solution under visible light irradiation. Adsorption-desorption experiments were conducted as displayed in Fig. 12. As shown in Fig. 12, the adsorption RhB into g-$C_3N_4$-550 increases up to 15 min. However, the amount of RhB adsorbed on g-$C_3N_4$-550 within 15 min was the same as that of adsorbed within 30 min. This indicates the adsorption-desorption equilibrium was obtained within 30 min in a dark place and almost 35% of the RhB was adsorbed on g-$C_3N_4$-550 before the visible light illumination (see inset in Fig. 12). RhB degradation of was not observed without the catalyst under illumination of visible light (Fig. 13a). Further, in the being of the g-$C_3N_4$ catalyst, no degradation was observed in dark. This confirmed that the degradation of RhB takes place only when g-$C_3N_4$ photocatalyst is present under light illumination. Figure 13 b-d shows a series of plots of absorbance versus wavelength for degradation of RhB over g-$C_3N_4$-470, g-$C_3N_4$-510 and g-$C_3N_4$-550 samples. As shown, as the irradiation time increased, absorption intensity decreased. But, shift of RhB absorption peak (centered at 554 nm) was not observed. The efficiency of RhB pollutant degradation over the g-$C_3N_4$-470, g-$C_3N_4$-510 and g-$C_3N_4$-550 were found to be 93.9%, 97.3%, and 100%, respectively. Furthermore, the photocatalytic performance of our g-$C_3N_4$-550 photocatalyst was compared with previously reported urea derived g-$C_3N_4$. The present procedure showed an excellent photocatalytic performance which required just 30 min for the complete degradation of RhB pollutant ($10 \text{ mg L}^{-1}$) under visible light irradiation (10 W LED lamp) using 55 mg of g-$C_3N_4$.

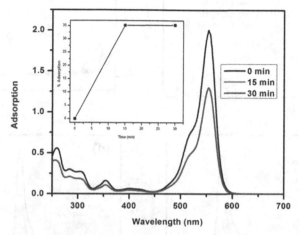

**Fig. 12.** Change of optical absorption of the RhB solution during adsorption in the dark. The inset shows the %Adsorption of RhB on the g-$C_3N_4$–550 in the dark.

According to the Langmuir–Hinshelwood model, the photodegradation of RhB over g-$C_3N_4$ photocatalysts fits pseudo-first-order kinetics (Eq. 5).

$$\ln\left(\frac{C_o}{C}\right) = k_{ap}t \tag{5}$$

Where, $C_o$ is the initial RhB concentration before irradiation and C is the RhB concentration at time t after irradiation and $k_{ap}$ is the apparent pseudo-first-order rate constant. It can be seen in Fig. 14, that there exists a linear relationship between $\ln(C_o/C)$ and t, confirming that the photodegradation reaction is definitely a pseudo-first-order reaction. The $k_{ap}$ of the photodegradation reaction were estimated to be 0.0933, 0.1223 and 0.1539 $\text{min}^{-1}$ for g-$C_3N_4$-470, g-$C_3N_4$-510 and g-$C_3N_4$-550, respectively. The highest value of $k_{ap}$ further proven that the g-$C_3N_4$-550 had the highest photocatalytic activity amongst the three catalysts. The superior activity was related to more visible-light absorption, large surface area and better suppression of electron-hole pairs from their undesirable recombination.

**Proposed Photocatalytic Degradation Mechanism.** The mechanism of photocatalytic activity of g-$C_3N_4$ was proposed from Active species trapping experiments. As presented in Fig. 15, the addition of benzoquinone (BQ, $\bullet O_2$ scavenger) acutely reduce the RhB oxidation on g-$C_3N_4$, suggesting that $\bullet O_2^-$ are the main reactive species for the photooxidation of RhB. As an alternative, no obvious depression in photocatalytic efficiency was observed in the presence of 2-propanol (2-PA, $\bullet$OH scavenger), suggesting that $\bullet$OH does not participate as active species on the photocatalytic degradation process. The large improvement of the RhB photooxidation after addition of formic acid

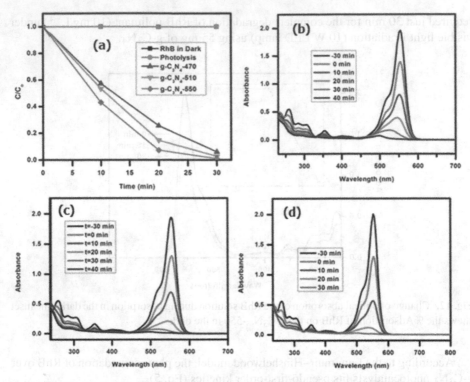

**Fig. 13.** (a) Photo-degradation of RhB over the g-$C_3N_4$-470, g-$C_3N_4$–510 and g-$C_3N_4$-550 photocatalysts. RhB degradation under irradiation of visible light (b) g-$C_3N_4$-470 (c) g-$C_3N_4$-510, and (d) g-$C_3N_4$-550. [RhB] = 10 mg L$^{-1}$, RhB volume 100 mL and catalyst dosage = 55 mg of reaction mixture.

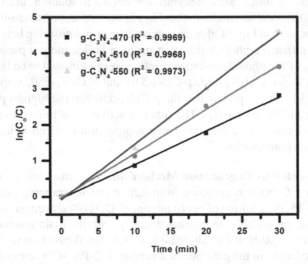

**Fig. 14.** Pseudo first-order kinetics of the RhB photodegradation reaction by the three photocatalysts.

(FA, $h^+$ scavenger) more confirmed that RhB is mainly oxidized by $\cdot O_2^-$, because the trapping of hole by FA would produce more photogenerated electrons by preventing the recombination of photogenerated $e^-/h^+$ pairs. The VB and CB positions for g-$C_3N_4$ are calculated and the values are +1.23 and −1.27 eV, respectively. The VB of g-$C_3N_4$ (+1.23 eV vs. NHE) is more negative compared with the $E°$ of OH $-/\cdot$OH (+1.99 eV vs. NHE) [29, 30]. That's why, the photogenerated $h^+$ in VB of g-$C_3N_4$ cannot oxidize the $OH^-$ to produce $\cdot$OH radicals. The CB of g-$C_3N_4$ (−1.27 eV vs. NHE) is more negative than the $E°$ of $O_2/\cdot O_2^-$ (−0.33 eV vs. NHE) and hence can reduce the adsorbed oxygen molecules so as to yield $\cdot O_2$ that can oxidize the RhB [31]. This agrees the $\cdot O_2^-$ is the main reactive species take part in the photocatalytic RhB degradation of in the presence of g-$C_3N_4$. Therefore, based on the obtained results from the active species trapping experiment, and VB and CB edge positions of g-$C_3N_4$ photocatalyst, the photocatalytic reaction mechanism of RhB over g-$C_3N_4$ shown in Fig. 16 was proposed.

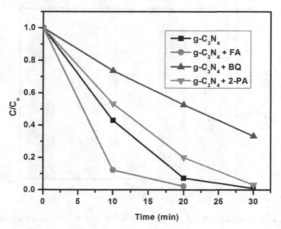

**Fig. 15.** Photocatalytic performance of g-$C_3N_4$ for the RhB degradation in the presence of different scavengers (BQ, 2-PA and FA).

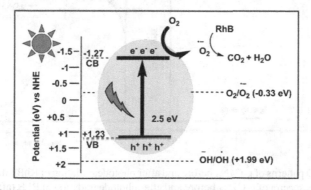

**Fig. 16.** Proposed mechanism of RhB degradation over the g-$C_3N_4$.

**Stability of the Photocatalysts.** The catalyst stability is very significant from the viewpoint of its practical application. So as to examine the stability of g-$C_3N_4$ photocatalyst, we accomplished the recycled RhB degradation in irradiation of visible light. As we can see in Fig. 17, the photocatalytic efficiency was almost the same for four successive cycles. But during the fifth consecutive cycle, it decreased by 5%, which may not be watched as a substantial decrease. Furthermore, the structural and optical properties of the g-$C_3N_4$ photocatalyst after catalytic reaction were examined using XRD, FTIR and DRS techniques. The XRD patterns, DRS and FTIR spectra of g-$C_3N_4$ before and after photodegradation of RhB are shown in Figs. 18 and 19. As shown in in Figs. 18 and 19, there were no appreciable changes in the structural and optical properties of the g-$C_3N_4$ samples before and after photodegradation experiments. It may then be decided that the g-$C_3N_4$ can be considered as a stable and highly active photocatalyst in visible light irradiation, suitable for use in photo-degrading organic pollutants.

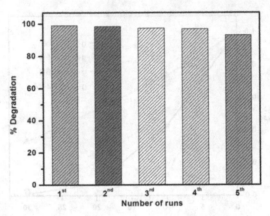

**Fig. 17.** Stability of g-$C_3N_4$ catalyst for five consecutive cycles.

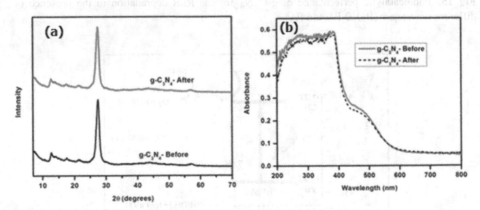

**Fig. 18.** (a) XRD patterns of g-$C_3N_4$ before and after photodegradation of RhB (after five cycles). (b) UV–VIS DRS spectra of g-$C_3N_4$ before and after photodegradation of RhB (after five cycles).

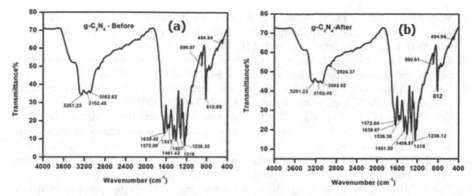

**Fig. 19.** The FTIR spectra for the g-C$_3$N$_4$ before and after photodegradation of RhB (after five cycles).

## 4 Conclusion

Graphitic carbon nitride (g-C$_3$N$_4$) materials with high surface area were excellently synthesized from urea via a polycondensation method at temperatures 470, 510 and 550 °C. Different characterization methods were used to investigate the physico-chemical and structural properties of the fabricated g-C$_3$N$_4$ materials. Photocatalytic activities of the samples were tested by the degradations of RhB in visible-light illumination. The g-C$_3$N$_-$–550 catalyst degraded the RhB pollutant within 30 min, with an efficiency of about 100%. Moreover, the prepared g-C$_3$N$_4$ photocatalysts had retained the same activity for five consecutive cycles. The outstanding photocatalytic performance of g-C$_3$N$_4$ was interrelated to a suitable band gap (2.5 eV) and high specific surface area (114.5 m$^2$ g$^{-1}$), in addition to low electron-hole recombination. Combined with a simple preparation method, a superior photodegradation activity and a durable photocatalytic stability of the g-C$_3$N$_4$ materials has generated significant interest in the photocatalytic degradation of organic poll utants.

## References

1. Xu, Y., Xu, H., Wang, L., et al.: The CNT modified white C$_3$N$_4$ composite photocatalyst with enhanced visible-light response photoactivity. Dalt. Trans. **42**, 7604–7613 (2013)
2. Gebreslassie, G., Bharali, P., Chandra, U., et al.: Hydrothermal synthesis of g-C$_3$N$_4$/NiFe$_2$O$_4$ nanocomposite and its enhanced photocatalytic activity. Appl. Organomet. Chem. **33**, e5002 (2019). https://doi.org/10.1002/aoc.5002
3. Wajid Shah, M., Zhu, Y., Fan, X., et al.: Facile synthesis of defective TiO$_{2-x}$ nanocrystals with high surface area and tailoring bandgap for visible-light photocatalysis. Sci. Rep. **5**, 15804 (2015)
4. Saputra, E., Muhammad, S., Sun, H., et al.: A comparative study of spinel structured Mn$_3$O$_4$, Co$_3$O$_4$ and Fe$_3$O$_4$ nanoparticles in catalytic oxidation of phenolic contaminants in aqueous solutions. J. Colloid. Interface Sci. **407**, 467–473 (2013)
5. Niu, P., Zhang, L., Liu, G., Cheng, H.M.: Graphene-like carbon nitride nanosheets for improved photocatalytic activities. Adv. Funct. Mater. **22**, 4763–4770 (2012)

6. Wang, A., Wang, C., Fu, L., Wong-Ng, W., Lan, Y.: Recent advances of graphitic carbon nitride-based structures and applications in catalyst, sensing, imaging, and LEDs. Nano-Micro Lett. **9**(4), 1–21 (2017). https://doi.org/10.1007/s40820-017-0148-2

7. Zheng, Y., Lin, L., Wang, B., Wang, X.: Graphitic carbon nitride polymers toward sustainable photoredox catalysis. Angew Chemie – Int. Ed. **54**, 12868–12884 (2015)

8. Sun, H., Zhou, G., Wang, Y., et al.: A new metal-free carbon hybrid for enhanced photocatalysis. ACS Appl. Mater. Interfaces **6**, 16745–16754 (2014)

9. Guo, F., Shi, W., Li, M., et al.: 2D/2D Z-scheme heterojunction of $CuInS_2$/g-$C_3N_4$ for enhanced visible-light-driven photocatalytic activity towards the degradation of tetracycline. Sep. Purif. Technol. **210**, 608–615 (2019)

10. Liu, J., Wang, H., Antonietti, M.: Graphitic carbon nitride "reloaded": emerging applications beyond (photo)catalysis. Chem. Soc. Rev. **45**, 2308–2326 (2016)

11. Xue, J., Ma, S., Zhou, Y., Wang, Q.: Au-loaded porous graphitic $C_3N_4$/graphene layered composite as a ternary plasmonic photocatalyst and its visible-light photocatalytic performance. RSC Adv. **5**, 88249–88257 (2015)

12. Zhao, Z., Sun, Y., Dong, F.: Graphitic carbon nitride based nanocomposites: a review. Nanoscale **7**, 15–37 (2015)

13. Gebreslassie, G., Bharali, P., Chandra, U., et al.: Novel g-$C_3N_4$/graphene/$NiFe_2O_4$ nanocomposites as magnetically separable visible light driven photocatalysts. J. Photochem. Photobiol. A Chem. **382** (2019)

14. Dong, F., Wu, L., Sun, Y., et al.: Efficient synthesis of polymeric g-$C_3N_4$ layered materials as novel efficient visible light driven photocatalysts. J. Mater. Chem. **21**, 15171–15174 (2011)

15. Cao, S., Low, J., Yu, J., Jaroniec, M.: Polymeric photocatalysts based on graphitic carbon nitride. Adv. Mater. **27**, 2150–2176 (2015)

16. Lee, S.C., Lintang, H.O., Yuliati, L.: A urea precursor to synthesize carbon nitride with mesoporosity for enhanced activity in the photocatalytic removal of phenol. Chem. - Asian J. **7**, 2139–2144 (2012)

17. Fang, H., Luo, Y., Zheng, Y., et al.: Facile large-scale synthesis of urea-derived porous graphitic carbon nitride with extraordinary visible-light spectrum photodegradation. Ind. Eng. Chem. Res. **55**, 4506–4514 (2016)

18. Shi, L., Liang, L., Wang, F., et al.: Higher yield urea-derived polymeric graphitic carbon nitride with mesoporous structure and superior visible-light-responsive activity. ACS Sustain. Chem. Eng. **3**, 3412–3419 (2015)

19. Zhang, Y., Liu, J., Wu, G., Chen, W.: Porous graphitic carbon nitride synthesized via direct polymerization of urea for efficient sunlight-driven photocatalytic hydrogen production. Nanoscale **4**, 5300–5303 (2012)

20. Ong, W.J., Tan, L.L., Ng, Y.H., et al.: Graphitic carbon nitride (g-$C_3N_4$)-based photocatalysts for artificial photosynthesis and environmental remediation: are we a step closer to achieving sustainability? Chem. Rev. **116**, 7159–7329 (2016)

21. Liu, J., Zhang, T., Wang, Z., et al.: Simple pyrolysis of urea into graphitic carbon nitride with recyclable adsorption and photocatalytic activity. J. Mater. Chem. **21**, 14398–14401 (2011)

22. Praus, P., Svoboda, L., Ritz, M., et al.: Graphitic carbon nitride: synthesis, characterization and photocatalytic decomposition of nitrous oxide. Mater. Chem. Phys. **193**, 438–446 (2017)

23. Pawar, R.C., Kang, S., Park, J.H., et al.: Room-temperature synthesis of nanoporous 1D microrods of graphitic carbon nitride (g-$C_3N_4$) with highly enhanced photocatalytic activity and stability. Sci. Rep. **6**, 1–14 (2016)

24. Shi, Y., Huang, J., Zeng, G., et al.: Stable, metal-free, visible-light-driven photocatalyst for efficient removal of pollutants: mechanism of action. J. Colloid. Interface Sci. **531**, 433–443 (2018)

25. Marchewka, M.K.: Infrared and Raman spectra of melaminium chloride hemihydrate. Mater. Sci. Eng. B **95**, 214–221 (2002)

26. Papailias, I., Giannakopoulou, T., Todorova, N., et al.: Effect of processing temperature on structure and photocatalytic properties of g-C$_3$N$_4$. Appl. Surf. Sci. **358**, 278–286 (2015)
27. Yan, S.C., Li, Z.S., Zou, Z.G.: Photodegradation performance of g-C$_3$N$_4$ fabricated by directly heating melamine. Langmuir **25**, 10397–10401 (2009)
28. Nagaraja, R., Kottam, N., Girija, C.R., Nagabhushana, B.M.: Photocatalytic degradation of Rhodamine B dye under UV/solar light using ZnO nanopowder synthesized by solution combustion route. Powder Technol. **215–216**, 91–97 (2012)
29. Li, Y., Zhang, H., Liu, P., et al.: Cross-linked g-C$_3$N$_4$/rGO nanocomposites with tunable band structure and enhanced visible light photocatalytic activity. Small **9**, 3336–3344 (2013)
30. Ye, L., Liu, J., Jiang, Z., et al.: Facets coupling of BiOBr-g-C$_3$N$_4$ composite photocatalyst for enhanced visible-light-driven photocatalytic activity. Appl. Catal. B, Environ. **142–143**, 1–7 (2013)
31. Mousavi, M., Habibi-Yangjeh, A., Seifzadeh, D., et al.: Exceptional photocatalytic activity for g-C$_3$N$_4$ activated by H$_2$O$_2$ and integrated with Bi$_2$S$_3$ and Fe$_3$O$_4$ nanoparticles for removal of organic and inorganic pollutants. Adv. Powder Technol. **30**, 524–537 (2018)

# Self-supporting Functional Nanomembranes of Metal Oxide/Polymer Blends

Anteneh Mersha[1,2(✉)] and Shigenori Fujikawa[3,4]

[1] Department of Industrial Chemistry, Addis Ababa Science and Technology University, Addis Ababa, Ethiopia
anteneh.kindu@aastu.edu.et
[2] Nanotechnology Center of Excellence, Addis Ababa Science and Technology University, Addis Ababa, Ethiopia
[3] Graduate School of Engineering, Kyushu University, Fukuoka, Japan
[4] International Institute of Carbon Neutral Energy Research, Kyushu University, Fukuoka, Japan

**Abstract.** Nanomembranes are important class of nanomaterials, with significantly advancing applications in a wide range of applications, including molecular separations, energy conversion and storage, sensing, catalysis and biomedical applications such as wound dressing, owing to their nano-scale thickness and high aspect ratios. However, in order to exploit the unique features of self-supporting nanomembranes (transferability onto any arbitrary substrate, high aspect ratio and unique interfacial properties), they need to have sufficient macroscopic stabilities. Conventional mechanical enhancement approaches, such as use of nanoparticle fillers often face material compatibility problems, limiting the range of material selection. In this work, a simple one-step strategy for developing functional free-standing nanomembranes (FS-NMs) from blended types of organic/inorganic composites has been presented. Such blending approach offers atomic scale *in-situ* interaction of organic and inorganic structures, ensuring nanoscale stability in membranes. Here, a hydroxyl-terminated polyethylene glycol (PEG-OH) was premixed with different metal oxide precursors for sol-gel assisted membrane formation, and the mechanical properties of the resulting FS-NMs were compared. The gas separation behavior of mechanically stable nanomembranes was also discussed. The presented strategy offers an alternative approach to develop functional self-supporting nanomembranes.

**Keywords:** Metal oxide · Polymer · Composites · Nanomembranes · Gas separation

## 1 Introduction

Polymeric films become weak upon thinning to a nanometer-scale and some polymers are difficult to spun into ultrathin films [1], making it unfavorable to prepare purely organic free-standing nanomembranes (FS-NMs). On the other hand, inorganic materials are rigid and fragile to handle as nanomembranes. Organic/inorganic composite materials

M. A. Delele et al. (Eds.): ICAST 2020, LNICST 385, pp. 442–452, 2021.
https://doi.org/10.1007/978-3-030-80618-7_30

combine these conflicting features of polymers and inorganics, and thus, enable the development of mechanically enhanced self-supporting nanomembranes [2].

In addition to incorporation of inorganic fillers into a polymer matrix, composite membranes are prepared by molecular scale integrations such as layer by layer (LBL) assembly [2, 3] and simply blending the organic and inorganic components prior to membrane preparation [4]. This molecular scale approaches enable atomic or molecular level interactions that are essential for the development of mechanically reinforced FS-NMs. Apart from mechanical reinforcement, composite membranes possess higher thermal stability [5], compared to the pristine polymer.

According to Kunitake's group [4], organic/inorganic hybrid interpenetrating networks are interesting pathways to prepare FS-NMs of only a few tens nanometer thickness with large macroscopic size and flexibility. They fabricated nanomembranes from blend formula of the corresponding metal oxide and polymer precursors. However, the membranes were not tested for any applications such as small molecule separation. Similarly, tough hydrogel membranes with micrometer-scale thickness have been developed via non-covalent double network strategy by Gong's [6] and other groups [7] for potential applications such as post-operative antiadhesive and biosensor membranes.

These mechanically robust materials are the motivations to the present work for preparing ultrathin separation membrane employing organic/inorganic hybrid materials. In this work, a metal oxide/polymer hybrid FS-NM was prepared by blending the components prior to membrane fabrication (Fig. 1). Blending approach can offer atomic scale in-situ interaction of organic and ceramic structures in a membrane. We previously reported the preparation of free-standing and ultrathin $PVA/TiO_2$ composite membrane via LBL assembly [2]. However, despite large lateral size and macroscopic flexibility of the nanomembranes, the $CO_2/N_2$ separation performance was not satisfactory. In addition to the low $CO_2$ affinity of PVA, the low separation performance (especially low selectivity) could be associated to pinholes formed either during membrane preparation or processing steps. This, in turn, may come from the hard nature of the nanomembrane where the PVA chain didn't soften the oxide phase sufficiently.

Thus, in addition to changing the membrane architecture, a softer polymer with more $CO_2$ affinity property was employed aiming to prepare mechanically stable, yet $CO_2$ selective nanomembrane.

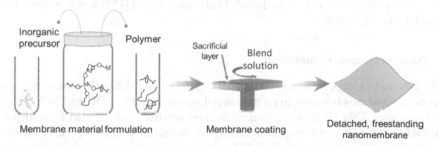

**Fig. 1.** General representation of hybrid nanomembrane preparation process.

Hydroxyl-terminated polyethylene glycols (PEG-OH) are potential candidates due to their compatibility with metal oxides for sol-gel reactions (Fig. 1), and their CO2 solubility selectivity behavior [8]. Alkoxides are often used as metal oxide precursors. In this study, however, silicon tetraisocyanate was utilized as a source of SiO2 due to its good reactivity, compared to alkoxides. Like alkoxides, the sol-gel reaction involving Si(NCO)4 goes readily to completion as confirmed by previous study [9] (Fig. 2).

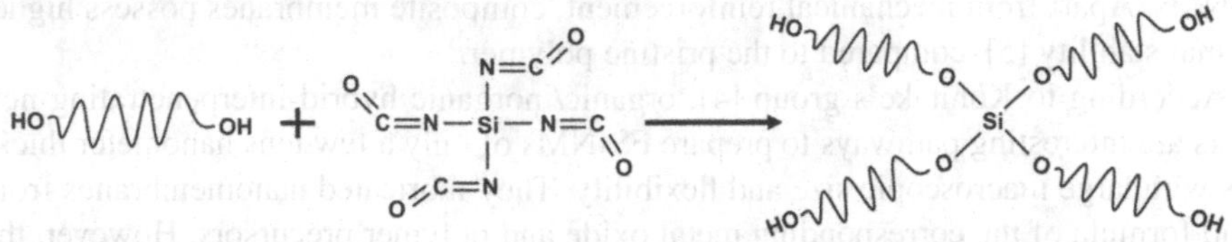

**Fig. 2.** Scheme for the formulation of organic/inorganic blend material.

In this chapter, the preparation of PEG-OH/SiO$_2$ hybrid nanomembrane with preferential selectivity to CO$_2$ over N$_2$ has been presented. In order to completely avoid gas leakage, a caulking layer of polydimethylsiloxane (PDMS), [10], was employed. To the best of my knowledge, gas permeation properties of such hybrid and free-standing ultrathin membranes have not been studied.

# 2  Experimental Section

## 2.1  Materials

Silicon wafer with 350 μm thickness and glass were used as substrates to spin-coat nanomembranes. Poly(4-vinylphenol) (PVP, Mw = 11000, Sigma-Aldrich) was used as a sacrificial layer. Polyethylene glycol (Mw = 2000, Wako Ltd.) was employed as a polymer precursor. Silicon tetraisocyanate (SiNCO)$_4$ (Matsumoto Fine Chemicals Co., Ltd.) and Titanium n-Butoxide (Ti(O$^n$Bu)$_4$, Gelest Inc.) were used as metal oxide precursors. Polydimethylsiloxane (PDMS, Sylgard® 184) was used as caulking material. Ethanol, chloroform and n-hexane were purchased from Wako Co., Ltd. and used as received. Deionized water (18.3 MΩ cm$^{-1}$, Millipore, Direct-QTM) was used for rinsing and solution preparation.

## 2.2  Nanomembrane Preparation

In the preliminary step, separate solutions of Si(NCO)$_4$ and PEG-OH were prepared in chloroform, and slowly mixed to prepare blend solutions of PEG-OH and Si(NCO)$_4$ in varying ratios (Table 1). In the meantime, a glass substrate was cleaned by sonication in EtOH for 60 min and subsequent rinsing by deionized water. The glass substrate was dried by air-blowing and treated with oxygen plasma for 4 min to hydrophilize its surface. The oxygen plasma treatment is described elsewhere [2]. Afterwards, a PVP (15 wt%, in EtOH) sacrificial layer was spin-coated (3000 rpm, 60 s) on the glass substrate and heated at 120 °C for 5 min.

**Table 1.** PEG-OH and Si(NCO)$_4$ ratio optimization from the view point of reactive sites and membrane formation tendency.

| S/N | | 1 | 2 | 3 | 4 | 5 | 6 |
|---|---|---|---|---|---|---|---|
| Molar ratio (PEG-OH/SiO$_2$) | | 9:1 | 4:1 | 2:1 | 1:1 | 1:2 | 1:4 |
| Concentration (Total=400mM) | PEG-OH | 360 | 320 | 268 | 200 | 132 | 80 |
| | SiO$_2$ | 40 | 80 | 132 | 200 | 268 | 320 |

Once cooled down to room temperature, a PEG-OH/SiO$_2$ blend solution was deposited on the pre-coated sacrificial layer at 3000 rpm for 2 min, and heated at 100 °C for 12 h. For membranes to be used in gas permeation test, a 10 wt% PDMS caulking layer was spin-coated. Finally, the glass substrate was immersed in ethanol to dissolve the sacrificial layer and release the free-standing nanomembrane. The overall membrane preparation process is illustrated schematically in Fig. 3.

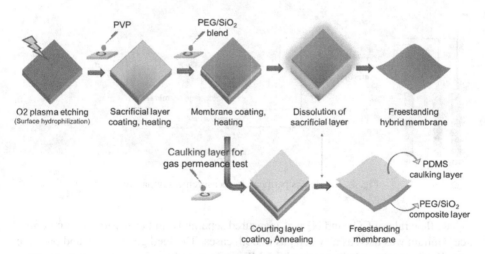

**Fig. 3.** Schematic representation of nanomembrane fabrication process by spin-coating.

Film thickness and surface morphology were investigated by scanning electron microscope (SEM, Hitachi S-5200). Specimen for surface observation was prepared by transferring the nanomembrane onto supports such as anodized porous alumina (Anodisc, G.E. Healthcare).

### 2.3 Gas Permeation Experiment

For gas permeation test, the prepared nanomembranes were transferred onto a porous polyimide support. After transfer onto a porous support, membrane area (space through which gas molecules pass) was limited by Kapton tape with the open hole of 1 cm diameter as illustrated in our previous work [2].

Subsequently, the membrane was placed in a home-made membrane cell, and gas permeation was measured using a bubble flow meter (Fig. 4). The pure gas flow rate in $cm^3/min$ of $CO_2$ and $N_2$ was measured and converted into permeance (P) using the following equation. Selectivity ($\alpha$) was also determined as the ratio of permeance.

$$P = \frac{N}{A \cdot \Delta P} \tag{1}$$

$$\alpha = \frac{P_{CO2}}{P_{N2}} \tag{2}$$

where $N$ ($m^3/s$) refers to the flow rate measured on the permeate side, $A$ ($m^2$) is effective membrane area and $\Delta P$ (Pa) is pressure difference between the feed and permeate side. In the experiment, effective area of gas permeation was 0.785 $cm^2$. For convenience, permeance was reflected in the common GPU unit, where $1 GPU = 7.5 \times 10^{-12} \, m^3/m^2 \cdot s \cdot Pa$, at standard temperature and pressure conditions.

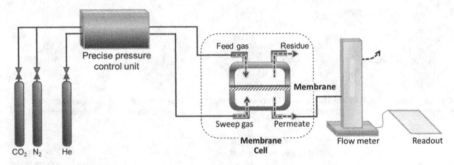

**Fig. 4.** Single gas permeation measurement apparatus.

The flow rate of $CO_2$ and $N_2$ was measured separately and transformed into permeance. Helium was used as a sweep gas in both cases. The feed gas volume and pressure conditions were set at 100 sccm and 0.2 MPa, respectively.

## 3 Results and Discussion

### 3.1 Membrane Material Selection and Preparation Conditions

In preparing a blend solution, suitable mixing ratio of the polymer and metal oxide ($MO_x$) precursor was very important for homogenous distribution of organic and inorganic structures. The PEG-OH/$SiO_2$ ratio was determined based on the sol-gel reactive sites of the PEG-OH and $MO_x$ precursor; i.e., the number of OH-groups per mole of PEGwas measured and converted into -OH and the number of NCO-groups in $Si(NCO)_4$. PEG-OH has two reactive sites and $Si(NCO)_4$ has four reactive sites per mole. Thus, stoichiometrically, 2 mol of PEG-OH react with 1 mol of $Si(NCO)_4$, i.e., PEG-OH/$Si(NCO)_4$ ratio of 2:1.

Based on this, wide range of ratios were prepared and evaluated for their film formation behavior. The result is summarized in Table 2. Also, the effect of temperature on membrane formation and stability was studied. Films were annealed at 100 °C to facilitate the sol-gel reaction.

**Table 2.** PEG-$(OH)_2$/$Si(NCO)_4$ ratio optimization from the viewpoint of membrane formation behavior.

| Annealing condition | PEG-$(OH)_2$/$Si(NCO)_4$ ratio* | | | | | |
|---|---|---|---|---|---|---|
| | 9:1 | 4:1 | 2:1 | 1:1 | 1:2 | 1:4 |
| Ambient, 12hrs | No film | | Film formed, but fragile | | Solution was not stable for film preparation (Fast hydrolysis) | |
| 100 °C, 12 hrs | Non-detachable film | | Stable free-standing film | | | |

*Molar ratio; PEG-OH : $Si(NCO)_4$

As can be seen in Fig. 5 and Table 2, there was an obvious enhancement in the chemical and mechanical stabilities of the prepared nanomembranes after thermal treatment, compared to ambient condition. This should be because heating facilitated the sol-gel crosslinking reaction. Accordingly, stable free-standing PEG-OH/$SiO_2$ hybrid nanomembranes were obtained from thermally annealed 2-to-1 and 1-to-1 combination of PEG-OH/$Si(NCO)_4$. The membranes maintained their shape and size after detachment from substrates.

### 3.2 Morphological and Mechanical Properties

In addition to blending ratio and annealing temperature, it is worth explaining that the reactivity of the $MO_x$ precursor affects the membrane formation and subsequent mechanical properties. As discussed in our previous work [2], $Ti(O^nBu)_4$ was used as a $MO_x$ precursor to prepare PVA/$TiO_2$ composite nanomembrane. However, when replacing PVA by polyethylene glycol (for its softer nature and $CO_2$ affinity property) to make PEG-OH/$TiO_2$ nanomembranes, the membranes became more fragile, even under heating at 70 °C for 12 h. The appearance of the nanomembranes is shown in Fig. 6. Although the annealing temperature of PEG-OH/$TiO_2$ (70 °C) was milder than that of PEG-OH/$SiO_2$ case (100 °C), the main reason for film fragility could be attributed

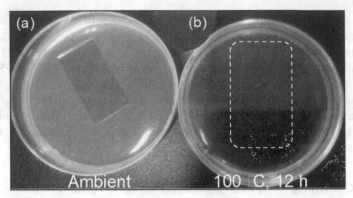

**Fig. 5.** Digital images showing the difference in the stability of the PEG-OH/Si(NCO)$_4$ films during immersion in EtOH for detachment. (a) PEG-OH/Si(NCO)$_4$ film directly immersed in EtOH. The murky appearance of the solution indicates the dissolution of membrane components. (b) PEG-OH/Si(NCO)$_4$ film immersed in EtOH after annealing at 100 °C. Solution remained clear implying that no new species was introduced into the solvent, except the PVP sacrificial layer.

to lesser sol-gel reactivity of PEG-OH relative to PVA. Apparently, this could be due to lesser proportion of -OH groups in PEG-OH than PVA. Therefore, Si(NCO)$_4$ was tested instead of Ti(O$^n$Bu)$_4$ as a MO$_x$ precursor to compensate the milder reactivity of PEG-OH.

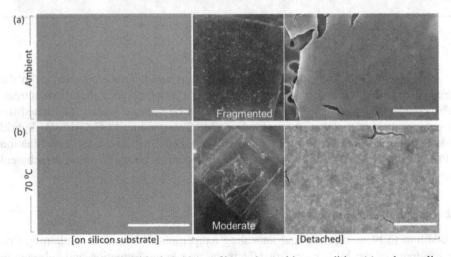

**Fig. 6.** Nature of PEG-OH/TiO$_2$ hybrid nanofilm under ambient condition (a) and annealing at 70 °C for 12 h (b). **Scale bar: 1 μm**.

Interestingly, a better integrity with PEG-OH has been observed, leading to the realization of large size (Fig. 7a), stable nanomembrane that can be detached and transferred onto a porous support without significant damage. As mentioned above, thermally annealed 2-to-1 and 1-to-1 molar ratios of PEG-OH/Si(NCO)$_4$ could form large size nanomembranes.

However, despite successful preparation of large size PEG-based nanomembrane, cracks were observed under SEM (Fig. 7b,c). It was seen from physical manipulation and SEM observation that the PEG-OH/SiO$_2$ nanomembrane showed rigid behavior. Although the mechanical property of this membrane was not pleasing, we considered evaluating its gas separation property as a proof of design concept.

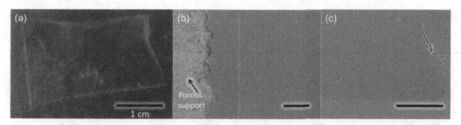

**Fig. 7.** (a) Digital image of the PEG-OH/SiO$_2$ nanomembrane while it was in the detachment solvent. (b,c) SEM image of the nanomembrane transferred onto a porous support. **Scale bar: 10 μm.**

### 3.3 Gas Permeation Property

Upon testing the gas permeation, the bare PEG-OH/SiO$_2$ membrane showed frequent gas leakage problem. On the other hand, although not consistently reproducible, the membrane randomly showed CO$_2$ selective separation behavior over N$_2$. In situations like this, a caulking layer is applied to alleviate the effects of structural defects [10]. Caulking materials need to have high gas diffusivities, so as not to hinder the performance of the separation layer. Accordingly, a PDMS caulking layer has been coated on PEG-OH/SiO$_2$ (Fig. 8) in order to seal the cracks and prevent simple gas leakage.

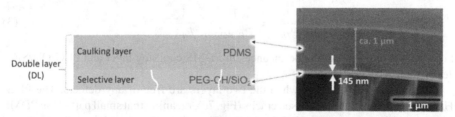

**Fig. 8.** Schematics (left) and cross-sectional SEM view (right) of PEG-OH/SiO$_2$ nanomembrane with PDMS caulking layer.

From the permeance and selectivity results in Table 3, the CO$_2$/N$_2$ selectivity of (PEG-OH/SiO$_2$)/PDMS membrane was approximated as ca. 15. This value is higher than the CO$_2$/N$_2$ selectivity of pristine PDMS (11.6) [11], signifying that the enhanced selectivity is due to PEG-OH/$SiO_2$. This is reasonable as the ethylene oxide group in PEG-OH could assist the solubility-selectivity of $CO_2$ over $N_2$. However, the improved $CO_2/N_2$ selectivity was compromised by a decrease in permeance relative to pristine PDMS. This might be because the PEG-OH/$SiO_2$ layer was very dense and had no molecular pathways. This, in turn, could be attributed to the presence of amorphous $SiO_2$ in the membrane, as well as the crystalizing nature of PEG [12] that restricts permeation pathways.

**Table 3.** Gas separation properties of pristine PDMS and PEG-OH/$SiO_2$ with PDMS caulking layer.

| Membrane | Permeance, GPU | | $CO_2/N_2$ selectivity |
|---|---|---|---|
| | $CO_2$ | $N_2$ | |
| Pristine PDMS | 3500.0 0 | 301.000 | 11.6 |
| PEG-OH/$SiO_2$ (with caulking layer) | 5.50 | 0.370 | 14.8 |
| PEG-OH/$SiO_2$ layer (Resistance model calculation) | 5.52 | 0.371 | 14.9 |

The effect of the caulking layer on gas separation behavior of PEG-OH/$SiO_2$ was examined by applying the resistance model [10, 13, 14]. According to the model, the permeance of the double layer ($P_{DL}$) membrane is related to the permeance of each layer as follows;

$$\frac{1}{P_{DL}} = \frac{1}{P_{PDMS}} + \frac{1}{P_{PS}}$$ (3)

where, $P_{PDMS}$ and $P_{PS}$ are the permeances of PDMS caulking layer and PEG-OH/$SiO_2$ selective layer, respectively.

This relation is valid only when the two layers are free of any defects. The PEG-OH/$SiO_2$ layer, however, possessed cracks (Fig. 7c), meaning that small part of the PDMS layer is not in contact with PEG-OH/$SiO_2$. Therefore, the experimentally measured permeance ($P_{meas}$) is not equal to $P_{DL}$, [14], but rather they are related as follows.

$$P_{meas} = P_{DL}\frac{A_{PS}}{A_{PDMS}} + P_{PDMS}\left(1 - \frac{A_{PS}}{A_{PDMS}}\right)$$ (4)

where, the $A_{PS}/A_{PDMS}$ refers to the area of the PEG-OH/$SiO_2$ layer covered by PDMS.

It is assumed (based on SEM observation) that the cracks in the PEG-OH/SiO$_2$ layer constitute about 5% and the rest 95% of the membrane was covered by PDMS. The calculated permeance and selectivity values are listed in Table 3. However, there was no significant difference between the experimentally measured and model-based calculated values. This means that the caulking layer has almost no resistance on gas permeation, and the results reflect the behavior of PEG-OH/SiO$_2$ layer. This, in turn, affirms that the PEG-OH/SiO$_2$ nanolayer has no serious cracks.

## 4 Discussion

The idea of PEG-OH/TiO$_2$ and PEG-OH/SiO$_2$ blend nanomembranes discussed in this paper was a follow up work of PVA/TiO$_2$ LBL nanomembrane discussed presented elsewhere, [2], with the aim to find out an alternative preparation route to integrate macroscopic mechanical property with CO$_2$/N$_2$ separation function.

Two possible ways were considered in order to overcome the low separation performance (where unsatisfactory mechanical stability could be a likely factor) of the PVA/TiO$_2$ nanomembrane; using a softer polymer with better gas separation properties, and changing the membrane architecture. Accordingly, a blended type of PEG-OH/SiO$_2$ FS-NM was developed from a blend formula of a hydroxyl-terminated polyethylene glycol (PEG-OH) and silicon tetraisocyanate. Although no significant mechanical property enhancement was seen, compared to the PVA/TiO$_2$ membrane, the PEG/SiO$_2$ hybrid nanomembrane demonstrated improved CO$_2$/N$_2$ selectivity.

## 5 Conclusion

Free-standing PEG-OH/SiO$_2$ blend nanomembranes were prepared by spin-coating. The sol-gel reaction between PEG-OH and Si(NCO)$_4$ was assisted by thermal annealing for improved mechanical property. Because the bare composite nanomembrane showed gas leakage due to cracks, PDMS caulking layer has been introduced and the gas separation property was estimated by employing the resistance model. Although no significant mechanical property enhancement was observed from physical manipulation, compared to the PVA/TiO$_2$ LBL nanomembrane discussed in our previous report, [2], the PEG-OH/SiO$_2$ hybrid nanomembrane demonstrated improved CO$_2$/N$_2$ selectivity.

## References

1. Koros, W.J.: Macromol. Symp. **188**(1), 13–22 (2002)
2. Mersha, A., Selyanchyn, R., Fujikawa, S.: CleanE **1**(1), 80–89 (2017)
3. Richardson, J.J., Bjornmalm, M., Caruso, F.: Science **348**(6233), 2491 (2015)
4. Vendamme, R., Onoue, S.-Y., Nakao, A., Kunitake, T.: Nat. Mater. **5**(6), 494–501 (2006)
5. Xu, Z.L., Yu, L.Y., Han, L.F.: Front. Chem. Eng. China **3**(3), 318–329 (2009)
6. Ye, Y.N., et al.: Adv. Funct. Mater. **28**(31), 1801489 (2018)
7. Fei, R., Means, A.K., Abraham, A.A., Locke, A.K., Coté, G.L., Grunlan, M.: Macromol. Mater. Eng. **301**(8), 935–943 (2016)
8. Liu, J., Hou, X., Park, H.B., Lin, H.: Chem. Eur. J. **22**(45), 15980–15990 (2016)

452     A. Mersha and S. Fujikawa

9.  Takaki, R., Takemoto, H., Fujikawa, S., Toyoki, K.: Colloids surfaces a physicochem. Eng. Asp. **321**, 227–232 (2008)
10. Dal-Cin, M.M., Darcovich, K., Saimani, S., Kumar, A.J.: Memb. Sci. **361**, 176–181 (2010)
11. Robb, W.L.: Ann. N. Y. Acad. Sci. **146**, 119–137 (1968)
12. Lin, H., Freeman, B.D.: Macromolecules **39**(10), 3568–3580 (2006)
13. Henis, J.M.S., Tripodi, M.K.J.: Memb. Sci. **8**(3), 233–246 (1981)
14. Ai, M., et al.: Carbon Nanomembranes (CNMs) supported by poly-mer: mechanics and gas permeation. J. Adv. Mater. **26**(21), 3421–3426 (2014)

# Investigating the Effectiveness of Liquid Membrane - Forming Concrete Curing Compounds Produced in Ethiopia

Rahel Ayalew[1]([✉]), Kassahun Admassu[2], and Solomon Dagnaw[3]

[1] Construction Technology and Management, Faculty of Civil and Water Resource Engineering, Bahir Dar Institute of Technology, Bahir Dar University, Bahir Dar, Ethiopia
[2] Ethiopian Institute of Architecture, Building Construction and City Development, Addis Ababa University, Addis Ababa, Ethiopia
kassahun.admassu@eiabc.edu.et
[3] Civil Engineering Department, Gondar Institute of Technology, University of Gondar, Gondar, Ethiopia
solomon.dagnew@uog.edu.et

**Abstract.** Liquid membrane-forming compound curing is a type of water retaining curing concrete technique by forming a membrane on the surface of the concrete. This study aimed to investigate the effectiveness of liquid membrane – forming concrete curing compounds produced in Ethiopia. The methodology include compressive strength and water absorption (on C-25 and C-40 grades of concrete) for samples examined under laboratory conditions and by exposing samples to external weather conditions which were cured through curing compounds, water sprinkling and plastic sheet covering. Additionally drying time and deleterious reaction tests were carried out. Liquid membrane – forming concrete curing compounds produced in Ethiopia are effective in compressive strength but not in water absorption, which water absorption was used to measure concrete quality in this study. Water sprinkling and plastic sheet covering methods were effective in compressive strength and water absorption than curing compounds. Regarding cost comparisons, water sprinkling method of curing is less costly than curing compounds and burlap coverings, and curing compound is more costly than the two.

**Keywords:** Curing compounds · Drying time · Deleterious reaction · Compressive strength · Water absorption

## 1 Introduction

Curing assures the maintenance of satisfactory moisture content and temperature in concrete for a period of time immediately following placing and finishing. Curing can be performed either by preventing evaporation of water from freshly placed concrete or by adding additional water to the concrete [1]. Liquid membrane-forming compounds

M. A. Delele et al. (Eds.): ICAST 2020, LNICST 385, pp. 453–466, 2021.
https://doi.org/10.1007/978-3-030-80618-7_31

enable concrete curing through retaining the water to the inside of concrete by forming a membrane on the surface of the concrete to prevent evaporation of water. In Ethiopia production of liquid membrane-forming compounds and application was started and still it is limited to few manufacturers and construction projects. Membrane-forming curing compounds typically consist of a wax or resin that is emulsified in water or dissolved in a solvent. The compound is applied to the concrete surface and then the water or solvent constituent evaporates leaving the wax or resin to form a membrane over the surface of the concrete [2]. ASTM C - 309 -07, classifies liquid membrane-forming curing compounds by the color of the compound and the solid constituent present for forming the membrane [3].

The Constructor- Civil Engineering Home [4] listed the following uses of curing compounds [4]:

• If wet curing is not possible, then the curing compound can be used to cure the concrete surface.
• For larger areas of concrete surfaces that are opened to sunlight, wind, etc. curing is a big task. But with the presence of the curing compound, it is easier.
• Curing of concrete pavements, runways, bridge decks, etc. can be cured to reach their maximum strength.
• A maximum durability of structure will be developed.
• Curing compound can be used for curing of canal linings, dams.
• Columns, beams, slabs can also be cured with curing compound.
• The membrane cane removed easily after complete curing.

Application of membrane-forming curing compounds is easy, short in time and not labor intensive [5]. Curing compounds should be applied as soon as finishing is completed, and bleeding has ceased [3]. At this stage, the bleed water has just left the surface and the texturing has increased the surface area resulting in increased evaporation. As the delay in the application of the curing compound under adverse conditions, plastic shrinkage cracking can result [6]. ASTMC 309 -07 specifies 200 ft$^2$/gal (5m$^2$/L) for testing purpose and noted that the application rate used for testing may, or may not, be the same as the rate to be used for field application. In a study conducted by researchers in Iowa department of transportation [5], results show that the specimens that were sprayed at 400 ft$^2$/gal (10 m$^2$/L) lost almost as much moisture as those that were sprayed at 100 ft$^2$/gal (2.5 m$^2$/L) [5].

For normal concrete with a water-cementitious materials ratio greater than about 0.45, because there is a water in excess of that needed for hydration and pozzolanic reactions membrane-forming curing compounds can be effective [7]. However, Copeland and Bragg [6], stated that membrane-forming curing compounds may not retain enough water in the concrete for concrete mixtures with high cement contents and low water-cement ratios (less than 0.40). In this case, concrete may require special curing needs [8]. Dinesh W. et al. [9], in their study of "Effectiveness of curing compound on concrete" conclude that the strength of membrane curing is not efficient as compared to conventional curing [9].

Even so the liquid membrane – forming curing compounds manufactured in Ethiopia, the competence of products on curing concrete was not investigated by researchers.

Accordingly, this study focus mainly on the effectiveness of products of liquid membrane – forming curing compounds produced in Ethiopia. The study investigates the compressive strength and water absorption of C-25 and C-40 grades of concrete cured by liquid – forming curing compounds and additionally, tried to answer the question does liquid membrane – forming curing compounds produced in Ethiopia effective than conventional curing methods. The purpose of selecting those two grades of concrete is to investigate the effectiveness of curing compounds with different concrete grades. This is because of curing compounds is more effective in the low grade of concrete only. To achieve the major objective of the research, the specific objectives are organized as follows:

- To examine the drying time of curing compounds and deleterious reaction of curing compounds with concrete.
- To examine the effectiveness of curing compounds through compressive strength and water absorption tests on C- 25 and C-40 concrete grades.
- Assessing sample conditioning effects by exposing specimens to various field water moisture retentions and water adding, and also to chemical curing compounds from the test results of compressive strength and water absorption capacity.
- To evaluate and compare the economical aspect of conventional curing practices with that of the chemical curing compound.

## 2   Materials and Methods

### 2.1   Materials

The concrete making materials used in this research were cement, fine aggregate, coarse aggregate and water. Four liquid membrane – forming concrete curing compound products which are produced in Ethiopia by three companies (one company produce two types of curing compounds) were used, product (1) a resin-based clear curing compound, product (2) a clear translucent, product (3) Clear Liquid –Emulsified paraffin wax, product (4) clear translucent which has sodium silicate and creates a film of adhering microcrystalline. The companies import raw materials for producing the curing compounds from Dubai and China. The type of cement used in this study was 42.5R Ordinary Portland Cement (OPC) equivalent to ASTMtype I (CEM I 42.5 R) cement from Derba Cement Factory and Lalibela sand. While, the coarse aggregate extracted from Meshenti aggregate crushing plant site with the maximum size of 25 mm was used. Material Property tests of the aggregates were carried out according to ASTMstandards and the water utilized in the concrete mix was drinkable water.

### 2.2   Experimental Procedures

**Testing Properties of Membrane Forming Curing Compounds.** Drying time and deleterious reaction tests were conducted in this study as evaluation of suitability of curing compounds to use these products of curing compounds as one of curing techniques in concrete. The tests were carried out as per ASTM C-309 [3].

**Casting and Curing of Concrete Specimens.** The required volumes of mix ingredients were measured and mixing was done thoroughly to ensure that a homogenous mix is obtained. The specimens were subjected to different curing techniques. For in laboratory samples the samples subjected to curing through soaking or immersion in a curing tank and curing compounds curing without exposing these samples. For field weather exposed samples curing was carried out through water sprinkling, plastic sheet covering and curing compounds curing techniques.

**Liquid Membrane - Forming Concrete Curing Compound Preparation and Application.** Application of curing compounds performed as per the specifications given by the manufacturers. For product (1), (3) and (4) curing compounds single layer application was done since there is no recommended double layer application. However, for the product (2) double coat application was recommended by the manufacturer and this also done. Even double coat is recommended, for economical effectiveness single layer applications were performed in this study. For all products, the curing compound was applied through spraying in a uniform manner as soon as the surface water disappears.

**Tests and Procedures for Compressive Strength and Water Absorption.** Concrete samples were casted for determination of compressive strength and water absorption and comparison is done with the control specimens. Laboratory experimental tests and tests for samples exposed to field weather conditions or samples outside the laboratory on C-25 and C-40 concrete grade were conducted. The purpose of selecting those two grades of concrete is to investigate the effectiveness of curing compounds with different concrete grades. This is because of curing compounds is more effective in the low grade of concrete. Copeland and Bragg [6], states that membrane-forming curing compounds may not retain enough water in the concrete for concrete mixtures with high cement contents and low water-cement ratios (less than 0.40) [6]. Field tests might be important to investigate the effectiveness of curing compounds when exposed to actual weather conditions. The time that concrete was casted, placed and cured was, Ethiopian spring time season which is on September. The room temperature were between 20 °C and 26 °C and temperature outside room was between 25 °C–28 °C of T max. and T min. was between 13.8°C–16 °C, relative humidity ranges from 62%–84% and wind run was recorded in between 0.28 m/s–0.72 m/s at the time.

*Compressive Strength Test.* The compressive strength tests for 3, 7 and 28 days were conducted for C-25 and C-40 concrete grades for samples in lab and field. Curing is essential to achieve expected compressive strength thus 3, 7 and 28 days compressive strength tests were conducted as per specification. This is used to examine early strength of samples of concrete and due to 99% of compressive strength achieved at 28 days. For tests exposed to field weather conditions two curing methods (water sprinkling and plastic sheet covering) were used for comparison with curing compounds. In lab samples also cured through immersion curing and curing compounds.

*Water Absorption Test.* The test conducted at 28 day as per ASTM C 642 [10]. Water absorption test method for hardened concrete used to see potential water absorption by concrete through full immersion of cube samples in the water. This test carried out for both samples exposed to field weather conditions and in lab.

**Curing Cost Comparison Between Two Locally Practiced Methods and Curing Compounds.** The curing methods used in this study for comparisons are water sprinkling, burlap covering and curing compounds. The cost of curing is compiled by considering the cost of materials and cost of labor for those curing methods. Material and labor costs for water and burlap curing depend on the current Bahir Dar city market price.

## 3 Results and Discussions

The results obtained from the; chemical properties of liquid membrane curing compounds, compressive strength and water absorption are discussed in this section.

### 3.1 Test results on membrane forming curing compounds

**Drying Time Test Results.** The drying time test is the test that the drying time of curing compounds after application. ASTM recommends that the curing compound shall be dry for touching in not more than 4 h.

The curing compounds of all the products drying time are less than 4h, indicating that all curing compounds fulfill standards of ASTM 309–07 [3]. Table 1 below shows that the drying time of each curing compounds.

**Table 1.** Drying time results of curing compounds

| Id | Drying time (Hr.) |
|---|---|
| Product (1) | 2 |
| Product (2) | 1 |
| Product (3) | 1.5 |
| Product (4) | 1 |

**Deleterious Reactions Test Results.** In case of all curing compounds, there was no deleterious reaction with the concrete. Hence, the result shows that no softening of concrete surface for the test done through scratching, after the surface of the concrete is dried properly. Any softening of the liquid membrane-forming compound-treated surface evaluated by such comparison shall be considered sufficient cause for rejection of the compound.

### 3.2 Compressive Strength Test Results

**C-25 Compressive Strength Test Results for Samples in the Laboratory.** The results of C-25 compressive strength for samples cured by curing compounds and immersion at 3, 7 and 28 days in the lab are also shown in the Fig. 1. As shown in figure the results of compressive strength of each curing methods are achieved the desired strength at 3, 7 and 28 days.

The three days compressive strength test results show that the immersion curing or control group has highest compressive strength than curing compounds. From those of curing compounds, at three-days, product (2) (with double coat), and results the highest strength from the remaining curing compounds. P (3), p (4) and p (1) compressive strength could be understood as in their decreasing order.

Similar to the three-day compressive strength test results, the seven day compressive strength of immersion curing (control group) also exceeds the results of the curing compounds. Product (2) curing compound has the highest compressive strength from the remaining. And product (2), product (4) and product (1) compressive strength could be understood as following those in their decreasing order.

The 28 - day's compressive strength of the C-25 grade of concrete shows that samples of immersion cured have highest compressive strength than curing compounds. At 28 - day's product (2) (with double coat) has highest compressive strength than the remaining curing compounds. And product (4), (1), (2*) and (3) compressive strength could be understood as in their decreasing order. Product (2)* is product (2) with single application and the compressive strength of this product resulted the desired strength. Double coat application for product (2) curing compound shows higher compressive strength, thus application of double coat influence the compressive strength without considering other factors. However, even double coat application of product (2) strength is higher, single coat application is achieved the desired strength. Due to this, except C-25 in lab compressive strength all tests considered single layer application of product (2).

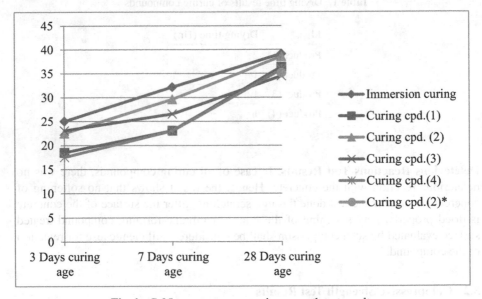

**Fig. 1.** C-25 concrete compressive strength test results

**C-40 Compressive Strength Test Results for Samples in the Laboratory.** In the Fig. 2, the results of compressive strength of each curing methods at 3, 7 and 28-days are shown. As shown in graph below P (3) shows high early strength at 3 days among curing compounds and at 28 days of P (3) is the lowest performer. Immersion curing results are the highest compressive strength at all the three testing ages.

For the three days C- 40 concrete grade compressive strength test results for immersion curing and curing compounds. And product (3), product (4), product (1) and product (2) compressive strengths could be understood as in their decreasing order.

The results of 7 and 28-days compressive strength show that the immersion curing (control group) exceeds the curing compounds compressive strength. From curing compounds product (4) is with the higher compressive strength followed by product (1), product (2) and product (3); respectively in both 7 and 28-days compressive strength results.

Generally, for samples conditioned in the laboratory, the samples with immersion curing scored higher compressive strengths than those with chemical compounds at 3, 7 and 28 days for both C-25 and C-40 concrete grades. As pointed out in various studies additional water curing is effective than water retaining method (such like curing compound curing method). This might be due to evaporation of water after placing of concrete. However, in this study the considered liquid membrane – forming concrete curing compounds are satisfying the required compressive strength.

Among the results of curing compounds, product (3) which is wax emulsion type, early compressive strength development was higher than the rest curing compounds, but the late age strength becomes lower and at 28 (in case of C-40) and at 7 ( in case of C-25) days registered less compressive strength than all curing compounds. As the Constructor - Civil Engineering [4], states, wax compound loses its efficiency with time increment [4]. Thus, product three's strength might be affected due to this reason.

QCL group [2], indicated that the different types of curing compounds could have different curing effectiveness ability; for example, Wax emulsion "compares as curing well with others", Hydrocarbon resins "excellent curing". However, under extreme weather conditions, the membrane becomes brittle and breaks down under the action of sunlight and weathering, thus reducing its effectiveness [2]. In this study also, hydrocarbons resin which is product (1) curing compound has very good compressive strength as evidenced by the test results. The study on "An experimental investigation on self-curing concrete using different curing agent" by Karthick R, Amrin Sulthana [11], found that the curing compounds with sodium poly acrylate which form crystalline structures when dry showed that 8%, 11% more compressive strength gains than the conventional at 7 and 14 days, respectively; and 6% lesser at 28 days than conventional. The study also investigated paraffin wax coated curing compound effect on compressive strength and the results show that 17.5%, 19.6% and 20% lesser compressive strength than conventional methods at 7, 14 and 28 days; respectively [11]. In this research also, the field weather exposed samples, curing compound (4) which form microcrystal and which has sodium silicate, also resulted the highest compressive strength amongst the rest.

In general, the compressive strength test results of all curing compounds were fulfilled the desired compressive strengths at all 3, 7, and 28 days.

**C-25 Compressive Strength Test Results for Samples Exposed to Field Weather Conditions.** The results of C -25 under field weather conditions in compressive strength for 3, 7 and 28 - days also shown in the Fig. 3. In this case, the conventional (water

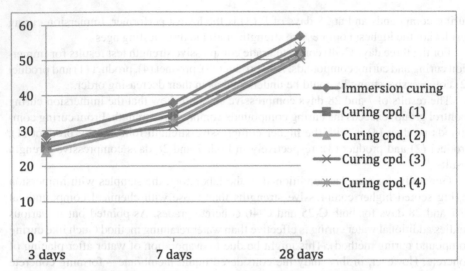

**Fig. 2.** C-40 concrete compressive strength test results

sprinkling and plastic sheet covering) curing methods have higher compressive strength at all the three testing ages.

At three day testing, from the two conventional curing methods, plastic sheet covering was found to score the highest compressive strength followed by water sprinkling, product (4) is with the highest compressive strength scorer among the curing compounds followed by product (3) and products (1) and (2) have less compressive strengths from all the curing compounds in their decreasing order.

The 7 and 28 days compressive strength also shows the highest strength for plastic sheet covering followed by water sprinkling method. From the curing compounds, curing compound (4) has the highest compressive strength; product (2) is the next one which is followed by product (1), and product (3) is the least in compressive strength series at 7 and 28 days. Figure 3 below shows C-25 compressive strength test results for samples exposed to field weather conditions.

**C-40 Compressive Strength Test Results for Samples Exposed to Field Weather Conditions.** Figure 4 shows the results of C - 40 under field weather conditions cured samples compressive strength for 3, 7 and 28 - days.

The 3, 7 and 28 - days compressive strength of C-40 concrete shows that plastic sheet covering have highest compressive strength followed by water sprinkling. From the curing compounds, product (4), (1), (2) and (3) compressive strengths followed in their decreasing order.

For the samples exposed to field weather conditions plastic sheet and water sprinkling have both registered higher strengths than curing compounds. Previous studies on curing compounds also reported that conventional curing methods are more effective than liquid membrane-forming curing compounds. According to a study by Dinesh W. et al. [9], in their study of —Effectiveness of curing compound on concrete conclude that the strength of membrane curing is not efficient as compared to conventional curing [9].

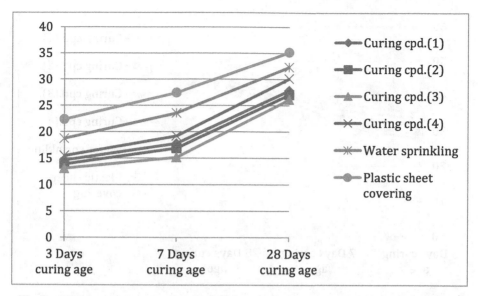

**Fig. 3.** C-25 concrete compressive strength for samples exposed to field weather conditions

Additionally, D. Gowsika, et al. [12], also in their study of -Experimental study on curing methods of concrete‖ investigated the effect of curing compound on strength for M 20 grade of concrete and the results of the comparisons between curing compounds and different other curing method for 7 and 28 days compressive strength was the membrane curing compound is the least effective method following air drying than those given conventional curing [12].

However, the compressive strength tests of all curing compounds achieved the desired compressive strength. Among the curing compounds in case of samples exposed to field weather conditions, product (4) which has sodium silicate which creates a film of adhering microcrystalline nature leading to highest compressive strength.

### 3.3 Water Absorption Test Results

Water Results of water absorption tests of C-25 grade of concrete on the in lab cured samples: Water absorption test results show that the immersion curing method has less percentage of water absorption than the curing compounds. Absorption is cause of degradation of concrete structures related with the quality and durability of concrete. One of the variables that control the degradation process in the concrete is effectively reduced water absorption. In unsaturated concrete, the rate of ingress of water or other liquids is largely controlled by absorption due to capillary rise [13]. Less water absorption indicates the ability of concrete to protect the entrance of liquids and other aggressive substances to its inside.

Products (1), (2) and (4) have less amount of water absorption value respectively from the curing compounds, with very close values to each other. Product (3) is the curing compound with higher absorption. According to Comite Euro-International du

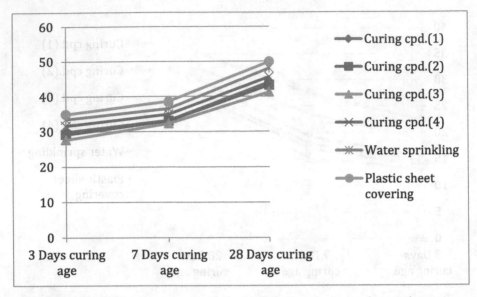

**Fig. 4.** For C-40 concrete compressive strength for samples exposed to weather test

Beton (CEB 192, 1989), concrete may be classified as good, average and poor, and the values of classification ranges proposed by CEB 192 are, from 0 – 3% good, >3% - 5% average and >5% - 7% poor concrete quality [14]. With the above in mind, Table 2 shows that immersion curing method with a result of 2.08% signifies a good concrete quality in the C-25 grade of concrete. Curing compounds (1), (2) and (4) have 4.05% and 4.06% absorption value respectively; which fall under average concrete quality. However, curing compound (3) has absorption value of 5.64%, which could be taken as a concrete of poor quality.

**Table 2.** Water absorption of C-25 samples cured in lab

| Description | Average mass after oven drying (g) | Average mass after immersion to water, (g) | % of absorption |
|---|---|---|---|
| Immersion curing | 8,926.33 | 9,111.66 | 2.08 |
| Curing cpd. (1) | 8,546.50 | 8,892.33 | 4.05 |
| Curing cpd. (2) | 8,506.16 | 8851.00 | 4.06 |
| Curing cpd. (3) | 8479.80 | 8958.80 | 5.64 |
| Curing cpd. (4) | 8378.30 | 8861.00 | 4.06 |

**Results of Water Absorption Tests of C-40 Grade of Concrete for the in Lab Cured Samples.** Medeiros – Junior et. al [13], had observed the relationship between water/cement ratio and water absorption through immersion, and the lower water/cement ratio results small water absorption value [13]. In this study also water absorptions in C-40 is less than in C-25 concrete grade. Where more water is not consumed by hydration reaction the microscopic pores cause higher water absorption thus, lower water/cement ratio result in lower water absorption [13].

As shown in Table 3, immersion curing method shows less percentage of water absorption. Curing compound product (4) has less water absorption than other curing compounds and product (1) and (2) results in the next less water absorption among the curing compounds; respectively. Product (3) shows the highest water absorption from all other. According to classification of Comite Euro-International du Beton (CEB 192, 1989) [14], immersion curing method which scored 1.86% is the range under good concrete quality, and curing compound (1), (2) and (4) have 3.84%, 3.93% and 3.07% absorption values respectively; which are under average concrete quality. Curing compound (3) has 4.46%, which is taken as an average among the established concrete qualities, but has the highest value.

**Table 3.** Water absorption for C-40 by samples cured in lab

| Description | Average mass after oven drying, (g) | Average mass after immersion to water, (g) | % of absorption |
|---|---|---|---|
| Immersion curing | 8846.25 | 9010.50 | 1.86 |
| Curing cpd. (1) | 8720.86 | 9,055.83 | 3.93 |
| Curing cpd. (2) | 8648.50 | 8,988.16 | 3.84 |
| Curing cpd. (3) | 8443.50 | 8905.17 | 4.46 |
| Curing cpd. (4) | 8451.30 | 8939.80 | 3.07 |

**Results Water Absorption Test on C-25 Grade of Concrete Field Weather Exposed Samples.** In the case of samples exposed to field weather, for C-25 grade of concrete, plastic sheet covering and water sprinkling techniques of curing show less percentage of water absorption. Also curing compound products (4), (1) and (2) have the sequential less absorption values; respectively. And product (3) result indicates high water absorption than the rest.

According to the classification of Comite Euro-International du Beton (CEB 192, 1989) [14], of concrete quality water sprinkling and plastic sheet covering curings are classified under good quality concrete; having 4.78 and 4.75% water absorptions; respectively. However all curing compounds have >5% absorption and these values show indicate poor concrete quality (Tables 4 and 5).

**Results of Eater Absorption Test on C-40 Grade of Concrete Field Weather Exposed Samples.** For C-40 grade of concrete, plastic sheet covering and water sprinkling techniques have lower water absorption values. Product (4), (1), (2) and (3) have the sequential less absorption values; respectively. Depending on (CEB 192, 1989) [14], concrete quality classification in regard to water absorption value [14], all curing compounds results come under poor concrete quality; whereas, water sprinkling and plastic sheet covering curing have absorption value classified as an average concrete quality.

**Table 4.** Water absorption of C-25 concrete grade for samples exposed under field weather conditions

| Description | Average mass after oven drying (g) | Average mass after immersion to water, (g) | % of absorption |
|---|---|---|---|
| Curing cpd. (1) | 8023.80 | 8540.70 | 5.94 |
| Curing cpd. (2) | 8068.30 | 8657.00 | 6.04 |
| Curing cpd. (3) | 8038.50 | 8541.50 | 6.76 |
| Curing cpd. (4) | 8125.20 | 8609.70 | 5.89 |
| Water sprinkling | 8349.70 | 8746.80 | 4.78 |
| Plastic sheet | 8351.80 | 8751.20 | 4.75 |

**Table 5.** Water absorption of C-40 grade of concrete for samples exposed under field weather conditions

| Description | Average mass after oven drying, (g) | Average mass after immersion to water, (g) | % of absorption |
|---|---|---|---|
| Curing cpd. (1) | 8252.80 | 8702.30 | 5.60 |
| Curing cpd. (2) | 8346.50 | 8780.70 | 5.46 |
| Curing cpd. (3) | 8191.00 | 8671.20 | 6.08 |
| Curing cpd. (4) | 8191.00 | 8591.30 | 5.20 |
| Water sprinkling | 8245.80 | 8618.50 | 4.51 |
| Plastic sheet | 8566.20 | 8937.80 | 4.33 |

## 3.4  Cost Comparison Between Curing Compounds and Conventional Curing Methods

The curing methods used in this study for comparisons are water sprinkling, burlap covering and chemical curing compounds. As shown in Table 6, water sprinkling curing method has less total cost than using burlap and curing compounds. The next one is covering with burlap and using curing compound is costlier than the rest. In places where water for construction is transported from far-off distances and for the additional curing days the cost of water sprinkling and burlap covering might be increased. Since where shortage of water is a challenge transport and water cost increase; and also if curing period increases by more than seven days (minimum requirements of ASTM 308 1-98 [15]) material and manpower cost increases as well. The costs shown in Table 6, are based on Bahir Dar City market and obtained through own survey.

**Table 6.** Cost of each curing methods

| Work item | Cost of each curing methods (Birr/m$^2$) | | |
| --- | --- | --- | --- |
| | Water sprinkling | Burlap covering | Curing compounds |
| Manpower cost (for curing) | 0.24 | 0.24 | 0.121 |
| Manpower cost (for covering) | – | 2.1 | – |
| Water cost | 2.94 | 2.94 | – |
| Burlap cost | – | 5 | – |
| Curing compound cost | – | – | 18 |
| Transport cost | – | – | 0.4 |
| Total cost | 3.04 | 10.52 | 18.5 |

# 4   Conclusions

Based on the results, analysis and discussion of all the performed tests and related complied relevant data the following conclusions are drawn.

- The drying time of curing compounds is from 1 h -2 h.
- All curing compounds did not deleteriously react with the concrete produced since there was no any softening of the liquid membrane-forming compound-treated surfaces.
- Based on the compressive strength test results, in case of both samples cured in laboratory and field weather conditions, all curing compounds were effective at 3, 7, and 28 days for both C-25 and C-40 concrete grades since all samples achieved expected strength.
- However, curing compounds have smaller compressive strengths and higher water absorptions than immersion (control group), water sprinkling and plastic sheet coverings curing.
- The compressive strength between mean of curing compounds and non-chemical curing method results show a statistically significant difference.
- All curing compounds results poor concrete quality at field and average in lab in both concrete grades, except Product (3) which results poor both at field and in lab, depending water absorption results.
- Water sprinkling and covering with plastic sheet results average concrete quality in both concrete grades and the control group results good concrete quality in both concrete grades.
- The cost comparison between those curing methods indicate that water sprinkling has less total cost than burlap covering and curing compounds. And cost of burlap covering is economical than curing compounds.

# References

1. Neville, A.: Properties of Concrete, 3rd edn. Longman Scientific and Technical, USA (1996)
2. QCL group: Technical note. The Curing of Concrete. Milton, Australia (1991)
3. ASTM C 309 -07 (2007): Standard Specification for Liquid Membrane-Forming Compounds for Curing Concrete1. ASTM International, West Conshohocken, PA (2007)
4. The constructor- Civil Engineering Home (2018). https://theconstructor.org/. Retrieved from https://theconstructor.org/
5. Wang, K., Cable, J.K., Zhi, G.: Iowa Department of Transportation. Investigation in to Improved Pavement Curing Materials and Techniques Part 1. Center for Transportation Research and Education, Iowa DOT Project TR-451, CTRE Project 00–77. IOWA STATE UNIVERSITY (2002)
6. Copeland, L.E., Bragg, R.H.: Self-Desiccation in Portland Cement Pastes. Portland Cement Association (1955)
7. Tech Brief: http://www.fhwa.dot.gov/pavement. Curing Concrete Paving Mixtures. FHWA-HIF-18–015 (2018)
8. Carino, K.W.M., Nicholas, J.: Curing of High-Performance Concrete. Report of the State of the Art. NISTIR 6295. National Institute of Standards and Technology, Gaithersburg, MD., 20899 (1999)
9. Gawatre, D.W., Sawant, K., Mule, R., Waydande, N., Randeve, D., Shirsath, T.: Effectiveness of curing compound on concrete. IOSR J. Mech. Civil Eng. 14(3), 73–76 (2017). https://doi.org/10.9790/1684-1403057376
10. ASTM C 642–06: Standard Test Method for Density, Absorption, and Voids in Hardened Concrete1. ASTM International West Conshohocken, PA (2006)
11. Karthick, R., Amrin, S.: An experimental investigation on self-curing concrete using different curing agent. Int. Res. J. Eng. Technol. 05(03), 429–431 (2018)
12. Gowsika, D., Balamurugan, P., Kamalambigai, R.: Experimental study on curing methods of concrete. Int. J. Eng. Dev. Res. 5(1) (2017). ISSN: 2321–9939
13. Medeiros – Junior, R.A., Munhoz, G.S., Medeiros, M.H.F.: Correlations between water absorption, electrical resistivity and compressive strength of concrete with different contents of pozzolan. Revista ALCONPAT 9(2), 152–166 (2019). ISSN: 2007–6835
14. Comite Euro-International du Beton, CEB Bull 192: Diagnosis and assessment of concrete structures _ state of the art report. Lausanne (1989)
15. ACI 308 1–98 (1998): Standard specification for curing concrete. Farmington Hills, MI American Concrete Institute (1998)

# Study on Effects of Process Parameters on Mechanical Behaviors of Injection Molded Glass Fiber Reinforced Polypropylene Matrix Composite

Eshetie Kassegn[1]([✉]), Frederik Desplentere[2], Temesgen Berhanu[1], and Bart Buffel[2]

[1] School of Mechanical and Industrial Engineering, Ethiopian Institute of Technology - Mekelle, Mekelle University, P.O. Box: 231, Tigray, Ethiopia
eshetie.kassegn@mu.edu.et
[2] ProPoLiS Research Group, KU Leuven Bruges Campus, Spoorwegstraat 12, 8200 Bruges, Belgium
{frederik.desplentere,bart.buffel}@kuleuven.be

**Abstract.** Currently, there is an expanding demand of composite materials for various engineering applications. Glass fiber reinforced polymer composites, prepared by injection molding, is among these composites. Injection molding method has basic process parameters which determine the mechanical behaviors of polymer matrix composites (PMCs). However, only few studies have been reported on the effects of injection molding process parameters for a typical short glass fiber reinforced polypropylene composites. In this study, process parameters such as melting temperature, mold temperature, packing pressure and flow rate were used for fabrication of the specimens. The modeled specimens, loaded by a compression force, were simulated and analyzed using moldflow (R2018) and ansys (R19.2) software. The specimens were also subjected to experimental studies of compression testing to study the effects of process parameters on mechanical properties of the composites. As a result, it is found that fiber orientation, deflection and mechanical properties of the composites are significantly affected by the injection molding process parameters. So, in pursuit of increasing the mechanical properties of the composite, set of injection molding process parameters of 80°C mold temperature, 240 °C melt temperature, 60 cm³/s flow rate and 40 MPa packing pressure are required. From the numerical and experimental studies, variations of melt temperatures significantly influence the mechanical properties of the short glass fiber reinforced polypropylene composite parts molded by injection molding.

**Keywords:** Polypropylene · Glass fibers · Mechanical properties · Process parameters · Injection molding

## 1 Introduction

Polymeric composite materials have extensive applications in many engineering areas due to their advantages of light weight, high specific strength and stiffness, good heat and

M. A. Delele et al. (Eds.): ICAST 2020, LNICST 385, pp. 467–481, 2021.
https://doi.org/10.1007/978-3-030-80618-7_32

sound insulation, excellent energy absorption, and good damping capacity [1]. Some of the application areas of polymer composites are aeronautic, automotive, naval, construction, sporting goods, home appliances, furniture, packaging and electronic devices [2]. Polymer composite processing methods are injection molding, hot press compression molding, vacuum assisted resin infusion, resin transfer molding, and so on. Among these methods, injection molding is widely used for the development of thermoplastic-based composite products [3, 4]. A composite of polypropylene with short glass fiber is one of the feedstock into injection molding process [5, 6]. Injection molding has fundamental process parameters that influence the mechanical properties of polymeric composite products. Injection molding process parameters also determine warpage of the polymeric composite parts in which warpage is an effect occurred during cooling. Process parameters also affect the level of residual stresses which also causes part warpage [5, 7]. Selection of gate location is also an important factor in ensuring uniform and complete mold filling with appropriate flow paths rapid as possible [6]. Uncontrolled deviations from the proper process parameters could significantly affect both morphology distributions and final material properties which in turn lead to the premature failure of a product/part [8]. The fiber orientation and fiber length, affected by process parameters, importantly determines the mechanical properties of composites [9–12]. Melting temperature, mold temperature, flow rate and packing pressure are process parameters for this study due to their high impact on part properties.

There is a kinetics creation and destruction of entanglements of the polymer molecules during the injection molding process which leads to a very complex shear thinning (non-Newtonian) fluid flow behavior a composite. This complex fluid flow behavior will influence the fiber orientation in the composite. Hence, the shear flow of the melt affects fiber orientation through aligning some of the fibers with the flow direction, and some other fibers with a typical skin-shell-core orientation distribution. Melt temperature changes viscosity of the matrix in the composite. At higher melt temperature, viscosity of the melt reduces and increases its flow velocity into the mold. This results the melt to enter to the mold and settle in an ordered manner of molecular orientations which provides reduced residual stresses but increased the yielding stresses. Consequently, the failure strain decreases. The residual stresses increase the failure strain of the composite part [8, 13, 14]. However, higher melt temperature results high molecular weight of melt in the molded part which maximizes energy consumption in molding and longer cycle time [15]. When a melt of the composite at high melt temperature enters to the mold at lower mold temperature, a frozen layer is formed between the surface of the mold and inner melt. The fibers in this frozen layer can't be oriented and are spread most randomly. The inner melt which is close to this frozen layer also experiences a large shear stress. This effect diminishes for the flow further away of this frozen layer and consequently the alignment is diminished. With increasing mold temperature, orientation of fibers can be higher but it shouldn't be too high for good quality of parts. If it is too high, weld-lines will occur and parts will stick to the mold and difficult to remove it [16]. Mold temperature has also an influence on the viscosity when in packing stage. In this case when the mold temperature is reasonably high, the flow of heat from the melt to the mold decreases and this leads to maintain viscosity of the melt to some extent [17]. Basically mold temperature is ranging from 10 °C to 95 °C as a standard

[5]. The other important process parameter is injection speed (flow rate). The injection time of an injection molding process is very short it which mostly less than one second. A too low injection speed (flow rate) can result in flow marks; whereas, a too high flow rate results less fiber orientation and incomplete mold filling, and can cause air to be trapped in parts which can lead to burn marks [18]. On the other hand, packing pressure tends to rotate fibers and the level of alignment of fibers tends to decrease. The viscosity of the melt determines the rate of this effect [17].

The injection molding process consists of two stages. In the first stage, the velocity is controlled and most of the cavity is filled. The pressure during this stage is variable and depends on the viscosity of the material. In the second stage, the velocity control is switched to pressure control and the pressure is lower as in the first stage. It is important to set the switching point correctly which shouldn't be too early or too late. Too early switching can lead to incomplete filling while switching too late can cause the part to flash and damage of mold and tools. The switch over from velocity controlled to pressure controlled is usually when the mold is 95% filled [13, 19].

To the understanding of this author, there are few studies conducted on investigation of effects of process parameters on injection molded glass fiber reinforced polypropylene (PP) matrix composites. But, similar studies haven't been studied on profile parts of the short glass fiber reinforced polypropylene (Sabic PP Compound G3220) matrix composites. Since Sabic PP Compound G3220 is designed for under-the-hood and structural applications [20], the influence of processing parameters should be studied for better performance of parts. Therefore, this study was conducted to investigate the effects of process parameters on mechanical performances of injection molded profile parts of short glass fiber reinforced Sabic PP Compound G3220 matrix composite.

## 2 Materials and Methods

### 2.1 Materials

The polypropylene (Sabic PP Compound G3220A) matrix and short E-glass fiber (1 mm length) were used for fabrication of the specimens. The density of the PP is 1.04 g/cm$^3$ and 210–270 °C process melt temperature. The shrinkage value of the PP is around 1% but this can slightly be changed with different sets of injection molding process parameters. The young's modulus of the PP is also 4.9 GPa [21, 22]. The glass fibers (GFs) have high strength (1,500 MPa), high young's modulus (72 GPa) and have a good thermal stability. In this study, 20% short glass fibers (SGFs) were used for fabrication of the composite specimens. This amount was used for the case of fast processing and providing good performer profiles [20].

### 2.2 Method

Injection molding process was used for fabrication of the specimens. The 80% PP matrix material and 20% short glass fiber were used for the composites development. Various sets of injection molding process parameters were applied for preparation of the composite. Hence, variable melt temperature and mold temperature, and constant injection speed (flow rate) and packing pressure were used for fabrication of the specimens. The switch over point was set at 95% filling of the volume.

## 2.2.1  Fabrication of Specimens

The specimens were fabricated with three profiles having different corners at the mid-point. The volume fractions used were 20% SGFs and 80% PP matrix. Silicon-free mold release agent (C-150) was used for demolding the specimens from mold cavity. Injection molding with various sets of process parameters was used for fabrication of the specimens. Accordingly, nine specimens of three profiles each were fabricated with various sets of process parameters shown on Table 1.

**Table 1.** The sets of process parameters of injection molding.

| Set of process parameters | Process parameters | | | |
|---|---|---|---|---|
| | Melting temp. (°C) | Mold temp. (°C) | Flow rate (cm³/s) | Packing pressure (MPa) |
| Set 1 | 210 | 20 | 60 | 40 |
| Set 2 | 210 | 50 | 60 | 40 |
| Set 3 | 210 | 80 | 60 | 40 |
| Set 4 | 240 | 20 | 60 | 40 |
| Set 5 | 240 | 50 | 60 | 40 |
| Set 6 | 240 | 80 | 60 | 40 |
| Set 7 | 270 | 20 | 60 | 40 |
| Set 8 | 270 | 50 | 60 | 40 |
| Set 9 | 270 | 80 | 60 | 40 |

The profiles of the specimen have a rectangular geometry cornered at the mid-point. The dimensions of profiles of the specimen were 30 mm width, 3 mm thickness and 90 mm² contact area. The three profiles of the specimen, however, have different inner radii at the corner positions. The dimensions were selected according to the European Standards of profile specimens. The left profile of the specimen shown on Fig. 1 has inner radius equal to halve its thickness. The middle profile of the specimen is a zero the inner radius. The right profile of the specimen has the inner radius equal to the thickness. The thickness of the three profiles of the specimen is 3 mm. The inner radius of the profiles of the specimen is the radii of them at the cornered parts (mid-point). The three profiles of the specimen were fabricated connectively together but experimentally tested separately.

## 3  Numerical Simulation Analysis

The inputs parameters used for numerical simulations were geometry of profiles of the specimen with dimensions and meshes, compression load and the various sets of injection molding process parameters (melt temperature, mold temperature, injection speed and packing pressure, and others such as cooling time kept as standard values).

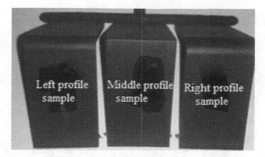

**Fig. 1.** The fabricated three profiles of the specimen.

## 3.1 Fiber Orientation

The properties of reinforced thermoplastic composites parts/products molded by injection molding depend on the state of fiber orientation and geometry of the part molded [23]. Fiber orientation is also affected by the injection molding process parameters and their sets. Increasing mold temperature delays heat transfer from the melt to mold walls (reduction of melt viscosity) which increases the degree of transverse alignment of fibers at the core layer during packing stage. This way, mold temperature affects fiber orientation of a composite. Packing pressure also increases the degree of transverse orientation of fibers at the core layer of the molded part [10]. This leads to rotation of fibers which increases transverse stress on fibers. The transverse stress also brings transverse orientation of fibers. Flow rate of the melt is also a factor influencing fiber orientations. At high flow rate (injection speed) of the melt, fiber loading content decreases and then fiber orientation gets decreased [24, 25]. Figure 2 illustrates effects of the melt temperature and mold temperature on orientation and alignment of fibers. The left-hand side figure indicates the specimen for the set of process parameters 1 (210 °C melt temperature and 20 °C mold temperature), and the right-hand side figure indicates the specimen for the set of process parameters 9 (270 °C melt temperature and 80 °C mold temperature). In this scenario, both melt temperature and mold temperature are increased for the set of process parameters 9 when compared with the set of process parameters 1, and the fiber orientations of the two specimens are different (as shown on Fig. 2 through color distributions indicating fiber orientations). The vertical bars representing ranges of fiber orientations on specimens are with merits of very high, high, medium, low and very low. As shown on Fig. 2 for example, the concentration and distribution of yellow color is higher for the right-hand side specimen (process parameters set 9) which means higher fiber orientation.

Another scenario was also examined to study the fiber orientation (as shown on Fig. 3). The left-hand side figure indicates the specimen for the set of process parameters 3 (210 °C melt temperature and 80 °C mold temperature), and right-hand side figure indicates the specimen for the set of process parameters 7 (270 °C melt temperature and 20 °C mold temperature). As shown on Fig. 3, the numerical simulation results indicate that fiber orientations of specimens are slightly different due to various sets of process parameters.

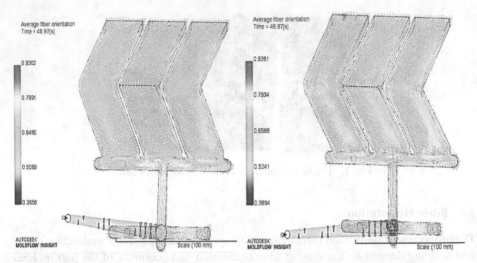

**Fig. 2.** Fiber orientation of specimens for sets 1 and 9 (Color figure online).

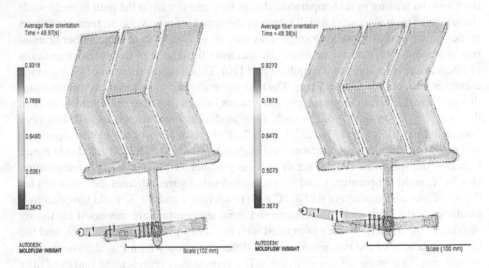

**Fig. 3.** Fiber orientation of specimens for sets 3 and 7 (Color figure online).

From Figs. 2 and 3, fiber orientations of the specimens for sets of process parameters 1 and 7 are different due to variation of the melt temperatures. Fiber orientation of the specimen for the set of process parameters 1 is lower than that of the specimen for the set of process parameters 7. At higher melt temperature of the part molded, there is high fiber orientation obtained. That means melt temperature has an effect on the fiber orientation of the part molded by injection. Again from Figs. 2 and 3, fiber orientations of the specimens for sets of process parameters 1 and 3 are different due to mold temperatures variation. This case, the two sets have the same melt temperatures but various mold temperatures. Fiber orientation of the process parameters set 3 is higher due to its higher mold temperature. Whereas when sets of process parameters 7 and 9 are compared, they have the same higher melt temperatures and variable mold temperatures. The numerical simulation results (Figs. 2 and 3) indicated that the two specimens seem has similar fiber orientations for sets of 9 and 7. From these analyses, it is possible to say that higher fiber orientation is achieved when either melt temperature or mold temperature is, or both are increased. But, melt temperature has slightly higher influence than mold temperature in fiber orientation (refer Fig. 3 of sets of process parameters 3 and 7).

Fiber orientations on faces of the specimens before and after the corner at the mid-point (gate location as a reference) are also different. It is higher result of fiber orientations on the faces of the specimens before the corner due to different reasons. This might be due to change of viscosity of the melt before and after the corner, incomplete mold filling and geometry of specimen molded.

## 3.2 Deflections

The magnitude and distribution of pressures on the core vary significantly during filling and packing; therefore, deflection will also vary with time. The maximum deflection occurs during filling and packing phases when the part is inside the mold [6].

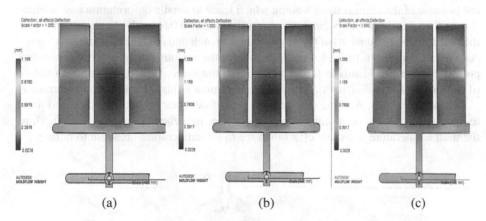

**Fig. 4.** Numerical deflections of specimens (Color figure online).

Figure 4a indicates deflection of specimen for the set of process parameters 3 (80 °C mold temperature and 210 °C melt temperature). Figure 4b also indicates deflection of specimen for the set of process parameters 7 (20 °C mold temperature and 270 °C melt temperature). Figure 4c also indicates deflection of specimen for the set of process parameters 9 (80 °C mold temperature and 270 °C melt temperature). As shown from the simulation results (Fig. 4), deflection is affected by mold and melts temperatures but mold temperature has less effect. That is why Fig. 4b and c seem similar due to the same values of melt temperatures for the two process parameters sets even if different mold temperatures. So, melt temperature has significant influence on part deflection. When melt temperature raises, the value of part deflection also increases. This can be exhibited from Fig. 4a and c which were simulated with the same mold temperature but different melt temperature.

When melt temperature increases, the viscosity of the melt decreases and allows fibers to freely rotate and develop inter-fiber internal shear stresses. These internal shear stresses produce residual deformations or deflections of parts. On the other hand, viscosity of the melt is low at high melt temperature and consequently the residual stresses and residual deformation of the part decrease [26].

### 3.3 Load-Displacement Curve

Ansys software (R19.2) was used for numerical simulation of applied load and displacement (extension) values. The applied loads and deformations (extensions) of the profile of the specimen (profile with inner radius of 3 mm which is the right profile sample) have been then drawn for various sets of injection molding process parameters (shown on Fig. 6). A compression load of 180.0 N was applied along the –z direction. This is illustrated on Fig. 5. As indicated on Fig. 5, the deformations (extensions) are varied along the profile in which the maximum value was found at the corner and ends of it. The deformation of the profile at the corner is maximum due to stress concentration is experienced there. The maximum deformations developed at the ends of the profile are because of the compression loading which leads to tensile deformation and in-plane shears. The profile of the specimen has been failed at 180.0 N loads. As shown on Fig. 6, the deformation (extension) of the profile at higher melt and mold temperatures is higher. As a result, the strains to failure of the profile for the various sets of process parameters are different but the loads at failure point seem the same. Hence, the strain to failure of the profile for higher melt and mold temperatures is higher due to the incremental elastic deformations. And the deformation even if depends on both the melt and mold temperatures, but the melt temperature have better influence (shown on Fig. 6). Thus, the melt temperature has more effect than the mold temperature on strain to failure.

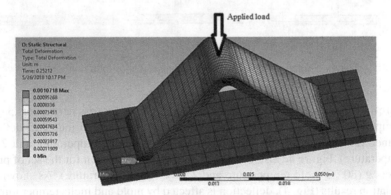

**Fig. 5.** Illustration on applied compression load on the profile (Color figure online).

Finally, the deformations and strains to failure of the profile of the specimen for the nine (9) sets of the process parameters have been determined and summarized in Table

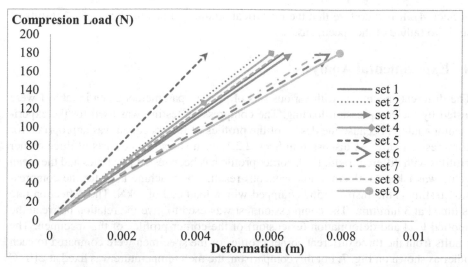

**Fig. 6.** Compression load versus deformation graph (Color figure online).

2. Table 2 shows that the strains to failure of settings 3 (low melt temperature and high mold temperature) and 6 (moderate melt temperature and high mold temperature) are the highest and lowest values, respectively. This seems very logical that the specimen molded by injection molding process with low melt temperature and high mold temperature has the maximum strain to failure which is tough. The specimen molded by moderate melt temperature and high mold temperature has the minimum strain to failure which is less tough but stiff one. So it is possible to conclude that the part molded by injection molding of moderate melt temperature and high mold temperatures performs the highest mechanical properties except the lowest strain to failure characteristics. Indeed, this conclusion was also aligned with the optimum conclusion of experimental results (shown

**Table 2.** Deformations and strains to failure of the profile of specimen for process sets.

| Set of process parameters | Compression load (N) | Deformation (mm) | Strain to failure (%) |
|---|---|---|---|
| Set 1 | 180.0 | 6.3634 | 4.4252 |
| Set 2 | 180.0 | 5.7753 | 4.4253 |
| Set 3 | 180.0 | 6.6065 | 4.4266 |
| Set 4 | 180.0 | 6.0356 | 4.4234 |
| Set 5 | 180.0 | 4.3046 | 4.4246 |
| Set 6 | 180.0 | 7.6924 | 4.4207 |
| Set 7 | 180.0 | 7.4078 | 4.4224 |
| Set 8 | 180.0 | 6.2909 | 4.4239 |
| Set 9 | 180.0 | 7.9483 | 4.4248 |

in Sect. 4). It is therefore that the numerical simulation has predicted good results of strain to failure of the specimens.

## 4  Experimental Analysis

The different specimens with various sets of process parameters given in table 1 were tested by the compression loading. The compression testing was used for the experimental analysis because the design of the profiles of the specimen was appropriate for compression only. As discussed in Sect. 2.2.1, each specimen consists of three corner profiles with different radii. Each corner profile has been tested five times and the mean value was taken to obtain a homogeneous result. The machine used for the compression testing is the Instron 5567 equipped with a load cell of 1 kN. The deflection rate is tuned at 3 mm/min. The compression test was used to give the relation between the applied load and deformation (extension) of the corner profiles of the specimen. The results from the three different corner profiles of the specimen were compared to each other as shown on Fig. 7. For this comparison, the melt temperature was fixed at 210 °C and the mold temperature was fixed at 20 °C. As shown on Fig. 7, the inner (internal) radius of the corner of the profile sample has great impact on the load carrying capacity. The bigger the inner radius, the larger compression load the profile of the specimen can sustain. This is because sharp corners will lead to the stress concentrations. These stress concentrations will lead to a premature failure of parts. Therefore, a good design rule is to make the inner radius of the part as large as possible. Accordingly, the middle profile (sample) not only failed at a load lower than the others two but it also failed under a smaller extension (shown on Fig. 7).

The effect of sets of the different mold temperatures was also examined. For this analysis, the profile of the specimen with the inner radius equal to half of the thickness (left profile sample) was used and the melt temperature was fixed at 210 °C. The results indicated that the effect of changing the mold temperature is less though the higher mold temperature has delivered slightly higher load carrying capacity which is better mechanical properties (shown on Fig. 8). Theoretically, a higher mold temperature improves the

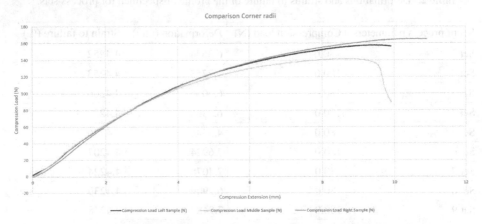

**Fig. 7.** Comparison of the three profiles of the specimen (Color figure online).

flow behavior of a melt and reduces the internal stresses but can make part demolding more difficult [5, 27].

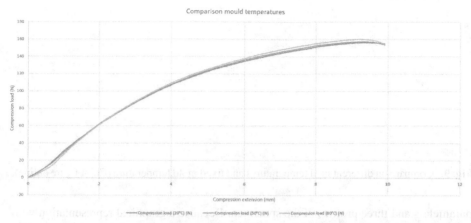

**Fig. 8.** Comparison of different Mold temperatures and fixed melt temperature (Color figure online).

The effect of changing the melt temperature was also investigated. Again the test profile of the specimen subject to this analysis was with the inner radius equal to halve of the thickness (left profile sample). The fixed mold temperature and various melt temperatures were used for the analysis. It is shown on Fig. 9 that the profile of the specimen performs different due to the change of the melt temperatures. This is because of the fact that the fiber orientation is one of the factors affecting the properties of composite parts. It is know that fiber orientation highly depends on melt temperature and geometry of the profile of the specimen. A higher melt temperature results higher orientation of fibers which also leads to an improved part performance.

Changing the melt temperatures has a larger effect than the mold temperatures on the mechanical properties of the profile of the specimen. This conclusion is evident just by looking the Figs. 8 and 9. The reason behind the larger effect of melt temperature on the composites is that the viscosity of the melt will be lower when increasing the melt temperature. The effect of lower viscosity will induce less residual stress but higher fiber orientation in the injection molded profile of the specimen. This means that the profile of the specimen manufactured by injection molding with higher melt temperatures can withstand a higher compression load (shown on Fig. 9). Though the profile of the specimen manufactured injection molding with higher melt temperature can withstand larger compression load, the profile of the specimen fails at lower compression extension (strain). This means that the profile of the specimen manufactured by injection molding at higher melt temperature is stiffer but less tough.

The three different setups were studied independently. The general comparison had been then done about the influence of the inner radii of the corner profiles of the specimen, melt temperatures and mold temperatures. In total, 27 load-extension (deformation) relationships were obtained for the various nine (9) sets of injection molding process

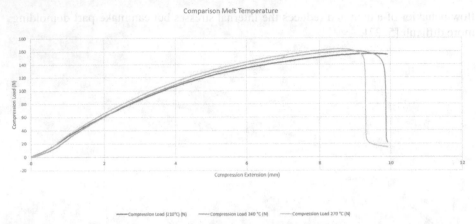

**Fig. 9.** Comparison different melt temperatures and fixed mold temperature (Color figure online).

parameters and three profiles of the specimen. Because a graphical representation with 27 lines would be varying chaotic, the authors of this paper have chosen to compare the maximum compression loads the specimens sustain and extensions (deformations) at which they occur due to the loadings (shown in Table 3).

**Table 3.** Comparison of load versus extension for profiles of the specimens.

| Set of process parameters | Load versus extension of the three profiles of specimens | | |
|---|---|---|---|
| | Left profile | Middle profile | Right profile |
| | N (mm) | N (mm) | N (mm) |
| Set 1 | 156.6 (9.37) | 141.5 (8.70) | 164.9 (10.62) |
| Set 2 | 157.3 (9.31) | 141.5 (8.59) | 168.0 (11.01) |
| Set 3 | 159.9 (9.21) | 141.7 (8.11) | 169.2 (10.18) |
| Set 4 | 160.2 (8.87) | 142.9 (7.98) | 169.0 (9.93) |
| Set 5 | 164.9 (8.81) | 139.9 (7.88) | 172.4 (9.48) |
| Set 6 | 163.6 (8.19) | 134.4 (7.06) | 174.0 (9.32) |
| Set 7 | 160.2 (8.55) | 141.4 (8.17) | 172.8 (9.74) |
| Set 8 | 161.4 (8.84) | 138.6 (7.85) | 174.7 (9.71) |
| Set 9 | 164.6 (8.58) | 126.3 (6.15) | 175.0 (9.36) |

When the maximum compression loads (shown in Table 3) are compared, some interesting facts are found. The geometry of profile of the specimen is the most important parameter for load carrying capacity. As said previously, the inner radius should be as large as possible to diminish the stress concentration. The right profile of the specimen has the largest inner radius and thus can withstand the largest compression loads (shown in Table 3). And as expected, the maximum load is proportional to the melt temperature and mold temperature. The inner radius of the left profile of the specimen is only half of the inner radius of the right profile of the specimen that leads the alignment of fibers in the left profile corner is more difficult. The left profile of the specimen shows that it is important to match the mold temperature and the melt temperature. A too large temperature difference between the melt and mold results in a larger frozen layer in which fibers will be orientated randomly and thus lower mechanical properties. The properties of the middle profile of the specimen seem to decrease with increasing mold temperature which can be explained by the transverse alignment of the fibers during the packaging stage. The small increasing properties with melt temperature could be due to a mismatch between melt and mold temperatures.

## 5 Conclusion

This paper contains a numerical and experimental analysis of three profiles of each specimen of the short glass fiber reinforced polypropylene (Sabic PP Compound G3220A) composite using various sets of injection molding process parameters. Following both the numerical simulations and experimental analysis of the profiles of specimens, the following conclusions have been drawn:

- The load carrying capacity of the specimen highly depends on the geometry of the profiled specimen. When the inner radius of the profile of the specimen is larger (less sharp at its corner), it sustains the maximum applied compression load.
- The extensions (deformations) values of the numerical analyses are less predicted than the extensions (deformations) values of the experimental extensions for the same profile (right profile sample). However, the numerical simulations of the right profile sample have predicted higher extensions (deformations) than the experimental extensions of the middle profile sample for sets of process parameters 6 and 9 (as shown in Tables 2 and 3).
- The mechanical properties of the specimens of the composite are slightly higher at high melt temperatures. This is because fiber orientation is higher at high melt temperatures whereas the residual stresses inside the injection molded part decreases as a result of viscosity reduction at higher melt temperatures.
- Melt temperature has more influence on the overall properties of injection molded parts when compared with other injection molding process parameters.

**Acknowledgments.** This research was supported by KU Leuven-Belgium in collaboration with the Ministry of Science and Higher Education-Ethiopia. The research has been conducted at KU Leuven campuses (Bruges, Heverlee and Diepenbeek). My grateful appreciation and thanks is to research group ProPoLiS members. Especial thank is to Cedric De Schryver who is a research assistant at KU Leuven, Bruges campus for his ultimate support in doing the research. I would like also acknowledge to Tim Evens who is project engineer at Cel Kunststoffen for his ultimate support of fabricating the specimens.

# References

1. Yang, J., Li, P.: Characterization of short glass fiber reinforced polypropylene foam composites with the effect of compatibilizers: a comparison. J. Reinf. Plast. Compos. **34**(7), 534–546 (2015)
2. Etcheverry, M., Barbosa, S.E.: Glass fiber reinforced polypropylene mechanical properties enhancement by adhesion improvement. J. Mater. **5**, 1084–1113 (2012)
3. Kassegn, E., Desplentere, F., Berhanu, T.: Mechanical properties of short sisal fiber reinforced polylactic acid (pla) biocomposite processed by injection molding. Branna J. Eng. Technol. **1**(1), 20–36 (2019)
4. Rajesh, G.: AV Ratna Prasad and AVSSKS Gupta: mechanical and degradation properties of successive alkali treated completely biodegradable sisal fiber reinforced poly lactic acid composites. J. Reinf. Plast. Compos. **34**(12), 951–961 (2015)
5. Vannessa, G.: Practical Guide to Injection Moulding. 3rd edn. Rapra Technology Limited, UK (2004)
6. Singh, A.K., Singh, D.K.: Modelling and analysis of mold filling parameters for PP and abs materials using software simulation. Int. J. Eng. Res. Technol. **1**(7), 1–6 (2012)
7. Mohd, A.: Ainul Ayunie Roslan and Nor Bahiyah Baba: Effect of Injection Molding Parameters on Recycled ABS (r-ABS) mechanical properties. Indian J. Sci. Technol. **9**(9), 1–6 (2016)
8. Dar, U.A., Xu, Y.J., Zakir, S.M., Saeed, M.-U.: The effect of injection molding process parameters on mechanical and fracture behavior of polycarbonate polymer. J. Appl. Polym. Sci. **134**, 1–9 (2016)
9. Liparoti, S., Speranza, V., Sorrentino, A., Titomanlio, G.: Mechanical properties distribution within polypropylene injection molded samples: effect of mold temperature under uneven thermal conditions. J. Polym. **9**(585), 1–18 (2017)
10. Parvin, S., Naresh, B.: Effect of packing pressure and mold temperature on fiber orientation in injection molding of reinforced plastics. In: The 8th International Conference on Flow Processes in Composite Materials 2006, vol. 8, pp. 1–8. Douai, FRANCE (2006)
11. DharMalingam, S., Mohd Zulkefli Bin Selamat, S., Said, M.R.B., Kalyanasundaram, S.: Effects of process parameters during forming of glass reinforced-PP based sandwich structure. J. Adv. Environ. Biol. **8**(8), 3143–3150 (2014)
12. Parveeen, B., Caton-Rose, P., Costa, F., Jin, X., Hine, P.: Study of injection moulded long glass fibre-reinforced polypropylene and the effect on the fibre length and orientation distribution. In: Proceedings of the Polymer Processing Society 29 Annual Meeting, pp. 1–4 (2013)
13. Farotti, E., Natalini, M.: Injection molding. Influence of process parameters on mechanical properties of polypropylene polymer. A first study. In: AIAS 2017 International Conference on Stress Analysis 2018, vol. 8, pp. 256–264. Elsevier, Pisa, Italy (2018)
14. Li, Y., Zhou, K., Tan, P., Tor, S.B., Chua, C.K., Leong, K.F.: Modeling temperature and residual stress fields in selective laser melting. J. Elsevier **136**(2018), 24–35 (2017)
15. Shrivastava, S.: Introduction to plastics engineering. J. Elsevier 1–262 (2018)
16. Li, X.-P., Zhao, G.-Q., Yang, C.: Effect of mold temperature on motion behavior of short glass fibers in injection molding process. Int. J. Adv. Manuf. Technol. **73**(5–8), 639–645 (2014). https://doi.org/10.1007/s00170-014-5874-8
17. Parvin, S., Naresh, B.: Effect of packing pressure on fiber orientation in injection molding of fiber-reinforced thermoplastics. J. Polym. Compos. **28**, 214–223 (2007)
18. Oumer, A.N., Mamat, O.: A study of fiber orientation in short fiber-reinforced composites with simultaneous mold filling and phase change effects. J. Elsevier **43**(3), 1087–1094 (2012)
19. Koffi, A., Koffi, D., Toubal, L.: Injection molding parameters influence on PE composites parts. Int. J. Eng. Res. Dev. **12**(10), 29–39 (2016)

20. Lin, J.-H., Huang, C.-L., Liu, C.-F., Chen, C.-K., Lin, Z.-I., Lou, C.-W.: Polypropylene/short glass fibers composites: effects of coupling agents on mechnical properties, thermal behavior and morfology. J. Mater. **8**, 8279–8291 (2015)
21. Colin, H.: Polypropylene (PP) (2019). https://www.bpf.co.uk//plastipedia/polymers/PP.aspx
22. PP short glass fiber reinforced (2019). https://www.sabicppppcompoundG3220A
23. Oumer, A.N., Mamat, O.: A review of effects of molding methods, mold thickness and other processing parameters on fiber orientation in polymer composites. Asian J. Sci. Res. **6**(3), 401–410 (2013)
24. Azaman, M.D., Sapuan, S.M., Sulaiman, S., Zainudin, E.S., Khalina, A.: Numerical simulation analysis of unfilled and filled reinforced polypropylene on thin-walled parts formed using the injection-moulding process. Int. J. Polym. Sci. **2015**, 1–8 (2015).
25. Kastner, C., Steinbichler, G., Kahlen, S., Jerabek, M.: Influence of process parameters on mechanical properties of physically foamed, fiber reinforced polypropylene parts. J. Appl. Polym. Sci. **136**, 1–11 (2018)
26. Kim, H.K., Sohn, J.S., Ryu, Y., Kim, S.W., Cha, S.W.: Warpage reduction of glass fiber reinforced plastic using microcellular foaming process applied injection molding. J. Polym. **11**(360), 1–12 (2019)
27. Vadori, R., Mohanty, A.K., Misra, M.: The effect of mold temperature on the performance of injection molded poly (lactic acid)-based bioplastic. J. Macromol. Mater. Eng. **298**, 981–990 (2013)

# Mechanical Properties Characterization of Water Hyacinth ("Emboch") Plant for Use as Fiber Reinforced Polymer Composite

Samrawit Alemyayehu[1,2], Yohannes Regassa[2(✉)], Bisrat Yoseph[3], and Hirpa G. Lemu[4] (iD)

[1] Dire Dawa University, Dire Dawa, Ethiopia
[2] Addis Ababa Science and Technology University, Addis Ababa, Ethiopia
[3] Defence Engineering College, Ethiopian Defence University, Bishoftu, Ethiopia
[4] University of Stavanger, 4036 Stavanger, Norway

**Abstract.** The aim of the research work reported in this article is to fabricate water hyacinth fiber reinforced polyester composites and characterize its mechanical properties. The fiber material was extracted manually after collecting the water hyacinth plant from Lake Koka in the Oromia Region, Ethiopia. Once the extraction was done, the fiber was treated by a chemical in different sodium hydroxide concentration, used for the improvement of bond and interfacial strength of the water hyacinth fiber. The composite of water hyacinth fiber is fabricated with polyester resin, using hand lay-up methods in different fiber/matrix ratios. The mechanical properties of the specimens were then measured according to ASTM standard recommendations experimental tests such as tensile, flexural and compressive tests were conducted on the prepared composite material samples. The results show that 20% fiber content is around optimum content for best mechanical behavior and all the mechanical properties are satisfactorily improved when the water hyacinth polyester composite is chemically treated using NaOH. Therefore, using water hyacinth fibers as reinforcement in a polymer matrix, it has been proved that successful composites can be developed.

**Keywords:** Natural fiber · Water hyacinth fiber · Polyester resin · Hand lay-up fabrication · Mechanical property

## 1 Introduction

Composite materials are combinations of two or more materials with different physical and chemical properties at distinct interfaces [1]. These materials have been in industrial applications for thousands of years. The most important reason for the selection of composite materials is the versatility in their properties including specific strength, high-temperature resistance, high specific modulus, and low thermal conductivity [2]. Among the areas where composite materials are widely used, the aerospace industry, marine sector, chemical industries, automotive industry, construction, electrical, and other application areas [3, 4] can be mentioned.

M. A. Delele et al. (Eds.): ICAST 2020, LNICST 385, pp. 482–492, 2021.
https://doi.org/10.1007/978-3-030-80618-7_33

The fibers used in reinforced composite materials can be classified as natural fibers and synthetic fibers [5]. Natural fibers are simple fibers found in plants and animals. Their advantages include high strength, durability, low thermal conductivity, lightweight, corrosion resistance, and dimensional stability [6]. The common drawback of almost all natural fibers is their relatively low dimensional stability, high moisture adsorption, and incompatibility with the binder matrix. Thus, chemical treatments and immersion techniques are needed to improve their mechanical performance [7]. The typical chemical treatments used on natural fibers are Alkali treatment, Acetic acid ($CH_2COOH$), Isocyanate, Silane treatment, Benzoylation, Peroxide, and other types of chemical treatments that are used for refinement of the natural fibers [8]. At present, many types of natural fibers are being investigated as reinforcement in the polymer matrix, including flax, hemp, jute straw, sisal, raphia, banana fiber, pineapple leaf fiber, and so on [9]. Table 1 shows the chemical composition and mechanical properties of selected plant fibers [10, 11].

**Table 1.** Chemical composition and mechanical properties of plant fibers.

| Fiber | Hemicelluloses (Wt. %) | Cellulose (Wt %) | Lignin (Wt %) | Density ($g/cm^3$) | Tensile strength (MPa) |
|-------|------------------------|------------------|---------------|---------------------|------------------------|
| Sisal* | 10–14 | 66–78 | 10–14 | 1.5 | 511–635 |
| Hemp | 17.9–22.4 | 70–74 | 3–5.7 | 1.48 | 690 |
| Flax | 18.6–20.6 | 71 | 2.2 | 1.5 | 345–1035 |
| Bamboo | 20.5 | 34.5 | 26 | 0.6–1.1 | 140–230 |
| Jute | 16 | 67 | 9 | 1.2 | 393–773 |

* The origin of sisal fiber is from leaves while the rest are from stem

One of the natural fiber sources is water hyacinth (WH), which contains lignocellulose materials. The water hyacinth (Eichhorniacrassipes) is a free-floating aquatic plant, a native of the Amazon basin, and belongs to the Pontederiaceae family, with different growth habits under different environmental conditions [12]. This plant is a noxious weed that has attracted worldwide attention because large water hyacinth mats prevent the transfer of oxygen from the air to the water surface or decrease oxygen production by other plants and algae [13]. The plant doubles its surface area indoors within two weeks, sometimes in a week. Water hyacinth covers 80% of Lake Victoria [14]. In Lake Tana, in Northern Ethiopia, water hyacinth recently invaded over 30% of the shoreline of the North-eastern part of the lake's shores [15].

Water hyacinth plant is used in animal feed and animal production, organic fertilizer (green manure or compost) or mulching materials, for making paper, biogas production, and the like. The use of this plant, for instance in Indonesian, as a raw material for handicraft and processed in a bag, basket, and tablecloth are the motivations of this study, which is aimed to convert this plant into engineering applications. Only limited previous studies and investigations are reported on the capabilities of this plant as a source of fiber and reinforcements to manufacture composite materials. For instance, Sawpan et al. [16] reported that the tensile strength of chemically treated (NaOH) fibers can be increased compared with the untreated hemp fiber. The reason is densification of fiber cell walls for the removal of the non-cellulosic components during treatment. The study reported by Bhuvaneshwari et al. [17] proved that the water hyacinth fiber has excellent absorbency, elongation and medium strength. The Scanning Electron Microscope (SEM) analysis shows that the fibers contain many hollow pores which can hold moisture and are suitable for high absorbency materials such as wipes and napkins.

Thus, the research reported in this article focuses on using this unwanted weed for useful engineering applications. Characterization of the mechanical properties of this plant as a source of fibers for composite materials demands an extensive research because the strength properties are affected by several parameters such as altitude, water quality, and water content. Thus, the current study aims only to develop some level of understanding on the possible applications of water hyacinth fiber as reinforced polyester composite as a source of fiber under limited conditions. A particular attention is given to the chemical treatments of WH fibers to improve the interfacial bonding between the WH fibers and the matrix.

## 2   Materials and Methods

The water hyacinth fiber was collected from Koka Lake in the Oromia region, Ethiopia and Phthalic Anhydride based TOPAZ-1110 TP unsaturated polyester resin with Luperox® K10 catalyst (purchased from World fiberglass engineering plc, in Addis Ababa, Ethiopia) was used as the matrix. Polyester resin, whose physical properties are given in Table 2, is the most widely used resin type particularly in the marine industry. This resin is low-cost and easily available in local market.

**Table 2.** Physical properties of polyester resin.

| | Properties | | | | | |
|---|---|---|---|---|---|---|
| | Density (g/cm$^3$) | Tensile strength (MPa) | Modulus of elasticity (MPa) | Elongation (%) | Flexural strength (MPa) | Flexural modulus (MPa) |
| Value | 1.2 | 50 | 3000 | 2.5 | 60 | 3000 |

To extract the fiber, the water hyacinth plant was collected and the root and leaves were separated from the stalk using knives. The stalk was then washed using tap water to remove dirt particles and soaked in water for seven days to remove lignin, any adhering dirty and hemicelluloses. The soaked fiber was washed by tap water and then dried. The steps used to collect the plant and extract the fiber are shown in Fig. 1.

According to the literature, treating the natural fibers with alkali solution has a good effect on their mechanical behavior. The chemical treatment was performed according to the following steps:

- Measuring the dry fiber and Sodium hydroxide (NaOH) amount according to the rule of mixture,
- Mixing the measured NaOH with distilled water,
- Soaking the fiber into alkali solution at room temperature for 3 h, and
- Washing the fiber thoroughly in distilled water.

Samples of fibers, both untreated and treated are given in Fig. 2.

**Fig. 1.** (a) Harvesting water hyacinth from Koka (b) sample of collected water hyacinth (c) washing samples by tap water (d) soaking in water (e) and (f) drying in open air.

**Fig. 2.** (a) Untreated fiber (b) 10% NaOH treated fiber and (c) 20% NaOH treated fiber

The test specimens were then prepared by using the hand lay-up method. This involved mixing the resin and the hardener, putting a plastic in the bottom and smearing a wax to remove adhesion between the sample and the mold, and finally, putting the mold in hydraulic pressing machine. The fibers collected and prepared according to the procedure presented above are then prepared for three types of tests according to the recommended ASTM standards (1) tensile test – ASTM D-3039/D-3039M [18], (b) flexural test – ASTM D-790 [19] and (c) compression test – ASTM D-695 [20].

To calculate the density of the water hyacinth, Pycnometer method was used. A Pycnometer flask with a capacity of 50 ml, oven-dry temperature at 105 °C and a sensitive balance were employed. The density was measured at Food Technology Laboratory of Addis Ababa University, Ethiopia.

First the mass of empty pycnometer flask was measured and record as $m_0$, then the flask was filled to $1/3^{rd}$ volume with chopped fiber and its mass was measured and recorded as $m_1$. Then, distilled water was added to the fiber-containing flask and measured ($m_2$) and the mass of distilled water was calculated ($m_3 = m_2 - m_1$). The density of distilled water varies depending on the temperature in the laboratory. Thus, for 20 °C, the density is 1.00 g/cm$^3$. Based on the recorded masses, mass fiber ($m_0 - m_1$) and measured volumes distilled water and the flask, the density of the chopped fiber was calculated. Finally, the pycnometer flask was dried for 20–30 min in an oven at 90–105 °C respectively before the next test.

# 3    Results and Discussions

## 3.1    Density

The density of water hyacinth was measured according to the procedure outlined in Sect. 2. The experiment was repeated five times and the average value was calculated. The linear density of untreated water hyacinth fiber was found to be 0.812 g/cm$^3$. When compared with the density of other natural fibers, hyacinth fiber is lower than the density of bamboo 1.20 g/cm$^3$ [21] but greater than Kenaf (core) 0.1- 0.2 g/cm$^3$ [22]. The density of natural fibers determines their application, for instance light weight applications prefer materials with low density.

According to the work reported by Bhuvaneshwari et al. [23], the density of water hyacinth is $1.37 \pm 0.05$ g/cm$^3$, and the density varies because of the drying temperature and moisture content of the fiber.

## 3.2    Tensile Tests and Results

To evaluate the in-plane tensile properties of the material, six different test groups were prepared with 5 test specimens each. The test groups are designated as follows:

1.. WHS1(T): Water hyacinth fiber reinforced polyester size one composite with fiber/matrix ratio of 30/70,
2.  WHS2(T): Water hyacinth fiber reinforced polyester size two composite with fiber/matrix ratio of 30/70,
3.  WHR20wt%(T): Water hyacinth fiber reinforced polyester composite with fiber/matrix ratio 20/80,
4   WHR10wt%(T): Water hyacinth fiber reinforced polyester composite with fiber/matrix ratio 10/90,
5.  WHT20%(T): 20% NaOH treated water hyacinth fiber reinforced polyester composite, and.
6.  WHT10%(T): 10% NaOH treated water hyacinth fiber reinforced polyester composite.

The tests were conducted at room temperature of 20 °C. For each test specimen, a cross-sectional area of 125 mm² was used. The tensile tests were conducted with focus on investigating the effects of cutting size, which are 10 mm and 2.5 mm for WHS1 (T) and WHS2 (T) respectively, fiber/matrix ratio (i.e. fiber content) and the chemical treatment of the composite on the stress-strain distribution (tensile strength). Table 3 shows the average values obtained from the tests.

**Table 3.** Tensile test results of the tested untreated sample groups.

| Specimen | Peak load (kN) | Max. deformation (mm) | Max tensile strength (MPa) |
|---|---|---|---|
| WHS1(T) | 0.21 | 5.62 | 1.68 |
| WHS2(T) | 1.38 | 6.52 | 11.28 |
| WHR20wt%(T) | 1.07 | 5.31 | 8.56 |
| WHR10wt%(T) | 0.78 | 4.28 | 6.24 |

As can be observed from the table (Table 3), higher average maximum tensile stress has been registered for the size two fiber contained composites (WHS2(T)) compared with the size one composite (WHS1(T)). In other words, the tensile strength of samples in the WHS2 group is about 85% higher than those in the WHS1 group. This can be attributed to the effect of fiber cutting size, 10 mm and 2.5 mm respectively, and this demonstrates the effect of weak internal interaction of large fiber size and an inability of a large fiber size to withstand the load transferred from the matrix. For the sake of better visualization, the comparison of the effect of the cutting size on the stress – strain distribution is plotted in Fig. 3(a). The tensile strength result obtained for size 2 water hyacinth fiber reinforced polyester composite in the current work (11.28 MPa) is close to the result obtained by Abral et al. [24], which is 14.9 MPa. The other observation is that fiber orientation is important for the performance of natural fiber composites where unidirectional long fiber or mat composites have higher tensile strength properties compared with randomly distributed short fibers.

Furthermore, to investigate the effect of fiber content on the tensile strength properties of the composite materials, the stress – strain distribution of the composites with fiber/matrix ratio of 30/70, 20/80 and 10/90 are plotted in Fig. 3(b). The plots show a clearly noticeable difference because of the fiber content. Though no particular trend is observed, the fiber/matrix ratio of 20/80 has the highest tensile strength compared with the rest in the comparison and this may be as a result of proper fiber distribution and dispersion that facilitated the strength of the composites. The plots also show that the fiber content highly influences the tensile strain. Composites with higher fiber content sustain higher strain.

The comparative results for the untreated (WHUT(T)) and alkali treated (WHT20%(T) and WHT10%(T)) fiber reinforced polyester composites are given in Table 4 and plots of the stress-strain distribution are given in Fig. 4. The results indicate that alkali treatment affects the tensile strength of the water hyacinth fiber reinforced polyester composite material. Treatment with higher percentage of alkali content leads to higher tensile strength and higher strain at failure.

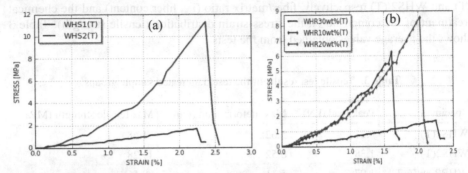

**Fig. 3.** Stress-strain distributions as functions of effects of (a) cutting size (WHS1(T) vs. WHS2(T)), and (b) fiber content (WHR30wt %(T), WHR20wt %(T) and WHR10wt %(T))

**Table 4.** Tensile test results of treated and untreated fiber reinforced polyester composites

| Specimen | Peak load (kN) | Max. deformation (mm) | Max tensile strength (MPa) |
|----------|----------------|------------------------|-----------------------------|
| WHUT(T) | 0.21 | 5.92 | 1.68 |
| WHT20%(T) | 0.55 | 6.28 | 4.4 |
| WHT10%(T) | 0.45 | 5.08 | 3.6 |

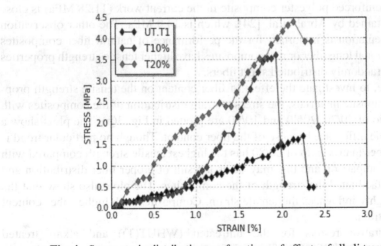

**Fig. 4.** Stress-strain distributions as functions of effects of alkali treatment

### 3.3  Flexural Test (3-point Bending Test)

Flexural strength is defined as a material's ability to resist deformation under load. The test is commonly conducted by a 3-point bend test, which generally promotes failure by inter-laminar shear. For this case, the test was conducted on 5 different test groups using 5 test specimens each. The test groups are designated as follows:

1. WHR30wt%(B): Water hyacinth fiber reinforced polyester composite with fiber/matrix ratio of 30/70,
2. WHR20wt%(B): Water hyacinth fiber reinforced polyester composite with fiber/matrix ratio of 20/80,
3. WHR10wt%(B): Water hyacinth fiber reinforced polyester composite with fiber/matrix ratio of 10/90,
4. WHT20%(B): 20% NaOH treated water hyacinth fiber reinforced polyester composite,
5. WHT10%(B): 10% NaOH treated water hyacinth fiber reinforced polyester composite.

Similar to the tensile test case, the flexural tests were conducted at room temperature of 20 °C. For each test specimen, a cross-sectional area of 125 mm$^2$ was used.

As the values given in Table 5 show, the maximum force and flexural strength was found in the sample with 20% alkali (NaOH) treated composite (i.e. sample WHR20wt%(B)). The results also indicate that the 20% fiber content among the untreated has highest load carrying capacity and flexural strength among the untreated composites. Furthermore, the 20%NaOH treated composite has 13.33% higher load carrying capacity than the 10%NaOH treated water hyacinth fiber reinforced polyester composite. The results, in general, show that chemical treatment improves the performance of the composite. This agrees with the work of Rokbi et al. [25] who studied the effect of NaOH treatment on natural fibers and identified that the flexural strength of treated composites improves likely due to bonding of the fiber with polyester matrix interaction.

**Table 5.** Tensile test results of the tested untreated sample groups.

| Chemical treatment | Specimen | Max. force (kN) | Flexural strength (MPa) |
|---|---|---|---|
| Untreated | WHR30wt%(B) | 70 | 26.6 |
| | WHR20wt%(B) | 340 | 137.70 |
| | WHR10wt%(B) | 270 | 109.35 |
| Treated | WHT20wt%(B) | 150 | 57.15 |
| | WHT10wt%(B) | 130 | 49.53 |

### 3.4 Compression Test

For this test, five different test groups were prepared with 5 test specimens each. The test groups are designated as follows:

1. WHR30wt%(C): Water hyacinth fiber reinforced polyester composite with fiber/matrix ratio of 30/70,
2. WHR20wt%(C): Water hyacinth fiber reinforced polyester composite with fiber/matrix ratio of 20/80,
3. WHR10wt%(C): Water hyacinth fiber reinforced polyester composite with fiber/matrix ratio of 10/90,
4. WHT20%(C): 20% NaOH treated water hyacinth fiber reinforced polyester composite,
5. WHT10%(C): 10% NaOH treated water hyacinth fiber reinforced polyester composite.

In accordance with the recommended standards, the specimens with the dimension of 25 mm × 12 mm × 3.2 mm were used and the tests were conducted at room temperature of 20 °C. Table 6 gives the test results.

**Table 6.** Compressive strength test results.

| Chemical treatment | Sample group | Peak load (kN) | Max. deformation (mm) | Max tensile strength (MPa) |
|---|---|---|---|---|
| Untreated | WHR30wt%(C) | 2.10 | 0.67 | 35.0 |
|  | WHR20wt%(C) | 6.39 | 1.66 | 106.50 |
|  | WHR10wt%(C) | 5.94 | 2.26 | 99.00 |
| Alkali treated | WHT20wt%(C) | 2.52 | 1.43 | 42.00 |
|  | WHT10wt%(C) | 2.44 | 2.17 | 40.67 |

Comparative stress-strain distribution for the untreated composites showing effect of fiber content on the compressive strength is given in Fig. 5(a). As the plots clearly show, highest compressive strength is obtained for 20% fiber ratio, similar to the previous test results for tensile and flexural tests. In a similar fashion as before, the failure strain decreases with increasing fiber weight percentage.

Furthermore, Fig. 5(b) indicates that alkali treatment has significant effect on the compressive strength of the water hyacinth fiber reinforced polyester composite material compared with the untreated water hyacinth fiber reinforced polyester composite (WHUT(C)). In general, the stress - strain plots indicate nonlinear segments caused by stick-slip behavior at the fiber-matrix interface.

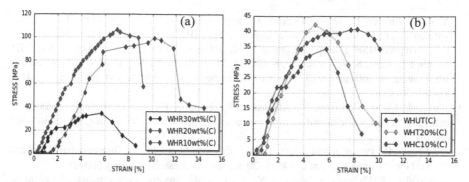

**Fig. 5.** Stress-strain distributions as functions of effects of (a) fiber content and (b) alkali treatment on compressive strength.

## 4 Conclusions

This article presented the study conducted on water hyacinth fiber reinforced polyester composite that was successfully extracted from the plant and fabricated. The article focused on limited mechanical properties of the composite which are studied using tensile, flexural and compression tests. Influences of parameters such as fiber cutting size, fiber content and alkali treatment are investigated in each case. The fiber cutting size is observed to improve the results of tensile strength. In general, it has been observed that the fiber content affects the results of tensile strength, compression, and flexural strength. It seems that fiber content of about 20% weight is optimum for all cases considered in the study. In addition, higher alkali (NaOH) treatment improves the mechanical properties because of better interface adhesion between the water hyacinth fiber and the polyester resin.

Future works of this research will focus on characterization of the mechanical properties with respect to different extraction methods, curing time and chemical treatment methods. Further investigations on hardness and impact properties will also be investigated.

## References

1. Tomar, S.S., Zafar, S., Talha, M., Gao, W., Hui, D.: State of the art of composite structures in the non-deterministic framework: a review. Thin-Walled Struct. **132**, 700–716 (2018)
2. Du, Y., Shen, S.Z., Cai, K., Casey, P.S.: Research progress on polymer – inorganic thermoelectric nanocomposite materials. Prog. Polym. Sci. **37**(6), 820–841 (2012)
3. Pop, P., Gheorghe, B.: Manufacturing process and applications of composite materials: Annals of the Oradea University. Fascicle Manage. Technol. Eng. **19**(9) (2010)
4. Arif, M., Asif, M., Ahmed, I.: Advanced composite material for aerospace application: a review. Int. J. Eng. Manuf. Sci. **7**(2), 393–409 (2017)
5. Sonar, T., Patil S., Deshmukh, V., Acharya, R.: Natural fiber reinforced polymer composite material: a review. IOSR J. Mech. Civil Eng. 142–147 (2015)
6. Tajvidi, M., Takemura, A.: Recycled natural fiber polypropylene composites: water absorption/desorption kinetics and dimensional stability. J. Polym. Environ. **18**(4), 500–509 (2010). https://doi.org/10.1007/s10924-010-0215-y

7. Yost, M., Shields, L.: Ethiopia's emerging apparel industry: options for better business and women's empowerment in a frontier market, BSR´s HERproject, Paris (2017). https://www.bsr.org/reports/BSR_Ethiopia_Scoping_Study_HERproject.PDF. Accessed on 30 Aug 2020

8. Mahir, F.I., Keya, K.N., Sarker, B., Nahiun, K.M., Khan, R.A.: A brief review on the natural fiber used as a replacement of synthetic fiber in polymer composites. Mater. Eng. Res. **1**(2), 86–97 (2019)

9. Baran, I., Cinar, K., Ersoy, N., Akkerman, R., Hattel, J.H.: A review on the mechanical modeling of composite manufacturing processes. Arch. Comput. Meth. Eng. **24**(2), 365–395 (2016)

10. Kozlowski, R.: Potential and diversified uses of green fibers. In: 3rd International Wood and Natural Fiber Composites, p. 1–14, 19–20 September, Kassel, Germany (2000)

11. Gurunathan, T., Mohanty, S., Nayak, S.K.: A review of the recent developments in biocomposites based on natural fibers and their application perspectives. Compos. A Appl. Sci. Manuf. **77**, 1–25 (2015)

12. Ramawat, K.G., Ahuja, M.R. (eds.): Fiber Plants: Biology, Biotechnology and Applications. Springer International Publishing, Cham (2016)

13. Villamagna, A.M., Murphy, B.R.: Ecological and socio-economic impacts of invasive water hyacinth (Eichhornia crassipes): a review. Freshw. Biol. **55**(2), 282–298 (2010)

14. Teygeler, R.: Water Hyacinth Paper: Contributions to a Sustainable Future, pp. 168–188. Gentenaar & Torley Publisher (2000)

15. Asmare, E.: Current trends of water hyacinth expansion and its consequence on the fisheries around North-Eastern part of Lake Tana, Ethiopia. J. Biodivers. Endanger. Species **5**, 189 (2017)

16. Sawpan, M.A., Pickering, K.L., Fernyhough, A.: Effect of various chemical treatments on the fibre structure and tensile properties of industrial hemp fibers. Compos. A Appl. Sci. Manuf. **42**(8), 888–895 (2011)

17. Bhuvaneshwari, D.K.S.M.: Investigation of physical, chemical and structural characterization of Eichhornia crassipes fiber. In: International Conference on Information Engineering, Management and Security, Association of Scientists, Developers and Faculties, pp. 92–96 (2016)

18. ASTM D3039: Standard Test Method for Tensile Properties of Polymer Matrix Composite Materials. ASTM International, PA USA (2010)

19. ASTM. D790–10: Standard Test Methods for Flexural Properties of Unreinforced and Reinforced Plastics and Electrical Insulating Materials, ASTM International, West Conshohocken, PA 19428–2959(2003)

20. ASTM. D 695 M: Standard test method for compressive properties of rigid plastics, ASTM International, West Conshohocken, PA 19428–2959 (2008)

21. Yusoff, R.B., Takagi, H., Nakagaito, A.N.: Tensile and flexural properties of polylactic acid-based hybrid green composites reinforced by kenaf, bamboo and coir fibers. Ind. Crops Prod. **94**, 562–573 (2016)

22. Xu, J., Han, G., Wong, E.D., Kawai, S.: Development of binderless particleboard from kenaf core using steam-injection pressing. J. Wood Sci. **49**(4), 327–332 (2003). https://doi.org/10.1007/s10086-002-0485-7

23. Bhuvaneshwari, M., Sangeetha, K.: Effect of blending ratio of water hyacinth fibers on the properties of needle punched nonwoven fabrics. Int. J. Tech. Res. Appl. **5**, 2320–8163 (2017)

24. Abral, H., et al.: Mechanical properties of water hyacinth fibers – polyester composites before and after immersion in water. Mater. Des. **58**, 125–129 (2014)

25. Rokbi, M., Osmani, H., Imad, A., Benseddiq, N.: Effect of chemical treatment on flexure properties of natural fiber-reinforced polyester composite. Procedia Eng. **10**, 2092–2097 (2011)

# Late Track

Late Track

# Practical Implementation of Geo-location TVWS Database for Ethiopia

Habib M. Hussien[1]($\boxtimes$), Konstantinos Katzis[2], Luzango P. Mfupe[3],
and Ephrem T. Bekele[1]

[1] School of Electrical and Computer Engineering, Addis Ababa Institute of Technology (AAiT),
AAU, Addis Ababa, Ethiopia
{habib.mohammed,ephrem.teshale}@aait.edu.et

[2] Department of Computer Science and Engineering, School of Sciences, 6 Diogenes Street
Engomi 1516, Nicosia, Cyprus
K.Katzis@euc.ac.cy

[3] CSIR Meraka Institute, Scientia Campus, Brummeria, Pretoria 0001, South Africa
Lmfupe@csir.co.za

**Abstract.** The beginning of TV white space (TVWS) for cognitive system is amongst the perceptible move towards solving the spectrum scarcity as well as rural connectivity problems. For the reason that this section of the spectrum band has higher bandwidth, good transmission characteristics and wide coverage. In this paper, we proposed a realistic implementation of the TVWS assignment simulation method focused on geo-location that solves the issue of spectrum under-utilization. The model is aided by the Calculation Engine of CSIR which is used in the radio frequency band of interest in Ethiopia to Intelligently quantify white spaces. More broadly, we aimed at the necessary input parameters, like radio propagation models suitable for the Ethiopian terrain environment, and calculation procedures to determine underutilized TVWSs. The models used by the Engine will approximate the contour coverage span of the incumbent TV station, separation distances for neighboring and co-channel locations, co-channel lists, as well as adjacent channels. In addition, using the planned implementation for the Ethiopia usage case; substantial amounts (87.9–98.23%) of geographically unoccupied broadcast TV channels are identified, such channels can be used for secondary provisioning of inexpensive broadband wireless networks.

**Keywords:** Calculation engine · Cognitive radio · Geolocation database · HAAT · Propagation model · Secondary user · TV white space

## 1 Introduction

These days, it has become difficult to allocate new spectrum for additional services. The spectrum has already been allocated for various wireless systems; thus, spectrum scarcity is nowadays one restrictive factor in incorporating more wireless services due to the fact that these systems have authorized users, users with exclusive access to the

© ICST Institute for Computer Sciences, Social Informatics and Telecommunications Engineering 2021
Published by Springer Nature Switzerland AG 2021. All Rights Reserved
M. A. Delele et al. (Eds.): ICAST 2020, LNICST 385, pp. 495–510, 2021.
https://doi.org/10.1007/978-3-030-80618-7_34

spectrum. However, studies indicate that white spaces, wide idle spectrum, exist amongst these exclusive bands [1]. Currently, White Spaces in the broadcast television band are the prime focus of studies. Digital Switch Over (DSO), migration from analog to digital broadcasting, is expected to increase the available White Space in the TV band. To realize secondary use for TVWS a technology called Cognitive Radio (CR) has been proposed [2]. CR allows secondary communication devices to access the spectrum, which is idle or underused by the authorized users. When countries like Japan [19], US [3, 35], South Africa [6, 7, 38], Ghana [39], UK [17, 32], Tanzania [37] switched to digital broadcast spectrum was left in the TV band that permitted use of CR.

The United States Federal Communications Commission (FCC) sanctioned the operation of unlicensed transmitters in broadcast TV spectrum according to set rules [3]. The European Conference of Postal and Telecommunications Administrations (CEPT) issued European Electronic Communications Committee (ECC) report 186 [4], which specifies the requirements for geo-location approach based operation of White Space Devices. The DSO is scheduled to be completed in Ethiopia by 2020 [5], after which some of the networks will be declared as digital dividends. Harmful interference is to be avoided in TVWS channels by using low power WSDs. The WSDs require techniques for authorized users services protection and TVWS sensing even though there is a large amount of TVWS available. Two strategies for the operation of TVWS networks have been proposed by many regulatory bodies worldwide, such as in the US, Europe and several African countries (South Africa, Malawi, Botswana, Mozambique, Ghana and so on).

These are (1) Geo-location White Spectrum Databases (GLSDs) (2) Spectrum sensing. From the two, GLSDs [6, 7] is better suited for the following reasons.

- It interprets the regulations of protective WS spectrum use issued by the national regulatory authorities for the spectrum.
- Primary user networks are protected from harmful interference when locally available spectrum is assigned.
- Techniques to access available local spectrum that are available for the WSDs.

It is expected that the database prioritizes incumbent users. Parameters such as location, antenna height, maximum effective radiated power (max ERP), site name, channel, frequency and other related information need to be sent to the system seeking WSD. Using the incumbent user information, the calculation engine defines the accessible channels and power levels at a particular location. The result is then forwarded to the device containing the available channels and powers, after which the device can start to transmit [8].

The remainder of the paper is arranged as follows: Related work is gggiven in Sect. 2; Sect. 3 includes Calculation Engine Specifications for White Space Calculation; Sect. 4 presents how the white space engine operates; Finally, the experimental findings and conclusion are discussed respectively in Sects. 5 and 6.

## 2   Related Work

The The FCC pioneered GLSD dynamic WS access [9]. Murty et al. [10] mobile users' convenience and stability may be increased by using GLSD assisted white spaces networking. Gao et al. [11, 13] designed GLSD based opportunistic spectrum use for vehicle-to-vehicle communication. Madhavan et al. [13, 14] applied in low range cellular network the utilization approach. Ameigeiras et al. [15] studied TV white space use in dynamically deploying small cells. In USA, the average UHF band can only accommodate 5 channels per person and 18% per person is available in Europe. In the United Kingdom [18], Japan [19], South Africa [6, 7, 38], Tanzania [37] and Ghana [39] similar studies have been conducted. In countries with poor spectrum utilization, such as Ethiopia where there is a single broadcaster transmitting two channels all over the country with each channel occupying a mere 8 MHz much of the spectrum is yet to be used. The digital switch over [5] is expected to avail a large number of unused bands, which may be used for rural communication [20].

## 3   White Space Calculation Engine Parameters

### 3.1   Terrestrial Television Planning Models

First, the planning strategy of Ethiopia must be understood to use the terrestrial television for TVWS. The desired parameters that can be included in the TV planning are allocation of frequencies, transmitters' status and their power limits [6, 7). The signal field strength or the appropriate calculations based on collected data can be expended to assure the received signal quality [21, 22]. The construction of the database is influenced by national terrestrial television planning. These are influenced by the recommendations of the ITU, by international and national conventions, and by multilateral ITU arrangements [23–25]. Transmitter-receiver pairs are configured in different modes. A fixed outdoor receiver antenna of 10 m and indoor/outdoor portable receiver antenna of 1.5 m are used. Transmitter-receiver pairs can be digital or analog. Digital technology can be used with transmitter-receiver pairs, which are outdoor or indoor. However, analog can only be used for fixed outdoor receivers. Reference values for receiver field strength, probability of location and level of interference are usually set forth in configurations of reference planning [6, 7].

### 3.2   Terrestrial TV Network Frequency

Secondary use of a network is only possible by knowing the frequencies used by a channel. A large power transmitter is surrounded by low-power repeaters in some situations. These repeaters may be property of TV planning authority or a village seeking better connectivity. Terrestrial TV networks may be single frequency transmitter or multiple frequency transmitters [6, 7].

*Single Frequency Transmitters:* Such transmitters broadcast over a single channel. This scheme might extend to a national level in which all TV information is transmitted over a single channel. To alleviate interference, enough gap must exist in transmission. To have multiple transmitters channel reuse is required [6, 7].

*Multiple Frequency Transmitters:* A single transmitter uses several frequencies to broadcast. Interference control scheme to limit co-channel and adjacent interference is essential for the transmitters. It is possible to reuse the channels which results in better channel utilization compared to single frequency transmission.

### 3.3   Terrestrian Television Coverage Determination Approaches

The power and/or field strength are used to determine the area of coverage of a TV transmitter. The further you go from the transmitter the signal quality degrades and at some point becomes undetectable. This field strength value is considered the minimum median field strength, the value of which is determined by the planning body. The region between the transmitter and points having a signal strength equal to the minimum median field strength is known as coverage area [6, 7]. There are two approaches.

*Noise Limited Contour:* The area for which the difference of minimum receivable signal power and noise floor are greater than the carrier to noise ratio threshold is taken as the coverage area.

*Interference Limited Contour:* The coverage is measured here as the noise-limited contour with the noise floor substituted by the interfering signal strength. It is assumed/considered that multiple frequency transmitters operate in the system. The CNR is about 8.05 dB higher for analogue TV than the SNR [22].

### 3.4   Protection for Terrestrial TV

The transmission by authorized users must be protected from interferers. Hence, the approved received signal protection ratio (PR) is defined to protect incumbent receivers from interferers. In the protection ratio equation [6, 7, 26, 27], CNR, CIR, NIR, and SNR may be used.

### 3.5   Path Loss Models for Terrestrial TV

There are propagation models for terrestrial TV broadcasting frequencies. The models may be categorized as deterministic, empirical and hybrid [6, 7].

*Empirical Models:* The data collected from location in the signal path is used to model the propagation. There will be less reliance on terrain modeling and other signal loss factors in this modeling, as the data is taken from the location of the signal path.

*Deterministic Models:* Here equations are formulated that predict the behavior of a signal on a path. These equations predict field strength and power at a particular distance. There are versions, too that use both strategies. These are known as combined versions (Table 1).

   Significant parameters which affect the WSD and transmission by incumbent users must be considered in the database design.

**Table 1.** Selected propagation models [6, 7, 28]

| Model | Frequency range (GHz) | Distance (km) | Category | Typical application |
|---|---|---|---|---|
| Extended Hata | 0.03–3 | Up to 40 | Empirical | Point-to-point short-to-medium spectrum preparation of short-to-medium height antennas for terrestrial television stations. Measured terrain information is utilized in the form of curves |
| Longley-Rice [29] | 0.02–40 | 1–2000 | Mixed: Empirical/deterministic | Point-to-averaged-radial and point-to-multipoint planning and generic coordination- planning of terrestrial broadcast stations. Uses terrain profile elevation and measured data |
| ITU-R P.1546-5 [34] | 0.03–3 | 1–1000 | Mixed: Empirical/deterministic | Point-to-multipoint generic coordination-Terrestrial radio station preparation. Using determined terrain details in the form of curves and elevation of the terrain profile 3–15 km from the transmitter |
| TM-91-1 [30] | 0.04–1 | <16 | Empirical | Point-to-point planning for short distances |
| ITWOM [31] | 0.02–20 | 1–2000 | Mixed: Empirical/deterministic | Point-to-point and point-to-multipoint planning of terrestrial broadcast stations. Elevation of the surface profile and measured data were used |

*Protection Ratio:* For the protection of incumbents from harmful interference there must a minimum signal threshold. Different regulators working at the national level have recommended safety ratios for co-channels and neighboring channels. Protection ratios have differing values depending on the ITU region of interest. For Ethiopia, which is in the ITU region 2 the values are given in Table 2 below.

**Table 2.** Protection Ratios (PR) [32]

| Regulatory body: Ofcom, UK (Class 1 WSD) | |
|---|---|
| Bandwidth of Channel (MHz) | 8 |
| The sort of channel which should be protected | PR (dB) |
| Co-channel ($\Delta F = 0$) | 17 |
| Adjacent channel ($\Delta F = \pm 1$) | $-36$ |

*WSD Emission Mask:* This is a limit for out of band emission for the operating WSDs. The emission mask is determined using emission power and frequency of operation [6, 7].

## 4   How White Space Calculation Engine Works

The figure below shows the Ethiopian GLSD front end which uses the CSIR calculation engine JSON RPC 2 [6, 7, 36]. The front end obtains unoccupied bandwidth, accessible channels and intermediate values via the API, such as distance of contour coverage, adjacent and co-channel separation distance, adjacent occupied and co-channel separation distance (Fig. 1).

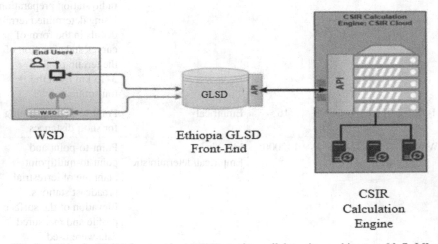

**Fig. 1.** Ethiopia GLSD front-end and CSIR engine collaboration architecture [6, 7, 36]

Implementation starts by identifying TV stations. The datasets/technical information for transmitters, which includes the location coordinates are obtained from the Ethiopian Broadcasting Authority (EBA). After preprocessing the data from EBA and converting to appropriate format, computation can take place. For each WSD the area in its vicinity is scrutinized. The calculation engine requires authentication, where the presence of the WSD in the allowed list is checked. If authenticated, the WSD forwards it GPS coordinates to the calculation engine. In addition, the WSD device sends the height of its antenna measured from the ground. The calculation engine then checks if the antenna height is above or below 30 m. In deciding the free channels, the following steps can take place.

- Following authentication, Height Above Average Terrain is computed
- Model of propagation TM-91-1 used for heights below 10 m [6, 7, 35]; use [6, 7, 30] to measure the distance of separation between the covered contour and the WSD.
- The ITU-R 1546-5 propagation model [34] for HAAT above 10 m is used for a given $E_{WSD}$ value using interpolation. The determined $D_{sep}$ is then used to compute the available channels.

### 4.1 Determination of HAAT/Effective Antenna Height

The calculation/computation requires the location coordinates of the antenna as an input. Then, starting from true north radials are taken with the desired resolution (typically 10 degree) to compute the average terrain. By measuring the terrain, height from 3.2 km to 16 km in equal step sizes the HAAT is determined. Similarly, by taking measurements from 3 km to 15 km at equivalent phase sizes, the effective antenna height is determined/calculated. The terrain closer than 3 km to the antenna does not affect coverage; hence, is neglected. The mean for the means of the radials is then taken as the HAAT. HAAT is not permitted to exceed 250 m.

### 4.2 Maximum Allowable WSD field strength (EWSD) Calculation

The protection ratio, protected contour median field strength and front-to-back ratio can be used to compute the maximum allowable field strength as follows.

$$E_{WSD} = E_{med} - R_p + R_{FP} \tag{1}$$

Where: $E_{WSD}$ is maximum allowable WSD field strength, $E_{med}$ is minimum median field strength $R_p$ is protection ratio of incumbent receiver, $R_{FB}$ is receiver's front to back ratio.

The TM-91-1 model [30], implies:

$$E_{WSD} = 1.414 + 20\log(h_1 h_2) - 40\log D_{sep} + 10\log P_{WSD} \tag{2}$$

Where: $h_1$ and $h_2$ are heights of antenna above average sea level, $D_{sep}$ is distance between WSD and incumbent contour and, $P_{WSD}$ is ERP of a WSD.

The separation distance may then be computed as:

$$D_{sep} = \frac{1.085 * \sqrt{h_1 h_2} * \sqrt[4]{P_{WSD}}}{10\exp\left(\frac{E_{WSD}}{40}\right)} \tag{3}$$

A minimum distance of $D_{sep}$ from the incumbent transmitter's protected contour is required if channels are to be available. For heights exceeding 10 m, the ITU-R 1546-5 propagation model is used at 50% location and 1% time in computing the $D_{sep}$. The field strength of the WSD may then be computed by taking into account the protection ratio, HAAT and path loss as follows:

$$E_{WSD} = 106.9 - 20 \log D \tag{4}$$

Where: $E_{WSD}$ is free space field strength for 1kW ERP, D is the distance in km [17].

It is now possible for each operating frequency to determine the distance value; however, interpolation and/or extrapolation may be required to do so.

### 4.3 Contour Distance for Incumbent Transmitter

The field strength can be computed/calculated by taking the normalized field strength at Half Power Beam Width or using depression angle to calculate the normalized field strength first. The square of normalized field strength is then multiplied by the maximum ERP of the incumbent transmitter. This value is known as the radial ERP. The radial power is then computed by converting the last value into dB using 1 kW as a reference. The difference between minimum median field strength and radial power yields radial field strength. By using this radial field strength at 95% location and 50% time the contour coverage can be computed using ITU-R 1546-5 propagation model. Interpolation according to the following formula may be necessary in case the values are not in the tables provided.

$$D_c = D_{inf} \left( \frac{D_{sup}}{D_{inf}} \right)^{\left( \frac{E_r - E_{inf}}{E_{sup} - E_{inf}} \right)} \tag{5}$$

where, $D_c$ is contour coverage distance, $D_{sup}$ is the distance for $E_{sup}$, $D_{inf}$ is the distance for $E_{inf}$, $E_r$ is radial field strength, $E_{sup}$ is the nearest field strength above $E_r$, $E_{inf}$ is the nearest field strength below $E_r$.

The incumbent transmitter's contour coverage and location should be saved in the database. Whenever a WSD requests for free spectrum, the database repackages the request and forwards it to the CSIR calculation engine. Upon receipt of the results from the calculation engine the database sends the results to the WSD. The detailed process is described as follows. The WSD begins by sending its HAGL, ERP, location along with its channel request. The GLSD authenticates the device. For a certified device, the GLSD computes HAAT by using HAGL and WSD location. The minimum median field strength, front to back ratio and protection ration are then used to compute the maximum allowed field strength for the WSD. The separation distance for the WSD is then computed from this information. The transmitters within 150 km of the transmitter are in the region where WSD causes interference. The separation distance is added to the contour coverage after which it will be deducted from the incumbent transmitter-WSD separation. If x, the last result, is greater than zero then the channels are available if not the channels shall not be used as it will cause interference.

## 4.4   Haversine Function Formula

With the following calculations, we have used the Haversine theorem to describe the locations that would be impacted by the WSD. The formula Haversine is also used to measure the WSD distance. The formula takes latitude and longitude inputs from the two positions for which the degree of separation between them is calculated [6, 7].

$$D = 2R arcsin\sqrt{haversine(\varphi2 - \varphi1) + cos(\varphi1)\,cos(\varphi2) haversine(\lambda2 - \lambda1)} \quad (6)$$

$$Haversine\,(\theta)\;=\;sin2\,(\theta/2) \quad (7)$$

Where, R is the radius of Earth, $\varphi1$ and $\varphi2$ are latitude of point 1 and 2, $\lambda1$ and $\lambda2$ are longitude of point 1 and 2 respectively.

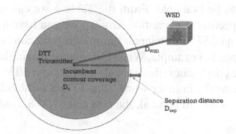

**Fig. 2.** Illustration of WSD and DTT transmitter location

For the illustration of parameters as seen in Fig. 2 above, the database will be built to operate as shown in Fig. 3 of the flowchart.

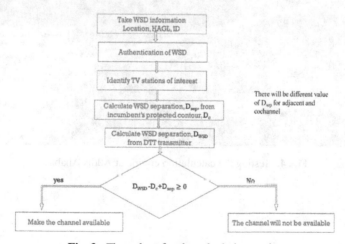

**Fig. 3.** Flow chart for the calculation engine

## 5   Experimental Results

We have taken the WSD to be located at a plateau near Tulu Dimtu (Addis Ababa) condominium site with transmitter HAGL to be 30 m. For DTT transmitters, we have also assumed to be 30 m HAGL. However, when we identified the transmitters which could be affected by the WSD, there was only Furi site (Addis Ababa) identified as depicted in Fig. 4. As it can be seen from Table 3 Using GLSD Calculation Engine, we have able to determine the coverage contour distance of the given free channels and the separation distance of the adjacent and the co-channel transmitters from the contour for protecting the incumbents from harmful interference. For instance for Furi Transmitter site, the adjacent and co-channel separation distance between the WSD and the incumbent coverage contour is 1.027 km and 58.48 km respectively. To be specific, the WSD must be 1.027 km away from the protected contour of adjacent incumbent transmitter and 58.48 km away from the protected contour of co-channel incumbent transmitter for TVWS free channels to be available. From the Table 4 we can see that, by using the Geo-location White Spectrum Calculation Engine, we can have a minimum of 51 free channels and maximum of 57 free channels among the total number of 58 TV transmitters' channels in Ethiopia. For example, When Calculation Engine has made a calculation for Furi transmitter site coordinates; there are about 3 occupied TV Transmitter channels and 55 free TVWS channels. In other words, the TVWS availability around Furi Area (Test Place) is around 94.8%. In general, the range of TVWS availability in Ethiopia is from 87.9%–98.23%.

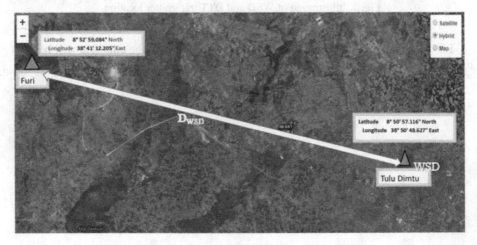

**Fig. 4.** Testing the calculation engine at Addis Ababa

**Table 3.** Coverage contour distance, adjacent and co-channel contour distances using the proposed calculation engine.

| Site name | Channel | Coverage contour distances (km) | Adjacent separation distance (km) | Co-channel separation distance (km) |
|---|---|---|---|---|
| Furi | 5 | 88.267 | 1.0207 | 58.48 |
| Furi | 7 | 88.267 | 1.0207 | 58.48 |
| Harar | 7 | 83.382 | 1.0207 | 58.48 |
| Dire Dawa | 5 | 84.495 | 1.0872 | 60.418 |
| Jijiga | 11 | 82.404 | 1.0207 | 58.48 |
| Nazireth | 11 | 85.423 | 1.0872 | 60.418 |
| Dessie | 9 | 79.91 | 0.9094 | 55.157 |
| Jimma | 5 | 79.302 | 0.9094 | 55.157 |
| Nekemte | 9 | 80.96 | 0.9625 | 56.737 |
| Shashemene | 5 | 81.552 | 0.9625 | 56.737 |
| Dila | 11 | 84.811 | 1.0872 | 60.418 |
| Gondar | 7 | 84.811 | 1.0872 | 60.418 |
| Bahirdar | 5 | 82.648 | 1.0207 | 58.48 |
| Mekele | 7 | 84.382 | 1.0528 | 59.423 |
| Axum | 9 | 81.552 | 0.9625 | 56.737 |
| Assosa | 11 | 79.91 | 0.9094 | 55.157 |
| Gode | 9 | 81.552 | 0.9625 | 56.737 |
| Adi Remest | 35 | 60.891 | 0.3885 | 35.087 |
| Ankober | 34 | 61.146 | 0.3932 | 35.325 |
| Assosa | 60 | 55.51 | 0.2977 | 30.793 |
| Debark | 57 | 56.061 | 0.3063 | 31.207 |
| Dessie | 48 | 57.864 | 0.3355 | 32.587 |
| Dila | 29 | 62.51 | 0.4191 | 36.59 |
| Kebridahar | 24 | 57.651 | 0.3316 | 32.422 |
| Fiche | 50 | 57.442 | 0.3285 | 32.261 |
| Furi | 42 | 59.216 | 0.3578 | 33.642 |
| Gore | 50 | 57.442 | 0.3285 | 32.261 |
| Jijiga | 43 | 58.981 | 0.3531 | 33.457 |
| Jimma | 45 | 58.524 | 0.3469 | 33.099 |
| Jinka | 46 | 58.3 | 0.3427 | 32.925 |

(*continued*)

**Table 3.** (*continued*)

| Site name | Channel | Coverage contour distances (km) | Adjacent separation distance (km) | Co-channel separation distance (km) |
|---|---|---|---|---|
| Kuni | 35 | 62.224 | 0.4138 | 36.326 |
| Maichew | 54 | 56.635 | 0.3158 | 31.643 |
| NefasMewca | 21 | 65.061 | 0.4684 | 38.927 |
| Shebel | 28 | 62.802 | 0.4246 | 36.86 |
| Tendaho | 43 | 58.981 | 0.3531 | 33.457 |
| Weldia | 25 | 63.723 | 0.4424 | 37.705 |
| Nekemte | 38 | 60.174 | 0.3744 | 34.418 |
| Gode | 28 | 62.802 | 0.4246 | 36.86 |
| Mekele | 54 | 56.635 | 0.3158 | 31.643 |
| Axum | 51 | 57.236 | 0.3241 | 32.102 |
| Dire Dawa | 42 | 59.216 | 0.3578 | 33.642 |
| Mega | 53 | 56.832 | 0.3182 | 31.794 |
| ChokeTeraa | 32 | 61.673 | 0.4033 | 35.815 |
| Abiy Adi | 24 | 64.046 | 0.4486 | 38 |
| Amentila | 40 | 59.698 | 0.3667 | 34.022 |
| Derba | 34 | 61.146 | 0.3932 | 35.325 |
| Warder | 47 | 57.014 | 0.3382 | 32.754 |
| Filtu | 41 | 56.759 | 0.3618 | 33.83 |
| Adigrat | 51 | 57.236 | 0.3241 | 32.102 |
| Ginir | 45 | 58.524 | 0.3469 | 33.099 |
| Dellomena | 40 | 58.6 | 0.3667 | 34.022 |
| Fik | 51 | 56.186 | 0.3241 | 32.102 |
| Maji | 36 | 59.605 | 0.3838 | 34.85 |
| Guba | 23 | 64.377 | 0.4555 | 38.302 |
| Yabello | 50 | 55.353 | 0.3285 | 32.261 |
| Samre | 47 | 58.081 | 0.3382 | 32.754 |
| Bella/Ghimi | 24 | 57.651 | 0.3316 | 32.422 |

**Table 4.** Identification of occupied adjacent and co-channels TV spectrums for each TV transmitter sites in Ethiopia for interference protection.

| Site name | Channel | Occupied adjacent | Occupied co-channel |
|---|---|---|---|
| Furi | 5 | 11, 38 and 42 | 11, 38 and 42 |
| Furi | 7 | 11, 38 and 42 | 11, 38 and 42 |
| Harar | 7 | 5, 11 and 42 | 5, 11, 42 and 43 |
| Dire Dawa | 5 | 5 and 42 | 5, 11 and 42 |
| Jijiga | 11 | 11 and 43 | 5, 11 and 43 |
| Nazireth | 11 | 11 | 11, 38 and 42 |
| Dessie | 9 | 9 and 48 | 9, 48 and 25 |
| Jimma | 5 | 5 and 45 | 5 and 45 |
| Nekemte | 9 | 9 | 9 |
| Shashemene | 5 | 5 and 11 | 5, 11 and 29 |
| Dila | 11 | 5, 11 and 29 | 5, 11, 29 and 34 |
| Gondar | 7 | 7 | 5, 7 and 57 |
| Bahirdar | 5 | 5 | 5 and 7 |
| Mekele | 7 | 7, 54, 24, 40 and 47 | 7, 9, 54, 24, 40, 51 and 47 |
| Axum | 9 | 9, 51 and 24 | 7, 9, 51, 24 and 51 |
| Assosa | 11 | 11 and 60 | 11 and 60 |
| Gode | 9 | 9 and 28 | 9 and 28 |
| Adi Remest | 35 | 35 | 7 and 35 |
| Ankober | 34 | 34 | 11 and 34 |
| Assosa | 60 | 11 and 60 | 11 and 60 |
| Debark | 57 | 7 and 57 | 7, 9, 35 and 57 |
| Dessie | 48 | 9 and 48 | 9, 48 and 25 |
| Dila | 29 | 5,11 and 29 | 5, 11, 29 and 34 |
| Kebridahar | 24 | 24 | 24 |
| Fiche | 50 | 50 | 50 and 38 |
| Furi | 42 | 11, 42 and 38 | 11, 42 and 38 |
| Gore | 50 | 50 | 50 |
| Jijiga | 43 | 11 and 43 | 5, 11 and 43 |
| Jimma | 45 | 5 and 45 | 5 and 45 |
| Jinka | 46 | 46 | 46 |
| Kuni | 35 | 35 | 5 and 35 |
| Maichew | 54 | 7, 54 and 47 | 7, 54, 40 and 47 |

*(continued)*

**Table 4.** (*continued*)

| Site name | Channel | Occupied adjacent | Occupied co-channel |
|---|---|---|---|
| Nefas Mewcha | 21 | 21 | 7, 5 and 21 |
| Shebel | 28 | 28 | 28 |
| Tendaho | 43 | 43 | 43 |
| Weldia | 25 | 25 | 9, 48 and 25 |
| Nekemte | 38 | 38 and 42 | 11, 38, 42 and 50 |
| Gode | 28 | 9 and 28 | 9 and 28 |
| Mekele | 54 | 7, 54, 24, 40 and 47 | 7, 9, 54, 24, 40, 51 and 47 |
| Axum | 51 | 9, 51 and 24 | 7, 9, 51, 24 and 51 |
| Dire Dawa | 42 | 5 and 42 | 5, 11 and 42 |
| Mega | 53 | 53 | 53 |
| Choke Terara | 32 | 32 | 5 and 32 |
| Abiy Adi | 24 | 7, 9, 24 and 47 | 7, 9, 24, 40, 47, 51 and 54 |
| Amentila | 40 | 7, 40, 47 and 54 | 7, 9, 24, 40, 47 and 54 |
| Derba | 34 | 34 | 11, 29 and 34 |
| Warder | 47 | 47 | 47 |
| Filtu | 41 | 41 | 41 |
| Adigrat | 51 | 7, 9 and 51 | 7, 9, 24, 51 and 54 |
| Ginir | 45 | 45 | 45 |
| Dellomena | 40 | 40 | 40 |
| Fik | 51 | 51 | 51 |
| Maji | 36 | 36 | 36 |
| Guba | 23 | 23 | 23 |
| Yabello | 50 | 50 | 50 |
| Samre | 47 | 7, 24, 40, 47 and 54 | 7, 9, 24, 40, 47 and 54 |
| Bella/Ghimbi | 24 | 24 | 24 |

# 6   Conclusion

This paper focused on the realistic application of GLSD modeling approaches to forecast the quantity of TVWS in the Ethiopian use case based on the CSIR engine. The experimental findings have shown that much of the spectrum of Ethiopian TV is underutilized or unused. From the performance of the results, we will note that the model applied is good at estimating the number of white spaces as well as the coexistence of primary and secondary devices. Rural areas in Ethiopia therefore have a promising future, given the usage of these free networks for rural broadband as well as for the resolution of spectrum shortages in urban areas.

**Acknowledgment.** The writers would like to thank the Institute of CSIR Meraka for providing access to the CSIR Calculation Engine and EBA for providing access to the data collection of the TV transmitter. In addition, we would like to thank Mr. Mofolo Mofolo of CSIR, Mr. Abrham Kahsay and Tessema Tariku of AASTU for their important contributions.

# References

1. Staple, G., Werbach, K.: The end of spectrum scarcity. IEEE Spectr. **41**(3), 48–52 (2004)
2. Fitch, M., Nekovee, M., Kawade, S., Briggs, K., MacKenzie, R.: Wireless service provision in TV white space with cognitive radio technology: a telecom operator's perspective and experience. Commun. Mag. IEEE **49**, 64–73 (2011)
3. FCC. Second report and order and memorandum opinion and order, no. FCC 08-260, November 2008
4. ECC Report 186. Technical and operational requirements for white space devices under geo-location approach, January 2013
5. Inview to provide middleware for Ethiopian Digital Switchover, 18 September 2017. https://www.telecompaper.com/news/inview-to-provide-middleware-for-ethiopian-dig ital-switchover--1212244. Accessed 18 Feb 2019
6. Mfupe, L., Mekuria, F., Mzyece, M.: Geo-location white space spectrum databases: models and design of South Africa's first dynamic spectrum access coexistence manager. Ksii Trans. Internet Inf. Syst. **8**(11), 3810–3836 (2014)
7. Mfupe, L., Mekuria, F., Mofolo, M.: CSIR Geo-location spectrum database: calculation engine application programming interface. https://glsdceapis.meraka.csir.co.za:8443/
8. Denkovska, M., Latkoski, P., Gavrilovska, L.: Geolocation database approach for secondary spectrum usage of TVWS. In: 19th Telecommunications forum TELFOR 2011 Serbia, Belgrade, 22–24 November 2011
9. Flores, A.B., Guerra, R.E., Knightly, E.W., Ecclesine, P., Pandey, S.: IEEE 802.11af: a standard for TV white space spectrum sharing. IEEE Commun. Mag. **51**(10), 92–100 (2013)
10. Murty, R., Chandra, R., Moscibroda, T., Bahl, P.: SenseLess: a database-driven white spaces network. IEEE Trans. Mobile Comput. **11**(2), 189–203 (2012)
11. Gao, B., Park, J.-M., Yang, Y.: Supporting mobile users in database driven opportunistic spectrum access. In: Proceedings of ACM MobiHoc, pp. 215–224 (2014)
12. Chen, X., Huang, J.: Database-assisted distributed spectrum sharing . IEEE J. Sel. Areas Commun. **31**(11), 2349–2361 (2013)
13. Zhou, H., et al.: WhiteFi infostation: engineering vehicular media streaming with geolocation database. IEEE J. Sel. Areas Commun. **34**(8), 2260–2274 (2016)
14. Madhavan, M., Ganapathy, H., Chetlur, M., Kalyanaraman, S.: Adapting cellular networks to whitespaces spectrum. IEEE/ACM Trans. Netw. **23**(2), 383–397 (2014)
15. Ameigeiras, P., Gutierrez-Estevez, D.M., Navarro-Ortiz, J.: Dynamic deployment of small cells in TV white spaces. IEEE Trans. Veh. Technol. **64**(9), 4063–4073 (2014)
16. Mishra, S., Sahai, A.: How much white space is there? Technical report UCB/EECS-2009-3, EECS Department, UC Berkeley, January 2009. http://www.eecs.berkeley.edu/Pubs/Tec hRpts/2009/EECS-2009-3.html
17. van de Beek, J., Riihijarvi, J., Achtzehn, A., Mahonen, P.: TV white space in Europe. IEEE Trans. Mob. Comput. **11**(2), 178–188 (2012)
18. Nekovee, M.: Quantifying the availability of TV white spaces for cognitive radio operation in the UK. In: Proceedings of IEEE International Conference on Communications, pp. 1–5 June 2009

19. Shimomura, T., Oyama, T., Seki, H.: Analysis of TV white space availability in Japan. In: Proceedings of IEEE Vehicular Technology Conference, September 2012
20. Mohammed, H., Katzis, K., Mfupe, L., Teshale, E.: How much TV white spaces is available in Ethiopia using geolocation spectrum white space database? In: ICT4DA2019, Bahirdar, 8–10 May 2019 (Accepted)
21. Damelin, J., Daniel, W., Fine, H., Weldon, G.: Development of VHF and UHF Propagation. Report R-6602, FCC, Office of Chief Engineer, Research Division, 07 September 1966
22. Brown, P.G., Tsioumparakis, K., Jordan, M., Chong, A.: UK planning model for digital terrestrial television coverage. R&D White Paper, WHP 048, BBC, 22 September 2002
23. GE-06: Final Acts of the Regional Radiocommunication Conference for planning of the digital, Vols. ITU, RRC-06.
24. Final Acts of Europe VHF/UHF Broadcasting Conference, ITU (1961)
25. The Chester 1997 multilateral coordination agreement relating to technical criteria, coordination principles and procedures for the introduction of terrestrial Digital Video Broadcasting (DVB-T), CEPT, Chester, 25 July 1997
26. Recommendation ITU-R BS.707–4. Transmission of multisound in terrestrial television systems PAL B, B1, D1, G, H and I, and SECAM D, K, K1 and L (1998)
27. Recommendation ITU-R BT.1895. Protection criteria for terrestrial broadcasting systems (2011)
28. Recommendation ITU-R p.1144–6. Guide to the application of propagation methods of radiocommunication (2012)
29. Longley, A.G., Rice, P.L.: Prediction of tropospheric radio transmission loss over irregular terrain. A Computer method-1968. ESSA Technical Report ERL 79-ITS 67, NTIA-ITS, July 1968
30. Daniel, W., Wong, H.: Propagation in suburban areas at distances less than ten miles. FCC/OET TM-91-1, 25 January 1991
31. Shumate, S.: Longley-rice and ITU-R P.1546 combined: a new international terrain-specific propagation model. In: Proceedings of 72ND Vehicular Technology Conference, IEEE, pp. 1–5, 6–9 September 2015
32. Ofcom, UK. TV white spaces: approach to co-existence. Technical report, 4 September 2013
33. Industry Canada. Spectrum management and telecommunications database requirements: white space database specifications, DBS-01, Issue 1, February 2015
34. ITU-R. Method for point-to-area predictions for terrestrial services in the frequency range 30 MHz to 300 MHz, International Telecommunication Union, Geneva, Recommendation, p. 1546-5, September 2013
35. Federal Communications Commission. DSA/white space interoperability work group geographic contour request for comment WINNF-11-RFI-0016-V1.0.0, 6 November 2011
36. The JavaScript Object Notation (JSON) Data interchange format RFC7159, JSON RPC 2.0. http://www.jsonrpc.org/specification
37. Lance Harris. Microsoft launches next TV white space pilot in Tanzania, 13 May 2013. http://www.zdnet.com/article/microsoft-launches-next-tv-white-space-pilotin-tanzania/. Accessed 27 March 2019
38. Song, S.: Studies on the use of television white spaces in South Africa: recommendations and learnings from the Cape Town television white spaces trial. http://www.tenet.ac.za/tvws/recommendations-and-learningsfrom-the-cape-town-tv-white-spaces-trial
39. Microsoft 4Afrika. Spectra Wireless and Microsoft 4Afrika Launched Africa's First Commercial Service Network Utilising TV White Spaces in Ghana, 26 January 2015. https://www.microsoft.com/africa/4afrika/Ghana_TVWS-PR.aspx

# Wind Turbine Control
# Challenges-A Comprehensive Survey

Endalew Ayenew[1](✉), Getachew Biru[2], Asrat Mulatu[1],
and Santoshkumar Hampannavar[3]

[1] College of Electrical and Mechanical Engineering, Addis Ababa Science and Technology
University, Addis Ababa, Ethiopia
asrat.mulatu@aastu.edu.et
[2] Electrical Power and Control Engineering, School of Electrical Engineering and Computing,
Adama Science and Technology University, Adama, Ethiopia
[3] School of Electrical and Electronics Engineering, REVA University, Bangalore, India

**Abstract.** To enhance wind energy technology, the present status and challenges
associated with the wind turbine controls have to be studied. The function of different wind turbine control strategies such as PID control, PI control, linear quadratic
optimal regulator, linear quadratic Gaussian optimal regulator, Robust Multivariable control, prognostic control or regulator and adaptive tuning of parameter are
comprehensively reviewed and limitations are presented. The challenges related to
wind turbine control are identified. Some of the required future works to improve
turbine energy capturing capacity and its lifetime are discussed.

**Keywords:** Wind turbine control · Energy capturing capacity · Challenges

## 1 Introduction

Since 3500 BC in Egypt wind energy technology was used to propel the boat. Later it
was used for water pumping in China, grinding in Persia, and for irrigation purposes
in France [1]. In 1888, Charles F. Brush created history by producing 12 Kilowatts of
electricity [2] using windmill in Cleveland, Ohio. Near the beginning 1900s, electricity
from wind turbines was used as a source of energy for peoples living in the country
side of Europe and America. In 1921 Agricco produced AC power and connected to
grid in New Zealand. In 1941 big turbine driven by wind (1.25 MW) was build in
Vermont and from 1977–1983 in the United State of America numerous turbines with
two blades were developed. Later upward oriented, variable speed and pitch controlled
three blades wind turbines were produced. In the 1990s, because of community became
more mature about environmental disaster such as increasing atmosphere contamination
index and worldwide temperature rise encouraged interests use of renewable energy
and hence wind turbine producers started manufacturing large-size wind turbines. The
biggest commercialized wind turbine has an average rating of 8 MW and blade length
of 81 m [3, 4]. 12 MW, 260 m tall, 107 m long blade wind turbine was Commercialized

M. A. Delele et al. (Eds.): ICAST 2020, LNICST 385, pp. 511–521, 2021.
https://doi.org/10.1007/978-3-030-80618-7_35

in 2017, while 15 MW wind turbines might be commercialised in 2030 [3]. Actually, when wind turbine dimension increases, there is large effect of loses due to driving train (gear box) which requires a cooling mechanism. One way to reduce lose is a direct coupling of the turbine to generators like a permanent magnetic synchronous generator (PMSG). One limitation of using PMSG is 100% of generated power passes through the two electronics convertors for frequency regulation which reduces overall efficiency. This limitation can be reduced when double-feed induction generator (DFIG) used in case convertors care only 30% of generated power even though the effect of gearbox exists in this case.

At the end of 2017 and 2018, about 539 GW and 600 GW of electric power were generated from wind power respectively [5]. As the report showed by [6, 7], by 2030s, 2,000 Giga Watt electric energy could be generated from wind. As the data on [8] PR China, USA and Germany respectively share 34.7%, 16.9% and 10.3% of the worldwide cumulative energy from wind. Even thought good potential wind resource exists in Ethiopia, the counter shared only 0.06% of global electricity from wind power. GWEO explores the upcoming of wind energy production until 2050. According to the IEA's guidelines, the state of affairs or scenario for wind energy and considering WEO as a reference, there are two states of affairs were specifically developed. These are GWEO modest scenario and the GWEO higher scenario. As per the higher scenario, the expected energy to be harvested from wind until 2030 is shown in Table 1; adapted from [6].

**Table 1.** Global wind power scenario [6]

| Complete capability in Mega Watt | 2013 | 2014 | 2015 | 2020 | 2030 |
|---|---|---|---|---|---|
| Latest guidelines state of affairs | 318,128 | 356,322 | 396,311 | 610,979 | 964,465 |
| Modest state of affairs | 318,128 | 363,908 | 413,039 | 712,081 | 1,479,767 |
| Higher state of affairs | 318,128 | 365,962 | 420,363 | 800,615 | 1,933,989 |

Energy from wind flow is recognized throughout the world as a cost-effective energy plant [3, 9] next to hydropower and biomass. It is an environmentally friendly solution to energy shortages, i.e. reduce climate change effect, greenhouse gas emission and protection for bio diversity. Wind power plant helps to reduce more than three Giga tons of carbon dioxide releases in a year [6]. The Wind is an inexhaustible power source that improves community health.

## 2   Wind Turbine Control Survey

As contemporary turbines driven by breeze become large by size they should have better power capture capacity and hence be more economical; they should have flexible parts that help turbine running under unsure surroundings. Mainly goals of wind turbine supervise and manage are improve turbine capacity of power capturing, enhance power quality, and reduce structural loading on the wind turbines. Wind turbines can be pitch controlled or stall angle types that is rotor blade can be rotate or may not be. Changeable blade-angle controlled turbine permits the entire or some of its blades to turn around its axis at the same time or individually. Also, turbines are of fixed- haste (speed) or of Variable- haste type. Variable-haste turbine runs near its highest aerodynamic performance for most of its operation duration, even though it needs power electronics converters to meet voltage and frequency requirement for gird connection.

Because of advancement in technology for generator and electronics development, variable-speed turbine is more accepted compared to fixed-speed turbine for gird connectable electricity generation from wind. This is due to the former capable to harvest more power than the later since it operates at higher performance for broad range of wind pace.

Ideal turbine can harvest approximately 59% of the energy in the wind (the Betz's Limit [10, 11]). But it is not possible to harvest total energy in the wind because of its fluid dynamics. As indicated in Fig. 1, operation goal of the turbine in the area 2 is to optimize power harvesting through rotor or generator speed control at most favorable tip-speed ratio. In area 3, generator speed is kept fixed by controlling blade angle. This is indicated in Fig. 2. Also, controller used to reduce vibrant loads on tower.

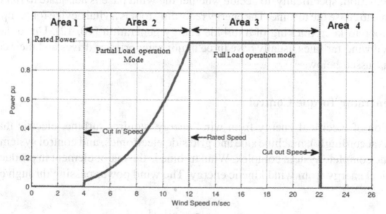

**Fig. 1.** Wind power characteristics of changeable haste and changeable blade angle controlled Wind Turbine.

Variations of the wind pace away from mean value in turbine rotor causes disturbance on turbine controller. Grid connectable wind turbine has supervisor and managing techniques. These are peak stage supervisory that acts on turbine to start or stop it against variation in wind pace, and examine turbine health; operation managing techniques that acts on turbine to accomplish its goals in the area 2 and area 3 as in Fig. 1. The third is components control system- controller that causes the machine side and grid side convertor electronics, yaw and pitch drive systems to execute what they intended to do. Figure 2 represents components control system diagram of wind turbines where $P_g(t)$, $T(t)$ and $\omega_g(t)$ are generator output real power, torque, and speed respectively. $\beta(t)$ is the rotor blade angle.

The turbine rotor speed sensor/measurement (in operational control) in feedback basic control loop is used in both Area 2 and Area 3. The other measurement device

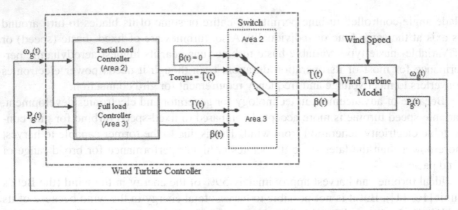

**Fig. 2.** Wind turbine supervisor and managing technique schematic for operation in area 2 and area 3

in the wind turbine control loop is an anemometer. It used for peak stage supervisory control function, specifically, to decide whether the wind pace is adequate to run turbine or extreme to cease the turbine. The energy recording tool is a vital device for components control loop to keep tracking of a turbine energy generation [10, 12]. Up to date grid connected wind turbines usually have three major categories of drives and their controls are as discussed below.

## 2.1 Generator Torque Control

Generation of electrical energy from wind energy requires turbine, electric machine, gearbox (accordingly), machine side and grid side electronics, and control systems. This makes the complete system complex. Wind turbine is the major element in production of mechanical energy from wind kinetic energy. The wind power passing through circular disc is

$$P_w = 0.5\rho\pi R^2 V_w^3 \tag{1}$$

for $P_w$ represents power [W], $\rho$ is atmosphere density [kg/m$^3$] and $V_w$ is space and time-varying wind velocity [m/s] passes in circular disc of $\pi R^2$ [m$^2$], and $R$ stands for blade length [m]. Wind turbine harvests some percent of energy that is accessible in wind pace. Power conversion coefficient is the division of harvested power – $P$ [W] to wind power passing through predefined circular disc. That is.

$$C_p = P/\left(0.5\rho\pi R^2 V_w^3\right) \tag{2}$$

$C_p$ is adjusted by $\beta$ and $\lambda$ [13].

$$C_p(\lambda, \ \beta) = 0.22((116/z) - 0.4\beta - 5)exp(-12.5/z) \tag{3}$$

$$1/z = 1/(\lambda + 0.08\beta) - 0.035(1 + \beta^3) \tag{4}$$

$$\lambda = \omega R / V_w \tag{5}$$

For $\lambda$, $\beta$, and $\omega$ represent fraction of rotor blade tangential tip velocity to the wind velocity, blade angle and rotor angular velocity respectively. The major goal of using controller is to maximize power conversion efficiency $C_p(\lambda, \beta)$. The power harvested using wind turbine is obtained when (2) is rearranged as

$$P = 0.5 \rho \pi R^2 V_w^3 C_p(\lambda, \beta) \tag{6}$$

According to the wind pace condition, $\beta$ can be control or adjusted in (3) and set to zero as shown in Fig. 2; and hence power conversion efficiency $C_p(\lambda, \beta)$ optimized at optimal $\lambda$. In this case, wind turbine operates in area 2 as indicated on Fig. 1. The maximum aerodynamic available power $(P_{wm})$ can be related to rotor speed $\omega$ and $C_{pm}$ as given by

$$P_w = 0.5 \rho \pi R^5 C_{pm} . \omega^2 / \lambda_{op}^3 \tag{7}$$

In (7) if $C_{pm}$ will become maximum conversion efficiency and then power is too. For machine security beyond the machine rated value, it should be restricted by controller. According to [18] maximum achievable value of $C_p$ ranges between 0.2 and 0.4 for wind turbines with three or more blades. In (7) for constant $P_{wm}$ and $\omega$, the torque acting on blade maintained fixed; though the wind haste varies and this can be achieved by the controller. Many electric machine drive system controllers are in application in different wind industries [14, 15].

## 2.2  Pitch Control

Most of the grid connected wind turbines are of three rotor blades and so that collective or independent pitch hydraulic actuators or drive motors are required, which are controlled as per wind speed situation. There are also turbines with two blades; in this case, there is teetering hinge that let the rotor to act in response to discrepancy in loads [16, 17]. The pitching speed is limited to about $5^0$/sec. The turbine is able to extract maximum power up to eclectic machine capacity and restrict power capturing when wind haste become more than the rating.

Usually, in group or independently blade angle controllers are implemented to restrict power when the pace is over nominal with electric machine torque is at its maximum.

As shown in (1), the wind power fluctuates as cube of haste; hence, the turbine must generate power at low wind haste; and withstand loading effect for extreme haste.

Beyond optimal wind haste, blades must be adjusted to feathering condition or pitched to active stall position using controller to limit power to the rated value. For most of wind turbines in market when operates in area 3, it is commonly carried out by proportional-integral-derivative (PID) collective pitch control [18]. The PI Controller gains are scheduled because of the nonlinearity in area 3. At moment, turbine will be operated in the area as indicated in Fig. 1 and Fig. 2. The turbine controller yields command to blade actuator. It alters blade position angle/ velocity at accordingly [11,

20]. Typically the pitch rates range from $8^0/s$ to $18^0/s$ for 5 MW and 600 kW turbines respectively [19].

Also, single input single output regulators are used for blade angle control [20]. A lots of recent grid connectable turbines controllers permit blades to be adjusted separately. This can be achieved employing extra sensors and multi input multi output feedback controller for individual blade [21, 22].

### 2.3 Yaw Control

The second actuator is a yaw motor that adjusts the nacelle into or away the wind direction according to wind status. But, because of risky due to gyroscopic torques, turbines are never yawed at higher rates. The majority of the big turbine turned for rate fewer of $1^0/s$ [19] and hence sophisticated controllers to yaw wind turbine is not must. When the wind direction is changed yaw controller points turbine nacelle towards wind direction. Even for extreme wind speed, yaw motion can be used to twist the nacelle to diminish the influence due to high wind haste (cut out action). Recent turbines could furthermore comprise independent blade twisting moment recorders and sensors for tower deflection and nacelle motion.

### 2.4 Existing Control Strategies

As it was seen in Sect. 2.1 to 2.3 several control techniques have been proposed for wind turbine. Article [23] describes goal of the control that aimed to attain best rotational speed, without considering large deviation in wind haste (stochastic behaviour of wind speed). In this article important action of control for structural load minimization is not considered. Many control approaches were indicated in journals focusing on time independent linear model. Linear quadratic regulators (LQR) [24, 25] and linear quadratic Gaussian (LQG) [26] form of controllers are also employed for wind turbine. Robust controllers were initiated in [25, 27] and recently nonlinear control laws were proposed [28]. The adaptive control is presented in [29]. All these control methods fail in addressing nonlinearity characteristics of wind turbine aerodynamics, structural behavior including stochastic nature of the wind. Model Predictive Control (MPC) was discussed in [30, 31] for upwind speed measurements, optimization of power capturing and reduce tower loading effect. MPC implementation was limited due to computational burden. The feed-forward control method alternative to MPC was dealt [19, 32–34] by pre-processing wind pace data with predicting the upcoming turbine loads [32].

## 3 Challenges in Wind Turbine Control

Although there has been rapid increase of establishments of wind farms, still there are engineering defies specifically in designing, selection of material and suitable control strategy. The control to be designed should address improving the competence of its efficiency, functioning, and life span of wind turbines [11]. From many challenges in wind turbine control, some of them are presented below.

a. Turbine structure loading problems are due to time to time increase in wind turbine sizes. Different load types on the wind turbines and their effect analysis are described in reference [16]. For the growing rotor dimension; there is the spatial weight deviation alongside of blade. It is essential to act in response to loading effects due to wind shear, and turbulence.The wind fluid is generally not uniform due to wind shear that is deviation in the wind speed magnitude and direction profiles. When rotor axis is unaligned to wind direction, twisted wind will be created and results in turbulent formation that affects turbine aerodynamics. Turbulent formation can get several forms, for instance wind speed may come into view as a rising and falling on the way to turbine. Different controllers are proposed to reduce such problems were presented in [22, 35] but still, suitable controller has to be developed to mitigate the structural loading. Logical turbulent kinetic energy can be reason for extreme stress on a wind turbine that is occurred and observed between 40 – 120m above the ground, which is found to be the usual for grid connected wind turbine rotor height [36]. MIMO structure for independently driven blade angle control may valuable to decrease major weight or load 0n turbine [21, 37, 38]. Only 20% of turbulence load reduction was achieved as reported by [39] and hence it is required to prevent premature breakdown of the turbine and improve energy capturing efficiency [40]. Wind turbine tower oscillations (sideway and fore-aft towers) cause fatigue loads on the tower and then reduce tower life. Therefore, a suitable control loop is required to damp sideway and fore-aft tower vibrations in area 3.

b. Representation of stochastic behavior in wind data profile for realizing the performance improvement of the turbine is essential. This is not only helps for speed regulation and maximization of the power output but also for structural load mitigation of wind turbines [35].

c. Due to the complication in a wind turbine for energy conversion, stability of fully established controller for it is frequently hard to found. Several control loops act together as do many degrees of freedom for turbine grow to be bigger, having smaller normal frequencies of oscillatory behavior [41, 42]. As reported by [41], wind turbine drive train oscillates between 0–10 Hz frequency which proportionate on blade rotational velocity; in turn affects output power. Controller should have a way to get separate blade position sensors together with electric machine speed that can also use data from strain gauges recording structural motion of tower. Modern control strategies are required to reduce structural oscillation [43].

d. Wind turbine control was handled by 2 separate controllers for Area 2 and Area 3. Switching among these areas controllers may difficult. In several occasions, highest structural injure of turbines happen because of great exhaustion loads through changeover of these two operation areas. The 2-blades Controls Advanced Research Turbine (CART2) baseline controller utilizes an extra control area named 'Area 2.5' for changeover from Area 2 to Area 3, or in reverse. The main purpose of Area 2.5' is to tie Area 2 with Area 3 controllers appropriately [20, 22]. Unluckily, the tie between these areas did not give even changeover. There is irregular gradient in torque control, which makes additional too much loading on turbine structure. For transition between the two regions as an option, a single controller that uses single reference for amplification of the two areas controller was developed. But reduced grading of performance of the areas occurred. Hence, the use of Area 2.5 is not much attractive [44].

e. There are causes for turbines hurt by decision-making control to act to stop the turbine while very small or extreme wind velocity and grid faults. But, incredibly small energetic control was fabricated and used for turbine stopping at time of turbine failure case [19].

f. Well developed turbine damage identification techniques with safety mechanisms were required. As it was discussed by [45], observation of parameter for damage indication using Rotational Invariance Technique (ESPRIT) technique followed by Root- MUltiple SIgnal Classification (R-MUSIC) technique has very high detection accuracy for wind turbine generator related faults. But, their computation is more complex and limits its real-time implementation. Therefore, either improvement for computation complexity of these technique or other simplest fault detection mechanisms for a wind turbine is required.

g. The controllers' recitals are affected by model incorrectness. As example, 5% of replica formulation mistake only in tip speed ratio of wind turbine blade results in about 1%–3% wastage of energy when turbine operates in area 2. In this case, consider Ethiopia electricity generation only from wind plant that is 324 MW, which is running at 32% capacity factor with annual energy production of 908.237 GWh; for estimated price of energy production is $0.09 per kWh, 1% -3% wastage of energy at this wind plant is equal with $817413–$2452240 wastage per annual [19, 46, 47]. The other point is even though plant replica formulation mistake is very little; dynamical performance of wind turbine may alter now and then because of wear, rubbish builds on blades, and so on. To overcome this inaccuracy, suitable control strategies are required [37, 46, 48–51].

# 4    Conclusion and Future Study Areas

## 4.1    Conclusion

The wind resource is available in abundant and sufficient for global upcoming energy wants. Wind turbine size and wind energy are fast-growing industries, which leads to a huge requirement for improved replica formulation with control structure of wind turbines for realizable power capture. Because of doubts and complexity in sensing and recording the wind fluid, developing control system is challenging. Wind turbine control is affected by different factors like turbine configuration and its operation modes within uncertain wind pace conditions. Different controllers were designed and implemented for wind turbines. For instance, PI and PID controllers, linear quadratic optimal, linear quadratic Gaussian optimal, and Robust Multivariable, Model predictive and adaptive controls. These controllers have limitation in structural load mitigation, structural vibrations in area 3, wind turbine fault detection and model error tolerance. Modeling using system identification and other sophisticated control techniques has to be discovered in order to decrease price of wind energy and improve efficiency, operation, and lifetime of wind turbines.

## 4.2 Future Study Areas

1. Development of superior control schemes for wind turbines, which allows the active suppression of mechanical vibrations in tower and drive-train/other structural vibrations in area 3 is required.
2. A novel control strategy for wind turbine since it operates in an uncertain environment that takes in to account robust steady-state stability of the overall system.
3. Stochastic modelling of intermittent wind speed is required for wind turbine structural load mitigation. These may include identification and prediction of particular load types and their related effect on wind turbine i.e. to reduce (possibly elimination) their effects. Also, suitable controller strategies can be developed for load mitigation.
4. The controller should have means to each blade position angle sensors along with electrical machine/ generator speed and that of tower motion and strain.
5. Fault detection and monitoring mechanism (a smart sensor that should be cost efficient, energy-efficient, offer an opportunity for deploying sensor in inaccessible locations in/on turbine, electrical noise environment) and also sophisticated control techniques required to reduce the turbine damage.
6. Novel commercially accepted signal processing techniques to take out the main features of a signal to forecast wind turbine components health are to be used.

# References

1. El-Shimy, M.: Modeling and control of wind turbines including aerodynamics. Ain Shams Uni. 41(2), 2 (2006)
2. Hennepin, E.: Wind Energy History. Recharges Lab, San Francisco (2010)
3. Schiffer, H.W.: World Energy Resources|2016, p. 660. World Energy Council, London (2016)
4. Renewable 2017: Global Status Report. REN21: Paris, France, pp. 87, 187–202 (2017)
5. World Wind Energy Association: Press Release statistics, 25 February 2019
6. Steve, S.: Global Wind Energy Outlook 2014, p. 10. GWEC, Brussels (2014)
7. Steve, S.: Global Wind Energy Outlook 2016. GWEC, Brussels (2016)
8. Fried, L.: Global Wind Statistics 2016, p. 3. GWEC, Brussels (2016)
9. Robert, S.P.: Energy Source Cost Comparisons. p. 10 (2007)
10. Manwell, J.F., McGowan, J.G., Rogers, A.L.: Wind Energy Explained: Theory, Design, and Application, pp. 92–95. John Wiley and Sons Ltd., West Sussex, England (2002)
11. Silvio, S.: Advanced issues of wind turbine modeling and control. J. Phys. ACD. 659, 11–19 (2015)
12. Neil, D., Kelley, R., Osgood, M.: Using Wavelet Analysis to Assess Turbulence/Rotor Interactions, Wind Energ. pp. 121–134 (2000)
13. Ranjan, V.: Dynamic modeling, Simulation and Control of Energy Generation. Springer-Verlag, London 20, 180–183 (2013)
14. Kathryn, E.J., Lee, J., Fingersh, M.J., Balas, L.Y.P.: Methods for increasing region 2 power capture on a variable-speed wind turbine. In: ASME, pp. 1–4 (2004)
15. Fernando, D., Bianchi, H., De, B., Ricardo, J.M.: Wind Turbine Control Systems Principles, Modelling and Gain Scheduling Design, pp. 65–76. Springer, Heidelberg (2006)
16. Tony, B., David, S., Nick, J., Ervin, B.: Wind Energy handbook, pp. 272–276. John Wiley & Sons Ltd., Hoboken (2001)

17. Wind Turbines: How many blades, Danish Wind Industry Association (2003) www.windpo wer.org/en/tour/design/concepts.html
18. Hand, M.M., Mark, J.B.: Systematic controller design methodology for variable-speed wind turbines. Wind Eng. 24(3), 169–187 (2000)
19. Lucy, P.: A Tutorial on the Dynamics and Control of Wind Turbines and Wind Farms. In: Proceedings of American Control Conference, St. Louis, MO, USA, pp. 18–32 (2009)
20. Irving, P., Girsang, J., Dhupia, S.: Collective pitch control of wind turbines using stochastic disturbance accommodating control. Wind Eng. 37(5), 518–534 (2013)
21. Geyler, M., Caselitz, P.: Robust multivariable pitch control design for load reduction on large wind turbines. J. Solar Energy Eng. 130, 1–12 (2008)
22. Jason, H., Laks, L., Pao, Y., Alan, D.W.: Control of Wind Turbines: Past, Present, and Future. American Control Conference, pp. 6–7 (2009)
23. Biegel, B., Juelsgaard, M., Kraning, M., Boyd, S., Stoustrup, J.: Wind turbine pitch optimization. In: IEEE International Conference on Control Applications (CCA), Part of 2011 IEEE Multi-Conference on Systems and Control, Denver, CO, USA, September 28–30, pp.1328–1334 (2011)
24. Abdin, E.S., Xu, W.: Control design and dynamic performance analysis of a wind turbine-induction generator unit. IEEE Trans. Energy Convers. 151, 91–96 (2000)
25. Alan, D.: Wright: Modern Control Design for Flexible Wind Turbines, NREL, pp. 82–85 (2004)
26. Pintea, A., Christov, N., Popescu, D., Borne, P.: LQG control of horizontal wind turbines for blades and tower loads alleviation. In: Proceedings of the 18th World Congress. The International Federation of Automatic Control, Milano (Italy) August 28–September 2, pp. 1721–1726 (2011)
27. Connor, D., Iyer, S.N., Leithead, W.E., Grimble, M.J.: Control of horizontal axis wind turbine using $H_\infty$ control. In: Proceedings of the First IEEE Conference on Control Applications, Dayton, OH, pp. 117–122 (1992)
28. Battista, H.D., Mantz, R.J., Christiansen, C.F.: Dynamical sliding mode power control of wind driven induction generators. IEEE Trans. Energy Convers. 15(4), 451–457 (2000)
29. Song, Y.D., Dhinakaran, B., Bao, X.Y.: Variable speed control of wind turbines using nonlinear and adaptive algorithms. J. Wind. Eng. Ind. Aerodyn. 85, 293–308 (2000)
30. Biegel, B., Juelsgaard, M., Kraning M., Boyd, S., Stoustrup, J.: Wind turbine pitch optimization. In: IEEE International Conference on Control Applications (CCA), Part of 2011 IEEE Multi-Conference on Systems and Control, Denver, CO, USA. September 28–30, pp.1328–1334 (2011)
31. Soltani, M., Wisniewski, R., Brath, P., Boyd, S.: Load reduction of wind turbines using receding horizon control. In: IEEE Conference on Control Applications (CCA), Part of 2011 IEEE Multi-Conference on Systems and Control, Denver, CO, USA. September 28–30, pp. 852–857 (2011)
32. Stotsky, A., Egardt, B.: Model based control of wind turbines: look-ahead approach. In: Proceedings of the 7th IFAC Symposium on Robust Control Design, Aalborg, Denmark, June 20–22, pp. 642–644 (2012)
33. Wang, N., Johnson, K., Wright, A.: FX-RLS-based feed forward control for Lidar-enabled wind turbine load mitigation. IEEE Trans. Control Syst. Technol. 20(5), 1212–1222 (2012)
34. Laks, J., Pao, L., Wright, A., Kelley, N., Jonkman, B.: The Use of preview wind measurements for blade pitch control. Mechatronics 21, 668–681 (2011)
35. Hand, M.: Mitigation of Wind Turbine/Vortex Interaction Using Disturbance Accommodating Control. Ph.D. Dissertation, University of Colorado at Boulder, pp. 11–21 and 37–69 (2003)
36. Banta, R., Pichugina, Y., Kelley, N., Jonkman, B., Brewer, W.: Doppler Lidar measurements of the great plains low-level jet: applications to wind energy. In: Proc. 14th International Symposium for the Advancement of Boundary Layer Remote Sensing, p. 4. (2008)

37. Moriarty, P., Butterfield, C.P.: Wind turbine modelling overview for control engineers. In: Proceedings of American Control Conference, St. Louis, MO, pp. 2094–2095 (2009)
38. Kausihan, S.: Individual Pitch Control for Large scale wind turbines: Multivariable control approach. M.Sc. thesis at TU Delft, pp. 4–5 & 32 (2007)
39. Stoyan, K.: Extreme Turbulence Control for Wind Turbines, pp. 18, 20–25 (2016)
40. Casctillo, L., Torres-Nieves, S., Meneveau, C.: The Role of Turbulence on Wind Energy: from Single blade to Wind Array, pp. 4–6 (2012)
41. Escaler, X., Mebarki, T.: Statistical analysis of low frequency vibrations in variable speed wind turbines. IOP Conf. Ser. Mater. Sci. Eng. **52**, 1–5 (2013)
42. Luuk, M.: Sensitivity analysis of the first natural frequency of the offshore wind turbines in the Eneco Luchterduinen wind farm. M.Sc. thesis at TU Delft, pp. 19–38 & 66 (2017)
43. Mate, J., Nedjeljko, P., Ivan, P.: Damping of wind turbine tower oscillations through rotor speed control. International Conference on Ecologic Vehicles & Renewable Energies, pp. 1–10 (2007)
44. Freeman, J., Balas, M.: An investigation of variable speed horizontal-axis wind turbines using direct model-reference adaptive control. In: Proceedings of AIAA/ASME Wind Energy Symposium, Reno, NV, p. 70 (1999)
45. Chakkor, S., Baghouri, M., Hajraoui, A.: Performance analysis of faults detection in wind turbine generator based on high-resolution frequency estimation methods. IJACSA **5**(4), 140–147 (2014)
46. Kathryn, E., Johnson, L., Pao, Y., Mark, J.B., Fingersh, L.J.: Control of variable speed wind turbine: standard and adaptive techniques for maximizing energy capture. IEEE Control Syst. Mag. **26**, 74–75 (2006)
47. Fingersh, L., Carlin, P.: Results from the NREL variable-speed test bed. In: Proceedings of AIAA/ASME Wind Energy Symposium, Reno, NV, p. 4 (1998)
48. van Wingerden, J.W., Houtzager, I., Felici, F., Verhaegen, M.: Closed-loop identification of the time-varying dynamics of variable speed wind turbines. Int. J. Robust Nonlinear. Control. **19**, 20 (2008)
49. Frost, S.A., Balas, M.J., Wright, A.D.: Direct adaptive control of a utility-scale wind turbine for speed regulation. Int. J. Robust Nonlinear Control, John Wiley & Sons, Ltd. p. 70 (2009)
50. Song, Y.D., Dhinakaran, B., Bao, X.: Variable speed control of wind turbines using nonlinear and adaptive algorithms. J. Wind Eng. Indus. Aerodyn. **85**, 293–308 (2000). (Elsevier Science Ltd., pp. 293–308)
51. Johnson, K.: Adaptive Torque Control of Variable Speed Wind Turbines. Ph.D. Dissertation, University of Colorado at Boulder, pp.43–57 (2004)

# Optimization-Based Robust PID Controller to Enhance the Performance of Conical Tank System

Mulugeta Debebe[✉] and Beza Nekatibeb

College of Electrical and Mechanical Engineering, Addis Ababa Science and Technology University, Addis Ababa, Ethiopia
bezan.nekatibeb@aastu.edu.et

**Abstract.** This paper uses a particle swarm optimization (PSO) approach in order to identify nominal model parameters and to tune a Proportional- Integral - Derivative (PID) controller. In order to analyze the nominal model uncertainty, lumped multiplicative uncertainty structure is used to account unmodeled dynamics and nonlinearties. Moreover, first order weighting function through trial and error approximation method that limits the upper bound of the multiplicative uncertainty has been found. The Nominal model is used to design PSO optimized PID controller; and then the simulated results are compared with ACO based PI controller. The results show that the PSO optimized PID controller shows smooth and enhanced performance in terms of speed of response. And PSO based approach can efficiently applied in identifying the parameters of the system and tuning the PID controller for this particular system.

**Keywords:** PID controllers · Nominal model · Uncertain system · PSO

## 1 Introduction

Many food and chemical industries use conical tanks for their applications. In most of these industries, it is common the use a PID Controller for control of the conical tank system [1]. However, controlling the conical system is challenging as a result of the nonlinear nature of the system. There are many literatures on PID controller tuning for industrial process application based on the first order process with time delay (FOPTD) model. Different approaches have been introduced to tuning the PID controller for the past decades [2]. The approached which is proposed by Ziegler and Nichols (Z-N) has been proven to be successful to some level of control. The main weakness of the Z-N based approach is the necessity of previous knowledge about plant model. Moreover, there is still considerable disagreement regarding the possibility of the optimum coefficient of PID controller. Moreover, determination of PID controller tuning parameters is a vexing problem in many applications [3].

© ICST Institute for Computer Sciences, Social Informatics and Telecommunications Engineering 2021
Published by Springer Nature Switzerland AG 2021. All Rights Reserved
M. A. Delele et al. (Eds.): ICAST 2020, LNICST 385, pp. 522–531, 2021.
https://doi.org/10.1007/978-3-030-80618-7_36

Recently, modern optimization technique for complex engineering applications is becoming a research interest. Some of to mention are Genetic Algorithms (GA) [4], PSO [5, 6], ant colony optimization (ACO) [7] etc. These heuristic methods are the intelligence optimization algorithms that are based on natural behavior and characteristics. Mohideen K. Asan et al. [4] have used Labview to carry out a system identification technique to find the model of hybrid tank system and then used this model to tune off-line PID parameters by using Real-coded Genetic Algorithm (RGA). Wei-Der Chang et al. [5] proposed the PSO algorithm in order to optimally estimate the parameters for the Genesio-Tesi chaotic nonlinear systems. Mercy.D etal in [6] proposed improved PSO algorithm and made a comparison among the improved PSO, the conversional PSO and the classical PID. In [7], S.M.GiriRajkumar et al. ant ACO algorithm introduced to tune the optimal control parameters of a Proportional Integral (PI) controller for a nonlinear conical tank system. This work also presents system identification technique to estimate the parameters of the model based on open loop response of the system for four different heights of conical tank system. A key limitation proposed in [7] is that it does not suitable for analysis and practical implementation due to too many models and controller for a single system. In 1995 Kennedy and Eberhart were the first to propose PSO Algorithm. They inspired by nature based on the behavior of bird flocking. Group of birds find their food in a special way. More details of PSO algorithm can be found in Changhe Li PhD thesis [8].

The organization of this paper is as follows. The Sect. 2 gives a brief overview of the model formulation framework. The Sect. 3 examines the frequency analysis of uncertain system. Section 4 addresses PSO-PID tuning results. Conclusions are drawn in the Sect. 5.

## 2  PSO Algorithm- Based Model Formulations.

In the literatures various system identification methods have been proposed to obtain the model of the system both in linear and nonlinear structure. However, in this paper, an attempt has been made to address nominal model for the overall conical tank system as (FOPTD) shown in (1) by taking the models estimated from [7].

$$G(s) = \frac{Ke^{-Ts}}{\tau s + 1} \tag{1}$$

Where $\tau$ denotes the time constant, $T$ is the time delay and $K$ is the steady state gain.

In [7], various experiments were conducted for different operating ranges (flow) ranges and valve openings to get a typical response curve. The models of the conical tank were obtained by dividing the height into four levels to account the non-linearity in the shape of the conical tank: model-1 form 0 to 15 cm, model-2 from 15 to 27 cm, model-3 from 27 to 36 cm and 36 to 43 cm as model 4 as shown in (2) to (5) respectively

$$G(s)_{model1} = \frac{2.74e^{-10.64s}}{4.24s + 1} \tag{2}$$

$$G(s)_{model2} = \frac{2.19e^{-13.98s}}{8.9s + 1} \tag{3}$$

$$G(s)_{model3} = \frac{1.6e^{-15.51s}}{12.19s + 1} \tag{4}$$

$$G(s)_{model4} = \frac{1.36e^{-19s}}{15.56s + 1} \tag{5}$$

Therefore, by taking these models, one nominal model that adequately enough to describe the overall conical tank system can be obtained using the PSO algorithm. Before PSO is executed, the objective function must be defined properly. Here well-known 2-norm error signal in (6) is used as the performance index to select the adjustable parameters of the model so that the step response error between the given models shown in (1) to (4) and the desired optimum model is minimized. Accordingly $T^*$, $K^*$, and, $\tau^*$ are estimated parameters of the nominal model, $Y_{nom}$ is step response of the nominal model and $Y_i$ is step response of the given models. The search lower and upper bounds for parameters $\tau$, T and K are constrained in the interval (13, 20).

$$\|Y_{nom} - Y_i\|_2 = \overset{arg\,min}{\underset{T,K,\tau}{}} \left( \sqrt{\sum_{i=1}^{4}(Y_{nom} - Y_i)^2} \right) \tag{6}$$

If any resulting parameter outside the interval during the search, set it the corresponding bounds, i.e.

$$parameter\ value = \begin{cases} 1.3 \ if\ search\ value\ \leq\ 1.3 \\ 20 \ if\ search\ value \geq 20 \end{cases} \tag{7}$$

PSO is described by a well-known evolution equation and a particle $j$ at iteration $k$ is characterized by the following set of Eq. (8)

$$\hat{X}_k^j = \hat{X}_{k-1}^j + \hat{V}_k^j$$
$$\hat{V}_k^j = W * \hat{V}_{k-1}^j + C_1R_1 * \left(P_b^j - \hat{X}_{k-1}^j\right) + C_2R_2 * \left(G_b - \hat{X}_{k-1}^j\right) \tag{8}$$

$\hat{X}_k^j$ is the $j^{th}$ particle and $\hat{V}_k^j$ $j^{th}$ particle velocity. The coefficients $C_1$ and $C_2$ are learning terms, coefficients $R_1$ and $R_2$ are random numbers following a uniform distribution and the coefficient $W$ is the inertia factor. Where $P_b^j$ is personal best and $G_b$ global best. The detailed selection of the value of the coefficients can be found in (7). Here the adaptive scheme that decreases $W$ linearly with iteration (9) has been used.

$$W = 0.96 * W. \tag{9}$$

MATLAB simulation software package has been used to identify nominal model parameter. The following values: variable size(parameters) = 3, Number of population = 15, $C_1 = 1.821$, $C_2 = 2.6$, $W = 1$ are selected. The resulting estimated nominal model parametrs are illustrated in Table 1.

**Table 1.** Estimated nominal model parameters

| $T^*$ | $K^*$ | $\tau^*$ |
|---|---|---|
| 11.1914 | 1.9718 | 11.8531 |

Substituting the obtained parameters in (1), the nominal model becomes

$$G_{\text{nom}}(s) = \frac{1.9718e^{-11.1914s}}{11.8531s + 1} \tag{10}$$

## 3 Frequency Analysis of Uncertain System

Further analysis is needed to investigate model uncertainties of the system before designing a controller. This model uncertainty arises from the time delay, the gain and poles of the transfer function. In this section, within the framework of FOPTD model structure, multiplicative uncertainty of the real perturbed system is examined explicitly. According to Doyle et al. [9] multiplicative uncertainty of the transfer function of the real (perturbed) plant $G_P(s)$ is defined as:

$$G_P(s) = G_{nom}(s)(1 + W_I(s)\Delta_I(s)); \qquad |\Delta_I(jw)| \leq 1, \forall w \tag{11}$$

$W_I(s)$ is weighting function that represents an upper bound on the multiplicative uncertainty, $\Delta_I(s)$ is disturbance (perturbation) acting on the system. In [9, 10], the relative uncertainty can be given as (12)

$$l_I = max \left| \frac{G_P(jw) - G_{nom}(jw)}{G_{nom}(jw)} \right|,$$
$$\text{with } |W_I(jw)| \geq l_I(jw), \forall w \tag{12}$$

From Eqs. (2)–(5), it is clear to verify that time delay, gain and time constants are within the following boundaries: $10.64 \leq T \leq 19, 1.36 \leq K \leq 2.74, 4.24 \leq \tau \leq 15.5$ respectively. Taking this in to consideration, the parameter intervals are widening to capture a large number of multiplicative uncertainties. The intervals are selected as: $8 \leq T \leq 20, 1.2 \leq K \leq 4, 4 \leq \tau \leq 20$.

To determine the relative error of perturbed system with a different combination of $\tau$, T and K., simulation is carried out using MATLAB software. The multiplicative error of the pre-compensated frequency responses from the nominal model is shown in Fig. 1. Consequently, first order weighting function in (13) has been obtained through trial and error approximation that limits the upper bound of the multiplicative uncertainty.

$$w_I(jw) \cong \frac{0.89\left(\frac{s}{0.04} + 1\right)}{\left(\frac{s}{0.3335} + 1\right)} \tag{13}$$

As shown in Fig. 1, the frequency responses of the relative error of the perturbed system remain below the frequency response of the weighting function ($w_I(jw)$) almost in all frequencies. Also, it is shown how the relative error increases with frequency.

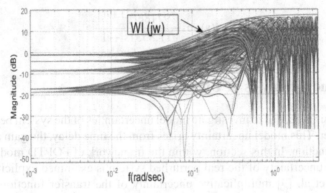

**Fig. 1.** Relative error of perturbed system

For this reason, the weighting function is increased with frequency to account the undesirable high-frequency unmodeled dynamics.

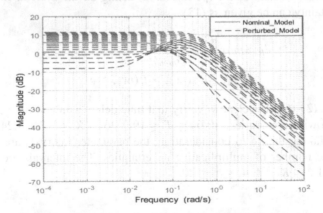

**Fig. 2.** Frequency response of nominal and perturbed model

Furthermore, the bode plot of the uncertain system with respect to weighting function is shown in Fig. 2. Obviously, most of the perturbed models show significant variation from the nominal model particularly at high frequencies.

## 4  PSO-PID Controller Design

Figure 3 demonstrates the designed implementation structure of PID-PSO controller. The optimal values of the controller parameters (Kc, $T_I$, and $T_D$) are tuned using PSO algorithm based on Integral absolute error (IAE) in (15) as a performance index.

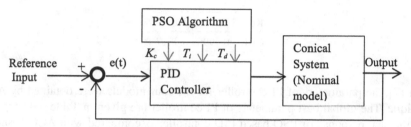

**Fig. 3.** PSO -PID Control Structure

$$I_{IAE} = \int_{0}^{T} |e(t)| dt \qquad (15)$$

In most cases the structure of the PID controller is pre-determined for a specific application. Many variations of PID controller structure have been proposed in [3]. The initial investigation was made using PID with the filtered derivative structure described by Eq. (14).

$$G_c = K_c \left[ 1 + \frac{1}{T_i s} + \frac{T_d s}{1 + \frac{T_d}{N} s} \right] \qquad (14)$$

The error, e(t) can be defined as, $e(t) = Y_{nom} - 1$. To run the PSO algorithm, different coefficient values and population sizes were chosen and investigated. The final selected values can be summarized as: variable size (parameters) = 3, number of population = 15, $C_1 = 2$, $C_2 = 2$, $W = 1$. The parameter Kc, Ti and Td are constrained with in the interval [0,1 to search for their upper and lower. Since at the beginning of each iteration, the difference between the actual output from the nominal model and the set point is large. Therefore, if the proportional part of the controller gain is too small during the PSO algorithm run time, the PID controller unable to respond adequately to the set point changes. To overcome this problem, an attempt was made by modifying the proportional part of the structure of the PID controller as shown in (16).

$$G_c = K_c \left[ \left( 1 + \frac{0.15}{K_c} \right) + \frac{1}{T_i s} + \frac{T_d s}{1 + \frac{T_d}{N} s} \right] \qquad (16)$$

## 5 Result and discussion

### 5.1 PSO-PID Controller

The PID controller coefficients that minimizes the integral absolute error are identified and given in Table 2 for N = 50. The performance of the PSO based PID controller was evaluated by computing the step response of the nominal model, model1, model2, model3 and model4, as shown Fig. 4.

**Table 2.** PSO based PID parameter values

| Kc | Ti | Td |
|----|----|----|
| 0.016 | 0.9996 | 0.9817 |

In [7], the parameters of PI controller for the four models were obtained by ACO technique. The global best parameters of PI controller are given in Table 3. Using this data, the step response of PSO based PID controller is compared with ACO based PI controller for different levels and the simulation results are depicted in Fig. 4, Fig. 5, Fig. 6, and Fig. 7. The results show that the nominal model demonstrates fast and smooth (nonoscillatory) response at level of conical tank system.

**Table 3.** ACO based PI parameter values [7]

| Parameters | Model1 | Model2 | Model3 | Model4 |
|------------|--------|--------|--------|--------|
| Kp | 0.21805 | 0.31813 | 0.4797 | 0.5502 |
| Ki | 0.02606 | 0.0227 | 0.0264 | 0.0252 |

**Table 4.** Comparison of time domain specifications

| Controller | Model 1 | | Model2 | | Model3 | | Model4 | |
|------------|---------|---------|--------|---------|--------|---------|--------|---------|
| | Over shoot (%) | Settling time (s) | Over shoot (%) | Settling time (s) | Over shoot (%) | Settling time (s | Over shoot (%) | Settling time (s) |
| ACO-PI | 23.28 | 73 | 19.44 | 102.4 | 16.2 | 95.6 | 15.36 | 120.2 |
| PSO-PID | 0.49 | 81 | 0.65 | 52.3 | 1.45 | 78.9 | 5.1 | 162 |

As can be seen from Table 4, PSO based PID controller shows better performance compared to ACO based PI controller regarding to overshoot for all four models. Similarly, settling time result shows model2 and model3 have been improved.

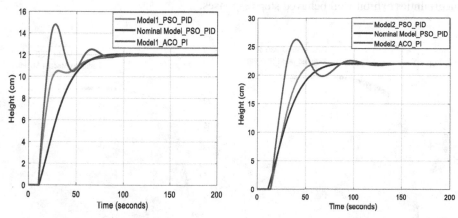

**Fig. 4.** ACO-PI and PSO-PID step response for model1

**Fig. 5.** ACO-PI and PSO-PID step response for model2

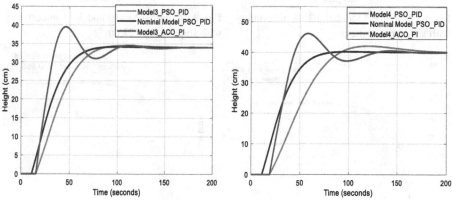

**Fig. 6.** ACO-PI and PSO-PID step response for model3

**Fig. 7.** ACO-PI and PSO-PID step response for model4

This section also investigates the degree of robustness of the PSO optimized PID controller to model uncertainty. These step response simulations are depicted in Fig. 8, Fig. 9, Fig. 10, and Fig. 11. The simulation results show that the designed PSO optimized PID controller is robust to the given uncertainties, since all the models and their uncertainties exhibit well behaved step responses.

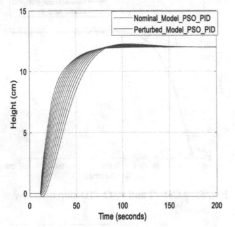

**Fig. 8.** Nominal Model and 30% uncertainty with step input of 12 cm

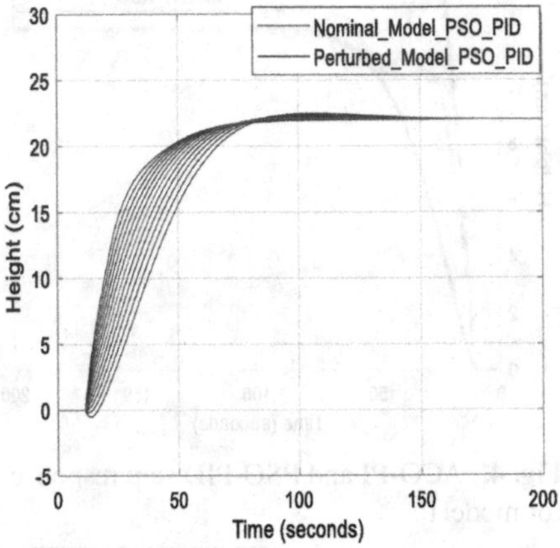

**Fig. 9.** Nominal Model and 30% uncertainty with step input of 22 cm

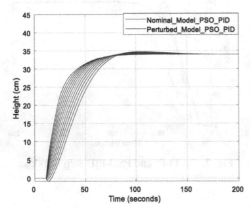

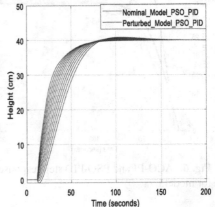

**Fig. 10.** Nominal Model and 30% uncertainty with step input of 34 cm

**Fig. 11.** Nominal Model and 30% uncertainty with step input of 40 cm

## 6    Conclusion

This paper has presented the PSO algorithm to solve the optimal parameters of nominal model that sufficiently enough to describe the overall height of conical tank system. In the proposed approach, a 2-norm is adopted as the performance index to minimize the error between the nominal model and the given four models. The unknown nominal model parameters can be obtained using the proposed PSO algorithm. The first order weighting function that limits the upper bound of the multiplicative uncertainty has been found. Moreover, an optimal value of PID controller parameters also obtained by using PSO algorithm. From the simulation results, one can to observe that PSO optimized PID controller has shown good performance. Additionally, the PID controller has shown robustness that able to reject model uncertainty up to 30%.

# References

1. Pushpaveni, T., Srinivasulu Raju, S., Archana, N., Chandana, M.: Modeling and Controlling of Conical tank system using adaptive controllers and performance comparison with conventional PID. IJSER **2013**, 629–635 (2013)
2. Ziegler, J.G., Nichols, N.B.: Optimum settings for automatic controllers. Trans. Asme **64**, 759–765 (1942)
3. O'Dwyer, A.:"Handbook of PI and PID Controller Tuning Rules. 2nd Edition, Dublin Institute of Technology, Ireland (2006)
4. Asan, K., Saravanakumar, G., Valarmathi, K., Devaraj, D., Radhakrishnan, T.K.: Real-coded Genetic Algorithm for system identification and tuning of a modified Model Reference Adaptive Controller for a hybrid tank system. Appl. Math. Mod. **37**(6), 3829–3847 (2013). https://doi.org/10.1016/j.apm.2012.08.019
5. Mercy. D., Girirajkumar, S.M.: Real time implementation of improved PSO tuning for a conical tank process used in biodiesel production. Int. J. Pure Appl. Math. **118**(18), 2051–2062 (2018)
6. Chang, W.-D., Cheng, J.-P., Hsu, M.-C., Tsai, L.-C.: Parameter identification of nonlinear systems using a particle swarm optimization approach. In: IEEE International Conference on Networking and Computing. https://doi.org/10.1109/ICNC.2012
7. GiriRajkumar, S.M., Ramkumar, K., Sanjay Sarma, O.V.: Real time application of ants colony optimization. Int. J.Comput . Appl. **3**(8), 3446 (2010). https://doi.org/10.5120/753-1054
8. Li, C.: Particle Swarm Optimization in Stationary and Dynamic Environments, PhD thesis, University of Leicester, Department of Computer Science (2010)
9. Doyle, J.C., Francis, B.A., Tannenbaum, A.R.: Feedback Control Theory. Macmillan Publishing, New York (1992)
10. Skogestad, S., Postlethwaite, I.: Multivariable Feedback Control Analysis and Design. Norwagian University of Science and Technology, Jhone Wiley & Sons

# Author Index

Printed in the United States
by Baker & Taylor Publisher Services